Impact of ICTs on Event Management and Marketing

Kemal Birdir
Mersin University, Turkey

Sevda Birdir
Mersin University, Turkey

Ali Dalgic
Mersin University, Turkey

Derya Toksoz
Mersin University, Turkey

IGI Global
PUBLISHER of TIMELY KNOWLEDGE

A volume in the Advances in Marketing, Customer Relationship Management, and E-Services (AMCRMES) Book Series

Published in the United States of America by
IGI Global
Business Science Reference (an imprint of IGI Global)
701 E. Chocolate Avenue
Hershey PA, USA 17033
Tel: 717-533-8845
Fax: 717-533-8661
E-mail: cust@igi-global.com
Web site: http://www.igi-global.com

Library of Congress Cataloging-in-Publication Data

Names: Birdir, Kemal, editor. | Birdir, Sevda, 1969- editor. | Dalgic, Ali, 1987- editor. | Toksoz, Derya, 1990- editor.
Title: Impact of ICTs on event management and marketing / Kemal Birdir, Sevda Birdir, Ali Dalgic, and Derya Toksoz, editors.
Description: Hershey, PA : Business Science Reference, 2021. | Includes bibliographical references and index. | Summary: "This book explores the impact of new information and communications technologies on event management and marketing"-- Provided by publisher.
Identifiers: LCCN 2020012893 (print) | LCCN 2020012894 (ebook) | ISBN 9781799849544 (hardcover) | ISBN 9781799857013 (paperback) | ISBN 9781799849551 (ebook)
Subjects: LCSH: Special events--Planning--Technological innovations. | Special events--Marketing--Technological innovations.
Classification: LCC GT3405 .I56 2021 (print) | LCC GT3405 (ebook) | DDC 394.2--dc23
LC record available at https://lccn.loc.gov/2020012893
LC ebook record available at https://lccn.loc.gov/2020012894

This book is published in the IGI Global book series Advances in Marketing, Customer Relationship Management, and E-Services (AMCRMES) (ISSN: 2327-5502; eISSN: 2327-5529)

British Cataloguing in Publication Data
A Cataloguing in Publication record for this book is available from the British Library.

For electronic access to this publication, please contact: eresources@igi-global.com.

Advances in Marketing, Customer Relationship Management, and E-Services (AMCRMES) Book Series

Eldon Y. Li
National Chengchi University, Taiwan & California Polytechnic State University, USA

ISSN:2327-5502
EISSN:2327-5529

Mission

Business processes, services, and communications are important factors in the management of good customer relationship, which is the foundation of any well organized business. Technology continues to play a vital role in the organization and automation of business processes for marketing, sales, and customer service. These features aid in the attraction of new clients and maintaining existing relationships.

The Advances in Marketing, Customer Relationship Management, and E-Services (AMCRMES) Book Series addresses success factors for customer relationship management, marketing, and electronic services and its performance outcomes. This collection of reference source covers aspects of consumer behavior and marketing business strategies aiming towards researchers, scholars, and practitioners in the fields of marketing management.

Coverage

- Electronic Services
- CRM strategies
- Cases on Electronic Services
- Mobile CRM
- B2B marketing
- Text Mining and Marketing
- Cases on CRM Implementation
- Ethical Considerations in E-Marketing
- Legal Considerations in E-Marketing
- Customer Relationship Management

IGI Global is currently accepting manuscripts for publication within this series. To submit a proposal for a volume in this series, please contact our Acquisition Editors at Acquisitions@igi-global.com or visit: http://www.igi-global.com/publish/.

The Advances in Marketing, Customer Relationship Management, and E-Services (AMCRMES) Book Series (ISSN 2327-5502) is published by IGI Global, 701 E. Chocolate Avenue, Hershey, PA 17033-1240, USA, www.igi-global.com. This series is composed of titles available for purchase individually; each title is edited to be contextually exclusive from any other title within the series. For pricing and ordering information please visit http://www.igi-global.com/book-series/advances-marketing-customer-relationship-management/37150. Postmaster: Send all address changes to above address.

Titles in this Series

For a list of additional titles in this series, please visit:
http://www.igi-global.com/book-series/advances-marketing-customer-relationship-management/37150

Building Consumer-Brand Relationship in Luxury Brand Management
Paula Rodrigues (Lusíada University of Porto, Portugal) and Ana Pinto Borges (Instituto Superior de Administração e Gestão, Portugal)
Business Science Reference • © 2021 • 318pp • H/C (ISBN: 9781799843696) • US $225.00

Innovations in Digital Branding and Content Marketing
Subhankar Das (Duy Tan University, Vietnam) and Subhra Rani Mondal (Duy Tan University, Vietnam)
Business Science Reference • © 2021 • 311pp • H/C (ISBN: 9781799844204) • US $195.00

Handbook of Research on Applied AI for International Business and Marketing Applications
Bryan Christiansen (Global Training Group, Ltd, UK) and Tihana Škrinjarić (University of Zagreb, Croatia)
Business Science Reference • © 2021 • 702pp • H/C (ISBN: 9781799850779) • US $295.00

Handbook of Research on Technology Applications for Effective Customer Engagement
Norazah Mohd Suki (Universiti Utara Malaysia, Malaysia)
Business Science Reference • © 2021 • 391pp • H/C (ISBN: 9781799847724) • US $295.00

New Techniques for Brand Management in the Healthcare Sector
Ana Pinto Borges (ISAG - European Business School and Research Group of ISAG (NIDISAG), Portugal) and Paula Rodrigues (Lusíada University of Porto, Portugal)
Business Science Reference • © 2021 • 300pp • H/C (ISBN: 9781799830344) • US $225.00

Leveraging Consumer Behavior and Psychology in the Digital Economy
Norazah Mohd Suki (Universiti Malaysia Sabah, Malaysia) and Norbayah Mohd Suki (Universiti Utara Malaysia, Malaysia)
Business Science Reference • © 2020 • 299pp • H/C (ISBN: 9781799830429) • US $195.00

Analyzing the Strategic Role of Neuromarketing and Consumer Neuroscience
Dincer Atli (Uskudar University, Turkey)
Business Science Reference • © 2020 • 304pp • H/C (ISBN: 9781799831266) • US $225.00

Managing Customer Experiences in an Omnichannel World
Taşkın Dirsehan (Marmara University, Turkey)
Business Science Reference • © 2020 • 300pp • H/C (ISBN: 9781799850069) • US $195.00

IGI Global
PUBLISHER of TIMELY KNOWLEDGE

701 East Chocolate Avenue, Hershey, PA 17033, USA
Tel: 717-533-8845 x100 • Fax: 717-533-8661
E-Mail: cust@igi-global.com • www.igi-global.com

Table of Contents

Detailed Table of Contents

Festivals have become one of the most popular types of events. Many factors need to be brought together for the festivals so that people can get rid of the stress of daily life and have different, life-enriching experiences. These factors, which are brought together in the planning and organization stages of the festivals can be considered as key success factors. Although the research shows different results regarding the festival success factors, the most important factors are cited as the festival program, the festival area, accessibility, information, employees and volunteers, souvenirs, convenience, food, and security. In addition to these factors, the festivals organized in recent years have benefited from many technological applications which have increased the participants' experiences. Robots, internet of things (IoT), virtual reality (VR), augmented reality (AR), artificial intelligence (AI), and self-service technology applications may be among the key factors that will play a role in the success of future festivals.

In the globalizing world, the use of social media as a marketing tool has been frequently discussed in academic researchers in recent years. It is possible to examine that the usage of these social media channels in the management and marketing of tourism-related activities is increasing. From this perspective, social media is considered as an important marketing tool for event organizers in the event industry in terms of some aspect of event studies. Besides, it provides significant benefits for visitors about deciding whether they participate in an event or not. In this framework, the aim of this chapter is to build a conceptual framework for revealing relation between social media and events. This conceptual study indicated that social media is one of the important digital tools for customer engagement, online experiences, and promoting events. Managerial implications and future research recommendation presented.

Electronic human resources management is the use of information technologies for human resources applications that enable easy interaction between employees and employers. Therefore, through electronic human resources management, information about recruitment, performance management, strategic orientation, and education is provided. Competitive business environments have made institutions and organizations to take into account innovations and superiorities to survive. In this context, one of the biggest obstacles that the human resources department has to overcome is the rapidly changing technological environment. The possibilities of technology for human resources management are infinite. In principle, all human resources processes are supported by technology. One of the areas where communication and information technology can be used effectively is events. This chapter describes how communication and information technology can be used effectively when planning and managing human resources in event organizations.

Digitalization has affected many areas as well as management and marketing areas. In the digital age, through ICTs, the ways of searching and accessing information about the event by the users have been developed and transformed. Besides, the developments in the digital age have also affected many sectors such as the production, design, software, management, and marketing sector. The opportunities offered by digital marketing make life easier for users and provide easy access to information. Likewise, businesses can facilitate their management and marketing events through digitalization. Businesses sustain their events by organizing and diversifying new events according to the customer base and the type of event for the management and marketing of events. ICT tools have spread to all functions and events of the tourism industry in terms of business, marketing, and management. In this chapter, which mentioned the opportunity and challenges of ICTs, the opportunities and challenges posed by ICT are also mentioned.

The development of information communication technologies and the increase in use have made it utilized as a tool for cultural and artistic production. Digital art, where technology and art coexist, has created a free working space for the artist. Digital art is a contemporary type of art that includes many different art methods such as sound art, computer graphics, virtual art, internet art, robotics, video, interactive art, computer animation, and it distinguishes itself from the old visual arts. The cities that have come to the fore with art in the world become the tourist attraction centers. In this context, tourist attraction centers can be created by developing digital art. The development of digital art and the increase in the number of artists interested in this art have led to the emergence of tourist attraction centers. In this chapter, digital art events and digital art museums are determined. And finally, digital art events and museum examples are given where digital art is an attraction.

Globally, the number of the internet and social media users is increasing day by day. The event industry has been affected by that popularity of social media and so event management and event marketing activities have changed radically. In this research, the importance of the social media in the events, management of the event, and finding how to take advantage of the social media by the marketing of the event are explored. Using of the social media in events was examined in these three parts: before, during, and after the events. Today it is regarded as an important tool used by the event managers of social media platforms and so social media has become an indispensable part of the events.

Event marketing has become an increasingly important role as a marketing tool for marketers. Nowadays, the ability of event marketing to provide deeper consumer participation with new, creative, unique, tailored, interactive, and compelling events attracts great interest among marketers. The enormous impact of digital development on our daily lives is now more important than ever. Digital technology, from a facial recognition app for easy recording to creating an event app or using virtual reality for realistic demonstrations, can help deliver a superior experience to participants. As key technological practices matured, a number of important trends and developments in event marketing emerged. The event industry enriches the experiences of the participants by using technological applications and creates new applications. All these activities that are vital to a successful event are an important part of the marketing function because event marketing strategy and planning is a whole with general event planning.

Digital technologies, such as virtual reality (VR), will have an increasing influence on the way events are experienced and managed. To date, scholarship has focused predominantly on the possibilities that VR presents for event experiences by event attendees, and there has been limited consideration of the application of VR for event planning and management. In this chapter, the authors provide a brief overview of the growth and application of virtual reality technology in events. A case study of a private sector start-up in the Australian setting is examined with a focus on VR technologies, it is developing as an aid in event planning and logistics. Key opportunities and challenges of VR pertinent to event planning and management are identified, and the authors suggest a number of implications for industry practice and event education, alongside avenues for future research to support the development of VR in event management and education.

The current use of artificial intelligence technology in the event industry, its effects on the industry, and future trends are discussed within the scope of this section. The use of artificial intelligence technology that provided by big data draws attention. In the event industry, it is known that robotic applications (telepresence robots, robotic concierge, robot bartenders, robot peacekeepers, robot servers, robot deliveries, and entertainment robots), digital assistants, and chatbots are used within the scope of artificial intelligence technology. It has been determined that artificial intelligence technology offers the stakeholders opportunities to gain competitive advantage, to obtain information that can be used in marketing efforts, to enable digitalization in manual processes, to improve customer interactions, to increase event participation with lower costs, and to create added value with new products and services. It is predicted that this progress will continue in the future and the use of artificial intelligence technology in the event industry will expand.

Today, with digital marketing communication, it has become easier to reach and persuade both existing and potential customers. The aforementioned situation is also valid for event applications which are one of the digital marketing communication tools. Indeed, with the technological power, brands began to offer participants almost unlimited options for events and participation takes place regardless of the venue. This study aims to provide information about the new event trends as a digital marketing communication tool. For this purpose, a literature review was made in the study. Accordingly, it can be argued that the new event trends used in digital marketing communications consist of real-time events, social events, storytelling, virtual reality and augmented reality applications, influencers, and virtual communities.

Industry 4.0 plays a role in meeting the demands of the global market in food and beverage activities with more efficient, harmonious, reliable, and sustainable production processes. In the recent years, enterprises have started taking advantage of augmented reality technology in the design phase; three-dimensional printers, internet of things technology and robot chefs during the production phase; and robot waiters in the presentation phase. In this context, in this chapter, the transformations experienced in the design, production, and presentation processes of banquet organizations as the result of the Gastronomy 4.0 concept, which emerged as a result of the reflections of Industry 4.0 on the field of gastronomy, were examined. It is thought that in the near future, if the prevalence of Gastronomy 4.0 applications increases, the personnel responsible for running banquet organizations will need to be trained and also informed about the equipment of the new age.

Preface

The first decade of the twenty-first century and in all corners of the world, there has been same interest and participation in events as they play a significant role in the development of culture, arts, education and tourism (Bowdin et al., 2011). In the history, events always played an important role in society, either to get out of the routine of daily life, or to celebrate some important things or persons (Shone & Parry, 2010). Events have long played an important part in everyday life of people and societies. The term event is used for describing different activities designed for different purposes. These activities can be art, sports, recreation and social activities, and can also be activities organized by giant organizers at a more professional and national or international level. According to Getz & Goldblatt, events are unique moments in time and aside from everyday occurrences (Berridge, 2007). Nowadays, the ability of event marketing to provide deeper consumer participation with new, interactive and interesting events attracts great interest among event planners (Close et al., 2006).

The events industry, including festivals, meetings, conferences, exhibitions, carnavals, sports and a range of other events, is rapidly developing and gains a significant contribution to business and recreation related tourism. O'Toole & Mikolaitis (2002) identify that, as growth in the demand for events has occurred and the events themselves have become increasingly complex, the event organizations have become also increasingly professional (Daniel, Bogdan & Daniel, 2012: 5410). Event marketing is a group of activities aimed at high level of participation. The events include the target group, company and products, as well as giving the target group an experience that appeals to be memorable (Martensen & Grønholdt, 2008). The impact of technology can be clearly seen in our daily life and all the facets of businesses and event organizations. Technological innovations have changed equipment, made them more sophisticated and impactful, and have led the way to develop and present better and memorable events (Flowers, & Gregson, 2012). There has been huge advances in technology and were applied to more business functions with the inclusion of Information & Communications Technology (ICTs) recently. All these technological developments with the growth of government and corporate involvement in events also affect the event industry. Information & Communication Technology is now offering advanced, fast and reliable communication possibilities all over the globe. Events industry has adopted itself to these changes as powerful tools to improve its services and products rapidly, and has attracted considerable attention which has caused it to be largely expanded. The newly emerged communication tools and media have made it possible for event planners to engage easily with their customers on network or the other way around. More interestingly, the use of social media, email, mobile, and other platforms enable the messages to be better delivered throughout the duration of the event (Mahdzar, Muhammaddin & Zulkepli, 2017).

While Information and Communication Technologies create a difference for event planners around the world, it is important to consider how it changes the event industry. Events become some of the top priority businesses for marketers. There is a continuously increasing demand and supply of events. They help to generate new businesses at destinations, create new jobs and help improve the image of destinations. Some of the most successful festivals and carnivals, for example, are the most important business activities such as Venice, in Italy, Sturgise in United States and Rion Carnival in Brazil. Like any other sector, technology is altering the way event marketers/organizers do, develop and present business. For example, event organizers are now able to capture data from preferences of interest in various sessions at a congress and develop products and services accordingly. Successful event management needs distinct sets of activities from each other and needs different skills to develop, plan, structure and run an event, what are widely regarded as the functions of management. Efficient management of large crowded events has been always a challenging situation. Successful management of such events largely depends on the effective use of technologies (Yamin et. al., 2008). The advances in technology, communication technology, the linking of information and the internet (Goldblatt, 2008) along with other innovations, have affected the marketing of events and created a global opportunity to enter new markets (Bowdin et al., 2011; Getz, 2012). There are many business cases where the use of latest technology can vastly improve their management. In recent times, many types of artificial and sensor devices, including RFID tags, have been developed and effectively used in event environments. Such technologies, combined with appropriate systems, can be used to improve the crowds and flow of event at every step (Yamin, et. al., 2008). It is important that event developers employ advance technology to gather insights, use this information to improve customer experience, and monitor and track results. In order to achieve this end, businesses need a detailed digital strategy that covers all aspects of the event (Regalix, 2019). As a result, Sherlock & O'Connor (2014) state that the positive impacts of effective utilization of technology in event business is the growth, development and feasibility of events.

Particular attention is given in the book to the concept of ICT evaluation and examination in the context of events. Such an effective utilization offers the event participants a more personalized experience and an increase in practitioners' level of professionalization. This book presents deep and broad information on ICT technologies used at events and also incorporates the most up-to-date thinking in event marketing. All the book chapters examine the issues of new technological subjects on the event sector. Some book chapters include best practices in event. The chapters in the book lead the reader gently through the new technological applications and practices. This book provides for practitioner both conceptual underpinnings of this field and the practical requirements for selling and ensuring the future success of events. The broad approach of this book makes it useful to academic researchers, students, and practitioners and all those with an interest in the field of event marketing.

EMERGING TECHNOLOGICAL TOOLS IN EVENT MARKETING

Knowing event technology trends and adopting the most valuable and effective ones to run various types of events successfully gives planners and developers new approaches and venues for a competitive advantage over their rivals. Technology makes more versatile applications to appeal to all kind of event consumers. Meetings become more interesting with various applications, concerts are more exciting with holographic presentations of past stars such as Michael Jackson or Elvis Presley, and weddings are more memorable with live broadcasting all over the world for family members and friends. The technology also can improve organized events, attract more customers and allows automation at a certain access points. Apps help event planners create a customized visitor experience. The event companies are changing their mindset for transforming themselves to suit and appeal the consumers with new event technology. Companies are using technology to stay closer to their customers, using social media to create awareness and using websites to share information and improve and grow collaboration among partners and stakeholders (Kang, Tang & Fiore, 2014). Due to the rapid growth, development and competition surrounding of many events (Goldblatt, 2008) technological applications are being widely used throughout all the phases of event management (Sherlock & O'Connor, 2014).

ON the other hand, technology is constantly evolving. Digital transformation using digital technology to automate standard processes is an essential and viable trend in every phase of our daily life and life of all businesses. Technology is not only transforming the way we do business but also helping people to lead more comfortable lifes with more affordable gadgets and applications. With technology becoming increasingly dominant in society and in the events industry, the shape and procedures have changed due to the innovations and developments in event technologies (Bizzabo, 2019). The role of technology in the events industry is becoming increasingly important with the dominance of technology. Technology in recent years has gained a dominant role in developing and planning events (Peacock, 1995) and had a major part to play in the growth, development and feasibility of many events (Goldblatt, 2008). Utilizing technology in the events industry means more professional planning, more reliable and flexible execution, new products, services and offerings for every needs and expectations of costumers and superior transport along with the benefit of globalization (Krugman & Wright, 2007). Recent development in technology has been incomparably astonishing, cutting across all area of human lifestyle. It ranges from series of events like technology meetings and trade shows to techno shows where robots, artificial intelligence and new equipments meets the every expectation of attendees. And many of these event trends keep exhibiting new innovations (Hindman, 2018).

Event organizers are now attempting to adapt their style and methods, in order to embrace the new era where digitalization, artificial intelligence and virtual reality will become the ruler of the industry. Advanced technology is on the way of improved visualization and application, as well as speedy and seamless accessibility for better customer experience. The CEO of Mbooked organizations, Michnowski express that one of the most important trends for 2020 that event planners need to watch out for using of social media for communications, event promotion, and community building (Michnowski, 2019). Technology allows event developers and organizers for automation of various elements of planning and managing events whilst it presents both opportunities and challenges for the events industry. As event technology continues to develop and be refined, it becomes easier to implement whatever the customers wants and expects, even exceeds their expectations in various instances and make accessibility to events all over the world better than ever. The latest event technology trends are Virtual Reality, Artificial Intelligence, 5G Technology, Chat Bots, Internet of Things, Big Data, and Augmented Reality are changing and will continue to change the shape, structure and rivalry in the event industry. New marketing platforms and technological innovations create comprehensive experiences around events by using social media and digital communities. With easy access to data and technology, human will also witness a shift in versatility of events instead of uniform products and services to highly personalized events.

ORGANIZATION OF THE BOOK

This book is a combination of concepts and practices related to management and marketing of events in regard to ICTs and consists of 16 chapters in total. The organization of the book follows a general to specific approach to event management and marketing, and technology process. A brief description of each of the chapters follows:

Chapter 1 reviews the factors which can affect the success of events activities in the context of ICT. The authors of this chapter provide a roadmap to the target audience for the success of future events. They stress the fact that technological applications that may be among the key factors in future festivals.

Chapter 2 presents a deep view between social media and events based on literature and build a conceptual framework of this relationship. The author elaborates the integration of social media and new event practices with studies and research reports in the field.

Chapter 3 examines marketing innovations in industry 4.0 and their impacts on events marketing. The chapter identifies the effects of the development process and components of the Industry 4.0 concept on event marketing. It explains marketing innovations in the Industry 4.0 perspective and evaluates event marketing to meet the expectations of the target groups.

Chapter 4 evaluates the new emerging technologies from the event industry perspective and contains conceptual approach. To provide information, existing literature and related websites have been reviewed. Some of the main applications frequently used in events are expressed with examples.

Chapter 5 presents the concept of digital marketing and the digital marketing methods are discussed in the first part of the study. The chapter also is described and digital marketing applications in event tourism and also goes into great detail on how ICT can play a role in effective marketing activities for events.

Chapter 6 describes the importance of ICT in human resources management and evaluation in terms of event. Chapter addresses the issue of how organizations will perform the functions of selection and recruitment, job analysis, education, compensation, planning, and motivation of volunteer employees, performance evaluation and occupational health and safety, which must be carried out in order to manage the human resource at events.

Chapter 7 presents a broad overview of the opportunities and challenges of event marketing in the digital era. It states the effect of digitalization on event marketing. It also focuses mainly on the opportunities and challenges created by ICTs and ICT in the tourism industry.

Chapter 8 which examines organized events within the framework of art activities offers a new perspective on digital art and digital museums. The author argues that development of digital art has led to the emergence of tourist attraction centers.

Chapter 9 describes the relationship between the social media and event. Suggestions are provided for event planner about keep the participants' interest alive by establishing uninterrupted two-way communication during the event and use social media to ensure that the effect lasts longer when the event is over, to reach potential participants in the future and to make strategic evaluations about the event.

Chapter 10 provides a general perspective of event marketing and new event trends the author examines some advantages of event marketing. They also covered in details the new challenges and new opportunities in event marketing.

Chapter 11 presents at the roles of virtual reality (VR) in order to create a quality event planning and management and it provides the underpinning implications for event practitioners about VR. The chapter ends with three main implications for event practitioners, including improving event management work, enhancing event volunteer performance and experience and acquiring VR competencies.

Chapter 12 is concerned with artificial intelligence applications for event management and marketing. The author explains the artificial intelligence applications used in the event industry and the contribution of these applications to the event stakeholders.

Chapter 13 covers the new event trends in the context of communication digital marketing communication. It highlights the new event trends used in digital marketing communications such as real-time events, social events, storytelling, virtual reality and augmented reality applications, influencers and virtual communities.

Chapter 14 brings a new perspective and evaluates the applicability of industry 4.0 at events organized in the context of gastronomy. The authors focused on the emphasis on new technology in banquet organizations. The author examines augmented reality in restaurant menus.

Chapter 15 is concerned with importance of social media in terms of the effective and efficient marketing of events. In addition, the section discusses why social media has become so important for today. Conclusions have been made about the future of the social media and events industry.

Chapter 16 is concerned with effective using of website in large-scale event with an example and provides a general perspective of properties of the event websites and express that what benefits will website offer to event users. The author of this chapter contends that large-scale mega events are more easily noticed by the participants through the effectiveness of web marketing. The effectiveness of web marketing in the perspectives of the participants of the event becomes an important element and positively affects the preferences of the visitors.

Kemal Birdir
Mersin University, Turkey

Sevda Birdir
Mersin University, Turkey

Ali Dalgıç
Isparta University of Applied Sciences, Turkey

Derya Toksöz
Mersin University, Turkey

REFERENCES

Berridge, G. (2007). *Events Design and Experience, Events Management Series* (1st ed.). Elsevier. doi:10.4324/9780080468112

Bizzabo. (2019). *Event Marketing 2019. Benchmarks and Trends Report*. Retrieved from https://welcome.bizzabo.com/hubfs/White-Papers-and-Ebooks/Event-Marketing-2019.pdf. 12.10.2020.

Bowdin, G., Allen, J., O'Toole, W., Harris, R., & McDonnell, I. (2011). *Events Management* (3rd ed.). Butterworth-Heinemann.

Close, A. G., Finney, R. Z., Lacey, R. Z., & Sneath, J. Z. (2006). Engaging the consumer through event marketing: Linking attendees with the sponsor, community, and brand. *Journal of Advertising Research, 46*(4), 420–433. doi:10.2501/S0021849906060430

Daniel, M., Bogdan, G., & Daniel, Z. (2012). The use of event marketing management strategies. *Procedia: Social and Behavioral Sciences, 46*, 5409–5413. doi:10.1016/j.sbspro.2012.06.448

Flowers, A. A., & Gregson, K. (2012). Decision-making factors in selecting virtual worlds for events: Advocacy, computer efficacy, perceived risks, and collaborative benefits. *Event Management, 16*(4), 319–334. doi:10.3727/152599512X13539583375054

Getz, D. (2012). Event studies: Discourses and future directions. *Event Management, 16*(2), 171–187. doi:10.3727/152599512X13343565268456

Goldblatt, J. (2008). *Special Events: A New Generation and the Next Frontier*. John Wiley & Sons.

Hindman, B. (2018). The event marketing evolution an era of data, technology, and revenue impact. *Harvard Business Review Analytic Services Research Report/Splash*. Retrieved from https://hbr.org/sponsored/2018/09/the-event-marketing-evolution

Kang, J., Tang, L., & Fiore, A. M. (2014). Enhancing consumer—brand relationships on restaurant Facebook fan pages: Maximizing consumer benefits and increasing active participation. *International Journal of Hospitality Management, 36*, 145–155. doi:10.1016/j.ijhm.2013.08.015

Krugman, C., & Wright, R. (2007). *Global meetings and exhibitions*. John Wiley & Sons.

Law, R. (2005). *Technology strategies for the hospitality industry*. Taylor& Francis. doi:10.1080/10941660500136033

Mahdzar, M., Muhammaddin, M. H., & Zulkepli, Z. Z. Z. (2017). Does Technology Affect Event Management in Malaysia? A Case Study of Stair Climb Sporting Race. *e-Academia Journal, 6*(2), 241-249.

Martensen, A., & Grønholdt, L. (2008). How events work: Understanding consumer responses to event marketing. *Innovative Marketing*, *4*(4), 44–56.

Michnowski, N. (2019). *The Biggest Trends in Event Technology for 2020 Per 10 Top Events Experts.* Retrieved from https://www.g2planet.com/blog/the-biggest-trends-in-event-technology-for-2020-per-10-top-events-experts

O'Toole, W., & Mikolaitis, P. (2002). *Corporate Event Project Management*. Wiley.

Peacock, M. (1995). *Information technology in the hospitality industry: managing people, change and computers*. Cassell.

Regalix. (2019). *The CMO Guide Event Marketing*. Retrieved from https://www.regalix.com/insights/the-cmo-guide-event-marketing-2019/

Sherlock, J., & O'Connor, N. (2014). Research into the Impact of Technology in the Events Industry. *International Hospitality and Tourism Student Journal, 7*(1), 88–102.

Shone, A., & Parry, B. (2010). *Successful event management: a practical handbook* (3rd ed.). Cengage Learning EMEA.

Yamin, M., Mohammadian, M., Huang, X., & Sharma, D. (2008). RFID Technology and Crowded Event Management. In M. Mohammadian (Ed.), *International Conference on Computational Intelligence for Modeling, Control and Automation*, (pp. 1293-1298). IEEE, Institute of Electrical and Electronics Engineers.

Chapter 1
Which Key Factors Will Be Effective in the Success of Festivals?
An Evaluation in the Context of Information and Communication Technology

Ali Dalgic
Isparta University of Applied Sciences, Turkey

Kemal Birdir
https://orcid.org/0000-0003-1353-3618
Mersin University, Turkey

ABSTRACT

Festivals have become one of the most popular types of events. Many factors need to be brought together for the festivals so that people can get rid of the stress of daily life and have different, life-enriching experiences. These factors, which are brought together in the planning and organization stages of the festivals can be considered as key success factors. Although the research shows different results regarding the festival success factors, the most important factors are cited as the festival program, the festival area, accessibility, information, employees and volunteers, souvenirs, convenience, food, and security. In addition to these factors, the festivals organized in recent years have benefited from many technological applications which have increased the participants' experiences. Robots, internet of things (IoT), virtual reality (VR), augmented reality (AR), artificial intelligence (AI), and self-service technology applications may be among the key factors that will play a role in the success of future festivals.

DOI: 10.4018/978-1-7998-4954-4.ch001

INTRODUCTION

With the technology developing rapidly and exponentially, different technological applications are being used in different fields. There are technological applications that facilitate our life and allow us to have different experiences. They are part of our daily life, from the houses we live to the hotels we have vacation, and from the shopping malls to the events we participate to get away from the stress of daily life (Dalgıç and Birdir, 2017).Today, robots have evolved into a structure that can act autonomously and perform tasks. They can perform data while simultaneously storing data (Smart Hotel Technology Guide, 2018). "Internet of things (IoT)", which enables objects to work in coordination with each other and turns objects into smart assets, makes human life easier. IoT can be easily controlled via sensors and mobile devices and enables the use of this data in subsequent applications by helping to obtain data. Virtual reality (VR) enables individuals to have real experiences with the virtual world (Desai, Desai, Aimera and Mehta, 2014), and augmented reality (AR) enables interaction between objects by combining the virtual and real world. These two technological applications frequently take place in our daily lives (Chung, Han and Joun, 2015: 589) such as in our homes, entertainment centers, hotels, marketing activities of businesses, etc. Another technological application, artificial intelligence (AI), is an application that enables machines to work like humans by sensing, understanding and learning. Through AI, machines can interact with people and react to people (Smart Hotel Technology Guide, 2018). Finally, self-service technology meets the needs of people without involvement of any human representative and provides individual experiences (Smart Hotel Techology Guide, 2018).

These technologies are mostly used in information & communication area using their data, autonomous and data processing functions (Dalgic and Birdir, 2020).These technologies come to the fore in the context of events in recent years, and that each of them is used in event themes. The organization of the festivals with a technological theme, has been increasing in recent years. Therefore, technology will become an important key factor in offering different experiences to the participants by successfully integrating robots to the events and using technologies such as IoT (Akiyama, Murata, Tsuchiya, Yokoyama, Maggio, Ciulla, Santana, Zhao, Nascimento and Gürgen, 2017; Groenli, Flesch, Mukkamala, Vatrapu, Klavestad and Bergner, 2018), VR (Wang and Tsai, 2019), AR (Cimbaljević, Stankov, Demirović and Pavluković, 2019), AI (Yang, Henthorne and George, 2020) in the non-technological festivals. For the festivals to be held successfully, it is necessary to bring together many factors in the planning and organization stages. When the studies on key factors that make the festival successful are examined, elements such as festival program, festival area, accessibility, information, employees and volunteers, souvenirs, convenience, food, and security come to the fore (Dalgıç, 2018), but there are limited findings about technological factors. There are uncertainties about which of the technological applications are included in the festivals and which technological applications influence the experiences of participants. This chapter sheds light on the technological applications that may be among the key factors in future festivals. First, the results of the research on the key success factors of the festival will be explained to the readers. This will be followed by elaboration of technological applications in the success of the festivals with sample applications. The chapter concludes with recommendation for future research and conclusion.

BACKGROUND

Festival's Key Success Factors

In order to perform the festivals successfully and to offer unique experiences to the festival participants, some elements must be brought together in the organization and execution of the festivals. Factors such as festival program, festival area, accessibility, information, employees and volunteers, souvenirs, convenience, food, security may affect the success of the festival (Dalgıç, 2018; Dalgıç and Birdir, 2019; Dalgiç and Birdir, 2020). In addition, The factors that have an impact on the success of the festivals and the participants' experiences can be listed as follows; adequate facilities around the festival area (Getz, 1997), food and beverages quality (Saleh and Ryan, 1993), appropriate festival activities (Cole and Illum, 2006), direction signs (Lee, Petrick and Crompton, 2007), toilet facilities and car park with sufficient capacity (Taylor and Shanka, 2008), festival ambience (Wan and Chan, 2013), adequate recreation areas (Kim, 2015). These studies suggest that festival program, festival area, facilities, activities, information resources, suitability, festival staff, food, and souvenirs play key roles in the success of the festivals. Table 1 presents key success factors of the festivals.

Previous studies show that "information" or "information opportunities" are among the key success factors of the festivals. This dimension includes elements such as announcing the dates of the festivals, informing potential participants about the festival area, and giving details about the festival program. It is not clear what information and communication technologies are used in festivals other than the use of "social media". Considering the festivals organized in recent years, the internet of things, virtual reality, augmented reality, artificial intelligence and self-service software technologies and applications are becoming more popular.

MAIN FOCUS OF THE CHAPTER

A comprehensive literature review shows that previous studies do not have a clear focus on the information and communication technologies utilized in the festivals. It is well-known that social media plays a key role in promoting the festivals. It is possible that robots may show up in future festivals; especially service and dance robots are expected to take part in festivals. In addition to these, we may expect technologies and applications such as internet of things, virtual reality, augmented reality, artificial intelligence, self-service software technology to take place in festivals. The internet of things will be an indispensable technology in the participant data storage and the synchronous operation of objects in festivals. On the other hand, virtual reality and augmented reality applications will be used to give the participants experiences as if they were real, to increase their experiences of the festival, to get information about the destination and the environment where the festival is held. Likewise, self-service software technology will undoubtedly be beneficial for participants in using food and beverage services, parking and toilet services. Below each of these important technological developments will be discussed related to festival organizations and applications.

Table 1. Festival's Key Success Factors

Scholar(s)	Festival's Key Success Factors
Bitner (1992)	"Ambient conditions" (weather, temperature, air quality, noise, smell etc.), "spatial order and function" (layout of equipment and furniture), "signs", "symbols and works" (signs and decor used for communication, symbols and works that can upgrade the image and mode etc.)
Lade & Jackson (2004)	"Good planning and organization", "the area where the festivals organized", "facilities", "activities", "marketing strategies"
Leenders, Telgen, Gemser & Van der Wurff (2005)	"Content of the program", "festival venue", "ticket prices"
Cole & Illum (2006)	"Activities", "amenities", "entertainment", "theme", "socialization"
Lee, Petrick & Crompton (2007)	"Special entertainment activities", "information resources", "opportunities to relax"
Taylor & Shanka (2008)	"Facilities" (crowd control, security, services, toilet facilities, etc.), "atmosphere" (uniqueness, atmosphere, knowledge, attractions, etc.), "convenience" (location, time, park availability etc.), "gastronomy" (food and beverage variety, quality of food and beverage, etc.), "accommodation facilities" and "adequate transportation facilities"
Yuan & Jang (2008)	"Facilities" (entertainment, art, ideal space, knowledgeable employees, suitable parking spaces, etc.), "organization" (short waiting time, good food, good organization, reasonable price, etc.)
Lee, Lee, Lee & Babin (2008)	"Suitability", "information", "facilities", "employees", "program content", "souvenirs" and "food"
Morgan (2008)	"Physical organization" (accessibility of tickets, venue and time of event, sound quality, seating facilities, shopping opportunities, food and drinks, etc.), "social interaction" (with employees, local people, new and old friends, family, etc.), "design" (image and professionalism, diversity, environment, etc.), "culture" (society, region, activity itself, etc.), "personal benefits" (relaxation and entertainment, self-development, sense of accomplishment, etc.) and "symbolic areas" (authenticity, becoming a tradition, nostalgia, donation collection, etc.)
Cole & Chancellor (2009)	"Festival program", "facilities" and "entertainment"
Esu & Arrey (2009)	"Event organization and marketing", "facilities and gastronomy", "shopping opportunities"
Marais (2009)	"Quality and good management" (adequate accommodation facilities, suitable facilities, reasonable prices, sufficient parking space, etc.), "effective marketing" (website, adequate information, effective reservation etc.), "entertainment and activities" (entertainment variety, variety of activities, friendly employees etc.), "accessibility" (comfort of facilities, directions, good management of the festival, etc.), "security".
Özdemir & Çulha (2009)	"The content of the festival program", "employees", "facilities", "food and beverage", "souvenirs", "suitability" (recreation area, toilet and parking places) and "information" (information on the signs, information in the brochures, etc.)
Yoon, Lee & Lee (2010)	"Information services", "festival program", "souvenirs", "food" and "facilities"
Choi (2011)	"Festival program", "festival products", "natural environment", "suitable facilities", "information"
McDowall (2011)	"Quality / comfort" (price and quality of products, drinks and souvenirs, waste management, safety, cleaning, etc.), "activity / culture" (arts and crafts, entertainment, shows, festival duration, atmosphere and environment, sweepstakes, etc.) and "program / management" (quality of the festival program, friendliness of the local people, ticket prices, management and service etc.)
Anil (2012)	"Festival area", "food" (presence of traditional food, sufficient variety of food, good quality food, selling food at a reasonable price, etc.) and "suitability" (adequate toilets, adequate parking spaces, adequate rest areas etc.)
Manners, Kruger & Saayman (2012)	"General management", "souvenirs", "marketing activities", "space and technical features", "accessibility and park", "accommodation facilities" and "food&beverage businesses"
Mason & Paggiaro (2012)	"Food" (food quality, beverage quality, etc.), "entertainment" (entertainment, calendar of events, information, etc.) and "comfort" (safety, cleaning of toilets, availability of rest areas, etc.)
Saayman, Kruger & Erasmus (2012)	"Security and personnel", "marketing and accessibility", "venue of the event", "accommodation facilities", "activities and local people", "parks and restaurants"
Wan & Chan (2013)	"Place and accessibility of the event", "food", "facilities at the event" (enough number of places to sit, etc.), "environment and ambience" (without excessive sound and crowd etc.), "service quality"
Wu, Wong & Cheng (2014)	"Interaction quality" (interaction with employees) and "output quality" (atmosphere, entertainment, spending time with friends, etc.)
Kim (2015)	"Commercialization of the festival" (such as selling quality souvenirs, reasonable prices at the festival, having many local food), "accessibility to the festival" (clean toilets, parking lot, etc.), "interpersonal facilitators" (socializing with people, opportunity to rest, friendship with new people), "structural facilitators" (good weather, various experiential activities, local food etc.)
Kong (2015)	"Entertainment" (organized entertainment), "comfort" (security, cleaning, toilets, parking areas, etc.) and "product" (quality food-beverage, food-beverage prices, etc.)
Lee & Chang (2017)	"Festival program" and "facilities"
Dalgıç (2018)	"Program", "festival venue and accessibility", "souvenirs and convenience", "security", "food"

Robotics

The most recent robots have autonomous ability to perform tasks, and can provide a data-oriented perspective performing tasks (Smart Hotel Technology Guide, 2018). Robots are being used in almost every field, including the festivals. Robotex International Festival was held in Estonia on November, 29 - December, 1, 2019. Over 10,000 visitors from 38 different countries participated in the festival. The festival hosted robotic competitions. 2511 contestants participated in 20 different competitions. In addition, 66 workshops were held at this festival (Robotex, 2019). "York festival of ideas" is another activity where robots and artificial intelligence technologies can be discovered, offers its visitor's opportunities to meet and talk with various robots, participate in robot programming training, and learn how artificial intelligence works in an interactive game (York festival, 2019). In addition, film festivals about robots are also common. The robot film festival was held in Portland, USA in 2018. This festival covers short and normal films with a robot theme, and it is held regularly every year (Robotfilmfestival, 2019).

Besides robot-themed festivals, we can also see robots in different themed festivals. Makr Shakr is a bartender robot with a social sharing system and alcohol consumption monitor. Guests send their orders through the monitor in Makr Shakr and track their orders on this monitor. Makr Shakr can inform guests about the estimated preparation time of the beverage, the number of pending orders, how long it will take to receive the order, and what are the most popular alcoholic beverages by gender. It offers visitors unique experiences at festivals. In addition, there are robots that act as stand attendees at festivals. These robots can talk to the participants, give information about the events, and invite them to the activities via the iPad in front of them. Such intriguing activities can increase the perception of the festival experience and contribute to the perception that the festivals are successful (Sorrells, 2013). Drones bringing alcoholic drinks to the participants took part in the Oppi Koppi music festival in South Africa. Participants ordered alcoholic beverages with an application on their smartphones. The application determined the location of the participants after the order was taken and delivered the order to the participants with the help of a parachute by giving the coordinates to the drones (Sorrells, 2013). We can also see the robots that can cook and serve the food in recent years (Daly, 2010).

It is also possible to see robots in different styles, especially in music festivals. The pianist robot "Teotronica" can play many pieces of songs at the piano (Chinadaily, 2017). Robot YuMi took the stage and became famous as the conductor at the International Robotic Festival in Pisa, Italy (Ong, 2017). During the 26th International Beer Festival held in China in 2016, 1007 robots danced simultaneously and entered Guinness World Records (BBC, 2016). Similarly, 540 robots performed together in the Spring Festival held in Guangdong, China (Gilbert, 2016). In addition to the robots dancing together, robots also dance with people. Two dancers and a dance robot performed together at the Trayectos International Dance Festival in Zaragoza in 2017. They have exhibited almost flawless performance in this show (Abad, France, Castillion, Alonso, Cambra, Sierra, Riozuelo, Montano and Murillo, 2017: 85). In addition to dance robots, another type of robot we can see at festivals is player robots. These robots can offer unique experiences to festival participants by playing certain games with people. A robot capable of playing "Jenga" was produced in early 2019 (Petkov, 2019). In recent years, robots are also frequently used in the field of security. It is possible to see the security robots in hotels, car parks and restaurants at festivals. These robots are constantly collecting data using face recognition systems, cameras and recording systems; therefore, they will help the authorities to instantly deliver any negative events to the authorities (Vincent, 2019).

Internet of Things (IoT)

IoT is a technology that connects objects and allows data exchange. It can be described as interconnections that enable devices such as sensors, identification tags, mobile devices to work effectively with other objects directly or indirectly (Kansakar, Munir and Shabani, 2017: 1). The information and data acquired by smart objects plays a key role in shaping up the experiences of the individuals. It is now possible to see this technology at homes, in workplaces, hotels or even parking lots or festivals. It may emerge as a key factor that affects success and experience in the following years. Wristbands/sensors provide faster and smoother access to the festivals, enable contactless payments and they can be supported by applications such as navigation (for food delivery or emergency services) or real-time crowd heatmaps. (İq-mag, 2016). IoT was used at Dubai Shopping Festival in 2018. Visitors passing by the shops received personalized digital promotions to their phones. Through the smart mirrors in the changing cabinets, individuals demanded other sizes of the clothes without leaving the changing cabin. Visitors were able to express their opinions and suggestions about the store and staff through the application on their mobile phones (Illum, 2018).

40,000 people attended the Music Festival held in Ontario, Canada in 2016. During the 3-day festival, most of the participants camped. IoT was used to help the participants pay their tickets through Ipad and they got little bracelets. After the login process, mails detailing all kinds of transactions started to drop into the mailbox. These small bracelets also presented a huge amount of data to festival organizers. They stored information such as how much beer was consumed or how many bottles of water will be needed next year. For 3 days, the participants took part in a large joint network via a tiny sensor on each person's wrist (Powell, 2016). In the Tomorrowland festival, social networking sites, blogs, video sharing sites and forums were used to allow participants to have a better experience. In addition, IoT technology was used to collect and analyze data to create a comprehensive "map" of what was happening at the event. Through IoT, a safe, smooth and experience-enhancing festival was held for the participants. With the data obtained, potential problems were solved beforehand. The CityMind 6.5 platform played an important role in creating a fun and safe environment. Thanks to CityMind 6.5, real-time maps were created by analyzing the bracelets and participants' social media shares, and more police teams and security personnel were directed to crowded areas (Weijman, 2014). In 2012 Scarecrow festival, digital scarecrow was designed, taking into account the drawings and models produced by children in the design workshop. Since most of the children's designs have a robot, ScareBot, which is 2.5 m long and weighted red-yellow colors, was shaped. ScareBot has "a wide range of technologies including an android tablet, a Raspberry Pi, an Arduino and LED lighting". ScareBot has a system that begins to interact with the festival participants sending messages and sends back a thank you message, including the current date, time and weather. ScareBot has a system where you can make various sounds as well as place your own face on the robot using the webcam on its arm. It is a fun IoT design that enhances the experience of visitors (Coulton, 2015: 166).

Festival participants can easily enter the event using IoT. In addition, it plays a guiding role for them to receive information with wearable devices and transfer data to the organizers for the next events. It can also provide insightful data during the event by creating heat maps for organizers. Heat maps can increase security. Finally, festival participants can have an active role in engaging with the festival through IoT-enabled devices. According to participants, IoT can be useful in mobilising the cars and organising the car park spaces (Saxena, 2016; Parker, 2018).

Virtual Reality (VR) and Augmented Reality (AR)

VR is "a technology that enables individuals to have real experiences with the virtual world in the computer environment" (Desai, Desai, Aimera and Mehta, 2014). AR is "a technology where the interaction between two types of objects is created by combining the virtual and real world". As a result of the integration of the objects created in the computer environment into the real world, it is possible to synthesize the real image and the virtual image (Chung, Han and Joun, 2015: 589). Both technologies have been used in festivals in recent years. For instance, you can take photos in front of or next to the icons of destinations with AR technology and immortalize this moment. You can appear and take photos in any destination you want to visit as if you were there. In addition to the destination application, it may be possible to have a photo side by side with any celebrity (basketball player, singer, etc.) (Eventsforce, 2016a).

One of the world's most beloved music festivals, "Tomorrowland" in Belgium offers technological innovations. It allows automate payments with wearable wristbands and interaction with other participants with the Tomorrowland app. At the same time, it offers unique experiences to those who participate in the festival with VR / AR (Medium, 2018). With VR technology, the opportunity to reach people with disabilities or people who cannot physically participate in an event can be provided (Eventsforce, 2016b). "Mutek", a technological music festival and held in Argentina combines digital music production and digital visual art. Participants maximize their experience and play games in a VR hall provided for them (Medium, 2018).

AR and VR were used at the Sundance film festival. Using AR and VR technologies, "holo-cinema" was presented to the participants. With the "holo-cinema", the participants can see the movie characters in different parts of the hall using smart glasses and experience as if they were in the movie. With the "holo-cinema" which will be developed further in the coming years, the participants will be presented with some portals and the opportunity to go to different areas within the film (Experenti, 2016). During the Scarecrow festival, visitors were given the opportunity to go to past festivals. Visitors experienced the present festivals and past festivals in an entertaining way through their mobile phones and tablets (Coulton, 2015: 166).

In general, VR and AR can offer many advantages. Before the organization, the event area can be evaluated by the organizers. Thus, organizers can save time and money without traveling physically. VR and AR can offer new experiences to the participants; therefore, they can attract people to the event. These practices can increase the number of new potential participants as participants exchange their different experiences after the event. In addition to these, such practices may offer remote participation opportunities for people with disabilities or those who have difficulty participating in the event. Finally, VR and AR applications can provide a gaming experience for festival participants and they can have a good time (Billetto, 2020; Morozova, 2020).

Artificial Intelligence (AI)

AI enables machines to perceive, understand and learn, work and react like humans (Smart Hotel Techology Guide, 2018). It provides machines with cognitive functions, enabling them to perform assigned tasks. AI can be a theme for festivals as well as a technology used in festivals. AI festival was held in India between 20-23 March 2019 for AI enthusiasts to showcase their projects to experts. This international event is a good opportunity for participants to achieve their goals and dreams, and to achieve personal development. Some musicians used AI to perform in the Sónar Festival held in Barcelona in 2019. Musicians incorporated computers into their own performances thanks to machine learning and increased the effect of their live performances by creating humanoid choirs in computer environment (Wired, 2019). Arts Electronica Festival was held in Linz, Austria, on 7-11 September 2017. During this festival, the current state of artificial intelligence was discovered by the participants. The participants lost themselves in a digital universe at the intersection of science and art. And social and cultural phenomenon were analyzed with the latest technological changes. Symposiums, exhibitions and shows related to AI were held. These symposiums focused on the growing integration of neural networks and the theoretical applications of machine learning. During the festival, the complex analysis of the paintings was performed with artificial intelligence and presented to the participants (ArtJaws, 2017).

In general, the use of artificial intelligence will provide many benefits for festival organizers and participants. Artificial intelligence can give information about participants and can store the information obtained during the festival for organizers to review. It contributes to security measures by means of face recognition devices created by the festival organizers at the entrance of the event. In addition to these, festival organizers can hire less staff by using artificial intelligence, therefore they can reduce costs and create new experience opportunities (Wilson, 2019). According to festival participants' opinions, it is possible to get information about the event program and get solutions to the problems encountered through Chatbots which works with artificial intelligence. In addition, artificial intelligence can help festival participants to have joint experience in activities by meeting with each other who share common interests (Wilson, 2019; Ideausher, 2020). Finally, artificial intelligence can also play an active role in overcoming the language barrier between participants (Ideausher, 2020).

Self-Service Technology

Self-service technology offers technological products and software that enable people to meet some of their needs without the support of a service representative. These products, which are mostly found in the form of kiosks, are technologies that ease people's lives (Smart Hotel Techology Guide, 2018). These technologies can be seen in all areas of life and they are one of the key factors in festivals. One of the most common self-service machines are ATMs (Automatic Telling Machines). It is important to have ATMs in the festival areas to ensure the continuity of participants' experiences (Lamasatech, 2019). Ticket purchases can be made using mobile technologies. Kiosks are important solution tools to ensure ticket validation and prevent the long queues at the entrances. Participants can scan the barcodes of the tickets, or they can check-in by buying tickets from kiosks (Eventbride, 2019). Another technology to be used in festivals is the self-ordering. With this technology, festival participants can purchase their food without waiting in a queue and place their orders without leaving the activity and event area. A further solution is to position food & beverage vending machines to the activity areas. Thus, participants can meet their eating and drinking needs without missing the events (Carreirão, 2019).

In general, use of self-service technology has many advantages for festival organizers and participants. Registration and digital payments (cash, credit card, gift points, etc.) can be made for event tickets at the kiosks in entrance of the festival area. In addition, kiosks may reduce the queues and waiting times by making the entrance to the festival area faster. Also, self-service technology provides easy information transfer about the schedule and event details. Self-service technologies, which can meet consumers' expectations such as new experience, convenience and fast transactions, also allow them to participate in the survey or give feedback while leaving the event (Myers, 2020). It obtains data for the organizers.

Finally, it can reduce organizational costs and provide an advantage in terms of sustainability (using less paper, improving carbon footprint, etc.) (Aventri, 2020).

SOLUTIONS AND RECOMMENDATIONS

Developing technology facilitates the human lives in every arena. In terms of festivals, different experiences can be offered to the participants with new technological applications. When factors affecting the success of festival are considered, festival program, festival area, accessibility, information, employees and volunteers, souvenirs, convenience, food and security are some of the most important factors cited in the literature. The relevant literature suggest that technological applications are not considered among the success factors. However, there is no clarity about which technological application will be the leading factors in the success of the festivals. When we analyze the festivals, we can argue that robots, IoT, VR, AR, AI and self-service technology applications may be among the factors that will affect the festivals' success in the future. Paying attention to and integrating the following technological applications may increase the experience of participants and create a perception that the festival is carried out successfully.

- Using robots which can cook and serve food, and work as bartenders at food and beverage stands can prevent long queues and time loss. This usage of robots can offer a different and unique experience to the participants.
- Organisers who want to offer different experiences, especially in music festivals, can use dance robots. The recent technology makes it possible to see robots that can dance in coordination with each other or even with people. They will offer different experiences to the participants in future festivals.
- Security is one of the most important factors affecting success in festivals. Robots, which have been frequently encountered in the field of security can be effective solution to ensure the safety of festival participants. The robots' data collection features, facial recognition system and camera recording capabilities can be of great help for the organisers.
- IoT will be used frequently by festival organizers in the coming years because it is a technological application that allows coordinated work by connecting objects, collecting data and enabling objects to work in the light of this data. IoT can be used by participants to pay cashless at the entrance of the festival and to pass the entrance without waiting in long lines with wristbands and sensors.
- Real-time crowd heatmaps can be created with IoT. This can increase security in crowded areas and decrease the problems that the participants may experience. In addition, since IoT can collect data through sensors and wristbands, it will assist the organizers during the planning and organizing stages for the next festival.
- Different activities can be offered to the participants through VR and AR technology. With AR technology, participants can receive information using their smartphones or tablets, and can participate in activities without losing time. In addition, the opportunity for individuals with physical disabilities to participate in the festival from their homes is also possible using these technologies.
- With AI technology, it is possible for machines to learn and serve like people. In recent years, especially in music festivals, we saw machines that accompany the artists' performances and produce new music. This is important in terms of attracting potential participants to the festivals.

- Self-service technology can enable festival participants to print their tickets at the entrance, verify their tickets, withdraw money, and provide food and beverage services without any human involvement. These services can improve the experiences of festival participants and ease their participation in different activities.

FUTURE RESEARCH DIRECTIONS

Festivals can be expected to be successful to the extent that they offer unique experience to the participants. In this context, some elements need to be brought together in the process from the creation of festivals to the completion of the organization. However, the current literature shows that the technological applications are not included in the factors that play critical role in the success of the festivals. Factors such as "festival program", "festival area", "accessibility", "information", "employees and volunteers", "souvenirs", "convenience", "food", and "security" are among the most cited success factors for festivals. However, an important amount of technological applications are used in the festivals organised over the couple of years. It is important to investigate which technological applications affect success of a festival in the studies to be conducted. Moreover, it is significant to investigate how IoT, VR, AR, AI and self-service technology applications can take part in a festival and study successful applications. Finally, the festival participants' satisfaction with the technological applications and their opinions about these technological applications may be another research topic. Understanding the experiences of the participants can help organizers to create applications that increase satisfaction of the participants.

CONCLUSION

We can claim that future festivals will include more use of robots and these applications can be major success factors increasing satisfaction of the participants. The festivals (such as Robotex international festival, York festival of ideas) using robot technology as the theme of the festival has potential to be more successful and participants can follow the developments and increase their knowledge. In different themed festivals, it is possible to see bartender robots (Sorrells, 2013), service robots (Daly, 2010), dance robots (BBC, 2016; Gilbert, 2016), pianist robots (Chinadaily, 2017), orchestra conductor robots (Ong, 2017), robots that can play games (Petkov, A. 2019) or play an active role in security (Vincent, 2019).The active role of robots in festivals will provide great advantages for both organizers and participants. The robots will be among the important factors affecting the success of the festivals in the following years.

Apart from robots, IoT technology is often used in our daily lives and at festivals. This technology, which provides fast transition at the entrance to festival participants and allows cashless payments, enables different experiences even at the very early stages of the festivals. In addition to this, IoT can also offer navigation features and greatly easies the jobs of organizers in times of crowd for security control purposes with real-time heat maps (Iq-mag, 2016). The data to be obtained through IoT can play a key role in the success of the festivals and sheds lights on the preparations for the next festivals (Powell, 2016). This creates a great opportunity for both organizers and participants. In addition, AI, which has been used frequently in music festivals in recent years, creates opportunities via enabling artists to offer unique experiences to their audiences. Moreover, it can be used in the creation of choirs for concerts (Wired,

2019).With AI, the analysis of the paintings exhibited in artistic festivals can be done by the machines, offering different perspectives to the participants and providing different experiences (ArtJaws, 2017).

VR and AR technologies are technological applications can become some of the key factors in future festivals. These technological advancements, especially in the field of entertainment, allow participants to take photographs with different icons of different destinations and even celebrities, as well as allowing participants to play games (Eventsforce, 2016a; Medium, 2018).

In addition, they can offer opportunities for people with physical disabilities who are unable to attend the event and those who do not have any physical disabilities to experience as if they were at the event (Eventsforce, 2016b; Medium, 2018). Finally, self-service technology products are among the products that make people's lives easier. Self-service technology can be used during ticketing and passages at festivals, withdrawals, food and beverage purchases and food and beverage ordering. These processes are important for not interrupting the experiences of the festival participants (Lamasatech, 2019; Eventbride, 2019; Carreirão, 2019).

REFERENCES

Abad, P., Franco, M., Castillón, R., Alonso, I., Cambra, A., Sierra, J., Riozuelo, L., Montano, L., & Murillo, A. C. (2017, November). Integrating an autonomous robot on a dance and new technologies festival. In *Iberian robotics conference* (pp. 75–87). Springer.

Akiyama, T., Murata, S., Tsuchiya, K., Yokoyama, T., Maggio, M., Ciulla, G., Santana, J. R., Zhao, M., Nascimento, J. B., & Gürgen, L. (2017). Festival: Design and implementation of federated interoperable smart ICT services development and testing platform. *Journal of Information Processing*, *25*(0), 278–287. doi:10.2197/ipsjjip.25.278

Anil, N. K. (2012). Festival visitors' satisfaction and loyalty: An example of small, local, and municipality organized festival. *Turizam: znanstveno-stručni časopis*, *60*(3), 255-271.

ArtJaws. (2017). *The Ars Electronica Festival explores the realities and visions of artificial intelligence from september 7th to 11th in Linz.* https://www.artjaws.com/en/the-ars-electronica-festival-explores-the-realities-and-visions-of-artificial-intelligence-from-7-to-11-september-in-linz/

Aventri. (2020). *The 2020 event technology guide.* https://www.aventri.com/strategy/onsite-event-technology#

BBC. (2016). *Dancing robots break world record.* https://www.bbc.com/news/av/world-asia-china-37019690/dancing-robots-break-world-record

Billetto. (2020). *9 ways to use augmented and virtual reality for events.* https://billetto.co.uk/blog/augmented-virtual-reality-events/

Bitner, M. J. (1992). Servicescape: The impact of physical surroundings on customers and employees. *Journal of Marketing*, *56*(2), 57–71. doi:10.1177/002224299205600205

Carreirão, P. (2019). *Top 10 self-service technologies that we all love to use!* https://asksuite.com/blog/top-10-self-service-technologies/

Chinadaily. (2017). *53-finger robot plays piano with Italian pianist in Tianjin.* https://www.chinadaily.com.cn/china/2017-06/05/content_29614677.htm

Choi, R. I. (2011). A multiple regression analysis on developing the profitability model of local cultural festivals. *Journal of The Korea Society of Computer and Information, 16*(10), 229–239. doi:10.9708/jksci.2011.16.10.229

Chung, N., Han, H., & Joun, Y. (2015). Tourists' intention to visit a destination: The role of augmented reality (AR) application for a heritage site. *Computers in Human Behavior, 50*, 588–599. doi:10.1016/j.chb.2015.02.068

Cimbaljević, M., Stankov, U., Demirović, D., & Pavluković, V. (2019). Nice and smart: Creating a smarter festival–the study of EXIT (Novi Sad, Serbia). *Asia Pacific Journal of Tourism Research*, 1–13. doi:10.1080/10941665.2019.1596139

Cole, S. T., & Chancellor, H. C. (2009). Examining the festival attributes that impact visitor experience, satisfaction and re-visit intention. *Journal of Vacation Marketing, 15*(4), 323–333. doi:10.1177/1356766709335831

Cole, S. T., & Illum, S. F. (2006). Examining the mediating role of festival visitors' satisfaction in the relationship between service quality and behavioral intentions. *Journal of Vacation Marketing, 12*(2), 160–173. doi:10.1177/1356766706062156

Coulton, P. (2015). Playful and gameful design for the internet of things. In More playful user interfaces (pp. 151-173). Springer. doi:10.1007/978-981-287-546-4_7

Dalgıç, A. (2018). *Festival ziyaretçilerinin sadakatlerini etkileyen faktörlerin analizi: Adana Portakal Çiçeği Festivali örneği* (Doctoral dissertation). Mersin University.

Dalgıç, A., & Birdir, K. (2017). Otel işletmeciliğinde yeni trendler. In Y. Akgündüz (Ed.), *Otel İşletmeciliği* (pp. 311–328). Paradigma Akademi.

Dalgıç, A., & Birdir, K. (2019). Festival Anahtar Başarı Faktörlerinin Festival Sadakati Üzerine Etkisi: Portakal Çiçeği Festivali Örneği. *Journal of Tourism and Gastronomy Studies, 7*(4), 2718–2738.

Dalgic, A., & Birdir, K. (2020). Smart hotels and technological applications. In *Handbook of Research on Smart Technology Applications in the Tourism Industry* (pp. 323–343). IGI Global. doi:10.4018/978-1-7998-1989-9.ch015

Dalgiç, A., & Birdir, K. (2020). The effect of key success factors on loyalty of festival visitors: The mediating effect of festival experience and festival image. *Tourism & Management Studies, 16*(1), 28–38. doi:10.18089/tms.2020.160103

Daly, I. (2010). *Just like Mombot used to make.* https://www.nytimes.com/2010/02/24/dining/24robots.html

Desai, P. R., Desai, P. N., Ajmera, K. D., & Mehta, K. (2014). A review paper on oculus rift-a virtual. *Int. J. Eng. Trends Technol, 13*(4), 175–179. doi:10.14445/22315381/IJETT-V13P237

Esu, B. B., & Arrey, V. M. E. (2009). Tourists' satisfaction with cultural tourism festival: A case study of Calabar Carnival Festival, Nigeria. *International Journal of Business and Management*, *4*(3), 116. doi:10.5539/ijbm.v4n3p116

Eventbride. (2019). *Tip #3: newest technology trends to spruce up your festival*. https://www.eventbrite.com/blog/academy/festival-newest-technology-trends/

Eventsforce. (2016a). *5 ways you could use virtual and augmented reality at events*. https://www.eventsforce.com/blog/5-ways-you-could-use-virtual-augmented-reality-at-events/

Eventsforce. (2016b). *6 technology trends from experts at Europe's largest event tech show*. https://www.eventsforce.com/blog/6-technology-trends-from-experts-at-europes-largest-event-tech-show/

Experenti. (2016). *Augmented and virtual reality hit Sundance Film Festival*. https://www.experenti.eu/ar/augmented-and-virtual-reality-hit-sundance-film-festival/

Getz, D. (1997). *Event management & event tourism*. Cognizant Communication Corporation.

Gilbert, B. (2016). *540 robots dancing in sync looks just as insane as you'd think*. https://www.businessinsider.com/this-is-540-robots-dancing-in-sync-2016-2

Groenli, T. M., Flesch, B., Mukkamala, R., Vatrapu, R., Klavestad, S., & Bergner, H. (2018, December). Internet of Things Big Data Analytics: The Case of Noise Level Measurements at the Roskilde Music Festival. In *2018 IEEE International Conference on Big Data (Big Data)* (pp. 5153-5158). IEEE.

Ideausher. (2020). *How can Artificial Intelligence (AI) benefit the events industry in 2020?* https://ideausher.com/blog/artificial-intelligence/how-can-artificial-intelligence-ai-benefit-the-events-industry-in-2020/

Illum, M. (2018). *How IoT could transform the experience for Dubai Shopping Festival season*. https://www.iotevolutionworld.com/iot/articles/436340-how-iot-could-transform-experience-dubai-shopping-festival.htm

İq-mag. (2016). *The internet of things: The future of event tech*. https://www.iq-mag.net/2016/10/internet-of-things-future-event-tech/#.XiALmpIzYdU

Kansakar, P., Munir, A., & Shabani, N. (2017). *Technology in hospitality industry: Prospects and challenges*. arXiv preprint arXiv:1709.00105

Kim, B. (2015). What facilitates a festival tourist? Investigating tourists' experiences at a local community festival. *Asia Pacific Journal of Tourism Research*, *20*(9), 1005–1020. doi:10.1080/10941665.2014.957222

Kong, Y. (2015). *Understanding group cohesion of festival and events attendees satifaction and intention to revisit* (Unpublished doctoral dissertation). Clemson University, Güney Carolina.

Lade, C., & Jackson, J. (2004). Key success factors in regional festivals: Some Australian experiences. *Event Management*, *9*(1), 1–11. doi:10.3727/1525995042781066

Lamasatech. (2019). *5 innovative self-service technology examples*. https://www.lamasatech.com/blog/5-innovative-self-service-technology-examples/

Lee, S. Y., Petrick, J. F., & Crompton, J. (2007). The roles of quality and intermediary constructs in determining festival attendees' behavioral intention. *Journal of Travel Research, 45*(4), 402–412. doi:10.1177/0047287507299566

Lee, T. H., & Chang, P. S. (2017). Examining the relationships among festivalscape, experiences, and identity: Evidence from two Taiwanese aboriginal festivals. *Leisure Studies, 36*(4), 453–467. doi:10.1080/02614367.2016.1190857

Lee, Y. K., Lee, C. K., Lee, S. K., & Babin, B. J. (2008). Festivalscapes and patrons' emotions, satisfaction, and loyalty. *Journal of Business Research, 61*(1), 56–64. doi:10.1016/j.jbusres.2006.05.009

Leenders, M. A., van Telgen, J., Gemser, G., & Van der Wurff, R. (2005). Success in the Dutch music festival market: The role of format and content. *International Journal on Media Management, 7*(3-4), 148–157. doi:10.1080/14241277.2005.9669431

Manners, B., Kruger, M., & Saayman, M. (2012). Managing the beautiful noise: Evidence from the Neil Diamond Show! *Journal of Convention & Event Tourism, 13*(2), 100–120. doi:10.1080/15470148.2012.679612

Marais, M. (2009). *Key success factors in managing the Wacky Wine Festival* (Unpublished doctoral dissertation). North-West University, Potchefstroom.

Mason, M. C., & Paggiaro, A. (2012). Investigating the role of festivalscape in culinary tourism: The case of food and wine events. *Tourism Management, 33*(6), 1329–1336. doi:10.1016/j.tourman.2011.12.016

McDowall, S. (2011). The festival in my hometown: The relationships among performance quality, satisfaction, and behavioral intentions. *International Journal of Hospitality & Tourism Administration, 12*(4), 269–288. doi:10.1080/15256480.2011.614528

Medium. (2018). *The 10 most tech-forward music festivals of 2018*. https://medium.com/singulardtv/the-10-most-tech-forward-music-festivals-of-2018-44a3189f33fe

Morgan, M. (2008). What makes a good festival? Understanding the event experience. *Event Management, 12*(2), 81–93. doi:10.3727/152599509787992562

Morozova, A. (2020). *How event organizers can apply virtual reality in the event industry*. https://jasoren.com/how-event-organizers-can-apply-virtual-reality-in-the-event-industry/

Myers, B. (2020). *What self-service technology means for the future of events*. https://pheedloop.com/blog/self-service-technology-the-future-of-events

Ong, T. (2017). *YuMi the robot makes debut as orchestra conductor in Italy*. https://www.theverge.com/2017/9/14/16306528/yumi-robot-abb-debut-orchestra-conductor-italy

Özdemir, G., & Çulha, O. (2009). Satisfaction and loyalty of festival visitors. *Anatolia, 20*(2), 359–373. doi:10.1080/13032917.2009.10518914

Parker, R. (2018). *Internet of things in events: What's in it for event planners*. https://readwrite.com/2018/03/18/internet-things-events-whats-event-planners/?__cf_chl_jschl_tk__=88d032fbae466d085c6f3c21bd4605f8c266fe93-1597857303-0-AZAJqw3s2ph3LFX-mKqK85rPsPPSJsypJ9ESxG-WN_UeYGr5BGpSV8Bvv7dbF1iLj7eLe4tFk5hfihM32ASFe_T7qpyTScMQ8KFjl8_AOgCHGy-1HcJZVkTTP-b5QWaVoOdH4XHPHhYeBNgX4cTBhTVlxJGFZHBLhJAX3k3V5oCApoN_wEg-wVF0BImeTZhMko3PY96d45RPXEIQW9AuDtsETWHQc_yH9Z3BY3aEx5ZU5Q_TGpE_TBTj0l-ZrmaCn7UVf3vtnfrMG02UFFh27l_yZslI18Q4kl7YcDez6Ug6HIghGmeVROpCQHKzD1l6TYI21m-cxjoHZz3r3e6Pqdj2e9LVsWDucEk1RH1R7laj4mk3IA3rzTkoaw9Lb4yuyfQsW0cWwm9hxQDke-EXIFNmq81FY

Petkov, A. (2019). *A robot plays Jenga, physics enters the graphic novel, and London hosts a chemistry festival*. https://physicsworld.com/a/a-robot-plays-jenga-physics-enters-the-graphic-novel-and-london-hosts-a-chemistry-festival/

Powell, M. (2016). *IoT in action…at a music festival*. https://www.plant.ca/insights/162614/

Robotex. (2019). *Event information*. https://robotex.international/information/

Robotfilmfestival. (2019). *Robot film festival*. http://robotfilmfestival.com/

Saayman, M., Kruger, M., & Erasmus, J. (2012). Finding the key to success: A visitors' perspective at a National Arts Festival. *Acta Commercii*, *12*(1), 150–172. doi:10.4102/ac.v12i1.142

Saleh, F., & Ryan, C. (1993). Jazz and knitwear: Factors that attract tourists to festivals. *Tourism Management*, *14*(4), 289–297. doi:10.1016/0261-5177(93)90063-Q

Saxena, P. (2016). *The advantages and disadvantages of Internet of Things*. https://e27.co/advantages-disadvantages-internet-things-20160615/

Smart Hotel Technology Guide (2018). *Using technology to navigate the guest experience journey*. https://sha.org.sg/userfiles/ckeditor/Files/Smart%20Hotel%20Technology%20Guide%202018.pdf

Sorrells, M. (2013). *5 ways robots are being used at events*. https://www.bizbash.com/production-strategy/event-management-tech-tools/media-gallery/13479962/5-ways-robots-are-being-used-at-events

Taylor, R., & Shanka, T. (2008). Cause for event: Not-for-profit marketing through participant sports events. *Journal of Marketing Management*, *24*(9-10), 945–958. doi:10.1362/026725708X381984

Vincent, J. (2019). *Security robots are mobile surveillance devices, not human replacements*. https://www.theverge.com/2019/11/14/20964584/knightscope-security-robot-guards-surveillance-devices-facial-recognition-numberplate-mobile-phone

Wan, Y. K. P., & Chan, S. H. J. (2013). Factors that affect the levels of tourists' satisfaction and loyalty towards food festivals: A case study of Macau. *International Journal of Tourism Research*, *15*(3), 226–240. doi:10.1002/jtr.1863

Wang, C. P., & Tsai, C. H. (2019, February). Application of virtual reality to the study of festival culture in aboriginal literature. In *Proceedings of the 2nd International Conference on Image and Graphics Processing* (pp. 136-139). 10.1145/3313950.3313975

Weijman, J. (2014). *AGT leveraged the internet of things to improve attendees' experience at Tomorrowland.* https://www.agtinternational.com/agt-leveraged-the-internet-of-things-to-improve-attendees-experience-at-tomorrowland-2/

Wilson, C. (2019). *Artificial intelligence is changing the event industry — Here's how.* https://blog.swapcard.com/artificial-intelligence-and-events

Wired. (2019). *How artificial intelligence is influencing creativity at this year's Sónar Festival.* https://www.wired.co.uk/article/artificial-intelligence-creativity-sonar-festival

Wu, H. C., Wong, J. W. C., & Cheng, C. C. (2014). An empirical study of behavioral intentions in the food festival: The case of Macau. *Asia Pacific Journal of Tourism Research, 19*(11), 1278–1305. doi:10.1080/10941665.2013.844182

Yang, L., Henthorne, T. L., & George, B. (2020). Artificial Intelligence and Robotics Technology in the Hospitality Industry: Current Applications and Future Trends. In Digital Transformation in Business and Society (pp. 211-228). Palgrave Macmillan. doi:10.1007/978-3-030-08277-2_13

Yoon, Y. S., Lee, J. S., & Lee, C. K. (2010). Measuring festival quality and value affecting visitors' satisfaction and loyalty using a structural approach. *International Journal of Hospitality Management, 29*(2), 335–342. doi:10.1016/j.ijhm.2009.10.002

Yorkfestival. (2019). *About the festival.* http://yorkfestivalofideas.com/about/

Yuan, J., & Jang, S. (2008). The effects of quality and satisfaction on awareness and behavioral intentions: Exploring the role of a wine festival. *Journal of Travel Research, 46*(3), 279–288. doi:10.1177/0047287507308322

ADDITIONAL READING

Chuah, J. W. (2014). *The internet of things: An overview and new perspectives in systems design.* In: In *2014 International Symposium on Integrated Circuits (ISIC).* Singapore: IEEE Computer Society. pp. 216–219. 10.1109/ISICIR.2014.7029576

Fonseca, D., Reis, J. L., Teixeira, S., & Peter, M. K. (2020). Mobile Applications at Music Festivals in Portugal. In *Marketing and Smart Technologies* (pp. 190–201). Springer. doi:10.1007/978-981-15-1564-4_19

Ivanov, S., Gretzel, U., Berezina, K., Sigala, M., & Webster, C. (2019). Progress on robotics in hospitality and tourism: A review of the literature. *Journal of Hospitality and Tourism Technology*, JHTT-08-2018-0087. doi:10.1108/JHTT-08-2018-0087

Ivanov, S., & Webster, C. (2019).*Perceived appropriateness and intention to use service robots in tourism.* In Pesonen, J. & Neidhardt, J. (Eds.) Informationand Communication Technologies in Tourism 2019, Proceedings of theInternational Conference in Nicosia, Cyprus, 30.01-01.02.2019, pp. 237-248. 10.1007/978-3-030-05940-8_19

Silva, P. A., Tymoshchuk, O., Renó, D., Almeida, A. M., Pedro, L., & Ramos, F. (2018, May).*Unraveling the Role of ICT in Regional Innovation Networks: A Case Study of the Music Festival 'Bons Sons'*. In *Conference on Smart Learning Ecosystems and Regional Development* (pp. 47-61).Springer, Cham.

Van Winkle, C. M., MacKay, K. J., & Halpenny, E. (2018). Information and communication technology and the festival experience. In *The Routledge Handbook of Festivals* (pp. 254–262). Routledge.

Wei, W. (2019). Research progress on virtual reality (VR) and augmented reality (AR) in tourism and hospitality: A critical review of publications from 2000 to 2018. *Journal of Hospitality and Tourism Technology*.Vol. ahead-of-print No. ahead-of-print.

Yang, L., Henthorne, T. L., & George, B. (2020). Artificial Intelligence and Robotics Technology in the Hospitality Industry: Current Applications and Future Trends. In Digital Transformation in Business and Society (pp. 211-228). Palgrave Macmillan, Cham. doi:10.1007/978-3-030-08277-2_13

KEY TERMS AND DEFINITIONS

AI: This application enables machines to perceive, understand and learn, it is possible for machines to work and react like humans.

Dance Robots: They are robots that we can often encounter in music festivals and can dance in coordination with each other and with people. At a festival held in China in 2016, 1007 dance robots managed to enter Guinness World Records by dancing at the same time. This increased the consciousness of dance robots.

Festival Key Success Factors: These are the factors that are brought together in the planning and organizing stages of the festivals and affect the perception that the festival has been successful. Factors such as "festival program", "festival area", "accessibility", "information", "employees and volunteers", "souvenirs", "convenience", "food", "security" can be counted among the factors affecting the success of the festival.

IoT: IoT enables objects to connect with each other and work in a coordinated way, IoT facilitates human life by working directly and indirectly with devices such as "sensors", "identification tags", and "mobile devices".

Self-Service Technology: This technology can meet the needs of people and make their lives easier and fulfill the demands of people without the need for any representative.

VR and AR: VR is a technological application that creates entertainment and experience by presenting the virtual world to the computer environment. AR, on the other hand, presents an integration of both virtual and real world to individuals.

Chapter 2
Web Revolution and Events:
Development and Progress

Betül Kodaş
Mardin Artuklu University, Turkey

ABSTRACT

In the globalizing world, the use of social media as a marketing tool has been frequently discussed in academic researchers in recent years. It is possible to examine that the usage of these social media channels in the management and marketing of tourism-related activities is increasing. From this perspective, social media is considered as an important marketing tool for event organizers in the event industry in terms of some aspect of event studies. Besides, it provides significant benefits for visitors about deciding whether they participate in an event or not. In this framework, the aim of this chapter is to build a conceptual framework for revealing relation between social media and events. This conceptual study indicated that social media is one of the important digital tools for customer engagement, online experiences, and promoting events. Managerial implications and future research recommendation presented.

INTRODUCTION

Due to the phenomenal growth in virtual environment, where geographical boundaries disappear, the interaction intense and simultaneous, the number of users reaches very high numbers and continues to increase day by day, traditional media presentations and implementations became inadequate and social media has started to become an important marketing medium for tourism industry. The most important purpose of promotion which is one of the important elements of the marketing mix is to communicate with potential and existing customers without the time and place constraints and to create a positive image in the minds of consumers (Barutçu, 2011). Today, social networks are considered as a very powerful new marketing channel to realize this aim of promotion and to make marketing activities more effective (Shih, 2009).

Digital-based applications for social media integration in activities are coherent with social media and designed specifically for the activities. The digital-based applications are easy, understandable, and fast. These favorable futures of the social media provide important advantages for event organizers for

DOI: 10.4018/978-1-7998-4954-4.ch002

reaching more potential participants. It is possible to list some of the most preferred digital applications in terms of social media integration in the activities as follows: QR code, rfid (radio frequency identification), tweet wall (twitter share wall), 360 selfie, prestagram (memory of Instagram), social break (hot drink vending machine with tweet), social goal (foosball table working with tweet), event-branded emojis and stickers, and social media walls for events. As the opportunities offered by social media increase, such practices used in events will develop and increase in number. In this respect, the fact that event management is a dynamic, creative and highly competitive business, it seems to continue to depend on the rapid development of technology and at the same time the power of social media. Therefore, the use of information and communication technology, which is widely used in the field of accommodation, transportation and food and beverage management, is also considered important for event management and marketing, especially in terms of reaching more participants through social media.

BACKGROUND OF THEORETICAL FRAMEWORK

Information and Communication Technologies

Information and communications technology provided set of applications for tourism industry. After the development of computer reservations systems (CRSs), global distribution systems (GDSs) emerging internet changed operational practices in all the industries (Buhalis, 2003; Buhalis and Law, 2008) as well as tourism industry which was highly influenced from a range of Web 1.0 to Web 4.0. Buhalis (1998) describes information technologies as a concept that expresses all the latest developments in computer, electronic and communication technologies that are used in obtaining, analyzing, storing, dissemination and implementation of information. Today, with the phenomenon of Tourism 4.0, deep-rooted innovations have emerged in tourism with the development of data mining, big data analysis, internet of things, cloud computing, intelligent technology and artificial intelligence concepts (Buhalis and Amaranggana, 2013). These developments in technology has great influence on tourism industry. Sari and Kozak (2005) define tourism as an information and global industry, suggesting that consumers buy products they can't touch or see with the help of information technologies, and that an effective communication network should be established with the help of information technologies. With an effectively established network, better service can be carried out both for tourists and practitioners. Thanks to the changes in information technologies, the establishment of central reservation and global distribution systems, the changes and developments that the Internet (from Web 1.0 to Web5) has undergone to date have brought about important changes in the production and management structure of the travel industry (Buhalis, 2003). For example, travel agencies are reorganizing their systems according to their customers' requirements and needs. With their websites, they are communicating with their customers interactively, so they can co-create experiences and individualized production together. Social media applications are also utilized for this co-creation in experience and production.

As rapid development of ICT infrastructure and software applications in the tourism and hospitality industry are crucial for tourism development, the information and communications Technologies (ICT) plays a major role in tourism, travel and hospitality industry (Bethapudi, 2013). E-marketing, web site marketing strategy, digital marketing, social media marketing, viral marketing, e-Wom, search engine marketing, online marketing, mobile communication technologies are effectively used in business and destination marketing facilities such as hotels, accommodation firms, events companies etc. Parallel to these ICT developments, firms and destinations have reshaped their marketing and management strategies in order to gain competitiveness because of reducing transaction and operational cost (Buhalis and O'Connor, 2005; Buhalis and Kaldis, 2008). Social media applications are one of basic elements of ICTs and are popular in tourism and hospitality industries (Zeng and Gerritsen, 2014).

Social Media Extended of Web 2.0

Social media channels that maximize interpersonal communication and interaction and thus constitute a great potential power (Büyükşener, 2009) have enabled people to produce their content and started to transform users from passive audience to active producer role (Yaylagül, 2017). A word is written and/or a photo/video is shared by a user who produces content on social media, can easily spread to the masses and at the same time, it can be reshaped by every user who shares it (Uraltaş, 2012).

The most important benefit of the Internet is that provides access to information at any time and directs businesses to marketing and promotional activities on the internet. Through social media networks, which are emerging with development of internet and provide mutual communication opportunities, businesses can strengthen their mutual connection with the consumer and increase customer brand loyalty to the business (Davis et al., 2010:42). Unlike other online channels, social media, which paves the way for one-to-one communication with the advent of the Internet globally, can offer an interactive environment for customer to customer communication and business to business and business to customer communications. Because of this feature of social media, tourism businesses can also create one-to-one relationships with their customers by maximizing customer service through social networking sites. (Pamukçu and Tanrısever, 2019). Social media provide tourism business with paramount opportunities to understand their customer preferences and requirement through analysis the comments on social media application tools (Dellacoras, 2003). Thus, they can understand easily what their customers like and dislike about them and their product and service (Leung et al., 2012).

Kaplan and Haenlein (2010: 61) define social media as "*a group of Internet-based applications that build on the ideological and technological foundations of Web 2.0, and that allow the creation and exchange of user-generated content*". Social media on the other hand, defined by Brake and Safko (2009: 6) as "*activities, practices and behaviors among communities of people who gather online to share information, knowledge, and opinions using conversational media*". it is possible to define the social media as a social platform that user share their information, manners, interests via the Internet or mobile system. These social platforms are generally; chat rooms, discussion forums, location-based services, social networking services, social guides, social reputation networks, weblogs, blogs, podcasts, videocasts, wikis, facebook, twitters, trip advisors and other tools in a a collaborative way (Eröz and Doğdubay, 2012; Leung et al., 2013). It is known that high number of people are users of social media and are always in communication with other people for different purpose and motivations. The fact that people have the ability to produce content the way that they want to post on social media and to follow and comment on content shared by others lead up to the development of unofficial communication channels. Communication barriers between businesses and individuals disappear through social media, thus making mutual interaction and communication as much as possible in social media networks (Cetinkaya, 2019: 176). Thus, social media in considered to be source of information exchange among people who are interested in digital world.

With the advent of Web 2.0, social media which is one of essential component of digital world and marketing for company practitioners are considered to be a way of communication between consumer and company. Therefore, it can be signed that social communication networks, which were used individually only for social purposes such as socializing, communicating and meeting new people, are now considered as powerful marketing tool for businesses (Cetinkaya, 2019:181).

It has been stated that the internet and social media effects on the whole stages of purchasing behaviors of the consumer in tourism (Eröz and Doğdubay, 2012). We can see examples from wide range of literature focused on travel planning process such as phase of before trip (Burgess et al., 2011; Cox et al., 2009; Fotis, Buhalis, and Rossides, 2011), during trip (Cox et al., 2009; Fotis, Buhalis, and Rossides, 2011; Lee, 2011; Sparks and Browning, 2011; Lee, Xiong, and Hu, 2012) and after trip (Cox et al., 2009; Fotis, Buhalis, and Rossides, 2011; Huang, Basu and Hsu, 2010; Lee, 2011; Parra-López et al., 2011; Yoo and Gretzel 2011; Scott and Orlikowski, 2012). Consumers are searching for information about that product which they interest before purchasing. The information obtained about the tourism product during the search for information affects the consumer purchasing process .With the benefits of the Internet consumers can learn about the product before purchasing it by focusing on comments, reviews posted and consumer-generated content on social media networks. Meanwhile, it can also influence other consumers' purchasing intentions by sharing their reviews on the post-experience product. To state their positive or negative reviews about holiday destinations, travel experiences or food and beverage businesses through social media or to share anything can be an important reference source for other people who wants to positive experience of a tourism during their trip (Xiang and Gretzel, 2010). To illustrate, Wong Lai and Tau (2020) tried to examine the relationship between sharing memorable ethnic minority tourism experiences on mobile social media and intentions to visit other ethnic destinations. And they found that memorable ethnic minority tourism experiences affect tourists' behaviours in sharing tourism experiences on mobile social media and travel intention to other destinations.

The widespread realization of word-of-mouth communication by consumers electronically (E-wom) or making conversation through technological ways such as social media tools is of vital importance to the tourism industry, where it is difficult to evaluate the product without experience (Litvin et al., 2008). Because tourists generally try to find information about different destinations, based on electronic word-of-mouth communication (eWOM) on various social media (Burgess, Sellitto, Cox, and Buultjens, 2011; Wong, Lai and Tao, 2020) and also seeing social media as a crucial information source for travel planning and decision-making (Jacobsen and Munar, 2012; Fotis, Buhalis, and Rossides, 2012). Hence, firms in hospitality and tourism industry are constantly communicating with consumers through social media, positively affecting consumers' recommendation towards their own products and by doing so they are trying to reach targeted customers.

MAIN FOCUS OF THE CHAPTER

In preparing this chapter, comprehensive literature review was conducted to investigate use of social media in event studies and business. Relevant literature indicates that impacts of social media on event management and marketing are well established in some aspects of event studies such as involvement, online experience (also means digital experience), engagement, advertising and promoting events. Although ICT is key factor in hotel business and destination activities related tourism for implementing services efficiently focusing tourist satisfaction, limited studies has been employed in event tourism studies by adopting ICT in their business product and services. Besides social media which is one of the important digital tools that so many people use actively, has provided some insights for both event attendees and event organizers for how people are engaged and experiences in digitally with events that take place. Therefore, this book chapter focuses on relation to social media and events conceptually. By doing this, the relevant literature investigated comprehensively via google scholar database.

Relation with Social Media and Events

"We Are Social and Hootsuite" prepared a report called "Digital in 2018" which includes data on the usage rates of digital channels in January 2018. According to this report, 53% (4.02 billion people) of the world's population are now internet users and 42% (3.19 billion people) are social media users. Compared to the previous year, the number of internet users increased by 7% and the number of social media users increased by 13%. The age range at which digital channels are most used is 18-34 with a rate of almost 60%. Another highlight of the report is that people spend an average of 7 hours a day on the Internet and 2 hours 48 minutes a day on social media (We Are Social-Hootsuite, 2018). When the internet penetration rates by country are reviewed it can be seen that the United Arab Emirates comes first with 99%, followed by Sweden (97%) and the Netherlands (96%). Turkey is the 28th (67%) in this ranking. When internet usage rates in Turkey were examined as an example of a large country, it can be clearly said that there are 54,33 million internet users in Turkey corresponding to 67% of the population. The social media users account for 63% of the population and comprise 51 million people. 84% of users report that they use digital channels every day. The most frequently visited social media channels in Turkey are Youtube, Facebook, and Instagram respectively (We Are Social-Hootsuite, 2018). It is possible to state that many people use social media for different motivations and purposes. From the tourism industry perspective, many customers use social media efficiently to search information about tourism products and services and examine people's experiences which they shared in social media channels.

Today, in parallel with the intensive use of social media by billions of people all around the world, companies are changing their strategies for interacting and connecting with their customers. As with any business, tourism firms and destinations have started to use information communication technology tools extensively. For modern and postmodern tourists, social media as an effective way of communication, tourism and destination practitioners have started to use it more frequently to reach their customers. Thus, today social media has become one of the most important information and communication technologic tools to reach prospective customers. Besides traditional mass communication tools, new tools, equipment and software based on computer technology (virtual chat facilities, voice and video e-mail services, CD-rom databases, virtual shopping, entertainment and communication services, video mobile phones) creates social and cultural consequences providing mass production and consumption of information (Babacan and Göztaş, 2011: 152). As a result of social media which shows rapid development, event marketers have discovered the importance of social media as a marketing tool and strategies, and started using social media so as to enhance mutual communication and create social interaction (Harb et al., 2019). Facebook event pages are considered as an effective marketing channels where social media users create user generated contents (UGC), include photos, videos, or post comments about their experience of mega and local events (Lee, Xiong and Hu, 2012).

The advent of internet-based social media technologies has provided tourists and travelers to share travel experiences, and through social media sites, potential tourists can make easier and informative travel planning by acquiring information about travel destinations, tourism activities, events and festivals etc, (Zeng and Gerritsen, 2014). So, the use of social media tools has been dramatically increased in tourists' travel planning, tourist destination management and tourism marketing activities Social media, as one of most powerful digital marketing tools, has been increasingly growing in the tourism industry. In tourism papers, assessment of the visual perspective of tourism was not studied enough to understand tourist behavior (Urry, 1990). It was emphasized that tourists tend to seek unique experiences, which tourism organizations should take in consideration in planning and developing new products and services fort he potential customers (Pine, Pine and Gilmore, 1999).

As a marketing strategy, many businesses integrate social network media into their marketing actions which provide their customer to create user generated contents and by giving feedback about these UGCs such as forums, online reviews, photos and videos. They are trying to be enable their customers to develop positive E-WOM, trust and loyalty behaviors (Zeng and Gerritsen, 2014; Hudson et al., 2015). Social media provides companies and organizers with great advantages such as in co-creating experiences with customers, enhancing value of services and managing information and knowledge through social media applications and metrics (Cova and Cova, 2002; Kaplan and Haenlein, 2009). Social media enable to obtain a collaborative marketing tool, where they can receive feedback, interact with and influence their consumers (MacKay et al., 2017; Hvass and Munar, 2012). Besides social media application tools are being much more trusted sources of information than official tourism web sites, travel agents and mass media advertising (Fotis et al., 2011), people find individually posted comments to be more trustworthy/beneficial for their buying behaviors. Facebook may be a good information acquisition tool to obtain the details about an event such as the date, time and location and post-event details such as viewing photos and videos about events and comments of the attendees (MacKay et al., 2017).

By organizing successful events or festivals, destinations can gain advantages in terms of competitiveness against their rivals. As events, festivals or special events have been considered as part of destination promotion policies, these activities have been important part of destination attractions and products and are now crucial tool that contribute to the destination branding. Events and festival have been basic element of hospitality and tourism industry as attracting tourist, creating positive image for the destination, contributing place marketing by making cities more liveable and attractive, acting as a catalyst for other forms of desired developments like urban development (Getz and Page, 2016). For the aforementioned reasons, if a tourism destination wants to utilize the events as a marketing strategy, it should closely follow developments such as technologic changes in their macro environment. In line with, developments in information and communication technologies (ICTs) have had enormous impact on marketing strategies which businesses conduct. Therefore, marketing has been influenced uttermost by the development of ICT like other managerial functions. Social media is one of best way to interact with the customer for the event organizer. Marketing through social media is vital for event's organizers to reach and attract targeted potential customer.

To answer the question of why social media and social media marketing are important for events tourism, we must look through impacts of social media on some aspect of events. There are limited conceptual studies in relation with social media and events. One of them conducted by Ngernyuang and Wu in 2020. The study findings and the comprehensive literature review showed the impact of social media on different variables related to events. In this study findings revealed that social media effects destination image in a positive way and strengthen the destination image, ease potential customers' search for information, help advertising activities, builts and strengthens trustworthiness, consumer loyalty, and e-wom and increase social interaction, and emotional engagement. Hence, it can be said that social media applications play an important role in events and festival marketing and management practices. Solaris (2018) indicated that there are some important areas that event planners should focus on event planning and management benefiting from social media. These features of event planning are crucial to have better and well-organized events and festivals. Some of these important elements of event planning are listed as; customer service, marketing, online reputation management, research, sales, event management, event feedback all are essential for successful organization of events and festivals and festival goers today can be very selective and critical in case these important characteristics are not well-organised, executed and managed.

Some limited researches indicates that social media plays a significant role in some aspects of events such as information search and decision-making behaviors, online practices for interacting with consumers (Zeng and Gerritsen, 2014), co-creating experiences (Hoksbergen and Insc, 2016) engagement (Hudson and Hudson, 2013; MacKay et al., 2017; Laurell and Björner, 2018), promotion to events (Paris, Lee and Seery, 2010; Lee, Xiong and Hu, 2012; Ngernyuang and Wu, 2020), festival destination image (Hanan and Karim 2015) building festival brand personality in social media environment (Maisello, Bonetti and Izzo, 2020) gain importance in the recent years. For example, Hoksbergen and Insc, (2016) examined to understand how younger music festivalgoers use and engage with a music festival's Facebook page, and how they perceive this social networking service as a potential online platform for value co-creation. This study found that five value types (functional, social, emotional, interactive and aesthetic) that festival-goers perceive from a music festival's Facebook page was identified. In this context, social media and its related contents such as photos and videos (Becker et al., 2009) of events and organizations can be useful for many event and festival organizers in terms of developing successful and attractive products for tourism and events industry (Lee, Xiong and Hu, 2012).

Customer engagement in digital word, online experiences and promoting events in the social network applications are important developments for event management. Social media offers the best way to promote a large festival, regardless of kinds of events or festival, that is it can be music, conference, meeting, art, corporate, or other events (Hanan and Karim, 2015). For example; Paris, Lee and Serry (2010) investigated that the influence of trust, expected relationships and perceived enjoyment in figuring consumer attitudes towards Facebook and consumers intentions to attend an event using Facebook 'events' as a medium for promoting special events for customers. And they found that users" trust and expected relationship through Facebook had a significant effect on users" acceptance of Facebook and their intended offline behavior to attend the event. Since usage of social media has become increasingly disseminated, empirical researches in which consumer engagement is increasingly performed is conducted in different fields such as tourism, healthcare service, and events (Kozinets, de Valck, Wojnicki and Wilner, 2010; Chathoth et al., 2016; Hudson and Hudson, 2013). For example, hotels can interact and engage with their customers before, during, and after the travel experience through social media (Tatar and Erdoğmuş 2016). This is the same in events and festivals. Pine and Korn (2011) suggest that social media is an accessible tool to augment the digital experience before during and after the festival or events.

Before the events take place, customers are trying to search information about the program, venue, facilities and cost of the events. Through social media applications such as facebook, twitter, youtube, and Instagram, event organizers give detailed information to their current and potential attenders to engage and involve them to the events. For example, according to Mintel, (2013) and Hudson et al., (2015) music festival tourist are using social media applications intensively to find out information about events to blog and engage. In the evaluation stage of festivals, consumers are concentrating on user-generated content to evaluate various festivals, and blogging web sites (Hudson and Hudson, 2013). During the festival, it is stated that social media enhances the consumer experience, and that activities and consumers interact better with events. (Hudson and Hudson, 2013). Hudson et al. (2015) revealed that the impact of social media on the customers' emotion and attachment to festival brands positively and social media relationship lead to customers to be eager for spreading a positive word of mouth. Similarly Laurell and Björner (2018) investigated 77,034 user-generated contents published in social media in the context of digitization of festival management and they found that festivals attract engagement levels in the social media network tools before, during, and after festivals takes place. Thus, social media is essential for engaging customers towards to events and for creating digital experiences. It is possible to posit from the previous discussions that customer engagements with the online social content of events increase their online event experiences and this experiences effects on consumers' future behavioral intentions of event (Kharouf et al., 2020). Therefore, digital engagement of events and festivals should be taken in consideration by event and festival organizers.

Social media has great influence customers for future behavioral intentions such as attend festival, recommendations online behavior and all stages customer decision making process (pre-during-after) (Hudson & Hudson, 2013). Previous studies noted that most of tourism and social media studies has been focused on just pre trip decision making process (MacKay et al., 2017). With growing interest on ICT, especially in event studies, papers which examine the relationship between social media and events and festival are rapidly increasing. Most of these papers seem to focus on various aspect of events such as engagement, promoting events, attend classification, online experiences, and marketing (Lee, Xiong and Hu, 2012; Hudson and Hudson, 2013; Moise and Crucero, 2014; Hudson et al., 2015; Laurell and Björner, 2018; de Lira et al., 2019; Kharouf et al., 2020).

For event and festival organizers, social networks are important and dominant digital communication instruments to announce the details of the events to their customers before the actual events venue occurs (Mintel, 2013; Chappuis, Gaffey, and Parvizi, 2011). Once event organizers announce a new event on its Facebook event page, online fans could answer to the organization and interact with other fans unmediated before attending the event (Lee, Xiong and Hu, 2012). For instance, International Gaziantep Gastronomy Festival which takes place in Gaziantep located Southeast of Turkey hold every year (except pandemic period). This festival has great number of Facebook fans (25.696 followers), İnstagram fans (27500 followers) and announce information about festival in advance and uses social media network efficiently to reach their potential attender. Among the social media network application, Facebook and Twitter are popular for promoting events and tourist destinations (Hays, Page and Buhalis, 2013; Jabreel, Moreno and Huertas, 2017). It is clear that social media offers some great opportunities for both organizers and customers; between the company and their customers (business-to-consumer) as well as between consumer-to-consumer (Mangold and Faulds, 2009). For event organizers and online users social network media is a two-way communication tool which they talk and listen each other (Pino et al., 2019). To interact with customer is crucial for event organizer and engaging customers with event or festival through social media have positive influences in terms of customers' future attending intention to event (Hudson et al., 2015; Pino et al., 2019).

SOLUTIONS AND RECOMMENDATIONS

In relevant literature, there are several studies examining that ICT tools, especially usage of social media used in tourism and hospitality industry; but existing studies on investigating on relation between social media and events is at an early stage and still in its infancy. So, to enhance number of event attender and to build attender engagement, which in turn affected loyalty haviour toward event, event organizer has to use social media network more actively, especially focusing on Y generations. Because young people become interested in social media applications more than other generations.

In related managerial implications, this study's conceptual results show that social media has gained attention of the event organizers and practitioners to online experiences, involvement and engagement. By doing so, event organizers can improve customer relation management, gain a more in- depth understanding of their customer's needs and demands about their planned events. Event organizers must have websites, Facebook, and Instagram pages so as to announce events and keep in communication with their customer to serve them and their needs better. They can manage information using big data from social media applications and develop effective marketing and management strategies for targeted potential attenders for events. In addition, an event organizer should use social media to promote and build successful events, and encourage many current and potential attender to involved, engaged in the event. Besides, if event marketers wants to promote events or festival via social media, they must learn wanted and potential customers preferences to fulfill their requirement and change behavior (Moise and Crucero, 2014).

FUTURE RESEARCH DIRECTIONS

This study discussed the importance of usage of social media for online event engagement, online experiences and promoting events. These are main aspects of event studies according to current study findings. there is a need for further research to investigate other variables empirically in different studies. Taking in consideration the popularity of social media in the tourism and hospitality industry and events, it is need to explore the antecedents and desired outcomes of social media in the content of events. It is considered that social media will play a very important role in the future of marketing events and festivals (Hudson and Hudson 2013). Thus, social media marketing in event studies may help to understand customer online behavior, motivations so as to have better event planning and management. For instance, ıf event marketers post event information and updates in detailed in social media, Facebook or Instagram event pages are valuable tools for information acquisition which customer has. So it is needed for further research to understand customer insights while they were using social media networks for searching event or festival. To illustrate, such as motivation to event in social media, online engagement, online experience, involvement, satisfaction, loyalty behavior, recommendation intentions etc. need to search both empirically and theoretically.

CONCLUSION

The aim of this chapter is to investigate the link between social media and events based on a comprehensive literature review and to build a conceptual framework of this relationship. This conceptual study shows that there is a considerable amount of academic papers related to the relationship between ICT and, tourism and hospitality industries. However, limited research has been performed to analyze the relationship between social media and event business both conceptually and empirically.

This study show that social media is efficient way to promote the events to the people and engage the customers to the event in online. Build an online experience of customer will affect their future behavioral intentions. Social media continues to be popular in all disciplines. In the tourism and hospitality framework, especially in events, social media increasingly positively impacts on event marketing and management issues. So event organizers should use social media as a marketing tool to reach their customer directly for fulfilling their requirements and satisfy them and affect behavioral intentions positively.

REFERENCES

American Marketing Association. (2017). *Definition of Marketing*. https://www.ama.org/AboutAMA/Pages/Definition-of-Marketing.aspx

Babacan, E., & Göztaş, A. (2011). *Etkinlik Yönetimi*. Detay Yayıncılık.

Barutçu, S. (2011). Mobil Viral Pazarlama. *İnternet Uygulamaları ve Yönetimi Dergisi, 2*(1), 5-14.

Becker, H., Naaman, M., & Gravano, L. (2009). *Event identification in social media*. Paper Presented at the *2009 ACM International Conference on Web Search and Data Mining (WSDM 2009)*.

Bethapudi, A. (2013). The role of ICT in the tourism industry. *Journal of Applied Economics and Business, 1*(4), 67–79.

Blackshaw, P., & Nazzaro, M. (2006). *Consumer-generated media (CGM) 101: Wordof-mouth in the age of the web-fortified consumer*. Nielsen Buzz Metrics.

Brake, D., & Safko, L. (2009). *The social media bible*. John Wiley and Sons, Inc.

Buhalis, D. (1998). Strategic use of information technologies in the tourism industry. *Tourism Management, 19*(5), 409–421. doi:10.1016/S0261-5177(98)00038-7

Buhalis, D. (2003). eTourism: Information technology for strategic tourism management. Pearson Education.

Buhalis, D., & Amaranggana, A. (2013). Smart tourism destinations. In *Information and communication technologies in tourism 2014* (pp. 553–564). Springer. doi:10.1007/978-3-319-03973-2_40

Buhalis, D., & Kaldis, K. (2008). eEnabled internet distribution for small and medium sized hotels: The case of Athens. *Tourism Recreation Research, 33*(1), 67–81. doi:10.1080/02508281.2008.11081291

Buhalis, D., & Law, R. (2008). Progress in information technology and tourism management: 20 years on and 10 years after the Internet—The state of eTourism research. *Tourism Management, 29*(4), 609–623. doi:10.1016/j.tourman.2008.01.005

Buhalis, D., & O'Connor, P. (2005). Information communication technology revolutionizing tourism. *Tourism Recreation Research, 30*(3), 7–16. doi:10.1080/02508281.2005.11081482

Burgess, S., Sellitto, C., Cox, C., & Buultjens, J. (2009). User-generated content (UGC) in tourism: Benefits and concerns of online consumers. *Proceedings of the 17th European Conference on Information Systems*, 1–14.

Büyükşener, E. (2009). Türkiye'de Sosyal Ağların Yeri ve Sosyal Medyaya Bakış. In *XIV. Türkiye'de İnternet Konferansı Bildirileri (12-13 Aralık 2009)* (s. 39-43). Bilgi Üniversitesi, İstanbul: inet-tr'09.

Çetinkaya, F. Ö. (2019). Sosyal Medya ve Turizm. In Turizm 4.0 Dijital Dönüşüm (pp. 173-184). Ankara: Detay Yayıncılık.

Chappuis, B., Gaffey, B., & Parvizi, P. (2011). *Are your customers becoming digital junkies?* Academic Press.

Chathoth, P. K., Ungson, G. R., Harrington, R. J., & Chan, E. S. (2016). Co-creation and higher order customer engagement in hospitality and tourism services. *International Journal of Contemporary Hospitality Management, 28*(2), 222–245. doi:10.1108/IJCHM-10-2014-0526

Cova, B., & Cova, V. (2002). Tribal marketing: The tribalisation of society and its impact on the conduct of marketing. *European Journal of Marketing, 36*(5/6), 595–620. doi:10.1108/03090560210423023

Cox, C., Burgess, S., Sellitto, C., & Buultjens, J. (2009). The role of user-generated content in tourists' travel planning behavior. *Journal of Hospitality Marketing & Management, 18*(8), 743–764. doi:10.1080/19368620903235753

Davis Mersey, R., Malthouse, E. C., & Calder, B. J. (2010). Engagement with online media. *Journal of Media Business Studies, 7*(2), 39–56. doi:10.1080/16522354.2010.11073506

De Lira, V. M., Macdonald, C., Ounis, I., Perego, R., Renso, C., & Times, V. C. (2019). Event attendance classification in social media. *Information Processing & Management, 56*(3), 687–703. doi:10.1016/j.ipm.2018.11.001

Eröz, S. S., & Doğdubay, M. (2012). Turistik Ürün Tercihinde Sosyal Medyanın Rolü ve Etik İlişkisi. *Dokuz Eylül Üniversitesi İktisadi İdari Bilimler Fakültesi Dergisi, 27*(1), 133–157.

Fotis, J., Buhalis, D., & Rossides, N. (2011). Social media impact on holiday travel planning: The case of the Russian and the FSU markets. *International Journal of Online Marketing, 1*(4), 1–19. doi:10.4018/ijom.2011100101

Gaziantep Uluslararası Gastronomi Festivali. (2020). https://www.facebook.com/GastroAntepFest/?__tn__=%2Cd%2CPR&eid=ARA0Y4KSs3RnjPx3yI7fTNjYQwA1oZEQiKe_y2tqdLIULhG25IA-HEmz1GhqBpY2S8EsW9_lTWbvDlbr8

Getz, D., & Page, S. J. (2016). Progress and prospects for event tourism research. *Tourism Management, 52*, 593–631. doi:10.1016/j.tourman.2015.03.007

Hanan, H., & Karim, S. A. (2015). Influence of social media in food festival destination image. In *Proceeding of International conference on tourism and ethnicity in ASEAN and beyond* (pp. 15-16). Academic Press.

Harb, A. A., Fowler, D., Chang, H. J. J., Blum, S. C., & Alakaleek, W. (2019). Social media as a marketing tool for events. *Journal of Hospitality and Tourism Technology, 10*(1), 28–44. doi:10.1108/JHTT-03-2017-0027

Hays, S., Page, S. J., & Buhalis, D. (2013). Social media as a destination marketing tool: Its use by national tourism organisations. *Current Issues in Tourism, 16*(3), 211–239. doi:10.1080/13683500.2012.662215

Hoksbergen, E., & Insch, A. (2016). Facebook as a platform for co-creating music festival experiences. *International Journal of Event and Festival Management*, *7*(2), 84–99. doi:10.1108/IJEFM-02-2016-0012

Huang, Y., Basu, C., & Hsu, M. K. (2010). Exploring motivations of travel knowledge sharing on social network sites: An empirical investigation of US college students. *Journal of Hospitality Marketing & Management*, *19*(7), 717–734. doi:10.1080/19368623.2010.508002

Hudson, S., & Hudson, R. (2013). Engaging with consumers using social media: A case study of music festivals. *International Journal of Event and Festival Management*, *4*(3), 206–223. doi:10.1108/IJEFM-06-2013-0012

Hudson, S., Roth, M. S., Madden, T. J., & Hudson, R. (2015). The effects of social media on emotions, brand relationship quality, and word of mouth: An empirical study of music festival attendees. *Tourism Management*, *47*, 68–76. doi:10.1016/j.tourman.2014.09.001

Hvass, K. A., & Munar, A. M. (2012). The takeoff of social media in tourism. *Journal of Vacation Marketing*, *18*(2), 93–103. doi:10.1177/1356766711435978

Jabreel, M., Moreno, A., & Huertas, A. (2017). Semantic comparison of the emotional values communicated by destinations and tourists on social media. *Journal of Destination Marketing & Management*, *6*(3), 170–183. doi:10.1016/j.jdmm.2016.03.004

Kaplan, A. M., & Haenlein, M. (2009). The fairyland of Second Life: Virtual social worlds and how to use them. *Business Horizons*, *52*(6), 563–572. doi:10.1016/j.bushor.2009.07.002

Kaplan, A. M., & Haenlein, M. (2010). Users of the world, unite! The challenges and opportunities of Social Media. *Business Horizons*, *53*(1), 59–68. doi:10.1016/j.bushor.2009.09.003

Kharouf, H., Biscaia, R., Garcia-Perez, A., & Hickman, E. (2020). Understanding online event experience: The importance of communication, engagement and interaction. *Journal of Business Research*. Advance online publication. doi:10.1016/j.jbusres.2019.12.037

Kozinets, R. V., De Valck, K., Wojnicki, A. C., & Wilner, S. J. (2010). Networked narratives: Understanding word-of-mouth marketing in online communities. *Journal of Marketing*, *74*(2), 71–89. doi:10.1509/jm.74.2.71

Laurell, C., & Björner, E. (2018). Digital festival engagement: On the interplay between festivals, place brands, and social media. *Event Management*, *22*(4), 527–540. doi:10.3727/152599518X15300559276930

Lee, S. (2011). To tweet or not to tweet: An exploratory study of meeting professionals' attitudes toward applying social media for meeting sessions. *Journal of Convention & Event Tourism*, *12*(4), 271–289. doi:10.1080/15470148.2011.621586

Lee, W., Tyrrell, T., & Erdem, M. (2013). Exploring the behavioral aspects of adopting technology. *Journal of Hospitality and Tourism Technology*, *4*(1), 6–22. doi:10.1108/17579881311302329

Lee, W., Xiong, L., & Hu, C. (2012). The effect of Facebook users' arousal and valence on intention to go to the festival: Applying an extension of the technology acceptance model. *International Journal of Hospitality Management*, *31*(3), 819–827. doi:10.1016/j.ijhm.2011.09.018

Leung, D., Law, R., Van Hoof, H., & Buhalis, D. (2013). Social media in tourism and hospitality: A literature review. *Journal of Travel & Tourism Marketing*, *30*(1-2), 3–22. doi:10.1080/10548408.2013.750919

Litvin, S. W., Goldsmith, R. E., & Pan, B. (2008). Electronic word-of-mouth in hospitality and tourism management. *Tourism Management*, *29*(3), 458–468. doi:10.1016/j.tourman.2007.05.011

MacKay, K., Barbe, D., Van Winkle, C. M., & Halpenny, E. (2017). Social media activity in a festival context: Temporal and content analysis. *International Journal of Contemporary Hospitality Management*, *29*(2), 669–689. doi:10.1108/IJCHM-10-2015-0618

Masiello, B., Bonetti, E., & Izzo, F. (2020). Multiple identities of a festival. *International Journal of Contemporary Hospitality Management, 32*(2), 749-768.

Mintel. (2013). Music festival tourism worldwide. *Travel and Tourism Analyst, 10*. London: Mintel Group Ltd.

Moise, D., & Cruceru, A. F. (2014). An empirical study of promoting different kinds of events through various social media networks websites. *Procedia: Social and Behavioral Sciences*, *109*, 98–102. doi:10.1016/j.sbspro.2013.12.426

Munar, A. M., & Jacobsen, J. K. S. (2014). Motivations for sharing tourism experiences through social media. *Tourism Management*, *43*, 46–54. doi:10.1016/j.tourman.2014.01.012

Ngernyuang, K., & Wu, P. (2020). Using Social Media as A Tool for Promoting Festival Tourism. *International Journal of Computer Science & Information Technology*, *12*(3), 17–32. doi:10.5121/ijcsit.2020.12302

Pamukçu, H., & Tanrısever, C. Y. (2019). Turizm Endüstrisinde Dijital Dönüşüm. In Turizm 4.0 Dijital Dönüşüm (pp. 2-29). Ankara: Detay Yayıncılık.

Paris, C. M., Lee, W., & Seery, P. (2010). The role of social media in promoting special events: acceptance of Facebook 'events. In ENTER2010 eTourism Conference, Lugano, Switzerland.

Parra-López, E., Bulchand-Gidumal, J., Gutiérrez-Taño, D., & Díaz-Armas, R. (2011). Intentions to use social media in organizing and taking vacation trips. *Computers in Human Behavior*, *27*(2), 640–654. doi:10.1016/j.chb.2010.05.022

Pine, B. J., Pine, J., & Gilmore, J. H. (1999). *The experience economy: work is theatre & every business a stage*. Harvard Business Press.

Pino, G., Peluso, A. M., Del Vecchio, P., Ndou, V., Passiante, G., & Guido, G. (2019). A methodological framework to assess social media strategies of event and destination management organizations. *Journal of Hospitality Marketing & Management*, *28*(2), 189–216. doi:10.1080/19368623.2018.1516590

Sari, Y., & Kozak, M. (2005). Turizm pazarlamasına internetin etkisi: Destinasyon web siteleri için bir model önerisi. *Akdeniz İİ BF Dergisi*, *9*, 248–271.

Scott, S. V., & Orlikowski, W. J. (2012). Reconfiguring relations of accountability: Materialization of social media in the travel sector. *Accounting, Organizations and Society, 37*(1), 26–40. doi:10.1016/j.aos.2011.11.005

Shih, C. (2009). *The Facebook Era: Tapping Online Social Networks to Build Better Products, Reach New Audiences, and Sell More Stuff.* Prentice Hall Direct.

Solaris, J. (2018). *Social Media For Events (2019 Edition): A Complete Guide To Marketing Your Events Using Social Media.* https://www.eventmanagerblog.com/social-media-events

Sparks, B. A., & Browning, V. (2011). The impact of online reviews on hotel booking intentions and perception of trust. *Tourism Management, 32*(6), 1310–1323. doi:10.1016/j.tourman.2010.12.011

Tatar, Ş. B., & Eren-Erdoğmuş, İ. (2016). The effect of social media marketing on brand trust and brand loyalty for hotels. *Information Technology & Tourism, 16*(3), 249–263. doi:10.100740558-015-0048-6

Uraltaş, N. T. (2012). lektronik Perakendecilik ve Bir reklam Mecrası Olarak Sosyal Ağ Siteleri. In Sosyal Medya - Akademi (pp. 21-56). İstanbul: Beta Yayınları.

Urry, J. (1990). The consumption'of tourism. *Sociology, 24*(1), 23–35. doi:10.1177/0038038590024001004

We Are Social-Hootsuite. (2018). *Digital In 2018.* Hootsuite. http://www.mediacatonline.com/wp-content/uploads/2018/05/we-are-social-digital-in-2018.pdf

Wong, J. W. C., Lai, I. K. W., & Tao, Z. (2020). Sharing memorable tourism experiences on mobile social media and how it influences further travel decisions. *Current Issues in Tourism, 23*(14), 1773–1787. doi:10.1080/13683500.2019.1649372

Xiang, Z., & Gretzel, U. (2010). Role of social media in online travel information search. *Tourism Management, 31*(2), 179–188. doi:10.1016/j.tourman.2009.02.016

Xiang, Z., Wöber, K., & Fesenmaier, D. R. (2008). Representation of the online tourism domain in searchengines. *Journal of Travel Research, 47*(2), 137–150. doi:10.1177/0047287508321193

Yaylagül, Ş. (2017). Sosyal Medya Fenomenlerine Bağlanmışlığın Belirlenmesi: Yükseköğretim Öğrencileri Üzerine Bir Uygulama. *Adnan Menderes Üniversitesi Sosyal Bilimler Enstitüsü Dergisi, 4*(3), 219–235. doi:10.30803/adusobed.349934

Yoo, K. H., & Gretzel, U. (2011). Influence of personality on travel-related consumer-generated media creation. *Computers in Human Behavior, 27*(2), 609–621. doi:10.1016/j.chb.2010.05.002

Zeng, B., & Gerritsen, R. (2014). What do we know about social media in tourism? A review. *Tourism Management Perspectives, 10*, 27–36. doi:10.1016/j.tmp.2014.01.001

ADDITIONAL READING

Alalwan, A. A., Rana, N. P., Dwivedi, Y. K., & Algharabat, R. (2017). Social media in marketing: A review and analysis of the existing literature. *Telematics and Informatics*, *34*(7), 1177–1190. doi:10.1016/j.tele.2017.05.008

Backman, K. F. (2018). Event management research: The focus today and in the future. *Tourism Management Perspectives*, *25*, 169–171. doi:10.1016/j.tmp.2017.12.004

Law, R., Bai, B., Ip, C., & Leung, R. (2011). Progress and development of information and communication technologies in hospitality. *International Journal of Contemporary Hospitality Management.*

Nusair, K. (2020). Developing a comprehensive life cycle framework for social media research in hospitality and tourism. *International Journal of Contemporary Hospitality Management*, *32*(3), 1041–1066. doi:10.1108/IJCHM-09-2019-0777

Van Winkle, C. M., MacKay, K. J., & Halpenny, E. (2018). Information and communication technology and the festival experience. In *The Routledge Handbook of Festivals* (pp. 254–262). Routledge.

KEY TERMS AND DEFINITIONS

Online Event Experience: Online experiences represent a key connection point between the event and consumers with social networks media (Kharouf et al., 2020).

Social Media: Social media can be generally described as Internet-based applications that carry consumer-generated content which encompasses ''media impressions created by consumers, typically informed by relevant experience, and archived or shared online for easy access by other impressionable consumers (Blackshaw, 2006).

Social Networks Media: Social networking media can be generally defined as internet-based applications which are created, initiated, circulated and used by consumers so as to educate each other about products, brands, services, and issues (Xiang and Gretzel, 2010; Lee, Tyrrell and Erdem, 2011).

Chapter 3
Marketing Innovations in Industry 4.0 and Their Impacts on Events Marketing

Mısra Çakaloğlu
https://orcid.org/0000-0002-2493-2385
Antalya AKEV Üniversitesi, Turkey

ABSTRACT

Industry 4.0 is a concept that creates the phenomenon of globalization due to technological advances, increased digitalization, and capital accumulation. This chapter presents the effects of the development process and components of the Industry 4.0 concept on event marketing. Also, it influences businesses' industrial-strength, production factors, and marketing strategies through information and communication technologies (ICTs). Various marketing innovations are offered with the positive impact of these factors on companies. These innovations create an impact on the target audience of event marketing in a way to increase social welfare. The purpose of this chapter is to create marketing innovations in the Industry 4.0 perspective and evaluate event marketing to meet the expectations of the target groups. Therefore, it is significant to create an understanding of goods and services with high added value by utilizing ICTs.

INTRODUCTION

The concept of globalization, which has begun to develop in international markets, requires that companies in global markets benefit greatly from the economics of scale in production, marketing, distribution, and management. In order to increase the competitiveness of the countries that benefit more from the economies of scale, the events organized within the scope of technological advances and the development of the socioeconomic structure have been accelerated. In this context, digital transformation and Industry 4.0 concepts have emerged. Developments in ICTs in these two concepts increase competitiveness in the long run in the production, consumption and marketing stages of goods and services.

ICT developments increase the market size of goods and services in events. Moreover, there is a potential to have an impact on social welfare in events. Based on these developments, it is known that

DOI: 10.4018/978-1-7998-4954-4.ch003

digital transformation contributes to the national economy such as productivity, employment, and income growth. These contributions are more common in sectors that track changes in digital transformation the fastest, such as the chemical, automotive, machinery and white goods industries. Besides, the telecommunications and financial services sectors are among the priority sectors for digitalization (Erdil, 2018: 59-60). In order for these sectors to adapt to current developments, they need to develop industrialization policies. In this regard, Industry 4.0 concept comes to the agenda. With this concept, dependence on the labor force is significantly reduced within the industrialization policies of countries (Ulusoy, 2018: 63). Decreasing the need for workforce Industry 4.0 is due to the increased value-added in the manufacturing industry and the share of high-tech products in exports. Consequently, efforts to increase competitiveness in the industry have gained importance. Some of these studies are to be used effectively in ICTs and to eliminate the understanding of asymmetry in the markets of manufacturers and consumers. Others are in the direction of developing countries to use their R&D expenditures in the fields required by digitalization to close the technology gap. Based on these policies, Industry 4.0 offers an opportunity for developing countries, with a stable innovation roadmap for sustainable development and growth.

In addition to digital transformation and Industry 4.0 concepts, another concept that has been developing and changing recently is the concept of Marketing 4.0. It has many features. Marketing 4.0, which is a virtual marketing-oriented approach, is an investment from today to the future. This understanding based on human refers to a series of researches about machines and other organisms. Playing an active role in the development of Web 4.0 and cybernetic revolution applications, Marketing 4.0 has production and timely production policies according to the consumer. It also has functional, emotional, spiritual and self-creativity features. These features show that Marketing 4.0 is related to event marketing and experiential marketing. Event marketing can be expressed as a marketing event that is major for brands and is carried out within various organizations. These events strengthen communication between the brand and the consumer and provide examples of experience-oriented interaction (Yalçın, 2017). Moreover, event marketing provides an additional advantage in the interaction of the consumer and the active brand and allows the brand to be positioned in the target market (Sneath et al., 2005: 374). Experiential marketing is an approach that enables the experience of the product before purchasing the product in order to make the loyalty of the consumers permanent (Arıca, 2016). In this context, manufacturers focus on the idea of their brands to provide the desired benefit for the consumer. For instance, in recent years, manufacturers carry out marketing events by telling the story of their brands. Therefore, they will be more successful than competitor brands, as they are more likely to convince consumers to purchase their products. For instance; manufacturers try to attract the attention of consumers to other products by doing many events on some special days (Okay, 2017). Taste tests at local product fairs and test drives in the automotive industry are among the first applications of experiential marketing.

Companies that provide good and detailed information about the content of the product in a competitive environment, increase the product sales and profit margins, will increase the chances of their brands to remain active in the market. On the other hand, in these cases, the consumer pays attention to the sustainability of the marketing events in which they want to participate by making a rational decision according to the characteristics of the product. This will strengthen the link between consumer and marketing effectiveness. These events are referred to as "Marketing 4.0". Marketing 4.0 is an approach that takes the consumer deeply into human-centered marketing. The ultimate goal of Marketing 4.0 is to move consumers from awareness to advocacy and develop various strategies to adapt consumers to changing market conditions in the digitalization process. These strategies are based on the philosophy of "Creating and Collaborating from Many to Many" (Tarabasz, 2013: 130; Büyükkalaycı and Karaca,

2019: 467). Since cooperation requires a certain specialization, the importance of the brand is revealed in Marketing 4.0. So, it is possible to explain Marketing 4.0 with the concepts of brand identity, brand image, brand integrity, and brand interaction. Brand identity is to determine the position of the brand in consumers' minds. Also, it is expressed as a set of features that create value by defining products that meet the demands and needs of consumers (Jara et al., 2012: 855). Brand image is the whole of beliefs such as product structure, quality perception formed in the consumer mind with the perception of brand associations in memory and perceptions about the reflected brand. Brand integrity is the ultimate point in the branding process while attaining the business goals, at the same time, having the desired brand image. As a result, brand interaction occurs when the manufacturers follow the innovations in other brands and their brand creates the best in the target market. Based on all these concepts, with the events of Marketing 4.0, the consumer seeks a brand that the technical developments and brand trends change very quickly and the versatility of the ads can trust and risk. Besides, brands can be preferred because of the emotional dimension of advertisements and create additional value for them (Çakaloğlu ve Çağatay, 2015: 8).

Consumers benefit from other marketing mix elements in the most appropriate and necessary way to make an informed brand choice. The consumer chooses the product by making use of affordable, various advertising activities and turns to well-known brands for easy distribution of the product. These brands enable the consumer to make a more informed choice as it gives confidence and loyalty to the consumer. Businesses do not only have sales policy but also strive to add value to their products for consumers. In this context, companies that value brand value is more conscious about the corporate responsibility, social and environmental aspects of the brand. Selecting a product suitable for the target market is possible by using the information communication technologies suitable for the end consumer. Consumers create awareness for other consumers by expressing their opinions about the product they purchase through ICTs. This is expressed by the transition of Marketing 4.0 from the traditional to the digital process. With the digitization process, the IT sector is one of the focus sectors in the transition program to high technology in industry. In this regard, scale capacity needs to be improved in order to increase exports of goods and services in information and processing technologies. With the development of scale capacity, production and accordingly, entrepreneurship increases the efficiency of the ecosystem. Thus, the development of human capital will increase the effectiveness of Marketing 4.0.

In this book chapter, the development process of the concept of event marketing within the context of marketing innovations is examined based on the concepts of digital transformation and Industry 4.0. Therefore, in this chapter, it is stated that the common point of Industry 4.0 and event marketing concepts are ICTs. On the other hand, the relationship between experiential marketing and event marketing is supported by various examples. So, in Industry 4.0, within the scope of marketing innovations and the digitalization process, the development of economic events and event marketing are accelerated by developing consumer relations with the brand. Besides, the importance of ICTs in marketing is emphasized with systematic event management for the development of event marketing.

BACKGROUND

Industry 4.0 and Event Marketing

Globalization occurs with the increasing integration of the internet into the industrial value chain, using information technologies to increase the competitiveness of countries in the industry. With globalization, event marketing is becoming the focus of attention for manufacturers and consumers in terms of various marketing innovations offered by Industry 4.0. This feature of Industry 4.0 is related to big data including the mobile and cloud information operating system. Mobile and cloud computing operating systems are significant in providing globally-oriented services over the internet through the globalization process. These systems ensure the coordination of services with each other thanks to their technological infrastructure (Roblek et al., 2016: 6). It provides a coordinated event marketing with a strong technological infrastructure. This aspect of event marketing is about the interactive participation of target groups in the communication process. This feature is a substantial feature of event marketing that differs from traditional communication strategies (Drengner et al., 2008: 138).

Many national and international studies have been published in the literature on Industry 4.0 and event marketing. During the transition to Industry 4.0, Germany is developing a strategic plan to provide a better transformation to the industry. This plan has four major points. These are defined as: networking, researching two main themes, realizing three integrations and achieving eight planning goals (Luo, 2014: 125-128). In creating a new network, a specialized network known as the Cyber Physical System, the core component of Industry 4.0, is created. This specialized network has many features such as computing, communication, coordination, and so intelligent manufacturing techniques are developed. Another stage of the plan is to investigate smart factory and smart production issues. While the smart factory is a future component of smart infrastructure, smart manufacturing systems and processes focus on the implementation of networked distributed production facilities. In this regard, combining ICTs and smart devices are components of two main topics. Within the strategic plan, three integrations are horizontal integration, vertical integration, and end-to-end integration. Horizontal integration refers to the integration between a resource that offers real-time products and services and an information network within the value chain. Vertical integration means customized production as an alternative to traditional fixed production processes. End-to-end integration means numerical integration with a digital value chain and integration between different companies, at a level that maximizes customization. Achieving eight planning goals is the last strategic plan created by Germany to provide a better transformation to the industry (Zhou et al., 2015: 2148).

Rojko (2017) presents many definitions of Industry 4.0 and the development process of Industry 4.0. In this context, it aims to understand and facilitate the driving forces, goals, and limitations of Industry 4.0. In this chapter, the Reference Architecture Model Industrie (RAMI 4.0) was used in the study. This model has the feature of a meta-model that plays a prominent role in the Industry 4.0 production system. It is also a compilation of the necessary technological components of Industry 4.0. This model is expressed as a model that examines, interprets and requires international acceptance as to whether German companies are ready for Industry 4.0. As a result of the study, it is stated that Industry 4.0 is considered as a disruptive technology that is different from the existing production systems and will open the way for the new generation industrial production systems.

Drengner et al. (2008) aim to provide information about the effects of event marketing in their study. The research findings include developing a model for consumers' attitudes towards advertising and explaining the effects of flow experience during marketing events. This model was tested by partial least squares structural equation modeling. As a result of this study, it was determined that the active participation of the target group had a positive brand image effect during the marketing process. Close et al. (2006) show that the sponsorship, event, and knowledge of sponsor products of a participant in the field of sponsorship activity positively affects a participant's desire to join the community. The result of this study shows that event marketing, together with consumers who are enthusiastic, active and knowledgeable about sponsors and events, acts as a valuable lever to interact with the consumer. It is related to many topics such as event marketing, lifestyle marketing, experiential marketing, relationship marketing, public relations, and marketing communications. It is concluded that a critical evaluation of existing methods to measure the effectiveness of experiential marketing techniques is not reliable because the existing methods are largely abstract because the event experience is abstract. In this regard, a framework has been developed to measure the effectiveness of experiential marketing events of subsequent research (Wood, 2009: 247-248).

Ertuğrul and Deniz (2018) studied aiming to conceptually analyze Marketing 4.0 and Industry 4.0. In this study, it is emphasized that information technologies and industry are integrated into the digital industrial revolution of Industry 4.0. The importance of social media is mentioned in Marketing 4.0 events. So, it is stated that businesses need to know their customers and develop appropriate goods/services in order to retain their existing customers or reach potential customers. Aksoy (2017), in his study, deals with the concept of technology in terms of Industry 4.0 and using dynamics specific to capitalism. In this regard, various questions are asked about understanding the concept of Industry 4.0. Yüksekbilgili and Çevik (2018), investigated the industrial revolution period of the Industry 4.0, in order to analyse the added values expected to be brought today and in the future both in the world and in Turkey in their studies. In this view, senior executives of 6 leading companies related to Industry 4.0 were interviewed. Common comments in the answers given to the interview questions were subjected to keyword analysis and interpreted. As a result of this study, it is determined that Turkey has formed an awareness of Industry 4.0. In this case, Turkey's road map in companies and government agencies are being set up and start working. In the study published by Yıldız (2018), the basic paradigms of Industry 4.0 were explained and an evaluation was made about smart factories. It was one of the conclusions drawn from the study that the Industry 4.0 trend should be adapted to the digitalization process in order to be followed and counted as an example in this context. In order to take advantage of smart specialization strategies, all companies belonging to Industry 4.0 must act according to a common country plan.

The study published by Göktaş and Kulga (2017) explores the opinions of consumers about event marketing. In this study, it has been determined how a brand that carries out event marketing practices has an effect on the main consumer group between the ages of 18-24 and what the opinion of the consumer about this brand is. As an event, an application that a brand started in 2016 and is still ongoing was preferred. Independent sample t-test, one-way variance and correlation analyzes were used in the study. As a result, it was found that consumers' having a positive opinion about the event caused brand loyalty. Also, it was concluded that event managers should be very careful about determining the name of the event, as the name of the event is effective in recognizing the brand. Altunbaş (2011) examines the effect of music and entertainment event on brand communication in relation to the relationship between marketing communication and event marketing. The other part of this study is mentioned that the contribution of Selçuk University to the companies in terms of event marketing of spring festivals. The brand's awareness, image, and purchasing behavior before and after the event were compared and the contribution of the event to brand communication was examined. As a result of the study, it was concluded that the brands that manage event marketing contribute to their brands in the event and the event is effective for consumers. Besides, it was emphasized that event marketing is effective in evaluating event marketing in comparison with brands and other promotional events.

This chapter shows various marketing innovations within the scope of digital transformation issues with Industry 4.0 and their effects on event marketing. Therefore, digital technologies lead the way in the development process of the concepts of experiential marketing and Marketing 4.0. Also, by examining the brand-consumer relationship dimension, we contribute to ensuring that event marketing is carried to a higher level.

MAIN FOCUS OF THE CHAPTER

Marketing Strategies in Industry 4.0 and Its Effects on Information Communication Technologies

Marketing Innovations

The main purpose of the chapter is to create marketing innovations by utilizing Industry 4.0 and to evaluate event marketing according to their meeting the expectations of the target audience. It is significant to clarify the strategies that businesses apply for Industry 4.0 and event marketing with appropriate ICTs. Industry 4.0 requires the optimal utilization of production processes at a time when ICTs are used intensively in the digitalization process. Bringing the innovation-oriented marketing approach, this concept is closely related to event marketing. Events are becoming significant component of target marketing. Planning and realizing the organizations that will give the most effective promotion result at the lowest cost are defined as event marketing (Kim and Chalip, 2004: 695). The event management as a component of the broader activity of event marketing, where the power of one-to-one communication is utilized. These marketing events created with the active participation of target groups are organized by businesses (Drengner et al., 2008: 138). The main purpose here is to organize events to meet the expectations of the target groups. So, the sustainability of the events is ensured by receiving positive feedback. Apart from meeting the expectations of the target groups, it is substantial to know the other potentials of Industry 4.0 in order to give a positive result in event marketing. The features of Industry 4.0 include providing flexibility and effectiveness, making the most appropriate decision, resource efficiency, creating value opportunities with new services, responding to demographic change in the workplace and ensuring work-life balance. These features form a significant perspective within the context of production technology and marketing innovations (Kagermann et al., 2013: 1516).

The globalization and the change of Industry 4.0 in technology have affected the marketing field and brought many innovations. These innovations greatly change the functioning of corporate and social life and the communication of businesses with their customers. Therefore, it brought with it different strategies and marketing methods. The transition from product-oriented marketing to virtual-oriented marketing has required the integrated use of all elements of marketing communication with the development of ICTs (Bulunmaz, 2016: 348). The fact that the virtual focused marketing approach is valid has enabled Marketing 4.0 to be associated with the concepts of event marketing and experiential marketing. In event marketing, companies will be able to organize face-to-face communication by organizing events such as training, seminars, fairs, and congresses about their brands, and will enable them to move their brands to a higher position (Kotler and Keller, 2009). Enterprises realize these events through various promotional events such as advertisement, personal sales, sales development, and public relations. Businesses try to connect their brands and consumers with experiential marketing strategies that are included in many marketing strategies. In this regard, since they have the chance to experience ICTs without purchasing the products, they are more likely to be satisfied with the product. As manufacturers create brand loyalty and customer loyalty through experiential marketing, they will increase their position in the market with the increase in competition. Based on these features, it continues to offer its customers the opportunity to experience their products or services on platforms such as experiential marketing and social media. So, experiential marketing is defined as one of the marketing strategies accepted by the masses. The fact that a store selling musical instruments gives weekly training to introduce new and different musical instruments to its customers creates the opportunity to experience that product. In this context, experiential marketing practices that enable companies to be in direct contact with their customers will have more opportunities to develop as brand recognition increases and there is no asymmetric information in the market. Schmitt (2003) argued that experiential marketing can give customers five basic experiences that differ from each other. These five types of experience consist of sensory (sense), emotional (feel), cognitive (think), physical (act) and social (relate) and are shown in Table 1.

Table 1. Dimensions of Experiential Marketing

Module	Content of the Customer Experience
Sensory Experience	Sensory experiences towards the five senses
Emotional Experience	Emotional experiences towards feelings and mood
Cognitive Experience	Intellectual experiences towards creativity and cognitive functions
Physical Experience	Behavioral experiences towards physical behavior and lifestyle
Social Experience	Relational experiences towards social and cultural groups

Source: Nagasawa, (2008: 314)

In the kind of sensory experience, it is expressed to create an experience with sensory perceptions towards five senses. So, product differentiation is made (Schmitt, 2003). Emotional experience builds a bond with customers about the brand, based on feelings. Analyzing the emotions of marketers and stimulants of customers is significant for the sustainability of emotional experience (Yu and Ko, 2012: 11). While cognitive experience is the experiential marketing dimension that appeals to the mind to create problem-solving experiences that concern customers' creativity, the physical experience dimension affects physical experiences and lifestyles (Nagasawa, 2008: 315). The social experience dimension includes experiences for social and cultural groups covering the sensory, emotional, cognitive and physical experience dimensions. The contribution of the individual to his individual experiences through his personal and private feelings associates the individual with his ideal self, other people or cultures (Schmitt, 1999). For instance, Starbucks creates different coffee types and the aroma of these coffees reflected in the environment, spatial design, various coffee materials and the opportunity to experience their coffees. In this regard, Starbucks, which has a self-service understanding and enables coffee sales, addresses all five senses of its customers (Aksoy, 2011). In this context, Starbucks is considered one of the best examples of experiential marketing. With these features, Starbucks strengthens the brand value more and gives different experiences to the target audience. Cyber Physical Systems, which further strengthens the communication network with the (IoT), diversifies the marketing innovations specific to Industry 4.0. When it is evaluated from this point of view, it creates customer loyalty and ensures that the event processes are managed well.

Evaluation of Event Management Within the Scope of Industry 4.0 and Event Marketing

Industry 4.0 is a concept that takes place in industrialized countries with production-oriented and advanced R&D activities, making industry and countries more proactive. This concept is known as the fourth stage of industrialization. It has three major elements. These are speed, width-depth, and system effect. Many new technological developments have occurred in terms of easy adaptation to recent industrial developments. The development of recent developments in the digital revolution is related to the width and depth dimension of Industry 4.0. This development in the digitization process creates changes in the production structure and the individual's living conditions. The last feature is the system effect, and it changes the systems of companies, countries, and sectors that have been operating recently. Thanks to these distinctive features, the ultimate aim of the companies is to produce quality products and to sell these products cheaply. Businesses that adapt to these three features continue to develop (Özsoylu, 2017: 46). In this regard, companies that want to make mass production are looking for ways to increase productivity in an increasingly competitive environment. Businesses that aim to respond to consumer expectations faster have the chance to seize Industry 4.0 opportunities, which are related to the Internet of Things and the Internet of Industrial Things. So, the opportunity to have good events in terms of event marketing is created.

In order to create innovation in marketing, it is necessary to follow globally-oriented strategies and make the most of ICTs. To this extent, the function of event marketing increases. In this context, there are many factors that affect the success of the event. These are (Yalçın, 2017);

- The compliance of the event with the target audience,
- The compatibility of the event with the product or brand,
- The location of the event,
- The form of the event,
- Time and duration of the event,
- Promotion network configuration,
- Current technology support,
- Process management,
- Source,
- Participants,
- Speakers,
- Invitees,
- Factors such as sponsors.

An integrated study of these factors increases the importance of the strategies of event marketing. Factors affecting the success of the event play a role in the evaluation of event marketing. In this sense, the measured properties, pros and cons of event marketing in Table 2 are examined in three stages.

Table 2. Three Levels of Event Marketing Assessment

Stage	Measured	Pros	Cons
1. Event	Participation, media, content, satisfaction	Focusing on the event	Not measuring the effectiveness
2. Consumer Experience (event experience)	Value = Benefit-Cost	Focus on the consumer Focus on experience	Assuming that the positive event experience is equal to the marketing event
3. Consumer Response (response to the experience) a. Attitude change as a result of experience b. Behavior change as a result of experience	Emotions, attitude, intention, behavior Perceived brand values, preference, liking Purchased behavior, Word-of-Mouth (WOM), recommendations, defense, trial	Focus on the results of the outputs	Difficult to separate the event for a longer period of time

Source: Wood, (2009: 265)

It can be mentioned among the advantageous aspects of event marketing that the process of adaptation to the activity, consumer, experience and the results of the outputs is short in event marketing. In this context, following up marketing innovations by making use of appropriate ICTs affects the management and performance of the event positively. On the other side, the high cost of resources resulting from the inaccurate positioning of the activity leads to an incorrect evaluation of the event. This can be a disadvantage to the event. Also, this affects the development process of event management negatively.

Industry 4.0 brings together a product and service approach with high competitiveness, efficiency and added value. Marketing innovations in Industry 4.0 are made possible by the digitalization process adapting to the changing structure of technology. The dependence on the workforce has decreased significantly with the experience of digitization in the industry in the industrialized countries of Industry 4.0. So, reducing their competitive advantage in the developing industrial zone countries such as Turkey, creating a trend towards increasing the competitiveness of the manufacturing industry (Ulusoy, 2018: 63). Increasing competitiveness enables the entrepreneurship sector to grow. This is because the ICTs that form the basis of Industry 4.0 guide the functioning of event marketing. This is possible thanks to good event management and ICTs in marketing. Event management is an applied science in which interdisciplinary studies are used the most. Therefore, event management has become a system that renews itself day by day with an advanced technological infrastructure system (Seyfi, 2017: 77). Event marketing has been one of the best examples of this. Event marketing has the feature that digital technologies should be used in production, as it is one of the methods used to reach the target audience. The selection of digital technologies suitable for the target audience reflects positively on the feedback received from event marketing. A decrease in the total cost and an increase in productivity can be counted as two features that support this (Balkır, 2018: 78). For example, since the demand for local fairs opened at certain times of the year is high, the sales price of some products decreases and productivity increases. So, the use of ICTs in value chains improves the level of development of the market, using the promotion mix elements optimally, such as advertising, personal sales, promotion, and sales development events. Thus, in the case of creating value in the production of goods and services, economic growth increases. The harmony of consumers and organizers for successful event management ensures that consumers' demands and needs are optimally met. In this context, the establishment of the communication program explaining the objectives of the event increases the applicability of the marketing innovations in Industry 4.0 (Tolan, 2014: 24). Therefore, the areas where digital transformation is provided must be defined. In this context, in Table 3, the stages of the development of digital technologies are included. Digital technologies are gathered in three groups as the core, complementary and software-oriented technologies. Software oriented technologies constitute the final stage of Digital 4.0. For instance, the blockchain system that forms the infrastructure of Bitcoin, which has been on the agenda recently, is of great importance for ICTs by attracting the attention of large companies (Hahn, 2019: 17).

Table 3. Development Process of Digital Technologies

Digital Technologies	Core technologies: Smart Human, Smart Object, Smart Organization
	Complementary technologies: Hardware oriented (manufacturing production, robots and drones), Software oriented technologies (blockchain technology)

Source: Hahn, (2019: 17)

In order to examine the relationship between digital technologies and Industry 4.0, Table 4 presents the stages that reflect the development process of Industry 4.0. Industry 1.0 is considered the beginning of the industrial revolution, and steam-powered machines are being used for the first time. Industry 2.0 has become the stage where mass production has emerged with the inclusion of electrical energy systems in water and steam energy production systems (Yüksekbilgili and Çevik, 2018: 423-424).

Table 4. The Development Process of Industry 4.0

Stages	Period	Features
Industry 1.0	The transition from the 18th century to the 19th century	Technology: Steam engines Traditional Market: Production Volume Production System: Labor-intensive production
Industry 2.0	The transition from the late 19th century to the 1980s	Technology: Electricity, electronics, mechanical devices, cars Stable Market: Production volume and production diversity Production System: Streamline, TPS, workplace, phone, FMS
Industry 3.0	The transition from the 1980s to the present	Technology: Information, analog to digital, modular integral Variable Market: Production volume, production diversity, delivery time Production System: Seru, Streamline, TPS, workplace, phone, FMS
Industry 4.0	Near future	Technology: Internet of Things (IoT), big data, electrical appliances, 3D printer, cloud communication system, artificial intelligence, cyber physical systems Intelligent Production: Customers attend in individual customization Production System: Seru, Streamline, TPS, workplace, phone, FMS

Source: Yin et al. (2018: 858)

With the developments in the digitalization process and ICTs, automation in production was the stage of Industry 3.0. The last stage used today is Industry 4.0. It is a concept where technological transformation adapts to the digital age and is a production stage that meets the demands and needs of consumers at the maximum level. Components of Industry 4.0 fall into five groups. These stages are;

1. **Cyber Physical Systems (CPS):** These are systems that reduce production costs and are major in meeting consumer expectations. It also has a simultaneous feature that reflects the integration process of computation and physical processes. The economic and social potential of such systems is much greater than realized. Large investments are made in these systems to improve technology worldwide (Lee, 2008: 363).
2. **Internet of Things (IoT):** It is a system of devices that enables the flow of information in communication with each other and allows the creation of an intelligent network. The IoT, which is expected to create many economic opportunities, contributes greatly to technological transformation with the network system it creates (Hofmann and Rüsch, 2017: 25).
3. **Internet of Services (IoS):** It is a web-based software components, which provides services and functionalities via the internet (Bartodziej, 2017: 54). This means that with the technology opportunities offered by Internet-based markets, the service society will play a critical role in the future industries.
4. **Cloud-Based Manufacturing (CBM):** It reduces product costs, increases efficiency and enables the most appropriate resource allocation by meeting customer demands. Networked production, ubiquitous access and virtualization, big data and data analytics, scalability, agility and the Internet of Things are the main features of cloud-based manufacturing (Yıldız, 2018: 550-551).
5. **Smart Factories:** At this phase, the products can have the chance to be identified and positioned easily by acting independently as part of their production processes. This is possible with optimum cost, flexible and individual mass production (Hofmann and Rüsch, 2017: 25).

Thanks to these components of Industry 4.0, there are six principles for businesses. These principles are (Fırat and Fırat, 2017: 15);

- Interoperability,
- Virtualization,
- Dissemination of responsibility,
- Real-time competence,
- Service orientation,
- Modularity.

The interoperability principle provided by all components is the most fundamental principle of Industry 4.0. Thanks to its features such as remote access, it eliminates time and space limitations. The principles of virtualization and dissemination are realized through cyber physical systems and smart factories. Real-time competence, service orientation, and modularity principles will speed up the technological transformation of Industry 4.0. The operation of these principles integrated with each other increases the function of organizational charts, management functioning, customer profiles (Lom et al., 2016: 1).

Based on these components, Industry 4.0 strengthens communication between the brand and the consumer. It also demonstrates the power of experience-based interaction. The production of products with brand value is possible with applicable marketing strategies. In these strategies, thanks to the innovation-oriented and globally moving structure of the ICTs sector, awareness is provided for the consumer in the digitalization era within the context of marketing. Consumers want to benefit from the marketing service with advanced industrialized policies and advanced technological opportunities that will provide maximum benefit in the ICTs sector. The high-tech marketing service is referred to as Marketing 4.0. The development process of Marketing 4.0 is given in Table 5. Marketing 1.0 is a product-oriented approach and begins with production concepts.

Table 5. The Development Process of Marketing 4.0

Stages	Approachs
Marketing 1.0	Product-oriented approach
Marketing 2.0	Customer-oriented approach
Marketing 3.0	Value-oriented approach
Marketing 4.0	Virtual marketing-oriented approach

Source: Tarabasz, (2013: 130)

In the early days of Marketing 1.0, the number of enterprises producing in the market was few and therefore the main purpose of the enterprises was to reach high efficiency with low cost (Kotler and Keller, 2006: 15). Therefore, businesses produce traditional products and disregard consumers' opinions. Along with economic developments, this situation has changed. With the increase in the variety of products in the market, businesses begin to produce goods and services and carry out marketing events to meet consumer expectations. In brief, the understanding of product diversity in marketing strategies begins to be adopted. High-quality understanding is formed and events are carried out to increase the competitive power in the market. Therefore, the products are supported by promotion events such as advertising, personal sales, sales promotion (promotion) and other sales increasing efforts (public relations, direct marketing) as the importance of the consumer is more understood in the market. Since Marketing 1.0 is a product-oriented approach, the management approach can be expressed as "I sell whatever I produce". In this understanding, managers act with the idea of "a good commodity is selling itself". The best example of this is the fact that "the consumer can choose the color he wants, provided that he is black", which the founder of the automobile industry, Henry Ford, said while producing a standard uniform and black colored cars, best describe this understanding (Mucuk, 2010: 8). With Marketing 2.0, a customer-oriented approach, which is formed by the further development of ICTs, is adopted. In this particular development, it has been given importance to use the elements of the marketing mix in the most appropriate way in order for consumers to reach the target market better. With the increasing purchasing power of consumers, product groups that benefit consumers from all aspects of the events started to be produced. Therefore, businesses have developed strong communication strategies to create loyalty instead of a consumer-oriented marketing strategy. Marketing 3.0 is a people-oriented period in which values originate from marketing (Kotler et al., 2010: 4). Businesses do not only have a sales policy but also strive to add value to their products for consumers. In this context, companies that value brand value is more conscious about the corporate responsibility, social and environmental aspects of the brand. Expressed as a virtual marketing-oriented approach, Marketing 4.0 is the last stage of marketing.

Marketing 4.0 increases the importance of event marketing as it can directly bring social events to the target audience through various social media channels. Salesforce in event marketing plays a significant role in having long-term relationships with customers. In this context, companies are one step closer to their marketing goals by expanding their production networks (Cruceru and Moise, 2014: 157).

Experiential marketing, as mentioned earlier, is closely related to event marketing. Organizing an event as a form of marketing communication is closely related to the experience experienced by the participants (Khotimah et al., 2016: 433). Experiential marketing is a process that determines and meets customer satisfaction of needs and requests through a useful activity (Smilansky, 2009: 9). The results of experiential marketing are directly proportional to the degree of identity that brands earn. For instance; when the Zara brand and an unknown brand are compared, it is seen that Zara appeals to a larger target audience. Because; consumers with brand addiction focus their attitudes on the brand they experience. Thus, it is about brands launching products that create added value and using ICTs in the most appropriate way. The evaluation of experiential marketing in terms of businesses has enabled various marketing insights to change and shape ICTs with globalization. This situation brings with it various electronic marketing events in an intensely competitive environment. So, businesses benefit from internet advertising (Çifterler, 2013: 1). Consumers like their products through internet advertising and they have the chance to experience the products whenever they want and shop online. In this context, Trendyol is one of the most used websites recently. Trendyol becomes the center of attention of consumers by making various discounts on some days of the year. Offering products that industrialize with different marketing strategies and shopping from Trendyol, which opens to the world, consumers increase their dependence on the brand with advanced ICTs. In this context, Trendyol is growing fast and strengthening its marketing networks.

SOLUTIONS AND RECOMMENDATIONS

Event marketing has five major features such as product, price, location, public relations and positioning (Hoyle et al., 2002: 13). Good coordination of these characteristics is among the common characteristics of economies that have reached the Industry 4.0 level. From this point of view, knowing the background of the event is important for producing products for the event. Apart from that, knowing the product value and the features that make the product unique will result in positive feedback on event marketing. In other words, it raises the question of how much participation should participate in the event. It is significant to understand the financial objectives of the sponsoring organization among the responsibilities of the event marketer. This is about how the price creates value on the other side. Knowing the corporate financial philosophy of the company that organizes the event, the cost of doing business and the financial demographics of the target audience is significant in the successful conclusion of the event. In particular, analyzing the payment capacity of the target audience will affect the planning of the event. The location element will increase the chance of successful marketing of events due to its easy accessibility feature. For instance, a congress held at a hotel near the airport attracts more attention from the participants, so participation in the congress will increase. The public relations element is part of the promotion mix, which is the subcomponent of marketing and creates positive perceptions of the participants. Businesses should act by paying attention to the current perception of the participants when creating a public relations campaign. In this case, the more the businesses' approach towards the participants develops, the more the public relations factor will contribute to the marketing of the event. Positioning, on the other hand, is another factor affecting event marketing and ensures the correct positioning of the product (Hoyle et al., 2002: 15-19). Niche markets are the best example of this. Niche markets that serve to fill the gap in the market are defined as positioning the business to meet unmet needs in these gaps (Cory, 1991: 241). The correct positioning of the business will contribute to the success of event marketing, as it will meet the gap in the market and meet consumer expectations. Based on all these factors, defining the product correctly selected in the activities helps the target audience to make decisions regarding the strategies to be used. In this case, it is more likely that the societies living in Industry 4.0 will direct the marketing of events with ICTs.

The globalization phenomenon that makes the world a single market and the changing understanding of production and marketing have led to the birth of different sales techniques. So, a tailor-made production approach is realized and the issue of consumer satisfaction becomes more important. Thanks to information communication and technologies, the number of events organized for the developing informatics sector is increasing, and quality and cheap production is becoming widespread (Özsoylu, 2017: 43). For instance, the Mediterranean Informatics Summit, which has been organized for the last few years, attracts the attention of many audiences. At this summit where new technologies are mentioned, participants have gained awareness about the IT sector. Many valuable speakers support participants to make the event productive by explaining their experiences. These types of events link mechanical and electronic components through information technologies. So, it ensures the communication and continuity of each of them in a network system. These systems reveal the existence of cyber physical systems in the development of Industry 4.0. Ensuring sustainability in production with the introduction of products developed based on these systems also contributes to further industrialization. This situation provides significant steps towards further technological transformation in marketing strategies.

Globalization leads to unprecedented increases in global innovation, competitiveness, and economic growth. This effect of globalization is more evident in the IT sector, which is one of the leading technologies. Industry 4.0 has a significant place in the IT sector as it is the digital industrial revolution. The IT sector takes over the production of robots that communicate with each other, can detect the environment with their sensors and perform data analysis, and reduce human errors with the development of artificial intelligence. Transfer of production from factories to homes through three-dimensional printers; enables a cheaper, higher quality and more economical production (Ertuğrul and Deniz, 2018: 168). Due to these features, Industry 4.0 is also related to the employment structure. With this revolution, the demand for employees equipped with ICTs will increase. Therefore, professions such as skilled labor and data analysts will gain importance (Özsoylu, 2017: 57). While the rights of old employees are protected, new employees need to make new planning and programming with structural adjustment programs (World Economic Forum, 2016). In this context, it is expected that with Industry 4.0, the production and logistics costs will decrease by 10-30% and quality management costs by 10-20% (Rojko, 2017: 80). Besides, production processes will accelerate as a result of using new production techniques with ICTs. This will also facilitate the provision of resource allocation.

Thanks to the digital transformation in the global economy, the economic dimension of Industry 4.0 is also affected by the increase in productivity. The economic dimension also reflects the sustainability dimension of Industry 4.0. Through smart specialization strategies, regional and global opportunities are addressed and information on market developments is obtained. This will accelerate economic growth by increasing digital investments thanks to the digitization process and transparent information provided in the market (Toker, 2018: 60). On the other hand, in order to increase the contribution of Industry 4.0 to the development of the information and communication sector, the production and marketing networks of the entrepreneurs must be expanded. Therefore, the Internet of Things is expected to have sufficient infrastructure for the event marketing of Industry 4.0 components such as smart factories.

FUTURE RESEARCH DIRECTIONS

The concept of Industry 4.0 contributes to the development of the digitalization process through ICTs. This development positively affected marketing innovations and event marketing. So, Industry 4.0, event marketing, ICTs, and event management are discussed together in this book chapter. Industry 4.0, the possibility of technology transfer from developed countries to developing countries such as Turkey is creating. So, the increasing number of events such as fairs, seminars, and workshops in developed and developing countries is considered as a positive result for the development and welfare of the countries' economies. Developing policies for these events to adapt to the development of technology standards and to play an significant role in the digitalization process of industrialization provides guidance for future studies.

CONCLUSION

Industry 4.0, digital transformation and ICTs concepts have been a very popular subject in recent years. This concept, which has many components such as the cyber physical system and the IoT, causes fluctuations in the socio-economic situation of countries. It greatly affects the returns of countries' production factors and the competitiveness of countries. Advances made with disruptive technologies such as big data and data analytics, nanotechnology, biotechnology, and intelligent specialization are evaluated in terms of the global economy in production, consumption, and distribution. With the effect of these opportunities, Industry 4.0 creates various innovations in the marketing sector and these innovations enable the marketing of events to gain momentum in the development process. Developed countries that are in a competitive monopoly position and developing countries trying to develop their technologies tried to determine the road map of Industry 4.0 through various global companies. In this context, factors such as innovation studies, R&D activities, ICTs, and digital transformation of the industry will affect regional development and public welfare. Thanks to the ICTs developed with globalization, developments in Industry 4.0 also play a major role in event marketing. The development of event marketing depends on the organizations and organizations that organize the event to coordinate their management processes about their brands well. The development of brand-consumer relationships also affects the success of the event. The development of brands in accordance with the wishes and needs of the consumers affects brand loyalty and enables the decision of the consumers to purchase the products quickly. On the other hand, the fact that the target audience has the chance to experience the products requires that consumers behave more rationally when purchasing the product. This enables the activity to be carried to a higher dimension.

Industry 4.0 affects company investments within the scope of value chains and ICTs. With smart specialization strategies, companies can find more growth opportunities by increasing their capital. This concept, which contributes to the development process of smart production, enables the creation of new business models thanks to the IT sector. The sectoral distribution of these business models will affect the marketing mix factors such as product, price, promotion, and distribution, and will lead to various marketing innovations. Increased recognition of these innovations is possible with the effect of ICTs. Addressing event marketing through digital transformation in areas such as experiential marketing and social media marketing increases the sustainability of the event. This enables the creation of events organized in real-time as a result of Industry 4.0 and the creation of value-added chain networks between events. These networks increase the potential for stability and efficiency by improving the quality of service in events. In this context, the efficiency potential increases by improving the service quality of events by means of information communication technologies. This situation reveals the global value chain concept with the development of production capacity and employment phenomena. Thus, companies in the global economy gain a cost competition function in activities.

ICTs constitute the most significant dynamics of developments in the technological field of globalization. The fact that the flow of information was more effective in producing information on the perspective of these developments led to revolutionary innovations. These innovations also had a significant impact on the acceleration of the ICTs process. Globalization dynamism also affects marketing innovations organized through Industry 4.0 and the event marketing process of these innovations. This effect is achieved through the use of advanced technologies in production processes, reducing costs and increasing productivity and profitability. Effective use of ICTs has required the organization of an automation system suitable for the activities by adapting the market needs to the target audience. In this context, the formation of an innovative event idea while determining the process in event management is the first step affecting the success of event marketing. The determination and compliance of the strategies by organizers and participants for a successful event marketing will reduce the risk to be faced during the event as the event has features such as quality, price, time and environmental friendliness.

REFERENCES

Aksoy, S. (2017). Değişen Teknolojiler ve Endüstri 4.0: Endüstri 4.0'ı Anlamaya Dair Bir Giriş. *SAV Katkı*, *4*, 34–44.

Aksoy, T. (2011). Deneyimsel Pazarlama. [https://www.myfikirler.org/deneyimsel-pazarlama.html]. Access date: January, 2020.

Altunbaş, H. (2011). Pazarlama İletişimi ve Etkinlik (Event) Pazarlaması 'Müzik Eğlence Etkinliğinin Marka İletişimine Etkisi'. *İstanbul Üniversitesi İletişim Fakültesi Dergisi*, *34*, 23-35.

Arıca, L. A. (2016). Deneyimsel Pazarlama ve Başarılı Örnekler. [https://www.dijitalajanslar.com/deneyimsel-pazarlama-ve-basarili-ornekler/]. Access date: January, 2020.

Balkır, B. (2018). Sanayi 4.0 Üzerine Görüşler. *İktisat ve Toplum Dergisi*, *92*, 77-82.

Bartodziej, C. J. (2017). The concept industry 4.0. In *The concept industry 4.0* (pp. 51–77). Springer Gabler. doi:10.1007/978-3-658-16502-4_4

Bulunmaz, B. (2016). Gelişen Teknolojiyle Birlikte Değişen Pazarlama Yöntemleri ve Dijital Pazarlama. *Trt Akademi*, *1*(2), 348–365.

Büyükkalaycı, G., & Karaca, H. M. (2019). Pazarlama 4.0: Nesnelerin İnterneti. *Üçüncü Sektör Sosyal Ekonomi Dergisi*, *54*(1), 463-477.

Çakaloğlu, M., & Çağatay, S. (2015). *Coğrafi İşaretler ve Değişen Tüketici Algısı: Finike Portakalı ve Antalya Tavşan Yüreği Zeytini Örnekleri*. Antalya: Yüksek Lisans Tezi. Akdeniz Üniversitesi Sosyal Bilimler Enstitüsü.

Çifterler, Ö. (2013). *Elektronik Pazarlamada İnternet Reklamcılığı: Özel Alışveriş Siteleri Üzerine Bir İnceleme*. İstanbul: Yüksek Lisans Tezi. Marmara Üniversitesi Sosyal Bilimler Enstitüsü.

Close, A. G., Finney, R. Z., Lacey, R. Z., & Sneath, J. Z. (2006). Engaging the consumer through event marketing: Linking attendees with the sponsor, community, and brand. *Journal of Advertising Research*, *46*(4), 420–433.

Cory, J. (1991). Niche marketing: What it is and how it works. *Chilton's Hardware Age*, *228*(8), 239–245.

Cruceru, A. F., & Moise, D. (2014). Customer relationships through sales forces and marketing events. *Procedia: Social and Behavioral Sciences*, *109*, 155–159.

Drengner, J., Gaus, H., & Jahn, S. (2008). Does flow influence the brand image in event marketing? *Journal of Advertising Research*, *48*(1), 138–147. doi:10.2501/S0021849908080148

Erdil, E. (2018). Dijital Dönüşüm/Endüstri 4.0 ve Türkiye. *İktisat ve Toplum Dergisi*, *92*, 57-61.

Ertuğrul, İ., & Deniz, G. (2018). 4.0 Dünyası: Pazarlama 4.0 ve Endüstri 4.0. *Bitlis Eren Üniversitesi Sosyal Bilimler Enstitüsü Dergisi*, *7*(1), 143–170.

Fırat, S. Ü., & Fırat, O. Z. (2017). Sanayi 4.0 Devrimi Üzerine Karşılaştırmalı Bir İnceleme: Kavramlar, Küresel Gelişmeler ve Türkiye. *Toprak İşveren Dergisi*, *114*, 10–23.

Göktaş, B., & Kulga, C. E. (2017). Tüketicilerin Etkinlik Pazarlaması Faaliyetlerine ve Düzenleyen Markalara Bakış Açısına Yönelik Bir Araştırma. *Global Journal of Economics and Business Studies*, *6*(11), 85–97.

Hahn, G. J. (2019). Industry 4.0: A supply chain innovation perspective. *International Journal of Production Research*, 1–17.

Hofmann, E., & Rüsch, M. (2017). Industry 4.0 and the current status as well as future prospects on logistics. *Computers in Industry*, *89*, 23–34. doi:10.1016/j.compind.2017.04.002

Hoyle, L. H. CAE., & CMP. (2002). Event marketing: How to successfully promote events, festivals, conventions, and expositions, John Wiley & Sons, Inc.

Jara, A. J., Parra, M. C., & Skarmeta, A. F. (2012, July). Marketing 4.0: A new value added to the Marketing through the Internet of Things. In *2012 Sixth International Conference on Innovative Mobile and Internet Services in Ubiquitous Computing* (pp. 852-857). IEEE. 10.1109/IMIS.2012.203

Kagermann, H., Wahlster, W., & Helbig, J. (Eds.). (2013). Recommendations for implementing the strategic initiative industrie 4.0: Final report of the industrie 4.0 working group. Academic Press.

Khotimah, K., Sari, D., & Kaltum, U. (2016). Event marketing and experiential marketing towards the formation of net marketing contribution margin (NMCM)(study at pt. garuda indonesia, tbk). *Procedia: Social and Behavioral Sciences*, *219*, 431–439. doi:10.1016/j.sbspro.2016.05.017

Kim, N. S., & Chalip, L. (2004). Why travel to the FIFA World Cup? Effects of motives, background, interest, and constraints. *Tourism Management, 25*(6), 695–707. doi:10.1016/j.tourman.2003.08.011

Kotler, P., Kartajaya, H., & Setiawan, I. (2010). *Welcome to marketing 3.0*. John Wiley & Sons, Inc. doi:10.1002/9781118257883.ch1

Kotler, P., & Keller, K. (2006). *Marketing management* (12th ed.). Pearson Prentice Hall.

Kotler, P., & Keller, K. (2009). *Marketing management* (13th ed.). Prentice-Hall.

Lee, E. A. (2008). Cyber physical systems: Design challenges. *11th IEEE International Symposium on Object and Component-Oriented Real-Time Distributed Computing (ISORC)* (pp. 363-369). IEEE. 10.1109/ISORC.2008.25

Lom, M., Pribyl, O., & Svitek, M. (2016, May). Industry 4.0 as a part of smart cities. In *2016 Smart Cities Symposium Prague (SCSP)* (pp. 1-6). IEEE. 10.1109/SCSP.2016.7501015

Luo, W. (2014). Germany industrial 4.0 strategic enlightenment to China's industrial transformation. *Fiber Reinforced Plastics/Composites*, 125-128.

Mucuk, İ. (2010). *Pazarlama İlkeleri*. Türkmen Kitabevi.

Nagasawa, S. (2008). Customer experience management influencing on human kansei to management of technology. *The TQM Journal, 20*(4), 312–323. doi:10.1108/17542730810881302

Okay, H. (2017). Helikopter Bakışı. [https://www.dunya.com/kose-yazisi/deneyimsel-pazarlama/345266]. Access date: January, 2020.

Özsoylu, A. F. (2017). Endüstri 4.0. *Çukurova Üniversitesi İktisadi ve İdari Bilimler Fakültesi Dergisi, 21*(1), 41-64.

Roblek, V., Meško, M., & Krapež, A. (2016). A complex view of industry 4.0. *Sage Open, 6*(2), 1-11.

Rojko, A. (2017). Industry 4.0 concept: Background and overview. *International Journal of Interactive Mobile Technologies, 11*(5), 77–90. doi:10.3991/ijim.v11i5.7072

Schmitt, B. H. (1999). *Experiential Marketing: How to Get Customers to Sense. Feel, Think, Act, and Relate to Your Company and Brands*. The Free Press.

Schmitt, B. H. (2003). *Competitive advantage through the customer experience*. The EX Group.

Seyfi, M. (2017). *Halkla ilişkiler perspektifinde dijital etkinlik yönetimi*. Der Yayınları.

Smilansky, S. (2009). *Experiential marketing: A practical guide to interactive brand experiences*. Kogan Page Publishers.

Sneath, J. Z., Finney, R. Z., & Close, A. G. (2005). An IMC approach to event marketing: The effects of sponsorship and experience on customer attitudes. *Journal of Advertising Research, 45*(4), 373–381. doi:10.1017/S0021849905050440

Tarabasz, A. (2013). The reevaluation of communication in customer approach-towards marketing 4.0. *International Journal of Contemporary Managament, 12*(4), 124–134.

Toker, K. (2018). Endüstri 4.0 ve Sürdürülebilirliğe Etkileri. *Institute of Business Administration-Management Journal/İşletme İktisadi Enstitüsü Yönetim Dergisi*, *29*(84), 51-64.

Tolan, S. (2014). *Spor Endüstrisinde Etkinlik Pazarlaması: Galatasaray Spor Kulübü Örneği*. Yüksek Lisans Tezi. Maltepe Üniversitesi Sosyal Bilimler Enstitüsü.

Ulusoy, G. (2018). İmalat Sektöründe Endüstri 4.0 Dönüşüm Çabaları. *Bazı Gözlemler, İktisat ve Toplum Dergisi*, *92*, 63–65.

Wood, E. H. (2009). Evaluating event marketing: Experience or outcome? *Journal of Promotion Management*, *15*(1-2), 247–268. doi:10.1080/10496490902892580

World Economic Forum. (2016). The future of jobs. [http://www3.weforum.org/docs/WEF_FOJ_Executive_Summary_Jobs.pdf]. Access date: January, 2020.

Yalçın, F. G. (2017). DijitalAge. [https://digitalage.com.tr/tum-yonleriyle-etkinlik-pazarlamasi-ve-etkinlik-pazarlamasinda-son-trendler/]. Access date: January, 2020.

Yıldız, A. (2018). Endüstri 4.0 ve Akıllı Fabrikalar. *Sakarya Üniversitesi Fen Bilimleri Enstitüsü Dergisi*, *22*(2), 546–556.

Yin, Y., Stecke, K. E., & Li, D. (2018). The evolution of production systems from Industry 2.0 through Industry 4.0. *International Journal of Production Research*, *56*(1-2), 848–861. doi:10.1080/00207543.2017.1403664

Yu, H., & Ko, H. T. (2012). Integrating Kano model with strategic experiential modules in developing ICT-enabled services: An empirical study. *Management Decision*, *50*(1), 7–20. doi:10.1108/00251741211194840

Yüksekbilgili, Z., & Çevik, G. Z. (2018). Endüstri 4.0 Bağlamında Türkiye'nin Yerine İlişkin Güncel ve Gelecek Eksenli Bir Analiz. *Finans Ekonomi ve Sosyal Araştırmalar Dergisi*, *3*(2), 422–436.

Zhou, K., Liu, T., & Zhou, L. (2015, August). Industry 4.0: Towards future industrial opportunities and challenges. In *2015 12th International conference on fuzzy systems and knowledge discovery (FSKD)* (pp. 2147-2152). IEEE.

ADDITIONAL READING

Bach, M. P. (2014). Exploring information and communications technology adoption in enterprises and its impact on innovation performance of European countries. *Ekonomicky Casopis*, *62*(04), 335–362.

Breukel, A., & Go, F. M. (2009). Knowledge-based network participation in destination and event marketing: A hospitality scenario analysis perspective. *Tourism Management*, *30*(2), 184–193. doi:10.1016/j.tourman.2008.05.015

Dalenogare, L. S., Benitez, G. B., Ayala, N. F., & Frank, A. G. (2018). The expected contribution of Industry 4.0 technologies for industrial performance. *International Journal of Production Economics*, *204*, 383–394. doi:10.1016/j.ijpe.2018.08.019

Daniel, M., Bogdan, G., & Daniel, Z. (2012). The use of event marketing management strategies. *Procedia: Social and Behavioral Sciences*, *46*, 5409–5413. doi:10.1016/j.sbspro.2012.06.448

Hudson, S., & Hudson, L. (2017). Marketing for tourism, hospitality & events: A global & digital approach. *Sage (Atlanta, Ga.)*.

Li, G., Tan, J. L., & Chaudhry, S. S. (2019). Industry 4.0 and big data innovations. *Enterprise Information Systems*, *13*(2), 145–147. doi:10.1080/17517575.2018.1554190

Ungerman, O., Dedkova, J., & Gurinova, K. (2018). The impact of marketing innovation on the competitiveness of enterprises in the context of industry 4.0. *Journal of Competitiveness*, *10*(2), 132–148. doi:10.7441/joc.2018.02.09

Witkowski, K. (2017). Internet of things, big data, industry 4.0–innovative solutions in logistics and supply chains management. *Procedia Engineering*, *182*, 763–769. doi:10.1016/j.proeng.2017.03.197

KEY TERMS AND DEFINITIONS

Cyber Physical Systems: It is an Industry 4.0 component that features an intelligent network system created in the entire value chain through ICTs.

Digital Transformation: It is the optimal use of technology in all processes for brands to adapt to digital time.

Event Marketing: It is a process where companies use ICTs in planning and implementing marketing mix events to meet the demands and needs of the participants.

Experiential Marketing: It is a form of marketing that contains many emotions and enables the connection between the brand and the consumer before purchasing the product and service.

Globalization: It is a concept that strengthens the integration of national economies and increases the competitiveness of these economies with each other as a result of increasing the functional income distribution among countries.

Industry 4.0: It is a concept that provides various innovative and technical features to industrialization with advanced ICTs and R&D events in production processes.

Internet of Things: It is a network that enables companies, which play a major role in the improvement of Industry 4.0 and make great use of ICTs, to make optimum decisions in their management.

Marketing 4.0: It is an effective marketing system that reflects the transition process from traditional product-oriented marketing to a customer-oriented virtual marketing-focused approach and reflects commercial transactions.

Chapter 4
Emerging Technologies at the Events

Cihan Cobanoglu
University of South Florida, USA

Seden Doğan
https://orcid.org/0000-0001-8547-7702
Ondokuz Mayis University, Turkey

Mehtap Yücel Güngör
Anadolu University, Turkey

ABSTRACT

Events are creating huge demand, have a vital role, and contribute to the tourism industry considerably. Whatever the objective or topic of the event, they are popular attraction to achieve diverse outputs. There are different types of events such as mega-events, special events, festivals, conventions, exhibitions, fairs, concerts, sporting events, and trade shows. They all have different purposes, different target audiences, and different planning processes. But the common thing that they need is to finish an event successfully and beneficially for both organizers and attendees. In this respect, they need to benefit from the advantages of technology. Technology use to plan, perform, and finalize an event is important. In this chapter, both academic studies and industrial articles have been reviews to provide information regarding the emerging technologies at the events with real-world examples. It has been seen that most music and sporting events used new technologies to attract and satisfy the attendees.

INTRODUCTION

The event industry has been one of the fastest evolving industries in the world. Even though COVID-19 pandemic impacted the event industry significantly, the trends in countries that controlled the pandemic such as China shows that event industry will recover quickly (Farazad, 2020). Oxford Economics and Events Industry Council pointed out that only the meetings generated 1294 USD spending per attendee

DOI: 10.4018/978-1-7998-4954-4.ch004

in 2018 (Event MB, 2019). Whether an event focuses on sport, luxury, entertainment, or music; event industry around the world is generating billions of revenues and changing the way of operation in the hospitality industry. A conference, a trade show, a concert, a sport event or a festival are samples of this important industry. Different destinations in many countries are realizing that the event industry is vital to attract visitors and they are trying to create new events (Glion, 2020) to gain more from this vibrant industry.

The event industry has the ability to utilize the emerging technologies before many other industries. There has been a growing trend of using more sophisticated technologies in event and meeting planning and production in recent years. The emerging technologies and applications transformed the nature of event planning and production (Yen, Wey, & Sullivan, 2016) in many attractive ways. Back in 1980s, event organizers were using basic computerized badge production and accept the reservation by a phone call or by walk-in customers. It was not possible to talk about any event technologies at that time. In 2000, first virtual tradeshow which was Expo Exchange has been organized by SpotMe in London. The show allowed the attendees to see pictures and contact information of other attendees. Following years, many technological developments have been presented such as wi-fi, iPhone, Skype, Face Time and others (Aksentyeva et al., 2020). With the emergence of Internet, the event planners started to build informative and up-to-date web sites to provide necessary information. Then, they started to create social media accounts to engage both stakeholders and attendees for more productive event experiences. Website of the events has always allowed one-way communication between organizers and stakeholders of the events but with the help of social media platforms, organizers were able to not only communicate but also interact with the people who were interested in to attend the event as participants or traders. Social media platforms were also beneficial to develop different strategies to promote the event. With the beginning of the fourth industrial revolution, new technologies have emerged into the business life in many different, attractive and productive ways. Automation, virtual reality applications, augmented reality, artificial intelligence development, Internet of Things and sensors, unmanned flying objects, driverless vehicles, and many other were started to be used by many industries such as automotive, medicine, retail, and agriculture as well as the tourism industry. Artificially intelligent robots are employed at hotels, restaurants, and airports to provide information and deliver items. Virtual reality and augmented reality are used in cultural heritage sites and museums to improve the visitor engagement. With the help of Internet of Things which can be defined as the connectiveness between devices with the help of internet protocol, contactless orders and contactless payments became possible. Wearable technologies help people to track the movements. Unmanned flying objects like drones provide nearly perfect visual ability to record videos and take photos (Ivanov et al., 2019; tom Dieck & Hyungsoo Jung, 2017; Stek, 2016). These technologies have also been started to be used effectively and creatively by the event industry. It is possible to experience augmented reality and hologram technologies at the sporting events or concerts. Massive events have started to use wearable technologies to provide constant information to the attendees and track their behavior. Facial recognition technology allows the organizers to perform the check-in process fast and more efficiently. However, academic studies about usage of these technologies at the events are very limited. In the existed literature, some of the authors evaluated the usage and role of social media in the events (Strickland et al., 2016; Severt, Fjelstul, & Breiter, 2013; Lee, Xiong, & Hu, 2012) while some of the others investigated the impact of mobile applications in the event industry (Ziyadin et al., 2019). From the attendee perspective, these technologies have also many advantages like saving time, securing personal information, watching a unique show, and exchanging information with other attendees. Wearable technologies help to terminate long lines on the different points of interest, facial recognition provides personalized service, hologram brings impossible performances on stage such as a deceased person (Social Tables, 2020; Schatz, 2019).

The new emerging technologies allow event planners to organize the event to satisfy the attendees in a cost-effective way also. With the help of different applications and tools, event planners can have more detailed information about the attendees. Thus, the ability to choose the appropriate tools, products and services can help the event planners to provide a more satisfying and enjoyable events for the attendees. Second, the emerging technologies such as wearable technologies help the attendees to enable to access all the information of an event from anywhere at any time. This helps them fulfill their objectives of attending an event and create a memorable event experience (Yen, Wey, & Sullivan, 2016). On the other hand, emerging event technologies create better opportunities for event organizer while working on the same event. Effective communication is crucial in determining the success of an event. Besides, it is more comfortable and convenient to collect data about the attendees which helps improve the event (Mehrotra & Lobo, 2020).

Event technologies can be defined as any digital tools and innovations that can help event organizers to provide a successful, secure, entertaining, and attractive event for the attendees (Event Brite, 2020). According to a recent research, 94% of event professionals are planning to invest in event technologies to boost engagement. About 75% of them will buy apps to increase audience engagement (Sitapara, 2017). According to the Global Event Industry Benchmarks Study conducted in 2016, 47% of the event organizers said that they used technology during events to be more efficient and to improve attendees' experience both in their offices and on-site. They claimed that technology usage helped them to reduce the costs, to save time, and to compete easier (Cvent, 2017). EventMB (2019) pointed out that 52.6% of event professionals invested more in technologies in 2018 comparing with the previous year. Another research conducted by Harvard Business Review Analytic Services showed that 90% of event technology adopters consider themselves well-positioned for future success (Shaw, 2019).

MAIN FOCUS OF THE CHAPTER

Artificial Intelligence, Robots and Chatbots

Artificial intelligence is defined as *"a technology or machine that can perform a task that, if conducted by a human, would require intelligence to complete"* (Buhalis et al., 2019, p. 487). The artificial intelligence applications significantly impact the operations, managerial issues, product and service development, finance, marketing and sales strategies, and relationships with the customers (Wirtz et al., 2018).

The artificial intelligence implementation may have a high impact on experiences and value formation at events. The events are rich to show how event organizers use smart access and payment systems to enhance their experiences and keep them up to date. The AI may support the event experience by providing personalized recommendations, assistance, and suggestions, and enhancing event organization in logistics, crowd management, and access systems (Neuhofer, Magnus, & Celuch, 2020). Moreover, the artificial intelligence helps the organizer to track and analyze the attendees' emotions by using their facial expressions. Emotional recognition is very helpful to determine how the attendees feel about a performance or product (Solaris, 2020).

Additionally, the concept of the robot has rapidly developed, and as of 2020, there is a wide variety of robots with different features, which can be categorized into two types as stationary and mobile. A robot can be defined as *"relatively autonomous physical device capable of motion and performing a service"* (Murphy et al., 2017, p. 106). Although the concept of "robot" was used for the first time in 1920, the existence of the first robot-like machines can be dated back to 3000 BC. Automatic water clocks of ancient Egyptian, Greek and Anatolian civilizations and similar machines may be some examples that have been developed by an engineer from Alexandria who lived around 1000 BC (Yildiz, 2019).

With artificial intelligence, mobile robots can interact with people in different ways, and this ability turns them into social beings. In this context, the service robots are employed to perform many service jobs in the front of the house and production jobs in the back of hotels, restaurants, airports, and event organizations. Some of the tasks performed by the robots are welcoming the guests, providing information, delivering food and drinks, and cleaning the toilets. Robotic receptionists, luggage holders, luggage storage robots, room assistants, robots using vacuum cleaners are some of the examples of robot technologies seen in hotel businesses. Various hotels use robots to provide food and beverage service and similar services to guests' rooms. With the widespread use of robot technology in different departments of hotels, it may reduce labor costs as well as increase efficiency in operations (Ibis, 2019).

Several hotels, restaurants, museums, shopping malls, conference centers, and airports around the world employ these robots. On the other hand, the industrial robots that look more like a machine with robotic arms are used to carry items, mix cocktails, and make different beverages. The robots developed by Bosch and Denso with two robotic arms make coffee and latte during massive events (Ellison, 2017). In the event industry, service robots can be used in different settings. A service robot can interact with and engage humans in a social setting such as a concert, an exhibition opening, or a gala. The main tasks of the service robots are to provide information and assist the human co-workers (Cain, Thomas, & Alonso, 2019). The service robots create new and entertaining forms of interaction and experience for both customers and employees (Rosete et al., 2020). Especially the leading event companies started to modernize their service with by combining services with this emerging technology. Robotic bartenders, robotic waiters and waitresses, robotic welcome staff, and many more are available to entertain the attendees at the events. Designed by the M.I.T. Senseable City Lab in collaboration with the Coca-Cola Company and Bacardi Rums and produced by Italian firm Carlo Ratti Associati, robotic bartender MakrShakr was perfomed at Google I/O conference in 2013. The attendees ordered the coctails via the MakrShakr mobile application and had chance to watch the robotic bartender mix the drinks. On the other hand, MantaroBots created a TeleMe which was integrated with an Apple device or Android tablet for the users to connect to an event via a video conference application. Similarly, Anybots QB robot has been developed with an integrated screen camera, and speaker to be controlled and activated via a web-based communication system. This robot can attend an event instead of human attendees (Sorrells, 2013). 24 robotic dogs named Jimu that have been developed by UBTECH performed at the Spring Festival Gala's opening in China. They danced, licked paws, and wagged tails during the show (Peng, 2018). Similarly, Mini Ada that was developed by a Turkish robotic company, was hired by an event organization to welcome the attendees and provide information at the opening ceremony different fairs and exhibitions (Akin Soft, 2019).

Robot photographers are being hired by event and especially wedding planners. For example, an artificial intelligence-powered robot named Eva was hired by the event planners in the UK. 5-foot-tall Eva that has a touchscreen panel on its torso, has been designed with facial recognition technology to take the photos. The photos taken by Eva are sent to the people's email address, can be shared through social media or can be printed out at a photo station (Zhang, 2019).

For the last days of the International Robotics Festival, which was held from in 2017 in Pisa, ABB has teamed up with the Lucca Philharmonic Orchestra for an atypical event because of replacing a conductor by a robot. The very sophisticated YuMi led the musicians to the baton. The grand finale of this festival was a world first for the Swiss robot, who made it into the classic by conducting the tracks "La Donna E 'Mobile" and "O Mio Babbino Caro" using his two mechanical arms, the 'one wagging the wand while the other made more bent gestures. Installed on his desk, he thus achieved this performance of six minutes, which will have required upstream nearly 17 hours of work (Boudet, 2017).

On the other hand, a San Francisco-based tech company developed robotic dolphins that looked like real dolphins to replace animals in show pools and theme parks. It is partially autonomous and partially remotely controlled. The people who experienced interaction with the robot dolphin could not tell that it was a robot not an animal (Graham-McLay, 2020). A Chinese company plans to use these robot dolphins in aquarium and shopping malls (Goodyear, 2020). The company says they will develop robot white shark and sea dragon (Meisenzahl, 2020).

Briefly, as per Ivanov, Webster, and Berezina (2020)'s latest article, robot integration into events can provide entertainment for the attendees, ensure safety and security, serve food and beverage, distribute merchandise and event amenities, and physical presence for the attendees who are not able to attend the event physically.

Chatbots are also used by the event planners. A chatbot is artificially intelligent software that can simulate a communication with a user in natural language through websites, messaging applications, and mobile applications. Chatbots provide a unique way to improve the customer engagement process and to reduce operational cost (Expert System, 2020). Event organizers integrate chatbots with the event website and mobile application to interact with the attendees instantly and to cut the temporary event staff cost. If the chatbot implementation is built successfully, the chatbots will provide fast and quick answers to the attendees' questions and save too much time of the organizers (Solaris, 2020). Chatbot software, which has many functions such as ordering food, arranging meetings, providing information, is expected to become one of the most important assets of the customer communication process (Yalcin Kayikci & Kutlu Bozkurt, 2018).

Hologram

Holography, from the Greek for whole and drawing, is "*a methodology which creates an exact visual replication of an object in three physical dimensions including all the depth cues, focal planes, and specific coordinates*" (Bruckheimer & Rotschild, 2019, p. 384) and conceived by Dennis Gabor in 1947 as a mean of improving electron microscopy. Gabor, who performed the hologram in 1963, announced his invention to the world with the book "Let's Create the Future." He named this technique "Holography" and won Nobel Prize in 1971.

A hologram is a reflection technology. It is a laser photo of any object. Firstly, 3D photographs are recorded with laser technology. Then they are stored, and the movement effect is added to the record. Finally, the record is transferred to a multidimensional environment (Durge & Jagtap, 2016). The hologram consists of a light-sensitive emulsion with a film or a thin sheet of glass. It is an incoming two-dimensional (2D) storage material. Interference patterns in this recording taken with laser help can also be transformed into a three-dimensional (3D) color and transparent light image (Leonardo, 2001).

John Henry Pepper, a British scientist and inventor, is best known for making a ghost appear on stage during an 1862 demonstration at the Polytechnic Institute in London. Pepper fitted an angled pane of glass on stage to reflect a brightly lit actor hiding beneath the stage. The actor's reflection was refracted through the angled glass and directed onto the stage. As a result, it looked as if a ghost was floating on stage (Engelking, 2015). The hologram technology was introduced to the whole world during the Coachella festival held in the USA in 2012. The famous musician Tupac Amaru Shakur who was shot dead in 1996, appeared on the stage (Tsukayama, 2012). While Snoop Dogg and Dr. Dre rapped behind the Mylar film, which was placed on the big stage at a 45-degree angle, a high-definition video feed was projected onto a reflective screen, and finally bounced off the Mylar film to create the illusion. Tupac's head was digitally recreated, then placed atop a body double (Engelking, 2015) and was projected on it using high-definition video projectors reflecting off mirrors below the stage (Khan, 2012). The cost of the hologram Tupac is estimated from $100,000 to $400,000. This performance also raised a new touring industry. Deceased artists like Frank Zappa, Roy Orbison, Buddy Holly, Amy Winehouse, and Michael Jackson have their hologram tour series (Nisancioglu, 2020). Buddy Holly, who died in 1959, and Roy Orbison, who died in 1988, have holographic versions developed by the BASE Company which created Amy Winehouse's hologram (Schatz, 2019). A holographic image of Michael Jackson performed on stage during the Billboard Music Awards at the MGM Grand Garden Arena in 2014 in Las Vegas (Gallo, 2014). Japanese composer and pianist Yoshiki performed a concert with his hologram. First, his hologram appeared on the stage, then Yoshiki himself came. Later, they played the piano together. This technology provides an opportunity that the performances can be performed more often and at more locations simultaneously (Meyer, 2014). Similarly, in 2019, during the annual League of Legends World Championship opening ceremony in Paris at the Accor Hotels Arena, hologram technology was featured. Circus Roncalli, which perform in Europe since 1976, is the first to introduce hologram animals instead of live performers. The Circus Roncalli has 11 Eleven ZU 850 projectors to create the 3D hologram elephants, horses, monkeys, and others (BBC, 2019; Miley, 2019). The dancing elephant is 20 feet tall. It is a 3D hologram and has six million pixels created by 15 engineers, more than 3000 processors, and 11 laser beams (Wolters, 2019).

Drones

Drones are widely known under various names, such as "*unmanned aerial vehicles (UAVs), unmanned aerial system (UAS), and remotely piloted vehicles (RPVs)*" and mean buzz. They can be categorized as fixed-wing, single-rotor multirotor, and fixed-wing hybrid (Li & Liu, 2019). The drones can be found in different sizes and shapes. They can be used indoor conferences and outdoor events. In this sense, they are accessible for the event organizers. For example, the organizers use drones to show the logo or motto of the event in the air (Hill, 2015). They provide colorful and memorable performances. The drones are also beneficial for the organizers to map the venue because they can capture images from non-accessible places (Drone Hive, 2019).

The drones are primarily used at sports events as they provide a broad landscape and pictures that are better than any photographer. They can also be combined with footage from traditional video cameras to capture corporate meetings (Thornley-Brown, 2018; Dodd, 2017). The drones were used during The Wooden Boat Festival to broadcast the event live (Kurgun, 2019). The CCTV Spring Festival Gala, China's famous festival that is being watched by hundreds of millions of people worldwide, started to use emerging technologies such as self-driving cars and boats, drones, and artificially intelligent robots. In 2018, 300 flying drones occurred over the Hong Kong-Zhuhai Macao Bridge in a dolphin shape. It was China's first 3D stereoscopic drone show (Peng, 2018). Similarly, 300 drones performed a choreographic show in the air in 2018 in Amsterdam. The project named as Franchise Freedom and developed by a tech company.

Drones are also becoming integrated into the production side of live events. In an aerial ballet, choreographed by event producer George P. Johnson at the Los Angeles Auto Show in 2015, a squadron of drones attached to translucent boxes hid the car from view at its press event. The drones then took off in a sequence that revealed the car on stage (Daley, 2019).The drone-based monitoring for the events has many advantages, especially in large territories. One of the advantages is obtaining a large-scale security. The drones have a high visibility range and may determine a dangerous or undesirable situation in the crowd. Another advantage is also security related. In any case, the drones may determine the situation's position and inform the security or paramedics to intervene in the situation, especially during a massive event (Robakowska et al., 2017). The drones provide a vast opportunity in advertising and entertainment. They are also seen as life savers regarding harmful and dangerous tasks for workers (Drone Hive, 2019).

Facial Recognition

Facial recognition is a technology that allows to identify or verify a person from a digital image or a video. Social media platforms and many mobile phone applications are using this technology. It works by training an algorithm, and the algorithm estimates to identify the face from the presented image (Sample, 2019). Facial recognition technology uses biometrics to map facial features from a photo or a video and compares them with a database. A recent example of this technology is Facedeals (Schmidt, 2020) which is a system in which a camera scans and detects the customer's face as he/she enters a store such as a restaurant. This scanned face is matched with social media networks such as Facebook to find a match. If a match is found, the customer's information is passed to the store computers to help the staff serve the customer in a more customized way. In addition, some customized deals can be sent to customer's cell phone if customer's phone number is publicly available on social networks.

This technology is instrumental in streamlining key attendee touchpoints. It makes the check-in faster to the event, improves the security process, and collects user data for event planners. It also helps to reduce cost (Social Tables, 2020), profile the attendees, track the traffic during the event (Tatulli, 2019), and provide contactless entrance (Accelevents, 2020). Besides, the organizers may have chance to deliver more personalized and customized event experience to the attendees (Solaris, 2020). Additionally, according to the IBTM World Trends Report published in 2018, Meetings Professionals International (MPI) pointed out that the security was one of the most important issues at the event. Especially during massive events, it might be difficult to obtain full security. Facial recognition technology is considered as a powerful and effective solution for this issue (Turner, 2019).

Wearable Technologies

Wearable technology, which creates interaction between people and computers, can be described as application enabled computing devices that accept and process inputs. Wearable technology products are special electronic monitoring devices synchronized to a computer or smartphone to provide long-term data monitoring wirelessly. They are networked devices that collect data, monitor activities, and be customized according to the users' requests and needs. The networked smart devices equipped with microchips, sensors, and wireless communication capabilities (Ozguner Kilic, 2017). They can be affixed to the body, placed inside clothing or accessories. They have access to some of the communication capabilities and real-time information of the wearer. They can store this information and data in their device memory and transfer it by connecting it to computers or other devices when necessary (Demirci, 2018). These transactions are made by RFID (Radio Frequency Identification) and NFC (Near Field Communication). RFID and NFC use radio waves to allow the attendees to make cashless payment, plan their daily program, order food, and get notification about the program instantly. RFID and NFC also allow the event organizers to track attendees, monitor their behavior, follow up important moments of the event, and reduce the cost (Solaris, 2020).

These technologies are combined with watches, wristbands, glasses, lenses, textile products, smart fabrics, rings, and hearing aids which are wearable devices (Sezgin, 2016). Wristbands and smart badges with NFC chip minimize the lines and increase attendee engagement. With this technology's help, it can be possible to access different event areas, exchange information, receive marketing materials, and make cashless purchases. Wearable technologies also provide fast check-in, control access, and monitor attendee behaviors. Hilton America used wristbands during the Leadership Conference in 2017. The attendees wore wristbands to exchange contact information with others. The wristbands also were incentivized with gamification to reward the attendee with bonus points (Social Tables, 2020).

Augmented Reality

AR can be defined as *"an integration of the real world and the virtual world, with the aim of providing additional information about something in the real world with information displayed in the virtual world"* (Nayyar et al., 2018). This technology, which combines real-world perception of a user with the computer to log in with the reality at the same time, provides visual experiences related to a place or object that they see directly which means without any delay (Gervautz & Schmalsteig, 2012). It covers the user experience with the digital information of advanced real application objects or places (Berryman, 2012). The ability to combine the physical environment with virtual elements such as information or image that can interact with the physical environment in real time provides customers with new possibility for content delivery (Javornik, 2016).

This technology is being used commonly in events, especially in sporting events. It allows attendees of the event to interact and connect to the event by gamifying it. Besides, it provides an opportunity to develop virtual tours and guides for the attendees (Cvent, 2019). It also makes easier for amateur and professional game players to monitor their performance improvement (Bielli & Harris, 2009). For the people who watch a game in the stadium, AR can provide information about restrooms, concessions, merchandise stores, or different places of interest. This technology played a huge role during the Rio 2016 Olympic Games. The OBS (Olympic Committee in charge of Broadcasting) let people watch the games in AR environment (Tremaud, 2017). Another good example has been seen during Korea Baseball Organization's opening in 2019. An image of the team's mascot which is a dragon was shown on the LED baseball scoreboard in the stadium. The flying dragon performed interactively when the attendees in the stadium pressed the cheer button on the mobile app (Hwaya, 2019).

AR is also used at concerts by the bands. The Irish band U2 used AR during their Experience and Innocence Tour. A giant iceberg was projected onto an 80-foot screen, but those who viewed the screen through their phone could see a giant projection of Bono towering over the audience. Maroon 5 also used AR to create a live karaoke experience by collaborating Verizon and Snapchat (Softjourn, 2020). Additionally, automotive events are using AR widely. Toyota Explore Augmented Reality application is one of the good samples (Tremaud, 2017). AR provides visual layers to the events which can enhance the sensory experience of the attendees. At the end of 2020, there might be 1 billion AR users (Deyan, 2020) and the event planners should benefit the advantages of this technology.

SOLUTIONS AND RECOMMENDATIONS

Considering that one of the main objectives of the event planners is to organize successful events and gather high number of attendees, it can be said that newly emerging technologies should be implemented in different steps of the event planning process. Among these technologies' robotics, hologram, drones, and wearable devices seem to have a significant impact on the success and efficiency of the event, satisfaction and engagement of the attendees, and performance of the event staff. Surviving in a competitive environment depends on how successfully the new trends and technologies are effectively used before, during and after an event. An event application which is basically a mobile app for the event, should be developed and used by the staff. The attendees also must be encouraged to use this app.

FUTURE RESEARCH DIRECTIONS

In this chapter, new emerging technologies have been evaluated from the event industry perspective and contains conceptual approach. To provide information, existing literature and related websites have been reviewed. In the future, data can be obtained from the organizers and attendees by using qualitative and/or quantitative methods. Research related robot usage in the hospitality industry mostly focused on hotels and restaurants. The important role of the robots at the events needs to be investigated. Similarly, impact of drones on an event's success or hologram technology's efficiency can be studied. Dark sides of these emerging technologies also need to be determined.

CONCLUSION

Events have become a part of our social life and effective management of events is a pressing need for organizers, developers and sponsors in this rapidly developing industry. The major events that take place around the globe like the Olympics, conferences, musical live concerts, corporate meetings as well as gala weddings need flawless management. A rapidly growing complexity and scale of events require innovative technology to organize them with ease and splendor (Mehrotra & Lobo, 2020). Emerging technologies which change the business environments, operations and the customer engagements can effectively be used in the event industry. The event organizers seek unique and creative ways to organize the events, satisfy the attendees, reduce the overall cost, and decrease the workload and stress level of the staff. Non-human workers like robots and chatbots can be employed to assist the human workers during especially massive events. These applications also might revolutionize the attendees' experience. Robot waiters, robot DJs, robot bartenders, and robot photographers can be very attractive for the attendees. Hologram technology can be saver for animals which have to perform during shows at pools, aquariums or circuses. This technology has also a great potential to bring a dead person back to perform at a concert. In this context, hologram technology is very attractive for both organizers and attendees. The unmanned aircrafts like drones provide many opportunities to improve the event quality. For example, these vehicles can take impossible footage and videos of the event. Facial recognition can provide fast check-in and personalized services. Wearable devices are great tools to track attendees' movements. They also can notify the attendees about the program instantly.

These new technologies have many benefits for both organizers and attendees. They provide opportunity to co-create the value. On the other hand, they help the organizers to plan the event in a time saving way, control the budget, organize the entertaining program, improve the catering services, provide high level of security, and reduce the cost. With the help of these technologies, event planners can obtain more data about the attendees to improve their product and services. Personalization and customization are other important benefits.

REFERENCES

Accelevents. (2020). *The Top 8 Event Technology Trends to Watch in 2020*. https://www.accelevents.com/top-8-event-technology-trends-2020/

Aksentyeva, N., Aminov, D.-S., Cayenne, J., Foo, J., Kammogne, G., Lum, A., & Zhou, H. (2020). *Technology Use in Meetings*. https://theirf.org/am-site/media/technology-in-offsite-meetings-and-incentive-events-full-paper.pdf

BBC. (2019). *A German Circus Uses Holograms instead of Animals and it Looks Amazing!* https://www.bbc.co.uk/newsround/48543263

Bellis, S., & Harris, C. G. (2009). *A Mobile Augmented Reality System to Enhance Live Sporting Events*. https://dl.acm.org/doi/pdf/10.1145/2735711.2735836

Berryman, D. R. (2012). Augmented Reality: A Review. *Medical Reference Services Quarterly*, *31*(2), 212–218. doi:10.1080/02763869.2012.670604 PMID:22559183

Boudet, A. (2017). *EnItalie, un robot chef d'orchestre a dirigé son premier concert* [In Italy, a robot conductor conducted his first concet]. https://www.numerama.com/tech/288927-en-italie-un-robot-chef-dorchestre-a-dirige-son-premier-concert.html

Brite, E. (2020). *10 Event Technology Trends for 2020*. https://www.eventbrite.co.uk/blog/10-event-technology-trends-2020-ds00/

Bruckheimer, E., & Rotschild, C. (2019). Holography in Congenital Heart Disease: Diagnosis and Transcatheter Treatment. In G. Butera, M. Chessa, A. Eicken, & J. Thomson (Eds.), *Atlas of Cardiac Catheterization for Congenital Heart Disease* (pp. 383–386). Springer. doi:10.1007/978-3-319-72443-0_44

Buhalis, D., Harwood, T., Bogievic, V., Viglia, G., Beldona, S., & Hofacker, C. (2019). Technological disruptions in services: Lessons from tourism and hospitality. *Journal of Service Management*, *30*(4), 484–506. doi:10.1108/JOSM-12-2018-0398

Cain, L. N., Thomas, J. H., & Alonso, M. Jr. (2019). From sci-fi to sci-fact: The state of robotics and AI in the hospitality industry. *Journal of Hospitality and Tourism Technology*, *10*(4), 624–650. doi:10.1108/JHTT-07-2018-0066

Cvent. (2017). *Second Annual Global Event Industry Benchmarks Study*. https://nsw.tourismaccommodation.com.au/files/2017/05/2nd-annual-global-event-industry-benchmarks-study.pdf

Cvent. (2019). *The Future of Augmented Reality at Events*. https://www.cvent.com/en/blog/events/the-future-of-augmented-reality-at-events

Daley, D. (2019). *Rise of the Event Drones*. https://www.avixa.org/insight/whitepapers/Details/rise-of-the-event-drones/

Demirci, S. (2018). Giyilebilir Teknolojilerin Sağlık Hizmetlerine ve Sağlık Hizmet Kullanıcılarına Etkileri. *Anemon Muş Alparslan Üniversitesi Sosyal BilimlerDergisi*, *6*(6), 985–992.

Deyan, G. (2020). *29+ Augmented Reality Stats to Keep your Sharp in 2020*. https://techjury.net/blog/augmented-reality-stats/?_ga=2.178951265.433351076.1602176151-113602177.1602176151

Dodd, K. (2017). *Using Drones at your Events*. https://www.eventtechsoftware.com/blog/using-drones-at-your-event

Durge, M. R., & Jagtap, H. P. (2016). 7D Holographic Technology. *International Journal on Recent and Innovation Trends in Computing and Communication*, *4*(1), 67–70.

Ellison, H. (2017). *Event tech: Robots*. https://www.campaignlive.co.uk/article/event-tech-robots/1421036

Engelking, C. (2015). *Beyond Tupac, Can Hologram Concerts Take Off?* https://www.discovermagazine.com/the-sciences/beyond-tupac-can-hologram-concerts-take-off

Event, M. B. (2019). *100 Event Statistics (2020 Edition)*. https://www.eventmanagerblog.com/event-statistics

Expert System. (2020). *Chatbot: What is a Chatbot? Why are Chatbots Important?* https://expertsystem.com/chatbot/

Farazad, K. (2020). *The Recovery Period Time for Hospitality Sector*. https://www.hospitalitynet.org/opinion/4101168.html

Gallo, P. (2014). *Michael Jackson Hologram Rocks Billboard Music Awards: Watch & Go Behind the Scenes*. https://www.billboard.com/articles/events/bbma-2014/6092040/michael-jackson-hologram-billboard-music-awards

Gervautz, M., & Schmalstieg, D. (2012). Anywhere Interfaces Using Handheld Augmented Reality. *Computer*, *45*(7), 26–31. doi:10.1109/MC.2012.72

Glion. (2020). *Why events are so important to the hospitality industry*. https://www.glion.edu/magazine/events-important-hospitality-industry/

Goodyear, S. (2020). *These hyper-realistic robot dolphins could replace live animals at aquariums*. https://www.cbc.ca/radio/asithappens/as-it-happens-monday-edition-1.5647594/these-hyper-realistic-robot-dolphins-could-replace-live-animals-at-aquariums-1.5647597

Graham-McLay, C. (2020). *Robot dolphins: The Cruelty-free 20m animal you can't tell from the real thing*. https://www.theguardian.com/environment/2020/jul/13/robot-dolphins-the-cruelty-free-20m-animal-you-cant-tell-from-the-real-thing

Hill, R. A. (2015). *How Drones may Propel your Event*. https://www.meetingstoday.com/magazines/article-details/articleid/26406/title/how-drones-may-propel-your-event

Hive, D. (2019). *How drones enhance events and event planning*. https://dronehive.com.au/news/26_how-drones-enhance-events-and-event-planning

Hwaya, K. (2019). *Augmented reality dragon wows baseball fans on opening day*. http://www.korea.net/NewsFocus/Sci-Tech/view?articleId=169492

Ibis, S. (2019). Turizmde robotlaşma [Robotics in the Tourism Industry]. *Türk Turizm Araştırmaları Dergisi*, *3*(3), 403–420.

Ivanov, S., Gretzel, U., Berezina, K., Sigala, M., & Webster, C. (2019). Progress on Robotics in Hospitality and Tourism: A Review of the Literature. *Journal of Hospitality and Tourism Technology*, *10*(4), 489–521. doi:10.1108/JHTT-08-2018-0087

Ivanov, S., Webster, C., & Berezina, K. (2020). Robotics in tourism and hospitality. In *Handbook of e-Tourism*. Springer. https://link.springer.com/content/pdf/10.1007/978-3-030-05324-6_112-1.pdf

Javornik, A. (2016). Augmented reality: Research Agenda for Studying the Impact of Its Media Characteristics on Consumer Behaviour. *Journal of Retailing and Consumer Services*, *30*, 252–261. doi:10.1016/j.jretconser.2016.02.004

Khan, S. (2012). *Tupac's rise from the dead was, sadly, not holography*. https://theconversation.com/tupacs-rise-from-the-dead-was-sadly-not-holography-6641

Kurgun, O. A. (2019). Kuresel Turizm Ekosistemi ve Turizm 4.0 [Global Tourism Ecosystem and Tourism 4.0]. In H. Kurgun & O. A. Kurgun (Eds.), *Turizm 4.0: Kavramlar ve Uygulamalar* [Tourism 4.0: Concepts and Applications]. Detay Yayincilik.

Lee, W., Xiong, L., & Hu, C. (2012). The Effect of Facebook Users' Arousal and Valence on Intention to Go to the Festival: Applying an Extension of the Technology Acceptance Model. *International Journal of Hospitality Management*, *31*(3), 819–827. doi:10.1016/j.ijhm.2011.09.018

Li, Y., & Liu, C. (2019). Applications of multirotor drone technologies in construction management. *International Journal of Construction Management*, *19*(5), 401–412. doi:10.1080/15623599.2018.1452101

Mehrotra, A., & Lobo, J. (2020). Technology Driving Event Management Industry to the Next Level. *8th International Conference on Reliability, Infocom Technologies and Optimization (Trends and Future Directions) (ICRITO)*. https://doi:10.1109/icrito48877.2020.9198025

Meisenzahl, M. (2020). *These $26 million robotic dolphins are coming to a Chinese aquarium soon and they look exactly like the real thing*. https://www.businessinsider.com/robot-dolphins-coming-to-chinese-aquarium-2020-7

Meyer, E. (2014). *Tupac's hologram ushers change in live concerts*. https://roundup.brophyprep.org/index.php/2012/05/tupacs-hologram-ushers-change-in-live-concerts/

Miley, J. (2019). *German Circus Replaces Animals with Stunning Holograms*. https://interestingengineering.com/german-circus-replaces-animals-with-stunning-holograms

Murphy, J., Hofacker, C., & Gretzel, U. (2017). Dawning of the age of robots in hospitality and tourism: Challenges for teaching and research. *European Journal of Tourism Research*, *11*, 104–111.

Nayyar, A., Mahapatra, B., Le, D. N., &Suseendran, G. (2018). Virtual Reality (VR) & Augmented Reality (AR) technologies for tourism and hospitality industry. *International Journal of Engineering & Technology, 7*(2.21), 156-160.

Neuhofer, B., Magnus, B., & Celuch, K. (2020). The Impact of Artificial Intelligence on Event Experiences: A Scenario Technique Approach. *Electronic Markets*. Advance online publication. doi:10.100712525-020-00433-4

Nisancioglu, B. (2020). *Coachella Highlights: Tupac Hologram in 2012*. https://festileaks.com/2020/04/coachella-highlights-tupac-hologram-in-2012/

Özgüner Kılıç, H. (2017). Giyilebilir Teknoloji Ürünleri Pazarı ve Kullanım Alanları [Wearable Technology Products Market and Usage Areas]. *Aksaray Üniversitesi İİBF Dergisi*, *9*(4), 99–112.

Peng, T. (2018). *China's Lunar New Year's Gala wowed Watchers with AI Innovations*. https://syncedreview.com/2018/02/16/chinas-lunar-new-years-gala-wowed-watchers-with-ai-innovations/

Robakowska, M., Tyranska-Fobke, A., Nowak, J., Slezak, D., Zuratynski, P., Robakowski, P., Nadolny, K., & Ładny, J. R. (2017). The Use of Drones during Mass Events. *Disaster and Emergency Medicine Journal*, *2*(3), 129–134. doi:10.5603/DEMJ.2017.0028

Rosete, A., Soares, B., Salvadorinho, J., Reis, J., & Amorim, M. (2020). Service robots in the hospitality industry: An exploratory literature review. In H. Nóvoa, M. Drăgoicea, & N. Kühl (Eds.), *Exploring Service Science. IESS 2020. Lecture Notes in Business Information Processing, 377*. Springer. doi:10.1007/978-3-030-38724-2_13

Sample, I. (2019). *What is Facial Recognition – and How Sinister is it?* https://www.theguardian.com/technology/2019/jul/29/what-is-facial-recognition-and-how-sinister-is-it

Schatz, L. (2019). *Roy Orbison and Buddy Holly holograms are going on tour together*. https://consequenceofsound.net/2019/03/roy-orbison-buddy-holly-hologram-rock-roll-dream-tour-dates/

Schmidt, R. (2020). *What is Facedeals?* http://shebytes.com/what-is-facedeals/#:~:text=Facedeals%20is%20a%20face%2Drecognition,sends%20you%20a%20customized%20deal.&text=Facedeals%2C%20which%20is%20a%20retail,connects%20data%20from%20social%20networks

Severt, K., Fjelstul, J., & Breiter, D. (2013). Information Communication Technologies: Usages and Preferences of Generation Y Students and Meeting Professionals. *Journal of Convention & Event Tourism*, *14*(2), 124–143. doi:10.1080/15470148.2013.781487

Sezgin, S. (2016). Eğitimde Giyilebilir Teknolojiler: Fırsatlar ve Eğilimler [Wearable Technologies in Education: Opportunities and Trends]. *Mehmet Akif Ersoy Üniversitesi Eğitim Fakültesi Dergisi, 40*, 405–418.

Shaw, T. (2019). *23 Event Marketing Statistics You Need to Know*. https://www.aventri.com/blog/23-event-marketing-statistics-you-need-to-know#:~:text=Engagement%20and%20Event%20Tech&text=An%20overwhelming%20majority%20of%20event,the%20success%20of%20their%20events.&text=90%25%20of%20event%20technology%20adopters,65%25%20of%20non%2Dadopters

Sitapara, J. (2017). *8 Event Technologies Every Organiser must Embrace*. https://medium.com/hubilo-officil-blog/8-technologies-all-event-planners-must-embrace-2910b1371ebf

Soft, A. (2019). *Mini Ada Expertika Açılış Organizasyonunda* [Mini Ada at the opening ceremony of Expertika]. https://www.akinsoft.com.tr/medya-merkezi/request.php?q=mini-ada-expertika-acilis-organizasyonunda-7097

Softjourn. (2020). *How to Elevate your Event with Augmented Reality*. https://softjourn.com/insights/how-to-elevate-your-event-with-augmented-reality

Solaris, J. (2020). *Event Technology: Trends and Strategy for 2020*. https://www.eventmanagerblog.com/event-technology

Sorrells, M. (2013). *5 Ways Robots are being Used at Events*. https://www.bizbash.com/production-strategy/event-management-tech-tools/media-gallery/13479962/5-ways-robots-are-being-used-at-events

Stek, T. D. (2016). Drones over Mediterranean Landscapes. The Potential of Small UAV's (Drones) for Site Detection and Heritage Management in Archaeological Survey Projects: A Case Study from le Pianelle in the Tappino Valley, Molise (Italy). *Journal of Cultural Heritage*, *22*, 1066–1071. doi:10.1016/j.culher.2016.06.006

Strickland, P., Williams, K. M., Laing, J., & Frost, W. (2016). The Use of Social Media in the Wine Event Industry. A Case Study of the High-Country Harvest in Australia. In G. Szolnoki, L. Thach, & D. Kolb (Eds.), *Successful Social Media and eCommerce Strategies in the Wine Industry*. Palgrave Macmillan. doi:10.1057/9781137602985_5

Tables, S. (2020). Top Event Technology Trends: 14 most-know. *Innovations: Technology, Governance, Globalization*. https://www.socialtables.com/blog/event-technology/event-technology-trends/

Tatulli, K. (2019). *The Top 9 Meeting & Event Technology Trends for 2020*. https://www.aventri.com/blog/meeting-and-event-technology-trends

Thornley-Brown, A. (2018). *5 Ways to Use Drones in the Event Industry*. https://www.mpi.org/blog/article/5-ways-to-use-drones-in-the-event-industry

tom Dieck, M. C., & Hyungsoo Jung, T. (2017). Value of Augmented Reality at Cultural Heritage Sites: A Stakeholder Approach. *Journal of Destination Marketing & Management*, *6*(2), 110–117. doi:10.1016/j.jdmm.2017.03.002

Tremaud, J. (2017). *Augmented Reality in Events: Examples and Benefits*. https://esculturaeventos.com/en/posts/augmented-reality-in-events/

Tsukayama, H. (2012). *How the Tupac Hologram works.* https://www.washingtonpost.com/business/technology/how-the-tupac-hologram-works/2012/04/18/gIQA1ZVyQT_story.html

Turner, A. (2019). *Trends Watch Report 2019.* https://www.ibtmworld.com/RXUK/RXUK_EIBTM/IBTM-World-2019/PDFs/13409_IBTM_TRENDS_WATCH_REPORT_2019_FINAL.pdf?v=637096812923316749

Wirtz, J., Patterson, P., Kunz, W., Gruber, T., Lu, V. N., Paluch, S., & Martins, A. (2018). Service Robots in the Front Line: Will it be a Brave New World. *Journal of Service Management, 29*(5), 907–931. doi:10.1108/JOSM-04-2018-0119

Wolters, C. (2019). *Holographic Elephants Shine New Light on Tradition—and Other Innovations.* https://www.nationalgeographic.com/science/2019/11/holographic-circus-elephants-naked-man-orchid-and-more-breakthroughs/#close

Yalcin Kayikci, M., & Kutluk Bozkurt, A. (2018). Dijital Çağda Z ve Alpha Kusagi, Yapay Zeka Uygulamalari ve Turizme Yansimalari [Generation Z and Alpha in Digital Age, Artificial Intelligence and Reflections on Tourism]. *Sosyal Bilimler Metinleri, 1*, 54–64.

Yen, T.-H., Wey, P.-S., & Sullivan, K. (2016). Classification of Event and Meeting Technology. *IIBA International Interdisciplinary Business-Economics Advancement Conference.* https://core.ac.uk/download/pdf/216960107.pdf#page=94

Yildiz, S. (2019). Turist Rehberligi Mesleginde Robot Rehberlerin Yukselisi [The Rise of Robot Guides in Tourist Guidance Profession]. *Vizyoner Dergisi, 10*(23), 164–177. doi:10.21076/vizyoner.481225

Zhang, M. (2019). *Couple hires robot photographer for their wedding.* https://petapixel.com/2019/04/11/this-robot-photographer-just-shot-her-first-wedding/

Ziyadin, S., Koryagina, E., Grigoryan, T., Tovma, N., & Zharaskyzy Ismail, G. (2019). Specificity of Using Information Technologies in the Digital Transformation of Event Tourism. *International Journal of Civil Engineering and Technology, 10*(1), 998–1010.

ADDITIONAL READING

Chanaron, J. J. (2014). Technology and economic impacts of Mega-Sport Events: A Key Issue? Exploratory Insights from Literature. *Megatrend Revija, 11*(4), 9–30. doi:10.5937/MegRev1404009C

Joy, J., Dadwal, S. S., & Pryce, P. C. (2020). *Innovative Trends in Technology for Marketing of Events.* IGI Global. doi:10.4018/978-1-7998-0131-3.ch018

Kassens-Noor, E., & Fukushige, T. (2016). Olympic Technologies. *Journal of Urban Technology, 25*(3), 83–104. doi:10.1080/10630732.2016.1157949

Lee, S. S., Boshnakova, D., & Goldblatt, J. (2017). *The 21st Century Meeting and Event Technologies: Powerful Tools for Better Planning, Marketing, and Evaluation.* Apple Academic Press, Inc.

Montgomery, B. (2019). 5 Event Technology to Look out for in 2019. *Meetings, 83*, 17.

Talantis, S., Shin, Y. H., & Severt, K. (2020). Conference mobile application: Participant acceptance and the correlation with overall event satisfaction utilizing the technology acceptance model (TAM). *Journal of Convention & Event Tourism*, *21*(2), 100–122. doi:10.1080/15470148.2020.1719949

KEY TERMS AND DEFINITIONS

Artificial Intelligence: The simulation of human intelligence processes by machines, especially computer systems.

Chatbot: AI based computer program that simulates human conversations.

Drone: An unmanned aircraft.

Facial Recognition: A system is a technology capable of identifying or verifying a person from a digital image or a video frame from a video source.

Hologram: A photographic technique that records the light scattered from an object, and then presents it in a way that appears three-dimensional.

Robot: Any automatically operated machine that replaces human effort, though it may not resemble human beings in appearance or perform functions in a humanlike manner.

Chapter 5
The Integration of Social Media Into Event Tourism

Cigdem Unurlu
https://orcid.org/0000-0001-5653-6013
Trakya University, Turkey

ABSTRACT

The aim of this study is to discuss digital marketing applications in event tourism with conceptual developments, to present examples of digital marketing applications in event tourism, and to explain the principles of these two disciplines in a clear and interrelated manner for students and marketing experts. Prepared in the light of academic resources and contemporary marketing practices, in this chapter, the conceptual developments in the field as well as the change in event tourism are comprehensively discussed, and applications with digital infrastructure in event tourism have been explained, and event management and the integration of events on social media have been comprehensively discussed.

INTRODUCTION

With the effect of both globalization and technological developments, digital marketing has started to attract the attention of service providers more, and this situation has made consumers the dominators of the market. The development of digital marketing opportunities has transformed the communication between producers and consumers. The realization of traditional marketing efforts in digital media has forced businesses to be more creative and flexible in their marketing efforts and increased their sensitivity to consumers. In short, these digital opportunities have radically transformed the lifestyles of consumers and the way businesses carry out their work. In an increasingly online world, businesses have the opportunity to carry out their marketing events in digital media in a more creative and fun way. Today, digital media has turned into environments where tourists tell about their travel experiences and evaluate the touristic goods and services they have purchased. Therefore, the tourism sector, which brings together different business processes and has its own structural characteristics, has been significantly affected by digital transformation. In this sense, the pressure that digital developments will create on the sector must be foreseen and managed. In event tourism, a separate digital transformation strategy

DOI: 10.4018/978-1-7998-4954-4.ch005

should be created for each organization, and investments should be made in this direction. Because in digital marketing, as long as the specific motivations of events are not highlighted and personalized, digital opportunities can harm the nature of the events. In a world where consumers are mostly online for reasons such as obtaining information, researching, communicating and having fun, touristic events can be marketed more effectively. In short, explaining Web 2.0 applications, one of the stages of the Internet revolution, this study aims to evaluate the digital marketing strategies and digital marketing applications in event tourism. For this purpose, the concept of digital marketing and the digital marketing methods are discussed in the first part of the study. In the second part, event tourism is briefly described and digital marketing applications in event tourism are included.

BACKGROUND

The Concept of Digital Marketing

Digital marketing is also referred to as "online marketing", "internet marketing" or "web marketing" in the literature. Although the term digital marketing has gained popularity over time, the term "online marketing" appears to be more widely used in the United States, and similarly the term "web marketing" is more commonly used in Italy (Kaur & Sandhu, 2017; Erdoğan, 2020). While digital marketing can be described as the individualized format of mass marketing, it is actually the realization of traditional marketing mix elements in digital channels in a personalized way (Piñeiro-Otero & Martínez-Rolán, 2016). It provides unlimited possibilities and opportunities to personalize content. It is a user-focused marketing method where the interaction between producers and consumers is continuous and does not know any bounds in the spatial sense (Erdoğan, 2020). In a world that is increasingly online, producers can find unique possibilities with digital marketing opportunities. In digital marketing, there is a more flexible and adaptable marketing approach that combines all the online and offline activities of the producer, emphasizing the authentic values of the product. With the digital marketing opportunities, the 4P of marketing (product, price, promotion, place) has evolved into 5A (ask, advise, assess, assist and arrange) (Kurum, 2020). These digital marketing opportunities have some advantages including (Krishnan, 2019):

- Being cost-efficient,
- Being able to produce fast, reliable and traditional strategies,
- Increasing access opportunities,
- Providing high income for producers,
- A higher return on investment,
- Interactive communication with consumers,
- Allowing data analysis and being measurable,
- Increased consumer awareness.

Digital Marketing Tools

It is necessary to develop and implement the right strategies for digital marketing tools that are more effective and faster than traditional marketing methods. Digital marketing tools are as follows:

- *Content Marketing:* Content marketing is a marketing technique that involves the creation and distribution of relevant and valuable content in order to influence, attract and engage a clearly defined target audience in order to create a profitable customer movement. Content marketing is the notion that all brands should think and act like media companies to attract and retain customers. For consumers, products must have a "valuable", "fit for purpose" and "compelling" story in the digital medium (Çakırkaya, 2019). Businesses need to produce content and make it sustainable in order to survive online and attract the attention of consumers. In this method, which is also considered as an effort of businesses to communicate deeply with their consumers in digital environments, they carry out marketing efforts by using the content that consumers find valuable (Mediaclick, 2020).
- *E-Mail Marketing:* E-Mail Marketing is the use of e-mail in the promotion, information and celebration messages of brands to reach a specific target audience. It is one of the digital marketing methods with the highest ROI (return on investment) and the highest interaction with the target audience, enabling advertisement and promotion in accordance with the communication technologies of the age.
- *Mobile Marketing:* Mobile Marketing is a marketing channel that reaches the target audience via mobile devices. Today, the rapidly increasing number of mobile devices, especially smartphones, increases the importance and power of mobile marketing. Targeting can be done in the best way with mobile devices, which have many features such as targeting by location, using QR codes, recognizing and detecting the environment in which it is located (Mobile Marketing; 2020).
- *SMM - Social Media Marketing:* Social media marketing refers to digital marketing practices that contribute to the promotion of a product or service and the increase of product awareness and brand awareness. It involves digital marketing activities that businesses carry out directly or indirectly through social web tools such as social networks, blogs, social marking and content sharing (Gunelius, 2011; Alan, Kabadayı & Erişke, 2018). It is a pull strategy that facilitates consumer access to products of their interest.
- *Online Advertising Activities:* Online advertising, also called interactive advertising, is described as a Web 3.0 application. Online advertising is becoming more widespread and gaining new dimensions with the development of social media. Finally, with the spread of e-marketing and online retail sales, Internet advertising has reached its peak. Young, educated Internet users with a busy business life and high socio-economic level have started to shop online by choosing among the products of all possible global brands without being dependent on time and place (Hoffman, Novak & Chatterjee, 1995; Toros, 2016).
- *Search Engine Optimization (SEO):* Search engine optimization (SEO) refers to the whole of the work that is carried out in order for a website to rank at the top of the search engine results page. When a word is typed into the search engine, a comprehensive algorithm kicks in and starts working with all linked web pages. Thanks to this algorithm, the websites that are most associated with the word group are located at the top of the first page. There are many criteria for search engines to decide which pages to rank first in searches. The content on the web page and the contents taken from other websites are some of these criteria. Search engine optimization optimizes these criteria to rank them first in popular search engines (Giomelakis & Veglis, 2016; Alan, Kabadayı & Erişke, 2018).
- *Revenue Sharing:* It is a commission-based sales and marketing method that results from businesses selling their products to visitors through an electronic commerce site with which they

have an agreement. There are three types of revenue models in this system, also called affiliate marketing. These include pay per subscription (Cost-Per-Lead), pay-per-sale (Cost-Per-Sale) and pay-per-click (Cpc: Cost-Per-Click) (Alan, Kabadayı & Erişke, 2018).

MAIN FOCUS OF THE CHAPTER

Event Tourism

Getz (1997) defines event tourism as "planning, developing and marketing activities that are considered as primary or secondary tourist attractions in order to maximize the number of tourists participating in events". The pressures of globalization, the problems brought about by economic restructuring, as well as the need to create new urban identities, have prompted cities to be different, to revive the urban texture and to make the most of cultural values and resources to ensure economic, social and cultural prosperity. Creating and promoting events such as festivals, shows, fairs, exhibitions and olympics has become part of the urban development strategy around the world (Richards & Palmer, 2010; Timur, Çevik & Kıcır, 2014). Events are classified in two groups in terms of their size and content. Events in terms of their sizes are presented below.

- *Mega Events:* Events with a large number of participants and requiring a large-scale organization are called "mega events". For example, the FIFA World Cup held every 4 years or the EURO tournaments held every 4 years are examples. Since there is a high level of participation in these events, they contribute significantly to the economy of the region (Tozlumikrofon, 2019).
- *Hallmark Events:* It is the global organization of a regional or city event or the arrival of a large number of participants globally to these events. These types of events are called "hallmark" events. For example, the Rio Carnival can be cited as the best example of this. A carnival in Rio, the starting point of the event, later became popular all over the world, and participants from abroad also came to the carnival (Tozlumikrofon, 2019).
- *Major Events:* Events with a large number of participants are called major events. For example, the Italian leg of Formula 1 is considered as a major event with 115 thousand people coming to watch it. These events attract great attention with reflections in the media (Tozlumikrofon, 2019).
- *Local Events:* Events that are not global, but rather refer to a small place or region, are called local events. The purpose of these events is to contribute to the economy of the region and the region itself from various aspects. For example, rafting on the Çoruh River or the wrestling competitions held every year in Kırkpınar are examples of this type (Tozlumikrofon, 2019).

Events according to their themes are evaluated under eight categories including cultural celebrations, political-official events, arts and entertainment events, business and commercial events, educational and scientific events, sportive competitions, recreational events and special events. In this part of the study, the classification in the study conducted by Getz (2008) is the basis. The eight categories of events are evaluated separately below (Ciderol, 2020):

- Cultural celebrations include festivals, carnivals, religious celebrations and commemoration ceremonies (Getz, 2008: 404).

- Political events usually take place in well-known cities that have a developed infrastructure and that do not distress the parties in terms of security. Political event attendees are usually pre-determined, and attendees participate by invitation. Summits, official celebrations and VIP visits are part of political events.
- Arts and entertainment events such as concerts and award ceremonies are considered in a separate category.
- Events such as meetings, congresses, consumer and trade fairs are included in the scope of business and commercial events.
- Conferences, seminars and symposiums are considered as educational and scientific events.
- Local, national, international, continental and global sporting events are considered as a separate activity type.
- Recreational sports, games and fun events are considered as recreational events.
- Organizations such as birthdays, New Year's Eve, graduation ceremonies, weddings and circumcision are included in the scope of special events.

Digital Applications in Event Tourism

Thanks to the development of information and communication technologies and improvements in the Internet speed infrastructure, a rapid transition from traditional marketing methods to digital marketing is observed in many sectors. In recent years, this rapid transition in the tourism sector has been adopted by many tourism businesses. Internet is known as a powerful marketing tool in tourism. The sector considers Internet technology as a continuous, uninterrupted and valuable tool for providing information and communication. Technological developments have been affecting business models for centuries and increasing human capabilities. Technological developments have also strengthened the consumers in the tourism sector, and applications such as the Internet of things, augmented virtual reality, artificial intelligence, and blockchain have started to rearrange social norms.

- *Destination Web Portals:* Destinations have created web portals where they can offer many services at the same time to make the most of online routes to get more shares of the international tourism cake and reach more visitors. In tourism, web portals help a destination to promote itself and reach more people. Web portals allow consumers to quickly access the information they need and make comparisons. Since these web portals reflect the image of the destinations, they must be open to innovations and constantly updating themselves. In terms of the visitors' research on destinations, the content and presentation of the information presented has an important place to convince them (Özdemir, 2007). In terms of event tourism, information about congresses, festivals, cultural and artistic events to be held on certain dates in the destination should be given on the portal. The portal has language options, and information on promotions of businesses and applications such as 360 virtual tours contribute to the promotion of the events.
- *Social Media:* Event management has a great importance in destination marketing, and events are easily organized and managed with applications and arrangements carried out over the Internet (Hoyle, 2002; Sönmez, 2020). Modern tourists rely more on other travellers' opinions by using social media rather than social marketing suggestions. Social media has made it more popular for consumers to share their ideas and experiences due to its increasing use and contributed others to use social media more effectively. Social media as a medium is an advantage for marketing in the

field of communication as it is cost-efficient and without prejudice (Fotis, Buhalis & Rossides, 2012). Social media also allows businesses to interact directly with their customers through various online platforms (Sönmez, 2020). Events can be marketed more effectively with applications such as personalized experience, data-oriented approach, multi-channel customer experience, real-time marketing, mobile integration, messaging platforms, chatbots, artificial intelligence, the Internet of things and virtual reality (Hanlon, 2019; Sönmez, 2020). This platform, where users can create content, is a Web 2.0 application and provides users with the necessary environment for marketing their own events. For example, from businesses such as Starbucks, Burger King, IBM to local ice cream shops, many businesses use social media in the marketing of events. In this sense, Burger King has come up with its creative and viral social media marketing many times. Burger King has given Facebook users a free Whopper coupon in exchange for removing 10 people from their social network connections (Hoffman & Fodor, 2010; Barutçu & Toma, 2013).

- *Video Protection Mapping Application:* Applications called 3D and 4D mapping video shows are very popular in the promotion of events. For example, a 3D Mapping stage was established in the celebrations held within the framework of the 565th anniversary of the conquest of Istanbul, and the conquest was animated with a theatrical show using 3D animations and real-size ship models in the show designed for this stage. In the events to be organized in this respect, special buildings in the place where the event will be held, areas such as the street where the event will take place, and the hotel hall can be animated with video mapping applications. These animations provide a visual feast to the audience.
- *QR Codes:* QR codes carry the encoded content of the shares such as any information and images wished to be presented in events. When QR codes are offered to participants in an integrated manner with social media, events can be announced and spread more easily with the support of social networks (Akay, 2014). Thanks to QR codes, events can be introduced extraordinarily. All the details that guests may need can be provided via a barcode. It is possible to access the barcode data from a cloud information system via any mobile device. Participation in the events can be controlled with these codes. Modern mobile applications provide highly effective solutions in event management. Thanks to cloud technology, all data related to events can be stored in the cloud and events can be audited and controlled more easily.
- *Radio Frequency Identification:* Radio Frequency Identification (RFID) technology is used to create a standard quality in events. Participants and their supervision in applications is facilitated with a chip-containing wristband or cards given to them. This system, which can be integrated into social networks, supports the promotion and popularity of events (Akay, 2014).
- *Tweet Wall:* It is a technology preferred in events such as congresses and conferences. The Tweet Wall refers to the screens located in the areas where all participants can see the event. With this technology, tweets posted using some hashtags and keywords during the event are reflected on this screen with a specially designed visualization (Akay, 2014).
- *360° Selfie:* It is a powerful digital application that spreads the event slogan through Instagram and enables participants to share it having fun. This system allows the participants to enter a video field placed in the event area, take a 360 ° video and share it via Instagram (Akay, 2014).
- *Presstagram (Instagram Memory):* Presstagram is a digital application that prints the photos of the participants shared with the hashtag determined on Instagram, with a specially designed frame, including the advertisement of the brand. While the application is a means of popularizing the

event through hashtags on social media, it also serves to present the photograph to the participant in a concrete way.

- *Search Engines:* Search engines are a frequently used method in event management to create digital advertising and influence a specific target audience. Search engines have the ability to determine the target audience based on the criteria of location, the device used, and previous visits to the site. Thanks to search engines, customers who have the potential to participate in events can be reached easily. While there are hundreds of millions of pages on the Internet, search engines are used to reach the desired information if the address is unknown. While the possible websites are listed on the search engine as a result of the search, advertisements with a link on a part of the page can also be displayed (Yavuz, 2011).
- *Applications:* Applications such as Biletix, IKVS Mobile, Arts & Culture and MyBilet have a large event database, and they can filter the events taking place at a certain distance for their users thanks to their 'near me' features. With these applications, popular events can be visited 360 °, museums and artworks can be viewed on mobile, and tickets can be purchased. On the other hand, applications such as Lonely Planet, Google Search, Google Maps and Google Trips are applications developed to find events as well as interesting and popular places in a geography. With these applications, tourists can personalize their travels and plan the events they can participate in with the places to be visited on a predetermined route. These applications are considered as a creative digital opportunity for event tourism (Gülal, 2019).
- *Search Engine Optimization:* With Search Engine Optimization (SEO), a website can rank high in search results, thereby increasing potential customer traffic to the website. In general, SEO is a digital marketing strategy based on keyword implementation. In order to attract potential customers of the event to the website, it is important to create keywords that will make the event easy to find. With SEO, the location and visibility of an event or organization's website can be improved.
- *Digital Content Marketing:* Significant amount of content should be created and consistently presented to enable events to communicate directly with potential customers on social networks such as blogs, Youtube, Facebook, Instagram and Twitter. Digital content is not the event itself exactly, and it is based on the principle of presenting information about the event in digital environment. It is possible to create content with videos, news, and visual training tools about the event. In other words, they are the by-products of the event in the digital environment and contribute to its promotion (Özçit, 2015). In digital content marketing, it is necessary to tell stories about events, to attract the attention of potential customers and to ensure that potential customers are listeners. With effective content, events will easily reach not only existing customers but also potential customers (Yıldız & Karagöz).

The Integration of Social Media in Event Tourism

Events have become creative, fun and extraordinary with digital applications. Through such applications, a warmer atmosphere is created in event tourism, events make more noise and reach more masses. In this sense, social media networks have become a very entertaining and important medium for event tourism (Akay, 2014). In this study, the integration of social media in event tourism has been discussed and examples from the sector have been presented. Akar (2010) evaluated social media as a web 2.0 technology and considered it as a concept that allows users to interact deeply and to form a community. Networks such as Instagram, YouTube and Facebook are brand new channels that are at the centre of many users' lives. Geray (2003) stated that social media emphasizes individuality and allows rapid feedback, adding that social media has three basic features (depersonalization, interaction, asynchronization) (Akay, 2014). Social media users have a high level of interaction thanks to the content they produce, and thus, social media turns into a strong communication environment where users share their knowledge and experiences (Aktan & Koçyiğit, 2016).

Social media can create information exchange between social units such as individuals, groups, organizations and provide users with the opportunity to share information, thoughts, and interests, and also individuals can create content on social media (Sabuncuoğlu & Gümüş, 2008). Social media, which is considered as a very comprehensive network including blogs, chat rooms, e-mails between consumers, product and service evaluation websites, social networking websites and forums, guides people of all ages in their activities and ways of doing business from shopping to politics, sports fanatism, activism, cultural events, voting behaviour, and political information process. It directs many activities and ways of doing business, and it affects their attitudes and behaviours in social life. Social media, which provides participants with a natural, sincere and mutual communication environment, is also a medium where users can produce content. Social networks are online platforms where users can create profiles, transfer their comments on written information, share information and maintain communication with the people they are connected to (Flynn, 2012; Duğan & Aydın, 2018).

Recent studies also prove that the impact of social media on the tourism industry is increasing day by day (Bayram, 2012). Literature reviews have revealed that the studies that deal with social media integration in event tourism in a clear and comprehensive way are very limited. In this respect, the effects of social media on event tourism and the consequences of these effects should be foreseen. In this study, in which the integration of social media, one of the new generation digital technologies, into event tourism is comprehensively evaluated, the main purpose is to reveal the necessary conditions to effectively integrate event tourism into social media, thus contributing to the literature, practitioners, industry and students. For this purpose, the social media phenomenon has been comprehensively evaluated, and afterwards, applications related to event tourism were discussed on social media. Antony (2018) classified the social media tools that are widely used today under the following headings:

Social Networks

These websites allow users to create personal web pages and then connect with other people to share content and communicate with each other. For example, social networks such as Facebook and Myspace open up new fields for tourism professionals in digital marketing. While the assessment of reaching the target audience can be made on a limited sample in traditional media, this assessment is made much more effectively and easily on social networks. Providing an advantage in the context of guest communication, which is of great importance in the tourism industry, social media contributes indirectly to reservations, not directly. The traffic on hotels' websites can increase with social media channels, which can directly affect sales. Thanks to visual or verbal content, an effective marketing strategy can be applied to the participants (Sanay, 2017). In this part of the study, Facebook, which is one of the most popular social media applications, was discussed (Doğan, Pekiner & Karaca, 2018).

- *Facebook:* Facebook is the most popular social platform website, has more than a billion users, and enables people to communicate with their friends, to share entertainment, information, and videos, and to be up to date. With over a billion users, this social platform has become a social market for companies to promote their brands (Doğan et. al, 2018). Facebook, the first medium that comes to mind when it comes to social networking, was created by Mark Zuckerberg on February 4, 2004 to form a communication network among Harvard University students. Since it has a high number of users and a spreading use all over the world, it is more well-known and mentioned compared to other social networks. Used extensively by people of all ages, Facebook has become an effective marketing tool for businesses. The tourism sector, which is open to innovation, has not remained indifferent to this development (Eryılmaz & Zengin). The applications carried out on Facebook in event tourism are as follows:

- Special offers related to events can be announced on Facebook. Applications such as discounts and promotions related to events can be promoted through social media tools.
- Some special arrangements can be done for those who like and follow the Facebook page of events.
- Facebook and other social networks should be used interactively to promote events and to raise awareness about them.
- Surveys can be conducted over social networks in order to learn about the demands and needs of the participants in events.
- Social networks where events are announced are considered as an invitation for fans and followers. Therefore, it should be possible to make reservations or buy tickets on event pages.

- *Blogs:* Blogs are online environments where the most up-to-date information is shared. They are online publications where people or institutions share their thoughts. Travel blogs are one of the social media tools that have an important place in tourism marketing. Travel blogs written by real people containing real travel experiences are taken very seriously by travellers today. This makes travel blogs an important platform that will improve the awareness of the participants in terms of event tourism (Sanay, 2017).
- *Wikis:* A Wiki is a website that allows all users to create a common database where they can add or edit information on various topics. The most important example of this is Wikipedia. On this platform, volunteering authors provide information about the content and subjects they are knowledgeable about to articles on specific topics. However, unlike other types of social media, users who are not members of the platform are only allowed to participate as readers. Wikis serve as the largest encyclopaedia of today. The most prevalent views about the meaning of the word wiki include its English meaning referring to "what I know is" (the abbreviation of "as far as I know"), or it being inspired by the word "wiki" in the Hawaiian language which means "fast". Furthermore, Wiki travel, another new application of Wikipedia, aims to create an up-to-date, free and reliable travel guide in the field of tourism and includes thousands of destination-related guides and articles (Sanay, 2017).
- *Forums:* Forums, which are online discussion areas, are online communities where users can exchange ideas about specific topics or interests. Online discussion communities are the result of people spending more and more time online. Forums are a specialized type of online discussion groups. Defined as one of the earliest examples of social networks, they are also called modern billboards. They are an important marketing tool for users to get involved in an ongoing discussion on a particular topic (Sanay, 2017).
- *Content Sharing Communities:* These are communities that organize and share certain types of content. The most popular content communities include Flickr on photography and YouTube on videos.

- *Microblogs:* It allows users to share small-sized content (sentences, photos, videos) online. Twitter and Instagram are the most used applications in this area.
- *Twitter:* Twitter is a social media and microblogging website. It is a social media website that allows users to write texts of 140 characters and can be used more effectively with various materials. It was used a lot by Barack Obama in the elections held in the USA in 2008. It has also become one of the most popular tools of social media. The number of Twitter users reached 328 million as of April 2018 (Doğan et. al, 2018). On Twitter, it is necessary to target people who will be interested in the content of the events organized. In this regard, targeting should be made in accordance with the demographic characteristics of the followers such as age and gender. Retweeting of the comments made on the event pages will also provide a separate motivation for the participants. Frequently used hashtags related to the events will increase the interaction regarding those events. The visuals on the page of the events will contribute to their prominence, and the questions or polls directed to the followers will increase their interaction. In addition, campaigns such as coupons and promotions related to the events will keep the interest in them alive.
- *Instagram:* Instagram is a photo sharing and editing application that allows filters and voiceovers on photos. This application, which was first made for iPhone, can also be used on devices with Android operating system. It is possible to obtain professional photos with Instagram, which is an application that is frequently used among young people. Photos with quite different appearances can be obtained with filter and sound applications in a very short time. The Instagram application, which has reached more than 100 million users worldwide as of 2017, can be used on both IOS and Android devices. Thus, the usefulness of the application has been increased. The number of Instagram users reached 800 million as of the end of 2017. In event tourism, the followers on the page of the event should be analysed, a correct targeting strategy should be developed, and the frequency of the content on Instagram should be maintained and shared regularly.
- *Experience, Comment and Voting Platforms:* In tourism marketing, reputation management, experience evaluation and price comparison websites such as HolidayCheck, TripAdvisor, Review Center, Triphub, Holiday Watchdog and Zoover are also used as social media. While the positive comments made on these platforms are effective in the decisions of potential consumers, the increasing number of comments is important in terms of recognition. These comments turn into an impressive, cost-efficient and faster marketing tool for businesses. For example, TripAdvisor, an international tourism and travelling social platform, provides market information that can be used independently by businesses as well as consumers, and also offers the ranking of businesses (Sanay, 2017).
- *Location Based Platforms:* With the widespread use of mobile devices today and the development of the GPS technology, it is evident that social networks increasing social communication opportunities suitable for people's locations have emerged. These applications facilitate access to instant information about events happening in the environment and provide location information on social networking websites. The Foursquare application, which is the most frequently used example of location-based services with 10 million subscribers registered around the world today, has changed consumer preferences by setting the location information it provides via GPS with a game-based structure (Altındal, 2013).

Social Media Marketing Strategies in Event Tourism

In order for soon-to-be-organized events to be effectively marketed through social media, the target audience should be observed systematically and regularly. In addition, the purpose of using social media in events is extremely important in determining the social media marketing strategy. The purpose of social media may be to promote events to be organized, to increase the number of visitors or to increase awareness of the nature of events. A strategy suitable for the purpose of the events should be determined through social media. As a matter of fact, each goal requires a different strategy (Çelen, 2018).

A strategy should be determined according to the social media platforms' characteristics and purpose of use, and the continuity of the event-related promotional-service contents should be ensured. Whichever social platform the event management will take place on, an intense content presentation plan for that platform should be prepared. Dominy (2016) stated that in order to achieve the desired goal on social media, posts should be short and interesting. In this respect, in order for the events to attract the attention of the followers, the publications and content should be arranged in accordance with the nature of each platform (Çelen, 2018). In event tourism, the social and demographic characteristics of the participants (age, gender, marital status, education, income, etc.) lead the participants to different purchasing behaviours. In this respect, events should be promoted on social media by segmenting the market. The event content for each segment of the market need to be designed differently.

SOLUTIONS AND RECOMMENDATION

As in many other fields, reasons such as social media taking on a more important mission in our lives every day, its strengthening by increasing the number followers, and the opportunities offered by technology beginning to unleash its possibilities make social media an important channel for events. While social media motivates event participants with its entertaining, informative and sharing aspects, it also lays the groundwork for the realization of different applications, becoming an important promotional tool for event brands or companies (Akay, 2014). The points to be considered in integrating events with social media are presented below:

- Despite all the contributions of social media, it is not widely used and known by experts and practitioners in promoting events (Leung et. al., 2013). In this regard, it should be considered that social media plays an important role in event tourism and should be used as much as possible in the management of events. The image and reputation of events will be reinforced with social media achievements such as the consumer opinions, dissemination of information and positive word of mouth (Aktan & Koçyiğit, 2016).
- Historical and cultural places or photos related to the event should be shared frequently on social media, and messages shared on social media should be translated into different languages. Some organizations can be arranged to increase the number of followers, and posters for the promotion of the events should be introduced on social media using famous people.
- With social media marketing, awareness about events can be created, consumer behavior can be examined, ideas can be developed for new marketing strategies, redirection to the websites of events can be done, specific messages can be virally disseminated, the display time of messages

about events can be extended, the reputation and image of events can be increased, and the target audience can be made to internalize events (Özgen & Doymuş, 2013).

- All marketing and promotional activities related to events can create effective results on the target audience in a short time with the right method on social media. In order for the promotion of events to be made accurately, the shared posts made by the authorized units should be audited, and supervision should be ensured against false statements regarding the events. The information flow should be constantly updated, and the promotional and marketing activities should be kept under control. It should be ensured that the events are found on frequently used social media platforms with their corporate identities and they share up-to-date and accurate information on these platforms (İmre, 2020).
- Emphasizing the visual richness of the events on social media and creating content that uses visuals intensely will contribute to the creation of the viral effect required for the promotion of the events more easily. In order for the event-related content to create more interaction, its specific features should be embodied.
- Airlines, agencies and accommodation establishments in the tourism sector have a structure that is interconnected and influencing each other. Considering the fact that consumers actively benefit from social media tools, social media campaigns to be carried out by these businesses should be supportive and not conflicting with each other (Bayram, 2012).

FUTURE RESEARCH DIRECTIONS

Based on social and demographic criteria such as age and the internet/social media use time, it is suggested for this study to be investigated in different channels of the tourism sector. It is also expected that these studies will contribute to the academic literature regarding the use of social media in the tourism sector. In future studies, the content and length of posts about events on social media can be investigated. In addition, posts can be classified in terms of their content being informative, entertaining and sales-oriented, and in this sense, they can contribute to the literature. Future studies can also explore creative digital applications related to event tourism on each platform of social media thoroughly.

CONCLUSION

Events can be more colorful, interesting and creative thanks to information and communication technologies. While digital opportunities provide participants with the opportunity to communicate more sincerely, it also has the potential to create behavioural change on them in event tourism. Technological developments have transformed events beyond being ordinary organizations into creative and recreational organizations. With the integration of technological opportunities with social media, events have managed to be more innovative, creative and extraordinary. Social media highlights the fun, informative and sharing aspects of events. This situation motivates the participants and contributes to events turning viral. Technological developments and social media increase the creativity and attractiveness of events and turn them into dynamic organizations in every aspect. In the future, it will be possible to see more creative digital applications in event tourism. In this sense, it is necessary to invest more in digital facilities than ever before in event management.

The tourism industry is one of the most easily obtainable sectors for big data communities. In this sense, tourism businesses can carry out marketing communication in marketing the events organized within the business by using some data about their customers. In this respect, information such as guest comments, data obtained from survey studies, general habits of customers, special days such as birthdays and wedding anniversaries, allergies, and room types frequently preferred by customers can be used as a digital database in event management. In this sense, it is extremely important to receive help from professionals. In order for the events to rank high in search engines, SEO studies can be carried out, and 360 ° virtual reality applications can be used. Moreover, live broadcasts made on the company's own website or on the destination's web portal will provide the customers an original, transparent, sincere and objective visual feast in the promotion of events.

REFERENCES

Akar, E. (2010). *Sosyal medya pazarlaması*. Efil Publishing.

Akay, R. A. (2014). Creative competition event management practices and social media integration. *The Turkish Online Journal of Design. Art and Communication*, *4*(4), 55–70.

Aktan, E., & Koçyiğit, M. (2016). A theoretical analysis for role of social media on tourism activities. *Journal of Social Sciences*, 62–73.

Alan, A. K., Kabadayı, E. T., & Erişke, T. (2018). The new face of communication: Digital marketing and social media marketing. *Electronic Journal of Social Sciences*, *17*(66), 493–504.

Altındal, M. (2013). Brand management and effects of social media in digital marketing. Academic Informatics 2013, 1-6.

Barutçu, S., & Toma, M. (2013). Sustainable social media marketing and measuring effectiveness of social media marketing. *Journal of Internet Applications & Management*, *4*(1), 5–23. doi:10.5505/iuyd.2013.69188

Bayram, A. T. (2012). *Importance of social media that is a current element of marketing database in hotel marketing* (Unpublished Master's Thesis). Gazi University, Ankara.

Çakırkaya, M. (2019). The effect of digital content marketing applications on perceived quality. *Journal of Turkish Studies*, *14*(5), 19–35.

Çelen, S. (2018). *A research on the use and efficiency of social media in food marketing* (Unpublished Master's Thesis). Ege University, İzmir.

Ciderol, M. (2020). *Evaluation of event tourism from local perspective and its role on destination marketing: International Manisa Mesir Macunu Festival case* (Unpublished Master's Thesis). Selçuk University, Konya.

CRM. (2019). *Otelcilik sektöründe 2019 dijital pazarlama trendleri nelerdir?* https://www.crmturizm.com/otelcilik-sektorunde-2019-dijital-pazarlama-trendleri-nelerdir/

Doğan, M., Pekiner, A., & Karaca, E. (2018). The effect of social media on tourism and tourist choices: Case of Kars-Doğu Express. *Journal of Travel and Hotel Management, 15*(3), 669–683.

Duğan, Ö., & Aydın, B. (2018). Publicity Aimed Usage of Social Media in Tourism: Sample of TR Ministry of Culture and Tourism. *International Journal of Turkic World Tourism Studies, 3*(1), 1–13. https://dergipark.org.tr/tr/pub/tdtad/issue/38069/347607

Erdoğan, Y. (2020). *Sales effect of digital marketing in small and medium-sized accommodation enterprises in core Cappadocia* (Unpublished Master's Thesis). Nevşehir Hacı Bektaşi Veli University, Nevşehir.

Eryılmaz, B. & Zengin, B. (2014). Sosyal medyada konaklama işletmelerine yönelik tüketici yaklaşımları üzerine bir araştırma. *İşletme Bilimi Dergisi*, 147-167.

Eryılmaz, B., & Zengin, B. (2014). A research on the botique hotels'social media use: Facabook Sample. *Journal of Kastamonu University Economics and Administrative Sciencies, 14*(2), 42–59.

Etkinlik Nasıl Pazarlanır. (2020). https://blog.adgager.com/etkinlik-nasil-pazarlanir-9-adimda-etkinlik-pazarlama/

Flynn, N. (2012). *The social media handbook: Rules, policies and best practices to successfully manage your organization's social media presence, posts and potential risks*. Pfeiffer Publishing.

Fotis, J., Buhalis, D., & Rossides, N. (2012). Social media use and impact during the holiday travel planning process. In Information and Communication Technologies in Tourism. Springer. doi:10.1007/978-3-7091-1142-0_2

Getz, D. (1997). *Event management & event tourism*. Cognizant Communication Corporation.

Getz, D. (2008). Event tourism: Definition, evolution, and research. *Tourism Management, 29*(3), 403–428. doi:10.1016/j.tourman.2007.07.017

Giomelakis, D., & Veglis, A. (2016). Investigating search engine optimization factors in media websites: The case of Greece. *Digital Journalism, 4*(3), 379–400. doi:10.1080/21670811.2015.1046992

Gülal, S. (2019). *Seyahatlerinizi kolaylaştıracak 20 mobil uygulama*. https://www.turizmgunlugu.com/2019/01/05/en-iyi-20-seyahat-uygulamasi/

Gunelius, S. (2011). *30-minute social media marketing: Step-by-step techniques to spread the word about your business*. McGraw-Hill.

Hanlon, A. (2019). *Digital marketing: Strategic planning & integration*. SAGE Publications.

Hoffman, D. L., & Fodor, M. (2010). Can you measure the ROI of your social media marketing? *MIT Sloan Management, 52*(1), 41–49.

Hoffman, D. L., Novak, T. P., & Chatterjee, P. (1995). Commercial scenarios for the web: Opportunities and challenges. *Journal of Computer-Mediated Communication, 1*(3), 0. doi:10.1111/j.1083-6101.1995.tb00165.x

Hoyle, L. (2002). *Event marketing: How to successfully promote events, festivals, conventions and expositions*. John Wiley and Sons.

İmre, N. (2020). An evaluation of using social media in tourism sector. *Journal of Turkısh Tourism Resarch, 4*(2), 1655–1670.

Kaur, A., & Sandhu, G. (2017). Opportunities and challenges to digital marketing in developing countries. *International Journal of Science Technology & Management, 6*(1).

Kocabaş, B. (2020). *Sosyal Medya Yönetiminin Olmazsa Olmazları*. http://www.sosyalmedya.co/sosyal-medya-yonetimi

Krishnan, A. (2019). *Quora, what are the basic features of digital marketing?* https://www.quora.com/What-are-the-basic-features-of-digital-marketing

Kurum, B. (2020). *Pazarlama 4.0: Gelenekselden Dijitale Geçiş*. https://medium.com/türkiye/pazarlama-4-0-gelenekselden-dijitale-gecis-e2a4cabea825

Mediaclick. (2020). *İçerik Pazarlaması Nedir?* https://www.mediaclick.com.tr/tr/blog/icerik-pazarlamasi-nedir

Mobil Pazarlama Nedir? (n.d.). https://www.dijitalfakulte.com/mobil-pazarlama-nedir/

Özçit, H. (2015). *The implementation of content marketing in the hotel industry: The example of hotels in İstanbul* (Unpublished Master's Thesis). İstanbul University, İstanbul.

Özgen, E., & Doymuş, H. (2013). A communicational approach to content management concepts as a differentiating factor in social media marketing. *Online Academic Journal of Information Technology, 4*(11), 91–103.

Piñeiro-Oter, T., & Martínez-Rolán, X. (2016). *Understanding digital marketing-basics and actions*. Springer. doi:10.1007/978-3-319-28281-7_2

Richards, G., & Palmer, R. (2010). *Eventful cities: Cultural management and urban revitalization*. Butterworth-Heinemann.

Sabuncuoğlu, Z., & Gümüş, M. (2008). *Örgütlerde iletişim*. Arıkan Publishing.

Sanay, G. Y. (2017). *Current approaches in electronic tourism marketing and analysis of the effects of social media on tourists' destination selection* (Unpublished Master's Thesis). Haliç University, Istanbul.

Sönmez, H. (2020). *Proposal of a common tourism portal model in Turkic World countries* (Unpublished Master's Thesis). Kastamonu University, Kastamonu.

Timur, M. N., Çevik, S., & Kıcır, G. K. (2014). Event Tourism: An Evaluation on Success Components of Capital of Culture Events. *The Journal of Academic Social Science, 2*(1), 56–83.

Toros, S. (2016). Reklam iletişiminde dönüşümler: Çevrimiçi reklam ve tüketiciler. *Journal of Economy and Society, 71*, 30–36.

TozlumikrofonB. G. E. N. (2020). https://www.tozlumikrofon.com/boyutlarina-gore-etkinlikler-nelerdir-etkinlikler-kaca-ayrilir/

Tunçalp, O., & İrge, N. T. (2018). The customer reviews and scoring system effects for sales price of choice hotels in online site of tourism marketing. *International Journal of Global Tourism Research, 2*(1), 43–57.

Yavuz, B. (2011). *Investigation of electronic marketing methods: A research made through surveying on three, four- and five-star hotels in Antalya region* (Unpublished Master's Thesis). Gazi University, Ankara.

Yıldız, A., & Karagöz, Ş. (2018). İçerik pazarlaması. In Değişen Pazarlama Anlayışı. Gazi Publishing.

ADDITIONAL READING

Anandh, U., Basu, G., Bajpai, D., Shingada, A. K., Lerma, E. V., Bek, S. G., Lopez-Almaraz, E., Granado, R. C., Arce-Amare, F., Dheerendra, P., & Conjeevaram, A. (2020). Social Media Coverage of the International Society of Nephrology World Congress of Nephrology 2019: Exploring Novel Strategies, Kidney International Reports, 2020.

Barutçu, S., & Toma, M. (2013). Sustainable social media marketing and measuring effectiveness of social media marketing. *Journal of Internet Applications & Management, 4*(1), 5–23. doi:10.5505/iuyd.2013.69188

Fotis, J., Buhalis, D., & Rossides, N. (2012). *Social media use and impact during the holiday travel planning process. Information and Communication Technologies in Tourism.* Springer.

Harb, A. A., Fowler, D., Chang, H. J., Blum, S. C., & Alakaleek, W. (2019). Social media as a marketing tool for events. *Journal of Hospitality and Tourism Technology, 10*(1), 28–44. doi:10.1108/JHTT-03-2017-0027

Hays, S., Page, S. J., & Buhalis, D. (2013). Social media as a destination marketing tool: Its use by national tourism organizations. *Current Issues in Tourism, 16*(3), 211–239. doi:10.1080/13683500.2012.662215

Hoyle, L. (2002). *Event marketing: How to successfully promote events, festivals, conventions and expositions*. John Wiley and Sons.

Laing, J. (2018). Festival and event tourism research: Current and future perspectives. *Tourism Management Perspectives, 25*, 165–168. doi:10.1016/j.tmp.2017.11.024

Mota, V. T., & Pickering, C. (2020). Using social media to assess nature-based tourism: Current research and future trends. *Journal of Outdoor Recreation and Tourism, 30*. Advance online publication. doi:10.1016/j.jort.2020.100295

Roig, M. E., Fuentes, M. E., & vRamon, D. N. (2017). User-Generated Social Media Events in Tourism. *Sustainability, 9*(12), 2250. doi:10.3390u9122250

Sönmez, H. (2020). Proposal of a common tourism portal model in Turkic World countries (Unpublished Master's Thesis). Kastamonu University, Kastamonu.

Yavuz, B. (2011). Investigation of electronic marketing methods: A research made through surveying on three, four- and five-star hotels in Antalya region (Unpublished Master's Thesis). Gazi University, Ankara.

KEY TERMS AND DEFINITIONS

Blogs: They are online environments where the most up-to-date information is shared. They are online publications where individuals or institutions share their thoughts.

Content Sharing Communities: They are communities that organize and share specific types of content. The most popular content communities include Flickr on photography and YouTube on videos.

Experience, Review, and Voting Platforms: In tourism marketing, reputation management, experience evaluation and price comparison websites such as HolidayCheck, TripAdvisor, Review Center, Triphub, Holiday Watchdog and Zoover are also used as social media.

Forums: They are online discussion areas and communities where users can exchange ideas about specific topics or interests.

Location-Based Platforms: These applications facilitate access to instant information about events happening in the environment and provide location information through social networking websites. The most frequently used location-based service example is the Foursquare application.

Microblogs: They allow users to share minimum amount of content (sentences, photos, videos) online. Twitter and Instagram are the most commonly used examples.

Social Networks: These websites allow users to create personal web pages and then connect with other people to share content and communicate with each other.

Wikis: They are websites that allow all users to create a common database where they can add or edit information on various topics. The most important example is Wikipedia.

Chapter 6
Importance of ICT in Human Resources Management and Evaluation in Terms of Events

Pınar Uçar
Antalya AKEV University, Turkey

ABSTRACT

Electronic human resources management is the use of information technologies for human resources applications that enable easy interaction between employees and employers. Therefore, through electronic human resources management, information about recruitment, performance management, strategic orientation, and education is provided. Competitive business environments have made institutions and organizations to take into account innovations and superiorities to survive. In this context, one of the biggest obstacles that the human resources department has to overcome is the rapidly changing technological environment. The possibilities of technology for human resources management are infinite. In principle, all human resources processes are supported by technology. One of the areas where communication and information technology can be used effectively is events. This chapter describes how communication and information technology can be used effectively when planning and managing human resources in event organizations.

INTRODUCTION

The developments in information technologies in recent years have led to changes in the field of business management, as in many other fields. Therefore, businesses have had to combine all their events with information and communication technologies to gain superiority in competitive and adapt to changes in technology. Human resources management is one of the business functions that are affected by these changes and developments. The human resources function has always been at the forefront of integrating technology within the organization. In this context, one of the business processes that have been automated long ago in organizations is payroll management. Human resources continue to combine old technology with new processes. While human resources management, which was previously

DOI: 10.4018/978-1-7998-4954-4.ch006

carried out administratively, was in the foreground, many human resources applications are now made electronically. Also, every year institutions spend a significant part of their budgets for digital human resources management solutions. An increasing number of organizations continue to invest in information and communication technology in human resources management. In this respect, using information and communication technologies while planning human resources in events provides convenience and superiority for businesses (Ucar, 2019:184).

Human resources management is a process that controls the human resources functions of an institution and an organization such as planning, organizing, leadership, recruiting, and control (Bingöl, 2017: 4). These basic functions need to be considered to achieve a functional standard of the event. Human resources management cooperates with the strategy of achieving the mission and goals of an organization. The main functions of human resources management are to determine the qualifications of the personnel needed, to select and recruit the appropriate personnel, to create the desired business culture, to train the personnel for managerial positions, to provide and develop communication. Human resources management tries to strike an effective balance between the employees and the strategic goals of an institution or organization (Bingöl, 2017: 4-6). In this regard, events are one of the areas where human resource management is necessary and important.

Events create a context for human resources management. Events include business events, conferences, festival, street parades, community and entertainment events, andsports. These events can be both commercial organizations and non-profit organizations. These events can be for collecting money or a big party only. Most events can also be project-based, which only happens once a year. An event is an event that occurs at a certain place at a certain time. Every event has a beginning and an end. Events have a predetermined plan and size (Akay, 2004: 55-56, Getz, 2008: 404-406). Eventually, events started to develop and change as more professionally organized events. This also required a new skill set in managing and organizing human resources at events. Due to the dynamics of the event industry, Human Resources Management requires special attention in the context of the event. First, unlike other more permanent and stable commercial operations, events can be classified as projects. Projects are defined as unique, temporary efforts with specific goals that need to be completed in a limited area. Consequently, each event is treated and managed as a separate entity (Bladen et al., 2012: 23). This definition applies to professional event organizations that continually plan and deliver countless events as part of their daily business processes, as well as occasional events elsewhere.

Even if some events share similar features, each event creates a unique project due to the event-specific needs and different outdoor environments and influences. This uniqueness and distinctive feature of each event is a special challenge for Human Resources Management, as each organization has different staff. Also, not only the need for staff differs from event to event, it is variable and dynamic for each event project. The need for human labor in the planning and conceptualization phase of an event can be very small. However, the number of collaborators may increase significantly while the event is taking place. At the same time, human resource managers may have a big task. For example, one of the most difficult tasks for the human resources manager is to manage people who design and organize events such as festivals, exhibitions, street parades (Shone and Parry, 2004: 186-189). Conducting a detailed business analysisfor the event, developing purpose or a vision, meeting the communication needs of everyone and responding to continuous changes in operational planning involved are just a few of the tasks of the human resources manager. This dynamic and challenging environment is the environment that tests the limits of people's management skills. As an event manager states, it is important how to respond when something goes wrong. When planning human resources for events, the key point is to determine the vision and mission, goals and strategy of the event. Human resources planning and management for events should include some business processes and tools (Van der Wagen, 2009: 11). Personnel selection, recruitment, education and performance management in human resources management is one of the most important jobs for every event organizer. Therefore, the purpose of this book chapter is to reveal how organizations will perform the functions of selection and recruitment, job analysis, education, compensation, planning and motivation of volunteer employees, performance evaluation and occupational health and safety, which must be carried out in order to manage the human resource at events. Also, it is to explain the effect of using information communication technology while performing all these functions.

As a result, this book chapter will be a guide for anyone who manages people in events such as festivals, carnivals, exhibitions, shows, contests, races, shows, matches, concerts or congresses. Everything changes constantly; the structure (organizational and physical) is often incomplete until hours ordays before the event begins. In this controlled confusion, decisions must be made quickly and open communication must be ensured and at the same time, people must be constantly optimistic.

BACKGROUND

The Importance of Information Communication Technology in Human Resources Management

Rapid changes and developments in information technologies in recent years have led to changes in the field of business management, as in many other fields. In this context, businesses have to combine all their events with computer technologies in order to gain an advantage in the competitive environment and adapt to changes in technology. One of the business functions affected by these changes and developments is human resources management. The human resources function has always been an important issue in the integration of technology in organizations. When considered from this point of view, one of the earliest business processes automated in organizations is payroll management. Since then, human resources continue to combine old technology with new processes. While administrative human resources management was in the foreground, it is seen that human resources applications are now carried out electronically. Besides, every year institutions allocate a significant part of their budgets to digital human resources management solutions. An increasing number of institutions and organizations continue to invest in electronic human resources management. Application of electronic human resources management solutions; it has applications that can be divided into transformational, relational and operational. Operational applications have been extensively researched in terms of providing efficiency and effectiveness for human resource management, cost and time savings. Relational practices make improvements in human resources communication and relationships for both employees and managers. Transformational applications; it focuses on strategic redirection, strategic information management, strategic competence management and human resource planning (Strohmeser and Kabst, 2014: 339, Démeijer, 2017: 11-12).

The term electronic human resources were first recognized in 1990 when it was included in electronic commerce and it started to be used. Electronic human resources, such as electronic commerce, required commercial transactions to use the Internet. So, the human resources department had to use the Internet. The Internet has provided human resources department managers and employees with the opportunity to provide information whenever they need it and at any moment with a computer. Eventually, however, human resources professionals have begun to explore all the possibilities of using the Internet. Today, technologies such as corporate resource planning software (ERP), interactive voice response (IVR), human resources service services, web applications, voice recognition systems (VRS) and executive and employee portals are used within the total electronic human resources system (Hall and Maritz, 2003: 365).

At the present time, there are some changes in the employee profile. The characteristics of the generation, especially called the Y generation, being talented, self-activating, technologically oriented and innovative distinguishes them from the X generation. So, institutions and organizations want to retain their new generation-oriented employees and take advantage of their talents. To achieve this, they have to use technology in every field and integrate it into every field. In this respect, electronic human resources systems offer effective applications for them. Considering that Y-generation employees are willing to interact with technological systems, it is more likely that they adopt electronic human resources management and are satisfied with the service they receive from the human resources department (Bissola and Imperatori, 377-382). So, institutions and organizations should gradually adapt their electronic human resources management practices to their businesses.

The human resources department has been using information technology since the 1940s. However, with the increasing importance of information technology, it is seen that digitalization has been affecting human resource management processes and practices more in the last 20 years. In these 20 years, human resources management has changed in various ways. It also utilized different types of information technologies to support business function and achieve goals. Electronic human resources management is expressed as the integration of information technology and the scientific research area of human resources management (Bondarouk et al., 2015: 2). In this respect, electronic human resources management is defined as both sharing and supporting human resource management functions and preparing, implementing and operating information technology for networking (Strohmeier and Kabit, 2014: 333). Moreover, electronic human resources management aims to make processes different and consistent, more efficient, high quality. It also focuses on all human resource management content shared through information technologies that create long-term opportunities between institutions and organizations for targeted users (Bondarouk et al., 2015: 2).

Electronic human resources consisted of a combination of some important changes in society and the business world. First of all, easy access to computer technology provided the necessary environment for managers and employees to perform human resources transactions online. In this context, personal computers provided a critical part of the infrastructure that electronic human resources can make. Second, widespread computer literacy was an important stage for managers and employees to take advantage of opportunities in the technology offered. Because having the necessary technology was not enough, people also needed to know how to use it. Third, the Internet; has enabled the computer literacy of managers and employees to be interconnected in real-time. Uniting people and data have eliminated many of the physical barriers that previously disrupted interactions and slowed business processes. Fourth, institutional resource planning made it possible to link all the operations of an organization. Fifth, together with information technology experts, human resources professionals have developed computer software that enables information to be transferred from the drawers to the computer (Hall and Maritz, 2003: 366-367).

Information technologies were used in computer calculations from the 1940s to the mid-1980s. In these years, digital human resource management solutions emphasized primarily the automation of basic human resource management functions such as payroll and record keeping. In this period, digital human resources management focuses on cost savings, faster reporting, greater sensitivity, and reduction of administrative burden with few staff. Client-server computing was supported from the mid-1980s to the mid-1990s. In this process, the delivery of business applications started. These applications have enabled important information to be provided to managers and human resources professionals for human resource management and human resources planning and critical employment decisions. In the period from the mid-1990s to 2010, using the web-based corporate planning systems, the enterprises provided many functions of the human resources department such as training, recruitment and selection, performance management and remuneration. Cloud-based software systems have been used since 2010. The transition to cloud computing has increased the use of mobile and social technologies. Consequently, the selection of potential employees has changed towards an electronic choice with the increasing use of social media (Bondarouk and Furtmueller, 2012: 1-6, Ruel et al. 2015: 21, Johnson et al., 2016: 537-541).

The way to use electronic human resources applications is possible through the full use of web-based technological channels and the conscious and directed support of human resources policies, practicesand strategies. Electronic human resource management can be expressed as a choice in human resource management, but not as a specific stage in the development of human resource management (Ruel et al., 2004: 368). Wright and Dyer (2000) describe three human resource management areas where there are organizations where they can choose to offer human resources services face to face or electronically: Traditional, operational and transformational human resource management. According to a similar distinction made by Lepak and Snell (1998), human resource management types are divided into three as operational, relational and transformational. When Strohmeier and Kabst (2014) consider the dominance of the three categories in the literature; they suggested that the three categorizations were an early typology of the electronic human resource management configuration. In this book chapter, operational, relational and transformational electronic human resources management, which are the prominent types of research, ınstead of will explained. Electronic human resources applications; is the way to implement human resources strategies, policies and practices through the full use of web-based technological channels and its informed and guided support. Electronic human resource management is not a specific stage in the development of human resource management, but it is a choice for an approach to human resource management (Ruel et al., 2004: 368). Wright and Dyer (2000) distinguish three human resource management areas with organizations where they can choose to offer human resources services face-to-face or electronically: traditional, operational and transformational human resource management. Lepak and Snell (1998) make a similar distinction and divide human resource management types into transformational relational andoperational human resource management. When Strohmeier and Kabst (2014) consider the dominance of the three categories in the literature; they suggested that the three categorizations were a premise typology of the electronic human resource management configuration. In this book chapter, transformational, operational and relational electronic human resources management, which are the prominent types of research, is explained.

- **Operational Electronic Human Resources Management:** It focuses on human resources management and aims to increase the efficiency of the human resources department. Also, automation of administrative human resources tasks is provided in order to reduce costs, speed up processes and increase efficiency. Payroll applications, electronic records, and personnel data management are examples of this (Bissola and Imperatori, 2014: 37, Strohmeser and Kabst, 2014: 335-336).
- **Relational Electronic Human Resources Management:** It aims to bring employees and managers together in order to increase the quality of cooperation and service level. Thanks to the communication and cooperation opportunities of information technologies, it develops stakeholder relations (manager and employee). The emphasis is not on management, but on human resources tools that support key business processes. Examples include web-based recruitment, e-pricing,

talent management systems, newsletters, e-learning, performance management and evaluation, training (Bıssola and Imperatori, 2014: 378-379, Strohmeser and Kabst, 2014: 336, Ruel et al., 2004: 368).

- **Transformational Human Resources Management:** It enables administrative human resources functions to support the strategy and create theoretical value. It aims to transform the human resources function by developing it towards strategic orientation. Strategic talent management, information management systems, web communities are examples (Gani and Anjum, 2017: 425, Strohmeser & Kabst, 2014: 339).

The use of information systems in human resources provides many advantages for institutions and organizations. These are (Mamoudou and Joshi, 2014: 35, Nenwani and Roj, 2013: 427);

- Contributes to better service delivery of managers,
- It links personal policies and personal processes, thereby facilitating the personal management of the company,
- It provides critical data for strategic decision making. It also allows for the rapid acquisition and analysis of information for human resource assistants,
- It reduces the costs of personnel events,
- Provides the collection and storage of workforce information that will form the basis for strategic decision making,
- Provides easy access to human resources data and ease in the classification of data,
- It reduces process and administrative costs.

Electronic human resources management applications have some disadvantages as well as advantages for institutions and organizations. These are (Marıtz, 2003: 368, Nenwani and Roj, 2013: 427, Selvan, 2015: 473);

- Security must be guaranteed. In order to feel "safe" when using web-based human resources tools, it is necessary to guarantee the security and privacy of the login data.
- Electronic human resources management requires expert knowledge, which increases the need for qualified technical personnel on information technology.
- While entering data, errors can be made.
- All employees' personal computers must be connected to the Internet to ensure access to the human resources system for everyone. In this sense, workers must have personal computers and Internet connections at home and at work to take full advantage of electronic human resources. This is a cost that institutions and organizations need to bear extra.
- There may be costs of transition from traditional human resources to electronic human resources management.
- Job opportunities may decrease due to technological changes so that many employees can remain unemployed.

Researches in the literature have concluded that the use of information and communication technology in human resources management increases the performance and effectiveness of enterprises. In his research, Saldamlı (2008) compared the situation three years ago with the current situation in the use of electronic human resources management functions. Saldamlı (2008) concluded that the number of enterprises that did not use this function three years ago was 7 and today the number of enterprises using this function is 13. He also concluded that the number of enterprises using the "e-performance management" function is only 1, but today it is 6. Another result of the study was found that "e-learning", "e-pricing" and "e-talent profiling" functions were performed at a very high level in 9 (28%) of the enterprises. Again, in this study, it was concluded that the majority of enterprises have a very high time-saving and cost-reducing effect on electronic human resources management practices. Orphan (2011), Turkey's top-rated 20 companies in the study that examined the website, to publicize human resources policies and practices, and reached to publish job postings and online websites in terms of making reference to the conclusion that use effectively. Türen et al. (2013) concluded that human resources management practices and information and communication technology capability directly affect the performance of the company and information communication technology capabilities have an intermediary effect in their research on the enterprises operating in Ankara OSTİM Industrial Area.

The effective use of information and communication technology in human resources management will facilitate the management and planning of the personnel in the events and the easier progress of the works. In this context, events require an inclusive understanding of information and communication technology when managing human resources. The requirements of all event stakeholders must be qualified in terms of common platforms and fully managed operations. Event information and communication technology security are only about technological issues, a qualified team is a key to management's success. Qualified human resources will be very useful in promoting open platforms, increasing cooperation with stakeholders and planning and following up activities. Compliance management (for example, following the rules) is also a key factor for success.

Event Management

Examples to be given to the events include an opening and welcome ceremony, congress, show, concert, food, festival-feast fair organizations, competition, roadshow, dealers meetings, launch, art-culture-sports organizations. These events are not spontaneous events. These are events planned in line with all these specific strategies. Strategically managing events that have special importance today is the most important factor in achieving the target's goal. Event management defines performances, presentations celebrationsor rituals all of which are planned in advance to serve social, cultural or institutional purposes (Getz, 2008: 404).

Event management goes through the stages of research - design - planning, editing, and evaluation. The process can be summarized in three stages as follows: (Akay, 2004: 57, Brown and James, 2004: 58-59):

- In the Research-Design-Planning (Pre-Event) stage, the goals of the event are determined in line with the expectations of the customer. Within the framework of the 5W rule (Why? Who? When? Where? What?), answers to questions about how to produce the event are sought.By performing a SWOT analysis, all risks and advantages regarding the effects are evaluated. The plan of the event is determined in line with all the data obtained, designs are prepared according to the concept of the event and the budget required for the event is determined.
- It is the process in which the preparations are made before the event, before the target audience, in the arrangement (During the Event) phase. Depending on the type of event, the application phase

may take less than 24 hours, or it may take several days or more. At this stage, it is aimed to carry out the event perfectly as planned.

- In the Evaluation (Post-Event) phase, a general evaluation of the event is made by determining how far the goals are achieved by comparing the results of the application with the planned goals.

At the present time, there are many institutions and organizations that frequently demand and perform event organizations. Among these are the first professional associations and institutions. Great importance is attached to event management by institutions that develop training programs and many professional associations. However, associations tend to focus on specific types of events for the exclusion of others, especially on the one hand, open to conventionsand meetings, and on the other hand open to special events and festivals. Moreover, some training programs seem to focus on tourism, while others see event management as a career path in their own right. It will be easy to conclude that the important and planned types of events are different enough to guarantee their own associations and education or training programs (Brown and James, 2004: 54-56). It is allied with easily. Associations organize regular meetings and periodically include fairs (exhibitions) and symposiums. Festivals often include a wide range of events, such as concerts, sports, participating recreation, sales, andconsumer shows, entertainment venues for educational events andsponsors. The main sports competitions include other types of events. Special interest groups and agencies and produce many types of events to raise money. With regards to event environments, there are a wide variety of events produced or facilitated by convention centers: meetings, congresses, exhibitions, special events, festivals, concerts. Resortsand hotels are also in the event area, and many resorts have increased their reputation and attractiveness by developing full programs of special events that appeal to many target audiences. Professional consultants offer their services to all kinds of events, even if they are called 'meeting planners'. Some jobs will focus on some kind of event or environment, but excessive specialization is undesirable. The event manager should be adaptable and flexible because the distinctions between events and environments are getting more and more blurred. Its main basis is a secondary consideration of the type of event and a thorough understanding of the nature of the event and basic management functions of the concentration in one or more types of events (Getz, 2000: 11).

The things to be done to use information and communication technology effectively and beneficially in event management are listed as follows (Leonard, 2002: 55-56):

1. Promoting and announcing: Using the Web resources to promote its effectiveness, attention can be drawn to its effectiveness. Web advertising can direct attention to your website.
2. Modern Services: Event management software can help manage many tasks related to meeting planning. Stakeholders from all over the world can stay in touch by organizing online meetings.
3. Communicating: There are a variety of resources for event managers to communicate on the Web. These include discussion groups, list presentations, Websites, e-mail, search engines, website links and online advertisements.
4. Doing research: The web is full of valuable resources and can answer almost any question. Managers canresearchtarget markets, vendors, and venues without even leaving the office.
5. Convenience: Important aspects of event management can be done directly from the table. Information can be accessed from anywhere in the world without leaving the office.

6. Reducing Costs: Lower phone bills and with no postage costs, event managers can reduce the costs of their events. In this context, the Internet offers a wide range of cost-saving methods for event organizations.

As can be seen, information and communication technology provides many advantages to businesses in event management. The use of information communication technology in areas such as recruiting, informing employees, providing the necessary training and establishing performance standards while managing human resources in event management will provide organizations with superiority and difference in competition.

MAIN FOCUS OF THE CHAPTER

Key Tasks of Human Resource Management in Events: Importance of Information and Communication Technologies

Recruitment

Personnel recruitment in human resources management is a strategic event for the events to be carried out. It is necessary to use application forms that collectlegally and necessary appropriate information during recruitment. Then, it is necessary to scan the applications according to the field and qualifications of the job. Interviews are conducted in the light of what has been learned about the applicant's skillsand personality, using open-ended and legally permitted questions. If necessary, it is necessary to involve content experts (customer service, food and beverage industries, technical production, etc.) when discussing applicants for skill-specific jobs (Van Der Wagen, 2009: 29). The applicant should be thanked and given information on when the final result will be announced. Candidates should be selected by reviewing and rating the applications, prioritizing the references of the candidates and final checks. Then it is necessary to make a proposal to the appropriate candidates and to include them in the organization. It is necessary to make sure that the result is reported to unsuccessful applicants. When a staff member or new employee administratively starts on the event team, it is necessary to create a staff file or record for the person. It is necessary to make sure that the available contact information is available and that all appropriate forms are filled. If it is not insured, voluntary disclaimer and confidentiality agreements may be required from volunteers (Silvers, 2012: 375).

Institutions and organizations have started to receive e-applications in the recruitment of the staff. At the present time, the Internet has become the main tool for employers to search for job candidates and for candidates to search for jobs. Institutions and organizations are making recruitments by establishing career-oriented websites. As e-recruitment methods; professional career websites, employer websites, job boards are used (Mamoudou and Joshi, 2014: 38, Nenwani and Roj, 2013: 425). Another way is to recruit employees who can take part in events through the ex-employee profile, by looking at their profiles. The e-employee profile web application provides a central access point for employee contact information. It also provides a comprehensive employee database that simplifies human resource management and team building by providing employee skills, organizational chart, and even visuals. E-employee profile; reward, assignment, past work experience, honor, education, skills, membership, certification, competence, job information, etc. covers areas (Deshwai, 2015: 608). When developing an online recruitment website, applicants should be provided with an opportunity to enter their data. This is absolutely necessary for volunteers, otherwise, someone must enter data for each written application. Organizations can thus reach volunteers and paid employees who can take part in every event, using information and communication technologies when needed. The factors that managers need to consider include the number of staff needed (paid and volunteers), skills requirements for staff, the experience needed by staff members, and the time needed. Moreover, the positions and numbers of supervisory staff should be considered when recruiting volunteers. Information obtained from past events should be used to obtain an operational volunteer and paid staff. The need for an increase in the number of both paid and volunteer workers should be evaluated in detail. One of the most important issues to be avoided for the event organization is to avoid the high turnover of staff. It would be very costly to employ and find different employees for each event. Information about the location of the event, possible changes of the venue or the number of venues should be taken into consideration. If the organizer does not have enough information about the event, they should look for similar events.

Job Analysis

Job analysis is a process in which job information is gathered to identify the tasks that make up the job, and the process of identifying the various aspects of the jobs, determining the skills required to perform the job. Moreover, it is the process of determining the characteristics of each job and the environmental conditions in which it is done by examining and recording information about them (Çelikten, 2005: 128). The manager, therefore, should define roles and responsibilities based on the skills and special skills of the staff to achieve reliable results. Job analysis is followed by a job description. It states what are the reasons for the existence of a particular job and what details are available about it. A job description consists of a title, salary, a summary of responsibilities, a relationship with other duties, performance standards, skill requirements, and authority. Information with such details focuses on the duties of paid staff. The job description for volunteers is less detailed and informative. Event organizers; realizing the human resources planning facilitates the manager's job by giving instructions that can be followed while making decisions regarding the rights of the employees. These questions may comprehend issues such as fair treatment of employees or determination of employment. Once these policies are well defined, they are not required to be renewed annually. Employment of employees is vital for an organization, so it is necessary to choose the right people for the right job. Therefore, thoroughness ensures the best results from recruitment (Van Der Wagen, 2007: 104-106).

Various methods can be used to make business analysis in event organizations. The first of the business analysis methods are focus groups. Most event organizations consist of a group of qualified individuals at the management level. Using their experience, detailed project planning can be carried out. This group can contribute to something vital and in this context, they can identify things that have worked in the past and have not worked. Furthermore, members of the group have experience in recruiting their own staff, organizing contracts with volunteer management andsuppliers. Using this experience, which can be internationalor local, is an important part of business analysis. The second of the job analysis methods consists of interviews. In this context, individuals may have rich ideas to contribute. The third of the job analysis methods is the survey (Bingöl, 2016: 90-94). The fourth of the job analysis methods are industry research. Similar professions and events may have similar roles. Legal requirements, such as an alcohol service certificate, may be part of a person's specification. Information about food safety systems and procedures will be required for catering managers. The final job analysis method is critical events. There is nothing stronger than a critical event analysis to address planning deficiencies. As an example, it can be determined that an access control monitor allows people to enter an area that should not be there and leads to bomb search and fear of security. This could mean inadequate training for the access tracker, and in turn, should lead to a review of training materials and possibly to develop an assessment task to check the volunteers' understanding of the various codes in their accreditation passes. By analyzing critical events, deficiencies in recruitment, training, job design, and job analysis can be highlighted (Van Der Wagen, 2007: 107-108).

Training and Development

Training programs provide the necessary tools to contribute to the success of the event by offering a consistent level of service to human resources. In order for the training to be effective, it is necessary for the intern to recognize the benefits of the intern as well as the event organizers and provide sufficient resources for the training program. These benefits includeincreased skill levels and productivity, progress, activity ownership, enthusiasm, improved guest and customer servicedecreased stress and absenteeism, greater commitment to pleasure and teamwork. In addition to job-specific training, general event training can also be provided. Individuals working in full or large groups can be trained before the event. It is necessary to determine the necessary training topics and measurable targets for training and evaluation measures. Besides, it is necessary to determine the time, place, instructors and method of delivery for the training program. In training, multiple communication mechanisms should be used that allow trainees to internalize and understand the information and instructions provided. Staff should be given the opportunity to apply procedures at an appropriate pace and should be implemented in an environment similar to the event conditions to be carried out. It is also necessary to encourage volunteers and staff to seek training and additional guidancewhen necessary (Silvers, 2012: 375). Education can play a role in the promotion of an event and can be an event on its own. It is unique as a motivating force. Educating the workforce in an event is a difficult task. Planning the training to be held in the context of human resources management is also very important for events.

Each training that will benefit the event organizers can be carried out electronically through information and communication technologies. Education programs, which are very comprehensive thanks to e-education, are made in less time, less cost and less effort. E-learning; it covers a wide range of applications such as web-based learning, computer-based learning, and virtual classroom room. In this way, the necessary information about the events can be given at any time of the day by bringing all the employees together electronically before the events (Yılmaz, 2007: 166).

Planning and Motivation of Volunteer Workers

For most of the events, volunteers constitute a very important part of the workforce (Goldblatt, 2011: 141). Volunteers commit their time, skills and efforts to the benefit of an event without financial compensation. It is important to know why they volunteer to recruit, reward and retain volunteers effectively (Shone and Parry, 2004: 195). Volunteers should be planned and motivated. In this respect, volunteers play an important role in many events from sports events to street crossings. Their participation should be the budget adjusted and planned. The motivation of the volunteers is important in the success of the event, as it contributes in many ways to the ambiance. There are many reasons for an event organizer to recruit volunteers as a full workforce (Van Der Wagen, 2009: 65):

1. Expanding the workforce at a low cost: The contribution of the volunteers is crucial for the total number of hours contributed since many distinctive events will not work in existing formats without the contribution of the volunteers.
2. Contributing to the community spirit: While it is true that events can significantly contribute to improving the community spirit, this is not usually the only reason an event is run by volunteers.
3. Establishing an event: the efforts of a group of individuals are needed to run and develop an event. In this respect, volunteers form a committee. Many music festivals, historical celebrations, organizations, etc. it starts from small beginnings and grows over time. At this step, volunteers have a big impact.
4. Making a social impact: Improving the qualifications and employment prospects of volunteers can create a social impact in the long run.
5. Contribution to diversity: event volunteers have a remarkable history and can help provide different languages and cultures for world music festival or sports competitions. Volunteers with different backgrounds can bring new ideas that can be enlightening during any negative situation during the event.
6. Belief in volunteering morality: some institutions and organizations contribute to the belief in volunteering by providing volunteers to work at events. This can lead to improved organizational development and learning.
7. Increasing the level of customer service: volunteers are primarily employed in customer contact roles and can contribute significantly to the environment of an event.
8. Extend the network: volunteers are generally preferred by friends andfamily. In this way, the volunteer network can grow and get in touch with new sponsors.

Occupational Health and Safety

Human resources management should take necessary measures for occupational health and safety for events. Security is a mandatory training element for everyone in the field and needs to be documented. Moreover, all employees should be informed about occupational health and potential safety (Van Der Wagen, 2009: 30). Employers should make every effort to prevent accidents and injuries at the workplace of employees, and in general, health and safety legislation should provide employers with; It includes permanent personnel, temporary personnel and agency workers in the workplace as well as public protection duties. An employer should provide (Bingöl, 2016: 612):

- A safe working place
- Safe equipment, facilities, and machinery
- A safe working system
- Educational program
- Action plan and checklist
- Safe and equipped employees

Workers are responsible for the behavior of managers and employees. Also, a manager should conduct risk assessments and take steps to control oreliminate risks. Workers should be informed about any potential risks associated with any work process, chemical. Training, supervisionand education are key elements of workplace safety. There are some special risks in event organizations that require special attention. One of the common injuries that can occur is manual reasons for which a risk assessment is required depending on the load and the person's capacity. Furthermore, in some cases, personal protective clothing is required. Material data sheets and instructions should be provided for workers using equipment and chemicals. When workers need to obtain a license, it should be checked if their licenses are current and relevant to the work at hand - this is related to the need for workers to work with competent others (Reid and Ritchie, 2011: 331).

Particular attention should be paid to breaksand total working hours, as fatigue is an important risk factor. A risk analysis should be carried out especially for occupational health and safety. Risk analysis includes defining the risk, analyzing the risk, evaluating the risk and controlling the risk (Silvers, 2009: 95). The situations with the highest risk level due to the possibility of injury and death in the risk analysis are fire, armed warehouse, and bomb threats. Other risks identified includemanual use injuries, incompetent personnel, crowd control issues, injuries caused by antisocial audiences, and diseases caused by heat and dehydration. In both cases, preventive measures should be taken, and in case of such risks, unexpected situation responses should be given. In this context, the following information about occupational health and safety should be addressed during labor training (Van der Wagen, 2009: 94):

- The plan of the place
- The command structure in the incident (especially to report serious and minor incidents)
- Case-specific risk examples likely to be encountered
- Noise exposure
- Protective clothing and equipment
- Prohibited products (flares and bottles etc.)
- Suspicious articles and bomb inspections
- Personal risksand potential hazards
- İnjuries andpersonal accidents
- Public accidents and injuries
- Maintenance and insurance task
- First aid treatment
- Access control
- Evacuation procedures

Performance Management

Performance evaluation system; consists of the stages of development, planning, evaluation and development of performance standards. Performance evaluation system; consists of the stages of development, planning, evaluation and development of performance standards. The goals and objectives of performance management include: (1) establishing fair performance standards, (2) measuring employees' performance on a timely and regular basis through fair criteria, (3) informing employees on performance results, (4) measures to improve employee performance within the scope of results. and (5) to increase the effectiveness of the organization (Saylı and Kızıldağ, 2007: 246). Performance evaluation and monitoring are critical elements of any human resource management process. The process begins with clearly defined job descriptions and goals, followed by appropriate guidance and training. Then come the checkpoints and effective feedback systems. The result, performance evaluations are made that encourage the development of the individual. In this context, when performance evaluation standards are correctly determined and measured, the event will contribute to the success of the organizations and improvement. Employees want to do a good job and succeed. Moreover, employees want to know how well they are performing and how they can do things better. The event manager should implement a systematic approach that supports bidirectional communication and commitment to improvement (Silvers, 2012: 375). Also, the effective use of information and communication technology in human resources management will ensure a healthy performance evaluation. In this context, the web-based performance evaluation system means that the Internet effectively evaluates the knowledge, skills, and performances of the employees (Nenwani and Roj, 2013: 425). So, various software programs enable human resources specialists to examine employee performance using the criteria to ensure that they meet performance standards (Selvan, 2015).

Wage Management

The first stage of wage management is to analyze the job and make a job evaluation. At this stage, it is necessary to act objectively in determining the characteristics of the work and the characteristics that the people who will do the work must-have. Therefore, the features that are necessary to fulfill the job and which should be available to the employees who will perform the job should not be exaggerated. The job valuation process after the job analysis is very important in ensuring wage justice. One of the important responsibilities of organizations in the sound functioning of the business valuation process is the determination of equal pay. If objective criteria are used in the business valuation process, wages will be determined fairly and wage justice and equality will be ensured. Thus, the job evaluation made in line with objective criteria will lead to a fair distribution of wages and wage ethics will be provided (Bayraktaroğlu and Yılmaz, 2015: 15).

Performance management also plays an important role in determining salary. The fact that performance evaluation results are fair and the evaluation is carried out in an ethical framework affects the wage management's ethical success. Another stage of wage management is wage research. Salary research is the study of the jobs in the market and the wages given to these jobs. Comparing wages thought to be given to jobs in the organization to provide wage justice and wages for similar jobs in the market will provide a control mechanism in determining fair wages (Saylı and Kızıldağ, 2007: 246-247).

The last stage of wage management gives feedback to the employees on the criteria according to which criteria they receive and how they are calculated. Employees should be correctly identified according to what criteria the salary is determined. Furthermore, it should be transparent and open at every stage. It is an ethical responsibility for the manager to keep an equal distance to all employees and to treat them fairly.

Employees may not expect special rewards for routine work in their daily work. In fact, the awards given may conflict with the moral behavior of some employees, and if rewarded, there may be a decrease in moral behavior. Therefore, symbolic rewards (praise and recognition) can be given instead of long-term rewards or material payments. Thus, the ethical behavior of the person who acts ethically will not decrease (Christy and Brown, 2009: 75). In general, employees of human resources with high ethical standards need strong organizational support, so that the desired language of a value-oriented ethics program can be addressed in a friendly and meaningful way. If the business says that it wants employees to "be as good as possible," it should reward extra to do so but take care not to reduce the intrinsic value of their behavior in this process (Weaver and Trevino, 2001: 125).

SOLUTIONS AND RECOMMENDATIONS

In order to effectively provide and coordinate human assets of an event, the following are required: establishing guidelines for managing human resources, identifying procedures and policies, responsibilities and roles, performance evaluation techniques and communication mechanisms and defining them. In order for the event organization to be successful, managers can follow the suggestions below (Van Der Wagen, 2009: 29-30, Silvers, 2012: 575):

- In order for the personnel to perform the necessary duties, it is necessary to show the appropriate information and directions. There should be procedures to enable them to grasp the experience, expertise, and effectiveness of the event and ways to reward these contributions.
- The event manager can be directly involved in the process or be responsible only for certain aspects of the process. However, appropriate tools, training, motivation, and recognition should be provided to those working in the event organization.
- Communication is very important from the planning and funding stages to the demand and selection stages, from the first meeting to the trainingand orientation program. Moreover, communication from the job description to performance evaluation will be the key to success in dealing with your human resources. You need to be clear to your employees about expectations, responsibilities, wages and the goals and results required for a successful event organization.
- Policies and procedures regarding all aspects of staff management, including code of conduct and disciplinary policy, need to be written. Procedures need to be extremely detailed for issues such as, shift allocation, re-hiring, incident reporting, update information, interruptions, and absenteeism.
- Lack of staff and lack of motivation are nightmares for the event organizer. It is essential to focus on organizational behavior with programs designed to reward and retain paid volunteers and staff, such as motivation and leadership analysis in the context of specific behavior.
- Everyone working in the event area should be trained. This includes all workforce, for instance, sponsor employees and emergency services. For each visitor, employees are likely to ask uniform questions, and everyone plays a customer relationship role.
- Volunteers play a important role in many event organization, from exhibitionsto conferences. Their participation should be planned and the budget adjusted. The motivation of the volunteers paid and unpaid staff contributes to the ambiance created in many ways.

FUTURE RESEARCH DIRECTIONS

Event practices increase their importance and are preferred more and more with the opportunities offered by changing and developing technology. The fact that events became an important tool enabled the increase of event agencies and organizations. Besides, it paved the way for a large sector related to the event. Competition between agencies and organizations in the growing sector has also reached very high levels. The diversity of growth and technology has brought an extraordinary and creative dimension to event practices. In this respect, benefiting from information and communication technologies while managing human resources in event management will provide an advantage to organizations. In this context, when digitalization is so prominent and its importance is emphasized, future researchers can uncover how and where organizations use information and communication technology while empirically managing human resources in event organizations.

CONCLUSION

Electronic human resources management is used as a web-based tool to automate and support human resources processes in an electronic environment. The application of electronic human resources is an important opportunity to hand over data entry to employees. Electronic human resources can be expressed as an advanced business solution that provides online support in the management of all processes, data, information andactivities needed to manage human resources in a company. It is an easy-to-use tool, reliable and efficient that can reach a large group of different users. Electronic human resources management is a way to realize human resources policies, practices, andstrategies in organizations with full use of web-technology based channels and conscious and directed support. Human Resources Management; recruitment process, job descriptions, education and training, corporate organization, career development, personal pages of the employee and annual meetings with employees, such as human resources management. Moreover, with the implementation of electronic human resources management, employees can identify their talents and help them improve their performance. So, these events can be supported and made more efficient with electronic human resources management while organizing events.

This book chapter provides a context for human resources management in events. Events include festivals, community and entertainment events, business events (conferences and exhibitions), sports, and arts. These events may be not for profitable or commercial. They can be just large parties orfund-raising events. These are project-based events that occur once a year. Human resources management –training, selection, performance management and recruitmentare important parts of the work of any event organizer. Also, the use of communication and information technology will provide superiority in the competition while performing functions in human resources management in event organizations. In this context, the fact that managers integrate the technology and use it properly while managing and planning the human resources in events will provide them with speed and advantage.

REFERENCES

Akay, R. A. (2014). Etkinlik Yönetimi Uygulamalarında Yaratıcı Rekabet ve Sosyal Medyanın Entegrasyonu, *The Turkish Online Journal of Design. Art and Communication*, *4*(4), 55–70.

Bingöl, D. (2016). *İnsan Kaynakları Yönetimi*. Beta Yayınevi.

Bissola, R., & Imperatori, B. (2014). The unexpected side of relational e-hrm: Developing trust in the hr department. *Employee Relations*, *36*(4), 376–397. doi:10.1108/ER-07-2013-0078

Bladen, C., Kennell, J., Abson, E., & Wilde, N. (2012). *Events Management*. Routledge. doi:10.4324/9780203852972

Bondarouk, T., & Furtmueller-Ettinger, E. (2012, August). Electronic human resource management: four decades of empirical evidence. *72nd academy of management annual meeting 2012*. 10.5465/AMBPP.2012.245

Bondarouk, T., Harms, R., & Lepak, D. (2015). Does e-hrm lead to better hrm service? *International Journal of Human Resource Management, 28*(9), 1–32.

Brown, S., & James, J. (2004). Event design and management: ritual sacrifice? In *Festival and Events Management:Ritual Sacrifice*. doi:10.1016/B978-0-7506-5872-0.50009-0

Çelikten, M. (2005). Neden İş Analizi Yapılmalı? *Erciyes Üniversitesi Sosyal Bilimler Enstitüsü Dergisi, 1*(18), 127–135.

Démeijer, D. (2017). *Making digital hrm work: A study in changes in perceived consequences of e-hrm in the past decade* (Master's thesis). University of Twente.

Deshwal, P. (2015). Role of e-hrm in organizational effectiveness and sustainability. *IJAR, 1*(12), 605–609.

Gani, R., & Anjum, D. (2017). E-human resource management (e-hrm). *International Journal of Emerging Research in Management &Technology, 6*(6), 184–188.

Getz, D. (2008). Event tourism: Definition, evolution, and research. *Tourism Management, 29*(3), 403–428. doi:10.1016/j.tourman.2007.07.017

Goldblatt, J. (2011). *Special events: a new generation and the next frontier*. John Wiley & Sons.

Jago, L., Veal, A. J., Allen, J., & Harris, R. (2000). Events beyond 2000: setting the agenda: proceedings of conference on event evaluation, research and education. Australian Centre for Event Management.

Johnson, R. D., Lukaszewski, K. M., & Stone, D. L. (2016). The evolution of the field of human resource ınformation systems: co-evolution of technology and hr processes. CAIS, 38, 28.

Lengnick-Hall, M. L., & Moritz, S. (2003). The impact of e-hr on the human resource management function. *Journal of Labor Research, 24*(3), 365–379. doi:10.100712122-003-1001-6

Leonard, H. H. (2002). *Event marketing. how to successfully promote events, festivals, conventions and expositions* (Vol. J). Wiley.

Lepak, D. P., & Snell, S. A. (1998). Virtual hr: Strategic human resource management in the 21st century. *Human Resource Management Review, 8*(3), 215–234. doi:10.1016/S1053-4822(98)90003-1

Mamoudou, S. E. Y. N. I., & Joshi, G. P. (2014). Impact of ınformation technology in human resources management. *Global Journal of Business Management and Information Technology, 4*(1), 33–41.

Nenwani, P. J., & Raj, M. D. (2013). E-hrmprospective in present scenario. *International Journal (Toronto, Ont.), 1*(7).

Öksüz, B. (2012). E-İşe Alım Sürecinde Kurumsal Web Sitelerinin Kullanımı ve Konu Üzerine Bir Araştırma. *Uluslararası Yönetim İktisat ve İşletme Dergisi, 7*(14), 267–283.

Reid, S., & Ritchie, B. (2011). Risk management: Event managers' attitudes, beliefs, and perceived constraints. *Event Management, 15*(4), 329–341. doi:10.3727/152599511X13175676722528

Ruël, H., Bondarouk, T., & Looise, J. K. (2004). E-hrm: Innovation or irritation. An explorative empirical study in five large companies on web-based hrm. *Management Review*, 364–380.

Ruël, H., Magalhães, R., & Chiemeke, C. C. (2011). *Human resource ınformation systems: an ıntegrated research agenda. In electronic hrm in theory and practice*. Emerald Group Publishing Limited.

Saldamlı, A. (2008). İnsan Kaynakları Yönetiminde Bilişim Teknolojisinin Kullanımına Yönelik Bir Araştırma. *Tekirdağ Örneği, İstanbul Ticaret Üniversitesi Sosyal Bilimler Dergisi*, *7*(13), 239–263.

Saylı, H., & Kızıldağ, D. (2007). Yönetsel Etik Ve Yönetsel Etiğin Oluşmasında İnsan Kaynakları Yönetiminin Rolünü Belirlemeye Yönelik Bir Analiz. *Afyon Kocatepe Üniversitesi Sosyal Bilimler Dergisi*, *9*(1), 231–251.

Selvan, V. T. (2015). Study on role of technology in human resource management. *International Journal Of Applied Research*, *1*(7), 472–475.

Shone, A., & Parry, B. (2004). *Successful event management: a practical handbook*. Cengage Learning EMEA.

Silvers, J. R. (2009). *Risk management for meetings and events*. Routledge.

Silvers, J. R. (2012). *Professional event coordination* (Vol. 62). John Wiley & Sons.

Strohmeier, S., & Kabst, R. (2014). Configurations of e-hrm–an empirical exploration. *Employee Relations*, *36*(4), 333–353. doi:10.1108/ER-07-2013-0082

Türen, U., Gökmen, Y., & Tokmak, İ. (2013). İnsan Kaynakları Yönetimi Uygulamalarının İşletme Performansına Etkisi: İşletmelerin Sahip Oldukları Bilgi ve İletişim Teknolojileri Kabiliyetlerinin Aracılık Rolü. *Business and Economics Research Journal*, *4*(4), 103.

Uçar, P. (2019). Elektronik İnsan Kaynakları Yönetimi: Kavramsal Bir Çerçeve. *Yönetim. Ekonomi ve Pazarlama Araştırmaları Dergisi*, *3*(5), 182–191.

Van der Wagen, L. (2009). *Human resource management for events*. Routledge.

Weaver, G. R., & Treviño, L. K. (2001). The role of human resources in ethics/compliance management: A fairness perspective. *Human Resource Management Review*, *11*(1-2), 113–134. doi:10.1016/S1053-4822(00)00043-7

Wright, P. M., & Dyer, L. (2000). *People in the e-business: new challenges. new solutions*. Working paper 00-11, Center for Advanced Human Resource Studies, Cornell University.

Yılmaz, Y. (2007). İnsan Kaynakları Yönetiminde E-Dönüşüm. *İktisadi ve İdari Bilimler Fakültesi Dergisi*, *9*(1).

ADDITIONAL READING

Abson, E. (2017). How Event Managers Lead: Applying competency school theory to event management. *Event Management*, *21*(4), 403–419. doi:10.3727/152599517X14998876105747

Brown, S., & Gunnervall, M. A. (2012, September). An event design body of knowledge research framework. In Australian Event Symposium 2012 (p. 50).

Ekuma, K. J., ve Akobo, L. A. (2015). Human resource management ethics and professionals' dilemmas: A review and research agenda. *Human Resource Management Review*, *5*(3), 47–57.

Elstad, B. (2003). Continuance commitment and reasons to quit: A study of volunteers at a jazz festival. *Event Management*, *8*(2), 99–108. doi:10.3727/152599503108751757

Nelson, K. B., & Silvers, J. R. (2009). Event management curriculum development and positioning: A path toward professionalization. *Journal of Hospitality & Tourism Education*, *21*(2), 31–39. doi:10.1080/10963758.2009.10696942

Rynes, S., Bretz, R. Jr, & Gerhart, B. (1991). The importance of recruitment in job choice: A different way of looking. *Personnel Psychology*, *44*(3), 487–521. doi:10.1111/j.1744-6570.1991.tb02402.x

Silvers, J. R., Bowdin, G. A., O'Toole, W. J., & Nelson, K. B. (2005). Towards an international event management body of knowledge (EMBOK). *Event Management*, *9*(4), 185–198. doi:10.3727/152599506776771571

KEY TERMS AND DEFINITIONS

Electronic Human Resources Management: It is the execution of human resources events through computer and communication technology. E-recruitment and selection, e-learning, etc.

Event Management: It refers to the presentations, performances, or celebrations in which all details have been previously planned and planned to serve social, cultural, or corporate purposes.

Human Resources Management: It means managing people in organizations as effectively as possible for the benefit of the company and its employees.

Job Analysis: It is the technique that examines the qualities, requirements, quantity, responsibilities and working conditions of each work in the organization with scientific methods in order to realize the right, effective and healthy work.

Performance Evaluation: It is a system of measuring, evaluating, and influencing the job attributes, behaviors, and outputs of the employees.

Recruitment and Selection: It is the process of creating a pool of candidates for the vacant positions and choosing the most qualified candidates.

Training and Development of Human Resources: These are events aimed at gaining knowledge and skills with the necessary attitude and behavior change in order to make it easier for the employees to realize the strategic goals of the career and institution or organization. These events are training and development, career planning and development, and performance evaluation.

Volunteers: People who commit their time, skills, and efforts to the benefit of an event without any income.

Chapter 7
Management and Marketing Events in a Digital Era:
Opportunities and Challenges

Gökhan Akel
Antalya AKEV University, Turkey

ABSTRACT

Digitalization has affected many areas as well as management and marketing areas. In the digital age, through ICTs, the ways of searching and accessing information about the event by the users have been developed and transformed. Besides, the developments in the digital age have also affected many sectors such as the production, design, software, management, and marketing sector. The opportunities offered by digital marketing make life easier for users and provide easy access to information. Likewise, businesses can facilitate their management and marketing events through digitalization. Businesses sustain their events by organizing and diversifying new events according to the customer base and the type of event for the management and marketing of events. ICT tools have spread to all functions and events of the tourism industry in terms of business, marketing, and management. In this chapter, which mentioned the opportunity and challenges of ICTs, the opportunities and challenges posed by ICT are also mentioned.

INTRODUCTION

Changes and developments in ICT in recent years have caused radical changes in tourism, management, and marketing areas as well as in many other fields. In this context, businesses had to combine all their events with ICTs to gain an advantage in competition and to adapt to the digital changes. Digitalization has affected many areas as well as management and marketing areas. Digitalization, which has radically changed marketing strategies and understanding of businesses, is known as the digital age. In the digital age, through ICTs, the ways of searching and accessing information about the event by the users have been developed and transformed. Changing advertising, communication policies, management strategies, and marketing events in the digital age affect all businesses and their approach to marketing events, as well as changing event marketing specifically in terms of event management, promotion, and announcement.

DOI: 10.4018/978-1-7998-4954-4.ch007

ICT is a significant tool to use in the management of events and marketing, as well as in planning, organizing, and running the events. It is necessary to obtain and develop the advantages offered by this event to organize a successful event by using information and communication technologies in the digital era. Besides, it is necessary to increase the quality of life of the audience, to target a competitive strategy, and to organize by determining priority market trends. Also, competitive strategies should be established in determining the priority market trends of the business, strengthening the basic advantageous aspects of the business, and increasing the quality of life of the population. Because digitalization affects competition strategies and digitalization changes the understanding of competition. The effectiveness of marketing communications is very crucial for the success and sustainability of the events in a competitive environment. The significance of marketing communication in ICTs in the digital age is an undeniable fact. The variety of marketing communication tools is high and their effect levels are quite different. The tools to be used in the management and marketing of the events are selected based on the scope of the event, target markets, and cost criteria. Examples include radio, SMS sending, outdoor advertising, targeted advertising, and social media.

One of the most important reasons for the rapid development and spread of ICTs is the development of information-seeking behavior. So, digitization has led to a new knowledge economy. The development of ICTs has led to changes in the contemporary business environment and efforts are continued to integrate into all sectors. Therefore, tourism a highly information-intensive industry, as ICTs have a potential impact on the tourism industry. It has emerged with the fact that the social structure includes information in a contemporary structure and the positive impact of ICTs in the tourism industry. Therefore, social interaction arises between the service and experience provider and the consumer. ICTs are significant in the tourism industry, can't be neglected in running the businesses, and serving the guests, and is a crucial driving force in the existing information-oriented society.

Developments in ICT contribute to the economy of the digital transformation in terms of productivity, employment, and an increase in income. As a result of the developments in ICTs, health economics, communication, economy, etc. changes have occurred in many areas. Quickly affecting almost all sectors, ICT has become an important milestone of economic and social order in general terms.

The rest of this chapter states that the effect of digitalization on event management and marketing. It also focuses mainly on the opportunities and challenges created by ICTs and ICT in the tourism industry. Finally, solutions and recommendations and future research directions are presented in the last.

BACKGROUND

New technologies have emerged with the quick outspread of the Internet to large masses. The new technologies existing in the light of current developments have affected all sectors, as well as caused some changes in the tourism sector. In addition to the increase in direct sales to the customer via the Internet, this new technology was also used in the sales of tourism products. Customers can access distribution channels used by tour operators, hotels, and airline companies over the Internet. As a result of interactions with the customer via the Internet, companies can change and even tailor the goods and services according to the needs and expectations of the customers. Thanks to the Internet, efficiency in transparency and relationships between customers and management increases. Among the benefits of the Internet brings, consumer service expectation is also increased. The specification of consumers in the search for information and content caused some changes in consumer behavior, such as being more conscious about cost and providing an environment of comparison. With the benefits of ICTs, new technologies in the tourism industry adapt to tourism value, lifestyle in tourism, and tourism products. Along with the change in economic navigation and the expansion of the industrial structure, ICT has influenced consumer behavior research, as well. Attracting potential consumers is possible by using ICTs successfully on a sectoral basis. ICT tools such as radio, television, computer, mobile phone, printer, and scanner (Sezer & Bröchner 2019: 116) are very important in attracting the attention and interest of consumers.

Individuals with a sense of curiosity and discovery in a globalizing world benefit from the opportunities of the digital age. When evaluated from a sectoral point of view, the gains of the digital age have created significant opportunities for tourists. The digital age creates development and change both in the economy of the country and in the socio-cultural values of the country rather than in individual opportunities. It is beneficial to follow the improvements and innovations in the tourism sector seriously through the opportunities offered by the digital age. Although it is not an industry that produces goods, tourism, which is in the service sector, operates in and interacts with many industries. The tourism sector, like other sectors, contributes to both the economy of the country and the economy on a global scale in terms of employment and job creation. At present, the tourism industry keeps up with the digital age with advanced and new technologies. Apart from all the possibilities offered by ICTs, the growth of the personalization infrastructure, the speed of information transfer, and the increase in the security of e-commerce transactions have also affected the tourism sector positively (Argyropoulou et al., 2011: 369).

Recent developments in the field of ICT technology have caused some changes in event management and marketing. New approaches, new techniques, and strategies have emerged in this field. There is a gap in literature examining the impact and role of ICTs in the tourism marketing and industry. The major effects of ICTs have been the subject of the marketing function in the tourism industry. Although there are not enough studies in the literature, it is possible to come across studies on tourism experience, design, and management. According to Neuhofer et al. (2014), it increases the persuasion and satisfaction level of the technologies that improve and strengthen the interaction of businesses and visitors in tourism. ICTs, which offer a range of technological tools, have changed both business practices and marketing strategies in the tourism industries, as in other industries. Besides, ICTs have created many areas of innovation in the tourism industry as in all industries. ICTs increase the attraction and experience as well as their contributions that develop and transform business models in tourism. ICTs also increases efficiency (Go et al., 2003). Changes and innovations in ICTs give the tourism sector significant momentum. The digital age is used in the tourism sector, where consumers are in information marketing, providing goods and services, managing their communication channels with consumers, and offering convenience and experience. ICTs are used in choosing the tourism destination, planning, and determining the alternative tourism type.

If an example needs to be given based on the use of ICT tools in tourism, the use of ICT tools is required for the technical and legal infrastructure that is substantial in the establishment, management, and success of any hotel or theme park. In this context, it can be said that advertisement and publicity are possible with ICTs along with the legal infrastructure in marketing events. ICTs are also used in the success of customer service interaction with visitors, reservation management, and follow-up. It is also easy to manage and track tourism destinations with tools such as GPS. Successful use of all ICT tools and management through ethical rules are possible with qualified and trained information technology (IT) personnel.

Industry 4.0, a concept that reveals the phenomenon of globalization due to technological advances, increased digitization and capital accumulation, affects the industrial power, production factors, and marketing strategies of companies through ICT. ICT is significant for the spreading and sustainability of globalization. It facilitates commercial transactions by increasing the efficiency of doing business in global markets, providing networking in a global atmosphere, and distributing goods and services. Globalization is a concept that increases the competitiveness of countries in their industries and arises with the integration of the Internet with the industrial value chain using the most appropriate ICT. Along with globalization, various marketing innovations offered by Industry 4.0 make event marketing the focus of attention. Mobile systems, cloud computing systems, and big data are substantial in coordinating the services offered through the internet.

Marketing 4.0, which entered our lives with digitalization and Industry 4.0 and affects all industries, is expressed by its understanding of online marketing. Marketing 4.0 also has an understanding of production and timely production according to the consumer. This concept, which includes functional, sensory, and emotional features, is related to event marketing and experiential marketing. Event marketing provides an advantage with the interaction of the brand to the consumer and allows the brand to be positioned in the target market (Sneath et al., 2005: 374). Events, which have become a widespread subject in recent years, strengthen the communication between the brand and the consumer and are focused on experience. In short, ICTs are the common point of Industry 4.0 and event marketing concepts. In Industry 4.0, within the scope of marketing innovations and digitalization process, the development of economic events and event marketing are accelerated by developing consumer relations with the brand.

Event management, strategy, and marketing can be mentioned in every field with marketing functions. Event marketing can be mentioned in the development and promotion of events in creating experiences in addition to industrial goods and services. In the tourism industry, events such as concerts, fairs, or festivals are examined within the scope of event marketing. These different themed events are considered cultural events and they provide a lot of benefits since they have a higher utilization capacity compared to traditional tourism events (Getz, 2005). The use of events in the tourism industry is spreading rapidly all over the world. So, technological innovations have positively affected the tourism sector as other sectors. It provided sectoral figures to gain momentum upwards rapidly. It will have an unbearable progress thanks to its potential. The size of marketing has changed in the tourism industry thanks to advanced technologies such as digital maps and virtual reality. In line with these changes in marketing, strategies have changed in the planning and marketing of events.

Event marketing can be expressed as the integration of marketing mix elements to help businesses achieve their strategic goals. Since the main and clear target audience of event marketing is customers, it is useful to take advantage of the power of communication. Events should be organized and applied in a way to increase satisfaction, loyalty, and word of mouth. Taking advantage of the opportunities created by social media in marketing understanding is based on the past, but it never seems to be out of date. Marketing of interactive and interesting events has reached a different dimension with the change and development brought by Marketing 4.0 and social media. Social media has increased the importance of consumption in different simulated worlds, the number of social media users increasing day by day, the fact that businesses allocate more shares to social media in their marketing budgets, and want to establish new and stronger connections with customers. It was provided to present innovative and exciting ideas through social media, to announce to the masses, to create transparency, and to support the power of persuasion with visual content and music. As it operates as a platform that provides communication, collaboration, and consumption opportunities based on social media, it mediated the organization and organization of the events mostly thanks to ICTs. When looking at the role and effects of ICT in tourism marketing, it is seen that websites, social media tools, and search engines are at the center (Law et al.,

2014). In a recent study, Wang et al. (2012) investigated the role of mobile technologies and social media in tourism marketing. In addition to the rapid development of social media and mobile technologies, the easy integration of ICTs into the tourism industry has also changed the course of tourism marketing. With social media technology that facilitates the way of globalization, it is now very easy to communicate with people at one end of the world with a mobile phone and computer connected to the Internet. Event marketing in social media has emerged as the type of marketing that businesses have recently applied for the promotion of their goods, services, and brands (Li and Duan, 2018). Using social media in event marketing has increased efficiency in publishing marketing events and announcing it to large groups (Li & Duan, 2018). Easy, fast, and smooth communication is provided with social media that create a global impact. Sharing has become easier, including establishing connections with the business and immediate surroundings, and sending photos and videos. It ensures that transactions are carried out quickly and with less error rate. Besides, ICT has been rapidly adopted for service quality and the customer experience in tourism. The use of social media has also helped to improve the experience of communicating, interacting, trading, and maintaining customers more easily. ICTs should be used effectively for experiential marketing in tourism.

Businesses have to combine all their events with ICTs to gain an advantage in the competitive environment and adapt to changes in technology. One of the business functions affected by these changes and developments is management such as marketing. The management function has always been a significant issue in the integration of technology in organizations. Tools such as planning, organizing, staffing, coordinating, and control are important processes for management. From the past to the present, management combines old technology with a new process. While many management-based applications come to the fore, event management has also been highly developed with new technology and has become the focus. Businesses that organize and manage events invest efficiently in both management and marketing.

There are web pages, blogs, wikis, podcasts, social media tools among the platforms that carry out tourism events and can be contacted by sharing the contents. These tools and applications, which mediate the delivery of event announcements to customers, are used to meet the needs and expectations of customers. ICT creates a more violent competition environment. New technologies have an impact on the emergence and spread of areas such as event marketing and e-commerce and create many opportunities. these technologies have had positive effects such as mass communication, rapid market management, electronic business execution, and efficiency. The development of the Internet, the increase in the number of smartphone users, has added variety in sharing and promoting marketing events. So, these developments have changed the functioning and structure of the tourism industry. Also, the opportunities offered by ICTs subscribe to the improvement of the tourism economy. In the tourism industry, customers can quickly access and communicate the right information through the right channel. Businesses benefit from ICT's blessings such as speed, convenience, and flexibility as well as customers. However, these developments have caused stiff competition among businesses.

MAIN FOCUS OF THE CHAPTER

The Effect of Digitalization on Event Management and Marketing

With digitalization, there have been great changes in their understanding and strategies regarding the field of management. The adoption of ICTs in the digital age means the transformation of processes in the tourism industry into a digital environment. Thanks to ICTs, businesses can develop their management functions and also improve them with technological support. So, it becomes easier to maintain event management. Also, ICTs affect competition strategies and change the understanding of competition in the field of event management. Effectiveness of management strategies is very important for the success and sustainability of events in a competitive environment. The tools to be used in the management of the events are selected according to the scope of the event, target markets, and cost criteria.

The effect of digitalization has not only led to any business that has adapted to technology, but also the digital transformation of the business environment. In the digital age, the management of tourism businesses is possible by integrating with ICTs. Being technology-oriented in the management of events has changed management and marketing strategies. The effective management of technology by tourism enterprises with technological infrastructure enables them to cope with the opportunities and threats of the changing order. In brief, businesses should align the opportunities and threats brought by technology with management, strategic planning, coordination, control, and human resources processes, and use technology more beneficially by focusing on meeting customer needs in terms of marketing.

Digitalization enables ICTs to obtain and develop the main advantages for successful management and organization events and to improve the quality of life of the target audience of the event. Competition strategies aimed at acquiring and strengthening the company's core strengths for a successful business and improving the quality of life of the population enable the company to identify the best market trends. The effectiveness of management functions is very important for the success and sustainability of events in a competitive environment. The importance of management functions benefiting from ICTs in the digital age is an undeniable fact. The effectiveness levels of management functions are quite different. Effective and integrated management functions in the management of events are very important in the success of businesses.

With digitalization, there have been major changes in marketing understanding and strategies. Thanks to ICTs, the ways of searching and accessing information about the event by the users have been developed. The main reason for the developments in ICT is that they have the potential to have an impact on social welfare in events. Businesses can facilitate their marketing events through digitalization. Digitalization affects competition strategies and changes the understanding of competition on event marketing. The effectiveness of marketing communications is very crucial for the success and sustainability of the events in a competitive environment. The tools to be used in the marketing of the events are selected based on the scope of the event, target markets, and cost criteria.

Digitalization provides ICTs to achieve and develop the main advantages for successful organizing events, to improve the quality of life of the target audience of the event, to target a competitive strategy, and to identify and organize. Competitive strategies aimed at achieving and strengthening the company's core strengths for accomplished work and improving the quality of life of the population enable the company to identify the top market trends. The effectiveness of marketing communications is very important for the success and sustainability of the events in a competitive environment. The significance of marketing communication benefiting from ICTs in the digital age is an undeniable fact. The variety of marketing communication tools is high and their effect levels are quite different. So, while the risk is reduced by using a general marketing communication tool in the marketing of events, a wide audience is targeted.

Businesses in the fields of tourism and marketing combine all their events with ICTs to gain an advantage in competition and to adapt to the digital changes. Digital transformation contributes to the national economy in terms of productivity, employment, and an increase in income. Quickly affecting almost all sectors, ICT has significantly affected the economic and social order in general terms. The modern information society has made tourism a rather information-intensive industry due to the impact of ICTs on tourism.

Opportunities and Challenges

In the digital age, management and marketing events have many opportunities as well as challenges. Opportunities and challenges are experienced in many industries as well as in tourism. Many factors, from business to customer, from marketing communication and management to service, from traditional to digital, have created opportunities or difficulties.

Increased cost and low efficiency in traditional marketing communication have created opportunities for effective marketing (Gupta, 2003: 87). Unlike traditional communication strategies, event marketing includes online marketing features to expand the involvement of customers in marketing communication and to expand event cognizance of customers. Improving the count of event participants is the same as the development of service awareness (Ozawa, 2017: 1354). Digital transformations provided by the private sector and the government have been substantial strategies for adapting and applying technological innovations. The digital capabilities of tourism businesses in the digital age are decisive for events that create value. The natural and acquired abilities of the strict followers of the digital age make a difference in the industry. The new tourism industry has replaced the events that took place in the traditional tourism sector that existed in the distant past. New technology brings new value, lifestyle, and inevitably new tourism products. The values and innovations that the new technology adds to the sector should be examined from the strategic management perspective and the marketing perspective. In this chapter, tourism is mentioned in ICTs and more concentrated on event management and marketing.

Event marketing, which has become widespread in the last decade, is expressed as a communication tool, which is to spread the marketing messages of a company by including the target groups in experiential events (Drengner et al., 2008: 143). It tries to draw the attention of customers to new products and brands through events such as event marketing, concerts, sports events, shows, and parties that establish a communication bridge between the brand and the customer (Liu et al., 2018: 465). The different types of events include business events, entertainment, arts, and community events, and festivals. All mentioned events may be commercial or not for profit. Events expressed as events occurring at a specific time and place have a predetermined plan and dimension (Akay, 2014: 55-56; Getz, 2008: 404-406). These face-to-face events are expressed as live in experiential organizations. While providing mutual communication with products and brands in event marketing, the grounds for creating interesting and unforgettable experiences are also prepared (Close et al., 2006). The significance and impact of event marketing in the digital age are more comprehensive and effective than traditional tools.

ICTs have a great influence on the development of the tourism industry. In parallel with the developing and changing technology, effective management and marketing of the events are possible with the effective use and management of ICTs. ICT tools are used in realizing, managing, and maintaining event management and marketing in tourism. ICTs can benefit the identification, customization, and purchase of products and services. Using ICT tools makes it easier to address different market segments by adding innovation and creativity to event managers. Event marketing, as in all industries, contributes to creating a brand image and improving the existing brand image in the tourism industry. All the events taking place in the tourism industry paves the way for the popularization of businesses in social, cultural, and artistic terms. In the literature, four different types of events are mentioned under the name of corporate, public relations, entertainment, and exhibitions (Gupta, 2003: 88). While these are evaluated under the name of dealer meetings, sales conferences, promotion and factory tours, and training programs, product launches, press meetings, and charitable events are evaluated under the umbrella of public relations. Entertainment events are classified as concerts, festivals, theater, dance, cinema, and sports events.

Artistic events such as museums, art galleries, and exhibition halls appear in hotels and theme parks integrated with the tourism sector. It is possible to develop customer experiences by managing artistic and cultural events with event marketing strategies. Businesses should determine the strategies to serve this purpose. The participation rate is used to measure the success of the events in terms of management and marketing. Traditional media channels are also used for an effective event. However, social media tools will be a better option for reaching a wide audience and low-cost process (Del Río et al., 2001). It is common to use marketing strategies in the organization and execution of events and to use social media tools in their promotion and announcement. The success of events in the digital age is in a way based on technology-based digital applications such as social media.

In the digital age, access to the data of the event participants is possible thanks to many database technologies. It is very significant to analyze the traces left by the participants in digital media and to analyze their contact information as user behavior and to evaluate this in management and marketing events. Accessing users' data in the digital age is very easy thanks to the technological infrastructure and adds value. Businesses follow the steps of the consumers and the traces they leave and create a database with the events they organize. Thanks to big data, businesses organize and classify customer data. The data obtained are then analyzed and interpreted. Businesses' main benefits that they hope to gain from analyzing customer data include (1) data-driven sales volume (2) promoting innovation (3) increasing customer engagement, and (4) creating stronger brand loyalty (Leeflang et al., 2014: 5).

Management and marketing strategies and marketing communication are major as they should be in a one-to-one relationship between events, businesses, and customers. The events are aimed to be related to the mission, vision, positioning, and image of the businesses and to establish significant contacts with the target group and to please them. The motivation and success of the event managers increase by increasing the satisfaction of the participants with a successful target group segmentation. The events to be carried out by following the main objectives of the business should also include experience by addressing the excitement, entertainment, and sensory aspects of the target group. The effectiveness of all events can also be measured by sales data, its position in the market share, and the number of visitors. Businesses use social media to promote and announce events, raise awareness, and increase sales and market share.

It is very critical to interact with potential participants and develop social relationships in social media strategies. In each event to be held, businesses need to know which social media tools they can find, and they have to master the habits of the participants. Success can be achieved by determining the power of an effective social media tool. Customer loyalty and intention to re-join can be created with successful social media and event marketing strategies. The power of social media cannot be denied at events, but the power of word of mouth marketing is an effective way of event marketing. It is known that there are social media users who share their experiences and comments on social media and do so as if they are professions. By choosing a social media tool suitable for the target audience to announce and promote the effectiveness of the event, it is ensured that the event's general and specific objectives, the content it wants to create, and its content is conveyed to consumers. The extent to which the event includes consumers in a two-way conversation is also related to the social media tool to be chosen. While blogs are an effective way for consumers to develop high-quality, meaningful content and express a specific message clearly, Facebook and Twitter are among the most effective ways to attract consumers to speech. YouTube can benefit according to the event to be organized with the visual and audio platform it offers. All social media formats have the potential to turn consumers into loyal customers by uniting consumers to one level and developing meaningful relationships with them. Besides, all components of marketing communication for organized events must nurture and strengthen each other and deliver the same consistent message to the participant. Social media tools, which serve as a tool in which all marketing communication efforts are connected to an easily accessible, integrated consumer space, are carried out in a coherent strategy with the goals of social media and business, to coordinate all efforts of the right application and event marketing in a coordinated manner.

Reviews of the events and referral pages are frequently followed by users and researchers. Consumers evaluate these comments and recommendations before participating in the events. With the use of social media in the digital age, it is very substantial and necessary to reveal the interests of users for the events they share and the events they attend and follow. In an environment where social media is used so much, its contribution to customer comments and recommendations about the events is undeniable. Blogs and chat rooms for events are also environments where customers collect information, share experiences, and conduct reviews, ratings, and evaluations for goods or services. The significance of this information on consumer behavior and their impact on their behavior is quite high (Onishi & Manchanda, 2012). As a marketing strategy, it is necessary to follow up on all behaviors of the customers to be aware of the event, to participate in the event, and to join in the event.

Many developments, expressed as digital innovation and revolution, also cause some difficulties for businesses. Numerous digital channels, increasing data prevalence, etc. cause businesses with difficulties in marketing events in the digital age. It faces the challenges of monitoring and controlling businesses in more complex and rapidly changing markets. In response to the challenges, businesses must actively participate in social media tools and develop solutions to the challenges they face to keep up with the development of the digital revolution.

With Industry 4.0, fundamental digital changes and innovations have emerged. Revolutionary innovation and opportunities have emerged with the benefits of Industry 4.0 and digitalization. With Industry 4.0, the Internet of Services (IoS), cloud computing technologies, the Internet of Things (IoT), and smart urbanism have become key technologies (Lom et al., 2016: 1). Industry 4.0 is a concept that focuses on consumer demands and needs, also referred to as the 4th industrial revolution. Besides, it is the understanding of meeting the consumer demands and needs at the maximum level. These radical changes and innovations will bring with it a change in power, wealth, and knowledge (Xu et al., 2018: 90).

It is essential to follow the marketing strategies and policies that adopt Industry 4.0 and ICTs in a changing and developing world. Industry 4.0 has four different components: IoT, IoS, Cloud-Based Manufacturing (CBM), Cyber-Physical Systems (CPS), and Smart Factories. The IoT attributed as a second industrial revolution and a pioneering subject in the field of information systems has a significant impact on the world (Shim et al., 2017: 1). IoT which was first applied by Kevin Ashton in supply chain management in 1999 (Gubbi et al., 2013), includes many applications such as smart transportation, smart health services, and smart vehicles. The IoT is divided into two as industrial and consumer exist in various industries such as public services, transportation, and logistics, consumer electronics, smart cities and buildings, and industrial automation (Shim et al., 2017: 2). It is a system of devices that enables the flow of information in communication with each other and allows the creation of an intelligent network. The IoT is a pioneering topic in the information systems field, with the ability to radically transform a business or event, improve efficiency, reduce the problem of operations, reduce operating costs, and develop new products (Shim et al., 2017: 1). The IoT, which is expected to create many economic opportunities, contributes greatly to technological transformation with the network system it creates (Hofmann & Rüsch, 2017: 25). The IoS provides a functioning order in the service society. It also makes it possible to make services easily available via web technologies (Wahlster et al., 2014). This means that the service society is going to play an important act in the next industries with the technology opportunities offered by Internet-based markets. IoS, which sees the Internet as a tool to provide and sell services, is seen as a new business model that can fundamentally change the way they discover and search for services (Cardoso et al., 2008: 15). Therefore, the IoS ensures the business and technical basis for advanced business models in which service providers and consumers create business networks for the service. CPS is significant in meeting consumer expectations and reducing production costs. It reflects the process of computation and integration of physical processes (Lee, 2008: 363). Major investments are made in these systems to improve technology worldwide. These systems, which support a new computational wave and become a theory, can offer new levels of performance and efficiency thanks to the advanced control-computing code mark (Wolf, 2009: 89). With the increase in production developed based on these systems, it will contribute to the sustainability of production and the development of industrialization. CBM is expressed as a decentralized and networked form of production that develops from other related production systems such as web-based production (Wu et al., 2014: 94). It is an Industry 4.0 component that provides benefits in meeting customer demands, reducing product costs, increasing efficiency, and enabling optimum resource allocation. Networked production, ubiquitous access and virtualization, big data and data analytics, scalability, agility, and the IoT are the main features of cloud-based production (Yıldız, 2018: 550-551). With Smart Factories, products can act independently within the scope of their production processes and find the chance to be easily identified and positioned. This is possible with optimum cost, flexible and individual mass production (Hofmann & Rüsch, 2017: 25). The above mentioned Industry 4.0 creates various innovations in the marketing sector with the effect of these opportunities and these innovations enable the marketing of events to gain momentum in the development process.

The impact of ICT on society and increasing individual needs create both opportunities and challenges for the future development of the accommodation industry (Breukel & Go, 2009: 188). In the digital age, ICT provides opportunities such as protecting existing customers and acquiring new customers as it provides ease of communication. There are many opportunities offered by technological innovations and developments in the marketing of events in the digital age. Malhotra (2001) and Ndou (2004) emphasize the potential of ICT tools for efficiency, cost reduction, service quality, convenience, innovation, and learning.

In the digital age, in management types and marketing trends in tourism, ICTs are becoming widespread, transaction costs are reduced and online services contribute to efficiency. ICT tools do not only increase productivity but also reduce the error rate and production cost. According to Ndou (2004), information is produced, transferred, accessed, and shared at a minimum cost. There is also a decrease in the level of inefficiency and uncertainty with a decrease in transaction costs. ICT tools overcome the distance and geographical constraints, eliminate the concept of distance, and offer opportunities such as removing borders. ICT has crossed the geographical boundaries of nation-states, enabling rapid market management and the ability to run electronic business. Buyers and sellers are informed along national borders of information, specification, production process, etc. allows everyone to know the comparative advantage in the market economy. It provides greater access to larger markets and global supply chains. In short, ICT provides rapid growth of event marketing with more security, convenience, precision, flexibility, diversity, and reliability in processes, thereby increasing total efficiency. ICT brings transparency in transactions and processes (Ndou, 2004: 1). Networking and information sharing certainly lead to demands for greater clearance and transparency. ICT, which has created new markets for goods and services, has benefited economic development in many aspects such as the ability of local businesses to operate in the global market, the opportunity to export a wider range of goods and services and increase the company's internal efficiency. Moreover, it is obvious that technology saves costs. Thanks to much technological equipment, it is provided to process, process, and control quickly and effectively.

The success and sustainability of ICT will change depending on its power to adopt digital technologies. Businesses will survive by adapting to the changes brought by ICT. The literacy levels of societies and low skills in electronic media can be expressed as challenges. These shortcomings are among the challenges facing digital transformation and digitalization. Also, countries that are not ready for ICT in the world may face the problem of not being able to keep up with innovation and change. The insufficiency of information and communication infrastructures slows down technological development and the effective use of technology. All infrastructures and networks must be of high quality, reliable, and comprehensive.

As with all electronic transactions, the need for the ICT infrastructure to be sufficient to meet current demands and needs is stated as one of the major challenges (Ndou, 2004: 5). An infrastructure foundation is required for all kinds of technological operations to be carried out in the management and marketing of tourism events. Every technological equipment that comes to mind in the tourism industry is subject to this classification, including computers and kiosks. It is also difficult to create trust, reputation, and loyalty for a brand in ICT (Leeflang et al., 2014: 4). Among the challenges, e-information proficiency can be mentioned (Ndou, 2004: 5). Although the proficiency of the technical and technological infrastructure is necessary and important, the human resources to manage it are just as important and essential. So, e-information proficiency is an important and vital need for the effective use of ICT and the quality of goods and services in the management of tourism events. Another challenge can be mentioned in internet access capability. As with tourism or any other industry, there are some limitations to Internet access. In addition to this limitation, technology adaptation and technology usability challenges across generations are among the technological challenges. It can also be said that there is a challenge, such as the rapid change of technology. This challenge is important as it affects the ability to respond to changes in management and marketing. Among the challenges, the issue of cost should also be mentioned. Costs can increase in a competitive market and are difficult to control.

The ability of tourism enterprises to obtain, store, and process much information provides them with a competitive advantage in the industry. In the daily activities of the enterprises, the evaluation of information within the company and its transmission to the relevant units are very necessary for effective management and marketing. Obtaining all the necessary information quickly and accurately is not sufficient alone. Information technologies play an active role in meaningful reading and analysis of these collected data. The use of information technologies required to collect and analyze large amounts of data is important in identifying potential customers and retaining existing customers (Mutch, 1995). For customer satisfaction, accurate and up-to-date information must be provided by customer expectations. So, information technologies have caused radical changes in the communication methods of tourism enterprises, information seeking and processing, and the way of purchasing touristic products and services. The use of management systems such as technology-based reservation systems and electronic sales points by tourism enterprises has changed the management approach. Therefore, in the digital age, technology is important in the production and quality processes of tourism businesses, especially in management and marketing.

The spread of information technologies in the digital age has brought globalization with it. The development of e-commerce thanks to ICTs has changed the course of marketing events. The necessity of good management in the background for the marketing of events has also changed the functioning of management tools. In addition to e-commerce, it has increased the effectiveness of new marketing and new management and organization techniques such as mobile marketing applications, digital advertising.

In the digital age, there are some challenges in the management of their events. Confusion and contradictions can occur when large amounts of data are not well managed and processed. This is due to information redundancy (Chong et al. 2000: 372). In addition to information redundancy, Chong (2000) mentioned challenges such as employee motivation to share information, whether tourism enterprises have a technological infrastructure suitable for the digital age. Also, he stated that the interaction of current information technologies with the new developing and changing digital age, the security of technological network systems, and old data are disadvantageous points. In addition to these, there are some challenges such as customer privacy, transaction security, and confidentiality against cyber-attacks, business integrity risks.

SOLUTIONS AND RECOMMENDATIONS

Businesses in the tourism industry should invest resources to appeal to a wide audience and to carry out a comprehensive tourism event. All players who play a role in the industry should apply the most appropriate event management and marketing strategies according to their workflow programs within an action plan. Management and marketing events should be used to gain a competitive advantage in the market and for long-term sustainability. Considering the short life of events, it is major not to ignore the management and marketing strategies that are affected by changing and developing technology.

Tourism, which was described as a labor-intensive sector in the past, has now become information-intensive and technology-intensive. It is impossible to carry out management and marketing events independently from technology in an environment where it is necessary to focus solely on customer requests and needs, and quality of service and experience. One of the points to be considered in all events is the consistency and reliability of management and marketing events. Efficiency can only be achieved through consistency and reliability.

Societies that adopt Industry 4.0 should direct their event marketing and management efforts through ICTs. To increase the contribution of Industry 4.0 to the development of ICTs, entrepreneurs need to expand their production and marketing networks over the Internet. So, Industry 4.0 components such as the IoT and Smart Factories must have adequate infrastructure for event management and event marketing.

FUTURE RESEARCH DIRECTIONS

It is very difficult for companies that cannot benefit from the opportunities offered by ICTs to be successful in a competitive environment. Compared to businesses, countries that do not adopt ICT tools to keep pace with globalization and meet their development needs will suffer significant disadvantages in the form of information poverty, which can further weaken the economic situation and competitiveness (Ndou, 2004).

The number and variety of conferences, festivals, exhibitions, meetings, and sports events in the tourism industry have increased in recent years. Event managers operating in the tourism industry need to make new arrangements and additions according to customer needs and wants. For these arrangements and additions, the market and customer structure should be well known. Due to the competitive environment and the necessity of event management and marketing strategies, it is necessary to understand and evaluate customers' behavioral characteristics. Events such as concerts, festivals, competitions, tournaments, and shows can be transferred to more people through word-of-mouth communication.

The use of events in the tourism industry is spreading rapidly all over the world. Therefore, technological innovations have positively affected the tourism sector as in other sectors. It provided sectoral figures to gain momentum upwards rapidly. It will have unbearable progress thanks to its potential. Developing policies for tourism industry events to adapt to technology will be a guide for future studies.

Industry 4.0 contributes to the digitization process with the development of ICTs. Therefore, it will be beneficial in terms of the integrity of the subject in future studies in terms of Industry 4.0, event management and marketing, and ICT. Tourism strategies and practices may differ in many countries. Although all kinds of innovations and changes that occur within the scope of ICT affect the whole world, the understanding of each country to adopt and apply the changes in ICTs may be different. In the tourism industry, there may be differences from business to business as well as application differences from business to consumer. In this context, challenges and obstacles may arise in the adoption of ICTs. This may require searching and finding some solutions in the future. For ICT and the tourism industry to work integrated into the long term, access, infrastructure, education, and adequate capacity must be available. Examining event management and marketing through digital transformation in areas such as human resources, experiential marketing, and social media marketing will be substantial for the sustainability of the event.

CONCLUSION

The adoption of ICTs in the digital age means the transformation of processes in the tourism industry into a digital environment. The effect of digitalization has led not only to any business that has adapted to technology but also to the digital transformation of the business environment. Businesses in the fields of tourism and marketing combine all their events with ICTs to gain an advantage in competition and to adapt to the digital changes. Digital transformation contributes to the national economy in terms of productivity, employment, and an increase in income. Some changes have occurred in many areas such as some developments in ICTs, health economics, management, and communication. Quickly affecting almost all sectors, ICT has significantly affected the economic and social order in general terms. The modern information society has made tourism a rather information-intensive industry due to the impact of ICTs on tourism.

ICTs are a substantial tool in the use and management of event marketing, as well as in evaluating events, determining methods, and systematizing actions. In the digital age, it provides ICTs to achieve and develop the main advantages for a successful event in organizing events, to improve the quality of life of the target audience of the event, to target a competitive strategy, and to identify and organize by prioritizing market trends. In the evaluation of ICTs, event management, event marketing, communication, and economic outcomes should be considered in an integrated manner and events should be organized accordingly. Meanwhile, competitive strategies aimed at achieving and strengthening the company's core strengths for accomplished work and improving the quality of life of the population enable the company to identify the top market trends. Because digitalization both affects competition strategies and changes the understanding of competition. The effectiveness of marketing communications and management is very important for the success and sustainability of the events in a competitive environment. The significance of marketing communication and management benefiting from ICTs in the digital age is an undeniable fact. The variety of marketing communication and management tools is high and their effect levels are quite different. So, while the risk is reduced by using a general marketing communication and management tool in the marketing of events, a wide audience is targeted.

This chapter focuses on ICTs and their opportunities and threats in the tourism industry. Moreover, the management and marketing events in the tourism industry by taking advantage of the opportunities of digitalization and the opportunities and challenges created are among the significant topics. There are many opportunities offered by technological innovations and developments in the management and marketing of events in the digital age. Ease of communication, efficiency, cost savings, service quality, convenience, innovation are mentioned among opportunities. In the digital age, in marketing trends in tourism, ICTs are becoming widespread, transaction costs are reduced and online services provided contribute to efficiency. Besides, ICTs are not only increasing efficiency but also reduce the error rate and production cost. Furthermore, ICTs overcome the distance and geographical constraints, eliminate the concept of distance, and offer opportunities such as removing borders. Therefore, it has enabled mass communication to develop mega-events that are aiming for the whole world. ICTs have crossed the geographical boundaries of nation-states, enabling rapid market management and the ability to run electronic business. Buyers and sellers are informed along national borders of information, specification, production process, etc. allows everyone to know the comparative advantage in the market economy. It provides greater access to larger markets and global supply chains. In brief, ICTs provide rapid growth of event marketing with more security, convenience, precision, flexibility, diversity, and reliability in processes, thereby increasing total efficiency. Networking and information sharing certainly lead to increasing demands for greater clearance and transparency. ICT has enabled new markets to emerge, helping local businesses to exist in the global market, exporting a wider range of goods and services, and enhancing a company's internal efficiency. Therefore, ICTs are believed to be a powerful tool to overcome some of the major barriers and challenges for the global economy and future growth potential.

Infrastructure is required for all kinds of technological processes to be carried out in the management and marketing events in tourism. Therefore, e-knowledge adequacy is substantial for ICTs and the quality of goods and services in the management of events in tourism. Another challenge can be mentioned as internet access capability. As with tourism or all other industries, there are several limitations to internet access. Besides this limitation, technology adaptation and technology availability differences among generations are among technological challenges. It can also be mentioned that such a challenge such as the rapid change of technology. This challenge is significant for its ability to respond to changes in technology and marketing. Among the challenges, the issue of cost should also be mentioned. Costs can rise in the competitive market and are difficult to control. In brief, challenges to the success of knowledge management mostly stem from technology, organizational structure, and cultural elements. Since businesses give importance and priority to technology to keep up with change, it can be thought that the challenges in this field can be overcome relatively easily. However, it is a fact that removing challenges arising from organizational structure and culture requires more care and time.

Industry 4.0 provides various innovations and opportunities in management and marketing events and other tourism products enable the development of event marketing to gain momentum. Thanks to the ICTs, developments in Industry 4.0 also play a major role in event management and marketing. Besides, the development of event management and marketing depends on the organizations that organize the event to coordinate their management processes about their brands well. The ability of tourism enterprises to obtain, store, and process much information provides them with a competitive advantage in the industry. In the daily activities of the enterprises, the evaluation of information within the company and its transmission to the relevant units are very necessary for ineffective management and marketing. Obtaining all the necessary information quickly and accurately is not sufficient alone. Information technologies play an active role in meaningful reading and analysis of these collected data.

REFERENCES

Akay, R. A. (2014). Etkinlik Yönetimi Uygulamalarında Yaratıcı Rekabet ve Sosyal Medyanın Entegrasyonu, *The Turkish Online Journal of Design. Art and Communication*, *4*(4), 55–70.

Argyropoulou, A., Dionyssopoulou, P., & Miaoulis, G. (2011). Tourist destination marketing and management using advanced ICTs technologies. *Advances on Information Processing and Management*, 365-369.

Breukel, A., & Go, F. M. (2009). Knowledge-based network participation in destination and event marketing: A hospitality scenario analysis perspective. *Tourism Management*, *30*(2), 184–193. doi:10.1016/j.tourman.2008.05.015

Cardoso, J., Voigt, K., & Winkler, M. (2008). Service engineering for the internet of services. *International Conference on Enterprise Information Systems*, 15-27.

Chong, C. W., Holden, T., Wilhelmij, P., & Schmidt, R. A. (2000). When does konowledge management add value? *Journal of Intellectual Capital*, *1*(4), 366–380. doi:10.1108/14691930010359261

Close, A. G., Finney, R. Z., Lacey, R. Z., & Sneath, J. Z. (2006). Engaging the consumer through event marketing: Linking attendees with the sponsor, community, and brand. *Journal of Advertising Research*, *46*(4), 420–433. doi:10.2501/S0021849906060430

Del Río, A. B., Vázquez, R., & Iglesias, V. (2001). The Effects of Brand Associations on Consumer Response. *Journal of Consumer Marketing*, *18*(5), 410–425. doi:10.1108/07363760110398808

Drengner, J., Gaus, H., & Jahn, S. (2008). Does flow influence the brand image in event marketing? *Journal of Advertising Research*, *48*(1), 138–147. doi:10.2501/S0021849908080148

Getz, D. (2005). *Event Management and Event Tourism*. Cognizant.

Getz, D. (2008). Event tourism: Definition, evolution, and research. *Tourism Management*, *29*(3), 403–428. doi:10.1016/j.tourman.2007.07.017

Go, F. M., Lee, R. M., & Russo, A. P. (2003). E-heritage in the globalizing society: Enabling cross-cultural engagement through ICT. *Information Technology & Tourism*, *6*(1), 55–68. doi:10.3727/109830503108751225

Gubbi, J., Buyya, R., Marusic, S., & Palaniswami, M. (2013). Internet of Things (IoT): A vision, architectural elements, and future directions. *Future Generation Computer Systems*, *29*(7), 1645–1660. doi:10.1016/j.future.2013.01.010

Gupta, S. (2003). Event marketing: Issues and challenges. *IIMB Management Review*, *15*(2), 87–96.

Hofmann, E., & Rüsch, M. (2017). Industry 4.0 and the current status as well as future prospects on logistics. *Computers in Industry*, *89*, 23–34. doi:10.1016/j.compind.2017.04.002

Law, R., Buhalis, D., & Cobanoglu, C. (2014). Progress on information and communication technologies in hospitality and tourism. *International Journal of Contemporary Hospitality Management*, *26*(5), 727–750. doi:10.1108/IJCHM-08-2013-0367

Lee, E. A. (2008). Cyber physical systems: Design challenges. *2008 11th IEEE International Symposium on Object and Component-Oriented Real-Time Distributed Computing (ISORC)*, 363-369.

Leeflang, P. S., Verhoef, P. C., Dahlström, P., & Freundt, T. (2014). Challenges and solutions for marketing in a digital era. *European Management Journal*, *32*(1), 1–12. doi:10.1016/j.emj.2013.12.001

Li, X., & Duan, B. (2018). Organizational microblogging for event marketing: A new approach to creative placemaking. *International Journal of Urban Sciences*, *22*(1), 59–79. doi:10.1080/12265934.2017.1343155

Liu, L., Zhang, J., & Keh, H. T. (2018). Event-marketing and advertising expenditures: The differential effects on brand value and company revenue. *Journal of Advertising Research*, *58*(4), 464–475. doi:10.2501/JAR-2017-043

Lom, M., Pribyl, O., & Svitek, M. (2016). Industry 4.0 as a part of smart cities. *2016 Smart Cities Symposium Prague (SCSP)*, 1-6. 10.1109/SCSP.2016.7501015

Malhotra, Y. (2001). *Enabling next generation e-business architectures: balancing integration and flexibility for managing business transformation.* Intel e-Strategy White Paper. www. brint. net/members/01060524/intelebusiness.pdf

Mutch, A. (1995). IT and small tourism enterprises: A case study of cottage-letting agencies. *Tourism Management*, *16*(7), 533–539. doi:10.1016/0261-5177(95)00056-T

Ndou, V. (2004). E–Government for developing countries: Opportunities and challenges. *The Electronic Journal on Information Systems in Developing Countries*, *18*(1), 1–24. doi:10.1002/j.1681-4835.2004.tb00117.x

Neuhofer, B., Buhalis, D., & Ladkin, A. (2014). A typology of technology-enhanced tourism experiences. *International Journal of Tourism Research*, *16*(4), 340–350. doi:10.1002/jtr.1958

Onishi, H., & Manchanda, P. (2012). Marketing activity, blogging and sales. *International Journal of Research in Marketing*, *29*(3), 221–234. doi:10.1016/j.ijresmar.2011.11.003

Ozawa, T., Sekiguchi, A., & Tsuda, K. (2017). A method for the construction of customer behavioral modeling knowledge for B2B event marketing strategy. *Procedia Computer Science*, *112*, 1353–1360. doi:10.1016/j.procs.2017.08.027

Sezer, A. A., & Bröchner, J. (2019). Site managers' ICT tools for monitoring resources in refurbishment. *Engineering, Construction, and Architectural Management*, *27*(1), 109–127. doi:10.1108/ECAM-02-2018-0074

Shim, J., Avital, M., Dennis, A. R., Sheng, O., Rossi, M., & Sørensen, C. (2017). Internet of things: Opportunities and challenges to business, society, and is research. *Proceedings of the 38th International Conference on Information Systems.*

Sneath, J. Z., Finney, R. Z., & Close, A. G. (2005). An IMC approach to event marketing: The effects of sponsorship and experience on customer attitudes. *Journal of Advertising Research*, *45*(4), 373–381. doi:10.1017/S0021849905050440

Wahlster, W., Grallert, H. J., Wess, S., Friedrich, H., & Widenka, T. (Eds.). (2014). *Towards the internet of services: The THESEUS research program*. Springer. doi:10.1007/978-3-319-06755-1

Wang, D., Park, S., & Fesenmaier, D. R. (2012). The role of smartphones in mediating the touristic experience. *Journal of Travel Research*, *51*(4), 371–387. doi:10.1177/0047287511426341

Wolf, W. (2009). Cyber-physical systems. *Computer*, *42*(3), 88–89. doi:10.1109/MC.2009.81

Wu, D., Rosen, D. W., Wang, L., & Schaefer, D. (2014). Cloud-based manufacturing: Old wine in new bottles? *Procedia CIRP*, *17*, 94–99. doi:10.1016/j.procir.2014.01.035

Xu, M., David, J. M., & Kim, S. H. (2018). The fourth industrial revolution: Opportunities and challenges. *International Journal of Financial Research*, *9*(2), 90–95. doi:10.5430/ijfr.v9n2p90

Yıldız, A. (2018). Endüstri 4.0 ve akıllı fabrikalar. *Sakarya Üniversitesi Fen Bilimleri Enstitüsü Dergisi*, *22*(2), 546–556.

ADDITIONAL READING

Brougham, D., & Haar, J. (2018). Smart technology, artificial intelligence, robotics, and algorithms (STARA): Employees' perceptions of our future workplace. *Journal of Management & Organization*, *24*(2), 239–257. doi:10.1017/jmo.2016.55

Dalenogare, L. S., Benitez, G. B., Ayala, N. F., & Frank, A. G. (2018). The expected contribution of Industry 4.0 technologies for industrial Performance. *International Journal of Production Economics*, *204*, 383–394. doi:10.1016/j.ijpe.2018.08.019

Guo, Y., Liu, H., & Chai, Y. (2014). The embedding convergence of smart cities and tourism internet of things in China: An advance perspective. *Advances in Hospitality and Tourism Research*, *2*(1), 54–69.

Witkowski, K. (2017). Internet of things, big data, industry 4.0: Innovative solutions in logistics and supply chains management: 7th International Conference on Engineering, Project, and Production Management. *Procedia Engineering*, *182*, 763–769. doi:10.1016/j.proeng.2017.03.197

KEY TERMS AND DEFINITIONS

Big Data: Is a set of data that enables the coordination of the services offered through the Internet, organizing and classifying customer data.

Event Marketing: Is expressed as a process in which ICT marketing tools use marketing mix events to meet the demands and needs of businesses and participants.

Industry 4.0: Is expressed as a concept that reveals the phenomenon of globalization due to technological developments, increasing digitalization and capital accumulation. It also affects the industrial-strength, production factors and marketing strategies of companies through ICT.

Information and Communication Technologies: Can be expressed in the digital age as the technology system that enables users to develop and transform ways to search and access information about the event.

Internet of Things (IoT): Can be expressed as a network that ensures optimum decisions in the management of companies that benefit greatly from information and communication technologies and enables data exchange and analysis.

Chapter 8
Digital Art Events and Digital Art Museums

Evrim Çeltek
https://orcid.org/0000-0002-2722-5256
Tokat Gaziosmanpasa University, Turkey

ABSTRACT

The development of information communication technologies and the increase in use have made it utilized as a tool for cultural and artistic production. Digital art, where technology and art coexist, has created a free working space for the artist. Digital art is a contemporary type of art that includes many different art methods such as sound art, computer graphics, virtual art, internet art, robotics, video, interactive art, computer animation, and it distinguishes itself from the old visual arts. The cities that have come to the fore with art in the world become the tourist attraction centers. In this context, tourist attraction centers can be created by developing digital art. The development of digital art and the increase in the number of artists interested in this art have led to the emergence of tourist attraction centers. In this chapter, digital art events and digital art museums are determined. And finally, digital art events and museum examples are given where digital art is an attraction.

INTRODUCTION

The development of information communication technologies and the increase in use have started to be used as a tool for cultural and artistic production. Digital art, where technology and art coexist, has created a free working space for the artist. Digital art provides an opportunity for direct communication with the viewer and creates an opportunity for interaction between the artist, the viewer and the work. Digital art is a contemporary type of art that includes many different art methods. Digital art using methods such as; sound art, computer graphics, virtual art, internet art, robotics, video, interactive art, computer animation, and distinguishes itself from the old visual arts. Today, new media is often used as an alternative to older nomenclature such as 'digital art', 'computer art', 'multimedia art' and 'interaction art'. Also, new genres such as 'net art', 'software art' and 'pixel art' are also referred to as new digital art. As stated in Çokokumuş (2012) the first use of the term digital art was in the early 1980s

DOI: 10.4018/978-1-7998-4954-4.ch008

when computer engineers devised a paint program that was used by the pioneering digital artist Harold Cohen. This became known as AARON, a robotic machine designed to make large drawings on sheets of paper placed on the floor. Many cities are not interested in the cultural or commercial dimension of art. Nowadays the cities that came to the forefront with art became the center of attraction in terms of tourism. New York, Paris, Milan are examples of these cities. In this context, tourist attraction centers can be created with developing digital art. The development of digital art and the increase in the number of artists interested in this art have led to the emergence of tourist attraction centers. In this chapter, digital art events and digital art museums determined. And finally, digital art events and museum examples are given where digital art is an attraction.

BACKGROUND

Digital Art

Digital art has undergone many naming changes since its inception. Computerized productions, which were started by the artists in the 1970s, were mentioned as computer graphics in the literature studies until the 1990s and "Computer Art" was later gathered under the title of "Multimedia Art". In the late twentieth century, film, video, sound art and other mixed art forms were evaluated under the term "New Media Art" (Arapoğlu, 2012; Atmaca 2011).

Digital art is generally referred to as the art form in which intangible and virtual objects produced with digital technology are created with aesthetic values (Ak, 2013; Türker 2011). Digital art is a form of art, which is realized by the production of non-physical objects, in which the computer plays a role in the general production. Digital art can be defined as "sense of art used in digital production as a tool and / or medium in its production or exhibition" (Avcı, 2013).

In the production of digital works of art, imagination and creativity that cross the boundaries of thought, as well as point, line, light, form, texture, color, etc. basic art elements are used with technology. Also, there is a need for computer use, programs and tools such as cameras, video cameras and scanners where digital art will be produced. Digital art is a form of computer aided art. Artists who are interested in digital art can produce new products by using computer programs and changing the pictures in various techniques. Although digital art is also named as computer art or computerized art, these terms do not fully meet the scope, but the computer has a very important role in digital art (Sağlamtimur, 2010).

From the first graphics using computer technologies to today's engineering wonder, interactive real and virtual environments, almost all works are defined as digital artwork. Christiane Paul states that digital art samples were first called "computer art", and later the name "multimedia art" was used. At the point reached today, she emphasizes that all these works are known as "new media art" (Paul, 2003).

According to Gültekin Çizgen, digital art is "the creation of visuals developed on the screen with a mathematical calculation, the technical language created by the 0's and 1's, and then the reflection of this infrastructure as a new technical tool in artistic expression and production" (Çizgen, 2007).

Digital art, formed by the combination of digital media and art, is called the art form in which the computer plays a role in its production. In this process, the computer can be found anywhere in the development, ranging from a traditional tool to a creative position. The works where only the usual use of the computer plays a role in the process are generally not included in this classification (Purves, 2005; Akten, 2008).

Digital art; it uses the internet, network connections, unique software, virtual reality, virtual environments, artificial life and organisms, GPS technologies, databases, robots, headgear, prostheses, machine extensions. Artificial intelligence, data display and mapping, hypertextual narratives and games are accepted as digital artworks. Experiencing in digital art has turned into a mental and physical act, and has become an art form that includes all senses. Digital art basically questions the interaction of man with his environment, knowledge, technology, aesthetics and, consequently, self-consciousness. The role of artistic expression in this interaction is important, just as in conceptual art, with its diversity of meanings and actionable orientations. Digital artwork often starts with the participation of the audience, continues with interactive methods, can change direction, end or transform into an infinite process. The predominantly spreading environment of digital art is the internet. The Internet offers people the opportunity to store, share and access the information that is increasingly produced day by day. Since digital art is spread on the Internet in general, this branch of art is more intensely known and accepted by a technology-prone audience. Today, many important exhibitions for digital art have been held in important art galleries and have been watched with interest by art lovers. Digital artworks are collected by museums, institutions and private collectors. However, issues such as the collection, presentation and protection of digital works of art, virtual museum, property and copyright are still under discussion. (Sağlamtimur, 2010; Sağlamtimur, 2017).

Identification and classification can help define the distinctive features of a field, but it can be dangerous to impose predetermined limitations on expressing emerging forms of art, especially digital art. On the one hand, it is seen that the naming and classifications such as computer art or electronic art will be inadequate as a result of the change and diversification of the tools and methods used in an art branch that changes constantly due to technological developments (Avcı, 2013).

Digital art products, which are directly or indirectly involved in social life, by artists; it is tried to be understood most effectively by using concepts such as copying, simulation, artificial life forms, databases, digital images, activism. The new media systems that emerged with the development of computer technologies in the 90s affected media artists. In this period, artists dealing with digital arts started to turn towards computer-based art. Artists with many different professional and artistic backgrounds have created a rich artistic environment. In the early days of the new media, people engaged in computer-based art were scientists who worked with artists rather than artists. The artists, who started to be interested in new media, started to establish different collaborations. Engineers, technicians, and artists began to produce artworks together (Toy, 2017).

MAIN FOCUS OF THE CHAPTER

Traditionally, art tourism involves tourists whose mobilities were determined by their motivation to see and enjoy art, often consumed within confined spaces such as exhibition halls, galleries, museums, etc. However, with the digitalization of art and space, and evolving visitor demands, mobility patterns have significantly changed for both the artist and the admirer of art. Digitization (conversion of physical into virtual content), digitalization (processing of digitized content), and (Tavakoli, Wijesinghe, 2020) now digital art, have transferred the traditional physical art museums and events to that of digital art museums and events. Many cities are not interested in the cultural or commercial dimension of art. Nowadays the cities that came to the forefront with art became the center of attraction in terms of tourism. New York, Paris, Milan are examples of these cities. In this context, tourist attraction centers can be created by

Figure 1. Digital Art

Features of Digital Art

- In digital art works, the audience has opportunity to experience working one to one.
- Works in digital art are shaped, changed and developed with the participation of people, interdisciplinary and collaboration.
- Even when digital art is exhibited in a museum, it is a work that is constantly changeable with commands given by people from different parts of the world.
- Digital art samples realized with the help of the Internet broaden the boundaries of the concept of interaction and make the audience a user.
- Digital art creates a hybrid form of expression by combining different art forms and different media technologies under one roof.
- Immersion, which is one of the most important features of digital art, is defined as a decrease in the awareness of the physical self as a result of the person's being completely involved in an experience.
- The common point of digital artworks is using computers. Besides; internet, network connections, software specific to projects, augmented reality, virtual reality, artificial reality, cyberspace, artificial intelligence, artificial life and organisms, GPS (Global Positioning System) technologies, databases, robots, cyborgs, wearable technologies are used.
- Futurism, Dadaism and Constructivism are trends that affect digital art.
- Digital art is a contemporary art form that includes new media technologies such as digital media, video, interactive art, computer graphics and animations.
- Digital art brings together studies such as art, science, technology and design that destroy the interdisciplinary boundaries and bring together research and development laboratories and academies.

Techniques of Digital Art (www.architecturelab.net, 2019)

- **Photography:** By using photographs from a conventional or digital camera, photos are digitized then manipulated on a computer, making modifications which range from sharpening the image to drastically re-creating the image in assorted colors, arrangements, and even breaking the photograph down to multiple parts.
- **Photo painting:** In this technique, the artist takes a photograph and uses computer tools to virtually "paint" the picture, modifying it from its original form, but often maintaining the general layout of the subject matter.
- **Digital collage:** By taking multiple images, artists layer and edit pictures to create unique works of art.
- **2D digital painting:** With 2d painting, artwork is created with virtual painting tools in an editing program using two-dimensional models. Video experiences.
- **3D digital painting:** More like sculpture, this technique utilizes modeling software to essentially sculpt on the computer. Items traditionally created by hand or machine can be re-created on the computer.
- **Vector drawing or dynamic painting:** Software created specifically for this use allows the artist to create details within shaped outlines, creating a graphic design. Andy warhol led this type of work, agreeing to be a representative for the fledgling commodore computer in 1985.
- **Algorithmic:** Also called fractals, this type of art is based on mathematical computations. This allows mathematicians to use software, calculations, and color graphics to create both patterned and realistic images.
- **Mixed media (integrated digital art):** Simply put, this is a combination of any other named digital techniques.
- **Video art & interactive digital installations:** Using computerized video imaging, this more recent style of digital art is a more immersive experience, often combining audio, video, and even movement within one presentation.

developing digital art. The development of digital art and the increase in the number of artists interested in this art have led to the emergence of tourist attraction centers.

EXAMPLES OF DIGITAL ART EVENTS FROM THE WORLD

Machine Hallucination Exhibition by Refik Anadol

Refik Anadol creates various installations using light, data and artificial intelligence. The artist works on the visualization and spatialization of the data. While designing his works, Refik Anadol creates unusual space experiences by using data and machine intelligence as a tool. Anadol offers its audience the opportunity to imagine new functions and space alternatives with both indoor and outdoor works. (Burçoğlu, 2018). In 2017, Refik Anadol grouped more than 1 million 700 thousand documents in SALT Research archive collections according to their common features with artificial intelligence and machine learning algorithms, then visualized these groupings and turned them into a media installation. He presented the resulting works in his exhibition Archive Dream (Dadanizm, 2019). In his second solo exhibition, "Melting Memories", Anadol has made an impressive work in the neurology laboratory of the University of California by transforming the data collected through algorithms that measure the processes between the human brain and consciousness into algorithms. Refik Anadol visualized the memories, which include many different emotions such as happy, sad and sorrowful in the Melting Memories exhibition, by separating them with algorithms. Finally, Anadol has achieved international success by digitizing the archives of the LA Philharmonic orchestra and placing it on the facade of Walt Disney Concert Hall, one of the most recognized buildings in Los Angeles.

"Machine Hallucination" by Refik Anadol is his first large-scale digital exhibition in New York. An underground gallery area of 6,000 square meters in the historic boiler room of Chelsea Market was used for the exhibition. In the Machine Hallucination exhibition, he used machine learning to display architectural hallucinations from the dataset of more than 3 million images. The installation focused on the architectural images of the city of New York, revealing the context between the city's iconic architectural culture and its memories in its history. Refik Anadol has provided the most famous buildings of New York with a stunning experience that reflects the city's architectural past, present and future. "Machine Hallucination" takes visitors into the mind of a machine: viewers stand in a vast room with moving projections on three walls and the floor. (Aydın, 2019).

Lyon Festival of Lights (Fête des Lumières)

The Festival of Lights emerged from the popular tradition going back to 8 December 1852, when the residents of Lyon placed candles in colored glasses on their window sills to celebrate the installation of a statue of the Virgin Mary on the Fourvière Hill. The entire districts of the city were lit up, transforming the facades of buildings in a show of lights. To commemorate this event, on the days surrounding 8 December every year the people of Lyon celebrate the lighting up of their city, showcasing its living heritage. During the festival of lights, all parts of the city are lit up with lively lights, and the facades of some historical buildings (with artworks created by artists) are transformed into a complete work of art with spots and slide shows accompanied by classical music. In this unique Lyon tradition, candles are lit outside the windows of each house to create a lavish effect on the streets. For four nights a variety of different artists light up buildings, streets, squares and parks all over the city. Over 40 light installations create a magical atmosphere. At 2018 Festival of Lights visited by totaling 1.8 million visitors over the 4 Festival evenings. 100,000 foreign visitors came to Lyon for the Festival of Lights. 260,000 hotel nights

Figure 2. Machine Hallucination Exhibition (Refik Anadol)
Source: Banks, N. (2019) Man And Machine: New Rolls-Royce Artwork By Refik Anadol Uses Complex Data To Provoke Dialogues, Retrievedfrom https://www.forbes.com/sites/nargessbanks/2019/09/09/rolls-royce-art-refik-anadol/#56debf8733b5.

were booked in Lyon over the 4 days. In 2019 Festival visited by 1.8 million visitors during the four-day event (https://www.fetedeslumieres.lyon.fr/en/page/story-behind-festival, 2020).

The Treachery of Sanctuary by Chris Milk

In his art, Chris Milk brings together experimental art types and different environments; he uses new technologies, web browsers, events and even physical human gestures and facial expressions in his works. Combines his work with interactive technology and art. He is the founder and CEO of the virtual reality media company Within (Vrse). In recent years, Milk has been using cross media innovations and technologies to develop emotional human storytelling. Chris Milk creates many projects using virtual reality as a canvas. The installation "The Treachery of Sanctuary" was exhibited in the "Digital Revolution" exhibition. "The Treachery of Sanctuary" is an interactive work that tells the story of birth, death and metamorphosis, which uses the shadows and body movements of the participants' body (Milk, 2019). "The Treachery of Sanctuary" installation consists of three digital panels. When a viewer gets in front of the screen, the system starts. The Kinect camera, located behind the panels, recognizes the outline of the person and uses several image filtering techniques to soften their edges before they are shown as shadows and turn the viewer's shadow into a bird. Inside the first panel; birds representing processes such as artistic inspiration, birth and pregnancy are scattered from the body. In the second panel; birds begin

Figure 3. Lyon Festival of Lights (Fête des Lumières)
Source: www.archdaily.com (2020) Light Matters: Europe's Leading Light Festivals Retrieved from https://www.archdaily.com/443556/light-matters-europe-s-leading-light-festivals

to eat the human body, which moves with their beaks. This panel represents the human body consumed by life's brutality, fatigue or ill-treatment. The third panel; it represents rebirth, with a magnificent voice, your huge wings are formed and as you flap your wings, you rise to the sky. The artist tried to convey a long spiritual journey or death with this work (George, Meyers, and Chasalow, 2012).

Van Gogh Alive Digital Art Exhibition (Turkey)

Van Gogh Alive Digital Art Exhibition, offered to visitors 'an unforgettable experience' of vibrant color, light, and sound. Van GoghAlive Digital Art Exhibition reached a wide audience in Turkey with 215,000 visitors. The exhibition explored the work and life experiences of the renowned artist from 1880 to 1890 through his artwork characterized by vibrant colors and vivid detail. Synchronized to a powerful classical score through a rich surround sound system, more than 3,000 digital images of Van Gogh's most celebrated works created a thrilling display that fills giant screens, walls, columns, ceilings and the floor, creating an unforgettable display that immersed visitors (www.abdiibrahim.com.tr/en, 2020).

Figure 4. The Treachery of Sanctuary (Chris Milk)
Source: George, J., Meyers, A., ve Chasalow, B. (2012) How It Works: Chris Milk's The Treachery Of Sanctuary, Retrieved from https://www.vice.com/en_us/article/3dpg9v/how-it-works-chris-milks-ithe-treachery-of-sanctuaryi.

DIGITAL ART MUSEUMS

MORI (Tokyo-Japan)

The world's first digital art museum MORI is located on Odaiba, a man-made island in Tokyo Bay in Japan. The Digital Art Museum takes visitors from the real world and drags them into a digital world with 520 computers and 470 projectors in a three-dimensional area of 10 thousand square meters (Wood, 2019; Bosnalı, 2019a). The museum reached 1 million visitors five months after its opening in June 2018 (Xinhua, 2019). The world's first digital art museum; it is a collaborative initiative of the group of artists called TeamLab Borderless, which has been working on digital art for a long time with Mori Building, which is an important supporter of culture and art. In the MORI Building Digital Art Museum, the digital artworks connect with people and create different perceptions of time. Sometimes, even the works mix with other works of art. Thus, the museum becomes an unlimited world for digital artworks. In the museum, artworks found in different museums of the world are exhibited with advanced projectors. Digital works that interact with them by perceiving and reacting to the movements of the viewers show magnificent animations of light, color and different graphic elements. The works exhibited do not consist of cyclical, pre-recorded and repetitive digital images. The works show organic change and development by being affected by mobility in the environment due to their software. The museum, which uses digital technologies to emphasize art, consists of 5 interconnected regions. If these areas are briefly explained as follows: (Akçay, 2019; borderless.teamlab.art, 2019):

1. "Borderless World" is designed as an interactive digital nature landscape. In this region, where there are many different digital works, the audience is moving between digital waterfalls, birds, flower fields and forests.
2. "Athletics Forest" is an area designed to train the brain's spatial recognition abilities and move people. Visitors can climb shining poles in space in this area, jump on a trampoline in the galaxy simulation, or play balance games in incredible visual presentations.
3. Designed for children, "Future Park" is an area that connects children with art and allows children to make their designs and music with interesting applications. In this part of the museum, it is aimed to expand the scientific perspectives and imaginations of children.
4. "Forest of Lamps" is a section full of colorful lamps. Composed of lamps and mirrors that are completely hung from the ceiling, this section instills a sense of timelessness to man. When one lamp is touched, it is seen that the light passes to another lamp. With the color scheme that goes from warm to cold, visitors can feel themselves in infinity.
5. The last part is EN Tea House, which is more stagnant than others. 'EN Tea', which gave its name to this part of the museum, is a new type of green tea grown in Hizen near Nagasaki. In this area, viewers can chat with each other and evaluate their experience while sipping their tea decorated with digital flowers.

Dali Museum (St. Petersburg-Florida)

The Dali Museum in St. Petersburg, in partnership with Disney, created the exhibition "Disney & Dalí: Architects of the Imagination". Archeological Reminiscence of Millet's Angelus, the artist's classic work, is shown in a virtual reality tour on the theme of "Dreams of Dali" (Dorn, 2016, Marshall, 2016). "Dalí's Dreams", 360 degree virtual reality video takes the visitors who visit the museum to the world of Dalí's painting in 1935. Archaeological Reminiscence of Millet's painting 'Angelus,' gained tremendous popularity during Dalí's youth. The painting drawn at the end of the 19th century depicts a peasant couple standing in a bent field with prayer heads. The virtual reality video not only adds a spatial dimension to the painting but also includes the sound of Dalí. The video can be rotated in the desired direction by using the arrows that appear in the upper left corner of the video. (Marshall, 2016)

Artechouse (America)

Artechouse was founded in 2015 by artists Tati Pastukhova and Sandro Kereselidze. It is an environment consisting of floor-to-ceiling interactive video and augmented reality sticks. Artechouse opened its first location in Washington to D.C. in 2017 and opened its second location in Miami in 2018. In September 2019, opened its third technology-based art museum in the boiler room inside Chelsea Market in New York. For Artechouse, the aim is to make room for 21st century art that emphasizes the intersection of art, science and technology, and to inspire, educate and empower visitors to the museum by exploring the latest art and technology. Artechouse uses the latest technology to create an unprecedented exhibition space and platform for digital artists (Jordan, 2019). Artechouse in Washington D.C consists of 15,000 square meters. The museum, which was visited by more than 100,000 visitors from June 2017 to March 2018, consists of four separate digital exhibition areas (Hannon, 2018).

Carrières de Lumières (France)

Carrieres de Lumieres, an old quarry where stones were mined for Baux Castle, is exhibited to visitors with the technique of "scenography (meaning creating a new environment by projecting on the walls)", with the works of world-renowned painters with magnificent light plays on the walls of the quarry. Carrières de Lumières presented Van Gogh's masterpieces as a digital exhibition to art lovers. More than 2000 works that Van Gogh made in the last 10 years of his life are reflected on the walls with a magnificent visual and musical production. His most famous works such as The Potato Eaters, Starry Night, Sunflowers and The Bedroom, representing Van Gogh's unique style and reflecting his chaotic and poetic inner world, come to life on the nearly 20-meter long walls of Carrières de Lumières. Since the works are displayed on the walls with a thematic route, viewers can examine the time the artist spent in Arles, Paris and Saint-Rémy-de-Provence and various stages of his life (Bosnalı, 2019b). Following are the themes displayed at Carrières de Lumières by years (www.carrieres-lumieres.com, 2019):

- 2012: "Gauguin, Van Gogh: Painters in Color" exhibition opened in March. Works of Gauguin and Van Gogh were exhibited at the exhibition.
- 2013: Works of 16 different artists from the Mediterranean were exhibited in the exhibition "Monet, Renoir, Chagall Journeys around the Mediterranean".
- 2014: "Klimt and Vienna" exhibition provided an overview of 100 years of Vienna painting, with a special focus on the vibrant colors of Gustav Klimt.
- 2015: "Michelangelo, Leonardo de Vinci, Raphael: Giants of the Renaissance-Michelangelo, Leonardo de Vinci, Raphael: The Giants of the Renaissance" exhibition allowed the audience to discover some of the greatest works of the Italian Renaissance from a new perspective.
- 2017: Paintings by Bosch, Brueghel and Arcimboldo were exhibited at the exhibition "The Fantastic and Wonderful World of Bosch, Brueghel, Arcimboldo".
- 2018: Digitized works of Picasso, Goya and Sorolla were exhibited in the "Picasso and the Spanish Masters" exhibition.
- 2019: "Van Gogh, Starry Night" exhibited the work of the genius painter Vincent Van Gogh, who gained fame only after his death.

When it opened in 2012, 239,000 people visited the Carrières de Lumières. This number is 594,000 visitors in 2019. The projection surface of the museum, where digital exhibitions have been held since 2012, reaches a height of 7,000 m^2 from floor to ceiling and a maximum of sixteen meters (culturespaces.com, 2019).

Atelıer Des Lumıères (France)

L'Atelier des Lumières, Paris' first digital art museum, is operated by Culturespaces, a French museum foundation specializing in impressive art shows, and many artworks are on display at the museum. With the use of visuals and sound with the latest technology, the works of the artists and the images of their paintings are displayed on a wide surface of 3 thousand 300 square meters by using laser video projectors to 10 meters high walls. These projected images use an innovative motion design sound system with 50 speakers programmed to create the 3D visual experience. In the museum, a panoramic show is created in a wide area with the music of Wagner, Beethoven, Chopin and other musicians. The museum was established in a nineteenth century foundry. The metallic structure and elements characteristic of the old foundry, which constitute the authenticity of the building by adhering to its industrial architecture: long brick chimney, pool, tank and cellar have been preserved (culturespaces.com, 2019).

Bunker De Lumıères (South Korea)

Bunker de Lumières was opened jointly by TMONET (a Korean company specializing in technologies) and Culturespaces in 2018. Bunker de Lumières, a digital arts center similar to the Atelier des Lumières, offers a digital exhibition about Gustav Klimt. Thanks to the AMIEX® (Art and Music Interactive Experience) system, which includes the reflection of artworks on large surfaces, Bunker de Lumières presents an immersive exhibition dedicated to the main figures in the Vienna art scene, where Gustav Klimt is located. 90 laser video projector and 60 speakers are used to project images in the museum. The museum consists of an area of 1550 square meters and a projection area of 2500 square meters. Annually 500 000 visitors are estimated for the museum (culturespaces.com, 2019).

Figure 5. Atelıer Des Lumıères (Fransa)
Source: http://www.brandlifemag.com/ (2019) Işıktan Tabloların İçinde Kaybolun, Retrieved from http://www.brandlifemag.com/isiktan-tablolarin-icinde-kaybolun/.

Ars Electronica (Linz, Austria)

Ars Electronica (Museum of the Future), opened in Austria in September 1979, is an electronic arts center offering museums, art festivals, competitions and research lab activities. Art, technology and society are the main philosophy of this platform. Various mixes of various art genres, scientific fields and technological trends are exhibited in the museum. Exhibitions on themes of biotechnology and genetic engineering, neurology, robotics, prostheses and media art are displayed here. Digital presentations on space, universe and people, cultural heritage, astronomy, planet earth are made with a 16 x 9 meter wall projection, an equally large floor projection, laser tracking and 3D animations. All exhibits address the question of how people can cope with their environment and offer different perspectives on our nature, origins, our present. Exhibitions presented in the museum offer visitors interactive communication opportunities (ars.electronica.art, 2019). Ars Electronica evaluates thousands of applications from all over the world with its annual festival and Prix Ars Cyber Arts Competition. Ars Electronica organizes a festival once a year where conferences, workshops, exhibitions and symposiums are held, attended by artists, scientists and researchers from all over the world. Different themes are covered in each festival. In Ars Electronica's research lab (Futurelab), experts from a wide variety of disciplines work on ideas that shape the future. Media art, architecture, design, interactive exhibitions, virtual reality, real-time graphics constitute research topics. Ars Electronica Archive is one of the world's largest digital art and cultural documentary collections. Ars Electronica Archive has the task of preserving, digitizing and further developing the archive and the necessary technical infrastructure, as well as providing the most important content through an attractive online portal for a wide audience and research work. There is a Children's Research Laboratory for children aged 4 to 8, offering young visitors the opportunity to refine, make music, draw, program and experiment (Iinztourismus.at, 2019). One of the exhibitions shown at Ars Electronica is Mirages & Miracles, which works created by Adrien M and Claire B using augmented reality technology. Augmented drawings, holographic illusions and virtual reality glasses were part of this exhibition. The works in the exhibition transformed into animated animations with the augmented reality software installed on the tablet (ars.electronica.art, 2019).

SOLUTIONS AND RECOMMENDATIONS

The concept of art tourism sounds new, but it is as old as tourism itself because for centuries many societies had already given much appreciation for the arts and culture. Art tourism covers a big segment of the industry because around the globe people travel to visit, explore and engage in activities related to art festivals, concerts, wine and cuisine events and to explore famous museums. The cities that have come to the fore with art in the world have become tourist attraction centers. New York, Paris, Milan can be given as examples of these cities. In this context, tourist attraction centers can be established with developing digital art. To transform cities into digital art attractions, the following must be done:

- A digital art inventory should be prepared. Exhibitions and festivals that will create an element of attraction should be organized in cooperation with leading artists in this field.
- People who include artistic visits in their travel plans often have very high income levels. Research should be done on these tourists as a target market.

- Digital art and tourism partnerships should be established for marketing. The objectives of this partnership should be to seek international funds and to create a partnership between the arts and tourism societies. Both areas should consider where they can support the other.
- If the city has art galleries, they should be promoted in tourism enterprises. One of the biggest obstacles to combining art and tourism is not knowing where the exhibitions are. People do not know the exhibition times, where and how to get the tickets. To provide information on this subject, a cultural activity and art web page can be created and a calendar of events can be created according to months throughout the country.

FUTURE RESEARCH DIRECTIONS

In this chapter, digital art, digital art events and digital art museums have been examined. In this context, this study is conceptual. Digital art has the potential to be used in tourism industry events. A model proposal study on digital art event is recommended for the tourism industry. Digital art can be studied on independently for tourism and tourism sub-sectors such as festivals, museums, and tours or travel agencies. Also, the perceptions and expectations of the tourism sector regarding digital art can be determined through field studies or surveys with managers and tourists.

CONCLUSION

Through information systems, digital art products that are directly or indirectly included in the life of society are tried to be interpreted in the most effective way by the artists by using concepts such as copying, simulation, artificial life forms, databases, digital images, activism. Developments in the software world allow for the expansion of digital art forms. In the future, digital art types, digital art events and museums will increase in diversity.

Traditionally, art tourism involves tourists whose mobilities were determined by their motivation to see and enjoy art, often consumed within confined spaces such as exhibition halls, galleries, museums, etc. However, with the digitalization of art and space, and evolving visitor demands, mobility patterns have significantly changed for both the artist and the admirer of art. Digitization (conversion of physical into virtual content), digitalization (processing of digitized content), and now digital art, have transferred the traditional physical art museums and events to that of digital art museums and events.

Digital art is no longer the “new thing” as conceptual, virtual, and immersive works have appeared in museums and galleries worldwide. The new focus is more on the experiential nature of digital works, as visitors are invited to enter a virtual scene, participate in the presentation, and create an individual encounter each time. As technology is introduced rapidly, so will new aspects of this general “technique.”

To conclude it is important to recognize the role that digital art and digital art museums play in tourism development of any destination. Tourism destinations need strategies for partnership between digital arts museums and digital art festivals, because it is key to foster a strong tourism destination.

REFERENCES

Ak, A. (2013). Dijital sanat, Akademik Bilişim. XV. Akademik Bilişim Konferansı Bildirileri 23-25 Ocak 2013, Akdeniz Üniversitesi, Antalya.

Akçay, E. (2019). *Dünyanın ilk dijital sanat müzesi: MORI.* Retrieved from https://www.sophosakademi.org/dunyanin-ilk-dijital-sanat-muzesi-mori/

Akten, Z. (2008). Gelişen Teknolojilerin Dijital Sanat Alanında Oluşturduğu Yeni Temalar ve Mimarlığa Katkıları. İstanbul Teknik Üniversitesi, Fen Bilimleri Enstitüsü yayınlanmamış yüksek lisans tezi, İstanbul.

Arapoğu, F. (2012). Dijital Sanat Üzerine. *Artam Global Art & Design,* (16), 48-52.

ars.electronica.art. (2019). *What is Ars Electronica?* Retrieved from https://ars.electronica.art/about/en/

Atan, A., Uçan, B., & Bilsel, Ç. (2015). Dijital Sanat Uygulamaları Üzerine Bir İnceleme. *İstanbul Aydın Üniversitesi Dergisi, 7*(26).

Atmaca, A. E. (2011). Modern Sanat Ve Bilgisayar Destekli Sanat Çalışmaları (Dijital Art). *Elektronik Sosyal Bilimler Dergisi, 10*(37), 293–302.

Avcı, E. (2013). *Dijital Sanat Bağlamında Dijital Teknolojilerin Güzel Sanatlar Eğitimine Entegrasyonu: Bir Eylem Araştırması.* Anadolu Üniversitesi Eğitim Bilimleri Enstitüsü Yayınlanmamış Yüksek Lisans Tezi.

Banks, N. (2019). *Man And Machine: New Rolls-Royce Artwork By Refik Anadol Uses Complex Data To Provoke Dialogues.* Retrieved from https://www.forbes.com/sites/nargessbanks/2019/09/09/rolls-royce-art-refik-anadol/#56debf8733b5

Bosnalı, C. (2019a). *Dünyanın İlk Dijital Sanat Müzesi: teamLab Borderless.* Retrieved from https://www.Oggusto .com/blog/detay/1750/dunyanin-ilk-dijital-sanat-muzesi-teamlab-borderless.html

Bosnalı, C. (2019b). *Van Gogh'un Dijital Sergisi Fransa'da.* Retrieved from https://www.oggusto.com/blog/detay/1833/van-gogh-39-un-dijital-sergisi-fransa-39-da.html

Burçoğlu, Z. (2018). *Binaların İnsanlarla İletişim Kurma Biçimi ve Refik Anadol.* Retrieved from http://aura-istanbul. com/index.php/2018/11/16/binalarin-insanlarla-iletisim-kurma-bicimi-ve-refik-anadol/

Çizgen, G. (2007). *Sanat Köprüsü Sırat Köprüsü.* Arkeoloji Sanat Yayınları.

Çokokumuş, B. (2012). Art And Culture On Dıgıtal Medıa, International Journal of New Trends in Arts, Sports &. *Science Education, 1*(3).

Culturespaces.com. (2019). *Venues.* Retrieved from https://www.culturespaces.com/en/venues

Dadanizm. (2019). *Refik Anadol ve Hislerimizin Heykelleri.* Retrieved from https://kolektifhouse.co/komag/refik-anadol-ve-hislerimizin-heykelleri/

Dorn, L. (2016). *The Dali Museum Offers an Immersive Virtual Reality Tour Inside One of Dali's Most Famous Paintings.* Retrieved from https://laughingsquid.com/dali-museum-dreams-of-dali/

George, J., Meyers, A. & Chasalow, B. (2012). *How It Works: Chris Milk's The Treachery Of Sanctuary.* Retrieved from https://www.vice.com/en_us/article/3dpg9v/how-it-works-chris-milks-ithe-treachery-of-sanctuaryi

Hannon, K. (2018). *Artechouse Lights Up Washington's Museum Scene.* Retrieved from https://www. nytimes. com/2018/03/14/arts/artechouse-washington-dc-museum.html

https://borderless.teamlab.art. (2019). *MORI Mueum.* Retrieved from https://borderless.teamlab.art/

http://www.brandlifemag.com/. (2019). *Işıktan Tabloların İçinde Kaybolun.* Retrieved from http://www. brandlifemag.com /isiktan-tablolarin-icinde-kaybolun/

Jordan, E. (2019). *ARTECHOUSE: A Technology-Based Museum Shakes up D.C., Miami, and New York.* Retrieved from https://www.whitewall.art/art/artechouse-technology-based-museum-shakes-d-c-miami-new-york

linztourismus.at. (2019). *Ars Electronica Center.* Retrieved from https://www.linztourismus.at/en/leisure/discover-linz/museums-and-exhibitions/ars-electronica-center/. Access 15.09.2019

Marshall, C. (2016). *Walk Inside a Surrealist Salvador Dalí Painting with This 360° Virtual Reality Video.* Retrieved from http://www.openculture.com/2016/02/walk-inside-a-salvador-dali-surrealist-painting-with-this-360o-virtua l-reality-video.html

MilkC. (2019). *Bio.* Retrieved from http://milk.co/bio

Purves, T. (2005). *What We Want Is Free.* State University of New York Press.

Sağlamtimur, Z. Ö. (2010). Dijital Sanat. *Anadolu Üniversitesi Sosyal Bilimler, 10*(3), 213–238.

Sağlamtimur, Z., Ö. (2017). Yeni Medya Sanatı ve Fotoğraf. *Anadolu Üniversitesi Sanat & Tasarım Dergisi, 7*(2).

Tavakoli, R., & Wijesinghe, S. N. R. (2020). Digital Art and Virtual Tourism Mobility: A Critical Discussion in Contemporary Asian Artistic Expressions and Tourism (P. Mura, K. H. T. Keith, C. W. Choy, & S. Singapore, Eds.). Academic Press.

Toy, E. (2017). *Görsel İletişim Tasarımı ve Animasyon.* İçinde İnteraktif Sanatın Oluşum Süreci ve Günümüzdeki Durumu, Pegem Akademi.

Türker, İ.H. (2011). Tuvalden Sayısala, Anadolu Üniversitesi Sanat ve Tasarım Dergisi. *Güzel Sanatlar Enstitüsü Yayınları, 2419*(1).

Wood, B. (2019). *TeamLab launches the world's first digital art museum in Tokyo.* Retrieved from https://thespaces.com/teamlab-launches-the-worlds-first-digital-art-museum-in-tokyo/

www.abdiibrahim.com.tr/en. (2020). *Van Gogh Alive Digital Art Exhibit.* Retrieved from https://www. abdiibrahim.com.tr/en/responsibility/social-responsibility-at-abdi-ibrahim/van-gogh-alive-digital-art-exhibit

www.architecturelab.net. (2019). *15 Types of Digital Art to Consider.* Retrieved from https://www. architecturelab.net/types-of-digital-art/

www.carrieres-lumieres.com. (2019). *The Hıstory Of The Carrıères De Lumıères*. Retrieved from https://www.carrieres-lumieres.com/en/venue/history-carrieres-lumieres

ADDITIONAL READING

Dew, C. (2016). *An analysis of touring exhibitions practice in the UK. Economics of touring exhibitions survey report, Touring Exhibitions Group*. TEG.

Echeverría, J. (2009). Cultura digital y memoria en red. *Arbor, 185*(737), 559–567. doi:10.3989/arbor.2009.i737.313

Rinehart, R., & Ippolito, J. (2014). *Re-collection: art, new media, and social memory*. MIT Press. doi:10.7551/mitpress/7975.001.0001

KEY TERMS AND DEFINITIONS

2D Digital Painting: With 2D painting, the artwork is created with virtual painting tools in an editing program using two-dimensional models. Video experiences.

3D Digital Painting: More like sculpture, this technique utilizes modeling software to essentially sculpt on the computer. Items traditionally created by hand or machine can be re-created on the computer.

Artificial Intelligence: Artificial intelligence (AI) is an area of computer science that emphasizes the creation of intelligent machines that work and reacts like humans.

Augmented Reality: The process of taking and integration digital info either with a live streaming video or with the user's actual, real time atmosphere is called augmented reality (AR).

Big Data: Big data is defined as a large amount of data sets that cannot be analyzed and managed with traditional data processing tools.

Digital Art: Digital art is a form of art, which is realized by the production of non-physical objects, in which the computer plays a role in the general production. Digital art can be defined as "sense of art used in digital production as a tool and/or medium in its production or exhibition."

Internet of Things: The internet of things is a concept of creating online networks in part by placing chips, sensors, and communication modules in the everyday objects, and data in everything that surrounds people.

Virtual Reality: Represents three-dimensional (3D), interactive, computer-generated environments are represented by virtual reality applications. These environments will either be models of real or imagined worlds and that they aim at representing data through a synthetic experience.

Chapter 9
Social Media and Events:
Before, During, and After

Gulser Yavuz
Mersin University, Turkey

Kemal Enes
Mersin University, Turkey

ABSTRACT

Globally, the number of the internet and social media users is increasing day by day. The event industry has been affected by that popularity of social media and so event management and event marketing activities have changed radically. In this research, the importance of the social media in the events, management of the event, and finding how to take advantage of the social media by the marketing of the event are explored. Using of the social media in events was examined in these three parts: before, during, and after the events. Today it is regarded as an important tool used by the event managers of social media platforms and so social media has become an indispensable part of the events.

INTRODUCTION

The habits related to communication are changing. Especially in the last 10 years, the channels used in communication have evolved and new communication channels are becoming more popular. As one of the most striking examples of today, 13 million people followed the marriage of Prince William and Catherine Middleton on the official YouTube channel, rather than the usual communication channel, television. They preferred two-way communication instead of one-way communication of traditional media by making live comments during the entire marriage process.

Social media gained the throne of television, which is the most important communication tool due to the emerging technology and the rapid increase of people's use of internet and mobile technology. TV celebrities are being replaced by influencers and bloggers and people prefer to be in touch around the clock or even 24 hours a day, not just at the beginning, as on TV.

DOI: 10.4018/978-1-7998-4954-4.ch009

This emerging communication technology has a serious impact in many sectors. Especially the event sector is one of the most common areas of this impact. Without social media support, it seems unthinkable for events to take place. Therefore, event management is also evolving with this process and continues to develop in order to benefit from the benefits of social media at a high level.

Communications with participants, stakeholders, and sponsors through social media, especially before, during, and after the event, are supported by social media in some cases carried out only through social media.

BACKGROUND

Key Success Factors of Use of Social Media at Events

Social media is an environment that gives people opportunities at the online social life. Social media is an internet-based group of applications allowing user-centered creation and exchange of content built (Kaplan & Haenlein, 2012, p. 102). Events are a part of real social life. online social life unimaginable without the social media and this indicates social media has a magic role in the events. In order to reach, announce and manage the potential participants social media activities are very important for the success of the events (Grate, 2020). According to the research, although there are existing studies about the social media and events, there has not been enough studies about using social media for the events.

According to investigated the sources during the research process; it is indicated that the using of the social media in activities should be examined in 3 phases such as before the event, during the event and after the event. These phases play a key role in the social media management in the events.

MAIN FOCUS OF THE CHAPTER

Globally the number of the internet and social media users is increasing day by day. Social media is a current and popular topic, especially in recent years. The widespread and increasing popularity of social media has also left its mark on the event industry and social media has become an indispensable part of events. A comprehensive literature review shows that research on the use of social media tools within the scope of event marketing and management processes should be increased. In this context, in order to contribute to the literature, the importance of social media in events and how social media can be used in event management and marketing are tried to be revealed. In this chapter; using of the social media in events was examined in these three parts: before, during and after the events.

Events

Events are an important source of motivation for tourism and play an important role in the development and marketing of many destinations (Getz, 2008). In addition to serving various policy areas such as the recent growth in the number, size, cost, and impact of activities, such as urban and economic development, it also includes various social efforts to promote community integration (Getz, 2012). Activities seen as an integral part of the tourism sector also help to market goods, services, ideas, places or people (Fuchs, 2014, p. 248).

Table 1. Key Success Factors of Use of Social Media at Events.

Scholar(s)	Key Success Factors of Use of Social Media at Events
Atçeken, K., Doğrul, Ü., & Çabuk, S. (2018)	Facebook, Festival, Social Media, Promotion
Aventri. (2019)	Event Marketing, Community Management, Micro-Influencer Marketing, Social Media Management, Social Media ROI, Event Marketing of the Future
Barutçu, S., & Tomaş, M. (2013)	Social Media, Social Media Marketing, Sustainable Social Media Marketing, Efficiency Measurement.
Brooks, R. (2020)	Social Media Marketing, Tweeter marketing, Facebook Marketing, Blog marketing, Using Hashtags, Event Marketing
Bulut, E. (2012).	Social Media, Social Media Tools, Social Media Applications, Political Marketing, Internet
Fuchs, C. (2014)	Social media, Critical theory, Internet, Social media, Web 2.0, social media culture, Social Media and Communication power, Political economy of social media, Google, Facebook, Twitter, Wikileaks, Wikipedia, Social Media and its Alternatives
Getz, D. (2008)	Event tourism; Definitions; Theory; Research
Getz, D. (2012)	Event studies; Discourses; Policy implications; Interdisciplinary theory
Ghazali, A., & Ramli, N. (2014)	Social Media, Event Management, Attendee Satisfaction
Hede, A.-M., & Kellett, P. (2012)	Event marketing, online brand community, social media, Web 2.0
Hoffman, D. L., & Fodor, M. (2010)	Social Media Measurement, Social Media ROI, Social Media Metrics,
Hudson, S., Roth, M., Madden, T., & Hudson, R. (2015)	Music festivals, Marketing, Social media, Brand relationship quality, Emotions
Kaplan, A., & Haenlein, M. (2012).	Social media, Internet, Information exchange, Information, Information management
Lee, S. S., Boshnakova, D., & Goldblatt, J. (2017).	Meeting and Event Technology History, Using the technology, Meeting and Event Search Engine Optimization, Searc technology, Meeting and Event Design Technology, Marketing with wikis websites blogs and podcast, social media technology solutions for event, Mobile applications for event marketing,
Paris, C. M., Lee, W., & Seery, P. (2010)	Social Capital, Web 2.0, Marketing, Consumer Behavior
Potter, B. (2018)	Social media impact on events,
Preston, C. (2012)	Event Promotion, Elektronic event marketins strategies, Merketing events, Social media in events
Van der Wagen, L., & White, L. (2010)	Event Managemt, Marketing, Consept and design, Using social media for sponsorship, financial management for event
We Are social. (2020, 10 07).	Social media statistics,
Yalçın, F. G. (2017, 08 25).	Factors affecting event marketing

The event sector is a large sector affecting many sectors and continues to grow. In the world, many types of events are organized in regional, national, international and global characteristics. For example, in the USA, more than 2,500 music festivals are held annually, while the UK hosts over 70 different beer festivals each year (Preston, 2012, p. 142). Conferences and meetings constitute a large 20% of the direct spending in the UK event sector, and the sector where exhibitions and trade fairs, music and sports events are predominant is worth £ 41.2 million (Luty, 2020).

The business events market, called the Global MICE (Meetings, incentives, conferences and exhibitions) sector, is expected to be worth $ 882.84 Billion in 2018 and $ 1546.69 Billion by 2025. The event sector is attracted by rapid innovations in technology and supported by social media platforms and continues to grow and develop (Heraldkeepers, 2020).

Social Media

Social media is an internet-based group of applications built on the ideological and technological foundations of Web 2.0, allowing user-centered creation and exchange of content (Kaplan & Haenlein, 2012, p. 102). Social media is a new online media group that shares most or all of the features of participation, openness, conversation, community, and connectedness. "Participation" refers to encouraging the contributions and feedback from all interested parties, "openness" means that most social media services are open to feedback and participation, "conversation" refers to two-way communication, the rapid formation of communities that share common interests in "community", "connectedness" refers to developing their connections by making use of connections to other sites, resources, and people (Paris, Lee, & Seery, 2010, p. 533).

There are basically six types of forms of social media. These are social networks (Facebook etc.), blogs, wikis (Wikipedia), podcasts (Apple Itunes), forums, content communities, microblogging (Twitter). Today, the social media term is generally used for all of these platforms (Mayfield, 2020, p. 6).

Studies conducted over the years show that the ranking of the most accessed sites in the world has changes over time. For example, in 2000, the most frequently accessed sites were MSN, Yahoo, Excite, AOL, Microsoft, Daum, sites like eBay and Altavista, while in 2013 Google, Facebook, YouTube, Yahoo, Baidu, Wikipedia, Windows Live, QQ, Amazon, Twitter, Blogspot, LinkedIn, Wordpress websites have been accessed the most. The main reason for this difference is that these platforms now include social networking sites (Facebook, LinkedIn), video sharing sites (YouTube), blogs (Blogspot, Wordpress), wikis (Wikipedia) and micro blogs (Twitter, Weibo). What differentiates these social networking sites and promotes their popularity is that the web pages, web mail, digital image, digital video, discussion group, guestbook, link list or search engine are integrated platforms that combine many media and information and communication technologies (Fuchs, 2014, p. 6).

According to the Global Digital Report, the number of internet users is increasing every day. In 2019, there were 4,388 billion internet users and 5,112 billion unique mobile users worldwide, up 2 percent from the previous year. Although social media use is still not distributed evenly throughout the world, it is seen that the number of active social media users reaches 3.483 billion people. 3,256 of these people use social media through their mobile devices. It is noted that new users have increased dramatically over 10 percent over the previous year. While time spent on social platforms varies between cultures, the average social media user spends 2 hours and 16 minutes on social platforms every day. In terms of active user accounts, social media platforms such as Facebook, YouTube, Instagram and WhatsApp, Facebook Messenger, WBXIN / WeChat messaging applications maintain their top positions (we are social, 2020, p. 8).

It can be said that social media is now a priority for people and institutions from many areas around the world, from politicians to artists, musicians to business people. Traditional media tools, which also played an important role in event management and were the most important communication channel of the era, have changed due to today's technological changes and innovations, and the media tool that is the most effective channel of today has become social media. According to a comprehensive study of event professionals in 2018, 73% of event planners believe that social media is the most effective tool for marketing events (Aventri, 2019, p. 10).

This change is based on changing preferences for many reasons for users. Compared to social media and traditional media, communication in media such as newspapers, radio and magazines, which are traditional media tools, is one-way, while social media can be said to be two-way. For example, at a sporting event, fans share news, information and comments from social media beyond watching. The updating, speed and interaction structure of social media make it more preferable. Unlike traditional media, many journalists, artists, experts, educators, and students can raise themselves heard through blogs or social media networks without any personal or organizational investment (Bulut, 2012, pp. 29-31) .Thanks to social media, people draw their routes, participate in scientific, artistic, recreational, etc. activities, and recommend them. They are able to find knowledge, inspiration, like-minded people, communities and collaborators faster than ever. New ideas, services, business models and technologies are emerging and evolving at a dizzying pace in social media (Mayfield, 2020).

Social media has fundamentally changed the way users share their personal and professional lives and the way they receive, process and act on shared information and ideas, as well as the way events are designed, marketed and sold (Potter, 2018).

If we look at the examples of big events, the Olympic Games, a Special Event, maintains its connection with the Olympic movement and the volunteer community through online social network interfaces. While the Facebook page for the 2012 London Olympics contains around 36 thousand followers (Hede & Kellett, 2012, p. 242) the 2020 Tokyo Olympics Facebook page is followed by 849 thousand people, and the videos posted show thousands of views (Tokyo 2020, 2020). The 2014 FIFA World Cup generated a total of 3 billion Facebook interactions between June 12, 2014, and July 13, 2014. 1.5 billion for the 2016 Rio Olympic Games, 534 million for the Rio Carnival held in Brazil in 2015, and 67 million for the Academy Awards in 2016 interactions were made (Clement, Selected global media and sporting events with the most Facebook interactions as of May 2017, 2020).

Companies that create Facebook pages can promote their products or services through photos and videos, invite their followers to launch or similar large or small events, and carry some services on their corporate websites to Facebook pages with special tools (Bulut, 2012, p. 46). In fact, Facebook has an event application, allowing the event owners to share the event date, time and place, and the remaining time by sending an invitation.

Twitter, one of the most widely used networks and founded in 2006, is an online social networking service that allows users to send text-based status updates and messages up to 280 characters long. These messages are called tweets. As of the fourth quarter of 2019, Twitter has reached 152 million daily active users worldwide. This network, which is also used very actively by famous people, is an important access channel that allows them to communicate with their fans almost instantly, provide news/information and create a public image about themselves. Major sporting events and awards events such as the American Football League Super Bowl, Grammy Awards or Academy Awards bring a lot of raises on Twitter. Online discussions, photos, tweets, or comments allows the users to participate in the success of these events and celebrities (Clement, 2020).

Instagram, another of today's most popular social media platforms, is a photo-sharing social networking service that allows users to take photos and edit them with filters. The platform allows users to share their images online and directly with their friends and followers on the social network. There are more than 1 billion monthly Instagram users worldwide as of June 2018, and about 112 million active Instagram users in the United States, and experts predict that this figure will exceed 120 million users in 2023.

Brands are keen to reach the Instagram audience, as social network users show high engagement rates with the content displayed. Sports content such as the NBA and NFL, as well as sports sites have high-interest audiences on the platform (Clement, 2020) Therefore, it can be said that today's popular social media platforms constitute the most important communication channel that is also referenced for events.

Use of Social Media in Events

From the point of view of events, looking at the management process of social media, it seems that events are evaluated in three stages before, during and after the event.

Before the Event

In order to reach and announce potential participants of the event, social media activities prior to the event are very important and create an important doping for the success of the event. According to brand and content marketing expert Grate (Grate, 2020), bringing an event to the sales stage is no easy task, and half of the struggle to organize it is marketing the event. The inclusion of social media in event strategies and design from the beginning allows this marketing to be effective (Potter, 2018).

In order to effectively and efficiently use social media tools, which are included in the promotional tools in marketing activities, it is necessary to carry out the promotional activities in a planned manner and to take into account the increasing importance of social media in promotion (Atçeken, Doğrul, & Çabuk, 2018, p. 157).

Rozgonyi (2019), an event marketing consultant, states that there are new social media rules for Event Design. According to the author, 4D should be considered when creating an activity design strategy map. These are the concepts of Digital, Direct, Dynamic, Data. Under these topics, event organizers should answer some questions. These are the questions respectively; "How does your event look on social media and where does it live on social media?", "How do you connect with your community through social media?", "How will you tell stories during the event cycle?" and "How will you determine the event's response and return on investment?" (Rozgonyi, 2019).

When used correctly, social media allows the event to reach more people, attract attention and keep interest alive. According to Brooks (2010), social media can be a cost-effective way to recruit participants into a one-time event into a recurring event. The trick is to determine when to use which social media tools. In event management, each social network serves a different purpose and needs to be used correctly. Multiple social media platforms can be used in this process. The first step is to notify people of your activity, make them mark these in their calendars and register them. For this, it is necessary to turn to the place where there are potential participants in the first place. In which of the social networks mentioned above are the contacts included? Various organizations collect and analyze data about social media tools according to the most preferred regions, countries, demographics. These analysis reports will be able to help with which platforms should be weighted in order to promote the event by type (Brooks, 2020).

Events should have a high level of interest, humor or social cause that will allow them to be shared on social media, among friends or communities with similar ideas. If the event does not have a remarkable reason, then the event will have a limited success (Van der Wagen & White, 2010, p. 454). In the planning of the event, that is, before the event takes place and during the event process, it is necessary to make shares that will attract users. By seeing and sharing and interacting with content related to this event, users on social networks can be made more aware of the event.

The best way to get knowledgeable and experienced social media users into a conversation around a topic is to create a hashtag (#). Therefore, it is recommended to create a hashtag first for the event. Although hashtags have been used in Twitter posts, they are now used on all social media platforms. The blowup in the popularity of Instagram is partly due to the use of hashtags to attract people to chat around the images used on this visual platform. Event planners often have some confusion about copyright infringement by using a hashtag, but hashtags are not copyrighted. Since there is no copyright, the biggest problem that can be experienced is the use of duplicate hashtags, so to see if there is a conversation that has started in the process of creating a hashtag, it must be written in the search area and the status of use there should be observed. Related citation address can be examined for examples related to the subject (Hayes-Peirce, 2017).

Yalçın (2020) notes that Twitter also allows you to measure the topics, most influential people, and information density that get the most attention at the event in real time, without the need for an app, thanks to hashtags. Although Facebook is still a little weak in getting a clear result over the hashtag, it emphasizes that the event page feature remains unique, and is very valuable in terms of providing the calendar feature and all the information together. Facebook's Social VR app states that Facebook Spaces enhancements and new features for Facebook Groups will give a magic touch to events (Yalçın, 2017).

Taking advantage of "influencers" in event marketing is a common method. Influencers literally means "the person who affects". Having a large audience of followers on a social media channel, the power to influence their purchasing decisions due to their expertise, knowledge, location or relationship with their audience are called Influencer. Influencers are classified as mega (over 1 million followers), macro (40 thousand-1 million followers) and micro (1,000-40 thousand followers), content style can be described as youtuber, blogger, social media sharers (What is an Influencer?, 2020). It is of great importance to use these influential individuals over the target audience to market events. The story of the event is also enriched when the right influencers are selected and included in the event plans. However, there is a risk that an influencer in the field of activity can positively affect the return on investment, while an improper sharing may have negative consequences (Yalçın, 2017). For this reason, the right influencers should be selected, taking into account the scope, type and size of the event. For example, Mega-Influencers, who are generally movie stars, athletes, musicians, etc., can be used for a large-budget event on a global scale.

To create new eyes on social media posts about the event, PPC (pay per click), an internet advertising model used for direct referral, where advertisers pay advertisers when clicked on online advertisements on social media, can also be used. Publishing PPC ads on social media is not only cost-effective, but also direct guidance to the destination (Social Tables, 2020).

Today, event planners have become event strategists (Solaris, 2020, p. 14). The expectation of planners about the event is actually a great way to share information with potential guests at an early stage of the planned process. If used correctly, social networks can help spread news at a very low cost.

Event planners collect information about the needs and expectations of potential guests and establishes the activity process. Through social media and networks, guests can ask questions, gather ideas, and start a conversation long before the event, which will provide a unique opportunity to create an event that best meets the needs and expectations of their guests.

One of the main reasons people participate in special events is to get in touch with new people, to share ideas with like-minded people that is to be part of a community. If it is possible to create a community on social media platforms, those who intend to participate in the event can establish a good network and communicate with each other before. (Lee, Boshnakova, & Goldblatt, 2017, p. 211). However, as for event trends, networking is the most neglected element, according to a research report prepared by examining more than 2,000 events over two years and interviewing more than 3,000 event professionals. More and more participation in events is achieved because it is desirable to meet the people involved. The chaotic and over-information-laden world of social media offers opportunities to find new peers and partners. In creating networking, planners will need to make effective use of event technologies. In addition, audiovisual effects will continue to be important in providing high-engagement experiences with projection mapping, virtual reality (VR), augmented reality (AR), and mobile event apps, giving planners the chance to incorporate their audience into a story. Because now there are participants who want to be involved in the story. In addition, it is recommended in the report that planners should be more inclusive while networking at events, and they should create a comprehensive network to serve underrepresented audiences such as younger, introverted, disabled, etc. (Solaris, 2020, pp. 10-22).

Atçeken, Doğrul and Çabuk (2018) have followed the 27-day process on their Facebook page in their research on the 5th Mersin Citrus Festival, an international event. For the first time, social media planning was applied to this event and the festivals held in previous years were compared and found that social media had a very important impact on the announcement of the festival, informing visitors about the festival activities, the rate of interaction of visitors and reaching more visitors. As a result of the studies; "total likes" and "engaging users" and "total representation" of the variables identified, which had a very large increase in the proportional change compared to the previous year and moreover, despite the fact that the festival's social media spending was realized with a very low budget and was actively used shortly before the festival, it showed that it is the most known communication tool for visitors. Therefore, it can be said that the advertising and promotion process is more effective when a planned social media supported event is carried out and can be carried out with lower budgets.

During the Event

The sustainability of events increases in direct proportion to the strength of interactions with participants during the event. In order for a good event to be in demand in the future, organizers now encourage participants to use social media. 2 million people follow the Instagram account of the Coachella Music Festival, which is one of the largest music events in the world and lasts for 3 days. During the event, 7 million posts are sent at the end of each concert, and a total of 43 million posts are reached at the end of each day (Baglietto, 2019). In addition, information about new concerts, surprise participants, sponsorship activities that will take place during the festival is shared for 3 days, which allows participants to use the festival more effectively. As in this example, it is possible to increase the number of participants in future events by sharing videos or images of speakers or events to increase the number of potential guests during any event.

As mentioned in the pre-event activities, the purpose of meeting new people, which is one of the main reasons why people participate in events, can be realized more quickly with the use of social media. If this network can be established prior to the event, participants will be able to communicate with each other during the event.

In addition, by increasing interaction with existing participants through social media during the event, participants can be prevented from entering into false expectations, which is a serious mistake for each event planner (Ghazali & Ramli, 2014, p. 8). In this way, it will be possible for participants to leave the event more happily by meeting their expectations. Instant feedback from participants related to the event can also be provided, making small interventions that need to be done during the event, which allows the event to go smoothly (Hudson, Roth, Madden, & Hudson, 2015, p. 70).

By strengthening ties with participants, event social media accounts increase tracking numbers and strengthen the hand of event managers for future sponsorship deals (Lee, Boshnakova, & Goldblatt, 2017, p. 225). Posts made with hashtags, which are available to event participants, especially those starting with Twitter and on many social media accounts such as Instagram and Facebook can reach a very large audience by making them one of the most talked-about topics in a specific region or all over the world. This is a valuable promotion work that cannot be achieved with no advertising budget. All these exchanges increase the awareness of the event and encourage future participants.

The biggest music festivals in the world, Coachella, Tomorrowland, Glastonbury Festival, Sziget Festival, Amsterdam Dance Event, Bestival, manage to be among the trending topics in the world when they take place. Each festival has its own hashtags so that they can reach potential future festival participants (Glastonbury, Tomorrowland, Sziget & More: How Top European Music Festivals Use Social Media, 2020). In addition, Oktoberfest, Cannes Film festival provides information about all programs and instant events with this hashtag and official social media accounts and ensures that the participants have a more effective festival.

Another event-related study examined more than 25 million social media posts sent by the organizers and participants of the 50 most popular events, including everything from music festivals to endurance races, during the calendar year, especially before, during and after the events. As a result, it was found that many people also talked about the event before the event, with the most social media updates being quotes and multimedia shared during the event (36% of all updates). According to the research, one of the most important social media strategies is to create a photo booth (Grate, 2020). Photo booths are booths used in event areas, where participants take photos using various accessories, and these photos can be obtained in special design prints or in the form of social media shares. While these photos can be shared by the participants during or after the event on social media, it is also interesting to share them by the event owners using the event or sponsor hashtags.

Finally, participants ' enthusiasm can be kept alive with small quizzes, reward programs and similar activities that will be held during the event. By obtaining data about the event, strategic decisions can be made more effectively in future events. As an example, in 2019, 67% of social media posts were made by female participants at the Coachella event and the majority of them were between the ages of 25-34, and the invitation of the Blackpink group, which consisted of all women and the majority of the audience was this audience. This group is the first K-pop (Korean pop) supergroup to be invited to Coachella (Baglietto, 2019).

After the Event

The end of the event does not mean the end of social media activities. The most important and beneficial element here is getting feedback. When compared to traditional media and social media, the fact that social media is faster in feedback and measurement is an important factor in its preference. It may take weeks or months to receive or measure the feedback of the message sent in television, newspapers, magazines or open air advertisements, which are the most important tools of traditional media. However, feedback on social media is almost as fast as one-on-one communication (Bulut, 2012, pp. 29-31) This speed can make strategic decisions faster, especially after the event, and better preparation for the next event.

Social media can track how many people reach the desired message on many platforms, such as the number of views of videos on Instagram, the number of tweets posted about the event, or the number of reads of the blog. Observing and analyzing the frequency of use of tweets and hashtags, and the interactions of the tweets (like, commenting, retweeting) even in small events, can guide the organizers by providing a control opportunity.

Event technology allows planners who have now become strategists to save time and focus on creating engaging, interactive event experiences. Event stakeholders use event data and participant feedback from event planners to improve return on investment and achieve event goals. Event technology is used as a useful tool to collect meaningful data and measure participant satisfaction (Aventri, 2019).

When conducting research related to social media, it is necessary to measure the effects of data before and during the event. There are 7 criteria set for this (7-ways-to-measure-social-mediaeffectiveness, 2011): The first is the measurement of brand awareness. Businesses can measure this by the number of followers of their brands, the number of searches, the number of visitors to their websites through links, and the number of keywords searched for related to the brand. The second is the follow-up of honest discussions. Online discussions are honest, explicit discussions between consumers. From these discussions, businesses can receive positive, neutral or negative comments about their brands. Businesses should monitor comments made on their own brands and competing brands through monitoring programs. The third is the measurement of impact area. Businesses can access impact figures by the number of links to their websites. There may be individuals who comment on the brand of the business or like the product on microblogs such as Twitter and social networking sites such as Facebook and LinkedIn. Examining these social media tweets and likes can analyze why individuals like or dislike them. The fourth way of measuring activity is the interaction indicator. It should be aimed to measure the interaction of people between your site and your brand, it is important to see how interested people are in what you say or offer. This means ratings for your brand, the number of good or bad statements, retweets, photos, video views, and new pages of Facebook likes. The fifth way to measure efficiency is popularity. The number of people who subscribe to your email or RSS feeds is the number of followers on Twitter, members of LinkedIn groups, and people who like your Facebook page or other social media sites. Other places to watch include industry gatherings or content communities such as Flickr or YouTube. The sixth is the use of Monitoring Tools. If you don't measure, monitor, and track information you receive from social media sites, it doesn't make much sense to see a lot of activity on Facebook likes or Twitter tweets. Google Analytics and Measure map are two tools that can be used to track and analyze data. In this way, it will be possible to understand how people will react and what needs to be changed by event managers in terms of advertising. The seventh and final criterion is listening and learning. It is necessary to pay attention to any positive, negative or neutral feedback received from social media sites. It is necessary to see what can be learned from these notifications and what needs to be changed. It is necessary to be proactive in monitoring the data and making the necessary adjustments to the advertising and advertising method. It is possible to succeed when you listen carefully to what is being said and make some proposed changes. Event planners must first set criteria to evaluate social media data related to events.

It is seen that Web 2.0 platforms are adopted by event organizations. However, the lack of academic research on this issue cannot fully demonstrate the results of social media contribution in the event sector (Hede & Kellett, 2012, pp. 241-242)Today, many people or organizations agree that social media has somehow come back. However, the uncertainties about how this level of return should be measured will allow organizations to hesitate to actively use social media. (Attraction et al. 2018). The table above is a good guide to the elimination of this hesitation.

Table 2. Relevant Metrics for Social Media Applications

Social Media Application	Brand Awareness	Brand Engagement	Word of Mouth
Blogs	•number of unique visits •number of return visits •number of times bookmarked •search ranking	•number of members •number of rss feed subscribers •number of comments •amount of user-generated content •average length of time on site •number of responses to polls, contests, surveys	•number of references to blog in other media (online/offline) •number of reblogs •number of times badge displayed on other sites •number of "likes"
Microblogging (e.g.,twitter)	•number of tweets about the brand •valence of tweets +/– •number of followers	•number of followers •number of @replies	•number of retweets
Cocreation (e.g., nıkeid)	•number of visits	•number of creation attempts	•number of references to project in other media (online/offline)
Social bookmarking (e.g., stumbleupon)	•number of tags	•number of followers	•number of additional taggers
Forums and discussion boards (e.g., google groups)	•number of page views •number of visits •valence of posted content +/-	•number of relevant topics/ threads •number of individual replies •number of sign-ups	•incoming links •citations in other sites •tagging in social bookmarking •offline references to the forum or its members •in private communities: number of pieces of content (photos, discussions, videos); chatter pointing to the community outside of its gates •number of "likes"
Product reviews (e.g., amazon)	•number of reviews posted •valence of reviews •number and valence of other users' responses to reviews (+/–) •number of wish list adds •number of times product included in users' lists (i.e., listmania! On amazon.com)	•length of reviews •relevance of reviews •valence of other users' ratings of reviews (i.e., how many found particular review helpful) •number of wish list adds •overall number of reviewer rating scores entered •average reviewer rating score	•number of reviews posted •valence of reviews •number and valence of other users' responses to reviews (+/–) •number of references to reviews in other sites •number of visits to review site page •number of times product included in users' lists (i.e., listmania! On amazon.com)
Social networks (e.g., bebo, facebook, linkedın)	•number of members/fans •number of installs of applications •number of impressions •number of bookmarks •number of reviews/ratings and valence +/–	•number of comments •number of active users •number of "likes" on friends' feeds •number of user-generated items (photos, threads, replies) •usage metrics of applications/ widgets •impressions-to-interactions ratio •rate of activity (how often members personalize profiles, bios, links, etc.)	•frequency of appearances in timeline of friends •number of posts on wall •number of reposts/shares •number of responses to friend referral invites
Video and photosharing (e.g., flickr,youtube)	•number of views of video/ photo •valence of video/photo ratings +/–	•number of replies •number of page views •number of comments •number of subscribers	•number of embeddings •number of incoming links •number of references in mock-ups or derived work •number of times republished in other social media and offline •number of "likes"

Source: (Hoffman & Fodor, 2010)

In addition to evaluating events, event planners use social media to provide credibility by sharing suggestions and photos of previous events, creating interactive communities between participants before, during and after the event (Roig, Fuentes, & Ramon, 2017, p. 5). This allows your social media-related area to be active and maintain its influence at the end of the event.

Event technology is adopted as a tool used to collect meaningful data about the event and measure participant satisfaction, and it is expected to continue to be used by event organizers in the future (Solaris, 2020, p. 14). Although what needs to be done after the event is generally expressed in this way, advances in technology can open up new and different ways of evaluating it.

SOLUTIONS AND RECOMMENDATIONS

The event sector has many subtitles and is a large and dynamic sector that is in direct and indirect interaction with many sectors. Professionals who organize events that create significant competitive advantages for countries, regions and organizations need to constantly monitor and analyze the everyday life of society, current technology, science and connected sectors.

The source of this information is communication tools. The form of communication is changing in the world and one-way communication is not preferred anymore. It is not a realistic approach to think that activities in which two-way interaction is performed will not use social media, which again has the same feature and allows two-way communication. In this context, event managers should reach out to potential event participants before the event and attract them to their activities, keep the participants' interest alive by establishing uninterrupted two-way communication during the event and increase their level of satisfaction, and use social media to ensure that the effect lasts longer when the event is over, to reach potential participants in the future and to make strategic evaluations about the event. In addition, event organizers have to have a strong social media channel to have a stronger hand in their negotiations with sponsors, so that they can reach out to sponsors with a larger budget.

As of January 2020, today, where it is not possible to ignore an environment where 3.8 billion people in the world are all together, event owners must use social media effectively. Otherwise, event managers will be called dinosaurs by the next generation, like the first generations who refused to use computers, and they will slowly disappear in the future.

As a final word, people in many parts of the world prefer to spend more time in their homes due to the pandemic today. For this reason, internet usage is increasing for news, information, education, sharing and communication purposes. In addition, most of the canceled events have been transferred to virtual environments and as a result of the pandemic, the event sector also changed. This process signals us that the social media tools used as aids in the near future may turn into the main environment and scenes where the events will be held.

FUTURE RESEARCH DIRECTION

The relationship between social media, which has billions of active users and an indispensable part of daily life, and the event sector, which affects many sectors and continues to grow, should be more subject to scientific research. There is limited research in the literature about the effects of social media marketing on events. Especially, researches on ROI for social media activities will contribute to both event literature and event managers in terms of directing their investments correctly and providing time and cost efficiency. Will be able to create a proactive perspective for new events in future researches using social media prediction models regarding events Finally, Factors such as measuring participants' satisfaction during and after the event, how and through what tools they have knowledge of the event and its content, what they expect from the event survey, etc. must be revealed by scientific methods.

Lastly the research focuses on the positive aspects of social media in events. However, in future studies, the negative effects of using social media can be examined.

CONCLUSION

In the globalizing world, using of the social media is increasing rapidly and the period of the people express themselves face to face is getting over. Personal relationships are transferred to social media environments. People meet, have fun and even share their sorrows on these platforms. The YouTube concert of Andrea Bocelli in Italy's famous Duomo Square, where the empty streets of big cities are also reflected, has been watched by 41 million people and liked by 1 million people and became the symbol of the struggle against pandemic. This example shows us, it is not thought that social media should be ignored in the activities that people organize for gathering. Therefore, the importance of social media in activities is discussed in this study and using a social media before, during and after the events are discussed. As a result of the research, it is found that the use of social media in events is very important for the success of the events.

In addition, while the studies in the literature mostly examine the relations between social media and the event, this research makes suggestions on how event professionals will use social media before, during and after the event.

REFERENCES

Atçeken, K., Doğrul, Ü., & Çabuk, S. (2018). Tutundurmada Sosyal Medyanın Önemi: 5. Mersin ULuslararası Narenciye Festivali Örneği. *Akademik Araştırmalar ve Çalışmalar Dergisi*, *10*(18), 146–157. doi:10.20990/kilisiibfakademik.428624

Aventri. (2019). *The future of Event Marketing* (2nd ed.). Norwalk: Event.

Baglietto, M. (2019). *What Brands Can Learn From Coachella's Social Media Marketing Mastery*. Retrieved from netbasequid.com web site: https://netbasequid.com/blog/coachellas-social-media-marketing-mastery/

Barutçu, S., & Tomaş, M. (2013). Sürdürülebilir Sosyal Medya Pazarlaması ve Sosyal Medya Pazarlaması Etkinliğinin Ölçümü. *Journal of Internet Applications and Management*, 5-24.

Brooks, R. (2020). *12 Ways to Market Your Event With Social Media*. Retrieved from https://www.socialmediaexaminer.com/12-ways-to-market-your-event-with-social-media/

Bulut, E. (2012). *Pazarlama İletişiminde Yeni Yaklaşımlar Kapsamında Sosyal Medya Uygulamaları ve Etkili Kampanya Örnekleri*. İstanbul: Unpublished masters thesis.

Clement, J. (2020). *Instagram accounts with the most followers worldwide 2020*. Retrieved from Statista web site: https://www.statista.com/statistics/421169/most-followers-instagram/

Clement, J. (2020). *Selected global media and sporting events with the most Facebook interactions as of May 2017*. Retrieved from Statitas: https://www.statista.com/statistics/477371/facebook-sporting-events-interactions/

Clement, J. (2020). *Twitter accounts with the most followers worldwide 2020*. Retrieved from Sttista web site: https://www.statista.com/statistics/273172/twitter-accounts-with-the-most-followers-worldwide/

Fuchs, C. (2014). *Social Media a Critical Introduction*. Sage Publication Inc. doi:10.4135/9781446270066

Getz, D. (2008). Event tourism: Definition, evolution, and research. *Tourism Management, 29*(3), 403–428. doi:10.1016/j.tourman.2007.07.017

Getz, D. (2012). Event Studies: Discourses and Future Directions. *Event Management, 16*(2), 171–187. doi:10.3727/152599512X13343565268456

Ghazali, A., & Ramli, N. (2014). The Relationship Between Social Media Uzage and Event Attendees Satisfaction At Carnival Event. In *Proceedings of the Australian Academy of Business and Social Sciences Conference* (pp. 1-10). Dubai: Australian Academy of Business and Social Sciences.

Glastonbury, Tomorrowland, Sziget & More: How Top European Music Festivals Use Social Media. (2020). Retrieved from Ticketbooth web site: https://www.ticketbooth.com.au/ticketing/blog/glastonbury-tomorrowland-sziget-more-how-top-european-music-festivals-use-social-media/

Grate, R. (2020). *Event Marketing 101: How to Keep Attendees Engaged Before, During and After Your Event*. Retrieved from Buffer Lİbrary Web Site: https://buffer.com/library/social-media-event-marketing/

Hayes-Peirce, S. (2017). *Social Media Strategies for Sparking Event Conversations in 2018*. Retrieved from Mpi web site: https://www.mpi.org/chapters/southern-california/chapter-news/single-blog/article/social-media-strategies-for-sparking-event-conversations-in-2018

Hede, A.-M., & Kellett, P. (2012). Building online brand communities: Exploring the benefits, challenges and risks in the Australian event sector. *Journal of Vacation Marketing, 18*(3), 239–250. doi:10.1177/1356766712449370

Heraldkeepers. (2020). *MICE (Meetings, Incentives, Conferencing, Exhibitions) Market Size To Worth USD 1546.69 Billion by 2025 ndustry Analysis, Business Outlook, Current and Future Growth By 2025*. Retrieved from Marketwatch Web Sitesi: https://www.marketwatch.com/press-release/mice-meetings-incentives-conferencing-exhibitions-market-size-to-worth-usd-154669-billion-by-2025-industry-analysis-business-outlook-current-and-future-growth-by-2025-2020-08-17

Hoffman, D. L., & Fodor, M. (2010). Can You Measure the ROI of Your Scial Media Marketing. *MIT Sloan Management Review, 52*(1), 41–49.

Hudson, S., Roth, M., Madden, T., & Hudson, R. (2015). The effects of social media on emotions, brand relationship quality, and word of mouth: An empirical study of music festival attendees. *Tourism Management, 47*, 68–76. doi:10.1016/j.tourman.2014.09.001

Kaplan, A., & Haenlein, M. (2012). Social media: Back to the roots and back to the future. *Journal of Systems and Information Technology*, *14*(2), 101–105. doi:10.1108/13287261211232126

Lee, S. S., Boshnakova, D., & Goldblatt, J. (2017). *The 21st Century Meeting and Event Technologies Powerful Tools for Better Planning, Marketing, and Evaluation.* Oakville: Taylor & Francis Group.

Luty, J. (2020). *Direct spending in the events sector in the United Kingdom (UK) as of 2017, by event type*. Retrieved from Statista Web Sitesi: https://www.statista.com/statistics/426464/direct-spending-in-the-events-sector-in-the-united-kingdom/

Mayfield, A. (2020). *What is Social Media.* Retrieved from icrossing Web sitesi: https://www.icrossing.com/uk/sites/default/files_uk/insight_pdf_files/What%20is%20Social%20Media_iCrossing_ebook.pdf

Paris, C. M., Lee, W., & Seery, P. (2010). *The Role of Social Media in Promoting Special Events: Acceptance of Facebook 'Events'. In Information and Communication Technologies in Tourism 2010* (pp. 531-541). Lugano: Springer-Verlag/Wien.

Potter, B. (2018). *The Impact of Social Media on Meetings and Events.* Retrieved from Mpi Web site: https://www.mpi.org/blog/article/the-impact-of-social-media-on-meetings-and-events

Preston, C. (2012). *How to Successfully Promote Events, Festivals, Conventions, and Expositions.* Wiley Press.

Roig, E. M., Fuentes, E. M., & Ramon, N. D. (2017). User-Generated Social Media Events in Tourism. *Sustainability*, 1–23.

Rozgonyi, B. (2019). *New Social Media Rules for Engaging Event Design.* Retrieved from Mpi.org web site: https://www.mpi.org/chapters/chicago-area/chapter-news/single-blog/c-c-articles/2019/08/06/new-social-media-rules-for-engaging-event-design

Social Tables. (2020). *15 Tactics to Sell More Event Tickets Today.* Retrieved from Socialtables web site: https://www.socialtables.com/blog/social-media/drive-event-ticket-sales/

Solaris, J. (2020). *10 events trend for 2020.* Retrieved from eventmanagerblog web site: https://www.eventmanagerblog.com/10-event-trends

Tokyo 2020. (2020). Retrieved from Tokyo 2020 Facebook page: https://www.facebook.com/tokyo2020/about/?ref=page_internal

Van der Wagen, L., & White, L. (2010). *Event management: for tourism, cultural, business and sporting events* (4th ed.). Pearson Pub.

7ways-to-measure-social-mediaeffectiveness. (2011). Retrieved from before it's news web site: http://www.sitepronews.com/2011/09/06/7-ways-to-measure-social-mediaeffectiveness-for-your-company-a-spn-exclusive-article/

we are social. (2020). *Digital 2020: Global Digital Yearbook.* Retrieved from Hootsuite Web Site: https://datareportal.com/reports/digital-2020-july-global-statshot

What is an Influencer? (2020). Retrieved from influencermarketinghub.com web site: https://influencermarketinghub.com/what-is-an-influencer/

Yalçın, F. G. (2017). *Tüm yönleriyle etkinlik pazarlaması ve etkinlik pazarlamasında son trendler*. Retrieved from Digitalage Web site: https://digitalage.com.tr/tum-yonleriyle-etkinlik-pazarlamasi-ve-etkinlik-pazarlamasinda-son-trendler/

ADDITIONAL READING

Abuhashes, M., Al-Khasawneh, M., & Al-Dmour, R. (2019). The Impact of Facebook on Jordanian Consumers' Decision Process in the Hotel Selection, IBIMA. *Business Review*, 1–16.

Alghizzawi, M., Habes, M., & Salloum, S. A. (2018). The role of social media in tourism marketing in Jordan. *International Journal of Information Technology and Language Studies*, *2*(3), 59–70.

Chen, S. C., & Lin, C. P. (2019). Understanding the effect of social media marketing activities: The mediation of social identification, perceived value, and satisfaction. *Technological Forecasting and Social Change*, *140*, 22–32. doi:10.1016/j.techfore.2018.11.025

Dedeoğlu, B. B., Niekerk, M., Küçükergin, K. G., Marcello, D. M., & Okumuş, F. (2019). Effect of social media sharing on destination brand awareness and destination quality. *Journal of Vacation Marketing*, *20*(10), 1–24.

Feliciano, J. F. D. G. (2018). Social media networks in the third sector: the road to sustainability. Lisbon: Unpublished masters thesis.

Harb, A. A., Fowler, D., Chang, H. J., Blum, S. C., & Alakaleek, W. (2019). Social media as a marketing tool for events. *Journal of Hospitality and Tourism Technology*, *10*(1), 28–44. doi:10.1108/JHTT-03-2017-0027

Hede, A.-M., & Kellett, P. (2011). Marketing Communications for Special Events: Analysing Managerial Practice, Consumer Perceptions and Preferences. *Journal of Marketing*, *45*(6), 987–1004.

Hills, M. (2015). *Doctor Who: The Unfolding Event*. Palgrave Macmillian. doi:10.1057/9781137463326

Hoyle, L. H. (2020). *Event Marketing*. John Wiley & Sons.

Romero, N. L. (2011). ROI. Measuring the social media return on investment in a library. *Managing Library Finances*, *54*(2), 145–151. doi:10.1108/08880451111169223

Shen, C., Luong, T., Ho, J., & Djailani, I. (2019). Social media marketing of IT service companies: Analysis using a concept-linking mining approach. *Industrial Marketing Management*, *90*, 593–604. doi:10.1016/j.indmarman.2019.11.014

KEY TERMS AND DEFINITIONS

Hashtag: A word or phrase with the symbol "#" in front of it, used on social media websites and apps so that you can search for all messages with the same subject. This function was created on Twitter.

Influencer: Having a large audience of followers on a social media channel, the power to influence their purchasing decisions due to their expertise, knowledge, location or relationship with their audience are called Influencer.

ROI/Return on Investment: Interest or dividends shown as a percentage of the money invested.

Social Media: Forms of media that allows people to communicate and share information in two ways using the internet or mobile phones.

Chapter 10
New Trends in Event Marketing

Remziye Ekici
Isparta University of Applied Sciences, Turkey

Derya Toksoz
Mersin University, Turkey

ABSTRACT

Event marketing has become an increasingly important role as a marketing tool for marketers. Nowadays, the ability of event marketing to provide deeper consumer participation with new, creative, unique, tailored, interactive, and compelling events attracts great interest among marketers. The enormous impact of digital development on our daily lives is now more important than ever. Digital technology, from a facial recognition app for easy recording to creating an event app or using virtual reality for realistic demonstrations, can help deliver a superior experience to participants. As key technological practices matured, a number of important trends and developments in event marketing emerged. The event industry enriches the experiences of the participants by using technological applications and creates new applications. All these activities that are vital to a successful event are an important part of the marketing function because event marketing strategy and planning is a whole with general event planning.

INTRODUCTION

Events have played an important role in different societies and cultures long times. Throughout history, events have been used to promote cities and towns. Looking back on history, it can be seen that events always played an important role in society, either to break down the dullness with the events, to get out of the routine of daily life, or to highlight some important rites or persons. (Shone and Parry, 2010: 3-9).

In the modern age, events which are more strategic and complex activity (Smith, 2008: 4), are seen as an integral part of growth and development strategies, and event planning and marketing has become a common worldwide phenomenon. In particular, the globalization of the economy has greatly increased the volume of travel to international events (Rogers and Davidson, 2006: 24). The event industry is currently experiencing a renaissance period. Until recently, organizers have not had the proper tools to monitor event schedules from start to end. Thanks to technological development, they have proper and

DOI: 10.4018/978-1-7998-4954-4.ch010

actual tools to monitor event schedules (Hindman, 2018). Today, people come together to experience more unique interests, hobbies and passions from the latest animations to electronic dance music of Japan to experience a wide variety of drinks and targeted niche events. The most prominent is that participants and fans enjoy more personalized experiences than ever before (Eventbrite, 2013: 1). Thus, events have become an effective trend among businesses in terms of high return on investment, meaningful interaction among participants, positive perception and image (Ferdinand and Kitchin, 2012: 113).

Event marketing tools such as trade fairs, pop-up brand stores and sponsored events have been integrated into the consumers daily life (Tafesse, Narui and Korneliussen, 2014). Nowadays, the ability of event marketing to provide deeper consumer participation with new, interactive and interesting events attracts great interest among marketers (Close, Finney, Lacey and Sneath, 2006). The focus of the events is to create primarily customer loyalty by attracting customers to the relevant destination (Ravald and Grönroos, 1996: 19).

It is argued that all businesses are on the verge of "Experience Economy", a new economic period in which customers can organize unforgettable events (Pine, Pine and Gilmore, 1999). Therefore, event marketing, which expresses a promotion strategy in which a themed event is developed in order to create experience for consumers and to promote a product or service, has become increasingly widespread in the last few decades (Belch and Belch, 2004). Because the events that see themselves as an alternative form of marketing communication, are gaining popularity as big investments by marketers. This growth can be attributed to the increasing awareness of marketers about event marketing, which aims to reach potential customers by making use of creative communication tools in achieving marketing, brand and corporate objectives (Zarantonello and Schmitt, 2013; Gupta, 2003). In other words, the basis of event marketing focuses on current and potential consumers (Goldblatt, 2005: 220). In this case, business managers realize that face-to-face events are an effective way to raise awareness and persuade participants to purchase goods and services (Goldblatt, 2013: 13).

Event marketing resulting from integrated marketing communication is the communication tool that can best increase direct contact between businesses and consumers (Tafesse, 2016). The main reason for this is event marketing, which includes target groups in experiential activities, is an effective communication tool that offers the opportunity of social interaction between the participants and between the company and participants (Close, Finney, Lacey, and Sneath, 2006; Sneath, Finney and Close, 2005; Tafesse, 2016; Liu, Zhang and Keh, 2018). Also, event marketing activities increase the experiential value by helping consumers to achieve their goals while interacting with them. Therefore, experiential value is also an indispensable impact dimension and increases the satisfaction and trust of tourists (Wu, 2016: 53).

While the first basic feature of event marketing is high consumer participation (Drenger, Gaus and Jahn, 2008; Close, Krishen and Latour, 2009), the second feature is that events involve innovation (Geraghty and Conway,2016; Drenger, Gaus and Jahn, 2008; Wood, 2009). Thirdly, the most important feature of event marketing is the experiential wealth it offers. Not only that, but also the experiences and expectations of the participants, as well as their experiences, are always personal and unique (Getz, 2007; Jackson, 2013; Chalip, 1992; Silvers, 2004; Schmitt, 1999; Karpinska-Krakowiak, 2015). Accordingly, scientists refer to event marketing as "experiential marketing" (Wood, 2009; Martensen and Grønholdt, 2008; Close, Finney, Lacey and Sneath, 2006). Also, it must be admitted that technology key is for sustainability of events. In a study conducted by Bizzabo Event Company, it was investigated how the technology used in events changed the event marketing. Organizations that use event software have been found to be more productive and better. Almost all of the organizations that use event software

(95%) think that event software makes it easier to achieve business outcomes and increase productivity. It is stated that it is one of the most invested software, especially with the best results of holistic event software (Bizzabo, 2019).

Since event marketing is basically a communication tool that aims to appeal to customers emotionally (Martensen and Grønholdt, 2008), the stronger the active flow experience of the event participant, the more positive emotional perception is (Drenger, Gaus and Jahn, 2008: 138 -139). Because experience reflects the aspects of interaction, innovation and high participation with the participation of consumers in promotional activities (Wohlfeil and Whelan, 2006; Kumar, 1997; Drenger, Gaus and Jahn, 2008). Experiential marketing in this regard provides in-depth experiences about services for customers to make purchasing decisions (Rogers and Davidson, 2006: 112). As the moves towards experiential consumption increase, the power of event marketing will also develop due to changes in the marketing environment (Wohlfeil and Whelan, 2005b).

Experts on tourism marketing see events as important parts of tourism development and marketing plans and consciously turn these event activities into tourist attractions (Yoon, Daniel, Spencer and Dae-Kwan, 2000: 33). This book chapter aims to introduce the concept of event marketing to a wider audience and to present new event marketing trends offered to customers and advantages in the context of marketing communication.

BACKGROUND

Event Marketing

Events are a form of attraction. They act as a "pull factor" to the target destination (Getz, 1997). Commercial events require a large number of small private parties and restaurants, hotels or resorts and convention centers. Sports also require special-purpose facilities, including athletic parks, arenas, and stadiums. Festivals and other cultural celebrations use parks, streets, theaters, concert halls and all other public or private places. Also, many types of places are used for entertainment events such as concerts (Getz and Page, 2013: 594). These events can be called as fiesta, carnival, special event, mega event, holiday or even agricultural show (Getz, 1991). Therefore, companies and businesses adopt events as key elements in their marketing strategies (Bowdin, Allen, O'Toole, Harris, and McDonnell, 2006: 3). This trend shows that there is a shift from traditional passive marketing communications which involve receiving the message of the company in passive form using traditional media (Close, Finney, Lacey and Sneath, 2006: 422), to communication tools such as event marketing that deals with more customers (Sharp and Wind, 2009; Winer, 2009; Karpinska-Krakowiak, 2015; Pope and Voges, 2000). The reasons why event marketing is so accepted can be explained as follows: There is a lot more to celebrate with the aging of the world population and events provide opportunities for these celebrations. At the same time, with the advancement of technology individuals seek more "feel and touch" experience in their lives. Hedonism and desire for entertainment (Holbrook and Hirschman, 1982), the growth of the economy in the recreational sector, as well as more and more individuals in recent years choosing to take shorter and frequent holidays increase significantly the demand for a wide range of events around the world (Jago, Veal, Allen and Harris, 2000: 3). Event marketing is also globally seen as the best marketing tactic for ROI (Return on investment) (Berridge, 2007: 51).

Event marketing, including the design of event programs and promotional materials, public relations, media coordination, and effective presentations (Rogers and Davidson, 2006: 4) present various forms such as event sponsorships, sales promotions, fairs, pop-up brand stores, product launches, press conferences, contests, and street performances (Crowther and Donlan, 2011; Wood, 2009; Drenger, Gaus and Jahn, 2008). Event marketing, staging these diverse corporate and private events as reality, is seen as a new experience-oriented marketing communication strategy that aims to influence positively the familiarity and attitude of customers (Wohlfeil and Whelan, 2005b: 184-186).

The communicative innovation of event-marketing derives from its four constitutive features.

- *Experience orientation*: Personal life experience tends to be stronger than traditional media experiences in determining consumers' concept of reality.
- *Interaction* includes interactive and personal dialogues between participants, audience and brand representatives.
- *Self-initiation:* Event-marketing aims to influence consumers emotionally by staging self-initiated marketing-events.
- *Dramaturgy:* It requires a unique and creative dramaturgy that captures the imagination of the target audience in order for consumers to experience brand hyperreality emotionally (cited by Zanger and Sistenich; Wohlfeil and Whelan, 2006: 645-646).

Event marketing is a communication program that can stay in touch with its participants, know their needs and motivations, and develop products that meet their needs (Hall, 1992; Cruceru and Moise, 2014). As a pull strategy in marketing communications, successful event marketing strategies require understanding why consumers are motivated to participate voluntarily in these marketing activities (Wohlfeil and Whelan, 2005a: 125). Therefore, understanding the motivations and experiential needs of consumers is a key factor in the design of effective event marketing strategies (cited by Weinberg and Nickel; Wohlfeil and Whelan, 2006: 644).

MAIN FOCUS OF THE CHAPTER

Objectives in Event Marketing

In the 21st century, the fact that mega celebrations, festivals, sports competitions and the live private events take place on global social media makes the events a contemporary lifestyle (Getz and Page, 2016). Marketing events have an important potential in creating an extraordinary experience for the consumer, developing this relationship with customers, creating a positive brand image and strengthening it. Therefore, the goals of event marketing range from awareness, sales, loyalty and partnership (Wood, 2009: 253). Firms also use event marketing to achieve various goals such as brand awareness, sales and image development (Javalgi, Traylor, Gross and Lampman, 1994; Gardner and Schuman, 1987; Sneath, Finney and Close, 2005). Because companies investing in event marketing have the tools to create a hands-on experience for their target markets (Sneath, Finney and Close, 2005). So that, it has been a subject of research for many disciplines such as sport and business management, anthropology, tourism and leisure studies and regional planning as sport, culture, business events, etc. and gained momentum in the second half of the twentieth century (Mair and Whitford, 2013: 7).

In general, the objectives of event marketing are evaluated in two categories as "communication and sales". Communication goals include image development, brand awareness, reputation, relationship development, information about products, strengthening corporate communication, creating sales opportunities, public relations, increasing sales goals, market share and distribution (Taylor and Cunningham, 1999; Eckerstein, 2009; Zarantonello and Schmitt, 2013; Altunbas, 2008). At the same time, events acquire objectives such as supporting the community and strengthening relationships with consumers and other business organizations (Mount and Niro, 1995), increasing visits (Light, 1996; Ritchie, 1984; McDonnell, Allen and O'Toole, 1999), providing unique entertainment, social or cultural experience (Ayob, 2003), reducing the seasonality of the tourist flow (Higham and Hinch, 2002; Ritchie and Beliveau, 1974), providing tourism market positioning and a competitive marketing advantage (McDonnell, Allen and O'Toole, 1999) and following goal development (Bramwell, 1997; Chacko and Shaffer, 1993). Moreover, the events of a destination are aimed to bring direct and indirect economic income across local communities (Baloglu and Love, 2005). In this regard, Saget (2006) states that event marketing is all about facilitating and accelerating the sales cycle.

The purpose of event marketing is to deliver a message to the target audience through a planned event. This situation creates something valuable for the participant. At the event, organizers gather everyone at a certain time, in a specific place and success is based on how much customers are involved in the created social meeting (Kaspar, 2014: 16). Event marketing also aims to attract customers' attention to a company's new products or brands through special live events where customers interact face-to-face with a product or brand such as concerts, sports events, parades, and parties (Wood, 2009). This popular idea is summarized by Kotler (2002) as "events marketing" as "events designed to convey certain messages to the target audience". Hall (1992: 136) states other goals of event marketing as follows: "to discover customer needs and motivations, to develop products that meet these needs and to create a communication program that expresses the objectives of the event".

Research from the Bizzabo Company (2019) demonstrates persuasively that events can play a strategic role in driving business value. Findings from this year's report show that events are the most valued marketing channel and more effective for achieving business goals than ever before. And the most successful organizations are still those that are making aggressive investments in live events. At the same time, their work demonstrates that primary reason for organizing events is to support lead generation, attendee engagement, satisfaction and sales acceleration, followed by brand awareness for their company or products and revenue generation from ticket sales or sponsorships (Bizzabo, 2019).

Advantages of Event Marketing

Events are the stimulators of target attractiveness and come to the forefront as a key marketing factor in the promotion of destinations with increasing global competitiveness (Getz and Page, 2013: 593). In contrast to traditional communication strategies that offer high cost and low efficiency to meet their target audience and to convince them to consume their products and services, event marketing is an important factor in affecting brand image positively by ensuring active participation of target groups in the communication process (Drenger, Gaus and Jahn, 2008; Gupta, 2003; Jackson, 2013). In this respect, Crompton and McKay (1997) emphasize the significant positive effects of event marketing activities and the physical environment on the experiential value, satisfaction and trust of tourists. And they also consider event marketing as a crucial component in designing better products and services, ensuring satisfaction, and understanding visitors' decision-making processes. As the increasing number and variety of activities cause competition, the marketing factor is becoming more and more important.

The nature of communication that has changed from past to present made the concept of flow more important (Hoffman and Novak 2009). Today, the main themes are interaction and digital. This has led to many Internet and digital technology-based media. Consumers now interact with the company, the new media, and more importantly through social networks. The new media provides the ability to communicate with the targeted segments that traditional media cannot provide. It is difficult to do this with traditional media, one-way communication from the seller to the buyer. As a result, marketers are looking for ways to engage more with their customers (Winer, 2009). Therefore, direct contact with customers and creating a communication message adapted to their profile remains one of the most effective communication tools. (Spiro and Weitz, 1990). However, it is not just the interaction between the company and the event participants that need to be encouraged. Managers are also expected to pay attention to creating an environment that facilitates communication between the participants. As a result, the event, which can have a positive impact on brand image, can also promote word of mouth communication that positively affects sales or broadens the effects of communication strategies (Hogan, Lemon and Libai, 2004; Drenger, Gaus and Jahn, 2008; Liu, 2006). The most visible benefit is direct contact with consumers through sales forces and thus creating special moments (Cruceru and Moise, 2014: 155).

The Five P's of Event Marketing

Hoyle (2002: 12-19) emphasizes that regardless of the nature of the event, the success of event marketing depends on the "product, price, place, public relations and positioning" elements:

- **Product**: What is the value of the product? Marketing an event requires to highlight how the participant can benefit from the message. The promises to increase efficiency or have fun can be benefits that can persuade someone to buy the product or participate in the event.
- **Price**: What is the cost of doing business? What are the financial demographics of the target audience? Answering such questions is an important issue in event planning.
- **Place**: An event location for an event is an important part of the marketing strategy of destination.
- **Public Relations**: To determine what current perception is about the product or service.
- **Positioning**: It is the strategy of the consumer to determine the areas that the activity can fulfill through intuition, research and evaluation.

Goldblatt (2013: 220-224) interprets 5 P's of a successful event marketing as follows:

- **Product**: It combines history, quality and value to produce a unique program.
- **Promotion**: In addition to having the best quality event product, the effectiveness of the promotion, which will provide awareness of the product, is required.
- **Price**: Cost of doing business and competition in the market are the factors affecting the price. The price of the event must be equivalent to the purchasing power of your target market.
- **Public Relations:** Public relations help create the impression that others will develop about the event. In this context, as it means greater reliability, it is considered significantly more valuable than advertising, In this regard, Hoyle (2002) argues that public relations are the means by which an event organizer shapes what their audience thinks or feels about the event. It is designed to

reach a number of stakeholders, such as public relations, funders, consumers and media (Saget, 2006: 89).

- **Place**: The event planner cares about the location element when designing the marketing program for the event. Place does not only express the taste or style of the event; it is also one of the most important elements to be persuaded to invest in the event. Allen, O'Toole, McDonnell and Harris (2005: 210) expresses the concept of place as physical location and on-site processes where the event is organized and tickets are distributed. In this regard, Hoyle (2002) points out that when choosing the right place, the event marketer should be aware of the potential impact on consumers. In other words, the place should be included as a marketing concept. Because the place creates a structured opportunity to facilitate a strategically designed positive event experience (Crowther, 2011: 71).

New Trends in Event Marketing

Event marketing allows a company to overcome its advertising complexity and target an audience by creating an image through association with a particular event, strengthening the product or service and increasing sales (Gupta, 2003: 87). Organizers find ways to excite more people and increase participation by customizing event packages and adding more options. For example, some organizers customize the event by organizing a wine tasting event at an art festival. Technology also reshapes the sector as much as the demands and expectations of the participants. Advances in data collection, analysis and communication technology greatly improve the way events are planned and managed. Social networks have been an important tool for event marketing and promotions, as fans have created communities of similar-minded friends and shared their excitement in their own group (Eventbrite, 2013: 2).

As key technological practices matured, a number of important trends and developments emerged. These trends briefly are; *more disposable income, improved technological delivery, faster technology, new media outlets, emphasis on health benefits, seamless registration, multilingual communication* (Hoyle, 2002: 172). For the success of the events, they should start to use new techniques to reach the event participants in a low cost, high-impact way. Event organizers are also responsible for the safety of the event, just as they are responsible for the good experiences of the participants. Many organizers have also developed their competencies to include basic emergency and evacuation procedures and in closer contact with local authorities in case of adverse situations (Maritz Global Events, n.d.:3).

"Psychographic" profiles used to define buyer characteristics and priorities often affect the decision to buy or not to purchase and participate. When we look at Generation Y and new generations, it is seen that there is a significant difference in terms of social, cultural and consumption from previous generations. They don't want to "wait in line", instant response to faxes, emails and online messaging, tend to somewhat suspicious and impatient (Hoyle, 2002: 179-180). The event industry leverages technology by including virtual reality (VR) and artificial intelligence (AI) in many presentations (Maritz Global Events, n.d.:2). Using the digital revolution and social media as a key channel for messaging strengthens the value of participation, discussion and networking for all areas where events have triumphed (CWT Meetings and Events, 2019). Vallee and Westcott (2002) stated that creative event strategies are major trends that are shaping event marketing. Some companies unexpectedly create strategic partnerships and produce successful products and organize events. For example, Target/Saturn, Toyota/MGM, and Nintendo/ Smirnoff firms. Outside traditional media techniques, stopping traffic on Wall Street, flying cars and discoveries are just a few ways to offer unforgettable brand experiences.

The enormous impact of digital development on our daily lives is now more important than ever. Our way of communicating, meeting new people, doing business, having fun or buying food has forever been transformed by technology. Digital technology, from a facial recognition app for easy recording to creating an event app or using virtual reality for realistic demonstrations, can help deliver a superior experience to participants (Regalix Research, 2019). Friedman (2016) addressed the following issues in his report on new trends in event marketing. *Safety and Security of Events, 5G Technology, Artificial Intelligence and Bots, Experiential Design, Internet of Things (IoT), Big Data, Virtual Reality and Augmented Reality* issues are the main fundamental trends.

The implementation of a faster wireless service called **5G** will take place in the next few years. This high-level wireless technology will be able to penetrate the walls of the congress centers and provide full wireless service without the need for the cables of the congress centers. With 5G technology, marketers will be able to offer marketing services such as VR programming for users, multi-person two-way interactive conference, 3D participation (Friedman, 2016: 9). Many companies plan to use and enhance of using *chatbots,* including event companies in the advancing years. By using artificial intelligence (AI) chat bots in different areas, event planners can automate a range of tasks and serve their customers better. We can clearly see the uses of artificial intelligence in the event industry. For example, a new startup called Styckie, which was created an intelligent AI algorithm to match ideal vendors at your location based on all event requirements (Arnold, 2019).

Experiential design increases the participation and memories of consumers in the event process. The organizers consider that their one of the mission is to design memorable, meaningful, and valuable event experiences for attendees in their event journey. Organizers can customize events, e.g. attendees can meet with other attendees on their mobile devices with an event app (customization), Designing game elements into their events (gamification) (Chan, 2018). There is an increasing need for event organizers to use data to evaluate their own programs, develop appropriate marketing and production plans, and evaluate the results of a particular event. Organizers need quality *data* and data analysis in order to present demonstrations and events to be adopted by the progress of different population segments, different media consumption patterns and demographically changing target audiences (Friedman, 2016: 9). Two examples are given on how major events use data to gather high-quality and comprehensive information. The organizers gave participants badges with Radio Frequency Identification (RFID) technology that tracked their movements in C2 Montreal,. In this way, they could see where people gathered and which parts of the event were empty. When they observed that there were a large number of people gathered at a particular dining table, they sent more food service workers for help (www.superevent.com).

IoT is predicted that it will play a key role in revolutionizing the event industry. Event management is based on a large amount of data about venues, potential participants, catering, performances, exhibitors' check-ins and payments. There are some ways to use the IoT for event organizations. For example, iBeacon allows event organizators smoothly connect the event with the attendees; in this way, visitors can access the event schedule, check in time, and be directed to the event venue with a map (Pitman, 2019). Virtual reality is a tool for event organizers. The virtual world provides; information transmission (via video, audio), interaction, fascination (through games), long-term commitment through interactive and constantly changing content (Pinker, 2017) and enriched consumer experience. Many companies and travel sites have already started promoting VR in their marketing programs. The Los Angeles Convention and Visitors Bureau created a tour of VR sites at its meeting in 2016. Currently, VR apps are being included in the program of sports events such as Rio Olympics and Super Bowl LI. VR allows distant viewers to experience the event not only as if it were there, but also closer to the action than ever before.

Another example can be an event organized by Intel at CES 2017. In the opening speech of Intel CEO Brian Krzanich, the venue is equipped with more than 200 headsets and transformed a virtual world into a real-world event experience (Eventmb Studio Team, 2019; Friedman, 2016). Augmented reality is a view of the real, combines both computer-generated elements and reality to create an augmented world. Event companies aim to distinguish their brands and offerings from competition by using VR in their organizations. When the examples of VR applications in the sector are examined, it is seen that the developments in telepresence tools come to the fore. Telepresence makes it easier for people to participate in an event remotely and ensures that participants interact remotely with other event participants (Levine, Schutz and Epstein, 2018).

Safety and security remains a concern for event organizers. These topics include both natural disasters and human-initiated events such as civil unrest and acts of terrorism (Friedman, 2016: 8). The main issues that they pay attention to the factors that react quickly to the negative reactions of the public in times of security, emergency planning and national crisis. When today's marketing activities are examined, it is clearly seen that safety and security factors have become a part of the marketing message (Hoyle, 2002: 172). Organizers have a revised and updated crisis plan and have pre-event planning with the venue, and if necessary, local authorities (Friedman, 2016: 8). Increasing use of social media marketing in the event industry is among the prominent trends of today. Companies can create predictions and a community of participants even before the event via social media so they can expand the reach of their event. A lot of event organizers know all about the power of the hashtag, but many events create Instagram accounts / pages for their events. Pinknic, for example; the upcoming NYC Music Festival event uses a mix of Instagram ads through publicity to gain followers on its pages (Shaw, 2019).

New Challenges in Event Marketing

Technological advances in recent years have not only improved living standards in the industrialized world, but have also brought a variety of new challenges to marketers. Never before has so many different lines of business been in maturity or decline as in recent years (Wohlfeil and Whelan, 2005: 187). It's becoming increasingly difficult to attract the attention of visitors. At trade fairs or events there is often a wide range of products and services that you have to find new ways of interaction in order to be successful. Uniformization, similarization of products and changing consumer expectations are the main topics that marketers seek and find solutions. Apart from this situation, event marketers trying to find solutions for extensive challenges in their marketing efforts, for example, increased media and audience fragmentation, greater competition in the media market (Martensen and Grønholdt, 2008: 44).

The event industry can face especially challenge in the catastrophic situations and security issues. These present particular challenges for the economy and risk management, as they can have serious long-term economic and social consequences. Since these events are normally a low probability of happening, there is limited historical data on which the risks based on their estimates, and there is considerable uncertainty associated with the experts' estimates of risk assessment (Kunreuther and Michel-Kerjan, 2004: 2). Apart from the safety and health issues of people, activity marketing has challenges in different aspects. Consumers are exposed to hundreds of advertising messages per day. Businesses can make their advertising messages and activities identifiable using guerrilla marketing. For guerrilla tactics to be successful, organizers must have a surprise element, creating attention by doing something unique. Organizers should have something to pay attention for promoting and find an area where there is already a large resident audience (Hoyle, 2002: 166). Marketing within the events is largely based on communication, whether it is directly inform the potential customers or to create a brand image in the market (Masterman and Wood, 2007: 4-17). Event marketing involves examining the complexities of the brand, identifying the target audience, designing the event concept, planning logistics, and coordinating technical aspects before realizing the methods of the proposed event (Rajesh, 2014: 27).

The effectiveness of the event marketing strategies, as a strategy to attract visitors in the marketing process, largely depends on the voluntary participation of consumers. Media involvement, along with motivation to process brand-related information, is seen as an important prerequisite for influencing brand image perception and determining its effectiveness in any communication medium (Wohlfeil and Whelan, 2006: 644). Therefore, event organizers need to find elements that will motivate potential participants to participate voluntarily.

New Opportunities in Event Marketing

Event organizers face the challenge of consumers increasingly less sensitive to traditional advertising and still looking for new marketing communication tools. Furthermore, in recent years there has been a focus on consumers who are emotionally moving and seeking experience (Martensen, Grønholdt, Bendtsen and Jensen, 2007: 283). The event industry is one-step ahead of the mainstream in terms of incorporating new technologies into its structure. For example, the Twitch website, which is used for video game streaming, has developed an ongoing technology in the event industry by adding an interactive game to its streams this year. Event professionals understood the importance and affordable budget of interactive games to keep an audience engaged (Maritz Global Events, n.d.:2).

An important factor in event marketing is to find a sponsor. Through qualified sponsors/sponsors who are successful in the working site, the event organizer can achieve success in public awareness, corporate image building, community involvement, reaching target markets, brand positioning, increasing sales, generating awareness, enhancing add campaigns and generating publicity issues (Gupta, 2003: 89). Event organizers are looking for ways to engage participants in unique ways. In recent research, it has been found that when people are actively involved in interpreting material by stimulating multiple senses, people remember more than 90 percent of a presentation. For these reasons, the event industry is constantly researching to find new ways to incorporate new sensory experiences into the more mundane aspects of a conference or other events. These experiences contain *customized lighting*, *special seating*, *3-D imaging*, *surround sound audio*. Even 4-D time warping events are becoming constants for modern participants (Maritz Global Events, n.d.:3).

Management of the visitor experience is a very important issue for the events. It is the management of experiences that requires a carefully structured approach to the provision of services and activities. Buswell (2004: 3) mentioned three factors that play a key role for leisure experiences. These are; time, flow and expression. Time provides us with a chronological order, socially constructed, and also provides us with a period of carefully selected activities. It affects our experiences by limiting the availability of time or by providing an unlimited amount of time. Flow is associated with emotions that people feel at different stages within any experience; the goal is to achieve the best experience when the most satisfying is reached. Finally, it is decided which action to take and to come to a conclusion. This decision represents a vital aspect of the formation of experience (Berridge, 2007: 71-72). Considering that these 3 dimensions are related to the experience, it is necessary to focus on improving the participant's experience. A descriptive identity must be created to promote and secure an event brand. The first step is to create a logo for the event. Thus, the logo creates an image that the person respects and understands and helps to brand this event. If there is a successful branded event in an area or at a certain time of the year, the lifetime of that event will be extended (Hoyle, 2002: 166).

The events involve offering participants experiences, thus activating emotional responses and more. The nature and amount of communication created will always be in focus as participants choose between alternative activities. Event marketing is a group of activities aimed at high level of participation. The events include the target group, company and products, as well as giving the target group an experience that appeals to sensory and affective (Martensen and Grønholdt, 2008: 44-45). The success and uniqueness of the events depend on branding. Every event needs a strong brand and by creating strong brand awareness, the event can be clearly distinguished from millions of other similar events. Marketing is an endless efforts and it does not mean that a firm that succeeds today, which will succeed tomorrow (Hoyle, 2002: 168).

SOLUTIONS AND RECOMMENDATIONS

Community-based event are an important success factor for many businesses in an increasingly globalized world. In order to keep up with the increasing competitiveness of today's new media, it is observed that businesses focus on interaction, communication, innovation and experience-oriented event marketing. Thus, it will be possible to have a unique event marketing solution for each individual in terms of unique personal communication and experiences between businesses, marketers, society and customers. Therefore, following suggestions could be proposed for tourism companies and marketers:

- The event organizer should identify the event theme that concerns the target group, and provide the environment that meets the requirements and characteristics of the participants (Drenger, Gaus and Jahn, 2008). Considering the customer types of companies, the event needs to match the brand's target market by meeting the marketing goals defined for the brand.
- Consumer motivation and needs, how and by whom the decision to participate is made, the effects of event experiences on visitor satisfaction, intentions to visit again and word of mouth recommendations should be known (Jago, Veal, Allen and Harris, 2000: 19).
- What makes the events unique and valuable, and how to evaluate the unique qualities for marketing activities should be investigated.
- Marketing should integrate with other classic elements, such as advertising and promotional campaigns, to focus on the goals of the event itself.
- Event organizers need to take into account the types of customers they address through new events to ensure participant satisfaction and therefore need to develop new events or diversify existing events (Daniel, Bogdan and Daniel, 2012: 5409).
- "An ideal event" should have the feature that closely matches the ideal target market, attracts attention, contributes to other marketing activities and reflects or even develops the brand (Keller, 2013).

Davidson and Rogers, (2006) and Daniel et al. (2012) have several suggestions on the success of the organized events. These;

- Activities should be as interactive and engaging as possible, depending on their characteristics and type.
- Participants can be made proud by participating in the event via giving them promotions, gifts, awards or discounts and sweepstakes at the end of the event.
- It is important that the event program is very flexible and adapted to the needs and constraints of the target audience.
- In order to reach the target audience, communication channels should be used and the message of effectiveness should be transferred to the target audience in a healthy way.

Event organizers need to consider some issues when organizing events. The primary consideration in the selection of an event is the brand-event and personality fit. In summary, the events are unique and make the experiences memorable. Therefore, event marketing can be a very effective marketing tool if it is well planned and executed. It can also strengthen the company's image and deepen relationships with customers.

FUTURE RESEARCH DIRECTIONS

Event marketing activities are more common than before in tourism enterprises. Therefore, it is important to study the needs and motivations to know to market events more effectively through the use of new media and technological applications. The challenges of new media in event marketing should be also explored. Furthermore, research that investigate customers' motivations in detail will be important for destination managers and company leaders. Thus, company leaders will be able to see the needs of customers. Finally, it is important to understanding of the experiences about event and their impacts on the customers.

Eventbrite (2013) company expressed new event trends under the following titles;

- Fans expect more choices and more personalized experiences
- Hybrid festivals attract bigger audiences and bring in more revenue
- Online ticketing unlocks powerful data and insights like never before
- Mobile technology is dramatically improving the overall attendee experience
- Radio Frequency Identification (RFID) technology and smart cards add value once inside the event
- Social media provides hard cash benefits to event organizers.

Park and Park (2016) examined 541 articles and made evaluations on activity research. The results showed that topics for event studies have changed over time. Recent studies heavily focus on visitor experiences, investigating motivation, satisfaction, and behavioral intention, while past studies paid more attention to the economic impact of events or volunteer motivation. In Mair and Whitford's (2013: 6) research about the discovery of event research, they stated that there is a need for studies on the socio-cultural and environmental impacts of events, as well as a better understanding of the relationship between the public policy agendas of events rather than the definitions, types and event logistics of events.

CONCLUSION

Technology is getting more and more into our lives and operates in almost all areas. From the simplest, smartphones have more ability and connectivity in our lives so we can accomplish so many things with a smartphone. The event sector is also a sector that has benefited immensely from the development of technology. Event technology is more reasonably priced and targets individual needs. Due to the convenience that technology provides for both event marketing and event management, many event planners put technological applications the center of their services.

In general, event marketing includes all marketing activities that business managers can undertake to produce a successful festival or event (Goldblatt, 2005: 180). Event marketing activities, which are developed by paying attention to event product, price distribution, place, promotion activities and public relations, attract more customers in today's competitive conditions. In other words, the needs of the target market, marketing communication, including messages to reach the audience of the event, determining the degree of success in determining the choice and design of the venue, and especially from the design of the event experience to the presentation of the event. All these activities that are vital to a successful event are an important part of the marketing function. Because event marketing strategy and planning is a whole with general event planning.

Event marketer acts as a channel between what event organizers want to reach and the demands of customers (Saget, 2006: 54). Therefore, marketing activities can be successful through broader promotional opportunities and target awareness developed in accordance with different expectations of the target audience (Nicholson and Pearce, 2000: 237). In order for the event marketing activities to be successful, the local government should create the tourism experience together with the tourists. Because the process of creating joint participation and experiential value together can increase the satisfaction and loyalty of tourists (Vargo and Lusch, 2006). Especially different and unique experience values are obtained from the direct use of products, service and other interaction behaviors (Mathwick, Malhotra and Rigdon, 2001). Thus, different consumers will experience the event differently. Depending on the skills, knowledge and past experiences of the target audience, this experience can be seen as disturbing, frightening or exciting for someone else (Wood, 2009: 250). Extraordinary events can create the appropriate sense of experience and love for the customers and determine the experiential value of the customers (Smith and Colgate, 2007). Apparently, when consumers enjoy more marketing activities, their satisfaction and emotional commitment will be higher (Moliner, Sanchez, Rodriguez and Callarisa, 2007).

Event marketing tries to give and capture participant experiences. If the customer has good experience in connection with the product, it will strengthen the relationship between the participant and the organization. Research by Bizzabo in 2019 indicated that companies spend more of their marketing budgets on events, invest more in event technology, and as a result measure event performance and return on investment with unprecedented precision. For this reason, it has been observed that the most successful organizations are still organizations that invest aggressively in live events. Event marketers who want to achieve success in today's conditions have comprehended how to respond to their events quickly, effectively and profitably or how to form their demands. It is important to keep their ears and eyes open to the target and developing target markets to learn how to quickly influence potential participants in their events. Emphasis should be placed on the importance of gathering in such events, the experience of the event and the relationships with the participants (Hoyle, 2002: 172).

There may be many negative situations in business life such as economic downturn, rapid moves by competitors and negative media news. Nevertheless, when current trends in event marketing are evaluated, innovative design opportunities and new audiences will emerge (Hoyle, 2002: 178-179). In this way, the event sector will continue to grow and diversify until the threat of the supply of events in many areas or the threat of exceeding demand.

REFERENCES

Allen, J., O'Toole, W., McDonnell, I., & Harris, R. (2005). Festival and special event management. Milton, Qld: John Wiley.

Altunbas, H. (2008). Pazarlama iletişimi ve etkinlik (event) pazarlaması 'müzik eğlence etkinliğinin marka iletişimine etkisi'. Istanbul University Faculty of Communication Journal, (34), 23-36.

Arnold, A. (2019). *How AI is transforming the event planning space one conservation at time*. Retrieved from https://www.forbes.com/sites/andrewarnold/2019/02/25/how-ai-is-transforming-the-event-planning-space-one-conversation-at-a-time/#4f28510210b3

Ayob, N. (2003). An analysis of event tourism in Malaysia. *ASEAN Journal on Hospitality and Tourism, 2*, 92–102.

Baloglu, S., & Love, C. (2005). Association meeting planners' perceptions and intentions for five major US convention cities: The structured and unstructured images. *Tourism Management, 26*(5), 743–752. doi:10.1016/j.tourman.2004.04.001

Belch, G. E., & Belch, M. A. (2004). *Advertising and promotion: An integrated marketing communications perspective*. McGraw-Hill.

Berridge, G. (2007). *Events design and experience*. Routledge. doi:10.4324/9780080468112

Berridge, G. (2007). *Events design and experience*. Routledge. doi:10.4324/9780080468112

Bizzabo. (2019). *Event Marketing 2019 Benchmarks and Trends Report*. Retrieved from https://welcome.bizzabo.com/hubfs/White-Papers-and-Ebooks/Event-Marketing-2019.pdf

Bizzabo. (2019). *Event Marketing 2019. Benchmarks and Trends Report*. Retrieved from https://welcome.bizzabo.com/hubfs/White-Papers-and-Ebooks/Event-Marketing-2019.pdf. 20.02.2020.

Bowdin, G. A. J., Allen, J., O'Toole, W., Harris, R., & McDonnell, I. (2006). *Events Management* (2nd ed.). Elsevier. doi:10.4324/9780080457154

Bramwell, B. (1997). Strategic planning before andafter a mega-event. *Tourism Management, 18*(3), 167–176. doi:10.1016/S0261-5177(96)00118-5

Buswell, J. (2004). Sport and leisure service encounter. In Sport and Leisure Operations Management. Thomson.

Chacko, H., & Schaffer, J. (1993). The evolution of a festival: Creole Christmas in New Orleans. *Tourism Management, 14*(6), 475–482. doi:10.1016/0261-5177(93)90100-Y

Chalip, L. (1992). The construction anduse of polysemic structures: Olympic lessons for sport marketing. *Journal of Sport Management*, *6*(2), 87–98. doi:10.1123/jsm.6.2.87

Chan, H. (2018). *5 Tips: How to Use Experience Design to Create a Memorable Event*. Eventmobi. Retrieved from https://www.eventmobi.com/blog/5-tips-use-experience-design-create-memorable-event/

Close, A. G., Finney, R. Z., Lacey, R. Z., & Sneath, J. Z. (2006). Engaging the consumer through event marketing: Linking attendees with the sponsor, community, and brand. *Journal of Advertising Research*, *46*(4), 420–433. doi:10.2501/S0021849906060430

Close, A. G., Krishen, A. S., & Latour, M. S. (2009). The event is me! How consumer event selfcongruity leverages sponsorship. *Journal of Advertising Research*, *49*(3), 271–284. doi:10.2501/S0021849909090412

Crompton, J. L., & McKay, S. L. (1997). Motives of visitors attending festival events. *Annals of Tourism Research*, *24*(2), 425–439. doi:10.1016/S0160-7383(97)80010-2

Crowther, P. (2011). Marketing event outcomes: From tactical to strategic. *International Journal of Event and Festival Management*, *2*(1), 68–82. doi:10.1108/17582951111116623

Crowther, P., & Donlan, L. (2011). Value-creation space: The role of events in a service-dominant marketing paradigm. *Journal of Marketing Management*, *27*(13-14), 1444–1463. doi:10.1080/0267257X.2011.626786

Cruceru, A. F., & Moise, D. (2014). Customer relationships through sales forces and marketing events. *Procedia: Social and Behavioral Sciences*, *109*, 155–159. doi:10.1016/j.sbspro.2013.12.436

CWT Meetings&Events. (2019). *2019 Meetings & Events Future Trends*. Retrieved from https://www.levenement.org/wp-content/uploads/2018/12/Future-Trends-Report-2019-CWT-ME-Base-doc-%C3%A9tude.pdf

Daniel, M., Bogdan, G., & Daniel, Z. (2012). The use of event marketing management strategies. *Procedia: Social and Behavioral Sciences*, *46*, 5409–5413. doi:10.1016/j.sbspro.2012.06.448

Davidson, R., & Rogers, T. (2006). *Marketing Destinations and Venues for Conferences, Conventions and Business Events*. Publishing House Elsevier.

Drenger, J., Gaus, H., & Jahn, S. (2008). Does flow influence the brand image in event marketing? *Journal of Advertising Research*, *48*(1), 138–147. doi:10.2501/S0021849908080148

Eckerstein, A. (2009). Evaluation of event marketing. Important indicators to consider when evaluating event marketing. Käsikirjaline magistritöö. Graduate Business School, Göteborg University, Göteborg.

Eventbrite. (2013). *New trends impacting festival and consumer events*. Retrieved from https://eventbrites3.s3.amazonaws.com/marketing/britepapers/Britepaper_6newtrends_webVersion.pdf

Eventmb Studio Team. (2019). *5 Trends In Virtual Reality For Events*. Retrieved from https://www.eventmanagerblog.com/virtual-reality-trends-events

Ferdinand, N., & Kitchin, P. (2012). *Events Management: An International Approach*. Sage.

Friedman, F. (2016). *Future trends impacting the exhibitions and events industry 2016 update*. International Association of Exhibitions and Events. Retrieved from http://www.iaee.com/wp-content/uploads/2016/04/2016-IAEE-Future-Trends-Impacting-the-Exhibitions-and-Events-Industry-White-Paper.pdf

Gardner, M., & Shuman, P. (1987). Sponsorship: An important component of the promotions mix. *Journal of Advertising*, *16*(1), 11–17. doi:10.1080/00913367.1987.10673055

Geraghty, G., & Conway, A. (2016). *The Study of Traditional and Non-traditional Marketing Communications: Target Marketing in the Events Sector*. Paper presented at the 12th Annual Tourism and Hospitality Research in Ireland Conference, THRIC 2016, 16th and 17th June, Limerick Institute of Technology.

Getz, D. (1991). *Festivals, special events and tourism*. Van Nostrand Reinhold.

Getz, D. (1997). *Event management and event tourism*. Cognizant Communication.

Getz, D. (2007). *Event studies: theory, research and policy for planned events*. Elsevier.

Getz, D. (2008). Event tourism: Definition, evolution and research. *Tourism Management*, *29*(1), 403–428. doi:10.1016/j.tourman.2007.07.017

Getz, D., & Page, S. J. (2016). Progress and prospects for event tourism research. *Tourism Management*, *52*, 593–631. doi:10.1016/j.tourman.2015.03.007

Goldblatt, J. (2005). *Special Events: Event leadership for a New World* (4th ed.). John Wiley & Sons.

Goldblatt, J. (2013). *Special events: creating and sustaining a new world for celebration*. Wiley Global Education.

Gupta, S. (2003). Event marketing: Issues and challenges. *IIMB Management Review*, *15*(2), 87–96.

Hall, C. M. (1992). *Hallmark tourist events – Impacts, management and planning*. Belhaven Press.

Higham, J., & Hinch, T. (2002). Tourism, sport and seasons: The challenges and potentials of overcoming seasonality in the sport and tourism sectors. *Tourism Management*, *23*(2), 175–185. doi:10.1016/S0261-5177(01)00046-2

Hindman, B. (2018). The event marketing evolution an era of data, technology, and revenue impact. *Harvard Business Review Analytic Services Research Report/Splash*. Retrieved from https://hbr.org/sponsored/2018/09/the-event-marketing-evolution

Hoffman, D. L., & Novak, T. P. (2009). Flow online: Lessons learned and future prospects. *Journal of Interactive Marketing*, *23*(1), 23–34. doi:10.1016/j.intmar.2008.10.003

Hogan, J. E., Lemon, K. N., & Libai, B. (2004). Quantifying the ripple: Word-of-mouth and advertising effectiveness. *Journal of Advertising Research*, *44*(3), 271–280. doi:10.1017/S0021849904040243

Holbrook, M., & Hirschman, E. (1982). The experiential aspects of consumption. *The Journal of Consumer Research*, *9*(2), 132–140. doi:10.1086/208906

Hoyle, H. L. (2002). *Event Marketing. How to Successfully Promote Events, Festivals, Conventions and Expositions*. John Wiley & Sons, Inc.

Jackson, N. (2013). *Promoting and marketing events: Theory and practice*. Routledge. doi:10.4324/9780203583166

Jago, L., Veal, A. J., Allen, J., & Harris, R. (2000). *Events beyond 2000: setting the agenda: proceedings of conference on event evaluation, research and education*. Australian Centre for Event Management.

Javalgi, R. G., Traylor, M. B., Gross, A. C., & Lampman, E. (1994). Awareness of sponsorship and corporate image: An empirical investigation. *Journal of Advertising*, *23*(4), 47–58. doi:10.1080/00913367.1943.10673458

Karpinska-Krakowiak, M. (2015). Marketing events in a digital era–a comparative analysis of new and traditional events in terms of branding effectiveness. *Conference Proceedings, 11 Annual International Bata Conference*, 239-255.

Kaspar, R. (2014). The dimensions of events management. In The business of events management. Pearson Higher Ed.

Keller, L. K. (2013). *Strategic Brand Management: Building, Measuring, and Managing Brand Equity*. Pearson Education Limited.

Kotler, P. (2002). *Marketing management*. London: Pearson Education.

Kumar, R. (1997). The role of affect in negotiations: An integrative overview. *Journal of Behavioural Science*, *33*(1), 84–100. doi:10.1177/0021886397331007

Kunreuther, H., & Michel-Kerjan, E. (2004). *Dealing with extreme events: new challenges for terrorism risk coverage in the US. Center for Risk Management and Decision Processes*. Wharton School, University of Pennsylvania.

Levine, J., Schutz, S., & Epstein, D. (2018). *Virtual and Augmented Reality: What Event Organizers must Know*. Retrieved from https://blog.bizzabo.com/virtual-and-augmented-reality-for-event-organizers

Light, D. (1996). Characteristics of the audience for "events" at a heritage site. *Tourism Management*, *17*(3), 183–190. doi:10.1016/0261-5177(96)00005-2

Liu, L., Zhang, J., & Keh, H. T. (2018). Event-marketing and advertising expenditures: The differential effects on brand value and company revenue. *Journal of Advertising Research*, *58*(4), 464–475. doi:10.2501/JAR-2017-043

Liu, Y. (2006). Word of mouth for movies: Its dynamics and impact on box office revenue. *Journal of Marketing*, *70*(3), 74–89. doi:10.1509/jmkg.70.3.074

Mair, J., & Whitford, M. (2013). An exploration of events research: Event topics, themes and emerging trends. *International Journal of Event and Festival Management*, *4*(1), 6–30. doi:10.1108/17582951311307485

Maritz Global Events. (n.d.). *Evolving Trends in the Event Industry*. Retrieved from https://cdn2.hubspot.net/hubfs/2186839/trendswhitepaper11.17-1.pdf?t=1528340918401

Martensen, A., & Grønholdt, L. (2008). How events work: Understanding consumer responses to event marketing. *Innovative Marketing*, *4*(4), 44–56.

Martensen, A., Grønholdt, L., Bendtsen, L., & Jensen, M. J. (2007). Application of a model for the effectiveness of event marketing. *Journal of Advertising Research*, *47*(3), 283–301. doi:10.2501/S0021849907070316

Masterman, G., & Wood, E. (2007). *Innovative marketing communications*. Routledge.

Mathwick, C., Malhotra, N., & Rigdon, E. (2001). Experiential value: Conceptualization, measurement and application in the catalog and internet shopping environment. *Journal of Retailing*, *77*(1), 39–56. doi:10.1016/S0022-4359(00)00045-2

McDonnell, I., Allen, J., & O'Toole, W. (1999). *Festival and Special Event Management*. John Wiley and Sons.

Moliner, M., Sanchez, J., Rodriguez, R. M., & Callarisa, L. (2007). Relationship quality with a travel agency: The influence of the post-purchased perceived value of a tourism package. *Tourism and Hospitality Research*, *7*(3/4), 194–211. doi:10.1057/palgrave.thr.6050052

Mount, J., & Niro, B. (1995). Sponsorship: An empirical study of its application to local business in a small town setting. *Festival Management & Event Tourism*, *2*(3-4), 167–175. doi:10.3727/106527095792315576

Nicholson, R., & Pearce, D. G. (2000). Who goes to events: A comparative analysis of the profile characteristics of visitors to four South Island events in New Zealand. *Journal of Vacation Marketing*, *6*(3), 236–253. doi:10.1177/135676670000600304

Park, K., & Park, S. (2016). Topic trend of event management research. *Event Management*, *20*(1), 109–115. doi:10.3727/152599516X14538326024991

Pine, B. J., Pine, J., & Gilmore, J. H. (1999). *The experience economy: Work is theatre & every business a stage*. Harvard Business Press.

Pinker, A. (2017). *Virtual Reality in Event Management*. Retrieved from https://medialist.info/en/2017/10/17/virtual-reality-in-event-management/

Pitman, L. (2019). *Internet of Things – the Newest Wrinkle in Event Management*. Retrieved from https://datafloq.com/read/internet-of-things-newest-wrinkle-event-management/6431

Pope, N. K., & Voges, K. E. (2000). The Impact of Sport Sponsorship Activities, Corporate Image, and Prior Use on Consumer Purchase Intention. *Sport Marketing Quarterly*, *9*(2), 96–102.

Rajesh, R. (2014). Issues and Trends of Event Tourism Promotion in destination Puducherry- An Empirical Study. *International Journal of Safety and Security in Tourism*, *6*, 25–41.

Ravald, A., & Gronoos, C. (1996). The value concept and relationship marketing. *European Journal of Marketing*, *30*(2), 19–30. doi:10.1108/03090569610106626

Regalix Research. (2019). *Event Marketing*. Retrieved from https://www.regalix.com/wp-content/uploads/2019/05/CMO_Guide_Event_Marketing_2019.pdf

Ritchie, J. R. B. (1984). Assessing the impact of hallmark events: Conceptual and research issues. *Journal of Travel Research*, *23*(1), 2–11. doi:10.1177/004728758402300101

Ritchie, J. R. B., & Beliveau, D. (1974). The impact of a mega-event on host region awareness: A longitudinal study. *Journal of Travel Research, 13*(2), 14–20. doi:10.1177/004728757401300202

Rogers, T., & Davidson, R. (2006). *Marketing destinations and venues for conferences, conventions and business events*. Butterworth-Heinemann. Routledge.

Saget, A. (2006). *The Event Marketing Handbook*. Dearborn Trade.

Schmitt, B. H. (1999). *Experiential Marketing*. The Free Press.

Sharp, B., & Wind, Y. J. (2009). Today's Advertising Laws: Will They Survive the Digital Revolution? *Journal of Advertising Research, 49*(2), 120–126. doi:10.2501/S002184990909014X

Shaw, T. (2019). *How Social Media is Appealing to the Events Industry*. Retrieved from https://www.aventri.com/blog/how-social-media-is-appealing-to-the-events-industry

Shone, A., & Parry, B. (2010). *Successful event management: a practical handbook* (3rd ed.). Cengage Learning EMEA.

Silvers, J. R. (2004). *Professional event coordination*. John Wiley & Sons Inc.

Smith, A. (2008). *Using major events to promote peripheral urban areas: Deptford and the 2007 Tour de France. In International perspectives of festivals and events: Paradigms of analysis*. Elseveir.

Smith, J. B., & Colgate, M. (2007). Customer value creation: A practical framework. *Journal of Marketing Theory and Practice, 15*(1), 7–23. doi:10.2753/MTP1069-6679150101

Sneath, J. Z., Finney, R. Z., & Close, A. G. (2005). An IMC approach to event marketing: The effects of sponsorship and experience on customer attitudes. *Journal of Advertising Research, 45*(4), 373–381. doi:10.1017/S0021849905050440

Spiro, R. S., & Weitz, B. A. (1990). Adaptive selling: Conceptualization, measurement, and nomological validity. *JMR, Journal of Marketing Research, 27*(1), 61–69. doi:10.1177/002224379002700106

Tafesse, W. (2016). Conceptualization of Brand Experience in an Event Marketing Context. *Journal of Promotion Management, 22*(1), 34–48. doi:10.1080/10496491.2015.1107007

Tafesse, W., Narui, J., & Korneliussen, T. (2014). Branding goals and strategies at international auto shows. *International Journal of Marketing Studies, 6*(4), 23–34. doi:10.5539/ijms.v6n4p23

Taylor, S. F., & Cunningham, P. H. (1999). *"Event Marketing" The Advertising Business*. Sage Publications.

Tinnish, S. M., & Mangal, S. M. (2012). Sustainable event marketing in the MICE industry: A theoretical framework. *Journal of Convention & Event Tourism, 13*(4), 227–249. doi:10.1080/15470148.2012.731850

Vallee, R., & Westcott, M. (2002). *Trends in Event Marketing. The George P.* Johnson Company.

Vargo, S. L., & Lusch, R. F. (2006). Service-dominant logic: What it is, what it is not, what it might be. In R. F. Lusch & S. L. Vargo (Eds.), *The service-dominant logic of marketing: Dialog, debate and directions* (pp. 43–56). M.E Sharpe, Inc.

Winer, R. S. (2009). New communications approaches in marketing: Issues and research directions. *Journal of Interactive Marketing*, *23*(2), 108–117. doi:10.1016/j.intmar.2009.02.004

Wohlfeil, M., & Whelan, S. (2005a). Consumer Motivations to Participate in Marketing-Events: the Role of Predispositional Involvement. In K. M. Ekstrom & H. Brembeck (Eds.), *E - European Advances in Consumer Research* (Vol. 7, pp. 125–130). Association for Consumer Research.

Wohlfeil, M., & Whelan, S. (2005b). Event-marketing as innovative marketing communications: Reviewing the German experience. *Journal of Customer Behaviour*, *4*(2), 181–207. doi:10.1362/1475392054797214

Wohlfeil, M., & Whelan, S. (2006). Consumer motivations to participate in event-marketing strategies. *Journal of Marketing Management*, *22*(5-6), 643–669. doi:10.1362/026725706777978677

Wood, E. H. (2009). Evaluating event marketing: Eexperience or outcome? *Journal of Promotion Management*, *15*(1), 247–268. doi:10.1080/10496490902892580

Wu, S. I. (2016). Competing Model of Event Marketing Activities. *International Journal of Marketing Studies*, *8*(4), 52–66. doi:10.5539/ijms.v8n4p52

www.superevent.com. (n.d.). How Big Data Is Revolutionizing the Event Industry. Retrieved from https://superevent.com/blog/how-big-data-is-revolutionizing-the-event-industry/

Yoon, S., Spencer, D. M., Holecek, D. F., & Kim, D. K. (2000). A profile of Michigan's festival and special event tourism market. *Event Management*, *6*(1), 33–44.

Zarantonello, L., & Schmitt, B. H. (2013). The impact of event marketing on brand equity: The mediating roles of brand experience and brand attitude. *International Journal of Advertising*, *32*(2), 255–280. doi:10.2501/IJA-32-2-255-280

ADDITIONAL READING

Andersson, M., & Wesslau, A. (2012). *Organising for event marketing in order to change brand image and increase sales* (Doctoral dissertation, School of Economics and Commercial Law).

Cunningham, P., Taylor, S., & Reeder, C. (1993). Event marketing: the evolution of sponsorship from philanthropy to strategic promotion. In S. Hollander, J.B. Schmidt, T. Nevett & J.N. Sheth (Eds) *Contemporary Marketing History, Proceedings of the Sixth Conference on Historical Research in Marketing and Marketing Thought* (407-425). Michigan: Michigan State University.

Daniel, M., Bogdan, G., & Daniel, Z. (2012). The use of event marketing management strategies. *Procedia: Social and Behavioral Sciences*, *46*, 5409–5413. doi:10.1016/j.sbspro.2012.06.448

Davidson, R., & Rogers, T. (2007). *Marketing Destinations and Venues for Conferences, Conventions and Business Events*. Publishing House Elsevier; UK.

Eckerstein, A. (2002). Evaluation of Event Marketing. *International Management Master Thesis:* 25, Goteborg University.

Hoyle, H. L. (2002). *Event Marketing. How to Successfully Promote Events, Festivals, Conventions and Expositions*. John Wiley & Sons, Inc.

KEY TERMS AND DEFINITIONS

Artificial Intelligence (AI): It is a system that has the ability to perform operations analogous to learning and decision making by imitating biological processes, with special emphasis on human cognitive processes.

Augmented Reality (AR): It is a technology that allows computer-generated virtual imagery information to be overlaid onto a live direct or indirect real-world environment in real time.

Event: It is a form of attraction. It acts as a "pull factor" to the target destination (Getz, 1997).

Event Marketing: It is a communication program that can stay in touch with its participants, know their needs and motivations, and develop products that meet their needs (Hall, 1992; Cruceru and Moise, 2014).

Internet of Things (IoT): It is a new technology paradigm envisioned as a global network of machines and devices capable of interacting with each other.

Radio Frequency Identification (RFID): Radio-frequency identification (RFID) technology is a wireless sensor technology which is based on the detection of electromagnetic signals. RFID is an area of automatic identification that is gaining momentum and is considered by some to emerge as one of the most pervasive computing technologies in history.

Virtual Reality (VR): It is typically defined in terms of technological hardware. The definition of virtual reality is based on concepts of "presence" and "telepresence," which refer to the sense of being in an environment, generated by natural or mediated means, respectively.

Chapter 11
Virtual Reality for Better Event Planning and Management

Alana Thomson
Federation University, Australia

Ingrid Proud
Better Events – Virtual and Augmented Reality, Australia

Andrew L. J. Goldston
Real Serious Games, Australia

Rebecca Dodds-Gorman
Griffith University, Australia

ABSTRACT

Digital technologies, such as virtual reality (VR), will have an increasing influence on the way events are experienced and managed. To date, scholarship has focused predominantly on the possibilities that VR presents for event experiences by event attendees, and there has been limited consideration of the application of VR for event planning and management. In this chapter, the authors provide a brief overview of the growth and application of virtual reality technology in events. A case study of a private sector start-up in the Australian setting is examined with a focus on VR technologies, it is developing as an aid in event planning and logistics. Key opportunities and challenges of VR pertinent to event planning and management are identified, and the authors suggest a number of implications for industry practice and event education, alongside avenues for future research to support the development of VR in event management and education.

DOI: 10.4018/978-1-7998-4954-4.ch011

INTRODUCTION

Advances in information and communication technologies have impacted the event management sector in a multitude of ways. We have seen practical advancements and scholarly interest in event management and ICTs the areas of management (including planning, marketing, delivery and evaluation) and participation experiences (including design, interactivity and co-design), consistent with developments in the tourism sector (c.f., Beck, Rainaldi & Egger, 2019). While the tourism literature has reflected a burgeoning interest in information and communication technologies (ICTs) such as augmented reality, mixed reality and virtual reality (VR) (Beck et al., 2019), the event management literature has been slower to respond (Backman, 2018; Mair & Weber, 2019). The scholarly study of ICTs and their current and potential application for the event management sector have not kept pace with industry developments. As such, there is a limited body of scholarship pertaining to contemporary and practical applications of ICTs to reflect critically on these advancements in the event management sector and to inform teachings of event management.

Responding to such a gap in the event management scholarship is important from a management perspective particularly given ICTs present ways to realise a range of cost efficiencies for event managers and stakeholders, as well as contribute to the quality of experiences and provide new and interesting ways to access events. It is also important we are reflecting ICT advancements in our event education. All aspects have become increasingly pertinent during the challenges experienced world-wide by the events and education sectors during COVID-19.

This chapter has been developed to push beyond broad comments regarding the potential of VR for the event sector by demystifying VR for the event sector, highlighting concrete opportunities for innovation and providing enough detail – in lay terms – to help people along on the innovation journey. Our team of authors includes academics and practitioners, working across areas of event management and VR, who have worked together to develop this book chapter to enlighten both event managers and software designers – so they each know enough about the other to identify opportunities and work together to realise innovation. As such, event practitioners, ICT developers, educators and students in these fields will find this chapter a useful resource for locating event management and VR within the broader ICT scholarship, gaining insight into the potential applications of VR in event management, and understanding implications from a range of perspectives regarding the potential roles for VR in event education and industry practice.

The objectives of this chapter include:

- To provide an overview of the extant literature pertaining to VR in events;
- To examine a case study of a private sector start-up in the Australian setting which is developing VR technologies as a tool for event planning and logistics; and
- To outline implications from the case study to be considered in event education and industry practice into the future.

BACKGROUND

Virtual Reality and Event Management

Virtual reality (VR) has been defined in the tourism literature as "a virtual computer simulated world" (Beck et al., 2019, p.586). Beck et al. (2019) argue that understandings of VR in the tourism setting are very much based on ideas borrowed from other industries concerned with the topic of VR and that the potential of such technology is so far largely unrealised in tourism and related sectors, such as events. In addition, the pace of VR development across the board has been rapid, with the result that there is a confusing range of terms now in use (Beck et al., 2019), which can be alienating for practitioners and students in the event management sector.

As an aim in compiling this chapter was to demystify VR for the lay audience in event management, we acknowledge the need to paint a more detailed picture about what VR is. Turning to a very practical non-academic source, Dictionary.com, we elaborate and define VR as "a realistic and immersive simulation of a three-dimensional (3D) environment, created using interactive software and hardware, and experienced or controlled by movement of the body". These physical characteristics of reality, immersion and sensory interactions are undoubtedly why VR has been widely adopted across tourism management settings (Beck et al., 2019), particularly from tourism marketing and tourist experience perspectives.

More recently, event academics have acknowledge the role of VR in event management settings, specifically in areas of event experiences and event education. There has been a recent increase of articles that demonstrate an increased awareness of, and interest in, the utility of virtual reality experiences as part of onsite festival programs for event participants to engage with as activations (Buhalis et al., 2019; Mair & Weber, 2019; Robertson, Yeoman, Smith, & Mcmahon-Beattie, 2015; Van Winkle, Bueddefeld, Halpenny, & MacKay, 2019). An extension to this is the use of virtual reality technologies to provide opportunities for event participants to co-create their own experience (Brown, Donne, Fallon, & Sharpley, 2019; Robertson, Hutton, & Brown, 2018; Robertson et al., 2015). In relation to VR and event education, recent discussion has acknowledged the potential for immersive and interactive digital experiences to be critical to developing employability attributes of event management students (Lockstone-Binny & Ong, 2019).

However, beyond the acknowledgement that there is potential for VR in event management settings, the body of knowledge lacks in-depth exploration of the practicalities or processes involved in realising these 'potentialities' or 'benefits. There is a need for greater focus on such technologies in event management to enhance our understanding of potential and useful applications of the technologies (Backman, 2018; Mair & Weber, 2019). In this chapter, we contribute to the body of knowledge by considering a so far overlooked potential application in event management, by way of using VR as a tool for the planning and management of events by event organisers and stakeholders.

We have compiled the following case study of an Australian private-sector start-up, which is pioneering the use of VR in event contexts as a solution to the complexities presented by multiple stakeholders and staging of events in urban public spaces. First, we provide a brief overview of Better Events (BE) – Virtual and Augmented Reality, Australia, the start-up firm which is the focus of our case study. Second, using BE as the stimulus, we discuss opportunities and challenges presented by VR for event planning and management in relation to extant literature where applicable. Third, we discuss the implications that our case study presents in event practice and event management in relation to extant literature where applicable. Fourth, we suggest several worthwhile avenues for future research. Finally, we conclude the chapter with a summation of key points from the case study and highlight important takeaways for event managers, stakeholders and students.

MAIN FOCUS OF THE CHAPTER

Case Study Methodology

In responding to the knowledge gaps regarding the application of VR in the event management sector we took a pragmatic transdisciplinary approach to develop a purposive single-case study. Transdisciplinary approaches to research and knowledge creation seek to "overcome the mismatch between knowledge production in academia, and knowledge requests for solving societal problems" (Hoffman-Riem, Biber-Klemm, Grossenbacher-Mansuy, et al., 2008, p.3). Rather than following conventional academic approaches to the creation and confirmation of knowledge, transdisciplinary approaches favour alternate ways of producing knowledge (Schikowitz, 2020). Consistent with this approach, the motivation for this book chapter was driven by underpinnings that not only did our review of literature indicate limited in-depth exploration of ways forward to apply VR and realise benefits, but our team of collaborators also observed anecdotally through interactions with event industry practitioners a lack of understanding of VR, the possibilities and aspects of "how-to" to realise these possibilities. As such, this book chapter provided the impetus for a collaboration between an event academic and industry practitioners to co-create a resource that provides an in-depth insight into the opportunities, and challenges, of VR for the event sector, and to do this in a way that is accessible to an event sector audience that may have limited technical expertise and lexicon that we might commonly associate with ICT. This collaboration and case study are inherently linked, with co-authors playing critical roles in the focal organisation, meaning this case study provides valuable "insider" insights into VR applications and processes that event academics and practitioners may not otherwise have access to.

We acknowledge that alternative ways of knowing need to adhere to some conventions to ensure quality. In the interest of transparency and trustworthiness, our processes for co-creation included drawing on insights from previous knowledge-sharing discussions that took place before any intention to write a book chapter. The event academic also drew on insights and observations gained during a technology showcase hosted by BE in late 2019. Once the decision to collaborate on the book chapter was agreed by the authors in early 2020, the academic noted down some key questions about the potential of VR for events and ways the event management sector could better engage in this space and emailed them to the BE representatives. The BE representatives responded to the questions and added additional insights they thought relevant to the target audience of event educators, students and practitioners. The event academic then used his information into start to craft the book chapter and through this process identified further information gaps and areas for clarification, for instance, what would a reader with no experience in this topic need to know about VR concepts and processes to feel more knowledgeable about VR in the event management setting? The authors went through several iterations generating the case study, debating and clarifying the knowledge created and areas for future research endeavours that are presented here in this book chapter.

The Focus Organisation: Better Events – Virtual and Augmented Reality

Better Events (BE) – Virtual and Augmented Reality, is an Australian start-up venture, established in 2019, to bring VR and AR technologies to the world of major sport event planning and management. Ingrid Proud, Managing Director – Operations, Better Events – Virtual and Augmented Reality, Australia, worked for the City of Gold Coast, the local government council that played host to the Gold Coast 2018 Commonwealth Games (GC2018). During the three years leading up to GC2018, Ingrid managed the 'Out of Venue' operations, i.e., any public space precincts that were outside the boundary of official event venues and precincts, but adjacent to, or providing a thoroughfare for, the official event spaces. Managing these 'Out of Venue' operations involved working with and coordinating multiple stakeholders (including the GC2018 Organising Committee and external stakeholders such as emergency services) to:

- Establish the event-related activities that would occur in these out-of-venue precincts and spaces;
- Name any associated temporary overlay infrastructure requirements; and
- Manage a team to determine and calculate crowd capacities and movements of spectators in and around the out-of-venue precincts.

The information compiled by Ingrid's team was then used by other teams in the City of Gold Coast council to determine overall operational requirements and to communicate with the local community about potential temporary changes to these public precincts for GC2018 purposes. This information also helped in securing relevant land use permissions to ensure the Host City's event operations were compliant with local laws and/or regulations.

One of the key issues Ingrid experienced during this time related to the spatial awareness of multiple stakeholders at the out-of-venue precincts and surrounding spaces. Each stakeholder came to the planning process with their own plans and maps, utilising various design technologies and platforms. This mixture of visions and interests provided a significant barrier in setting up a true and central map for all stakeholders to establish accurate and realistic spatial awareness, and, therefore, to be able to plan for and implement necessary overlay infrastructure. Without a central true and actual foundation for spatial details, Ingrid experienced frustration with much time and effort spent having to negotiate and re-negotiate details with various stakeholders. One stakeholder's change of decision could have flow on consequences for many other stakeholder functions, presenting many planning and functional challenges, some of which became challenging to rectify as the event date approached.

After Ingrid's GC2018 experiences, she had a chance meeting with Karen Sanders, founder of the company Real Serious Games (RSG), specialising in VR and related technologies in settings of engineering, infrastructure and large capital works projects. Ingrid and Karen recognised the potential to translate RSG's technologies in VR to event planning, design, training and operations to deliver innovative, effective and efficient solutions to the kinds of challenges Ingrid had experienced first-hand in the build-up to GC2018. In response to the realities of event management experienced first-hand by Ingrid, BE uses state-of-the-art VR technologies to create true and actual event maps, designs and simulated physical event spaces to enable event planning and management. This technology has broad applicability for major events, stadiums, arenas and organisations in the event industry.

BE creates realistic, interactive and multi-functional virtual worlds allowing for a clear vision of how the event is to be designed and delivered, for efficient procurement scope and for effective workforce training to be developed from a central source of truth. BE technology allows event organisers and organisations to focus on continual improvement and innovation while saving time and money and ensuring efficient use of resources.

Building a VR Application for Event Planning and Management

BE's technological partner, RSG was founded by Karen Saunders and Andrew Goldson in Australia in 2009. This is an important element of BE, as RSG brings technical expertise and practical wisdom refined over the last decade. RSG was the first company in Australia to deliver a commercial VR based application with Tunnel Boring Machine Training for multi-national construction company John Holland. RSG takes pride in their history with VR technology, and below we identify some of the key considerations and characteristics they bring to their VR work collated via iterative discussions with BE and RSG representatives. These include: 1) Fundamentals of functional VR; 2) Core values; and 3) The unique factor – RSG's commitment to return-on-investment (ROI) maximisation.

Fundamentals of Functional VR

For a VR experience to be useful and functional, it must go through an iterative process, needing a range of inputs and considerable time and effort from a diverse team of specialists. For instance, a non-exhaustive list of individuals involved in VR design will include game designers, writers, subject matters experts, engineers, full stack developers, and 3D modellers.

Usually, VR companies do not have in-house subject matter experts (e.g., event professionals), which means it is critical for every team member to research a client's project in-depth and to be able to understand assumptions in the client's work and their operations, as well as the assumptions clients bring to VR. This in-depth engagement by the VR team with the client's concept and context assists with arriving at a point where the VR design team know how they can help the client, and assist with managing the expectations of the client. In line with these discussions between the VR team and the client, language and concepts are constantly being translated from practice to technical, and from the physical and to the virtual. Lots of hard thinking and discussion goes into determining what the most effective interface will be to transition across these various considerations. These processes provide an important foundation to ensuring the VR product and experience that is designed will be fit for purpose and a worthwhile investment for the client over the long-term.

Ongoing and purposeful communication throughout the design process is critical in achieving an effective result. This is underpinned by the ongoing involvement of the client, but also managing the involvement of key members of the VR team who will come in at certain points of the design process. RSG use a concept they call *white boxing* to assist with the communication and design process. White boxing entails the art team setting up a 360-degree play area which is informed by the initial pieces of information provided to them early in the design process. This provides a basis for the client and members of the VR team to talk about any assumptions identified and determine subsequent information needs, design features and ways forward. This is one of the first steps in what is a very iterative process.

Core Values of Better Events and Real Serious Games

There are two core values that inform the approach to VR by BE and RSG. First is the core value of *designing for purpose*, ensuring the final product and experience meets the client's desired objectives and outcomes. In delivering on this core value, BE and RSG follow an outcomes-based approach that includes understanding the scope, budget and desirables of a client's given project. This is usually achieved via workshops which are designed to arrive at an understanding of what a minimum viable product (MVP) looks like. RSG strives to build a VR experience which is useful for a client and will work with clients to ensure they are equipped with required knowledge and skills to manage technological change in their workplaces and benefit from the introduction of cutting-edge solutions.

A second core value is *accuracy*, that is, striving for the VR experience to mimic, or replicate, the physical world as much as possible to allow the user seamless transition between the physical and VR worlds. Accuracy is important because it determines the extent to which the user recognises, understands and engages with the virtual space, and can therefore translate their learnings in the VR world back in their real and physical world. A lack of accuracy can mean the user experiences distractions while in the virtual world, which limits their engagement and learning experience. When everything is built to scale and looks like it would in the real world, it reduces the gap between the real world and the virtual world. Similarly, when the mechanics of a VR experience behave and respond as they would in the real world (aligned with notions of *realism* in the arts and development setting) the reality of a VR experience is enhanced, and engagement and learning outcomes will be better.

The Unique Factor – Commitment to ROI Maximisation

Established in 2009, the RSG team have refined their approach to VR over a number of projects and years, and these experiences and insights underpin the company's commitment to develop VR products and experiences that provide strong business cases and return on investment for their clients. The RSG team are very aware that for a non-technical person, VR might just be considered as another piece of software. However, the potential of this software for commercial applications bring greater challenges than other technologies. RSG developers approach VR development as more than just creating content, instead, the team are focused on the creation of content that has real value and lessons that can be translated into the real world. For these reasons, RSG has spent years working to come up with a process that allows them to incorporate elements of neuroscience, specialised content and gaming expertise to create visually powerful tools that enhance knowledge acquisition and memory retention.

RSG also work continuously with clients throughout a design process to give them the best, not necessarily the most expensive solution on the market. RSG also strives to design VR products to integrate with existing resources and materials clients may have to enhance their resources. For instance, in the context of training, RSG will design VR products that integrate with existing videos, teaching notes, etc.

Opportunities of VR for Event Management

Drawing on the case study outlined above, we now focus on three key opportunities of VR for event planning and management, including: 1) enabling shared visions by event managers and stakeholders; 2) encouraging collaboration between stakeholders and efficient use of resources; and 3) equipping an event workforce with realistic training environments. We explore each of these opportunities below.

Enabling Shared Visions

Most event management and planning texts refer to the multiple stakeholders and network structures that surround events (Getz & Page, 2020). The stakeholder and inter-organisational interactions are complicated by stakeholders working across multiple sectors, having different specialisations and ways of working, and often representing more than one role or interest throughout the event lifecycle (Parent, 2008). Event scholars have highlighted the importance of developing shared visions among the various stakeholders to secure the success of an event and its legacies (Chalip, Green, Taks, & Misener, 2017).

From a theoretical perspective, the importance of knowledge transfer and sharing across networks of event stakeholders to encourage collaborative and shared visions has been acknowledged (Mallen, 2008), as well as ensuring effectiveness, efficiency and innovation in event planning and management. Mallen (2008, p.19) proposed a definition for *Event Management Knowledge* as: 'The synergy of common knowledge and advancement knowledge that leads to perspicacity (quick insights and understandings) for competence (in actions and ability).' However, there has been limited examination of the concepts and exercises of encouraging and achieving shared visions in the complex environment of event planning and management, even though achieving such shared visions has been found by many as being critical to event success.

From a practical perspective, our case study highlights the critical need for event partners to establish prerequisite knowledge in terms of event spaces and event design. This information is needed by all stakeholders to inform the planning for their component parts of event overlays and servicing. Such a process is extremely complex given the multiplicity of details that need to come together in a context such as Ingrid found herself working in for GC2018. For instance, when working in public spaces, the information needed by stakeholders includes such elements as the spatial dimensions, weight bearing loads, permissible uses of the space, access points and traffic control requirements.

In addition to such variables, there may also be issues of land tenure, who owns or manages different parts of public space, and what different considerations might come into play as a result. An example of this might be the local council owning a public park, a local school owning the adjacent playing fields and amenities block, a state or provincial government owning an adjacent nature reserve, as well as being responsible for the roadway which provides access to this potential event site. Each of these landowners will have laws or guidelines which govern the use of their land. Therefore, an event manager may have to abide by multiple requirements across the various sub-precincts within a potential event site. The event manager will then need to pass this information on to each of the stakeholders contributing to the staging of the event to ensure they are all compliant with the various land use requirements. The sharing of this information can take time and runs the risk of misinformation and/or misinterpretation, which can impact on event planning and management, as well as the end-user experiences of an event.

Ingrid and her team at BE have identified valuable, strategic opportunities to use VR technology to compile these various spatial and contextual details into a 'virtual' and 3D event site which would provide an accurate and comprehensive foundation for collaboration between stakeholders. Stakeholders can then access the simulated event site through an immersive experience and get to see and explore spaces in greater depth and familiarity than permitted by typical 2D planning. The VR simulation can be accessed in real time, and remotely, with the ability to simulate various conditions and configurations. Stakeholders can view the VR simulation either through technologies such as VR headsets, or even as simply as viewing remotely on their PC. By using VR in this way, event planners and managers are better positioned to communicate consistent messaging of event sites and associated overlay design and operational requirements, enabling Mallen's (2008) notion of 'perspicacity' by stakeholders translating event information to their individual planning activities. Another added benefit is that VR technology allows for the translation of data across different languages, making information accessible in cross-cultural contexts, particularly relevant to international events.

Encouraging Collaboration and Use of Resources

In addition to establishing shared visions, as discussed above, it is imperative that event networks can maintain effective collaborations and efficient use of resources throughout the event planning process to ensure successful event delivery. While the nature of events requires collaboration between stakeholders, there are at various times a range of inhibitors to collaborative interactions across the network of event stakeholders (Getz, Anderssen, & Larson, 2007). To date, there has been limited empirical research into technologies that can improve the way stakeholders work together and the benefit this might hold for the events sector.

From a practical perspective, some of the inhibitors to collaboration can include blockages in the flow of information between key stakeholders which can arise for a multitude of reasons. In Ingrid's experience of GC2018, the key stakeholders for her out-of-venue work came together from multiple backgrounds with varied interests, objectives and priorities in relation to the event. In essence, they brought a mix of approaches and working styles to the event setting meaning that before they could get to their productive planning for the event, the stakeholders needed to come to a common understanding about terminology being used, about how the event was planned and mapped, and about the technologies used by each of the stakeholders. Establishing a working relationship across diverse stakeholders takes time and the different working styles can impact on communication in terms of what is disseminated and how this is interpreted, and then what is done about it. At the same time, decision making and revisions to decisions are made at a rapid pace in the setting of event planning and management. Decisions made in terms of one stakeholder can have iterative effects across stakeholders. This can lead to complex situations where it can be difficult to keep track of the current and revised status of decisions and plans and ensuring that all relevant stakeholders are aware of these updates and the implications for their discrete contributions.

Designing, planning and managing with VR technology can assist collaborative processes and resource efficiencies in several ways. Firstly, establishing a central and accurate platform of relevant information, which all stakeholders can access, provides consistency and visibility across all stakeholders. This means decisions can be made quicker as all information is at the ready, and as changes are made, the platform can reflect these changes in real time. This is much more efficient than typical approaches whereby each stakeholder will run their own planning systems and software that do not interact with other systems or update automatically, running a risk of overlooking emergent details in the planning process. Second, VR provides the opportunity to support scenario testing and undertake readiness exercises and simulations prior to event environments being physically constructed. Event managers can bring stakeholders into an immersive VR setting where they can work through and test operational scenarios within a real-life environment. Stakeholders can work together in this virtual space to identify, monitor and assess operational issues and high-risk areas that can then be redesigned, allowing for a mitigation plan to be implemented prior to build. These redesigns can be applied within the VR asset, which is then updated in real time, so stakeholders have access to current versions of planning.

This real-time functionality of VR provides important advantages in terms of procurement, which has been explored previously in the construction industries (Chowdhury, Adafin, & Wilkinson, 2019;

Nicoletti, 2018). With every component in the VR program assigned a unique identifier, event managers and stakeholders can keep their procurement requirements up to date with the latest plans to ensure accuracy and avoid issues with over or under-ordering of relevant equipment and goods. Estimations for event workforce requirements (e.g., volunteers and security) can also be assisted with event site planning in VR. These advantages in procurement have flow on implications for managing an event's bottom line, with the added benefit of preparing budget forecasts and predictions with more realistic figures.

By making such information available through VR applications such as described here, event planning and management information becomes democratised across stakeholders and is accessible anywhere if stakeholders have access to basic computer devices (Buhalis, 2019). In line with Mallen's (2008) notion of *Event Management Knowledge*, this application of VR contributes to stakeholder 'competence' whereby they can deliver on their discrete components but are also well positioned to provide incremental feedback and communicate with other stakeholders in a dynamic fashion. This represents a significant advancement from more traditional methods where stakeholders may only interact in person during 'bump-in' and 'bump-out' periods immediately around an event, meaning very limited opportunities pre-event to test scenarios and implement mitigations if required.

Equipping an Event Workforce With Realistic Training Environments

Across all types and scales of events, the competence and confidence of an event's workforce, including paid staff and volunteers, is critical to the delivery of successful events (Getz & Page, 2020) and securing volunteer legacies from events (Benson, Dickson, Terwiel, & Blackman, 2014). Events pose unique challenges from a human resources perspective, with a diversity of roles, a range of contracted staff and volunteers, and a broad array of motivations involved (Muskat & Mair, 2019). Further factors adding to the challenge include the predominantly short-term project nature of much of the work, the pulsating nature of the event organisation, the pace of work and the high expectations of the end user (Muskat & Mair, 2019). While there is often much discussion of the potential for events to upskill host workforces and to leave volunteer legacies, there remains limited understanding of the procedural requirements which underpin the securing of such outcomes (Benson et al., 2014; Muskat & Mair, 2019).

Event scholars have suggested that event managers could structure volunteer training to better foster social interactions amongst volunteers so they experience greater satisfaction through their volunteer experiences, enhance commitment to the event and build confidence to perform tasks (Costa, Chalip, Green, & Simes, 2006). Others have suggested the need for volunteer training to better reflect real-life scenarios to ensure competence and confidence (Leigh, Lamont, & Cairncross, 2013). However, the unique short-term nature of events, combined with the increasing likelihood that event volunteers come from non-host regions (Chen, Zheng, & Dickson, 2018), present challenges to calls for bigger and better workforce training, such as the cost and logistics of delivering such training programs (Leigh et al., 2013). For instance, the GC2018 volunteer workforce consisted of 15,000 people, selected from an applicant pool of 40,000. Of the 15,000 contingents, only about 4,000 of those, or just under a third, were host city residents (City of Gold Coast, 2019). Most of the volunteer workforce were intra- or inter-state, or international visitors to the host city. This means bringing together these volunteers for extra sessions of traditional modes of face-to-face training would probably not have been feasible given the cost to both the event organising committee to stage trainings and the cost to the volunteer workforce to travel and attend the trainings.

From a practical perspective, our case study provides a viable solution to meet objectives of event managers, and in meeting needs and wants of event workforces in relation to workforce training. As an extension to using VR to build an event site, as described above, this 'asset' can also be adapted and utilised for event-related training, thus providing the event workforce with access to the 3D simulated environment for training exercises and simulations representing ROI for events and their VR technologies. The training asset could be set up to run training as a facilitated session and/or self-guided sessions. There are also opportunities to capture data in VR, meaning opportunities for participant assessment and result summaries while participants are in the VR simulation. Importantly, participants can join these sessions remotely. These options of training formats mean a much less costly exercise for both the event organising committee and event volunteers, and event workforces can be immersed in their practical environments much earlier than afforded by bricks and mortar event venues.

This option also addresses other considerations such as when site-specific training might be inhibited due to timelines of venue builds or bump-in of temporary overlays. This is particularly useful for training and familiarity of security staffers, who typically do not have an opportunity to orientate themselves with a venue until first shift deployment. Prior to this their only knowledge of the venue and their role is typically based on PowerPoint training sessions and 2D artistic imagery that might be available to include in the presentation. VR training in the lead up to an event is likely to improve the capacity of security staff to do their job effectively, as well as provide a safer environment for event attendees.

Training event workforces in the VR environment provides opportunities to address several suggestions in the academic literature for the enhancement of event workforce and event volunteer training and preparation. A VR setting allows for increased practical experience by immersing people in a simulated and realistic environment. There are also opportunities to run specific team training in a venue providing event staff and volunteers opportunities to interact and build familiarity with each other in the virtual environment, meaning social ties are established before arrival in the host city or event site.

In addition, studies from areas such as medical training and disaster response indicate students who have used VR simulations in training are able to take on more information during learning and are more likely to remember what they learned over a longer period, compared to students in traditional educational modes (Feng, González, Amor, Lovreglio, & Cabrera-Guerrero, 2018). These benefits in learning provided by VR simulations are particularly valuable in event settings with high-risk, high-stress and highly skilled components, and with multi stakeholder groups and temporary infrastructure builds/venues.

Challenges of VR for Event Management

Having considered the opportunities for VR, next we focus on two key challenges presented by VR for event planning and management, including: 1) a new way of operating; and 2) perceptions of cost and accessibility. We explore each of these challenges below.

A New Way of Operating

Technology has an increasing influence on the strategy and competitiveness of events (Emery, 2010). For the event sector to experience the full advantages presented by contemporary and emerging technologies, such as VR, event managers require paradigm shifts in how they approach their planning and management as well as a redesign of operational practices to benefit from technological advances (Buhalis, 2019). While the increasing importance of technology in the event sector has been acknowledged

(Emery, 2010), there has been limited research that considers the adoption of technologies in event management. Research into adoption of technology generally suggests organisations face challenges with privacy issues, the potential for inadequate or inappropriate systems and subsequent inefficiencies, and particularly pertinent to the event context, the elimination of the human touch (Townsend, 2017). We anticipate event managers are likely to experience challenges in the adoption and integration of technology both strategically and in the workforce similarly to these other sectors.

From a practical perspective, Ingrid's interactions thus far with event professionals have demonstrated some of the challenges to adopting new technologies and a degree of inertia in adopting new ways of operating. These responses may be justified at the individual level in terms of the pace of event management and inability to dedicate time to learning and integrating new technologies. In addition, the nature of event management means the event manager also needs to engage relevant stakeholders in the learning and adoption of the technology as well. Thus, challenges may well exist at both the intra- and inter- organisational levels, and in many cases, it makes complete sense that event managers will tend to focus on event delivery, and consider an exercise in adopting new technology a distraction from the main goal.

Ingrid has also reflected that in many cases where she has been able to demonstrate the VR technology to event professionals, their experiences have been generative, that is, once they have seen the technology and what is possible, they quite often think of further transferable applications in their work. However, given current levels of awareness and acceptance of VR across the event sector, Ingrid is very conscious of the difficulties for event managers and relevant stakeholders in contemplating the opportunities and advantages of VR until they have experienced the technology first-hand. From another perspective, Ingrid also anticipates that once event professionals have a greater understanding of the various applications of VR, the broad potentialities can then be quite overwhelming. This poses another challenge about learning the best way to engage with and roll out VR technologies so it provides return on investment, while simultaneously knowing where to draw the line with the technology.

Recent research suggests that large-scale events provide opportunities to introduce advanced technology and can leave a legacy of innovation and capacity for the event sector (Girgin & Tasci, 2019). Given the logistical challenges presented to a host city, it may be that large-scale events are more likely to seek innovation and new solutions to problems, rather than reverting to old ways of doing things. If we can provide more VR touchpoints for the event sector to experience the technology, this will go a long way to raising awareness of potential and realising advantages for the event sector and stakeholders.

Perceptions of Cost and Accessibility

Another challenge to the adoption of VR is perceptions of cost and accessibility of the technology. Research in health found concerns over the cost of new technologies in terms of the initial implementation, as well as additional and ongoing expenses such as personnel with the expertise to interpret and train other users, the hardware and software, ongoing upgrades, and maintenance (DePhillips, 2007). Research in environment found there can also be concerns over the ongoing use of new technology and if there are the funds and demand to continue its maintenance (Schaeffer, 2013). There has also been limited investigation of this challenge specific to the event management setting, however, this research in the areas of health and environment helps us understand the potential for this challenge to occur in the event setting.

In practical terms, Ingrid reflected that the majority of her discussions with event professionals have raised the issue of costs, with many assuming that VR technology will be beyond the modest budgets available to them for investment in hardware and software, as well as upskilling their workforce to use systems effectively. However, recent advancements mean that VR technology is not as costly as people may think (Gradinaru, Moldoveanu, & Moldoveanu, 2018), and - once designed - can be accessed on PCs which are now a standard hardware in most workplaces. Ingrid also outlines that VR solutions can be built to suit both purpose and budget, making it feasible for a range of event management operators.

The efficiencies and advantages gained through the adoption and integration of VR technology, such as described in this chapter for planning and management of logistics and event workforce training, mean returns on investment are seen by event managers very quickly. VR technology becomes an asset to the organisation. It can be used for a range of purposes for the one event, for instance as we have detailed in the chapter thus far in terms of planning for logistics, and then repurposing for event workforce training, amongst others. With subsequent re-designs, the same technology can be used for a different event altogether. In addition, the scalability of VR training enabling mass participant training either in real time or remotely presents a case worthy of comparison with traditional modes of event workforce training, particularly with the advantages of improved experience and workforce performance, as we have described in this chapter.

SOLUTIONS AND RECOMMENDATIONS

Implications for Event Practice and Education

Based on what we have outlined and discussed in our case study of VR for event planning and management and the opportunities and challenges of application, several implications for event practice and event education into the future are apparent and discussed below.

Implications for Event Practitioners

We focus on three main implications for event practitioners, including: 1) improving event management work; 2) enhancing event volunteer performance and experience; and 3) acquiring VR competencies.

Improving Event Management Work

The opportunities of VR for event planning and management that we identified earlier in the chapter go some way to alleviate common inefficiencies and stressors in the event management professions, and thus have the potential to contribute to improved job satisfaction and retention of event managers in the sector over the longer term. Being able to bring stakeholders and event workforces on board with the event vision by providing an opportunity to see and 'feel' an event site through an immersive VR experience has the potential to achieve substantial efficiencies of time and effort by event managers. In addition, having a central repository of information to inform planning, procurement and budget offers opportunities to save time, duplication of efforts, the potential for human error and a range of cost savings. Further, the increased opportunity for real-time engagement and up-to-date and correct communications between stakeholders can significantly enhance collaboration throughout the event planning and management process. It also brings the potential to reduce substantial workload in engagement and liaison for event managers.

Another factor worthy of consideration in this context is burnout. The fast-paced and high-profile nature of event planning and management, combined with the challenges and uncertainties of working with multiple stakeholders and planning and delivery partners, places event management professionals at increased levels of burnout compared to other professions (Chan, 2015; Morarji, V L N G Sharma, & Professor, 2015). There has been limited investigation of the 'event practitioner experience', but the potential for increased application of technology in the event sector has been identified as one way to reduce likelihood of burnout among event management graduates (Clark, Dimanche, Cotter, & Lee-Rosen, 2017).

Enhancing Event Volunteer Performance and Experience

As we outlined earlier in the chapter, there are rich opportunities for the application of VR for event workforces, particularly for event volunteers. In the case of many large-scale events, pre-event training sessions will be based on PowerPoint training sessions and 2D imagery that might be available for inclusion or based on artists' interpretations. Sometimes training will include venue tours prior to a first shift, and depending on the event, this could be the day of the first shift.

The use of VR for event volunteer training could be revolutionary both in terms of training processes and the impacts of such training. VR training has the potential to offer immersive experiences in the event setting, meaning higher quality and more realistic training environments which lead to improved knowledge retention and greater confidence and competence among trainees based on virtual familiarity with a worksite. There are also the benefits we outlined earlier including accessibility, that training can be conducted remotely, providing event managers the opportunity to rethink their current training provisions entirely, or to offer mixed modes of face-to-face and VR. For instance, VR experiences could provide an effective option for venue or task-specific trainings that may become too costly to deliver face-to-face across a volunteer workforce of several thousand.

The ability to capture data through aspects such as eye-tracking, engagement with assets in the virtual setting and built-in functionality such as quizzes, presents an unprecedented increase in sophistication for event volunteer training and management. In addition, the scenario testing we discussed in relation to event planning is also applicable for volunteers, providing opportunities to test risks and emergency procedures in a real-life setting.

Given that a large part of volunteer satisfaction has been found to be influenced by training experiences and perceptions of job-readiness (Costa et al., 2006; Leigh et al., 2013), these advantages of VR offer an important opportunity to enhance event volunteer performance as well as volunteer experiences. To achieve these outcomes, event managers will require capacities to consider how to integrate the technology into an event program, how to secure buy-in from across the organisations (i.e., VR is likely to be viable for volunteer training if it is already in place for event planning and management), and have training in how to adapt and operate systems for use in their events.

Acquiring VR Competencies

To experience the opportunities and benefits we have discussed so far in this chapter, event managers will need not only the skills to utilise VR technologies, but also an awareness of the potential applications of VR, now and into the future. This requires an investment of time and resources by event management professionals to familiarise and upskill in VR and other technologies. As with any advancement in technology, these initial stages of investment can seem daunting, however, they are necessary to be able to achieve the economies of scale into the future. An initial step towards VR competencies might include engaging with firms such as BE to consult or partner on event projects. As event education engages more with digital technologies, there are likely to be more opportunities for professional development by event managers in digital technologies to assist practitioners in identifying further potential for application and efficiencies.

Implications for Event Education

We next focus on three main implications for event education, including: 1) skilling students to work with VR in the workplace; 2) immersing students in real-life scenarios; and 3) ongoing professional development in VR for event managers.

Skilling Students to Work With VR in the Workplace

The balance of scholarly and practical skills that event students should graduate with has been an ongoing area of discussion for some time (Bladen & Kennell, 2014; Junek, Lockstone, & Mair, 2009). Recent research suggests that while event management graduates feel academically prepared for their event management careers, many feel they lack practical skills required when they enter industry (Barron & Ali-Knight, 2017). The case study we have presented here indicates that VR offers huge potential for application in event management, and we know it is important for students to be trained in technologies that are relevant to their careers (Clark et al., 2017; Lee, Shin, & Jeong, 2019). In preparing this article, we found only limited reference to VR in event management scholarship, and the authors hypothesise that this may also be indicative of a limited presence of VR in contemporary event management curriculum.

Given the potential of VR to revolutionise event management, it is crucial that that universities and educational institutions do more than merely acknowledge VR as one of many emergent technologies. Instead, event management qualifications need to incorporate specific units on what VR is and how it can be applied, with case studies on promising practice in the field. Peltz, Junek & de Ross (2018) provide a comprehensive overview of ways that VR can improve festival and event management education, across discrete areas including: 1) event marketing and promotion; 2) venue selection; 3) event concept development; 4) induction and training of staff; 5) sponsorship acquisition and management; and 6) risk management. Innovation in curriculum developments can be supported by further research, we elaborate this point below regarding future research directions. Related to these implications is the need for greater collaboration between academics and industry practitioners (Arcodia, 2009), such as that which led to the writing of this book chapter.

Of course, integrating any new technology into a curriculum requires educators to have abilities in using and teaching the technology, as well as facilitating learning within a VR environment. Most of the scholarly material on VR in education settings appears committed to showing the efficacy of VR in education settings, and there is a dearth of research that considers the perspectives of the educators. This means that while the idea to teach in VR might excite, there is a further big step to be taken to advance the idea and engage and deliver on it. O'Connor and Domingo (2017) supply a comprehensive collection of ideas and resources for educators who want to take the VR journey. We also emphasise the opportunities for educators to collaborate with event and VR specialists in the design and delivery of VR education experiences as a way of overcoming barriers to entry.

Immersing Students in Real-Life Scenarios

There is potential for the event education environment to engage with VR to deliver immersive experiences for students across a range of event applications (Peltz, Junek, & De Ross, 2018). This means students not only develop awareness of possibilities (as discussed above) but also gain experience using the technology integrated into their everyday learning environments. This means students are more likely to go into their careers equipped with knowledge and skills to add value to the event sector. At the individual level, it also means graduates are likely to have competence in using technology to balance the demands of their chosen careers and be less likely to experience burnout, as discussed earlier in the chapter.

The integration of VR technology experiences into event management education also offers potential for the kinds of advantages discussed earlier in terms of event workforce training, including higher satisfaction levels with the learning environment, improved knowledge retention, greater confidence and competence in real-life settings. Given the challenges of the effective facilitation of positive learning in work-integrated learning experiences (Peltz et al., 2018) and the increased propensity for universities and training institutes to offer online and flexible modes of learning, VR simulations seem to provide a logical and accessible complement to traditional modes of teaching and learning.

Ongoing Professional Development in VR for event managers

To be effective in using VR technology, as well as equipping others to use the technology (e.g. event staff and stakeholders), event managers will need to develop capacities themselves in using and teaching others to use the technology (Gradinaru et al., 2018). The event management sector is highly aware of the need for continuing development generally to contribute to the professionalisation and effectiveness of events, as well as the specific need to continue developing skills in digital technologies (Barron & Ali-Knight, 2017). However, there is limited scholarship available to suggest the best ways forward to diffuse technological skills across such a diverse sector. We suggest that in line with curriculum developments outlined above, universities and training institutes should consider partnering with industry specialists to offer professional development opportunities. These could range from general familiarisation sessions through to applied workshops supporting event professionals to think about ways VR might apply to their business and operations, as well as hands-on training sessions in how to best use VR technologies in practice.

FUTURE RESEARCH DIRECTIONS

VR represents an untapped opportunity in the event management sector, with many gaps in our knowledge and understanding of its potential. In compiling information for this book chapter, the authors identified many worthwhile areas for research, and have underscored the following as key priorities to move forward with VR technology in the event management setting. First, there seems to be a broad awareness of the variety of technologies that can play a role or influence event management with many event management texts making reference to ICTs and the importance of knowing more about them and preparing our students to use them in their future careers. There has also been a growth of interest in the influence that technology can have on event experiences by event attendees. However, there has been limited in-depth research carried out in the event management scholarship considering specific technologies, such as VR, and potential roles and influences of these on event professionals across the sector. There is a greater need for future research that seeks to understand the role and use of technology from the event professional's perspective (Emery, 2010). Investigations might look at current and anticipated uses of technology, attitudes towards digital technologies, and factors influencing the adoption of technologies.

Second, there is a need for further research to empirically explore the opportunities of VR for event management that have been identified in this chapter. For instance, case studies investigating the efficacy of VR for collaborative working between event stakeholders may help to uncover better practice while also addressing shortfalls in collaborative event networks. Case studies considering the cost-benefit of VR for workforce and event volunteer training would help with the continual improvement of training, as well as adding to our understanding of how to better manage the variety of human resources in events, contributing to job satisfaction in events. Finally, there is also a need for further research into VR and events education, both from the perspective of learning about VR, as well as learning with VR. Case studies providing accounts of a variety of educators and ways they have effectively worked with VR would be a valuable resource providing a foundation for more educators to embark on the VR journey.

CONCLUSION

This chapter had three main objectives. In relation to our first objective to provide an overview of the extant literature pertaining to VR in events, we suggest that while academics and practitioners are aware of ICTs and their potential application to event planning and management, there has been a limited in-depth engagement with these technologies across the event management sector. Most of the knowledge reflected in event management scholarship considers VR as it relates to event experiences, but there is very little that has been looked at from the perspective of the event professional for the purpose of planning, management and logistics. Event practitioners and academics may benefit from more proactive and transdisciplinary engagement in this area to experience operational benefits and share best practices moving forward.

Our second objective was to examine a case study of a private sector start-up in the Australian setting which is developing VR technologies as an aid in event planning and logistics to inform our understanding of the potential applications of VR for event planning and management. This case study provided a valuable source of information in terms of considering the event professional perspective at a more in-depth level than has been considered previously, including the potential application of VR and how event professionals might go about bringing it to their organisations. The case study helped to demonstrate the potential for holistic integration of VR technology in designing an asset for event managers that can be used in a multi-stakeholder setting, and for multiple functions such as securing shared visions across stakeholders, encouraging collaboration, securing resource efficiencies and equipping an event workforce with training in realistic work environments. The case study also provided insights into the challenges of adoption and the knowledge diffusion and paradigm shifts needed across the sector to fully capitalise on the opportunities of VR for the event sector. We emphasise the need for further transdisciplinary work in the field as a supporting factor for VR innovation in the event sector.

Finally, we provided key implications for event practitioners and educators as we move forward and hopefully see greater engagement and integration of VR in the event management setting. While we compiled this chapter pre-COVID-19, the authors believe that many of these implications have become even more pertinent in a post-COVID-19 operating environment where virtual and remote working has become much more normal than it was previously. For event practitioners, there are benefits to be realised in terms of improving event management work and managing the demanding nature of the event management job. VR also presents advantages for event volunteer experience, performance and satisfaction. However, we also acknowledge that to achieve these two benefits, event professionals need to invest in upskilling themselves to work with the technologies. There are also benefits for event education, on different levels. VR can be used in the learning experience to conduct skill-based activities (e.g. risk assessments), and it can also be used to provide immersive opportunities to learn, experience and test out event training in a simulated but realistic environment. Just like the sector more broadly, there is a need for educators and institutions do engage with the paradigm shift also, building skills to use VR in education design, for both current students, as well as offering professional development opportunities for those already in the profession and needing to upskill over the coming years.

We have outlined that in order to realise the valuable potentialities of VR, our current and future event professionals need to have the skills to best utilise, adapt and integrate VR technologies. These practical skills can be realised through transdisciplinary collaboration between educators, VR specialists and the event management industry. We also identified key areas for future research that will assist in providing an evidence base of best practice to inform practical decision-making, as well as ongoing curriculum development. Increased understanding of event professional's perceptions of the role and use of technology and factors influencing the adoption of technologies will help to identify key areas of focus for future innovation efforts. There is also a need to empirically examine VR opportunities for event management identified in this chapter to contribute to knowledge through critical analysis and help inform business cases for innovation across the event sector.

ACKNOWLEDGMENT

This research received no specific grant from any funding agency in the public, commercial, or not-for-profit sectors.

REFERENCES

Arcodia, C. (2009). Event Management Employment in Australia: A Nationwide Investigation of Labour Trends in Australian Event Management. In T. Baum, M. Deery, & C. Hanlon (Eds.), People and Work in Events and Conventions: A Research Perspective. CABI. doi:10.1079/9781845934767.0017

Backman, K. F. (2018). Event management research: The focus today and in the future. *Tourism Management Perspectives*, *25*, 169–171. doi:10.1016/j.tmp.2017.12.004

Barron, P., & Ali-Knight, J. (2017). Aspirations and progression of event management graduates: A study of career development. *Journal of Hospitality and Tourism Management*, *30*, 29–38. doi:10.1016/j.jhtm.2017.01.005

Beck, J., Rainoldi, M., & Egger, R. (2019). Virtual reality in tourism: A state-of-the-art review. *Tourism Review*, *74*(3), 586–612. doi:10.1108/TR-03-2017-0049

Benson, A. M., Dickson, T. J., Terwiel, F. A., & Blackman, D. A. (2014). Training of Vancouver 2010 volunteers: A legacy opportunity? *Contemporary Social Science*, *9*(2), 210–226. doi:10.1080/21582041.2013.838296

Bladen, C., & Kennell, J. (2014). Educating the 21st century event management graduate: Pedagogy, practice, professionalism, and professionalization. *Event Management*, *18*(1), 5–14. doi:10.3727/152599514X13883555341724

Brown, A. E., Donne, K., Fallon, P., & Sharpley, R. (2019). From headliners to hangovers: Digital media communication in the British rock music festival experience. *Tourist Studies*. Advance online publication. doi:10.1177/1468797619885954

Buhalis, D. (2019). Technology in tourism-from information communication technologies to eTourism and smart tourism towards ambient intelligence tourism: A perspective article. *Tourism Review*, *75*(1), 267–272. Advance online publication. doi:10.1108/TR-06-2019-0258

Buhalis, D., Harwood, T., Bogicevic, V., Viglia, G., Beldona, S., & Hofacker, C. (2019). Technological disruptions in services: Lessons from tourism and hospitality. *Journal of Service Management*, *30*(4), 484–506. doi:10.1108/JOSM-12-2018-0398

Chalip, L., Green, C., Taks, M., & Misener, L. (2017). Creating sport participation from sport events: Making it happen. *International Journal of Sport Policy and Politics*, *9*(2), 257–276. doi:10.1080/19406940.2016.1257496

Chan, G. (2015). Part-Time Event Management Employee Expected Quality of Work Life. *International Journal of Business and Management*, *10*(5). Advance online publication. doi:10.5539/ijbm.v10n5p233

Chen, S., Zheng, J., & Dickson, G. (2018). Volunteering for sports mega events: A non-host region perspective. *Managing Sport and Leisure*, *23*(3), 189–203. doi:10.1080/23750472.2018.1530609

Chowdhury, T., Adafin, J., & Wilkinson, S. (2019). Review of digital technologies to improve productivity of New Zealand construction industry. *Journal of Information Technology in Construction*, *24*(2019VMAR), 569–587. doi:10.36680/j.itcon.2019.032

City of Gold Coast. (2019). *Volunteering Legacy Action Plan*. Retrieved from https://www.goldcoast.qld.gov.au/documents/bf/volunteering-legacy-action-plan.pdf

Clark, H., Dimanche, F., Cotter, R., & Lee-Rosen, D. (2017). Human capital challenges in the events industry of Canada: Finding innovative solutions. *Worldwide Hospitality and Tourism Themes*, *9*(4), 424–432. doi:10.1108/WHATT-04-2017-0018

Costa, C., Chalip, L., Green, C., & Simes, C. (2006). Reconsidering the Role of Training in Event Volunteers' Satisfaction. *Sport Management Review*, *9*(2), 165–182. doi:10.1016/S1441-3523(06)70024-9

DePhillips, H. III. (2007). Initiatives and Barriers to Adopting Health Information Technology. *Disease Management & Health Outcomes*, *15*(1), 1–6. doi:10.2165/00115677-200715010-00001

Dictonary.com. (n.d.). *Definition of Virtual reality*. Retrieved December 15, 2019, from https://www.dictionary.com/browse/virtual-reality

Emery, P. (2010). Past, present, future major sport event management practice: The practitioner perspective. *Sport Management Review*, *13*(2), 158–170. doi:10.1016/j.smr.2009.06.003

Feng, Z., González, V. A., Amor, R., Lovreglio, R., & Cabrera-Guerrero, G. (2018). Immersive virtual reality serious games for evacuation training and research: A systematic literature review. *Computers & Education*, *127*, 252–266. doi:10.1016/j.compedu.2018.09.002

Getz, D., Anderssen, T., & Larson, M. (2007). Festival Stakeholder Roles: Concepts and Case Studies. *Event Management*, *10*(2–3).

Getz, D., & Page, S. (2020). *Event Studies: Theory, Research and Policy for Planned Events* (4th ed.). Routledge.

Girgin, F. A., & Tasci, O. E. (2019). Mega-Event Organization Considering Safety, Security and Resilience. *TeMA - Journal of Land Use. Mobility and Environment*, *12*(3), 249–264. doi:10.6092/1970-9870/6269

Gradinaru, A., Moldoveanu, A., & Moldoveanu, F. (2018). Designing a virtual reality learning management system. *ELearning & Software for Education*, *2*, 11–17. doi:10.12753/2066-026X-18-072

Hoffman-Riem, H., Biber-Klemm, S., Grossenbacher-Mansuy, W., Hirsch Hadorn, G., Joye, D., Pohl, C., Wiesmann, U., & Zemp, E. (2008). Idea of the Handbook. In G. Hirsch Hadorn, H. Hoffman-Riem, S. Biber-Klemm, W. Grossenbacher-Mansuy, D. Joye, C. Pohl, U. Wiesmann, & E. Zemp (Eds.), Handbook of Transdisciplinary Research (pp. 3-18). Bern, Switzerland: Springer.

Junek, O., Lockstone, L., & Mair, J. (2009). Two perspectives on event management employment: Student and employer insights into the skills required to get the job done! *Journal of Hospitality and Tourism Management*, *16*(1), 120–129. doi:10.1375/jhtm.16.1.120

Lee, S., Shin, H. H., & Jeong, M. (2019). Are Students Ready for Their Future Career in the Event and Meeting Industry? Lessons from a Comparative Study between Students and Event and Meeting Professionals. *Journal of Hospitality & Tourism Education*, 1–11. doi:10.1080/10963758.2019.1654886

Leigh, J., Lamont, M., & Cairncross, G. (2013). Towards a Process Model of Induction and Training for Young Event Volunteers. *International Journal of Event Management Research*, *8*(1), 1–20. www.ijemr.org

Lockstone-Binny, L., & Ong, F. (2019). Event studies: Progression and future in the field. In S. Beeton & A. Morrison (Eds.), *The Study of Food, Tourism, Hospitality and Events* (pp. 37–46). Springer. doi:10.1007/978-981-13-0638-9_4

Mair, J., & Weber, K. (2019). Editorial Event and festival research: A review and research directions. *International Journal of Event and Festival Management*, *10*(3), 209–216. doi:10.1108/IJEFM-10-2019-080

Mallen, C. (2008). The concept of knowledge in event management. In C. Mallen & L. Adams (Eds.), Sport, Recreation and Tourism Event Management (pp. 9–24). Butterworth-Heinemann. doi:10.1016/B978-0-7506-8447-7.00002-X

Morarji, B., & Sharma, V. N. (2015). A study on job stress in event management organizations with reference to Thrissur District, Kerala. *International Journal of Advanced Research*, *7*(4), 51–58.

Muskat, B., & Mair, J. (2019). Knowledge Sharing and Power in the Event Workforce. *Event Management*. Advance online publication. doi:10.3727/152599519X15506259856228

Nicoletti, B. (2018). The Future: Procurement 4.0. In Agile Procurement (pp. 189–230). doi:10.1007/978-3-319-61085-6_8

O'Connor, E., & Domingo, J. (2017). A Practical Guide, With Theoretical Underpinnings, for Creating Effective Virtual Reality Learning Environments. *Journal of Educational Technology Systems*, *45*(3), 343–364. doi:10.1177/0047239516673361

Parent, M. (2008). Evolution and Issue Patterns for Major-Sport-Event Organizing Committees and Their Stakeholders. *Journal of Sport Management*, *22*(2), 135–164. doi:10.1123/jsm.22.2.135

Peltz, P., Junek, O., & De Ross, J. (2018). Virtual Reality: The white knight of festival management education? In J. Mair (Ed.), *The Routledge Handbook of Festivals* (pp. 397–405). Routledge.

Robertson, M., Hutton, A., & Brown, S. (2018). Event design in outdoor music festival audience behavior (A critical transformative research note). *Event Management*, *22*(6), 1073–1081. doi:10.3727/152599518X15346132863157

Robertson, M., Yeoman, I., Smith, K. A., & Mcmahon-Beattie, U. (2015). Technology, society, and visioning the future of music festivals. *Event Management*, *19*(4), 567–587. doi:10.3727/152599515X14465748774001

Schikowitz, A. (2020). Creating relevant knowledge in transdisciplinary research projects – Coping with inherent tensions. *Journal of Responsible Innovation, 7*(2), 217-237.

Van Winkle, C., Bueddefeld, J., Halpenny, E., & MacKay, K. (2019). The unified theory of acceptance and use of technology 2: Understanding mobile device use at festivals. *Leisure Studies*, *38*(5), 634–650. doi:10.1080/02614367.2019.1618895

ADDITIONAL READING

Fuchs, P. (2017). Concepts of virtual reality. In P. Fuchs (Ed.), *Virtual Reality Headsets – A Theoretical and Pragmatic Approach* (pp. 9–21). CRC Press. doi:10.1201/9781315208244-3

O'Connor, E., & Domingo, J. (2017). A Practical Guide, With Theoretical Underpinnings, for Creating Effective Virtual Reality Learning Environments. *Journal of Educational Technology Systems*, *45*(3), 343–364. doi:10.1177/0047239516673361

Peltz, P., Junek, O., & De Ross, J. (2018). Virtual Reality: The white knight of festival management education? In J. Mair (Ed.), *The Routledge Handbook of Festivals* (pp. 397–405). Routledge.

KEY TERMS AND DEFINITIONS

Asset: The various components that constitute the VR experience. For instance, an individual brick in a virtual building is an asset, the building itself is an asset, and the overall virtual product is also referred to as an asset.

Effective Collaboration: Positive communication exchanges and working patterns between multiple stakeholders resulting in processes and outcomes of greater value than the efforts of stakeholders working individually. Characterised by open communication channels, limited tensions and mistakes, and maximisation of return on investment.

Event Education and Training: The institutional dissemination of knowledge and skills for event management students and professionals to support learning and development event practitioners.

Event Planning and Management: The range of tasks that go into the creative and logistical exercises of coordinating a range of activities in order to stage a one-off event.

Graduate Skills: The practical outcomes secured by event management students throughout their formal education.

Professional Development: Formal and informal methods to continue the acquisition of professional knowledge post-qualification.

Subject Matter Experts: People who have intimate knowledge, technical understanding and insight into a specific topic or area of interest. Specific to our chapter context, a subject matter expert might include an event manager, venue manager, stage performer, etc.

Virtual Reality: The mimicking of a real world setting in technology, which provides opportunities to immerse and/or interact in a virtual world in a realistic way.

Chapter 12
Artificial Intelligence Applications for Event Management and Marketing

Fatma Doğanay Ergen
Isparta University of Applied Sciences, Turkey

ABSTRACT

The current use of artificial intelligence technology in the event industry, its effects on the industry, and future trends are discussed within the scope of this section. The use of artificial intelligence technology that provided by big data draws attention. In the event industry, it is known that robotic applications (telepresence robots, robotic concierge, robot bartenders, robot peacekeepers, robot servers, robot deliveries, and entertainment robots), digital assistants, and chatbots are used within the scope of artificial intelligence technology. It has been determined that artificial intelligence technology offers the stakeholders opportunities to gain competitive advantage, to obtain information that can be used in marketing efforts, to enable digitalization in manual processes, to improve customer interactions, to increase event participation with lower costs, and to create added value with new products and services. It is predicted that this progress will continue in the future and the use of artificial intelligence technology in the event industry will expand.

INTRODUCTION

New technologies and artificial intelligence are a natural and inevitable fact of human development, and it seems that technological changes affect almost every part of our lives. Thanks to advances in communication and computer science, the way and speed of how we do our work have changed, as well as our personal lives. Technological developments are encountered in every field, either individually or institutionally. Therefore, it is necessary to follow these developments closely and to gain the necessary competencies to benefit, to establish the necessary data and information power to use and to conduct research which areas, how to use. Artificial intelligence is the intelligence displayed by machines. Artificial intelligence is an artificial operating system specific to human intelligence that is expected to display

DOI: 10.4018/978-1-7998-4954-4.ch012

higher cognitive functions or autonomous behaviors such as perception, learning, connecting multiple concepts, thinking, reasoning, problem solving, communicating, making inferences and decision making. Artificial intelligence is aimed to enable machines producing solutions to complex problems like humans. Thus, it is expected that artificial intelligence will be beneficial for humanity, save human life, increase productivity and life quality. Today, there are many application areas that have the potential to use artificial intelligence (Uludağ İhracatçı Birlikleri Genel Sekreterliği AR&GE Şubesi, 2017). One of these areas is the event industry. Organizations involved in the realization of events have to innovate in order to compete with their competitors. The use of technology is considered very important to increase the efficiency of events. Many improvements are made to the service, including time efficiency, productivity and efficiency delivery or processes, as a result of the use and application of new technologies. Helping customers make decisions through machine learning, networking opportunities, relevant presentation sessions, and recommendations on products aligned with business interests. Therefore, the interpretation of participant data is provided to improve the event experience. In the future, artificial intelligence technologies will be able to move events away from a dedicated event app and deliver all event content via a social media chatbot. At the same time, the ability of artificial intelligence-supported managers to identify event participants at the entry point and analyze the behavior of participants with seasonal ticket membership will proactively contribute to promotional marketing efforts and customer relations management (Ogle and Lamb, 2019).

There are new developments regarding the use of artificial intelligence technology in the event industry, but when the literature is examined, it seems that there are limited studies on the subject. In this context, it is aimed to contribute to filling this gap in the literature by examining the use of artificial intelligence technology in the event industry. The primary aim of the department is to provide information on the use of artificial intelligence technology in the event industry. In this context, first of all, information about artificial intelligence technology is given. In addition, the artificial intelligence applications used in the event industry and the contribution of these applications to the event stakeholders are among the aims of the section. It is also aimed to provide information about the future trends of artificial intelligence technology in event management and marketing.

BACKGROUNDS

Artificial Intelligence and Events

The first developments in artificial intelligence were experienced when Alan Turing, in an article published in 1950, raised whether machines could think or not. With the Turing Test proposed by Turing, whether a machine is intelligent or not could be distinguished. If a human cannot distinguish between a human or a machine behind an interaction, which means that it is an intelligent machine that can think. On the other hand, John McCarthy, not Alan Turing, is seen as the real name father of artificial intelligence. John McCarthy organized an academic conference on the subject in 1956 (Şener, 2019). The study of McCarthy, Minsky, Rochester, and Shannon (1955) titled "Proposal for the Artificial Intelligence Dartmouth Summer Research Project" is to proceed on the basis of the assumption that every aspect of learning or every feature of intelligence can be precisely explained and a machine can be built to simulate it. It is planned to make an attempt on how machines will use language, how to create abstractions and concepts, how to solve the types of problems that arise for people and how to improve themselves. Today, technology promises to enter our daily lives from research laboratories and help humanity cope with the difficulties they face (International Telecommunication Union, 2019). At the same time, artificial intelligence systems generally need to have the capacity to learn or adapt to new experiences or stimuli. Artificial intelligence is a new form of intelligence that can synthesize several different ideas at the same time (Zsarnoczky, 2017). When the concepts used in artificial intelligence are examined; Algorithm, which is a set of instructions for calculating or solving problems, and is the basis of artificial intelligence systems, the expert system that imitates a person's decision-making ability and is a computer system, a neural network consisting of artificial neurons that are interconnected in nodes and layers that enable data exchange, it is deep learning, a new variation of neural networks that is used to solve more difficult problems, classify information from texts or sounds, by connecting many layers of artificial neurons (Şener, 2019). However, when it comes to artificial intelligence, terms describing modern technologies such as machine learning and data mining are also widely used (Gümüş, 2019). Machine learning refers to the computer science techniques used to give machines the ability to learn without the need for explicit programming (Birer, 2020). Data science is the process of extracting relevant and necessary insights from data. Machine learning is a tool for artificial intelligence to achieve smart machines. In other words, machine learning is a subset of artificial intelligence that focuses on a narrow set of activities, and data science uses machine learning to analyze data and make predictions about the future, although it is not exactly a subset of machine learning. Machine learning combines other disciplines such as big data analytics and cloud computing to solve real-world problems (Gümüş, 2019).

It is predicted that there is a rapid progress in the development of artificial intelligence and this speed will continue progressively. At the same time, artificial intelligence has become an integral part of operations as it provides real value and this trend is expected to continue in the future (Çeltek and İlhan, 2020; International Telecommunication Union, 2019). Today's technological revolution also requires efficiency, sustainability and productivity. The use of artificial intelligence, which can be used in many different areas, is expanding in every sector (Zsarnoczky, 2017). It is seen that one of these areas is the event sector. The event is defined as "to meet certain social or individual needs that occur as a result of people acting together, or to achieve common goals as a group and organization, to share a common feeling or thought, and to be a social entity in social life, etc. events organized for purposes" (Ekin, 2011). Considering the event as a project; Conducting the pre-event, during and post-event processes (project planning, budgeting, whether or not to earn income, earnings of the institution, design, procurement, planning, operation, measurement and evaluation, reporting, etc.) based on strategic principles, in line with the determined targets, in a planned manner " is defined as "Event Management" The main goal in event management is to manage all event processes in a healthy way that will increase the prestige of the institution (Tontuş, 2019). Event marketing is the process of driving the marketing mix to achieve goals through creating value for customers. The organization should adopt a marketing approach that emphasizes mutually beneficial relationships and maintaining competitive advantage (Getz, 1997: 250). Van der Wagen (2005) also mentioned that promotion efforts in event marketing should be designed in a way that guarantees that people will have fun and have a good time (Timur, Çevik and Kıcır, 2014). In this context, artificial intelligence is seen as a powerful tool in strategy (Bethapudi, 2013). With machine learning and artificial intelligence, participants will be dealt with as if they have a personal assistant, and only content selected for them will be shown. Just as services like Netflix and Spotify are constantly improving the way they offer recommendations that fit our tastes perfectly, event apps will be able to do a similar situation (Wilson, 2019).

MAIN FOCUS OF THE CHAPTER

Artificial Intelligence Applications for Event Management and Marketing

Artificial Intelligence Applications

It is seen that artificial intelligence applications are cognitive robotic process applications and managers are working to integrate these applications into their value chains more successfully. In the field of tourism, artificial intelligence applications such as artificial intelligence robots, chatbots, digital assistants and robotic concierge services are used, and the applications enable the development of customer interactions. While robotic process automation applications in the tourism sector, finance, accounting, support functions, etc. provide digitalization in manual processes; artificial intelligence applications come up with chatbots and smart assistants where voice calls are made. The use of artificial intelligence and robotic process technologies in processes such as sales and customer relations that touch the customer make customers feel more special (EY Türkiye, 2019). In the industry, online travel agencies such as Expedia appear to use artificial intelligence applications for customer service, chatbots, a chat tool that automates Booking.com online travel searches, virtual assistants to learn unique preferences, robotic concierge to assist guests during check-in (tuyed.orgt.tr, 20.08.2020). In addition, artificial intelligence and tourism virtual assistants, specially developed for tourism and cultural protection zones, meet the expectations of tourists by increasing visitor satisfaction from the beginning to the end of visits, entertainment, travel, events and similar holiday actions. Thus, people can receive up-to-date information about visiting points such as artifacts, restaurants, services and events belonging to the relevant touristic region or can watch relevant promotional videos and reach any point they want to go within the scope of touristic areas with navigation guidance (Çakır, 2020).

As in the tourism sector, it is seen that artificial intelligence technology is used in event tourism management for similar reasons. Event organisers have important aims such as attracting the attention of the participants and arousing excitement in them. Therefore, it is seen that they try to use the latest technology to keep the interest and excitement alive. At this point, the use of artificial intelligence in event management and marketing draw attention. It is admitted that the best artificial intelligence in the event industry is artificial intelligence that enables customizing customer engagement and improving business processes to increase revenue. Artificial intelligence used in the event industry in 2019 is explained as the technology best used to provide personalized exhibitor experiences that delight event organizers, attendees and sponsors, enhanced by more meaningful interactions. At the same time, event organizers can gain a competitive advantage thanks to the personalized participant experiences (Groot, 2017). For example; Artificial intelligence and event assistants enable users to receive up-to-date information about events, movies and more, or to watch promotional videos on the subject. In addition, it offers people the opportunity to examine the details of weather and traffic conditions, to check the promotions in cafes and stores, and to get information about current campaigns (Çakır, 2020). At the same time, it is seen that artificial intelligence is used as chatbots and robots in exhibitions and events held in museums and is applicable to museums of all capacities in the world effort. Thanks to artificial intelligence, the number of visitors can be estimated, the quota of the museum can be determined accordingly, and the total number of visitors can be increased by preventing the loss of visitors. In addition, with artificial intelligence applications, museums have the opportunity not only to understand visitor behavior but also to improve their museum collections by better understanding visitors. More effective exhibitions can be planned for the visitors by measuring which types of exhibitions visitors interact with the most or which exhibitions they react positively to (Gümüş, 2019). It is seen that one of the most important parts of artificial intelligence in event management is deep learning. Thanks to deep learning, where a reasoning component is added to create new actions based on reasoning, a system in which recording data is interpreted can be used in the event. During the event, one can predict which logistics requirements are required in terms of food, beverage and crowd control in the venue. Although deep learning practice is available today, it requires complex systems that require expertise, so it may take several years for this system to become popular in the event industry (Groot, 2017). However, it is seen that artificial intelligence applications such as big data have an important place in the field because a big data is needed to develop artificial intelligence by realizing learning (tuyed.orgt.tr, 20.08.2020).

Big Data

Nowadays, almost every action such as watching movies, walking, sleeping, driving, talking and writing generates data, thanks to smartphones and internet connected items. The data stacks formed by the collection of these produced data in large data centers are called big data (Birer, 2020). More broadly, it is defined as "data sets that cannot be captured, managed and processed by public computers within an acceptable scope"(Chen, Mao and Liu, 2014; Song and Liu, 2017). The term big data is mainly used to describe massive datasets, compared to traditional datasets, big data often includes unstructured datasets that require more real-time analysis. Big data also brings new opportunities to discover new values and helps us to deeply understand hidden values. On the other hand, new challenges arise, such as how to organize and manage such data sets effectively (Chen, Mao and Liu, 2014). It can be said that this is due to the fact that what is meant by big data is not only volumetric size. There are different sources such as social media posts, blogs, photos, videos and all these data are not only digital, but also voice, text, location (GPS) information, etc. such as many varieties and each can be in various sizes. These data, which are collected in different forms, should be made meaningful and processable. Therefore, the important thing is to obtain meaningful and valuable information from such a large, fast and diverse data collection (Atalay and Çelik, 2017). On the other hand, in order for machine learning, which is one of the most frequently used methods for artificial intelligence, to be effective, a lot of data is needed and it is very difficult to develop artificial intelligence without data (Birer, 2020). Learning from the large amount of data generated to understand human behavior, machine learning algorithms can be developed to customize products and services according to the needs and conditions of each individual. All businesses or organizations with data-driven problems such as customer relationship management and diagnosing problems in complex systems can benefit from the application of analytics with the help of machine learning (Xiang and Fesenmaier, 2017). For example; Today, tourists also use many information and communication technologies before, during and after their travels to improve their overall experience. Therefore, many big data sources that make up the digital footprints of tourists are of great importance in terms of answering questions that cannot be handled with traditional methods such as tourist surveys and second-hand statistical data sources (Li and Yang, 2017). At this point, capturing, managing and processing the data produced by technologies such as artificial intelligence becomes easier than ever (EY Turkey, 2019).

Artificial intelligence and big data are inventively used to include event participants to the event and to provide services beyond their expectations with personalized service (Çeltek and İlhan, 2020). Improved data collection and the ability to analyze the collected data are among the important contributions of artificial intelligence (Arnold, 2019). Big data applications is used for new and competitive products / services, internal operations, personalization of services and pricing strategy development in revenue management (Çeltek and İlhan, 2020). Artificial intelligence helps event planners create valuable events and enhance the experience of attendees and gains insights that can be used for future marketing and engagement efforts. Chatbot interfaces, data analysis tools and recommendation engines can be used to make event planning a much more successful effort. Carried out correctly, these tools can provide very useful insights for event planners and their clients by creating better experiences (Arnold, 2019). With artificial intelligence, it is seen that digital marketers use big data on their potential customers as the driving force behind their marketing campaigns and social media strategies. Artificial intelligence extracts, analyzes and classifies text from places such as e-mail and social media. It turns this extracted and classified information into labels (e.g. price, product, emergency issues, etc.) that marketing teams can add to applications or workflows and collect new insights about their business. Artificial intelligence makes sense of consumer data to improve the participant's journey. Digital marketers can identify trends and tweak as needed to optimize their efforts. Demographic information allows them to create more efficient ads and use customized messages for different audiences. Another area where big data is used is seen in face recognition systems in the security part. When it comes to large events with thousands of visitors, security is very important. It is predicted that artificial intelligence will start to play a bigger role in hosting a safe event. For example; it is thought that a tool such as face recognition may be useful at the point of confirming the identity of the participants during the check-in process. Face recognition is already used as a tool to access smartphones or take a plane. In the events, there are self-check-in booths that can scan and recognize a participant's face and print their badge within a few seconds. In the coming years, it is anticipated that the self-check-in cabin will be used more (Wilson, 2019). Artificial intelligence also gives confidence in terms of data protection. It enables event organizers and sponsors to know which parts of their events are most effective and where they get the best return on their investment, while also protecting the privacy of participants (Groot, 2017).

As a result of the literature examined first in the study of Nilbe, Ahas and Silm (2014) on event visitors; Various models are seen to be used to study the spatial behavior of event visitors, including Global Positioning Systems (GPS) devices, bluetooth tracking (Versichele et al., 2012a, 2012b), and mobile positioning (Ahas et al., 2008). In the study of Nilbe et al. (2014), By analyzing passive mobile positioning data, new information about event visitors is presented in two aspects. Firstly, it was examined whether the distance traveled by foreign visitors visiting the events is different from the travels of regular visitors who come to Estonia but do not visit the events. Second, it was researched whether the distances traveled by event visitors and regular visitors to the attractions are affected by the characteristics of the visits (eg time, duration, previous visits, return and travel to other destinations). Observing and analyzing the experiences of tourists were enabled by the use of passive mobile positioning data. Passive mobile positioning data was used from a comparison group of regular visitors (199,859 visits) and 145 events visitors (119,288 visits) in Estonia between 2006 and 2009. The study showed that event visitors come from closer than regular visitors, and events bring more visitors from more distant countries off-season (winter). In the studies of Garcia, Lansley and Calnan (2017), location data collected from a mobile phone app at a music festival was used as a way to model spatial behavior for consumer analysis. The aim of the study is to collect geo-temporal variables from application data to model when individuals visit food and beverage services in the field. Using Random Forest and Artificial Neural Networks machine learning algorithms, an effective way to simulate the popularity of bar areas in the festival area over time has been presented. The time spent in the festival, the time elapsed since the last visit to the bar, and the distance to the nearest bar, especially as it approached the closing time of the festival, were effective. The popularity of the next artist to be watched shows a slight increase in food purchases of the participants before watching the artist. At the same time, it was determined that there were thin peaks in the visits to the bar after the performances of the big shows and there was a significant decrease at 17:00. The model shows that there are both spatial and temporal elements that can influence an individual's decision to visit bar spaces. This information will help event planners how to allocate their services according to time and place.

While the use of big data is still in its infancy, it is seen that there is a potential growth in applications. It is predicted that big data will be used by airlines, restaurants, accommodation and many related industries in the coming years. Thus, it will be possible to learn a lot about the macro level preferences of the customers and to gain much more benefit with relatively small investments (Song and Liu, 2017).

Robots

Artificial intelligence and robotic process applications are used in the tourism sector to improve customer interactions. It is seen that artificial intelligence and robotic processes provide many benefits to the tourism industry. Providing personalized service by processing the data obtained throughout the experience, providing 24/7 customer service, reducing customer representative effort for frequently asked questions, offering personal pricing and promotions, saving employee effort, increasing the added value of talents, immediate response to seasonal workforce needs and digitalization in manual progressive processes (finance, accounting, support functions, etc.) with robotic process automation applications in the tourism sector (EY Turkey, 2019). Within the scope of event management, it is seen that robots also benefit from artificial intelligence technology. Robots are electromechanical units programmed or controlled by someone, and they perform certain actions and tasks. It is used in many areas, from bartender robots that prepare participants' cocktails during the event, to robots presented as holograms that greet participants at the entrance of the event and provide information to the participants (Novak, 2017).

As the events industry is also intricately linked to catering and customer service, it has adopted many applications that hotels and restaurants have installed and automated many services. For example, applications such as various types of kiosks and information booths are widely used, especially at large events. However, several service applications, such as interactive booth attendants, concierge robots, robot bartenders, robot baristas, robot servers, delivery robots and entertainment robots help make events easier and more practical (Ivanov et al., 2017). For example; At an entertainment at an open-air rock festival in South Africa, participants were able to meet their thirst without queuing. After the participants placed their order using the smartphone app, a drone offered drinks by approaching 15 meters above the festival participants' heads to make delivery. The application was carried out by recording the locations of the participants using GPS satellite chips of their phones (Daily News, 2013). On the other hand, it is seen that artificial intelligence technology is changing the event industry by offering a wide range of products from robotic bartenders to holographic fair hosts. For example; Makr Shakr is a bartender, alcohol consumption monitor and social sharing system in robotic design. Guests submit their cocktail orders through the Makr Shakr app and then watch the three large robotic arms mix the desired combination of liquor, syrup, fruit mixer and ice. The large screen behind the bar also provides various statistics such as the number of drinks in the queue, approximate waiting time, drinks ready to be taken and the most popular alcoholic beverages by gender. In addition, the app allows users to see what kind of drinks others have ordered, rate drinks, and share photos on social networks. On the other hand, it is aimed to encourage responsible consumption by monitoring which drink and how often participants order. Another robotic application used in events is mobile telepresence. Mobile telepresence allows users to attend meetings and events remotely (Sorrels, 2013). Thus, telepresence robots allow virtual audience interaction with the presenter thanks to their remote positioning (Ogle and Lamb, 2019). Created by mounting a tablet on a long, rotating base, users can connect to this device via Skype or any other video conferencing application and control the movement of the device from their desktops. Another similar device is the telepresence robot, which has an integrated display, camera, and speaker positioned about two meters above the ground and on a mobile platform. Users can control and activate the robot using a web-based communication system. These robots can allow an off-site person to interact with visitors at the booth and explore the show area virtually at trade shows (Sorrels, 2013). Telepresence robots are particularly useful at conference-type events where it is not possible to actually be present at the venue. It is predicted that this audio-visual virtual presence will further expand the repertoire of event presentation by providing an enhanced simultaneous remote conference experience and will support live streaming platforms such as virtual reality (Ogle and Lamb, 2019). For example; It is seen that the robot barista, which is a detailed barista-bot system consisting of multiple robotic arms called Bubble Lab, took part in the showroom floors of various international industry events in 2017 (Bryman, 2018). An example of robots used as stand attendants is the use of a 3M holographic virtual server named Jenny at the South by Southwest Interactive Film and Music Festival. "Jenny" is able to perceive passing people and talk to them about panels and events (Briodagh, 2013). On the other hand, robots can provide information about upcoming events such as congresses, conferences or presentations to be held in hotels. With a website hosted by the robot, the staff the event description, meeting room, program, etc. allows them to enter event information. At the same time, thanks to an easy interface used for the staff to change the information content such as the menu of the day, events, meetings and conferences and to plan the event of the robot remotely, it will contribute to both the successful management and marketing of the events (Pinillos et. al, 2016).

It is seen that robots are also used for entertainment purposes in events. Used to greet and entertain consumers, robots are controlled by an invisible staff member who wears sensors that transmit their movements to the robot. The staff also has a microphone to conduct conversations with passersby via a robot (Sorrels, 2013). Another example is the robot named Titan, which is eight meters tall and weighs 770 pounds, built in the UK to promote the Toyota brand's new car model. On the other hand, there are robot cameramen who take photos of the event with a camera programmed to move on a tripod depending on the movements of the participants. Programmed to take photos from the best angle, these robot cameramen can also group photos according to themes and distinguish non-aesthetic photos (Novak, 2017).

Chatbots

When it comes to artificial intelligence, machines that can speak like a human are the first applications that come to mind. For this, it is necessary to analyze human language as text and sound and to reveal speech patterns. Chatbots, which can be called speech software with artificial intelligence, are used integrated with various messaging programs (Birer, 2020). Chatbots, which can be called speech software with artificial intelligence, are used integrated with various messaging programs (Birer, 2020). Chatbots developed for automatic communication have improved greatly since the first model was launched (Zsarnoczky, 2017). Chatbot software is a conversational tool that provides variety in a chat-driven process, and their primary function is to provide consistent answers to questions through programming (Cooper,

2018). Chatbots are also a program designed to simulate conversations with humans, and chatbots often use artificial intelligence to parse the user's responses (Hatch, 2017). It appears as pop-ups that appear in the lower corner of a website that help its visitors (Cooper, 2018).

Although the use of chatbots in the tourism sector is generally at the beginning level, industry players see that this technological development has the potential to reduce costs in operations and increase sales by positioning it as a new sales channel. It is predicted that the annual total cost savings to be provided by chatbots for companies in 2020 will be 8 billion dollars and the new business opportunity created by artificial intelligence will be 2.3 million dollars (EY Türkiye, 2019). In the event industry, it is noteworthy that chat support is used as a new communication tool, and the levels of artificial intelligence used differ from each other (Cooper, 2018). Event planners can use chatbot software in different areas to automate a range of tasks and provide better service to their customers. It is worth noting that in the event planning industry, 80% of businesses plan to use chatbots by 2020 (Arnold, 2019).

A chatbot can present information like buying tickets, booking locations and transportation, cabin rental, uploading and sharing presentation materials, sharing all kinds of issues that participants needs in terms of customer service, etc. (Hatch, 2017). At the same time, additional value added services such as informing about all permanent or temporary events in cities and regions supported by chatbots can be provided. Cultural and touristic information can be presented on subjects such as museums, opera houses, theaters, permanent exhibitions, cinemas, concert or opera halls, travel services. It is able to provide location information to interested customers based on trade fairs, markets, sporting events, cultural or musical events, temporary art or other exhibitions, folk festivals, restaurants and cafes (Zumstein and Hundertmark, 2017). Another usage area of the chatbot software is that it can increase the participation in the event by providing support for group chat sessions. By using a chatbot, large audiences attending the events for the opportunity to communicate with people of the same events and interests can significantly enhance these experiences. Many event planners encourage participants to interact more with each other through group chat sessions. The chatbot can provide 24/7 live support to the exhibitors whose products and services come as buyers as well as to the exhibitors who are presenter (Arnold, 2019).

Chatbot software appears to make the event planning industry better with lower costs. There is no price or technical barrier for event planners to implement artificial intelligence-based chatbot software. At the same time, chatbot software can be suitable for every event (Groot, 2017). The difference of chatbots from other applications is their level of flexibility. They can be designed to work in place of the event application prepared to provide a unique interaction experience to the participants without the need to download another application to their phones or within an application (Hatch, 2017). At the same time, chatbot software, Facebook and Messenger etc. can also be used through other popular applications that are widely used. Since the applications take up space, it is easier to use for the participants who do not want to download applications only for the event (Arnold, 2019). Various features including programs, agendas, surveys and much more can be embedded in chatbots. Conversations with chatbots can be personalized with the help of other event management software to suit the specific information needs of your participants (Hatch, 2017). Today, as the most successful chatbot software, chatbots that can understand and answer the questions asked are shown. For example, among the most popular versions of artificial chatbot software that shown are consultancy and personal assistance applications that can answer a question when asked for a place in the event venue (Cooper, 2018; Zsarnoczky, 2017).

In the event industry, the application areas of chatbots appear to be diverse and popular, such as calendar assistants (chatbots such as X.ai, Rhonda) and chatbots for booking or purchasing event tickets (eg Morph.ai) (Zumstein and Hundertmark, 2017). Popular chatbots created specifically for the event industry are Concierge EventBot-Sciensio, Eva-Event2Mobile, ConfBot, or Morph.ai (Hatch, 2017). Sciensio's Concierge Eventbot offers a range of text services, including event schedule, directions, floor plans, polls, crowdsourced questions, sessions, materials, event information about speakers, sponsors and attendees (www.corbinball.com, 23.08.2020). Event2Mobile's Eva claims to be the first chatbot in the industry for event applications. They offer surveys, live Q&A, meeting scheduling, directions, feedback, in-app messaging, gamification, and a full range of text services for speakers and attendees (www.corbinball.com, 23.08.2020; e2m.live, 23.08.2020). ConfBot chatbot helps with text services, agenda-related event information, personalized programs, participant messaging, feedback, surveys. Morph.ai chatbot, on the other hand, can communicate and live chat over channels such as Facebook Messenger, Twitter, Skype, SMS, and the website (www.corbinball.com, 23.08.2020). At the same time, Morph.ai allows users to sell more tickets by sending special offers directly to their inboxes. Participants can be divided into segments according to their preferences and interests and targeting the right segment (morph.ai, 23.08. 2020).

SOLUTIONS AND RECOMMENDATION

While the event industry has been based on automation for a long time, it has recently become an industry where artificial intelligence and machine learning technologies are used. How the artificial intelligence and robotic technologies that used help create and improve the efficiency experience is seen as an important issue. The fact that an event is an experiential service product based on human emotions and perspectives, which are primarily unpredictable, difficult to calculate and control, makes events different from many other services (Ogle and Lamb, 2019). What contributes to value creation should not be selling memorable experiences, but ensuring that the participant perfectly lives all moments of their relationship with a company beyond their expectations (Gentile, Spiller and Noci, 2007). It can be said that artificial intelligence contributes to providing services beyond the expectations of the participants in the event industry. In this context, it is seen that artificial intelligence provides many benefits for the event industry. Artificial intelligence can provide unexpected business intelligence for organizations, increase information about customers, and improve customer interaction with the company (Hussain and Manhas, 2016). On the other hand, using artificial intelligence for events is seen as a gain because of some simple benefits it provides for the environment. Chatbots and event apps are available online only. Therefore, this technology, calendars, maps, survey cards, etc. is much more green and sustainable than printed materials, which provides a significant benefit (Cooper, 2018). In some cases, it is predicted that smart, learning machines can replace all departments as they fulfill tasks that have been completely reserved for humans until now (Hussain and Manhas, 2016). On the other hand, it is another view that as a result of the control of many business and business processes by robots, people will have the opportunity to focus on more personalized services, thus leading to the emergence of new professions (İbiş, 2019). Applications of artificial intelligence and robotics have the potential to have a tremendous impact on the events and event industry in the future and deserve the intense attention of both academics and practitioners (Wirtz et al., 2018; Ogle and Lamb, 2019). In the light of this information, it is considered important to pay attention to the following suggestions for the successful use of artificial intelligence technology in event management and marketing. In this context, suggestions that are thought to contribute to the relevant literature, researchers and industry have been presented:

- It is worth noting that the ongoing evolution of mobile applications and hybrid meeting solutions, with potential applications for newer technologies such as artificial intelligence, has provided exciting results for meeting hosts and attendees. It is seen that modern participants expect an online experience to be available to enhance their face-to-face experience. It is also noteworthy that the participants are willing to use technologies that facilitate personal event participation goals such as networking and deeper interaction with content. Therefore, it is expected that technology will continue to transform meetings and events (American Express Meetings & Events, 2018). The use of these technologies is among the expectations of the participants and contributes to the industry. In this respect, it is considered that the use of artificial intelligence technology by event organizers is very important in order to maintain their existence and gain competitive advantage.
- It is thought that it is important to compare the events in which artificial intelligence technology is used and not used in order to see the effects of these technologies. Thus, both the development of the industry and the literature will be contributed.
- While it is seen that the use of artificial intelligence technology requires significant investments, it is noteworthy that some applications in artificial intelligence technology, such as chatbot, can be realized with lower costs. Therefore, for event organizers who are concerned about the costs of artificial intelligence technology, it is thought that it is important to know that this technology offers many options.
- It is inevitable that the rapid developments in technology will appear in every aspect of our lives individually or institutionally. Therefore, businesses that do not follow these developments are unlikely to survive and gain competitive advantage. For the development of the industry, it is especially important to know which applications are liked by the participants and which applications make significant contributions to the organizers. Thus, by including these applications in events, the contributions of artificial intelligence technology will be benefited in both event management and marketing.

FUTURE RESEARCH DIRECTIONS

With the rapid developments in technology, it is seen that artificial intelligence technology appears with more applications and services in the event industry every day. It is noteworthy that despite these rapid developments, research on artificial intelligence technology in the event industry has remained extremely limited.

Due to the rapid changes in technology, the applications used in the event industry are constantly renewed. It is predicted that there are many different applications in artificial intelligence technology, and at the same time, as a result of the rapid development of technology, different applications will come into our lives. When the literature is examined, it is seen that there are limited studies regarding the use of these applications in the event industry. It is thought that presenting these applications by researching them in detail in the studies carried out is significant both in terms of contributing to the development of technology in the event industry and to the literature. At the same time, it is seen also important to examine the factors affecting the use of artificial intelligence technology in the event industry and their effects on the industry. On the other hand, although it is seen that the use of artificial intelligence technology in the event industry contributes to the industry, it is noteworthy that it also brings some threats. A detailed study of the threats that artificial intelligence technology may bring to the industry will contribute to the minimization of negative situations that will be encountered in both the literature and the event industry.

CONCLUSION

Events are seen as celebrations of significant changes in a person's presence for attendees, while event technology is seen as the application of technology in the event industry to improve, assist and enhance an experience (Sherlock and O'Connor, 2015). It is noteworthy that the event industry has experienced a great growth in recent years, has undergone a significant change, and organizers have had to adapt to new trends and changing consumer preferences. It is considered important that event organiser need to understand how to use technology in this rapidly changing environment to attract the right audience. It is also clear that organizing an exciting event loses its meaning when there are not enough participants to fill the capacity (Green, 2018). As event organization businesses have begun to apply more and more artificial intelligence technology to events, many differences have begun to be seen in both event design and user experience. By understanding that each person is unique and needs personalized experiences, the organizers strive to maximize the value participants derive from holding an event with artificial intelligence technology (Blaisdell, 2018). Artificial intelligence technology provides important contributions to event organizers such as collecting and protecting data, providing important reports on the event, and realizing processes that can last for months in a short time by artificial intelligence (Arnold, 2019). Sherlock and O'Connor (2015) in their study on the impact of technology in the event industry "Social Network", "Internet", "World Wide Web", "Search Engines" and "Photo Sharing" were examined as the main types of technological applications used in the event industry. It has been determined that the positive effects of these practices in the event industry greatly exceed their negative effects. It is seen in the study that it has positive effects on "professional planning", "reliable application", "superior transportation" and "globalization" on "the growth, development and feasibility of events". It is also noteworthy that all the aforementioned effects change the "shape" of the event industry. As a negative effect in the study, it is revealed that the need for personnel may be eliminated due to technology replacing human beings and fear of technology occurring in the aging population known as technophobia.

It is seen that there is a need for comprehensive studies on many issues such as the current applications of artificial intelligence technology to the event industry and its positive and negative effects on the industry. Due to the rapid changes in technology, more research is needed on the subject in order to be aware of new applications and to be aware of the effects of these applications.

REFERENCES

E2m.live. (2020). *E2m Event Chatbot Industry-First Chatbot for Event Apps*. Retrieved July 23, 2020 https://e2m.live/chatbots

Ahas, R., Aasa, A., Roose, A., Mark, U., & Silm, S. (2008). Evaluating Passive Mobile Positioning Data for Tourism Surveys: An Estonian Case Study. *Tourism Management*, *29*(3), 469–486. doi:10.1016/j.tourman.2007.05.014

American Express Meetings & Events. (2018). *Global Meetings and Events Forecast, 2018*. Retrieved July 8, 2020. https://www.amexglobalbusinesstravel.com/content/uploads/2017/12/2018-Global-Meetings-Forecast-US.pdf

American Express Meetings & Events. (2020). *Global Meetings and Events Forecast, 2020*. Retrieved July 23, 2020 https://www.amexglobalbusinesstravel.com/content/uploads/2019/09/2020-Global-Meetings-Forecast-Final-US.pdf

Arnold, A. (2019). *How AI is Transforming the Event Planning Space One Conversation at a Time*. Retrieved February 1, 2020, from https://www.forbes.com/sites/andrewarnold/2019/02/25/how-ai-is-transforming-the-event-planning-space-one-conversation-at-a-time/#303aa94510b3

Atalay, M., & Çelik, E. (2017). Artificial Intelligence and Machine Learning Applications in Big Data Analysis. *Mehmet Akif Ersoy Üniversitesi Sosyal Bilimler Enstitüsü Dergisi*, *9*, 155–172. doi:10.20875/makusobed.309727

Bethapudi, A. (2013). The Role of ICT in Tourism Industry. *Journal of Applied Economics and Business*, *1*(4), 67–79.

Birer, C. G. (2018). Yapay Zeka Temel Kavramlar. *TÜBİTAK Bilim ve Teknik. Ocak*, *2018*, 2–11.

Blaisdell, R. (2018). *Is artificial intelligence good for the event industry?* Retrieved from September 5. https://rickscloud.com/is-artificial-intelligence-good-for-the-event-industry/

Briodagh, K. (2013). *3M Posts its Technical Chops in Interactive Lounge at SXSW*. Retrieved July 23, 2020. https://www.eventmarketer.com/article/sxsw-3m/

Bryman, H. (2018). *Bubble Lab Launching Drop Milk Dispenser and Drip Pourover Arm*. Retrieved July 28, 2020. https://dailycoffeenews.com/2018/08/15/bubble-lab-launching-drop-milk-dispenser-and-drip-pourover-arm/

Çakır, Ö. (2020). *Yapay Zeka ve Kullanım Alanları*. Retrieved July 20, 2020 https://www.yapayzekatr.com/2020/01/06/yapay-zeka-ve-kullanim-alanlari/

Çeltek, E., & İlhan, İ. (2020). Big Data, Artificial Intelligence, and Their Implications in the Tourism Industry. In E. Çeltek (Ed.), *Handbook of Research on Smart Technology Applications in the Tourism Industry* (pp. 115–130). IGI Global. doi:10.4018/978-1-7998-1989-9.ch006

Chen, M., Mao, S., & Liu, Y. (2014). Big Data: A Survey. *Mobile Networks and Applications*, *19*(2), 171–209. doi:10.100711036-013-0489-0

Cooper, K. (2018). *AI for Events: The Future is Here*. Retrieved February 3, 2020, from https://helloendless.com/ai-for-events/

Corbinball. (2020). *The Rise and Benefits of Text Apps and Chatbots for Events*. Retrieved July 23, 2020. https://www.corbinball.com/article/36-mobile-and-wireless-technology/212-rise-of-text-apps-and-chatbots-for-events

Daily News. (2013). https://www.nydailynews.com/life-style/eats/drone-drops-beers-not-bombs-south-africa-article-1.1422617

Garcia, M. F. L., Lansley, G., & Calnan, B. (2017). Modelling Spatial Behaviour in Music Festivals Using Mobile Generated Data and Machine Learning. *GISRUK 2017 Conference.*

Gentile, C., Spiller, N., & Noci, G. (2007). How to sustain the customer experience? *European Management Journal, 25*(5), 395–410. doi:10.1016/j.emj.2007.08.005

Getz, D. (1997). *Event Management & Event Tourism.* Cognizant Communication Corporation.

Green, R. (2018). *How technology is drastically shaking up the events industry.* Retrieved from September 10. https://www.verdict.co.uk/technology-events-industry/

Groot, T. (2017). *AI in 2019: How Artificial Intelligence Is Impacting Events.* Retrieved February 22, 2020, from https://www.eventbrite.com/blog/ai-in-2018-artificial-intelligence-events-ds00/

Gümüş, F. (2019). *Müzelerde Yapay Zeka Uygulamaları, Etkileri ve Geleceği* (Unpublished master dissertation). İstanbul Üniversitesi Sosyal Bilimler Enstitüsü, İstanbul.

Hatch, K. (2017). *The Who, What, and Why of Chatbots for Events.* Retrieved July 23, 2020 https://meetingpool.net/the-who-what-and-why-of-chatbots-for-events/

Hussain, M., & Manhas, J. (2016). Artificial Intelligence for Big Data: Potential and Relevance. *International Acadmey of Engineering and Medical Research, 1*(1), 1–5.

İbiş, S. (2019). Turizm Endüstrisinde Robotlaşma. *Türk Turizm Araştırmaları Dergisi, 3*(3), 403–420. doi:10.26677/TR1010.2019.169

International Telecommunication Union. (2019). *United Nations Activities on Artificial Intelligence (AI) 2019.* International Telecommunication Union.

Ivanov, S., & Webster, C. (2017). *Adoption of Robots, Artificial Intelligence and Service Automation by Travel, Tourism and Hospitality Companies – A Cost – Benefit Analysis.* International Scientific Conference "Contemporary Tourism – Traditions and Innovations", Sofia University.

Ivanov, S., Webster, C., & Berezina, K. (2017). Adoption of Robots and Service Automation by Tourism and Hospitality Companies. *Revista Turismo & Desenvolvimento, 27*(28), 1501–1517.

Li, D., & Yang, Y. (2017). GIS Monitoring of Traveler Flows Based on Big Data. In Analytics in Smart Tourism Design Concepts and Methods. (pp. 111-128). Springer. doi:10.1007/978-3-319-44263-1_7

McCarthy, J., Minsky, L. M., Rochester, N., & Shannon, E. C. (1955). *A Proposal for the Dartmouth Summer Research Project on Artificial Intelligence. August 31.* Retrieved February 1, 2020, from http://jmc.stanford.edu/articles/dartmouth/dartmouth.pdf

Morph.ai. (2020). *Events. Create a Chatbot for Your Event in Minutes without Coding.* Retrieved July 23, 2020 https://morph.ai/events

Nilbe, K., Ahas, R., & Silm, S. (2014). Evaluating the Travel Distances of Events Visitors and Regular Visitors Using Mobile Positioning Data: The Case of Estonia. *Journal of Urban Technology, 21*(2), 91–107. doi:10.1080/10630732.2014.888218

Novak, M. (2017). *Robots and Event Planning*. Retrieved February 22, 2020, from https://www.seebtm.com/en/robots-and-event-planning/

Ogle, A., & Lamb, D. (2019). The Role of Robots, Artificial Intelligence, and Service Automation in Events. In S. Ivanov & C. Webster (Eds.), *Robots, Artificial Intelligence, and Service Automation in Travel, Tourism and Hospitality* (pp. 255–269). Emerald Publishing Limited. doi:10.1108/978-1-78756-687-320191012

Pinillos, R., Marcos, S., Feliz, R., Zalama, E., & Bermejo, G. G. J. (2016). Long-term Assessment of a Service Robot in a Hotel Environment. *Robotics and Autonomous Systems*, *79*, 40–57. doi:10.1016/j.robot.2016.01.014

Şener, S. (2019). *Yapay Zeka, Makine Öğrenimi ve Derin Öğrenme Arasındaki Farklar.* Retrieved February 22, 2020, from https://www. endustri40.com/yapay-zeka-makine-ogrenimi-ve-derin-ogrenme-arasindaki-farklar/

Sherlock, J., & O'Connor, N. (2015). Research into the Impact of Technology in the Events Industry. *International Hospitality and Tourism Student Journal*, *7*(1), 88–102.

Song, H., & Liu, H. (2017). Predicting Tourist Demand Using Big Data. In Analytics in Smart Tourism Design Concepts and Methods. (pp. 13-30). Springer. doi:10.1007/978-3-319-44263-1_2

Sorrels, M. (2013). *5 Ways Robots Are Being Used at Events*. Retrieved July 28, 2020 https://www.bizbash.com/production-strategy/event-management-tech-tools/media-gallery/13479962/5-ways-robots-are-being-used-at-events

Timur, N., M., Çevik, S. & Kıcır, K., G. (2014). Etkinlik Turizmi: Kültür Başkenti Etkinliklerinin Başarı Unsurları Üzerine Bir Değerlendirme. *Akademik Sosyal Araştırmalar Dergisi*, *2*(2/1), 56-83.

Tontuş, Ö. (2019). *Etkinlik Yönetimi*. Retrieved August 8, 2020. file:///C:/Users/dogan/Downloads/EtkinlikYonetimi2.pdf

Türkiye, E. Y. (2019). *Turizm Sektörü Dijitalleşme Yol Haritası Seyahat Acentaları Dijital Dönüşüm Raporu*. TÜRSAB & TBV.

TUYED. (2020). *Turizm Sektörüne 5 Yapay Zeka Uygulaması*. Turizm Yazarları ve Gazeteleri Derneği. Retrieved August 20, 2020, from http://www.tuyed.org.tr/turizm-sektorune-5-yapay-zeka-uygulamasi/

Uludağ İhracatçı Birlikleri Genel Sekreterliği AR&GE Şubesi. (2017). *Yapay Zeka ve Yeni Teknolojiler.* Retrieved August 23, 2020. file:///C:/Users/dogan/Downloads/Yapay%20zeka%20ve%20yeni%20teknolojiler.pdf.

Van der Wagen, L. (2007). *Human Resource Management for Events: Managing the Event Workforce*. Butterworth-Heinemann.

Versichele, M., Neutens, T., Delafontaine, M., & Van deWeghe, N. (2012a). The Use of Bluetooth for Analyzing Spatiotemporal Dynamics of Human Movement at Mass Events: A Case Study of the Ghent Festivities. *Applied Geography (Sevenoaks, England)*, *32*(2), 208–220. doi:10.1016/j.apgeog.2011.05.011

Versichele, M., Neutens, T., Goudeseune, S., Bossche, F., & Weghe, N. (2012b). Mobile Mapping of Sporting Event Spectators Using Bluetooth Sensors: Tour of Flanders. *Sensors (Basel), 12*(10), 14196–14213. doi:10.3390121014196 PMID:23202044

Wilson, C. (2019). *Artificial Intelligence is Changing the Event Industry – Here's How*. Retrieved July 23, 2020. https://blog.swapcard.com/artificial-intelligence-and-events

Wirtz, J., Patterson, P., Kunz, W., Gruber, T., Lu, V., Paluch, S., & Martins, A. (2018). Brave new world: Service robots in the frontline. *Journal of Service Management, 29*(5), 907–931. doi:10.1108/JOSM-04-2018-0119

Xiang, Z., & Fesenmaier, R. D. (2017). Analytics in Tourism Design. In Analytics in Smart Tourism Design Concepts and Methods (pp. 1-12). Springer. doi:10.1007/978-3-319-44263-1_1

Zsarnoczky, M. (2017). How does Artificial Intelligence affect the Tourism Industry? *Journal of Management, 31*(2), 85–90.

Zumstein, D. & Hundertmark, S. (2017). Chatbots-An Interactive Technology for Personalized Communication, Transactions and Services. *IADIS International Journal on WWW/Internet, 15*(1), 96-109.

ADDITIONAL READING

Ivanov, S., & Webster, C. (2019). *Robots, Artificial Intelligence, and Service Automation in Travel, Tourism and Hospitality*. Emerald Publishing Limited. doi:10.1108/9781787566873

Kansakar, P., Munir, A., & Shabani, N. (2019). Technology in the Hospitality Industry: Prospects and Challenges. *IEEE Consumer Electronics Magazine, 8*(3), 60–65. doi:10.1109/MCE.2019.2892245

Nyheim, P., & Connolly, D. (2014). *Technology Strategies fort he Hospitality Industry* (International Edition). Pearson New.

Osawa, H., Ema, A., Hattori, H., Akiya, N., Kanzaki, N., Kubo, A., Koyamaa, T., & Ichise, R. (2017). *What is Real Risk and Benefit on Work with Robots?: From the Analysis of a Robot Hotel.* The Companion of the 2017 ACM/IEEE International Conference. 1-3.

Robinson, P., Wale, D., & Dickson, G. (2010). *Events Management*. CABI. doi:10.1079/9781845936822.0000

Shone, A., & Parry, B. (2010). *Successful Event Management*. Cengage Learning.

Xiang, Z., & Fesenmaier, R. D. (2017). *Analytics in Smart Tourism Design Concepts and Methods*. Springer. doi:10.1007/978-3-319-44263-1

Yeoman, I. (2004). *Festival and Events Management*. Elsevier Butterworth-Heineman. doi:10.1016/B978-0-7506-5872-0.50010-7

KEY TERMS AND DEFINITIONS

Artificial Intelligence: Is technologies capable of performing tasks that require human intelligence, such as visual perception, speech, recognition, and language translation (British Government Industrial Strategy White Paper, 2017).

Big Data: Is data sets that cannot be captured, managed and processed by general computers within an acceptable scope (Chen, Mao and Liu, 2014; Song and Liu, 2017).

Chatbot: Is a conversational tool that provides variety in a chat-driven process, and its primary function is to provide consistent answers to questions through programming (Cooper, 2018).

Event: Is to meet certain social or individual needs that occur as a result of people acting together, or to achieve common goals as a group and organization, to share a common feeling or thought, and to be a social entity in social life, etc. events organized for purposes (Ekin, 2011).

Event Management: Is conducting the pre-event, during and post-event processes (project planning, budgeting, whether or not to earn income, earnings of the institution, design, procurement, planning, operation, measurement and evaluation, reporting, etc.) based on strategic principles, in line with the determined targets, in a planned manner (Tontuş, 2019).

Event Marketing: Is the process of driving the marketing mix to achieve goals through creating value for customers (Getz, 1997: 250).

Machine Learning: Refers to computer science techniques used to give machines the ability to learn without the need for explicit programming (Birer, 2020).

Robots: Are electromechanical units programmed or controlled by someone, and they perform certain actions and tasks (Novak, 2017).

Chapter 13
New Event Trends as a Tool of Digital Marketing Communication

Dilaysu Cinar
https://orcid.org/0000-0002-5306-9031
Beykent University, Turkey

ABSTRACT

Today, with digital marketing communication, it has become easier to reach and persuade both existing and potential customers. The aforementioned situation is also valid for event applications which are one of the digital marketing communication tools. Indeed, with the technological power, brands began to offer participants almost unlimited options for events and participation takes place regardless of the venue. This study aims to provide information about the new event trends as a digital marketing communication tool. For this purpose, a literature review was made in the study. Accordingly, it can be argued that the new event trends used in digital marketing communications consist of real-time events, social events, storytelling, virtual reality and augmented reality applications, influencers, and virtual communities.

INTRODUCTION

Nowadays, where changes and developments are an inevitable necessity, even people at the back of beyond can be aware of all developments thanks to the transformation of communication channels with the internet. The increasing complexity of consumers, the dynamic nature of the market, broad marketing communication tools, and the consistency and reliability of messages first of all required companies to turn to the digital marketing communication approach in the face of achieving competitive clarity towards the target audience (Kehinde, 2009: 204). The main reasons for businesses turning to digital marketing communication and gaining importance of this type of communication in today's competition are seen as the decrease in the power of mass marketing and mass communication, the increase in advertising costs, the inability to create messages that will affect consumer behavior and the difficulties in conveying them (Bozkurt, 2002: 139).

DOI: 10.4018/978-1-7998-4954-4.ch013

With the increase in digital environments and thus the developments in communication technologies, changes in marketing communication are also occurring. Today, thanks to digital media, marketers can create close ties with consumers by implementing effective communication activities. In this way, businesses can affect consumers' purchasing orientation with the content they offer to consumers (Çelik, 2014: 29). Apart from that, reaching the target market, obtaining the optimum mix of digital communication elements, creating consistent brand messages from digital channels and helping communication marketers can be realized more easily through this communication type. (Valos et. al., 2016: 22) The diversity of growth and technology has also brought extraordinary opportunities to event applications. As a matter of fact, the importance of event applications in digital marketing communication is increasing day by day and for this reason, it has been used more frequently.

Event can be defined as all activities carried out at a specific place and time where a message is conveyed to the target audience or their attitudes and behaviors are tried to be changed on a particular subject. (Eckerstein, 2002). Event marketing is the process of creating a marketing mix to achieve organizational goals by creating value for employees and customers. Event marketing is a tool that exists to create an emotional and rational holistic experience that focuses on consumer experiences (Schmitt, 1999). Event marketing helps the consumer and the brand come together actively. Event marketing are activities such as public sporting events, public fairs (e.g. garden show), association events and franchise organizations to persuade participants with active participation. (Tinnish and Mangal, 2012: 233). The fundamental aims of event marketing are to market the event without making people noticeable to them when they are resting and having fun and ensuring that they participate in the events again and again with their experience and satisfaction from this experience. Marketers look for ways to give messages and experience without consumer noticing the messages, instead of squeezing customers by sending them a message bombardment, as traditional marketing does. Therefore, event marketing has been a marketing strategy that businesses use a lot. Meeting the expectations of those who want to enjoy the event, especially by creating free time, and even providing them with an unforgettable experience, making them loyal participants towards the event has become the main goal of event marketing (Yürük,2015:40). Event marketing in the digital environment has an important contribution to the creation of positive emotions in the digital environment, the promotion of the event to a wider audience and the attention of the event (Horo, 2015: 54).

In the light of the benefits discussed above, the main purpose of this study is to try to comprehend the new event trends as a digital marketing communication tool. For this purpose, a literature review was made in the study. Accordingly, it can be argued that the new event trends used in digital marketing communications consist of real-time events, social events, storytelling, virtual reality and augmented reality applications, influencers and virtual communities. These trends were examined in detail in the study and evaluated on the basis of efficiency.

BACKGROUND

Digital marketing communication covers all situations from pre-sales to consumption of the product and creates a continuous and active dialogue between consumers and the business. Digital marketing communication starts at the design stage of the product and continues through the communication process through digital channels. The interaction of customers with the business during the purchase is also a part of the digital marketing communication process. In addition, after-sales satisfaction or dissatisfaction of consumers and services to be offered to consumers after sales are also included in the digital marketing communication process (Çalık et. al., 2013: 139).

With the increase of internet users, the easiest and most cost-effective way for companies to communicate with their target audience has been digital media. Businesses can encourage their target audiences to buy with their communication activities in digital environments. Businesses can increase their follower day by day with remarkable content they will make to their target audiences in digital environments. These communication activities that businesses will do in the digital environment can increase the dependence of both existing and potential customers on the brand.

Digital marketing communication mix elements consist of public relations, advertising, direct marketing, event marketing and point of purchase communication. (Mucuk, 2012: 181). In this study, new trends used in event marketing, which is a digital marketing communication tool, are discussed.

Since event marketing is a mix of sales and marketing activities, the main purpose is actually to improve the marketing communication activities of the brand. (Stevens, 2005: 57). Events organized for this purpose are among the areas where sales can be made most easily. For this reason, it can be said that a kind of marketing communication work is applied with event marketing. Considering that events are an integral part of the basic marketing mix elements, event marketing allows companies to make serious breakthroughs in their strategic plans in the medium and long term. However, the correct determination of the goals and target audience of the event will directly affect the effectiveness of event marketing. For this reason, it is essential for brands to choose the right digital media tools in their event applications.

MAIN FOCUS OF THE CHAPTER

1. Digital Marketing Communication

Marketing communication is the name given to all of the marketing studies carried out in different channels in order to create a demand for the brand or product in the target market. Nowadays, with the change in marketing understanding, if businesses improve their marketing communications, they have the opportunity to convey their messages to their target audiences more accurately. This can cause a successful marketing communication by positively affecting the purchasing decisions of the consumers. Previously, it was not possible for businesses to try new methods in marketing communication, but with the increasing competition environment and the development of technology, businesses have come to the situation of keeping up with the current marketing communication methods (Karjaluoto et al., 2015: 703).

With the increase of internet users, the easiest and most cost-effective way for companies to communicate with their target audiences has been digital media. Businesses can encourage their target audiences to buy their products with advertisements and promotions in digital environments. Businesses can increase their followers day by day with the remarkable content they will make in digital environments to their target audiences and keep their current followers active in digital environments. The dependence of existing and potential customers on the brand can be increased with these works to be carried out by businesses. Businesses need to prepare a plan, determine the target audience they want to communicate with, and implement messages and applications in order to perform effective marketing communication (Odabaşı and Oyman, 2002: 45). It is possible for businesses to transfer their digital marketing communication activities to their target audiences with an effective digital marketing communication process.

The digital marketing communication process consists of the applications that businesses implement in order to create the brand identity and positioning they desire in the context of the goals and strategies they have set. Businesses transform the activities they want to convey to consumers in line with the goals they have set into messages and send these messages to their target audiences through digital channels. In order for these messages to be transferred to their target audiences by businesses in a very short time, digital channels should be selected in accordance with the business structure. This communication process takes place through a number of tools used in digital environments. These tools are; search engine optimization, search engine marketing, display advertising / marketing, google ad words, e-mail marketing, content and communication management, viral marketing, affiliate marketing, return on investment and social media (Tığlı, 2010: 4).

Digital marketing communication covers all situations from pre-sales to consumption of the product and creates a continuous and active dialogue between consumers and the business. Digital marketing communication starts at the design stage of the product. Then the communication process continues through digital channels. Promotion activities, such as price and advertising activities, continue the digital marketing communication. The interaction of customers with the business during the purchase is also part of the digital marketing communication process. In addition, after-sales services to be offered to consumers are also included in the digital marketing communication process (Çalık et al., 2013:148).

Digital marketing communication mix elements consist of public relations, advertising, direct marketing, event marketing and point of purchase communication. (Mucuk, 2012: 181). Public relations can be defined as the management organization that an organization implements in order to positively affect the interest of its target audience, to receive the support of the target audience and to make this situation permanent (Erciş, 2010: 193). Advertising, which is another digital marketing communication mix, can be defined as the delivery of the desired message to the target audience by acting as a mass communication tool for a fee (Pickton and Broderick, 2005: 593). The third marketing communication mix is direct marketing. Direct marketing can be defined as communicating directly with consumer channels at the point of delivery of products or services to consumers (Çakmak, 2011: 3). The fourth marketing communication mix is point of purchase communication. Point of purchase communication can be defined as the place where sales are made by using point of sale exhibitions, package designs, sales promotions, sales staff, window dressing arrangements, posters hanging in the store, announcements about the product, advertisement spots and other different communication tools in order to reach customers (Erdem, 2009: 47). The final digital marketing communication mix is event marketing. Event marketing can be defined as the interactive marketing communication where the customer takes an active role at a behavioral level before, during or after the purchase of the product or service and causes an emotional connection with the brand (Küçüksaraç and Sayımer, 2016: 78).

Factors affecting digital marketing communication are situational factors, environmental factors, target audience factors and technology factors. Situational factors are situations where customers are exposed to a number of messages and at the same time affect their purchasing orientation. In this context, it can be said that advertisements, programs and broadcasts that customers will be exposed to in digital environments form the basis of this scope (Bilgen, 2011: 42). It is possible to evaluate environmental factors, which are another factor affecting digital marketing communication, under the concept of competition. In this context, businesses can analyze competitors in the market within the framework of digital marketing communication activities and determine their financial status, new products or services and many similar activities. The target audience factor includes factors such as demographic factors, psychographic factors and economy. The last factor affecting digital marketing communication is the technology factor.

Businesses need to keep up with the ever-changing and developing technology environment. Technology contributes significantly to the daily activities of businesses. With the increase in technological developments, businesses have to allocate budgets for equipment and services to effectively implement digital marketing communication activities.

In this study, trends in event marketing included in the digital marketing communication mix are discussed. In the light of the above explanations, it is essential that event marketing should focus on technological factors as well as situational and environmental factors. In this direction, it is necessary to use social media effectively, to benefit from influencers, to create virtual communities, to benefit from augmented reality and virtual reality applications, to implement content marketing effectively and to benefit from real-time events. These trends are explained below with detailed and practical examples.

2. Social Events

Social events are the first type of event commonly used in digital marketing communication. Social events are organizations that a business organizes and advertises on social media for a specific purpose. Apart from traditional media channels, social media channels add a new dimension to the marketing approach. The innovations and features brought by the internet contain differences that traditional media do not have. These differences are not only due to technological features, but also to the opportunity to establish social relationships and communication (Sohn, 2005: 14). However, it is beneficial to consider social media as a complement to traditional media, not as an alternative to traditional media. Because social media participants are also influenced by traditional media, differently, they can add their comments to events and reflect their own perspectives (Evans, 2008: 33).

Although it is not a clear definition because it is a very broad concept in terms of the qualities of social media, Tuten (2008: 20) expressed social media as online communities aiming to establish a fluent communication with the participants or participants with the meeting of technology and internet. These communities enable members to create, publish, control, criticize, sort and interact with content online. Social media has many internet-based channels. Blogs, video and picture sharing sites, social networks, microblogs, wikis, podcasts and e-mailing are the main social media channels. Social media channels create great advantages for all small / large businesses, such as conducting cost-free events in these channels, contacting customers, accessing ideas and suggestions in a short time (Köksal and Özdemir, 2013: 325).

Features that help define the differences between social media and traditional media may differ according to the method used (Bulut, 2012: 38). Both traditional media and social media technologies allow anyone to reach a general audience. Producing for traditional media is often owned by private companies; social media tools, on the other hand, can be used by everyone in general, with little or no cost. Traditional media production often requires specialized skills and training. This is not the case with most social media, or in some cases the skills are completely changed and new, meaning anyone can produce content. The time difference that occurs in traditional media communications can be long compared to social media where immediate effects and reactions are observed. Traditional media is also adapting to social media applications, so this difference will disappear in the near future. In traditional media, content cannot be changed after it is created, whereas in social media, content can be changed instantly through comments or rearrangement. Being measurable is among the most important benefits of social media. It is difficult and costly to measure how many people watch an advertisement made with traditional media tools. However, it can be easily followed by how many people visited the video published on the social media site. Considering these differences, it can be stated that it is essential for brands to benefit from social media in event applications. As a matter of fact, brands that announce their activities through social media can differentiate themselves from their competitors, save time and cost, increase awareness of the event, reach people who are likely to participate in the event faster, and analyze the event through participant feedbacks.

The London Gin Festival, Sherlocked: The Official Sherlock Convention, Play Blackpool, Audacious, X Music Festival, Burger Bear and Jersey Live organizations can be shown as examples of social events ("8 Great Examples of Social Media Event Marketing", 2016). In the London Gin Festival, organizers organized International Kiss A Gin Day via social media in order to increase participation in the event. On the day in question, a hashtag was created on Twitter and they encouraged their followers to send pictures of themselves kissing with a bottle of gin using a hashtag. They also rewarded the best photo with a bottle of gin. In another example, Sherlock organizers increased the excitement of their followers by sharing information about the Sherlock event on social media. In the end, when the event day came, it enabled 1,231 posts about the event on Facebook and close to 1,000 on Twitter. In another example, Play Blackpool organizers carried out their social event on their own blog site. They asked the blog readers to vote in a range of categories such as best game, best movie and best album and gave voters the chance to win tickets and other prizes to the fair. In this way, they increased their participation in their event. To increase participation in a religious fair, an album was created focusing on the music of a rock band in a social event organized by the Audacious church. Afterwards, the album promotion was made by making a hashtag study on the subject. As a result of the event, the album took the second place in the iTunes list. X music festival organizers organized a competition by hiding the images of the artists on Instagram. Followers of the account have been forced to guess the identity of the player hidden in the photo to win VIP weekend tickets. Additionally, the organizers asked 300 fans to like and share the photo before revealing the identity of the actor in the picture. As a result of this social event, festival ticket sales have increased ("8 Great Examples of Social Media Event Marketing", 2016).

3. Influencers

Influencers are the second type of event that is widely used in digital marketing communication. Influencer is a person who influences, leads, inspires and guides people against a specific situation Influencer marketing emerges as the evaluation of influencers, who are effective in the digital environment, in marketing processes. Today, there is a significant consumer group using social media (Mert, 2018: 1302). It has become almost a necessity for businesses competing in intense competitive conditions to use social media in order to accelerate their marketing processes. At this point, businesses need social influencers to help them share their online marketing content (Singh and Diamond, 2012: 19). In fact, there are some beliefs that there have been significant changes in the purchasing habits of the consumer for a long time. Accordingly, consumers now have negative perspectives against both traditional advertisements and digital media advertisements that unexpectedly encounter in the digital environment and undermine the experience they actually want to experience. Influencer marketing comes into play at this point. Brands use influencer marketing to attract the attention of consumers, direct them to buy and enter their natural spaces (Eker et. al., 2017: 23).

According to McCracken (1989), a celebrity's contribution to a brand emerges when the cultural meanings of that celebrity are first transferred to the branded product or service promoted by the celebrity, and then transferred to the consumer who purchases that product or service. This approach is called the "meaning transfer model" and forms the basis of famous use in marketing. According to this approach, when marketers cooperate with influencers, they aim to carry the image and identity relationships of that person to their brands (Kıran et. al., 2019: 104). Influencers are content creators who build a solid foundation for their followers. Influencers convey their daily lives, personal experiences and opinions to their followers through blogging, vlogging or short form content. With the involvement of influencers (for example, testing a product, organizing a special event, or simply paying for them), brands aim to encourage those affected to approve their products. (Veirmen et. al., 2017: 802).

It is possible to divide influencers into two as micro and macro influencers. Macro influencers have a large audience and do not have detailed information about the characteristics and trends of their followers. Micro influencers, on the other hand, have a smaller number of followers, but are people who have a stronger communication between them and are directly influential in the social graph of the consumer. Influencers, which have become quite effective in recent years, significantly affect the purchasing decision of the consumers, at the same time they take the responsibility on the consumers (Brown and Hayes, 2008: 50). Influencers have various responsibilities such as informing the products and services of brands and increasing brand awareness, communicating with large communities, ensuring the interaction between the brand and its current and potential target audiences, directing and persuading the purchasing behavior of target audiences based on their own brand experiences. In addition, building trust and being sincere and genuine are the most important elements for influencer marketing to achieve its purpose (Köse and Çakır, 2019: 213).

Influencer marketing method can only benefit brands with effective selection and measurement tools. The purchasing power of influencer followers and their capacity to transform recommendations into consumption should be measured on the basis of product and influencer. In addition, it must be measurable which product can be more effective with which kind of sharing. Marketers should turn to influencers that

will tell them to the large masses they want to reach. They must also understand the nature of the influencer mass they are targeting for an efficient operation. (Brown and Fiorella, 2013: 39).

When managed effectively, influencer marketing creates an experienced and sincere opportunity for new generation consumers. In particular, in campaigns carried out with influencer marketing, brands provide their target audience with the opportunity to capture an instant relationship and insight. In addition, with the influencer marketing, brands have the opportunity to reach the niche audience they want to affect more easily (Alikılıç and Özkan, 2018: 45). In addition, with influencer marketing, apart from popular sectors such as fashion, sports, cosmetics and entertainment, it can also provide the opportunity to interact with by communicating with consumers from many sectors from healthy life to nutrition and automobiles. In short, influencer marketing, beyond satisfying the consumer, establishes a unity between the brand and its target audience (Kaya, 2015: 158).

There are many events that are organized or announced through influencers. For example, Subaru organized a #MeetAnOwner event to promote a car brand and hired a youtuber with five million followers to increase attendance at the event. The youtuber in question made interesting videos on the subject and advertised the brand and the video reached a large number of viewers. In another example, Swissper, a cotton brand, encouraged famous bloggers and their followers to take makeup-free photos, thereby increasing brand recognition. In another example, Sun Peaks, a ski resort, organized a social event with Canada's best adventure photographer and Instagram influencer to raise awareness about key winter attractions such as uncrowded ski slopes, seasonal festivals and the natural beauty of the region. In this way, Sun Peaks aroused great interest in its target market. In another example, the Marriott hotel hired a famous youtuber to celebrate reaching one million check-ins via its mobile app. In the application in question, mobile users encountered a surprise dance party after the check-in process was completed. This video then went viral and had nearly four million views this way. In another example, on International Women's Day, Microsoft partnered with National Geographic to highlight 30 photos of National Geographic's wildlife photographers, who are five Instagram influencers. The photos depicted female scientists and outdoor adventurers and garnered more than 3.5 million likes in one day. In this way, Microsoft has positively strengthened its brand image (Schachter, n.d.).

Today, it is of great importance to benefit from influencers in brand event applications. Brands can take advantage of influencers for any type of event. In this period, it can be stated that the connection between the brand and the consumer is enriched when the right influencers are selected and included in the event plans of the brand. In addition, the event to be carried out in this way can reach a large number of target audiences in a very short time. At this point, the brand should benefit from influencers that will bring it closer to its target audience in the event application. Another important issue is that these people associated with the event must have full knowledge of the event to be carried out by the brand. In addition, the brand should make use of influencers who trust the target audience, who are sincere to the target audience and who have high communication skills for the event announcement.

4. Virtual Communities

The third type of event commonly used in digital marketing communications is the virtual community. Virtual community is the generic name of the network that bringing together groups of people for a common purpose on the internet. According to the social identity theory, people classify themselves by putting them in social communities. Thanks to these communities, people define to their environment and try to take a place in the social environment (Ashforth, 1989: 22). Likewise, since virtual communities are social groups, a social identity formation can be mentioned. Rheingold was the first to describe virtual communities. According to Rheingold (1993: 14), virtual communities are social groups that computer aided, communicating with each other and even penetrated real-world communication. People who are members of this group are in the form of reference groups that communicate with each other and make various shares in line with their common goals and interests in an electronic communication environment (Romm, 1997: 261). People take part in virtual communities to share resources, build relationships, and trade (Armstrong and Hagel, 1996: 136).

Virtual communities include mailing lists, internet relay chat, shopping and auction sites, e-newsletters, blogs, online gambling communities, internet forums where interests are shared, and social networking sites (Finin et. al., 2005: 418). The appeal of online communities is due to the unique quality of online experiences, low cost, the ease of joining and leaving the community. It also makes it easier to be asynchronous. Most importantly, it provides interpersonal bonding by providing information and social support (Miller et. al., 2009: 312). In social communities, two or more people engage in social interaction and exchange in line with common interests and in a computer-mediated environment. Members in social communities are aware of the membership of others. There is an emotional connection and a sense of belonging among the members (Bagozzi and Dholakia, 2002:4). Members involved in virtual communities communicate with each other and provide information flow. In addition, the members present their own opinions by giving advice to each other on every subject. Virtual communities also often share their own consumption experiences with others. In line with these features, virtual communities have a feature that affects consumer knowledge and purchasing behavior (Valck, 2009: 185).

Marketing through virtual communities is seen as one of the advanced Web 3.0 marketing tactics that can be used to generate leads, make deals, and conduct internal communications (Tasner, 2010: 105). Marketers show an interest in both virtual community members and virtual community members' communications with other internet users. Because the virtual community participants contribute to each other in terms of product knowledge, learning about general consumption activities, sharing experiences and developing social relations with other members. Marketing events in these communities can be measured, observed and developed according to emerging needs. (Akar, 2010: 147).

Furthermore, marketing through virtual communities offers a number of values to businesses and consumers. The values it offers for consumers are about facilitating consumers' access to all kinds of information about goods or services, creating a rich source of information, conducting price research, accessing the experiences of other users and using the power of the community for more affordable prices. The values it offers for companies are increasing sales, increasing profit rate, diversifying marketing activities, facilitating customer relationship management, creating market research and database, contributing to effective market segmentation, creating a strong brand, supporting promotion efforts and helping product development (Argan, 2008: 307).

It is possible to find many creative examples of virtual community events. For example, Gilda's Club Madison organizes healthy life activities such as yoga for unhealthy groups through virtual environment in order to provide support especially to cancer patients. In another example, St. Louis Aquarium Foundation used the Facebook Live application to enable children to visit the aquarium from a virtual environment, and in this way brought the virtual community and animals together. In the last example, the National Deaf Children Association has supported their virtual community by offering a range of online programs for both parents and children (Soucy, 2020). Brands can do business with the support of virtual communities in both their traditional and virtual event applications. In this way, they can announce their activities to more audiences, inform those who do not know about the event, make the event more attractive and increase participation in the event.

5. Content Marketing

The fourth type of event commonly used in digital marketing communication is content marketing. Content marketing is a strategy to grow the brand and product by producing useful and interesting content, especially on the internet. Technological developments affecting consumer behavior in all aspects have manifested themselves most clearly in the digital platform. Brands, which have to shift their communication aspects to digital environments in order to interact with their target audiences, produce various contents taking into account the power of digital media. Additionally, they expose their target audience to thousands of different contents at each touchpoint. Although it is not easy to attract the attention of target audiences with the content produced under such a content bombardment, it requires differentiation (Köse and Çakır, 2019: 208). In a digital environment where content becomes so important and valuable, "content marketing" is another of the digital marketing tools of brands and it is more related to the consumer rather than the producer. (Sarıtaş, 2018: 232).

Content marketing is the marketing concept that aims the customer to find the product with the desired feature and quality and ensure the highest customer satisfaction. It aims to allow the consumer to determine the product he wants without confusing his mind and to buy the product that will meet his needs. It is seen that the content has basically two dimensions. The first dimension consists of the content prepared by the business and the second dimension is the content prepared by the consumers. Business contents are related to consumers' purchasing products. Consumers' content is about the voluntary promotion of the product on social media at the rate of satisfaction felt. In the content marketing technique, while preparing the content for the sale of the product, stages such as draft design, production drawing and modeling are followed after the design created in the mental dimension. At this stage, the product must be prepared by loading various features for the customer's area of interest (Karkar, 2016: 225). In this context, it is possible to create valuable content related to the field by training existing and potential customers. (Goldstein, 2013: 28).

Content marketing consists of the stages of preparation, determining the goals and strategies, determining the target audience, creating the brand story, determining the channels to be used, creating and publishing the content and measuring the content (Yıldız and Karagöz, 2018: 79). In the first stage, it should be determined who the people to be contacted with and how the measurements will be made for the targeted success. As a result of content marketing activities to be implemented in businesses, it should be revealed exactly what is actually desired in the context of issues such as increasing sales or lowering costs (Pulizzi and Barrett, 2009: 28). In the second stage, there is a need to determine the goals of digital media content to be created and to create a content strategy document. Within the scope of this document, there are drafts that reflect what, why and how the contents will be realized before the creation of the contents. As one of the parts used in content marketing studies, it should be taken natural that the content strategy document changes depending on the time passed. However, the digital content strategy to be determined must be in motion with all digital marketing channels (Ryan, 2016: 413).

The third stage for content marketing is about understanding the target audience. Determining the identity of the target audience is an important point in all marketing activities. From this point of view, determining the target audience in content marketing studies is an important factor that provides convenience for businesses and brings success (Handley and Chapman, 2012: 58). The fourth stage is about the ability to tell the brand story successfully. For this, it is necessary to know well which emotional needs of the brand products and services meet the consumers. The brand is unlikely to be successful if the story created does not differ from other stories, in other words, if it does not have originality (Bierman, 2010: 40). The fifth stage of content marketing is about determining the channel that should be used. In determining the channel, it is important to determine which sites the target audience spend their time on. Determining where consumers access the content in question will provide businesses with clues about the content they will publish (Handley and Chapman, 2012:58). In the sixth stage, the brand mission, values and philosophy should be conveyed using simple expressions and translated into language that the target audience will understand. However, using a language that is too simple is not appropriate. (Handley and Chapman, 2012: 212). At the last stage, evaluations are made about whether the digital content goals are reached, whether a relationship with the target audience is established, which strategic decisions are lacking or which channels have contributed to, at what stages the tactics cause success or failure, and comments from consumers. (Penpece, 2013: 98).

It is possible to list the advantages of content marketing as follows (Saruhan, 2018: 48);

- Content marketing increases the sharing of the brand's story.
- Customer loyalty can be achieved through content marketing.
- Content marketing enables information to be conveyed to the consumer about brands and products.
- Content marketing contributes to reaching large audiences by creating a viral effect.

- Through content marketing, the brand strengthens its reputation in the digital world.
- Brand advocates are formed in times of crisis through content marketing.

Content marketing is frequently used in events used as a digital marketing communication tool. For example, Coca Cola personalized the content with the "Share a Coke" event organized on its website. In this way, people gave the names of their loved ones on Coca Cola bottles and then shared it from their own accounts, which made the Coca Cola event popular in a very short time through viral means. The Game of Thrones series has organized the Game of Social Thrones event in order to increase the devotion to the series and made the content it created in this way fun and exciting. Mc Donald's Canada explained what is in the product ingredients one by one in order to increase brand trust and additionally answered questions from about 10,000 consumers. In addition to the written content, it can be claimed that it is effective in increasing consumer loyalty in visual content. For example, the GoPro brand has doubled its site traffic with its quality images. Additionally, it has 3.4 million subscribers on YouTube and 6.8 million followers on Instagram (Dholakiya, 2015).

In the light of the above information and examples, it can be stated that it is essential for businesses to benefit from content marketing in digital activity applications. In particular, it can be stated that especially tourism and media organizations frequently benefit from content marketing in order to provide information about when and where the event will be held and to increase participation in the event. At this point, especially many digital tools and environments provide great convenience for businesses. In this context, the first type of content marketing that businesses can benefit from in event applications is the visual or written content that businesses will prepare on their own pages. The second is the sharing of the company's event contents via the corporate social media account. Finally, event contents can also be presented via digital ads. When content marketing related to event applications reaches the right participants, from the right platforms and at the right time, it is inevitable for companies to gain competitive advantage and increase their market share.

6. Storytelling

The fifth types of event commonly used in digital marketing communication are storytelling. Storytelling is the narration of time and space through words, images and sounds. Stories have been used throughout human history for all kinds of social functions, from framing social order and laws to encouraging creativity. Today, stories have emerged as a new phenomenon as a result of developments in digital and electronic fields and are used to create emotional bonds with the consumer within the framework of marketing communication. Storytelling is the art of telling a specific event using words and images. The aim of storytelling is to convey a particular idea, value and perception to the listener or reader (Mathews and Wacker, 2007: 41). Today, individuals exposed to messages from thousands of sources need to original stories. (Lambert, 2013). Because through stories, individuals can be easily encouraged to research and discover (McDrury and Alterio, 2001: 65).

With the development of the internet, storytelling has become one of the most important parts of marketing communication activities. In today's marketing world, it is possible to see that the most popular brands are based on a good story. According to Moon and Millison (2003: 34), each brand tells a story, and stories add meaning to the consumer's relationship with the brand. In fact, the stories of some brands are like the stories of the consumers themselves. Defines it, acts like a label, and shapes the value judgments it shares with other people. Especially in Web 2.0, where technological products (such as

YouTube, Twitter, Instagram) are diversified day by day, it has been inevitable that stories become more attractive with enriched visual and audio elements. "Digital storytelling", known as the digitalization of stories, first emerged in 1993 with a non-profit organization called "The Center of Digital Storytelling". The name of the center has been changed to "Story Center" since 2015. The center delivers the stories to the target audience interactively through digital technology and media. The center also makes it possible to interact with the audience / audience regardless of place and time (Öztel and Öymen, 2019: 37).

Miller (2005: 34) lists the main features of web-based storytelling as follows;

- The predominance of the plot and protagonist of the story: An interesting subject and interesting characters constitute the basis of successful Web-based storytelling.
- Creating a series of Web sites: creating one or more Web sites that tell the story of the characters or institutions. The visual design of the site is very important. Characters should also appear in other views of the internet. The visibility of the story should also be ensured on other social media platforms such as Youtube, Facebook, Twitter, and Instagram.
- Interactivity: It often seems more natural to see that the story created is a game and the participants are a player. Therefore, it is necessary to minimize the evidence that reveals that the site design is a fiction.
- Telling the story by improving the content of the site: Instead of telling the story in a simple way, it is necessary to show the results of the events in the story and leave it to the participants to understand what these actions are.
- Watching and adapting: Web-based content needs to be watched and made sure that it reaches its objective.

In addition, Lambert (2013: 47) draws attention to the necessity of some elements to create an effective digital story. Accordingly, the narrator should tell about his experiences or a new insight using the first-person expression, using moving photos or images provided by digital media, using the soundtrack, and the story should last a maximum of five minutes. Web-based applications that brands utilize in their communication processes include websites, social networks such as Facebook, Twitter, or video-based applications with high visual efficiency such as YouTube. The effective use of these applications in the storytelling processes of brands has many opportunities to achieve the main objectives of brand communication, such as creating brand loyalty, brand positioning or brand awareness (Akbayır, 2016: 69). In addition thanks to the digitization of the stories, the information given is processed more effectively by the brain.

There are some examples of the inclusion of the storytelling application in the event. For example, Wedding organizers tell the bride and groom's love story through video and various photographs, distribute storytelling giveaways, and play interactive games. The Dear World brand is incredibly popular with the "Choose Your Own Adventure" book event, as it not only empowers the reader, but also allows the reader to discover many unique ways from the beginning to the end of the story. (Stanfield, 2017) In the "the Men thing" event organized by Dove, the brand included men in its story and shared this story on YouTube. In this way, Dove has increased emotional loyalty to its own brand. In another storytelling application, "Likeagirl", a hashtag was created on the subject and an additional video was posted on YouTube. With this practice, the expressions described as reddish were opposed and the power of women was emphasized. The mentioned event campaign reached large audiences through storytelling and attracted a lot of attention. In another example, TOMS shoes created a "day without shoes" event on social media and asked their followers to donate shoes to children without shoes, who participated in the event and shared a photo of bare feet. In this way, the brand both added a story to the event and differentiated itself from its competitors. Similarly, the Heinz brand organized the "Get Well Soon" event and encouraged fans on Facebook to buy a box of "Get Well Soon" soup. In this way, Heinz strengthened the brand story by allowing fans to send soup to their loved ones and differentiated himself from his competitors. In addition, it has increased its sales (Ashraf, 2018).

Considering the aforementioned benefits and examples of storytelling, it can be stated that the storytelling that will be applied in event applications will increase the emotional bond with the participants. It can be claimed that this method will be more effective especially in the events of non-profit organizations. In order to increase this effect, brands should not only tell stories, but also make the people participating in the event a part of this story. As a matter of fact, when the participants of the event are included in the story, an emotional bond will be established with the event and the event will be shared digitally. Increased sharing in the digital environment will increase the visibility of the event and will bring more participants in the next event.

7. Augmented Reality and Virtual Reality Applications

The term reality technology can be basically divided into virtual reality and augmented reality. With the augmented reality, a world that does not actually exist but is perceived as real by digital programs emerges. Sertalp (2017: 110) defines the concept of augmented reality as applications that combine real-time and physical environment and information produced in computer systems. In augmented reality, the environment is real and expanded with articulated information and images. In other words, augmented reality builds a seamless bridge between reality and virtuality (Lee, 2012: 13). Although augmented reality technology was originally used for military purposes, today it has become widespread in all sectors from education to health, from architecture to art. This technology, which is increasingly used in many fields and disciplines, can be used in different platforms such as desktop and laptop computers, tablet computers and smart phones. It is a field of study that covers the combination of real world and computer-generated data such as sound, video, graphics, animation, GPS location information (Zachary et al., 1997: 1119).

Cheng and Tsai (2013: 452) gathered the augmented reality systems under two categories, location-based and image-based, according to their technological infrastructure. Image-based methods are divided into two as pointer-based augmented reality systems and non-pointer-based augmented reality systems (Katiyar et. al., 2015: 443). Location-based augmented reality methods are the determination of the user's location with data from sensors, global positioning (GPS), wireless local area network (WLAN) and radio frequency identification (RFID) and are the addition of media enrichment data on real images. Among the advantages of location-based augmented reality systems are its compatibility with portable devices, its cost effectiveness and its effectiveness in outdoor applications. Location-based augmented reality can be used effectively in promoting areas such as education, architecture and tourism (İçten and Bal, 2017: 122). Image-based augmented reality systems use objects (picture, graphic, logo, photograph, motion and sound detection) defined in the augmented reality environment as pointers. Then it adds virtual data, graphics or 3d / 2d objects according to the determined points. When software and applications offered in the field of augmented reality are examined, image-based augmented reality studies are the most common (Abdüsselam and Karal,2012: 174).

Augmented reality technology enables users to create a participatory experience and increases the impact of the experience (Stapleton and Hughes, 2006: 333). Dunleavy et. al. (2009: 8) emphasizes that augmented reality technology is one of the most important features of providing an environment ready for use anywhere, anytime. Pavlik and Bridges (2013: 23) stated that augmented reality has storytelling potential.

Augmented reality enables customers to present impressive media products and advertisements of companies in an easy and entertaining way (Finkelstein et. al., 2005: 102). In addition, the use of augmented reality, which is currently an unknown form of marketing and advertising, will put the company one step ahead of its competitors as it is sensitive to technological developments. Users will start the communication themselves by choosing their own special content thanks to augmented reality. Therefore, they will experience an optional, volunteer and fun marketing experience. Augmented reality can appeal to all kinds of products and marketing tools. It has the opportunity to find itself on social media due to both gamification and advertainment. This means that in today's world, the company can reach very large audiences with a smart augmented reality project.

Coates (1992: 57) defines virtual reality as systems that enable users to experience three-dimensional experiences through various materials. There are three basic features that distinguish many applications from virtual reality (Pimental and Teixeira, 1993,97). First of all, it gives the participants a sense of reality. The users should feel that they are in control of this environment created by computers. This can only be achieved through mutual interaction. Virtual reality applications should include virtual reality glasses. The sense of vision in the virtual environment can be expanded to include the displacement of objects, touch, feeling physical properties and hearing sounds (Sui et. al., 2001: 33).

Virtual reality aims to change the real world, while augmented reality supports it well (Feiner, 2002: 50). Everything in virtual reality is a simulation of virtual, digital or reality. Augmented reality is the integration of digital with reality (Berryman, 2012: 213). Augmented reality technology does not cut the user's relationship with the real world, but the virtual reality technology completely immerses the user in the virtual environment and prevents developing communication with the real world. (Kounavis et.al., 2012: 2). Virtual reality replaces the real world with an artificially generated environment, while augmented reality enhances or changes the perception of the real world (Střelák, 2016: 2). Virtual reality and augmented reality technology are used to develop many fields such as medicine, education, design, education, museum, entertainment, advertising, gaming, marketing, online social networks, daily life, robotics, military, architecture, cultural heritage, travel and tourism (Azuma et. al., 2001: 42).

Marketing orientations in which individuals experience different experiences using virtual reality and augmented reality applications have also begun to be applied in Turkey. These applications are consumer oriented, not producer. The concept of prosumer that develops with technology is an indicator of personalized marketing trends. Applications provide individuals with the opportunity to see exactly what the products will look like by experiencing them in virtual ways, without experiencing them in real life. This situation brings along many positive factors for the consumer. These factors are such as; being able to compare comfortably, to try the product as if it were bought, to reduce instability and to be able to buy easily (Köse and Yengin, 2018: 101).

There is a general opinion that the participants should be where the event is organized. However, it can be stated that today, with the support of technology, the activities do not limit. At this point, brands have started to focus on augmented reality and virtual reality applications as well as making live broadcasts from their events. Thanks to augmented reality and virtual reality, event participants can physically feel that they are there and navigate within spaces or scenes. In this case, it increases the participants' experience of the event in a more interactive way and their interest in the event.

There are many examples of using virtual reality and augmented reality in event applications today. For example, the ArtScience Museum in Singapore, in collaboration with WWF, created an augmented reality application-based exhibition event titled "Into the Wild", highlighting the story of deforestation and what drives certain animal species and habitats to disappear. In another example, Dallas Cowboys and AT&T stadium cooperated and organized the "Pose with the Pros" event. In the event in question, people took photos with American football players they admire through augmented reality and shared them on social media. About 50 million interactions resulted as a result of the event and the emotional bond between the Dallas Cowboys football team and the fans deepened. In another example, Tramsheds mall sets out another creative example for augmented reality. Accordingly, by using physical markers in the shopping center, shoppers were able to find their way in the physical area, and in this way, the shopping center differentiated itself from its competitors. Another example In 2014, NRMA Insurance used virtual reality technology to allow a 'driver' to experience what it was like to be in a car accident, and in this way offered drivers a training event. In the last example, the Royal Flying Doctors Service Museum enabled Darwin to reenact the bombing of World War II via virtual reality and thus increased the number of people visiting the museum (Lee, 2019).

8. Real Time Events

The last type of event commonly used in digital marketing communications is real time events. Real time events are a type of evet that happens instantly to a specific customer at a specific time and place. For many years, alternative methods of marketing communication studies have been discussed by marketing communication experts in order to create a strong communication between brands and their target audiences. With the development of communication technologies that facilitate the collection and processing of information, some new trends have emerged in marketing activities. Especially with the widespread use of social web platforms, it has become possible to create an effective link between the brand and the consumer on a global scale (Macy and Thompson, 2011: 58). At this point, it can be said that web-based marketing strategies such as real-time marketing are an excellent way for brands to be catchy, create social audiences, and even influence consumers' purchasing decisions (Bazarcı and Mutlu, 2017: 3). Real-time marketing is a marketing approach in which personalized products or services are constantly updated by monitoring changing consumer needs without the conscious feedback of consumers. Therefore, the conceptual framework of real-time marketing is as follows: customization of products according to the needs of individual customers, maintaining flexibility to adapt to changes in consumers' preferences and needs, interact with individual customers on an ongoing basis and maintaining a sustainable relationship after the purchase. In addition, in real time marketing, it is important to match the changing needs and preferences of individuals and product-performance needs. Moreover, this product preference adaptation requires active practice to gather information about a consumer's product and service preferences. (Oliver et. al., 1998: 31).

Real-time marketing can be divided into two different elements. Kerns (2014: 32) named these two different contents as 'known' and 'unknown'. Due to the fact that the current situation can be predicted in terms of scope in real-time marketing created for known issues, preparation can be made in advance. "Planned" and "Watchlist" categories in the upper region of the matrix are two regions that allow content creation and approval before the event occurs. However, Unknown real-time marketing content is unpredictable. For this reason, any issue should be created reactively until it becomes a trend. Creating real-time marketing requires a fast-reactive process. The existing short time period is a time that brands need to create opportunities (Kerns, 2014: 32). Real-time issues create excellent opportunities for companies to raise awareness and interact (Kerns, 2014: 32). Real-time marketing has real-time power law, according to Scott. There is a total of 3 time periods under the power law. These; the peak period of events, the period of time in which the peak followed a rapid decline and the period when less frequent events form a "long queue" (Scott, 2011: 51). The event in question will decline after its peak and will lose its dominance on the agenda and the frequency of being mentioned in social media conversations. According to this; The peak phase becomes the most talked about moment, it begins to become out of date in the old news phase, and the past phase is experienced with the ending phase. Attention should be paid to the timing of content production for brands (Macy and Thompson, 2011: 39).

Dieguez (2015) mentions three important variables in turning real-time marketing into opportunity and achieving success. The first of these is that the work done should be about the business. It is important for real-time marketing that the vehicle and other elements used do not exceed the brand and the business. Another variable is that real-time marketing should be concerned with the users. The content to be created must have a feature that can be of interest to the target audience. The last variable is that real time marketing should be about time. Time is very limited to create a content and present it to target audiences. Since it is a strategy based on instant reactions, presenting the right content to the users at the right time is important for the effective implementation of real-time marketing.

Real-time marketing activities can also be applied effectively in event management. For example, brands can create instant marketing content for sports or special day events (such as Mother's Day or New Year's events). Social media events, such as music shows and conversation between celebrities are an excellent time for real-time events, as millions of people are following them on social media and live posting. For example, during the Superbowl 2013 power outage, Oreo tweeted by putting its own biscuit photo taken in the resolution, which quickly made Oreo a hit on social media. Similarly, when the news about the iPhone 6 being bent was shared intensely on social media, the KitKat brand's jokingly creating the "We don't bend we #break" hashtag made it into the agenda on Twitter. Another unusual example is the fast food chain Wendy's. In this example, a consumer who buys Wendy's products says, "how many retweets for a year of free chicken nuggets?" and Wendy's quickly answered that 18 million. With this response, Wendy's created its own real-time marketing event and rapidly increased its number of followers (Artug, 2019).

When such events are happening or are on the agenda, brands should determine their movements and always have a plan for instant sharing. Brands that make content arrangements by catching the event agenda can keep the relationship between consumer and brand dynamic, maintain interest and follow-up within the framework of continuity, have organic followers and become distinctive from their competitors. In this respect, in order to create an interactive environment with the consumer, the brand must establish a strategic infrastructure and adopt an open and transparent understanding by creating a coordinated work system (Bazarcı, 2017: 15).

SOLUTIONS AND RECOMMENDATIONS

Today, as a result of the widespread use of the internet and the use of digital marketing communication applications that are included in our lives with the internet, the use of digital marketing communication applications in corporate life has increased day by day. Including event applications in the digital marketing communication activities has become mandatory in today's world. As a matter of fact, brands have the opportunity to reach their event activities via digital marketing communication at a lower cost and faster, and also to a wider audience, compared to the event activities via traditional marketing communication.

Considering that the main purpose of brands is to reach wider audiences and increase sale data and considering the presence of target audiences in digital environments, it can be stated that brands should use to event marketing as a digital marketing communication tool. Among digital event tools, brands should observe user interaction values, which tool gets the most interaction and how much benefit is gained from the studies conducted. Brands should determine the most accurate event activities and contents that can meet the expectations and demands of customers in line with the data obtained. In this way, brands will reach the most suitable digital event tool for their target audience. It is thought that in order to increase market share, promote new products, gain competitive advantage and remind products that are about to be forgotten, companies should make more use of event applications, which are a digital marketing communication tool.

FUTURE RESEARCH DIRECTIONS

This study was conducted only to observe what new event trends are used in digital marketing communications. For this, only the literature review has been carried out. In future studies, a comparative study can be conducted on which of the activity trends included in this study are more effective in creating brand loyalty, promoting product or increasing product purchases. In future studies, event trends can also be analyzed by sector-based comparison. In addition, studies can be carried out on the attitude of consumers to each event trends.

CONCLUSION

Digital marketing communication, which creates a radical change in the lifestyles of consumers with the developing technology and communication network in the world, and digitalizes consumption habits from top to bottom, is a tool that has many components in itself. Digital marketing communication, which develops and progresses day by day, has begun to be at the top of the event implementation strategies of brands. Brands have started to appear on digital platforms in order to inform their target audiences about the events they have done and to receive feedback from them.

As a matter of fact, the reasons such as the digital marketing communication applications undertake a more important mission in our lives, increase the number of followers and offer endless options to consumers have made events an important medium of digital marketing communication as in many other fields. Digital marketing communication, which paves the way for the realization of different applications in today's events, is an important promotional tool for the event host brand or company. At the same time, it motivates the event participants with its entertaining, informative and sharing aspects. The main reason why event applications have become a creative, interesting and high-budget sector is the rapid development of technology and the power of digital marketing communication.

In this study, referring to the above-mentioned importance of the subject, the new event trends as a digital marketing communication tool applied by brands are examined. Certain applications stand out when these event trends are observed. The first of these is based on the organization and announcement of events via social media. Through this application, which is called social activities, brands that announce or arrangements their activities through social media can differentiate themselves from their competitors, save time and cost, increase awareness of the event, reach people who are likely to participate in the event faster, and analyze the event through participant feedbacks. The second application is the inclusion of influencers in events or the announcement of events through influencers. With this way, brands can take advantage of influencers for any type of event. In this period, it can be stated that the connection between the brand and the consumer is enriched when the right influencers are selected and included in the event plans of the brand. In addition, the event to be carried out in this way can reach a large number of target audiences in a very short time. The third application is the inclusion of virtual communities in events or the announcement of events through virtual communities. In this way, brands can announce their activities to more audiences, inform those who do not know about the event, make the event more attractive and increase participation in the event. Using content marketing to announce an event or to create a new event on social media is the fourth event trend. In this way brands can benefit from content marketing in order to provide information about when and where the event will be held and to increase participation in the event. It can be also said that when content marketing related to event applications reaches the right participants, from the right platforms and at the right time, it is inevitable for companies to gain competitive advantage and increase their market share. Announcing the event through storytelling or including the participants in the event story is the fifth event trend used by companies. It can be stated that when the participants of the event are included in the story, an emotional bond will be established with the event and the event will be shared digitally. Increased sharing in the digital environment will increase the visibility of the event and will bring more participants in the next event. The sixth event trend is related to augmented reality and virtual reality applications. It can be stated that thanks to augmented reality and virtual reality, event participants can physically feel that they are there and navigate within spaces or scenes. In this case, it increases the participants' experience of the event in a more interactive way and their interest in the event. The latest event trend is real time events application. An interactive interaction with the participants can be realized through real-time events. The visibility and sharing of the event can increase through social media. And brands can differentiate themselves from their competitors in this way.

As a result of the study, it can be argued that today's event practices are no longer ordinary organizations as they were in the past, and have become much more colorful, creative and interesting works. According to the literature analysis, it has been observed that different goods and services sectors have begun to develop a wide variety of ideas and applications related to events in the digital environment. It can be stated that the success of the results in these new event trends implemented within the framework of digital marketing communication increases the need for the application of events day by day and the differences in the events start to push the limits of creative minds. As a matter of fact, it has been observed that with the continuous development of technology, applications in event management have reached much higher levels and events that were ordinary in the past appear in a quite different way today.

REFERENCES

Abdüsselam, M. S., & Karal, H. (2012). Fizik öğretiminde artırılmış gerçeklik ortamlarının öğrenci akademik başarısı üzerine etkisi: 11. Sınıf manyetizma konusu [The effect of augmented reality environments on student academic achievement in physics teaching: 11th grade magnetism topic]. *Eğitim ve Öğretim Araştırmaları Dergisi, 1*(4), 170–182.

Akar, E. (2010). *Sosyal medya pazarlaması [Social media marketing]*. Efil Yayınevi.

Akbayır, Z. (2016). Bana bir hikâye anlat: Marka iletişiminde hikâyeleştirme ve internet [Tell me a story: Storytelling and internet in brand communication]. *Karadeniz Teknik Üniversitesi İletişim Araştırmaları Dergisi, 3*(12), 67–84.

Alikılıç, I., & Özkan, B. (2018). Bir sosyal medya pazarlama trendi, hatırlı pazarlama ve etkileyiciler: Instagram fenomenleri üzerine bir araştırma [A social media marketing trend, influencer marketing and influencers: A study on Instagram phenomena]. *Uluslararası Sosyal Bilimler Dergisi, 1*(2), 43–57.

Argan, M. T. (2008). Pazarlamada sanal topluluklar (Virtual communities in marketing). In İ. Varinli & K. Çatı (Eds.), *Güncel pazarlama yaklaşimlarindan seçmeler* (pp. 305–332). Detay Yayıncılık.

Armstrong, A., & Hagel, J. III. (1996). The Real Value of On-Line Communities. *Harvard Business Review, 74*, 134–141.

Artug, E. (2019). *4 Examples of Successful Real-Time Marketing*. Retrieved from: https://medium.com/better-marketing/4-examples-of-successful-real-time-marketing-4b55c089adac

Ashforth, B. E., & Mael, F. (1989). Social identity theory and the organization. *Academy of Management Review, 14*(1), 20–39. doi:10.5465/amr.1989.4278999

Ashraf, S. (2018). *7 Incredible Examples of Brand Storytelling on Social Media*. Retrieved from: https://locowise.com/blog/7-incredible-examples-of-brand-storytelling-on-social-media

Azuma, R. (1993). Tracking requirements for augmented reality. *Communications of the ACM, 36*(7), 50–51. doi:10.1145/159544.159581

Bagozzi, R. P., & Dholakia, U. M. (2002). Intentional social action in virtual communities. *Journal of Interactive Marketing, 16*(2), 2–21. doi:10.1002/dir.10006

Bazarcı, S. (2017). *Dijital çağda yeni bir pazarlama yaklaşımı olarak gerçek zamanlı pazarlama: Türkiye'de markaların sosyal medya paylaşımları üzerine bir inceleme* [Real-time marketing as a new marketing approach in the digital age: A review on social media sharing of brands in Turkey] (Unpublished master's thesis). İzmir Ege University, Social Science Institute, Turkey.

Bazarcı, S., & Mutlu, B. (2017, April). *Yeni bir pazarlama iletişimi yaklaşımı olarak gerçek zamanlı pazarlama: Markaların sosyal medyadaki paylaşımları üzerine bir inceleme* [Real-time marketing as a new marketing communication approach: A review of brands' shares on social media]. Paper presented at the meeting of the 1. Uluslararası İletişimde Yeni Yönelimler Konferansı, İstanbul, Turkey.

Berryman, D. R. (2012). Augmented reality: A review. *Medical Reference Services Quarterly, 31*(2), 212–218. doi:10.1080/02763869.2012.670604

Bierman, J. (2010, Nov.). Tell me a story. *NZ Business*, 40-42.

Bilgen, İ. (2011). *Tüketici davranışlarında durumsal faktörlerin satın alma niyeti ve memnuniyet üzerinedeki etkisi ve bir araştırma* [The effect of situational factors in consumer behavior on purchasing intention and satisfaction and a study] (Unpublished master's thesis). Marmara University, Social Science Institute, Turkey.

Bozkurt, İ. (2002). Bütünleşik pazarlama iletişimi sürecinde halkla ilişkilerin rolü. *Gazi Üniversitesi İletişim Fakültesi Dergisi*, (16), 139-154.

Brown, D., & Fiorella, S. (2013). *Influence marketing*. Que Publishing.

Brown, D., & Hayes, N. (2008). *Influencer marketing, who really influences your customers?* Elsevier Ltd.

Bulut, E. (2012). *Pazarlama iletişiminde yeni yaklaşimlar kapsaminda sosyal medya uygulamalari ve etkili kampanya örnekleri* [Social media applications and examples of effective campaigns within the scope of new approaches in marketing communication] (Unpublished master's thesis). Istanbul Kültür University, Social Science Institute, Turkey.

Çakmak, A. (2011). *Doğrudan satış ve şebeke yoluyla pazarlama sistemi [Direct selling and network marketing system]*. Türkmen Kitabevi.

Çalık, M., Altunışık, R., & Sütütemiz, N. (2013). Bütünleşik pazarlama iletişimi, marka performansi ve pazar performansi ilişkisinin incelenmesi [Integrated marketing communications, brand performance and market performance analysis]. *Uluslararası Yönetim İktisat ve İşletme Dergisi*, *9*(19), 137–161.

Çelik, S. (2014). Sosyal medyanın pazarlama iletişimine etkisi [The effect of social media on marketing communications]. *Erciyes İletişim Dergisi*, *3*(3), 28–42.

Cheng, K. H., & Tsai, C. C. (2013). Affordances of augmented reality in Science learning: Suggestions for future search. *Journal of Science Education and Technology*, *22*(4), 449–462. doi:10.100710956-012-9405-9

Coates, G. (1992). *Invisible site-a virtual sho*. Siggraph.

Dholakiya, P. (2015). *Content Marketing Done Right: 8 Examples You Can Learn From*. Retrieved from: https://marketingland.com/content-marketing-done-right-8-examples-can-learn-149088

Dieguez, V. S. (2015). *Are You Overlooking the Most Valuable Real-Time Marketing Strategy?* Retrieved from http://www.convinceandconvert.com/digital-marketing/are-you-overlooking-the-most-valuable-real-time-marketing-strategy/

Dunleavy, M., Dede, C., & Mitchell, R. (2009). Affordances and limitations of immersive participatory augmented reality simulations for teaching and learning. *Journal of Science Education and Technology*, *18*(1), 7–22. doi:10.100710956-008-9119-1

Eckerstein, A. (2002). *Evaluation of event marketing* (Unpublished master's thesis). Göteborg University, Graduate Business School, School of Economics and Commercial Law, Swedish.

Eker, M., Bayindir, M., Büktel, S., & Yilmaz, K. (2017). Influencer'ın hatırı kaç yıl sürer? [How many years does the Influencer respect?]. *Campaign Dergisi*, *69*, 22–24.

Erciş, M. S. (2010). *Pazarlama iletişiminde temel yaklaşımlar [Basic approaches in marketing communication]*. Nobel Yayıncılık.

Erdem, A. (2009). Firmalarda bütünleşik pazarlama iletişim stratejilerinin belirlenmesinde tüketici davranışlarının önemi [The importance of consumer behaviors in determining integrated marketing communication strategies in companies]. *Erciyes Üniversitesi İktisadi ve İdari Bilimler Fakültesi Dergisi*, 42-64.

Evans, D. (2008). *Social media marketing an hour a day*. Wiley Publishing Inc.

Feiner, S. (2002). Augmented reality: A new way of seeing. *Scientific American*, *286*(4), 48–55. doi:10.1038cientificamerican0402-48

Finin, T., Ding, L., Zhou, L., & Joshi, A. (2005). Social networking on the semantic web. *The Learning Organization*, *12*(5), 418–435. doi:10.1108/09696470510611384

Finkelstein, N., Perkins, K., & Adams, W. (2005). Can computer simulations replace real equipment in undergraduate laboratories? In *Physics Education Research Conference* (vol.790, pp. 101-104). New York: American Institute of Physics Conference Proceedings. 10.1063/1.2084711

Goldstein, J. (2013). Content marketing: The smart way to grab attention. *Bank Marketing*, 26–29.

8Great Examples of Social Media Event Marketing. (2016). Retrieved from https://www.eventbrite.co.uk/blog/social-media-event-marketing-ds00/

Handley, A., & Chapman, C. (2012). *Dijital çağda içerik yönetiminin kuralları [Content management rules in the digital age]*. Kapital Medya Hizmetleri.

Horo, S. (2015). *The role of social media on event marketing* (Unpublished master's thesis). Bahcesehir University, Social Science Institute, Turkey.

İçten, T and Bal, G. (2017). Artırılmış gerçeklik üzerine son gelişmelerin ve uygulamaların incelenmesi [Examining the latest developments and applications on augmented reality]. *GU J Sci, Part C, 5*(2), 111-136.

Karjaluoto, H., Ulkuniemi, P., & Hänninen, N. (2015). The role of digital channels in industrial marketing communications. *Journal of Business and Industrial Marketing*, *30*(6), 703–710. doi:10.1108/JBIM-04-2013-0092

Karkar, A. (2016). Değer ve güven ağlarının yükselişinde içerik pazarlaması [Content marketing in the rise of value and trust networks]. *International Journal of Social Sciences and Education Research*, *2*(1), 274–285. doi:10.24289/ijsser.279104

Katiyar, A., Kalra, K., & Garg, C. (2015). Marker based augmented reality. *Advances in Computer Science and Information Technology*, *2*(5), 441–445.

Kaya, İ. (2015). *Pazarlama bitanedir: Bir pazarlama ansiklopedisi [Marketing is solidarity: An encyclopedia of marketing]*. Babıali Kültür.

Kehinde, O. J. (2009). *Integrated marketing communications and consumers patronage of Nigerian beverage products* (Unpublished doctoral dissertation). Covenant University, College of Business and Social Sciences, Nigeria.

Kerns, C. (2014). *Trendology: Building an advantage through data-driven real-time marketing*. New York: MacMillan Press.

Kiran, S., Yilmaz, C., & Emre, I. E. (2019). Instagram'daki influencer'larin takipçiler üzerindeki etkisi [Influence of Instagram influencers on followers]. *Uluslararası Yönetim Bilişim Sistemleri ve Bilgisayar Bilimleri Dergisi, 3*(2), 100–111. doi:10.33461/uybisbbd.637155

Köksal, Y., & Özdemir, Ş. (2013). Bir iletişim araci olarak sosyal medya'nin tutundurma karmasi içerisindeki yeri üzerine bir inceleme [A review on the place of social media as a communication tool in the promotional mix]. *Süleyman Demirel Üniversitesi İktisadi ve İdari Bilimler Fakültesi Dergisi, 18*(1), 323–337.

Köse, G., & Çakır, S. Y. (2019). Markaların dijital pazarlama çağında tüketicileri etkileşime ikna etme yolları: Influencer pazarlama ve içerik pazarlamasına ilişkin kavramsal bir çalışma [Ways to convince consumers to interact with brands in the digital marketing era: A conceptual study on influencer marketing and content marketing]. *KOSBED, 38*, 205–222.

Köse, N. & Yengin, D. (2018). Dijital pazarlamadan fijital pazarlamaya geçişe örnek olarak artirilmiş gerçeklik ve sanal gerçeklik uygulamalarinin pazarlama üzerindeki katkilarinin incelenmesi [Examining the contribution of augmented reality and virtual reality applications on marketing as an example of the transition from figital marketing to digital marketing]. *İstanbul Aydın Üniversitesi Dergisi, 10*(1), 77-111.

Kounavis, C. D., Kasimati, A. E., & Zamani, E. D. (2012). Enhancing the tourism experience through mobile augmented reality: Challenges and prospects. *International Journal of Engineering Business Management, 4*(10), 1–6. doi:10.5772/51644

Küçüksaraç, B., & Sayımer, İ. (2016). Deneyimsel pazarlama aracı olarak arttırılmış gerçeklik: Türkiye'deki marka deneyimlerinin etkileri üzerine bir araştırma [Augmented reality as an experiential marketing tool: A study on the effects of brand experience in Turkey]. *İstanbul Üniversitesi İletişim Fakültesi Dergisi*, 73-95.

Lambert, J. (2013). *Digital storytelling* (4th ed.). Routledge. doi:10.4324/9780203102329

Lee, J. (2019). *6 Amazing Use Cases for AR/VR Technology within the Events Industry*. Retrieved from: https://www.virtualimmersive.com.au/post/6-amazing-use-cases-for-ar-vr-technology-within-the-events-industry

Lee, K. (2012). Augmented reality in education and training. *TechTrends, 56*(2), 13–21. doi:10.100711528-012-0559-3

Macy, B., & Thompson, T. (2011). *The power of real-time social media marketing*. Mc Graw Hill Press.

Mathews, R., & Wacker, W. (2007). Senin hikayen ne? [What's your story?] (A. Özer, Trans.). İstanbul: MediaCat Press.

McDrury, J., & Alterio, M. (2001). Achieving reflective learning using storytelling pathways. *Innovations in Education and Teaching International, 38*(1), 63–73. doi:10.1080/147032901300002864

Mert, Y. L. (2018). Dijital pazarlama ekseninde influencer marketing uygulamaları [Influencer marketing applications on the digital marketing axis]. *Gümüşhane Üniversitesi İletişim Fakültesi Elektronik Dergisi, 6*(2), 1299–1328.

Miller, J. (2015). Case study; Exococand the future of storytelling. *Interaction*, (January- February), 30–47.

Miller, K. D., Fabian, F., & Lin, S.-J. (2009). Strategies for online communities. *Strategic Management Journal, 30*(3), 305–322. doi:10.1002mj.735

Moon, M., & Millison, D. (2003). Ateşten markalar [Fiery Brands] (Ş. T. Kalkay, Trans.). İstanbul: MediaCat Press.

Mucuk, İ. (2012). *Pazarlama ilkeleri [Marketing principles]*. Türkmen Kitapevi.

Odabaşı, Y., & Oyman, M. (2002). *Pazarlama iletişimi yönetimi [Marketing communication management]*. Mediacat Kitapları.

Oliver, R. W., Roland, T. R., & Sanjeev, V. (1998). Real-time marketing. *Marketing Management, 7*(Fall), 28–37.

Öztel, T., & Öymen, G. (2019). Duygusal pazarlamada slogan kullanımının önemi: Pandora reklamları üzerine bir inceleme [The importance of using slogans in emotional marketing: A review on Pandora ads]. *Halkla İlişkiler ve Reklam Çalışmaları E-Dergisi, 2*(2), 31–53.

Pavlik, J. V., & Bridges, F. (2013). The emergence of augmented reality (AR) as a storytelling medium in journalism. *Journalism & Communication Monographs, 15*(1), 4–59. doi:10.1177/1522637912470819

Penpece, D. (2013). *Dijital içerik pazarlaması [Digital content marketing]*. Karahan Kitabevi.

Pickton, D., & Broderick, A. (2005). *Integrated marketing communications*. Pearson Education Limited.

Pimental, K., & Teixeira, K. (1993). *Virtual reality through the new looking glass* (2nd ed.). McGraw-Hill.

Pulizzi, J., & Barrett, N. (2009). *Get content- Get customers*. McGraw Hill.

Rheingold, H. (1993). *The virtual community: Homestanding on the electronic frontier*. Harper Collins.

Romm, C., & Plinskin, N. (1997). Virtual communities and society: Toward an integrative three phase model. *International Journal of Information Management, 17*(4), 261–270. doi:10.1016/S0268-4012(97)00004-2

Ryan, D. (2016). *Dijital pazarlama: Dijital kuşağa seslenmek için pazarlama stratejileri [Digital marketing: Marketing strategies to address the digital generation]* (M. M. Kemaloğlu, Trans.). Türkiye İş Bankası Kültür Yayınları.

Sarıtaş, A. (2018). İçerik pazarlamasına yönelik bir literatür taraması [A literature review on content marketing]. *Sosyal Araştırmalar ve Davranış Bilimleri Dergisi, 4*(6), 232–239.

Saruhan, O. (2018). Sosyal medya canavarı olmak ister misin? [Do you want to be a social media monster?]. İstanbul: MediaCat Press.

Schachter, H. (n.d.). *20 Killer Exanples of Influencer Marketing*. Retrieved from: https://www.travelmindset.com/20-influencer-marketing-examples/

Schmitt, B. H. (1999). *Experiential marketing*. The Free Press.

Scott, D. M. (2011). *Gerçek zamanlı pazarlama ve halkla ilişkiler [Real time marketing and public relations]* (A. Özer, Trans.). MediaCat Press.

Sertalp, E. (2017). Müzelerin tanıtım kitaplarında artırılmış gerçeklik (ag) teknolojisi kullanımı: Ankara Anadolu Medeniyetleri Müzesi kitabı örneği [The use of augmented reality (ag) technology in the promotional books of museums: An example of the Ankara Anatolian Civilizations Museum book]. *Hacettepe Üniversitesi Güzel Sanatlar Fakültesi Sanat Yazıları*, *36*(May), 107–120.

Singh, S., & Diamond, S. (2012). Social media marketing for dummies (2nd ed.). John Wiley and Sons, Inc.

Sohn, D. (2005). *Interactive media and social exchange of market information* (Unpublished doctoral dissertation). The University of Texas.

Soucy, C. (2020). *Stay Connected with Virtual Community Events*. Retrieved From: https://wiredimpact.com/blog/virtual-community-events-stay-connected/

Stanfield, J. (2017). *5 Ways to Harness the Power of Storytelling at Events*. Retrieved from: https://www.eventmanagerblog.com/the-power-of-storytelling-at-events

Stapleton, C. B., & Hughes, C. E. (2006). Making memories of a lifetime. In M. Haller, M., Billinghurst, & B. H. Thomas (Eds.), Emerging Technologies of Augmented Reality: Interfaces & Design (pp. 329-351). London: IDEA Group Inc.

Stevens, R. P. (2005). *Trade show and event marketing*. Thomson.

Střelák, D. (2016). *Augmented reality tourist guide* (Master's Thesis). Masarykova Univerzita Fakulta Informatiky. Czechia.

Sui, Y., Geng, D., Allen, C. R., Burn, D., Bell, G. D., & Rowland, R. (2001). Three-dimensional motion system ("data-gloves"): Application for Parkinson's disease and essential tremor. In *IEEE International Workshop on Virtual and Intelligent Measurement Systems* (pp.28-33). Budapest, Hungary: IEEE. 10.1109/VIMS.2001.924896

Tasner, M. (2011). *Anında pazarlama, web 3.0 pazarlama kılavuzu [Instant marketing, web 3.0 marketing guide]* (A. Özer, Trans.). MediaCat Press.

Tığlı, M. (2010). *Pazarlama iletişimde şöhret figürü [Fame figure in marketing communications]*. Beta Basım.

Tinnish, S. M., & Mangal, S. M. (2012). Sustainable event marketing in the MICE industry: A theoretical framework. *Journal of Convention & Event Tourism*, *13*(4), 227–249. doi:10.1080/15470148.2012.731850

Tuten, T. L. (2008). *Advertising 2.0: Social media marketing in a web 2.0 world*. ABC-CLIO.

Valck, K. D., & Bruggen, G. H. V. (2009). Virtual communities: A marketing perspective. *Decision Support Systems*, *47*(3), 185–203. doi:10.1016/j.dss.2009.02.008

Valos, M. J., Hajı Habıbı, F., Casıdy, R., Drıesener, C. B., & Maplestone, V. L. (2016). Exploring the integration of social media within integrated marketing communication frameworks: Perspectives of services marketers. *Marketing Intelligence & Planning*, *34*(1), 19–40. doi:10.1108/MIP-09-2014-0169

Veirman, D. M., Cauberge, V., & Hudders, L. (2017). Marketing through Instagram influencers: The impact of number of followers and product divergence on brand attitude. *International Journal of Advertising*, *36*(5), 798–828. doi:10.1080/02650487.2017.1348035

Yıldız, A., & Karagöz, Ş. (2018). İçerik pazarlaması (Content marketing). In Y. Akçi (Ed.), *Değişen pazarlama anlayışı- Yeni pazarlama yaklaşımları [Changing marketing understanding - New marketing approaches]* (pp. 75–102). Gazi Kitapevi.

Yürük, P. (2015). *Etkinlik pazarlamasinda sosyal etki algilamasinin etkinliğe katilim, tatmin ve sadakat üzerine etkisi: Kirkpinar festivali örneği* [The effect of social impact perception in event marketing on participation, satisfaction and loyalty: The example of the Kirkpinar festival] (Unpublished doctoral dissertation). Trakya University, Social Science Institute, Turkey.

Zachary, W., Ryder, J., Hicinbothom, J., & Bracken, K. (1997). The Use of executable cognitive models in simulation-based intelligent embedded training. In *Proceedings of Human Factors Society 41st Annual Meeting* (pp. 1118-1122). Santa Monica, CA: Human Factor Society. 10.1177/107118139704100287

ADDITIONAL READING

Çizmeci, F., & Ercan, T. (2015). The effect of digital marketing communication tools in the creation of brand awareness by housing companies. *Megaron*, *10*(2), 149–161.

Corniani, M. (2006). Digital marketing communication. *Symphonya: Emerging Issues in Management*, *2*, 41–61.

Dahiya, R. G. (2018). A research paper on digital marketing communication and consumer buying decision process: An empirical study in the Indian passenger car market. *Journal of Global Marketing*, *31*(2), 73–95. doi:10.1080/08911762.2017.1365991

Gagandeep, K. N., & Gopal, R. (2014). The effect of digital marketing communication on consumer buying. *International Journal of Management*, *5*(3), 53–57.

Hoyle, L. (2002). *Event marketing: How to successfully promote events, festivals, conventions, and expositions*. Wiley.

Tassiopoulos, D. (Ed.). (2000). *Event management: A professional and developmental approach*. Juta Education.

Tum, J., Norton, P., & Wright, J. (2006). *Management of event operations*. Butterworth-Heinemann/ Elsevier.

Uysal, M., Gahan, L., & Martin, B. (1993). An examination of event motivations: A case study. *Festival Management & Event Tourism*, *1*(1), 5–10.

KEY TERMS AND DEFINITIONS

Augmented Reality: Changing and enhancing the reality by the computer.

Content Marketing: It is a strategy to grow the brand and product by producing useful and interesting content, especially on the internet.

Influencer: Person who influences, leads, inspires, and guides people against a specific situation.

Real-Time Marketing: A type of marketing that happens instantly to a specific customer at a specific time and place.

Social Media: It is the whole of the dialogues and shares people make with each other on the internet.

Storytelling: The narration of time and space through words, images, and sounds.

Virtual Community: The generic name of the network that bringing together groups of people for a common purpose on the internet.

Virtual Reality: Combining fictions created using technology with reality and imagination.

Chapter 14
Applying Industry 4.0 on Management of Gastronomy Events

Asim Saldamli
Abant Izzet Baysal University, Turkey

Nurhayat Iflazoglu
Mustafa Kemal University, Turkey

Ipek Itır Can
https://orcid.org/0000-0003-4793-7151
Anadolu University, Turkey

ABSTRACT

Industry 4.0 plays a role in meeting the demands of the global market in food and beverage activities with more efficient, harmonious, reliable, and sustainable production processes. In the recent years, enterprises have started taking advantage of augmented reality technology in the design phase; three-dimensional printers, internet of things technology and robot chefs during the production phase; and robot waiters in the presentation phase. In this context, in this chapter, the transformations experienced in the design, production, and presentation processes of banquet organizations as the result of the Gastronomy 4.0 concept, which emerged as a result of the reflections of Industry 4.0 on the field of gastronomy, were examined. It is thought that in the near future, if the prevalence of Gastronomy 4.0 applications increases, the personnel responsible for running banquet organizations will need to be trained and also informed about the equipment of the new age.

DOI: 10.4018/978-1-7998-4954-4.ch014

INTRODUCTION

Technology can be defined as a practical process that reproduces human life via continuous development, affects the behavioral plane and living spaces, and is based on the ability to think and produce knowledge. Therefore, technology can be regarded as an important force that shapes the future and needs to be constantly monitored, that can change and transform people who are its creators, their nature and living spaces, and nature in general. The series of industrial revolutions, which started with the transition from manpower to machinery, evolved into the Technological Revolution with the emerging of the period when superior electrical technology produced larger scale production and more complex machines compared to the previous periods. On the other hand, it is known that the digital revolution started with the first computers in the 1950s. Computers laid the foundations for the industrial revolutions that would come after them. Machines have become able to manage themselves in many ways, often using internet technologies or internet objects. This technological stage is now called industry 4.0 and includes the use of cloud technology and applications of big data (Topsakal et al., 2018). It is an undeniable fact that the developments in information technologies are used in an innovative way by industrial companies, changing the production processes, production, value chain, household behavior and demand.. But of course, this process has gradually come to this level of advancement. Developments in different periods of history have contributed to the development of different industrial branches and other sectors.

Industry 1.0, the first industrial revolution, was realized as the transition from agricultural economy to industrial economy at the end of the 18th century with the discovery of steam and its use in machinery. Production has evolved from hand and body labor to machine power (Genc, 2018).

The foundations of Industry 2.0 were laid in the early 20th century after the previous revolution mechanized production. The leap of the superiority, knowledge and know-how gained by England with the first industrial revolution, to other countries had brought technological progress. This revolution is also known as "technology revolution". New techniques such as the use of electricity in factories, the substitution of coal with crude oil as the energy source, and mass production and the assembly line are the prominent features of Industry 2.0. Electrical technology that is more efficient than steam power has been used in production lines. Thus, production increased significantly and the world met with the Fordist mass production applications (EBSO, 2015).

Industry 3.0 is also known as "digital revolution" due to the inclusion of computer technology in production. It is a period that defines the transition from the industrial society to the information society. After the development of computers based on calculators powered by mechanical electricity, the search for a network that will enable the interconnection of machines within the computer system is regarded as the beginning of the history of the internet (Ziewitz & Brown, 2013). While the rapid increase in the processing power of computers gave birth to "smart machines", the sudden and rapid breakthrough of the robotic industry caused the decrease in manpower in production for the first time due to the use of robotic machines in production instead of humans. The integration of electronic and computer applications into the machinery applications has led to the automation of production systems, and the development of electronic, information and communication technologies has enabled the automation of production.

Developments in the Industry 3.0 era such as the development of the Internet, fiber optic networks and automation in production played a major role in the development of Industry 4.0's prominent smart production and Internet of Things technologies (Kabaklarlı, 2016). Germany is the leading country of Industry 4.0. It first came to the agenda with the Hanover Fair held in Germany in 2011. Following Germany, Spain started a national initiative under the name of "Advanced Factories", Italy - "Smart

Factories" and France - "Industry of the Future". Industry 4.0 can be defined as a smart production era where any animate or inanimate object that has economic value can communicate and interact with other objects through the developments in the areas of smart factories, artificial intelligence, 3D printers, robots, internet of things, big data, cloud systems, and bio, nano and space technologies. In this period of digitization in production, we can talk about a production system in which virtual and physical systems are integrated with each other and objects connected to the internet will act within the framework of a "mind" (TUBITAK, 2016). This system is the backbone of the new revolution and can be adapted to many different machines ranging from homes to factories. Smart factories can facilitate communication between millions of devices and machines using their own cloud storage unit on web-based services. Malfunctions in smart factories can be detected instantly and on site, and the system operates smoothly at full capacity (Ghafory, 2016). The Internet of Things is the physical and social communication of electronic devices with their environment over a digital network through the acquisition of a virtual identity. As can be seen, in the fourth industrial revolution, new technological breakthroughs have intertwined in various fields. According to Hooijdonk (2015), today smart technologies have started taking place in almost all areas of life, without the need for the users to consciously accepting their use. In this respect, it would not be wrong to say that Industry 4.0 technologies are rapidly being used in areas such as conducting business, communication, education, and began to change business environments and lifestyles.

Industry 4.0 also plays a role in meeting the demands of the global markets in food and beverage production with more efficient, harmonious, reliable and sustainable production processes. The food industry not only meets the food and beverage needs of people, but also affects people environmentally, socially and economically. Digital Gastronomy is a culinary vision that combines traditional cooking with Industry 4.0 technology. This is why digital gastronomy mainly results from innovations in the food and beverage industry. For example; when we examine industry 4.0, it is possible to talk about four basic technological developments (3D printers, the internet of things, augmented reality and robots) that can add a different dimension to the food and beverage industry. With 3D printers, there has been a radical change in food and beverage production systems, the coordination of all devices and robots has been ensured through the internet of things, the use of information in all these processes has been taken to a different dimension with augmented reality through cameras and sensors, and with the spread of robotic technology to every area, autonomous robots have entered the food and beverage industry (Bulut & Akçacı, 2017).

Banquet organizations are one of the most important activities considered within the scope of event management of food and beverage and accommodation businesses. Utilization of industry 4.0 technologies, more precisely Gastronomy 4.0 applications, is increasing day by day in banquet organizations. In banquet organizations, the process basically consists of design, production and presentation stages. Nowadays, businesses may use augmented reality technology at the design stage; three-dimensional printers, internet of things technology and robot chefs during production, and robot waiters in the presentation phase. In this context, in this section of the book; transformations experienced in the design, production and presentation processes of the banquet organizations in regard to the concept of Gastronomy 4.0 which emerged as a result of the reflections of industry 4.0 in the field of gastronomy, were examined with the aim to present a perspective on the use of Gastronomy 4.0 technology in banquet organizations in line with today's consumer needs.

BACKGROUND

Gastronomy 4.0 Applications in Event Management

In the Contemporary Turkish Dictionary by Turkish Language Association, the concept of an event is defined as "the actions and activities of an enterprise, or an institution in a certain field" (TDK, 2020). According to another definition, an event is "a series of events that occur as a result of the participation of individuals which is realized within a specific time frame, and has an organization and management style" (Tassiopoulus, 2005). Event management, on the other hand, is the planning, organizing, directing, coordinating and supervising the stakeholders of a large or small-scale event and activity, whether for profit or not, in order to achieve the goals of the event producer.

Banquet organizations, which are evaluated within the scope of event management, their basic element being gastronomy, are simply "mass catering organizations that are presented to a certain number of groups for a specific purpose and have a social character" (Kılıçhan, 2015). In a different definition, the banquet organization is described as "the organization of events that are organized in areas that serve a specific purpose, and have a predetermined menu, number of participants and a date of realization" (Kılıçhan, 2018). They are referred to as "banquet organizations" because of the word "banquette" which means banquet or feast in French.

The steps that the banquet organization manager is obliged to take at the basic level are outlined as follows (Kılıçhan, 2018; Çatalkaya, 2020).

- Menu planning,
- Menu pricing,
- Table layout planning,
- Determination of the service flow order,
- Planning of mise en place,
- Time planning for the banquet,
- Preparation of weekly /monthly banquet lists and allocation of halls,
- Other planning work.

There are two main departments related to the management process of banquet organizations. The first of these is the kitchen department that designs and produces the food and beverages in the menu; the second is the food and beverage (F&B) department, which offers products designed and produced in the kitchen. As a result of the increasing inclusion of technological developments in our lives and the application of Industry 4.0 to different sectors, various transformations have begun to occur in the aforementioned design, production and presentation processes of these departments that carry out banquet organizations. One of the main reasons driving businesses to this transformation is the differentiation of the consumers' eating and drinking habits and their expectations towards gastronomy in the information age encompassing industry 4.0. So much so that, today, food and beverage businesses that can meet the transforming and differentiating habits of consumers, and their requests and expectations by taking the right steps, have started to become places where people can have new and special experiences thanks to the products and services they design, produce and offer.

After Industry 4.0 started to be included in banquet organizations, food and beverage businesses have started to design banquet organization more creatively, running the processes faster and more effectively, providing different experiences to the customers, and leaving a much more reliable impression on the customers before the organization. Food and beverage businesses benefiting from these opportunities have started to gain a significant competitive advantage over their competitors.

MAIN FOCUS OF THE CHAPTER

Due to the existence of food and beverage businesses that want to gain competitive advantage and adapt to the requirements of the new age; besides cooks, waiters, and owners, technology experts as well have started to be included in the sector with robotic coding. Thus, in the gastronomy and food and beverage sector, new data-based digital business ideas have come to the fore and the concept of Gastronomy 4.0 has started to be mentioned.

Gastronomy 4.0 has created an online world that designs, produces and offers products and/or services regardless of time and place. With the introduction of Gastronomy 4.0; it is seen that food and beverage businesses create layered atmospheres by using technology, offer new services that combine virtual images with reality, try to appeal to all senses while serving, and provide a suitable environment for telematic dinners that make people feel that they are in the same environment despite being in different places. In addition to these, food and beverage enterprises benefit from innovations such as e-menus and edible menus and robot chefs in the Industry 4.0 period (Aksoy & Akbulut, 2017). In other words, today food and beverage businesses make various innovations in their services by using science and technology in order to make the eating and drinking experience unique and extraordinary.

Gastronomy 4.0 applications, which businesses use the most for banquet organizations, are categorized under the heading of design, production and presentation of elements of a banquet organization and are presented below.

A New Technology Accompanying the Design Process in Banquet Organizations: Augmented Reality in Restaurant Menus

Augmented reality (AR) is a system that provides a live view of a physical, real-world environment augmented with computer-generated input such as information, sound, video, graphics or GPS data (Kounavis et al., 2012; Özel & Uluyol, 2016). Augmented reality stands out as one of the most popular concepts of the age. Businesses can design creative works by investing in augmented reality technologies to better market their products. In the age of technology, one of the most effective ways to increase the experiences offered to consumers is to constantly follow the changing and developing technological developments and adapt them to their businesses (Aksoy & Akbulut, 2016). Augmented reality technology has strong effects on businesses where individual experiences are prioritized, and is among the 100 innovations that changed tourism industry (Güler, et al., 2015). In other words, augmented reality technology emerges as an "experience enhancing power" for food and beverage businesses. Furthermore it can be said that one of the recent trends is the "individual-focused experiences" in food and beverage sector. In recent years, businesses turn to technology-supported presentation and service in order to gain a competitive advantage in the market (Özgüneş & Bozok, 2017).

Foodpath, a vegetarian restaurant in Mumbai, created a design through the company SMACAR to attract potential customers and encourage them to come back to the business. It has integrated an augmented reality game that the customer can play by scanning the logo on printed materials (flyers, menu

Figure 1. QR Code 1: Augmented Reality of Menus

cards, logo on the website, etc.). The augmented reality spin wheel game based on a wheel design that allows players to spin a virtual wheel to win discount offers, providing interactive experiences alongside discount offers, created curiosity among customers and was instrumental in persuading customers to return to the restaurant (SMACAR Solutions, 2018). "Inamo" developed interactive projection supported applications at restaurant dining tables in London. Customers can interact with the desktop and choose their own table themes, order items from the multimedia-rich menu, or see a live video stream from the kitchen. These expanded surfaces use the richness of paintings and walls seen as canvases to provide both a physical co-working space and an interactive computer view of virtual information (Yovcheva & Buhalis, 2013). In addition, with the services provided in the virtual environment, customers are provided with AR interactive menus placed on the tables to order food and beverages, giving customers a pleasant and unique experience while eating. This restaurant, which applies the latest technological

Figure 2. QR Code 2: Augmented Reality of Menus

developments, in 2019 was deemed worthy of "Best Use of Technology" award at Restaurant Marketer & Innovator awards (www.inamorestaurants.london).

Burger chain Bareburger became one of the first to adopt AR technology by partnering with AR food menu application Kabaq. This new application made the meat of the impossible burger (a meatless burger) appear on the plates of the guests through a Snapchat application. Similarly, customers can now see realistic lunches before their meals are ready, so the restaurant benefits from the marketing advantages of being at the forefront of new technology and building campaigns around it (Future Restaurants, 2019).

New Technologies Accompanying the Production Process in Banquet Organizations: 3D Food Printers, Internet of Things and Robot Chefs

Figure 3. QR Code 3: Meatless Impossible Burger

Three Dimensional Food Printers

Three-dimensional (3D) printing is a controlled robotic process in which a product can be built layer by layer and a three-dimensional object can be created (Yang et al., 2017). Creating a 3D model of the product in a computer environment before the product is built is the first step of this process. After the 3D model is created, the design information is sent to the printer. The printer divides the 3D model into layers and combines them in the specified cross section (Dankar et al., 2018). 3D printing has a variety of applications that are constantly developing, such as medicine, food, gastronomy, engineering, manufacturing, arts and education. However, although its use in the field of food has gained importance in recent years, its use in gastronomy, which is a newly discovered and encouraged field, is also striking (Murphy & Atala, 2014; Rayna & Striukova, 2016; Dankar et al., 2018). Some successful results of new 3D printed shapes have been published where several parameters of the printing process (process chain, ingredients etc.) have been optimized and different food materials are used. Among these food materials are chocolate (Periard et al., 2007; Hao et al., 2010), cookie dough and cereals (Lipton et al., 2015; Severini et al., 2016; Hamilton et al., 2018), powdered sugar (Dankar et al., 2018; Holland et al., 2018;

Liu et al., 2018), processed cheese (Periard et al., 2007; Le Tohic et al., 2018), meat gels (Lipton et al., 2010; Wang et al., 2018) and in recent years some fruits and vegetables (Severini et al., 2018; Yang et al., 2018) (Dankar et al., 2018). In addition, 3D food printers, which print any object desired by the customer on coffee foam, lead the establishment of new and different concept businesses (Pallottino et al., 2016; Zeleny & Ruzicka, 2017). Artistic pasta production according to the shape and formulation requested by the customer is another field of gastronomy where 3D food printing is used (Zeleny & Ruzicka, 2017). Known as the first 3D restaurant in the world, the "Food Ink" Restaurant offers different experiences to its customers by preparing and serving the dishes chosen by the guests with 3D technology (Özgüneş & Bozok, 2017). The restaurant positions itself as a conceptual "pop-up" dinner series where "quality cuisine meets art, philosophy and the technologies of tomorrow". The restaurant, whose main purpose is to create a futuristic space, also uses other technologies such as VR.

Figure 4. QR Code 4: Food Ink at La Boscana Restaurant

Melisse, a stylish restaurant in Santa Monica, may not seem like a place where you will find a 3D printer, but it uses a 3D printer to give a modern twist to classic dishes. Loaded with various designs of croutons for use in onion soup, for example, the 3D printer makes fresh croutons using aromatic onion powder. Another restaurant is La Enoteca, a stylish Michelin-starred restaurant in the center of Barcelona. The restaurant stands out not only with fine cuisine but also for use of technology. It uses a 3D printer for dishes that are difficult to design by hand. For example, a sea coral meal is served with a flower-like shape using a 3D printer, then decorated with sea urchin and caviar. La Boscana, a stylish Spanish gourmet restaurant, offers its customers a unique dining experience using a 3D printer (Ahmed, 2017).

Internet of Things (IoT)

Internet of Things means that objects have a distinctive sign and they communicate with each other via the internet. In other words, the internet of things connects objects to each other, producing and sharing data. Internet of Things is considered as one of the most important technology fields of the

Figure 5. QR Code 5: 3D Food Printing

future (Holler et al., 2014). The most common example of the Internet of Things is the coffee machine. Engineers working at Cambridge University needed to go out of the laboratory to get coffee from the coffee machine, but since they could not return with coffee every time they went, they put a camera in front of the coffee machine and connected it to the computer, if the coffee was fresh, they went out of the laboratory and took the coffee from the corridor. This situation has attracted attention and with the spread of web browsers and the Internet, the image of the coffee machine has been published on the Web symbolically for 10 years. This example is considered as the first application of the Internet of Things (Doyduk & Tiftik, 2017).

The smart kitchen concept developed by Moley Robotics can cook with hands using multiple joints, multiple actuated degrees of freedom, tactile sensors and robotic arms with sophisticated control systems, and then clean the kitchen area. The Robot Chef, which can be managed via the application or touch screen on the smartphone, has more than 2000 recipes in its memory. With the 3D recipe recording feature, the robot has a system where the skills of chefs are taught by coding, so that the robot can cook by imitating the chefs' movements. It is noted that the consumer version set for release in 2020 will be supported by an iTunes-style recipes library (www.moley.com). In summary, providing the necessary technologies for the existence of the Internet of Things system and establishing a permanent communication between objects-people, and objects-objects, data is collected and processed, passed through control mechanisms and ultimately creates value for users.

The way we receive service from the restaurants changes every day. From car service to table service, after robotic waiters, a waiter-free ordering system has emerged with an application installed on a smartphone. In addition, the application allows customers to bid on the prices of food and beverages. Located in India, The Deccan Bid Capital is the country's first organization to use the application. The prerequisite for receiving service from this restaurant is that the application, which aims to eliminate paper waste and improve customer experience through the digital platform, is installed on smartphones (Brittow, 2018).

Figure 6. QR Code 6: Moley Robotics

A New Technology Accompanying the Production Process in Banquet Organizations: Robot Chefs

Today, human and machine work hand in hand in human-robot cooperation in many new applications as well as in unmanned smart factories. The use of robots in the manufacturing sector has also created a great revolution in the field of gastronomy. Chefs and service robots are the best examples of this situation. Chef Robot can learn and reproduce the cooking act of a human chef that is captured on a 3D camera and recorded on a computer to cook as needed (Gibson, 2015). The temperature and humidity settings of pre-cooked meals uploaded to the robot server preserve the food throughout the run-time through steam infusion so that the serving robot can serve the correct preset portions and temperatures for a variety of dishes ranging from rice bowl dishes (Kondo, 2018). Nestle is serving with robots in Japan to attract Chinese customers. The company chose Tokyo for cashless sales in the face of the rapid rise of Starbucks, and in an open booth on the third floor of a commercial complex in Tokyo's historic city center Asakusa, the company greeted the customers with the Chinese speaking humanoid robot Pepper who asked "How about a coffee?" (Obe, 2018). AUSCA was first introduced to the hospitality industry in November 2017 as the world's first robot chef prototype, where it prepared eggs for *M-Social Singapore Hotel* guests as part of the hotel's breakfast. While the first AUSCA prototype prepared eggs (sunny side up or omelet style) in an average of 2 minutes and 30 seconds, the current version offers the same products in just over a minute and allows guests to choose from a variety of ingredients for their omelets (Hospitality Net, 2018).

Automatic and robotic restaurants have started to be used in service in various parts of the world. In addition, restaurants want to continue their services with advanced technology by using smart technology to provide an excellent experience to their customers. Because dining out is not just about trying different types of cuisine, and customers are not afraid to pay high prices for a different experience while consuming the delicious food provided by courteous service staff in a good atmosphere (Khosla, 2019). The world's first robot-equipped Chinese restaurant has attracted a large number of customers after its official launch in the state capital of Guangdong. The restaurant has 46 different robots that can do virtually all the jobs at the restaurant, including welcoming customers, making fries, mixing wines, making desserts, cooking rice, operating a cloud rail and serving food. Moreover, customers have the opportunity to see how their food is cooked by robots in the kitchen separated from the dining room with transparent glass walls (The Star, 2020). On the other hand, leading countries of fast food chains such as the USA, Japan and China have cooperated with technology companies and integrated robot chefs into restaurant kitchens, thus gaining a great advantage in terms of speed. For example, a robot developed by the San Francisco-based company Momentum Machines, can prepare a hamburger from start to finish and can also prepare 400 burgers per hour. Developed by the Japanese robot manufacturer Kawasaki, the sushi robot prepares sushi consisting of fish, rice and fresh vegetables requiring delicate work in seconds. The robot of the American Zume Pizza Restaurant quickly spreads the tomato paste of the pizza on the dough, but other ingredients are prepared by the people in line with the restaurant's preference. The robot called Foxbot cuts noodle slices much faster than a human, and each slice that is cut rapidly is almost the same size as the others. Foxbot is actively used in a restaurant in China (Başöz, 2017).

A New Technology Accompanying the Presentation Process in Banquet Organizations: Robot Waiters

Figure 7. QR Code 7: Robot Chefs

According to Fırat and Fırat (2017), with the design of low-cost, hygienic and smart machines and systems in food and beverage businesses, the enterprises where these machines and systems are installed and operated well will come to the fore in the sector. One of these systems is undoubtedly robotization technology. While robot chefs accompany the production processes in food and beverage businesses, robot waiters accompany the presentation process. Robot waiters involved in the presentation process of food and beverage businesses can also entertain customers with activities such as dancing and singing in addition to their functions such as meeting, directing, taking food orders and serving customers (Jyh-Hwa & Su Kuo, 2008; cited in İbiş, 2019). In addition, in Moscow an enterprise that uses robots for service and in kitchen, also used them for promotion and marketing activities, saw a 40% increase in the sales figures. It is a clear indication that food and beverage businesses where robotization is used effectively attract more attention and gain more business from the guests (İbiş, 2019).

The first company on record to use robot waiters in food and beverage businesses is a fast food restaurant in Pasadena, California, USA, they started using robot waiters in 1983. The technologies of the time were not as advanced as today, and the robot made errors (such as dropping the food and drinks they carried when radio interfered with its signals) despite that the company created a great source of attraction in the relevant years and the business became popular thanks to robot waiters (Guinness World Records, 2020).

All operations are carried out by robots at Spyce Restaurant located in Boston, USA. Robot waiters serve the product produced by robot chefs in the kitchen. In other words, there are no people working in this restaurant. In the People's Republic of China, the use of robot chefs and robot waiters in food and beverage enterprises has been rapidly increasing. It is emphasized that one of the biggest reasons for this is that robots are much less costly than using human personnel (a robot costs about $ 1,200, which is the equivalent of only a few months worth salary of a human waiter). Another reason is that they are considered new and fun and therefore increase customer demand (Nguyen, 2016).

Hijime Robot Restaurant, which opened in Bangkok, Thailand in 2010, appears as a thematic restaurant where robots dressed like samurai perform the service (Wilson, 2010). Produced in Turkey's Konya province by Akın Robotics, a robot named "Ada", began to serve as a waitress in a Konya establishment in 2015 (NTV, 2015). In 2019, in Istanbul, Turkey, Touch Restaurant started to use robot waiters and does not have any human service personnel (CNN Turk, 2019).

Royal Palace restaurant, located in the town of Renesse in Zeeland province of the Netherlands, announced that it started to use robot waiters as a way to minimize human contact after the COVID-19 Pandemic. From this point of view, it is possible to say that the use of robot waiters will increase in the "new normal" social environment after the pandemic (Lyons, 2020).

The use of robot waiters today has become one of the factors that provides cost advantages to businesses in the long term, provides the benefit of minimizing the mistakes that may arise due to human nature, attracts customer attention, and highlights the business in promotion and marketing. Due to these

Figure 8. QR Code 8: Robot Servers at Royal Palace Restaurant, Netherlands

aspects, it is believed that the use of robot waiters in food and beverage businesses will increase significantly in the long term. In banquet organizations, it is aimed to establish a better running and error-free system with the use of robot waiters. In addition, in a period where people have become afraid of human contact due to the COVID-19 Pandemic, it has become very advantageous to use robots with zero risk of carrying the virus to service in enterprises.

SOLUTIONS AND RECOMMENDATIONS

Banquet organizations, which are considered under event management, are special events that are organized to serve a specific purpose and have a specific menu, place and time. Banquet organizations create important opportunities for businesses in terms of promotion, contribute to reducing stocking costs, increase the productivity of the workforce and creates high income for the businesses (Akgül, 2020). With the introduction of computer network systems, internet and smart phones in food and beverage activities, which were previously marketed and managed by physical strategies, perspectives shift towards virtual strategies. Digital gastronomy is a modern culinary vision that combines traditional cooking with industry 4.0 technology. This way, banquet organizations take place beyond only considering taste to cover all aspects of gastronomy. For this reason, many businesses have made various innovations in their services using industry 4.0 to make the eating and drinking experience unique and extraordinary. For example;, the reflections of industry 4.0 on gastronomy, or in other words, the leading technological innovations of Gastronomy 4.0 are augmented reality, three-dimensional printers, internet of things, robot chefs and robot waiters.

Augmented reality allows restaurants and the similar businesses to display food and beverages in three dimensions in menus, provide information about the nutrients (allergens, foods, calories, etc.) of the food and drink in the meal selection, and monitor the preparation of the meal. Augmented reality is also able to translate the menu according to the language preference of the guests (Bilici, 2015; Akram & Kumar, 2017). With augmented reality, a food and beverage business or restaurant can provide guests with a different experience, reduce costs, create a positive image, provide sustainable competitive advantage, improve and strenghten marketing and promotion activities, and can attract more customers (Cankül et al., 2018).

Banquet organizations are considered under event management and create a significant income for businesses. In banquet organizations which are arranged according to the personal wishes and expectations of the customers, it is of great importance to ensure the satisfaction of the customers who organize them. The processes of menu planning, table layout planning, determining the service flow and planning mise en place, which are among the basic stages of banquet organizations, can be presented to customers in advance and possible questions can be addressed thanks to augmented reality technologies. In other words, visuals and contents of the design of all the elements for the event can be presented to customers before the event, thanks to augmented reality. Problematic points can be redesigned before the event, so that the event can be presented to the customers in a perfect form.

It is possible to claim that businesses that can present all this information in full reality at the point of signing of the event agreement to customers through augmented reality will gain a competitive advantage over other businesses. Especially showing the contents, visuals, and presentation of the menus offered to the customers; innovations such as displaying the table layout, landscaping, and decorations placed in the designated area at the event can provide serious gains both for the businesses and for customers who request the events.

The use of three dimensional printers has great potential in the food industry in the development of personalized nutritional content, texture in foods, and production of 3D structures with complex geometries. From entertainment to automotive, medical to production industry, from education to the food sector, the usage areas of 3D printers are quite wide. In the areas where it is applied, it offers great advantages to its users (ease of design and production, low cost, etc.). The first issue that highlights 3D food printers is that this type of production does not require different equipment and molds used in traditional food production. The second is that production can be made only with raw material and computer design. Banquet organizations are special events with high expectations for those who demand the event. Especially in events such as weddings and engagements where people want to share their special days with other people, the desire for the event to have the best possible features is always high. At this point, in banquet organizations, it is seen that the usage rate of traditional methods is decreasing and the visuals and content can be changed depending on the requests of the customers. The use of new age technologies and the provision of personalized food and beverages are attractive factors for customers. For example, at a wedding event, roduction of food with the initials of the couple or with the company logo at a company meeting are details that make customers feel special and enable them to choose that business again. At this point, the use of 3D printers in the gastronomy sector stands out as an innovation that will increase customer loyalty.

Gastronomy and food and beverage industries are sectors that compete with time, require serious effort and many different tasks to be conducted at the same time. Especially in banquet organizations, high numbers of people need to be served simultaneously and a systematic operation becomes important. At this point, taking advantage of the Internet of Things technology in banquet organizations can provide great benefits to the businesses in terms of time and personnel management. It will also significantly alleviate the workload of both the kitchen and the F&B team.

The use of robotic chefs is one of the technological developments that accelerate the process and alleviate the workload of the kitchen staff in banquet organizations that generally serve large groups and require rapid action. In this respect, it is possible to predict that robotic chefs, who contribute to the production process of banquet organizations, will become much more common in the near future. The use of robot waiters today has become one of the factors that provides cost advantages to businesses, provides the benefit of minimizing mistakes that may arise due to human nature, attracts the attention of the customers, and highlights the business in promotion and marketing. Due to these aspects, it is predicted that the use of robot waiters in food and beverage businesses will increase significantly in the long term.

FUTURE RESEARCH DIRECTIONS

Technological innovations and applications developing in line with Industry 4.0 are becoming more common every day. In recent years, it is observed that these innovations have started to be used in the food and beverage, and gastronomy sectors, both are considered under the tourism industry. Although its prevalence is not very high yet, it is an undeniable fact that it will develop in the future and will provide significant benefits for food and beverage establishments. The benefits of these innovations, which are/ will be used in the events of food and beverage establishments, -banket organizations- are predictable. However, these benefits should be investigated with various scientific research techniques and customer satisfaction studies should also be conducted to monitor the effects of technology on customer preferences. In addition, the approaches of customers participating in banquet organizations should be investigated to developing technologies within the scope of industry 4.0. Also, research should be conducted on how these technologies can be better adapted to the food and beverage, gastronomy and event industries.

CONCLUSION

It is considered that these innovations, which are currently developing and newly implemented today, will be mentioned frequently in the near future. Increasing use of innovations in the fields of kitchen, and food and beverage operations will undoubtedly affect the design, production and presentation processes of banquet organizations. It will transform the promotion, marketing, and implementation phases. In the near future, as predicted, if the prevalence of gastronomy 4.0 applications increases, the personnel responsible for running the banquet organization will need to be heavily trained and become knowledgeable about the equipment of the new age. Also, it will be ineluctable that the methods used to influence customers will change and organizational agreements will be revised. When the related literature is examined, it is possible to claim that Gastronomy 4.0 applications are a new field of study to explore. Researchers should spent more time and dedicate more studies to understand how emerging technologies will affect the gastronomy and event organizations. Effects of these technological developments on customers, saisfaction, complaints and their loyalty should also be investigated and discussed in detail.

REFERENCES

Ahmed, R. (2017). *4 Famous restaurants that use 3D printers.* Retrieved August 2, 2020, from https://3dprinting.com/food/4-famous-restaurants-that-use-3d-printers/

Akgül, D. T. (2020). *Ziyafet servisi yönetimi.* Retrieved August 27, 2020, from https://obs.yasar.edu.tr/oibs/akademik/shr_files/FILE_zou07jrmmfn43fv12zofexnx5hnw3_duyuru.PDF

Akram, W., & Kumar, R. (2017). A study on role and applications of augmented reality in tourism: Its challanges and future prospects. *International Journal of Advanced Research in Computer Science, 8*(8), 168–172. doi:10.26483/ijarcs.v8i8.4633

Aksoy, M., & Akbulut, B. A. (2017). Restoranlardaki teknolojik yeniliklerin deneyim pazarlaması açısından değerlendirilmesi. In *International Congress on Cultural Herigate and Tourism (ICCHT)* (pp. 19-21). Academic Press.

Aydın, N. (2016). *Moore yasası ve geleceği.* Retrieved December 2, 2020, from https://www.endustri40.com/moore-yasasi-ve-gelecegi/

Başöz, İ. (2017). *Geleceğin robot mutfak şefleri.* Retrieved August 2, 2020, from https://www.itohaber.com/haber/teknoloji/205713/gelecegin_robot_mutfak_sefleri.html

BBC. (2018). *Future article.* Retrieved September 3, 2020, from https://www.bbc.com/future/article/20181204-the-chef-making-fast-food-even-faster

Brittow, R. (2018). *Digital dining: Is this the way forward for the restaurant industry?* RetrievedSeptember 5, 2020, from https://www.food24.com/News-and-Guides/News-and-Trends/digital-dining-is-this-the-way-forward-for-the-restaurant-industry-20180911

Bulut, E., & AKÇACI, T. (2017). Endüstri 4.0 ve inovasyon göstergeleri kapsaminda Türkiye analizi. *ASSAM Uluslararası Hakemli Dergi, 4*(7), 55-77.

Cankül, D., Doğan, A., & Sönmez, B. (2018). Yiyecek-içecek işletmelerinde inovasyon ve artırılmış gerçeklik uygulamaları. *Journal Of Business Research-Turk, 10*(3), 576–591.

Çatalkaya, Y. (2020). *Ziyafet ve ikram hizmetlerinde yönetim.* Retrieved August 25, 2020, from https://avys.omu.edu.tr/storage/app/public/yusuf.catalkaya/134619/Z%C4%B0YAFET%20 H%C4%B0ZMETLER%C4%B0%20Y%C3%96NET%C4%B0M%C4%B0%20HAFTA%202.pdf

Dankar, I., Haddarah, A., Omar, F. E. L., Sepulcre, F., & Pujolà, M. (2018). 3D printing technology: The new era for food customization and elaboration. *Trends in Food Science & Technology, 75*, 231–242. doi:10.1016/j.tifs.2018.03.018

Doyduk, H. B. B., & Tiftik, C. (2017). Internet of things: Future projections and business opportunities. *Third Sector Social Economic Review, 52*(3), 127–147.

EBSO. (2015). *Sanayi 4.0: Uyum sağlamayan kaybedecek.* https://www.inovasyon.org/pdf/EBSO.Sanayi4.0_Raporu.Ekim.2015.pdf

Financial Times. (2017). *World.* Retrieved August 2, 2020, from https://www.ft.com/content/9b72c5a6-d680-11e6-944b-e7eb37a6aa8e

Fırat, S. Ü., & Fırat, O. Z. (2017). Gıda ve İçecek Sektöründe Endüstri 4.0 Devrimi: Otomasyon ve Robotlar. *ST Robot Yatırımları, Robot Ürün ve Sistemleri, Ekim*, 214-220.

Genc, S. (2018). Turkey's proceed on industry 4.0. *Sosyoekonomi, 26*(36), 235–243. doi:10.17233osyoekonomi.2018.02.14

Gibson, M. (2015). *Meet the robot chef that can prepare your dinner.* Retrieved August 2, 2020, from https://time.com/3819525/robot-chef-moley-robotics/

Guinness World Records. (2020). *First restaurant with robot waiting staff.* Guinness World Records. Retrieved August 26, 2020, from https://www.guinnessworldrecords.com

Güler, O., Akdağ, G., Çakıcı, A. C., & Benli, S. (2015). Turizmi değiştiren 100 yenilik. (U. Gökovalı, Dü.). *Anatolia: Turizm Araştırmaları Dergisi, 26*(2), 290–317.

Güven, M. (2017). *Internet of things (nesnelerin interneti) nedir?* Retrieved August 2, 2020, from http://www.teknolojivetasarim.org/internet-of-things-nesnelerin-interneti-nedir/

Hamilton, C. A., Alici, G., & Panhuis, M. (2018). 3D printing vegemite and marmite: Redefining "Breadboards.". *Journal of Food Engineering, 220*, 83–88. doi:10.1016/j.jfoodeng.2017.01.008

Hao, L., Mellor, S., Seaman, O., Henderson, J., Sewell, N., & Sloan, M. (2010). Material characterisation and process development for chocolate additive layer manufacturing. *Virtual and Physical Prototyping, 5*(2), 57–64. doi:10.1080/17452751003753212

Holland, S., Foster, T., MacNaughtan, W., & Tuck, C. (2018). Design and characterisation of food grade powders and inks for microstructure control using 3D printing. *Journal of Food Engineering, 220*, 12–19. doi:10.1016/j.jfoodeng.2017.06.008

HospitalityNet. (2018). *Millennium hotels and resorts deploys robotic solutions to ıts singapore properties*. Retrieved August 2, 2020, from https://www.hospitalitynet.org/news/4090560.html

İbiş, S. (2019). Turizm endüstrisinde robotlaşma. *Türk Turizm Araştırmaları Dergisi, 3*(3), 403–420. doi:10.26677/TR1010.2019.169

Innovation, B. C. C. (2019). *Lab-e digital gastronomy lab*. Retrieved September 3, 2020, from https://innovation.bculinary.com/en/portfolio/labe-digital-gastronomy-lab/

Jyh-Hwa, T., & Kuo, S., L. (2008). The Development of the Restaurant Service Mobile Robot with a Laser Positioning System. *Chinese Control Conference*, 662-666.

Kabaklarlı, E. (2016). *Endüstri 4.0 ve dijital ekonomisi: Dünya ve Türkiye ekonomisi için fırsatlar, etkiler ve tehditler*. Nobel Bilimsel Eserler.

Khosla, S. (2019). *Watch: Robots serve food at east India's first-of-its-kind high-tech restaurant in Odisha; Twitter Reacts*. Retrieved April 3, 2020, from https://food.ndtv.com/news/watch-robots-serve-food-at-east-indias-first-of-its-kind-high-tech-restaurant-in-odisha-twitter-reac-2118340

Kılıçhan, R. (2015). *Ziyafet/banket organizasyonu menü çeşitleri, tanzimi ve takdimi kahvaltı çeşitleri oda servisi*. RetrievedAugust 23, 2020, fromhttp://www.gastronomi-mutfaksanatlari.com/FileUpload/ks241201/File/ziyafet-menu-kahvalti-oda_servisi.pdf

Kılıçhan, R. (2018). *Ziyafet organizasyonu ve yönetimi*. Retrieved August 25, 2020, from http://www.gastronomi-mutfaksanatlari.com/

Kondo, A. (2018). *Rice-serving robot dishes up sales*. Retrieved August 2, 2020, from https://asia.nikkei.com/Editor-s-Picks/Japan-Update/Rice-servingrobot-dishes-up-sales

Kounavis, C. D., Kasimati, A. E., & Zamani, E. D. (2012). Enhancing the tourism experience through mobile augmented reality: Challenges and prospects. *International Journal of Engineering Business Management, 4*(10), 1–6. doi:10.5772/51644

Le Tohic, C., O'Sullivan, J. J., Drapala, K. P., Chartrin, V., Chan, T., Morrison, A. P., Kerry, J. P., & Kelly, A. L. (2018). Effect of 3D printing on the structure and textural properties of processed cheese. *Journal of Food Engineering, 220*, 56–64. doi:10.1016/j.jfoodeng.2017.02.003

Lipton, J., Arnold, D., Nigl, F., Lopez, N., Cohen, D. L., & Norén, N., & Lipson, H. (2010, August). Multi-material food printing with complex internal structure suitable for conventional post-processing. *Solid Freeform Fabrication Symposium*, 809-815.

Lipton, J. I., Cutler, M., Nigl, F., Cohen, D., & Lipson, H. (2015). Additive manufacturing for the food industry. *Trends in Food Science & Technology, 43*(1), 114–123. doi:10.1016/j.tifs.2015.02.004

Liu, Z., Zhang, M., Bhandari, B., & Yang, C. (2018). Impact of rheological properties of mashed potatoes on 3D printing. *Journal of Food Engineering, 220*, 76–82. doi:10.1016/j.jfoodeng.2017.04.017

Lyons, K. (2020). *A restaurant in the Netherlands is using creepy robot waiters for social distancing*. The Verge. Retrieved August 26, 2020, from https://www.theverge.com/2020/5/31/21276318/restaurant-netherlands-robot-waiters-social-distancing-pandemic

Murphy, S. V., & Atala, A. (2014). 3D bioprinting of tissues and organs. *Nature Biotechnology*, *32*(8), 773–785. doi:10.1038/nbt.2958 PMID:25093879

Nguyen, C. (2016). *Restaurants in China are replacing waiters with robots*. Retrieved August 26, 2020, from https://www.businessinsider.com/chinese-restaurant-robot-waiters-2016-7

NTV. (2015). *Konya'daki bu kafede çay servisini robot yapıyor*. Retrieved August 25, 2020, from https://www.ntv.com.tr/teknoloji/caylar-robot-adadan,qa4oUOCklUGMjOeuU4Q6Sw

Obe, M. (2018). *Business trends*. Retrieved August 2, 2020, from https://asia.nikkei.com/Business/Business-trends/Nestle-serves-up-robots-in-Japan-to-woo-Chinese-customers

Özel, C., & Uluyol, Ç. (2016). Development of an augmented reality application and students' opinions. *Turkish Journal of Social Research.*, *20*(3), 793–823.

Özgüneş, R. E., & Bozok, D. (2017). Turizm sektörünün sanal rakibi(mi?): Arttırılmış gerçeklik. *Uluslararası Türk Dünyası Turizm Araştırmaları Dergisi*, *2*(2), 146–160.

Pallottino, F., Hakola, L., Costa, C., Antonucci, F., Figorilli, S., Seisto, A., & Menesatti, P. (2016). Printing on food or food printing: A review. *Food and Bioprocess Technology*, *9*(5), 725–733. Advance online publication. doi:10.100711947-016-1692-3

Periard, D., Schaal, N., Schaal, M., Malone, E., & Lipson, H. (2007). Printing food. *Proceedings of the 18th solid freeform fabrication symposium*, 564-574.

Rayna, T., & Striukova, L. (2016). From rapid prototyping to home fabrication: How 3D printing is changing business model innovation. *Technological Forecasting and Social Change*, *102*, 214–224. doi:10.1016/j.techfore.2015.07.023

Restaurants, F. (2019). *Bareburger's augmented reality strategy: AR menus*. Retrieved May 1, 2020, from https://restaurants.wbresearch.com/blog/bareburger-augmented-reality-technology-strategy-to-menus

Severini, C., Derossi, A., & Azzollini, D. (2016). Variables affecting the printability of foods: Preliminary tests on cereal-based products. *Innovative Food Science & Emerging Technologies*, *38*, 281–291. doi:10.1016/j.ifset.2016.10.001

Solutions, S. M. A. C. A. R. (2018). *Augmented reality case study for restaurants*.Retrieved February 15, 2020, from https://smacar.com/augmented-reality-case-study-restaurants-case-study-restaurants/

Tassiopoulus, D. (2005). *Events – an introduction. In Event Management: A Professional and Developmental Approach*. Juta Academic.

TheStar. (2020). *World's first robot-operated Chinese eatery opens in South China*. Retrieved February 8, 2020, from https://www.thestar.com.my/news/regional/2020/01/14/world039s-first-robot-operated-chinese-eatery-opens-in-south-china

Topsakal, Y., Yüzbasıoglu, N., Celik, P., & Bahar, M. (2018). Tourism 4.0 - tourist 5.0: Why the human revolution is one number bigger than industrial revolutions? *Journal Of Tourism Intelligence And Smartness*, *1*(2), 1–11.

TUBITAK. (2016). *Yeni sanayi devrimi, akıllı üretim sistemleri, teknoloji yol haritası*. https://www.tubitak.gov.tr/sites/default/files/akilli_uretim_sistemleri_tyh_v27aralik2016.pdf

Türk, C. N. N. (2019). *İstanbul'da robot garsonlar işe başladı*. Retrieved August 26, 2020, from https://www.cnnturk.com/turkiye/istanbulda-robot-garsonlar-ise-basladi

Türk Dil Kurumu. (2020). Etkinlik. *Sözlük maddesi*. Retrieved August 15, 2020, from https://sozluk.gov.tr/

Watkin, H. (2016). *World's first 3d printing restaurant opens in london*. Retrieved May 5, 2020, from https://all3dp.com/worlds-first-3d-printing-restaurant-coming-london/

Wilson, A. (2010). *Hajime robot restaurant*. Live Less Ordinary. Retrieved August 25, 2020, from https://www.live-less-ordinary.com/hajime-robot-restaurant-in-bangkok-yakiniku/

Yang, F., Zhang, M., & Bhandari, B. (2017). Recent development in 3D food printing. *Critical Reviews in Food Science and Nutrition*, *57*(14), 3145–3153. doi:10.1080/10408398.2015.1094732 PMID:26479080

Yovcheva, Z., & Buhalis, D. (2013). Augmented reality in tourism: 10 unique applications explained. *Digital Tourism Think Tank,* 1-12.

Zeleny, P., & Ruzicka, V. (2017). The design of the 3d printer for use in gastronomy. *Modern Machinery (MM). Science Journal, 1744-1747*. Advance online publication. doi:10.17973/mmsj.2017_02_2016187

Ziewitz, M., & Brown, I. (2013). A prehistory of internet governance. In *Research Handbook on Governance of the Internet*. Edward Elgar Publishing. doi:10.4337/9781849805049.00008

ADDITIONAL READING

Bregazzi, A. (2014, July). Digital gastronomy. In *Food & Material Culture: Proceedings of the Oxford Symposium on Food and Cookery 2013*. Oxford Symposium.

Güneş, E., Bayram, Ş. B., Özkan, M., & Nizamlıoğlu, H. F. (2018). Gastronomy four zero (4.0). *International Journal of Environmental Pollution and Environmental Modelling*, *1*(3), 77–84.

Özkul, E., & Kumlu, S. T. (2019). Augmented reality applications in tourism. *Uluslararası Güncel Turizm Araştırmaları Dergisi*, *3*(2), 107–122.

Rojko, A. (2017). Industry 4.0 concept: Background and overview. *International Journal of Interactive Mobile Technologies*, *11*(5), 77–90. doi:10.3991/ijim.v11i5.7072

Sun, J., Zhou, W., Huang, D., Fuh, J. Y., & Hong, G. S. (2015). An overview of 3D printing technologies for food fabrication. *Food and Bioprocess Technology*, *8*(8), 1605–1615. doi:10.100711947-015-1528-6

Witkowski, K. (2017). Internet of things, big data, industry 4.0–innovative solutions in logistics and supply chains management. *Procedia Engineering*, *182*, 763–769. doi:10.1016/j.proeng.2017.03.197

Zoran, A., & Coelho, M. (2011). Cornucopia: The concept of digital gastronomy. *Leonardo*, *44*(5), 425–431. doi:10.1162/LEON_a_00243

KEY TERMS AND DEFINITIONS

3D Food Printing: Is the process of manufacturing food products using a variety of additive manufacturing techniques. Most commonly, food grade syringes hold the printing material, which is then deposited through a food grade nozzle layer by layer. The most advanced 3D food printers have pre-loaded recipes on board and also allow the user to remotely design their food on their computers, phones or some IoT device. The food can be customized in shape, color, texture, flavor, or nutrition, which makes it very useful in various fields such as space exploration and healthcare (Kakuk, 2020).

Augmented Reality (AR): Is an interactive experience of a real-world environment where the objects that reside in the real world are enhanced by computer-generated perceptual information, sometimes across multiple sensory modalities, including visual, auditory, haptic, somatosensory and olfactory. AR can be defined as a system that fulfills three basic features: a combination of real and virtual worlds, real-time interaction, and accurate 3D registration of virtual and real objects (The Huffington Post, 2016).

Digital Gastronomy: Is a culinary vision that infuses traditional cooking with new computational abilities (Hbyrid Lab, 2020).

Event Management: Is the application of project management to the creation and development of small and/or large-scale personal or corporate events such as festivals, conferences, ceremonies, weddings, formal parties, concerts, or conventions. It involves studying the brand, identifying its target audience, devising the event concept, and coordinating the technical aspects before actually launching the event (Event Academy, 2020).

Industry 4.0: Refers to the transformation of industry through the intelligent networking of machines and processes with the help of information and communication technology (ICT). The term is used interchangeably with the 'fourth industrial revolution' in industry (I-Scoop, 2020).

Internet of Things (IoT): Is inter-connected objects of a giant network ranging from smartphones and corridor signs to room thermostats. This broad network enables the exchange and analysis of data. This data can help hotels to discover new business insights and see and act to new opportunities (Smart Hotel Technology Guide, 2018).

Robots: Can be defined as "actuated mechanism programmable in two or more axes with a degree of autonomy, moving within its environment, to perform intended tasks" (International Organization for Standardization, 2012).

Chapter 15
The Role of Social Media in Event Marketing:
Outcomes for Practitioners and Participants

Serap Serin Karacaer
Aksaray Universty Vocational School of Social Sciences, Turkey

ABSTRACT

Activities, which include events that are not all intangible, include large-scale service components, and hence, their marketing includes service marketing. From this point of view, it is possible to state that it is very difficult to market activities that the participants cannot take home and consume physically. In this context, it is very important that the event marketing activities convey the feeling to the target audience that they will have fun and be entertained. Therefore, social media is one of the most important tools used in the effective transfer of the organization to the target audience within the scope of event marketing activities. As the most effective current communication and interaction tool, social media has become the most important tool for event marketers who are trying to appeal to large audiences and promote a certain destination, product, or service.

INTRODUCTION

Events, whether they are public or private or organized for whatever reason such as commercial or aid, for celebration or commemoration, are organizations that bring people together to share an experience and achieve measurable results (Silvers, 2004). Furthermore, events that are organized for the protection and development of the social identity in the region where they are organized are also activities that are a tourist attraction for the destination (Derret, 2004: 39) have increased rapidly in number, variety and popularity in recent years. Therefore, the rapidly developing event industry is one of the industries with the biggest employment potential and positive economic impact in the world today (Theocharis, 2008). There is a multi-dimensional organizational network in direct proportion to the size of the event, such as

DOI: 10.4018/978-1-7998-4954-4.ch015

managing activities, managing financial affairs and staff, conducting public relations, ensuring security, advertising and promotion, decoration, organizing behind every event that is planned (Tassiopoulos, 2005). In this context, it is possible to provide this whole operation in a certain order with an organized event management and event marketing. Event management is the function of providing links between various sections of an event and organizing the flow of information between them (Bhe, Glasmacker, Meckwood, Pereira & Wallace, 2004). In other words, event management can be expressed as a way of dealing with the activities planned in an organization. Event marketing is the effort to coordinate the communication of an event. In other words, event marketing can be defined as an effort to coordinate communication around an event that occurs spontaneously or is organized by a professional sponsor (Behrer & Larsson, 1998). At this point, the purpose of organizing an event from the perspective of the sponsor is to announce the product to larger masses, to create an image and to increase participation (Lundmark, 1998).

Social media is one of the most important areas of communication, with its improved infrastructure facilities and its ever-increasing variety (Aktan & Çakmak, 2015). In today's internet age, social media has become a platform that allows people to turn themselves into "media" to collaborate and share information (Thevenot, 2007; Li & Wang, 2011). When evaluated from this point of view, it is possible to express social media as a communication tool that makes information sharing and communication very fast and easy (Koçyigit, 2015). However, the main strength of social media is its ability to enable two-way communication rather than information sharing (Chu & Kim, 2015). Furthermore, being mobile-based without time and space limitations, social media establishes a form of communication in which sharing, discussion and exchange of ideas is the main factor. Therefore, content sharing can take place instantly, quickly and easily, without the need for an intermediary, through social media (Vural & Bat, 2010) which consists of the dialogues and sharing that individuals have with each other on the internet (Kaynak & Koç, 2015). Hence, from this point of view, social media is seen as an important marketing tool to be used in event marketing.

Within the scope of the study, the concept of event marketing will be discussed in full detail, and the importance of social media will be emphasized in terms of the effective and efficient marketing of events. The role of social media in the promotion of events, enabling the participants to share their views with the target audience and receive feedback about events will be expressed in this context.

BACKGROUND

The Activity Concept

The concept of activity is a concept that can have different meanings depending on how it is defined. When the concept of activity is associated with the concept of "event", the meaning of the "event" concept also differs and is directly proportional to the purpose of each event (Eckerstein, 2002). In this context, in its most general form, an event can be expressed as bringing people together to influence them and create an experience for them (Silvers, 2004). From a wider perspective, an event is a series of activities that enable the revival of natural and physical resources in the cities or countries where it is organized, creating an image for that place and increasing the tourism attraction of the destination in question (Getz, 1997). The event concept, which expresses a unique time period (Berridge, 2007) apart from daily events, is also used to define activities designed for different purposes. These activities can be local involving art, sports, tourism and other social activities, but they can also be more formal and professional events organized by major organizers (Argan, 2007).

The reasons why people participate in activities can differ. Getz (1997) examined the incentive of individuals participating in activities by dividing them into three groups. Accordingly, individuals in the first group participated in activities in line with physical motives such as food, drink, exercise, relaxation and comfort. The incentives of the individuals in the second group participating in the activities were social and interpersonal motives such as socializing with family and friends, being included in groups, connections with cultural and ethnic origins, expressing feelings of socialism and nationalism, a desire to gain status and recognition. The third group participated in activities with personal motives such as seeking new experiences, information, a desire to be understood, and to realize their passions. Crompton and McKay (1997) addressed their study under six headings: innovation, cultural discovery, gaining balance, a desire to socialize as part of a certain group, the desire to socialize by interacting with other people, and family unity. One of the main motivating factors that affect individuals' participation in activities was the feeling of experiencing "a once in a lifetime" event. Neioretti et al. (2001) also concluded that the "once in a lifetime" experience was one of the main motives for individuals to participate in an event. Therefore, although the reasons for individuals to participate in events differ according to various motives, it is possible to state that these motives are also related to the personal characteristics of individuals (social, cultural, economic, etc.).

Numerous events are organized in different places and at different scales every year in the world to fulfill different purposes. In this context, two different classifications should be made regarding such events in terms of their scales as well as their form and content. Accordingly;

1. **Events by scale** vary according to criteria such as the number of participants, media influence, cost amount and benefits. However, there is a direct proportion between the size and scale of the event and its diversification. In other words, the higher the number of participants attending the event and the higher their spending, the greater the impact rate is and the classification according to scaling is made accordingly (Bowdin, G., Allen, J., O'Toole, W., Harris, R. & McDonnell, I., 2012: 16).
    a. **Mega events:** are those that have the highest number of participants in terms of event scales that generate the highest resonance and are the most talked about. Mega events require a more detailed planning and larger organization than others (Yürük, 2015: 12). Mega events are viewed as events that start with a cause-effect relationship, develop very rapidly, manifest their impact and results immediately, and show continuity (Hiller, 1998: 47). Global events such as the FIFA World Cup and the Olympic Games that have a strong global impact on society are examples of mega events (Arcodia & Robb, 2000: 156; Bowdin et al., 2006: 18).
    b. **Hallmark events:** Hallmark events can be defined as events planned to increase the attractiveness of a particular destination or region (Murphy & Carmichael, 1991: 32; Van der Wagen, 2005). The main purpose of holding Hallmark events is to increase awareness of the place where the event takes place and transform it into a special market (Derrett, 2011: 34). The most popular example that of such events is the Rio Carnival (Bowdin et al., 2006: 17). Other examples of hallmark events are the Kentucky Derby in America, the Chelsea Flower Show in Britain, Oktoberfest in Munich, the Edinburgh Festival in Scotland (Koh & Jackson, 2006: 21).

c. **Major events:** Major events are those that are smaller than mega and hallmark events with their scope and scale (Arcodia & Robb, 2000: 156). However, major events have cultural value as a result of the image effects they ensure for the host community or country (Richards & Wilson, 2004:1933). Formula 1 Grand Prix and Tennis Tournaments held in various cities or countries are examples of major events (Koh & Jackson, 2006: 21).

d. **Local events:** Local events that physically represent the narrowest geographic area can be defined as social and entertainment events organized for the local audience. Janiskee (1996: 404) defined local events as entertainment activities that are generated by institutions and organizations such as public institutions, non-governmental organizations, business associations utilizing public spaces such as streets, schools, parks where all the services are delivered voluntarily by the locals under the auspices and adopted by a certain host community. These events are events that evoke pride and strengthen the sense of belonging for the local community (Bowdin et al. 2012: 12).

2. **Events by format and content** are culture and festival-oriented events that have existed in many societies for years, have universal values and date back in history (Bowdin et al. 2012: 17).

a. **Cultural events:** Society has a social role in these events which are organized to ensure that the profile and image of a city and society are different and unique. Festivals organized for socio-cultural activities such as music, art and science in a city or across the country are examples of cultural events. Festivals, which are the most well-known forms of cultural activities are described as events which are mainly attended by local people and develop rapidly (Arcodia & Whitford, 2006: 3). In other words, festivals are celebrations involving the participants' experience and emotions that the local community wants to share. The main feature that distinguishes festivals from other events is that they have emerged as a result of society and celebration. Another aim of festivals is to reach maximum numbers in terms of participants who undergo a major experience that differs from daily life (Arcodia & Robb, 2000: 156).

b. **Sports events:** Involve sports activities that cover a full range of individual and multiple sports, such as the Olympic Games. These events benefit not only the management and sports organizers where the event is held, but also the players, coaches, officials, and viewers who come to enjoy and be entertained (Bowdin et al., 2006: 20).

c. **Business and operation events:** Include events such as conferences, congresses, symposiums, panels, fairs, and exhibitions that are organized with a business content. These events, organized by countries or businesses with a work-related content, also play an important role in the development of the city where the event is organized (Mackellar, 2008: 47).

d. **Other events:** Recently, events organized in areas referred to as theme parks or amusement parks are also very popular. Theme parks, in particular, are a new concept established to attract tourists and create an impressive atmosphere in a place. The primary aim of these parks is to combine the structure of the organization with the physical condition, and present visitors with an experience. Disneyland, which opened in Anaheim, California in 1955 and adds a new dimension to entertainment, is one of the most well-known examples of theme parks (Milman, 2010: 221).

Attention should be paid to avoid overlooking the negative effects of the "event" phenomenon, which has become increasingly important recently throughout the country and sometimes in cities, for many

Table 1. Positive and negative effects of events

Event Area	Positive Effects	Negative Effects
Socio-Cultural	· Sharing a common experience · Strengthening traditions · Enhancing social pride · Increased social participation · Introducing new and creative ideas · Expanding cultural perspectives	· Alienation of the society · Manipulating society · The formation of a negative social image · Negative behavior · Abuse of values · Change in the social structure · Loss of comfort
Physical and Environmental	· Displaying the environment · Presenting the best feasible models · Increasing environmental awareness · Infrastructure system to be inherited · Development of the transportation and communication system · Urban transformation and renovation	· Environmental destruction · Pollution · Damage to cultural heritage · Noise pollution · Traffic congestion
Tourism and Economy	· Promotion of the touristic area and increase in tourist numbers · Extention of their stay · Increase in income · Increase in tax revenues · Generating employment	· Resistance of society to tourism · Loss of originality · Damage to the image · Abuse by interest groups · Inflationary prices · Opportunity cost
Political	· International prestige · Advanced profile · Promotion of investments · Reciprocal social support · Development of administrative skills	· Risk of failure of the activity · Improper distribution of funds · Lack of responsibility in ownership and control · Legalization of ideologies

Source: (Mc Donnel, Allen & O'toole, 1998: 20)

reasons such as its economic return, advertisement and promotion opportunities, touristic attraction and appeal along with its positive effects. These effects can be listed as socio-cultural, tourism, economic, physical, environmental and political effects (Table 1). The many positive effects of events can be listed as the society having new experiences, learning and discovering new things (Delamere, Wankel & Hinch, 2001), creating a sense of togetherness in the host community (Arcodia & Whitford, 2006; Getz, 1993), contributing to the development of the city (Jeong & Faulkner, 1996), aiding in the promotion of attractions centers in the destination (Fredline & Faulkner, 2000) and enabling the exchange of thoughts and opinions between local people and visitors (Dwyer, Mellor, Mistilis & Mules, 2000).

On the other hand, events can have negative effects in a destination such as traffic congestion, crowds, increase in crime rate (Atci, Unur & Gursoy, 2016; Dwyer et al., 2000), destruction of natural, cultural and historical resources (Gursoy & Kendall, 2006), physical damage to the natural environment (Raj & Musgrave, 2009: 67), as well as a loss of identity that can be experienced in the society, as well as the deterioration of moral values (Leenders, Go & Bhansing, 2015).

MAIN FOCUS OF THE CHAPTER

Events designed for an audience and specially designed to enable people to interact with various goods and services are seen as an important market for many businesses today. Event marketing is a natural part of the marketing mix, and in fact, the concept of marketing has been around since its existence

(Eriksson & Hjalmsson, 2000). The main theme of event marketing focuses on providing the audience with positive experiences about the event (Lundmark, 1998). The event is a formation that includes "participants". Therefore, conveying messages about the event to the participants in question and transferring the experiences they can experience is related to the function of event marketing. In this context, event marketing can be defined as an effort to coordinate communication around an event that occurs spontaneously or is organized by a professional sponsor (Behrer & Larsson, 1998). At this point, the purpose of organizing an event from the perspective of the sponsor is to announce the product to larger masses, create an image and increase the number of participants (Lundmark, 1998). Another definition of event marketing is to support a brand and organizational interests of a business by associating it with different, unique and special organizations (Martensen et al., 2007).

At the point of explaining the concept of marketing and how it works for businesses, it is possible to use a statement such as "meeting the demands and needs that are valuable for the customer by exchanging goods, services or ideas" (Bowdin et al., 2006: 180). Although the concept of event marketing has been used frequently in marketing literature recently, its explanation is not as easy as the concept of marketing. This is because event marketing is a combination of "opening, facilitating, accelarating and closing the sales business" during an event (Toner & Walker, 2014, p.32). In other words, what makes event marketing different is that event planners include media elements in this process and connect them together with all other elements before, during and after the event (Close et al., 2006, p. 422). Therefore, it is important for managers who carry out the activity business to know the factors that the event should include while marketing the events. These elements help define and facilitate the marketing process.

In this context, although the venue and purpose of each event is different, three basic elements should be taken into consideration in terms of marketing. These are (Hoyle, 2012; 1-2):

1. **Entertainment:** The dictionary defines entertainment as something which offers "a joyful and enjoyable time" (www.sozluk.gov.tr). Although the concept of entertainment exists in the daily lives of societies, it is an integral part of events. So much so that nobody wants to be part of a social event that does not offer entertainment. The main objective of event planners is to provide the participants with positive feelings and experiences during and after the event. Although the positive feeling in question varies depending on the motivating element of each of the participants, the desire to experience the feeling of "having fun" is the same in the event for almost all of the attending participants. Therefore, in terms of event marketing, it is important to present the correct format and activities that will entertain the target audience saturated with home entertainment such as television, computer, CD, DVDs. At this point, the success of event marketing is directly proportional to making the participant group, who is the target audience, feel that they will be offered a different, unique and tailor-made entertainment.
2. **Excitement:** Excitement is a concept that does not appear concretely, but it is known to exist in every person. However, excitement is also the key to making an event unforgettable. Excitement, which is an element of event marketing, should not be confused with entertainment. Excitement is an item offered to participants with activities such as a surprise party, uninterrupted music and dancing within the scope of an event. The realization of the phenomenon of excitement during the event, which is an important part of an effective event marketing, that was promised before the event is an important point in the success of the event marketing.
3. **Initiative:** The third element of event marketing which is initiative, is to create and present innovative and new approaches in partnerships and negotiations related to the activities to be carried out

at the planned event. These initiatives should be designed in an exciting and desirable way by the participating group. In other words, in event marketing, the initiative should be the element that keeps the activity fresh, and surprises and affects the participants with the innovations it offers.

Events can have many different purposes such as attracting attention, promoting a particular brand and creating an image, creating brand awareness, and increasing sales. Furthermore, the target group of event marketing can be a more comprehensive framework such as a business, the employees of a business, the customers that the business offers products to. Therefore, activities are carried out for a small number of people gathering for a small event or thousands of people are catered to for a large organization within the scope of event marketing activities (Behrer & Larsson, 1998). Another purpose of event marketing can be to provide information about any goods or services. In order to meet the goals of event marketing, elements included in the marketing karma such as the media, communication, sponsorship are utilized in addition to the event itself. Therefore, it is possible to say that event marketing is a part of marketing strategy (Eckerstein, 2002: 2).

The basic concepts of event marketing are messages, interaction and integration. The primary purpose of event marketing is to convey a message about a planned event. At this point, as is the case with other marketing tools, the aim is not to establish communication but to provide a communication that has value for the customer. A correct and effective message in event marketing ensures that the target group gets together at a certain place at a certain time. The second aim in event marketing is to ensure interaction between the target group and the event. The third objective is to ensure the integration of event marketing as part of marketing strategies. It is not possible for event marketing that is kept apart from general marketing or business strategies to be successful (Luttorp, 1997; Eckerstein, 2002: 2; Milgrom, 2002).

Any business should focus on four main decision areas before planning a marketing strategy. These decisions, known as product, price, place and promotion and expressed as 4P in marketing literature, form a marketing karma that every business should have (McCarthy, 1960: 45). Marketing karma elements known as 4P are also valid in event marketing. However, at the point of making event marketing different from other types of marketing, the "positioning" element should also be included and event marketing should be evaluated with the 5P. (Hoyle, 2012: 12). Accordingly, the ***product*** is the service offered by the event. The ***Price*** is the amount of money expected from the target group for the services provided within the event. The ***Place*** is the area prepared for presenting the event to the participants of the event. ***Promotion*** is the process of informing, persuading and influencing the target group regarding the event. ***Positioning*** is a necessary marketing karma element to fulfill the expectations of the participants at the event venue. The areas of interest of the consumers should be determined within the scope of positioning studies, which is a karma element related to the audience and therefore the target group of the event and the event should be designed accordingly (McCarthy, 1960: 45-47; Hoyle, 2012: 16-19).

The focus of event marketing is to convey various activities related to the event to be carried out to the target group. The mentioned event can involve different topics such as sports, entertainment, concerts, fairs, music. Therefore, it is important to analyze various demographic and psychographic characteristics of the target group well in order to determine what they are like, what they like, what they care about to market the event successfully (Saget, 2006). It should also be taken into account that a well-organized and executed event generates great value in the target group and leaves a long-lasting impression on the participants (Wood, 2009). The participants, who leave the event with positive impressions, share this situation with their social environments such as their families, friends and business circles. Therefore, the importance of event marketing is understood even better considering that different festivals and events are held in different places every year in the world and these events bring a competitive advantage and image to the host destination.

Social Media

There are different definitions in the literature regarding the concept of social media, which is one of the most powerful online tools of recent times, and which has been rapidly integrated into the social and economic life (Zeng & Gerritsen, 2014). Boyd and Ellison (2004: 211) have defined social media as "virtual environments where users create a profile which is wholly or partially open as well as a list of people they are in contact with, display and share with, and where they can observe the profiles and relationships of other users". According to Kaplan and Haenlein (2010: 61) social media is a "group of internet-based applications created by the user, enabling the production and sharing of content, built on the ideological and technological foundations of web 2.0". According to Kietzmann, Hermkens, McCarthy and Silvestre (2011) social media is a highly interactive platform that uses mobile devices and other web-based technologies to facilitate individuals, groups and communities to develop, co-create, share, transform and discuss user-generated content. In the process, social media continued to develop and its usage areas expanded and hence its definitions changed and improved accordingly. In this context, Cohen (2011) gathered the important features and qualities of social media under three headings through his study which included nearly thirty social media definitions. Accordingly, (1) social media consists of online tools, applications, platforms and media and therefore depends on information technology; (2) the terminal-to-terminal communication channel using the social media web base enables interaction between various organizations, communities and individuals for information exchange, and brings significant and widespread changes in communication between those communities; (3) it is a tool that connects users to create a virtual community using social media cross platforms and therefore affects the behavior and real lives of people.

Nowadays social media is used for many different purposes. In other words, depending on the priorities of people, the utilization of social media differs from one person to another. Some people use this platform for entertainment, while others use it for organizational and business purposes. As a requirement of the current era, the popularity of social media is increasing day by day with the desire of people to stay in touch and interact with each other; it has become an excellent tool not only for entertainment purposes but also for businesses to realize their activities. Therefore, it is possible to state that the effective role of social media is active in all areas of life (Mangold & Faulds, 2009). One of these areas is marketing. In the field of marketing, social media is used as a great platform for customer orientation. Social media makes it easier for businesses to carry out their commercial activities and relieves their concerns about reaching customers (Wang, Carley, Zeng & Mao, 2007). However, the most important aspect of social media is that everything is related to people. Whether it is used for entertainment, mutual communication or commercial use, social media offers many possibilities such as the exchange of ideas, an energetic and dynamic discussion environment, perception of different thoughts, commercial coordination and cooperation on every platform (Bessenoff, 2006; Thompson, 2013). For all these reasons, the coverage of social media is expanding day by day and it is rapidly penetrating almost the whole world.

Social media tools such as Facebook, Instagram, Twitter, Youtube are the most widely known and recognized social media tools. While the common features of social media tools such as interaction, communication and sharing come to the fore in the conceptual definitions about social media, there are also some features that distinguish social media tools from each other. Although it does not seem possible to draw a systematic framework for the classification in question (Kaplan & Haenlein, 2010: 61; Fischer & Reuber 2011: 2-3), there are various classifications in the literature. Weinberg (2009: 9-11) classified social media in four groups, namely social news sites, social bookmarking sites, social networks and other social media sites. Kietzmann et al. (2011: 242) classified social media into seven groups as general mass sites, professional networks, media sharing sites, blogs, social news and bookmarking sites, microblogs, location-specific networks. Akar (2011: 25) classified social media blogs, microblogs as wikis, social networking sites, media sharing sites, social marking and tagging, podcasting and virtual worlds. While Fischer & Reuber (2011: 3) classified social media under eight different groups as social networks, social bookmarking, video sharing, photo sharing, professional networks, user forums, blogs and microblogs, Berthon et al. (2012: 263) distinguished them under five groups as blogs, microblogs, photo sharing sites, video sharing sites and social networks. An examination of the various classifications made in the literature reveals that the common denominator of social media tools appears to be social networks, blogs, microblogs and Wikis.

1. **Social networks:** According to Boyd and Ellison (2008: 211) social networks are internet-based services that allow people to create a public or semi-public profile within a limited system, to specify a clear list of other users with whom they share links, and reciprocally see the lists of others in the system and their activities". On the other, social networks are defined by Kaplan and Haenlein (2010: 63) as "Social networking sites are applications that create personal information profiles which can contain any kind of information such as photos, videos, audio files and blogs and invite friends and colleagues to access this profile, and send e-mails and exchange instant messages with each other, allowing users to connect with each other." Social networks have features that enable (1) user-owned profile pages and the sharing of text, video, music, (2) a higher user interaction than traditional media tools, (3) sharing that can be seen by all platform users at the request of the user, (4)) private messaging with other users and (5) is especially common among young internet users (Weinberg, 2009: 11; Kaplan & Haenlein, 2010: 63-64; Phua, Jin & Kim, 2017: 412-413).
2. **Blogs:** Blogs are a variant of websites with unique characteristics. Blogs are one of the first tools according to the chronological classification of social media. Blogs can be considered the equivalent of personal internet pages on social media (Kaplan & Haenlein, 2010: 63). Nardi, Schiano and Gumbrecht (2004: 222) have defined blogs as "websites that are usually sequenced in a reverse-chronological order, contain archived sharing series and are frequently updated". Akar (2011: 49) defines blogs as "a website, which is usually maintained by individuals or groups, recently by businesses which offers comments and ideas for a wide audience". Blogs include features such as (1) a reverse-chronological order in terms of sent content, (2) enabling interaction with readers, (3) frequently updated content, (4) it is comparable to a personal diary in terms of format, and (5) it is generally managed by a single person (Nardi et al., 2004: 222; Kaplan & Haenlein, 2010: 63).
3. **Microblogs:** Microblogs are smaller versions of social media compared to blogs. Berthon et al. (2012: 263) define microblogs as platforms where users exchange short text messages with character limitations. Microblogs are platforms that enable real-time updates (Kietzmann et al., 2011: 242), are faster to access and easier to use than blogs (Safko, 2012: 291). Features describing microblogs are indicated as (1) character limitation in the content sent, (2) posts are sorted in reverse chronological order, (3) users can establish friendships, (4) instantaneous news can be received, (5) messages, audio, images and files can be sent, and (6) they have features that enable product-service research and purchasing (Berthon et al., 2012: 263; Safko, 2012: 291).

4. **Wikis:** Wikis can be defined as internet-based information pages created and edited by users. Wikis are "Web sites that allow users to add, remove and modify text-based content" (Kaplan & Haenlein, 2010: 62). Wikis are noteworthy platforms in the context of users who connect to the internet with a decentralized system which generates results that are at least as good as those of an organization with a traditional hierarchical structure (Rigby, 2008: 11). Wikis are social media platforms (1) where their users can voluntarily add, remove or edit information-based content, (2) where the reliability of the content depends on the integrity of the contributors, and (3) that have an encyclopedic knowledge base (Rigby, 2008: 11; Kaplan & Haenlein, 2010: 62; Safko, 2012: 168).

Social media is a communication network that gives the opportunity to directly and precisely connect with many segments such as friends, family, relatives, acquaintances, colleagues, brand representatives, suppliers and customers (Gilbert and Karahalios, 2009). In recent years the importance of social media for businesses that have goods or services to offer in reaching and interacting with consumer masses is noteworthy (Hanna, Rohm and Crittenden, 2011). In this context, social media has become a prominent tool especially in the marketing activities of businesses. Marketing is a phenomenon that changes its rules and consequently its dimensions to develop according to constantly changing consumer expectations (Thackeray, Neiger, Hanson & McKenzie, 2008). Along with the globalization process ongoing throughout the world, the difference in the lifestyles of today's people compared to the previous generations has caused enterprises to turn to new searches in their marketing studies (Mulhern, 2009). Businesses, which have adopted many different marketing tools according to the periods they are in, have rapidly adapted to internet-based virtual usage that has developed with the advancement of technology in recent years. In this context, the increasing use of the internet, comfortable, fast and easy access to communication tools has also attracted marketers (Brown, Broderick & Lee, 2007; Saravanakumar & Suganthalakshmi, 2012). Therefore, today in many areas, social media is the focal point of individuals promoting and selling their products to giant multinational companies and corporate organizations.

Social Media in Event Marketing

Nowadays, it is possible to state that approximately half of the world's population, in other words, one out of every two people worldwide are social media users. It is possible to state that the main factor in increasing the use of social media in the world is that people have easier access to the internet. According to the January report of "2020 World Internet Usage and Social Media Statistics" published by "We Are Social", 59% of the world population (approximately 4.54 billion people) is internet, 49% (approximately 3.80 billion people) is an active social media user. Considering the previous year's data, the number of internet users in the world increased by 7% (298 million people) and the number of social media users increased by 9.2% (321 million people). When social media usage is ranked according to social media platforms, "Facebook" ranks first with its 2.49 billion users. "Youtube" with 2 billion users and "WhatsApp" with 1.6 billion users follow Facebook (Kemp, 2020). Therefore, from this point of view, it can be asserted that using social media is the fastest and most effective tool in the marketing studies of any product or a destination in the current world. In other words, social media is one of the platforms that are considered to be the most popular and fastest way of communicating and interacting with a large number of people (Evans, 2010).

Social media, which enables people to connect, interact and communicate with others virtually, provides these links with different social media tools and after a while the difference between virtual and real interaction decreases for people (Scott, 2009). From this point of view, the major and important role played by social media plays in the success of any event or activity is undeniable. Therefore, within the scope of the event marketing activities, the use of social media is very important in the process starting with the promotion activities of an event to the moment it starts and proceeds and subsequently to get feedback about the participant experiences. From this aspect, the basic elements of event marketing through social media need to be taken into account. These (Horo, 2015: 22-23):

1. **Provide Networking Opportunity:** Thanks to social media access, establishing potential connections with the event is enabled. These connections can be made before, during and even after the event. This will positively affect the course of the event and ensure a more efficient and productive process among the participants.
2. **Provide Informational Content:** Within the scope of marketing efforts for any event to be successful the preferences, tastes and similarities of the target audience must be analyzed well and planning should be done accordingly. At this point, social media tools (Facebook, Twitter, LinkedIn etc.) provide the advantage of following the likes and preferences of the target audience. Therefore, this advantage provides valuable information in creating the content of the event.
3. **Present Perfect Criticism:** Social media is a tool that encourages everyone to participate and be included in such an event. This does not only include the participants of the events, it includes a comprehensive range of speakers, staff, event planners and organizers. Therefore, all these participants will have a role in examining the event and presenting critical analysis. This will result in the participant groups undertaking the role of spreading the event all over the world via social media networks. An interaction of this size may also have disadvantages; however, it is a great opportunity for the event to be recognized and popular on a large scale. Furthermore, event organizers and planners will have the opportunity to carefully monitor participants' feedback and responses to be prepared for upcoming events.

Social media presents major advantages to enterprises practicing event marketing such as the opportunity to characterize the participants of the event, the potential of people to interact with each other by networking, and enabling the further dissemination of the effects related to the event even after its completion (Chalip, 2006; Williams & Chinn, 2010). The execution and success of an activity requires great effort. The success of an event is directly proportional to the number of participants as well as its attractiveness. Therefore, considering the potential of social media platforms to gather many people over network connections (Smith, 2006), its effectiveness in event marketing can be understood more clearly.

Mobile devices, which have emerged as a result of the rapid development of technology today, have also changed the dimensions of word of mouth marketing, one of the most common traditional marketing approaches. Word of mouth marketing is considered as one of the most effective, reliable and efficient marketing tools in the marketing literature. Nowadays, this category includes marketing with social media and social network usage. In fact, it can be argued that marketing activities through word-of-mouth communication are carried out on social media platforms (Williams & Chinn, 2010). This is accomplished by monitoring the sharing of different groups on social media sites, through social media, which plays an active role in determining the interests and expectations of businesses and event planners in the target market (Chalip, 2006). Sharing with mobile devices not only before the event but especially during the event increases the number of participants, and for those who cannot attend, it can create a feeling of following the event live and even being there. Therefore, the use of social media in event marketing is of great importance not only for the success of the event, but also for the reputation and brand awareness of the business organizer (Smith, 2006) as well as the event destination.

It is important that the studies on the use of social media tools in relation to event marketing are consistent with the studies on marketing activities with other communication channels. In other words, the content of the promotion, advertisement, informative activities carried out through various media such as television, posters and billboards related to the event and the content of the activities carried out on social networks such as Facebook, Instagram and Twitter should be similar. Messages with different contents to be given in different communication channels for any event may cause perception problems for the participants. However, the most important reason why social media tools are preferred more in event marketing is because while messages intended to attract the attention of participants in marketing studies conducted with traditional media wait for a reaction, transmissions made through social media tools generate value with instant participation and response (Gunelius, 2011: 11). In this context, there are clear differences between using social media in event marketing and using other marketing efforts such as continuous communication with the participants, involving the participants and, as a result, invoke a unique experience on the part of the participants (Kim & Ko, 2012: 1484). Some of the benefits of marketing efforts using social media can be listed as follows (Tuten, 2008: 19-20; Whiting & Deshpande, 2016: 84-85):

- As a result of the change which incurred in word of mouth communication with the development of the internet, the exchange of ideas about an event can spread very quickly.
- The interaction between event organizers and participants is strengthened.
- The message ensures that the target market is exposed longer to the message conveyed about the event.
- As a result, the target market, which is exposed to the message for a long time, is more likely to be involved in the event.
- Social media increases the internalization of the message about the event and strengthens the brand value.
- As a result of social media enabling closer and mutual communication with the participants, the expectations and desires of the target audience are understood more clearly and therefore the content of the event is shaped accordingly.
- Social media reduces the cost of communicating with the target market.
- Social media provides the opportunity to send personalized messages to the target audience.
- Social media offers the opportunity to reach a more specific target audience compared to other marketing tools.
- The positive impact of event marketing through social media lasts longer compared to other marketing tools.

SOLUTIONS AND RECOMMENDATIONS

In order to benefit effectively from the use of social media within the scope of event marketing activities, the elements of reading, creating, sharing and discussing that are important within the framework of the social media-based marketing approach should be taken into consideration. In this context, a detailed research should be carried out on social media on issues related to the activity planned as a priority. At this point, all posts, interactions, and conversations that might concern the event should be examined. While doing this, it should not be forgotten that social media is an active medium and the examinations in question should be continuous. Subsequently, content that might attract the attention of social media users and prepare the ground for their conversations should be created. Content related to the event to be organized and similar content related to the subject should be shared during the sharing process. Finally, it should not be forgotten that social media has a bi-directional communication network due to its dynamics and the comments on the posts should be taken seriously, answered if necessary, and the discussion environment should be kept robust by continuing the dialogue with the target audience.

FUTURE RESEARCH DIRECTIONS

Nowadays, it is possible to come across different studies in the literature regarding the activities realized with social media which is the fastest and most effective way of reaching large audiences and the participation of large masses. The role of social media in activity marketing studies has been discussed within the conceptual framework of the scope of the study. However, the subject of the study and similar issues has the potential to be a broader and more comprehensive field study. For researchers who want to work on a similar subject in the future, an efficient study result can be achieved by monitoring the process of a major event from the preparation stage to the feedback stage in the field. In addition, the effects of event marketing through social media on the awareness and image of the destination where the event is organized can be proposed as another subject to be studied.

CONCLUSION

Being involved in an event is invoked by the social aspects of people. Likewise, the essence of social media is about people being "social". Therefore, "social media", which is a social event, is also one of the most accurate tools that can be used for "event" activities, which are also social events. It is an accepted fact that social media enables people to connect and interact with each other and almost the whole world by using the innovations brought by technology. In this context, it can be said that businesses, organizations and agencies operating in all sectors, especially those that are involved in service marketing efforts, are very eager to use the communication and interaction power of social media. Consequently, the event industry, which has common characteristics regardless of type, purpose and scale, uses social media in almost every important step of their marketing activities such as promotion, advertising and publicity.

Reaching the target audience directly or indirectly is at the core of each event. In this context, the power of social media in reaching people directly, and especially the ability to get feedback from this outreach, makes this media indispensable in terms of event marketing activities. The fact that social media is a communication channel with the highest number of users in the world has made it an indispensable element of event marketing. Therefore, events that can act in integration with social media will benefit from all the technological opportunities offered by social networks. The activities and organizations related to an event activity reach large masses to be included in the event or to think about participating at a later time, talking about it to their inner circle such as friends, relatives, acquaintances through word of mouth and sharing their positive or negative opinions about the event with them as well as the event organizers makes social media the most effective tool in event marketing.

In conclusion, the reasons why social media is becoming a more and more indispensable element of human life with every passing day, the strengthening and increasing number of followers, and the opportunities enabled by technology which have started to offer limitless opportunities in social media in many areas have made social media an important channel for events as well. Whether it is a large mega event or a small local one, social media used in readying the groundwork for the preparation and presentation of practically every stage of events organized today motivates the participants of the event with its entertaining, informative, sharing, and interactive aspects and is also an important promotional tool for the brand or company and the destination where the event is organized.

REFERENCES

Akar, E. (2011). *Sosyal medya pazarlaması: Sosyal Web'te pazarlama stratejileri*. Efil Yayınevi.

Aktan, E., & Çakmak, V. (2015). Halkla ilişkiler öğrencilerinin sosyal medyadaki siber zorbalık duyarlılıklarını ölçmeye ilişkin bir araştırma. *Gümüşhane Üniversitesi İletişim Fakültesi Elektronik Dergisi*, *3*(2), 159–176.

Arcodia, C. & Robb, A. (2000). A future for event management: A taxonomy of event management terms. In J. Allen, R. Harris, L. K. Jago, & A. J. Veal (Eds.), *Events beyond 2000: Setting the agenda, proceedings of conference on event evaluation, research and education.* Sydney: Australian Centre for Event Management School of Leisure, Sport and Tourism, University of Technology.

Arcodia, C., & Whitford, M. (2006). Festival attendance and the development of social capital. *Journal of Convention & Event Tourism*, *8*(2), 1–18. doi:10.1300/J452v08n02_01

Argan, M. (2007). *Eglence pazarlamasi*. Detay Yayincilik.

Atçı, D., Unur, K., & Gürsoy, D. (2016). The impacts of hosting major sporting events: Resident's perceptions of the mediterranean games 2013 in Mersin. *International Review of Management and Marketing*, *6*(1), 139–145.

Behrer, M., & Larsson, A. (1998). *Event marketing att använda evenemang som strategisk resurs i marknadsföringen*. IHM Förlag AB.

Berridge, G. (2007). *Events design and experience, events management series* (1st ed.). Elsevier. doi:10.4324/9780080468112

Berthon, P. R., Pitt, L. F., Plangger, K., & Shapiro, D. (2012). Marketing meets web 2.0, social media, and creative consumers: Implications for international marketing strategy. *Business Horizons*, *55*(3), 261–271. doi:10.1016/j.bushor.2012.01.007

Bessenoff, G. R. (2006). Can the media affect us? Social comparison, self-discrepancy, and then ideal. *Psychology of Women Quarterly*, *30*(3), 239–251. doi:10.1111/j.1471-6402.2006.00292.x

Bhe, T., Glasmacker, P., Meckwood, J., Pereira, G. & Wallace, M. (2004). *Event management and best practices*. IBM.

Bowdin, G. A., Allen, J., O'Toole, W., Harris, R., & McDonell, I. (2006). *Events management* (2nd ed.). Publishing House Elsevier. doi:10.4324/9780080457154

Boyd, D. M., & Ellison, N. B. (2008). Social network sites: Definition, history, and scholarship. *Journal of Computer-Mediated Communication, 13*(1), 210–230. doi:10.1111/j.1083-6101.2007.00393.x

Brown, J., Broderick, A. J., & Lee, N. (2007). Word of mouth communication within online communities: Conceptualizing the online social network. *Journal of Interactive Marketing, 21*(3), 2–20. doi:10.1002/dir.20082

Chalip, L. (2006). Towards social leverage of sport events. *Journal of Sport & Tourism, 11*(2), 109–127. doi:10.1080/14775080601155126

Chu, S. C., & Kim, Y. (2017). The ınfluence of perceived interactivity of social media advertising and voluntary self-disclosure on attitudes and intentions to pass-along. In Advertising and Branding: Concepts, Methodologies, Tools, and Applications (pp.1388-1405). IGI Global. doi:10.4018/978-1-5225-1793-1.ch064

Close, A. G., Finney, R. Z., Lacey, R. Z., & Sneath, J. Z. (2006). Engaging the consumer through event marketing: Linking attendees with the sponsor, community, and brand. *Journal Of Advertısıng Research, New York, 46*(4), 420–433. doi:10.2501/S0021849906060430

Cohen, H. (2011). *30 social media definitions. Posted by Heidi Cohen on May 9, 2011 in actionable marketing social media, 101*. http://heidicohen.com/ social-media-definition/

Crompton, J. L., & Stacey, L. (1997). Motives of visitors attending festival events. *Annals of Tourism Research, 24*(2), 425–439. doi:10.1016/S0160-7383(97)80010-2

Delamere, T. A., Wankel, L. M., & Hinch, T. D. (2001). Development of a scale to measure resident attitudes toward the social impacts of community festivals, part 1: Item generation and purification of the measure. *Event Management, 7*(1), 11–24. doi:10.3727/152599501108751443

Derret, R. (2011). Festivals, Events and The Destination. In *Festival and events management an international arts and cultural perspective*. Routledge Taylor&Francis Group.

Derrett, R. (2004). Making sense of how festivals demonstrate a community's sense of place. *Event Management, 8*(1), 49–58. doi:10.3727/152599503108751694

Dwyer, L., Mellor, R., Mistilis, N., & Mules, T. (2000). A framework for evaluating and forecasting the ımpacts of special events. In J. Allen, R. Harris, L. K. Jago, & A. J. Veal (Eds.), *Events beyond 2000: Setting the agenda* (pp. 31–45). Australian Centre for Event Management.

Eckerstein, A. (2002). *Evaluation of event marketing important indicators to consider when evaluating event marketing* (Master thesis). Graduate Business School School of Economics and Commercial Law, Göteborg University.

Evans, D. (2010). *Social media marketing: the next generation of business engagement*. John Wiley & Sons.

Fischer, E., & Reuber, A. R. (2011). Social interaction via new social media: (How) can interactions on twitter affect effectual thinking and behavior? *Journal of Business Venturing*, *26*(1), 1–18. doi:10.1016/j.jbusvent.2010.09.002

Fredline, E., & Faulker, B. (2000). Host community reactions a cluster analysis. *Annals of Tourism Research*, *27*(3), 763–784. doi:10.1016/S0160-7383(99)00103-6

Getz, D. (1993). Festivals and special events. In M. A. Khan, M. D. Olsen, & T. Var (Eds.), *Encyclopedia of hospitality and tourism* (pp. 789–810). Van Nostrand Reinhold.

Getz, D. (1997). *Event management and event tourism*. Cognizant Communication Corporation.

Gilbert, E., & Karahalios, K. (2009). Predicting tie strength with social media. In *Proceedings of the SIGCHI Conference on Human Factors in Computing Systems* (pp. 211-220). ACM.

Gunelius, S. (2011). *30-Minute social media marketing*. McGraw-Hill.

Gursoy, D., & Kendall, K. W. (2006). Hosting mega events-modelling locals' support. *Annals of Tourism Research*, *33*(3), 603–623. doi:10.1016/j.annals.2006.01.005

Hanna, R., Rohm, A., & Crittenden, V. L. (2011). We're all connected: The power of the social media ecosystem. *Business Horizons*, *54*(3), 265–273. doi:10.1016/j.bushor.2011.01.007

Hiller, H. H. (1998). Assessing the impact of mega-events: A linkage model. *Current Issues in Tourism*, *1*(1), 47–57. doi:10.1080/13683509808667832

Horo, S. (2015). *The Role of Social Media on Event Marketing* (Master's Thesis). The Republic of Turkey Bahcesehir University, Istanbul.

Hoyle, L. H. (2012). *How to successfully promote events, festivals, conventions, and expositions*. John Wiley & Sons.

Janiskee, R. L. (1996). Historic houses and special events. *Annals of Tourism Research*, *23*(2), 398–414. doi:10.1016/0160-7383(95)00069-0

Jeong, G. H., & Faulkner, B. (1996). Resident perceptions of mega-event impacts: The Taejon International Exposition Case. *Festival Management & Event Tourism*, *4*(1-2), 3–11. doi:10.3727/106527096792232388

Kaplan, A. M., & Haenlein, M. (2010). Users of the world, unite! The challenges and opportunities of social media. *Business Horizons*, *53*(1), 59–68. doi:10.1016/j.bushor.2009.09.003

Kaynak, S., & Koç, S. (2015). Telif hakları hukuku'nun yeni macerası: Sosyal medya. *Folklor/Edebiyat*, *21*(83), 389-410.

Kemp, S. (2020). *Digital 2020: 3.8 Billion People Use Social Media*. https://wearesocial.com/blog/2020/01/digital-2020-3-8-billion-people-use-social-media

Kietzmann, J. H., Hermkens, K., McCarthy, I. P., & Silvestre, B. S. (2011). Social media? Get serious! Understanding the functional building blocks of social media. *Business Horizons*, *54*(3), 241–251. doi:10.1016/j.bushor.2011.01.005

Kim, A. J., & Ko, E. (2010). Impacts of luxury fashion brand's social media marketing on customer relationship and purchase intention. *Journal of Global Fashion Marketing, 1*(3), 164–171. doi:10.1080/20932685.2010.10593068

Koçyiğit, M. (2015). *Sosyal ağ pazarlaması marka bağlılığı oluşturmada bir pazarlama stratejisi.* Eğitim Yayınevi.

Koh, K. Y., & Jackson, A. A. (2006). Special events marketing. *Journal of Convention & Event Tourism, 8*(2), 19–44. doi:10.1300/J452v08n02_02

Leenders, M. A., Go, F. M., & Bhansing, P. V. (2015). The importance of the location in hosting a festival: A mapping approach. *Journal of Hospitality Marketing & Management, 24*(7), 754–769. doi:10.1080/19368623.2014.934981

Lundmark, M. (1998). Lys upp marknaden med Event Marketing. *Sälj och marknadsstrategi, 8*, 50-57.

Luttorp, E. (1997). Event marketing. *Ansikte Mot Ansikte Med Målgruppen,* 45-47.

Mackellar, J. (2008). Conventions, festivals and tourism. *Journal of Convention & Event Tourism, 8*(2), 45–56. doi:10.1300/J452v08n02_03

Mangold, W. G., & Faulds, D. J. (2009). Social media: The new hybrid element of the promotion mix. *Business Horizons, 52*(4), 357–365. doi:10.1016/j.bushor.2009.03.002

Martensen, A., Gronholdt, L., Bendtsen, L., & Jensen, M. J. (2007). Application of a model for the effectiveness of event marketing. *Journal of Advertising Research-New York, 47*(3), 283–301. doi:10.2501/S0021849907070316

McCarthy, E. J. (1960). *Basic marketing: A managerial approach.* R.D. Irwin, Indiana University.

McDonnel, I., Allen, J., & O'Toole, W. (1998). *Festival and special event management.* John Wiley & Sons.

Milgrom, J. (2002). *Two decades of event marketing and sponsorship, I have good and bad news. In Event Marketing Strategies.* EMS.

Milman, A. (2010). The global theme park industry. *Worldwide Hospitality and Tourism Themes, 2*(3), 220–237. doi:10.1108/17554211011052177

Mulhern, F. (2009). Integrated marketing communications: From media channels to digital connectivity. *Journal of Marketing Communications, 15*(2-3), 85–101. doi:10.1080/13527260902757506

Murphy, P. E., & Carmichael, B. A. (1991). Assesing the tourism benefits of an open access sports tournament: The 1989 B. C. Winter Games. *Journal of Travel Research, 29*(32), 32–36. doi:10.1177/004728759102900305

Nardi, B. A., Schiano, D. J., & Gumbrecht, M. (2004). Blogging as social activity, or, would you let 900 million people read your diary? CSCW'04, 222-231.

Neirotti, L. D., Bosetti, H. A., & Teed, K. C. (2001). Motivation to attend the 1996 Summer Olympic Games. *Journal of Travel Research, 39*(3), 327–331. doi:10.1177/004728750103900315

Phua, J., Jin, S. V., & Kim, J. (2017). Gratifications of using facebook, twitter, instagram, or snapchat to follow brands: The moderating effect of social comparison, trust, tie strength, and network homophily on brand identification, brand engagement, brand commitment, and membership intention. *Telematics and Informatics*, *34*(1), 412–424. doi:10.1016/j.tele.2016.06.004

Raj, R., & Musgrave, J. (2009). *Event management and sustainability*. CABI. doi:10.1079/9781845935245.0000

Richards, G., & Wilson, J. (2004). The impact of cultural events on city image: Rotterdam, Cultural Capital of Europe 2001. *Urban Studies (Edinburgh, Scotland)*, *41*(10), 1931–1951. doi:10.1080/0042098042000256323

Rigby, B. (2008). *Mobilizing generation 2.0: A practical guide to using web 2.0 technologies to recruit, organize, and engage youth*. Jossey-Bass.

Safko, L. (2010). *The social media bible: tactics, tools, and strategies for business success*. John Wiley & Sons.

Saget, A. (2006). *The event marketing handbook: beyond logistics and planning*. Kaplan Publishing.

Saravanakumar, M., & Suganthalakshmi, T. (2012). Social media marketing. *Life Science Journal*, *9*(4), 4444–4451.

Scott, D. M. (2009). *The new rules of marketing and PR: how to use social media, blogs, news releases, online video, and viral marketing to reach buyers directly*. John Wiley & Sons.

Silvers, J. R. (2004). *Professional event coordination*. John Wiley & Sons Inc.

Smith, W. A. (2006). Social marketing: An overview of approach and effects. *Injury Prevention*, *12*(1, suppl_1), 38–43. doi:10.1136/ip.2006.012864 PMID:16788110

Tassiopoulos, D. (2005). *Event management: A professional and developmental approach* (2nd ed.). Juta Academic.

Thackeray, R., Neiger, B. L., Hanson, C. L., & McKenzie, J. F. (2008). Enhancing promotional strategies within social marketing programs: Use of Web 2.0 social media. *Health Promotion Practice*, *9*(4), 338–343. doi:10.1177/1524839908325335 PMID:18936268

Theocharis, N. (2008). *Event Tourism: Examining the management of sports events from a physical approach*. Synenergy Forum, Athens.

Thevenot, G. (2007). Blogging as a social media. *Tourism and Hospitality Research*, *7*(3/4), 287–289. doi:10.1057/palgrave.thr.6050062

Thompson, J. B. (2013). *Media and modernity: A social theory of the media*. John Wiley & Sons.

Toner, L. & Walker, M. (2014). *The new age of event marketing: Increase event attendance and engagment with an inbound marketing strategy*. Https://cdn2.hubspot.net/hub/53/file-1298172927pdf/The_New_Age_of_Event_Marketing.pdf

Tuten, T. L. (2008). *Advertising 2.0: Social media marketing in a web 2.0 world*. Praeger.

Van der Wagen, L. (2005). *Event management for tourism, cultural, business and sporting events* (2nd ed.). Pearson Education Australia.

Vural, Z. B., & Bat, M. (2010). Yeni bir iletişim ortamı olarak sosyal medya: Ege Üniversitesi İletişim Fakültesine yönelik bir araştırma. *Journal of Yasar University*, *5*(20), 3348–3382.

Wang, F. Y., Carley, K. M., Zeng, D., & Mao, W. (2007). Social computing: From social informatics to social intelligence. *IEEE Intelligent Systems*, *22*(2), 79–83. doi:10.1109/MIS.2007.41

Wang, W. T., & Li, H. M. (2012). Factors influencing mobile services adoption: A brand-equity perspective. *Internet Research*, *22*(2), 142–179. doi:10.1108/10662241211214548

Weinberg, T. (2009). *The new community rules: Marketing on the social web*. O'Reilly Media.

Whiting, A., & Deshpande, A. (2016). Towards greater understanding of social media marketing: A review. *Journal of Applied Business and Economics*, *18*(4), 82–91.

Williams, J., & Chinn, S. J. (2010). Meeting relationship-marketing goals through social media: A conceptual model for sport marketers. *International Journal of Sport Communication*, *3*(4), 422–437. doi:10.1123/ijsc.3.4.422

Wood, E. H. (2009). Evaluating event marketing: Experience or outcome? *Journal of Promotion Management*, *15*(1-2), 247–268. doi:10.1080/10496490902892580

Yürük, P. (2015). Etkinlik pazarlamasında sosyal etki algılamasının etkinliğe katılım, tatmin ve sadakat üzerine etkisi: Kırkpınar festivali örneği (Doktora tezi). Trakya Üniversitesi Sosyal Bilimler Enstitüsü, İşletme A.B.D., Edirne.

Zeng, B., & Gerritsen, R. (2014). What do we know about social media in tourism? A review. *Tourism Management Perspectives*, *10*, 27–36. doi:10.1016/j.tmp.2014.01.001

ADDITIONAL READING

Chalip, L., & Green, B. C. (2001). Event marketing and destination image. In *American Marketing Association. Conference Proceedings*, 12, 346-351.

Kose, H., Argan, M. T., & Argan, M. (2011). Special event management and event marketing: A case study of TKBL all star 2011 in Turkey. *Journal of Management and Marketing Research*, *8*, 1.

Leung, D., Law, R., Van Hoof, H., & Buhalis, D. (2013). Social media in tourism and hospitality: A literature review. *Journal of Travel & Tourism Marketing*, *30*(1-2), 3–22. doi:10.1080/10548408.2013.750919

Wood, E. H., & Masterman, G. (2008, January). Event marketing: Measuring an experience. In *7th International Marketing Trends Congress*, Venice.

Zhang, J., & Wu, F. (2008). Mega-event marketing and urban growth coalitions: A case study of Nanjing Olympic New Town. *The Town Planning Review*, *79*(2-3), 209–227. doi:10.3828/tpr.79.2-3.4

KEY TERMS AND DEFINITIONS

Event: Event is a series of activities that enable the revival of natural and physical resources in the cities or countries where it is organized, creating an image for that place and increasing the tourism attraction of the destination in question.

Event Marketing: The main theme of event marketing focuses on providing the audience with positive experiences about the event. The event is a formation that includes participants. Conveying messages about the event to the participants in question and transferring the experiences they can experience is related to the function of event marketing.

Social Media: Social media consists of online tools, applications, platforms and media and therefore depends on information technology; the terminal-to-terminal communication channel using the social media web base enables interaction between various organizations, communities and individuals for information exchange, and brings significant and widespread changes in communication between those communities; it is a tool that connects users to create a virtual community using social media cross platforms and therefore affects the behavior and real lives of people.

Social Media in Event Marketing: It is possible to state that the main factor in increasing the use of social media in the world is that people have easier access to the internet. Therefore, from this point of view, it can be asserted that using social media is the fastest and most effective tool in the marketing studies of any product or a destination in the current world. Therefore, within the scope of the event marketing activities, the use of social media is very important in the process starting with the promotion activities of an event to the moment it starts and proceeds and subsequently to get feedback about the participant experiences.

Chapter 16
Effective Use of Website in Large-Scale Event Marketing:
25th East Mediterranean International Tourism and Travel (EMITT) Fair

Seda Derinalp Canakci
Sarikamis, Turkey

ABSTRACT

The Eastern Mediterranean International Tourism and Travel Fair (EMITT), which will be held for the 25th time in Istanbul in 2022, is preparing to host national and international industry professionals and thousands of tourists who want to take advantage of the new and exciting travel opportunities offered by holiday destinations and travel companies from all over the world. EMITT Fair will open its doors to visitors for the 25th time in 2022. A well-prepared website is of paramount importance to the event industry today. The Eastern Mediterranean International Tourism and Travel Fair is also one of the mega events considered among large-scale events within the scope of congress and fair organizations. Participation in events, which can result in national and international attention, usually begins with examining the websites prepared for the event. This study aims to examine the effectiveness of the website of the Eastern Mediterranean International Tourism and Travel Fair.

INTRODUCTION

Fairs are platforms that play an important role in helping businesses reach existing and potential buyers and intermediaries on the one hand and gathering information about the market and competitors on the other. For this reason, the participation of enterprises in national or international fairs is increasing (Çakıcı, 2009). Fairs, which provide an opportunity for participants to have quality and purposeful face to face communication with visitors and potential customers, help participants to introduce themselves in a short time and in the most effective way while enabling them to learn directly about customers' requests, expectations, complaints and satisfaction as well as capturing the related demand easily. As

DOI: 10.4018/978-1-7998-4954-4.ch016

one of the most common types of events, fairs are one of the oldest types of events that have positive effects such as introducing new products, collecting information about competitors, identifying potential customers, taking orders, and establishing commercial relations for the future (Getz, 1997; Getz, 2008; Zamzuri, Awang & Samdin, 2011; Chen & Mo, 2012).

Events create social and cultural, physical, environmental, political and marketing effects on stakeholders such as local people, businesses, local governments, and destinations. These effects can be positive or negative. In this direction, a good planning and management process are necessary for the activities to be successful, to ensure their sustainability, to increase their positive effects and to reduce their negative effects. However, a comprehensive knowledge of activities is required for a correct and effective planning (Hall 1989; Turco, 1997; Zou & Ap, 2009; Getz, 1997; Bastida & Huan, 2014).

Today, internet technology is widely used in all segments of society. The internet technology has affected people as consumers as well as their normal lives and changed their habits and behaviors. Thanks to the websites, consumers have the opportunity to pre-examine goods and services. They can also find preliminary information about goods and services. Internet technology, which draws attention of many different sectors, also finds a place in the event industry. Internet technology provides various benefits to businesses in the marketing of the goods and services offered in the event industry (Tierney, 2000; Hung & Law, 2011). The most important internet technology marketing tools are websites. Websites can affect consumers' decision-making and their attitudes towards the business. Therefore, the websites are so important. E-consumers want websites that offer fast, user-friendly and high-quality service (Zhao & Gutierrez, 2001; Liu & Arnett, 2000).

A well-prepared website is of paramount importance to the event industry today. The Eastern Mediterranean International Tourism and Travel (EMITT) Fair, which will be held for the 25th time in Istanbul in 2022, is one of the mega events considered among large-scale events within the scope of congress and fair organizations. Participation in events, which can result in national and international attention, usually begins with examining the websites prepared for the event. This study aims to examine the effectiveness of the website of the Eastern Mediterranean International Tourism and Travel Fair.

BACKGROUND

The Concept of Event Marketing

Events first emerged as a marketing communication strategy in 1980 in Germany in response to significant changes in both the marketing environment and consumer behavior (Wohlfeil & Whelan, 2005). Because the mass media used by national and international companies are more expensive and less effective, it has been revealed that event marketing offers a suitable alternative when used in coordination with other elements in integrated marketing communication and plays an important and key role in establishing direct contact with consumers (Fan & Phitzenmaier, 2002; Liu, Liu, Liu, & Huang, 2019). Event marketing is based on the creation of a strong communication program that explains the goals of the event, and event management, organizers, and service marketing that keeps consumers together, determines the demands and needs of consumers and produces products and services to meet those needs (Tolan, 2014). Therefore, it is possible to define event marketing in its broadest form as follows: Event marketing is the process of integrating various communication channels within an event theme. The motivation that is effective in marketing the event is to reach the target market in the most effective way in order to achieve the sales objectives through marketing communication. Expenses are mostly covered by sponsorship fees through various advertising and promotions related to the event theme. Expected returns in event marketing are measurable increases in sales and marketing communications (Tuckwell, 1991; Liu, Zhang, & Keh, 2018).

Three Es are important in event marketing these are: Entertainment, Excitement, and Enterprise. These three elements are the common ground of all activities. The concept, which is compatible with the marketing and communication plans of the enterprises, requires an integrated application with the creation of project mechanics, visual and three-dimensional design and application, artist and supplier relations, purchasing, field application, workshop production, operation and logistics, audit and activity evaluation analysis (Tolan, 2014).

Event marketing makes the business that organizes the event and therefore its brand, visible. It plays an active role in raising brand awareness. It also provides convenience to the consumer in remembering the brand. Every creative and successful event is also a memorable experience for the consumer (Tığlı, 2008). The main reason for brands to carry out event marketing is that the direct experience provided by the event is used to encourage interaction between consumers and brands and to increase the connection between consumers and the brand (Hsu & Wang, 2009). On the other hand, Wood and Masterman (2008) argue that three levels should be taken into consideration in order to perform an event marketing evaluation. These levels are the event level, consumer experience in the event and consumers' response to experience. *Event level*: During the event, it is possible to achieve all the experiences and all emotions related to the event, but the main goal is to focus on the event. *Consumer experiences in the event:* The experiences of the consumers in an event and the value of the event are found by subtracting the costs from all the benefits of the event. The main goal is to focus on the event and consumer experience. *Consumers' responses to experience:* It is possible to understand whether the consumers are satisfied with the event or not through their feelings, attitudes and behaviors after the event. The main goal is to focus on results. If there are negative consequences, it takes a long time and effort to distance participants from these negative thoughts. After participating in the event, it is very difficult to change the brand preference, value, and interest they perceive, as well as changing the resulting purchasing behavior and recommendations, suggestions, objections. In other words, word-of-mouth marketing activities after the event are difficult. However, if there are positive results, it is very easy for these results to spread among the participants.

Event Marketing Process and Planning

Event marketing is a strategic management of the event that will help to create magnificent events that will meet the expectations of both the participants and the customers interested in the product or service in the event (Pira, 2004; Müller, 2015b). Krugman and Wright (2007) describe the most effective event marketing development steps to communicate the strongest and lasting responses from the event as follows: First, event organizers conduct research on target participants to meet the needs and expectations of the participants. Then a program appealing to this target audience is prepared. A theme for the event is created in the program content. This theme with an eye-catching graphic and a title describing the event will be an important marketing element to raise awareness of the event. Using the media to disseminate program content plays an important role in the event. Lastly, event planners and relevant committees will have created the program in the most effective way for communication. In order for an effective event marketing to be successful, the process must have a structure that can vary depending on the events and situations. Choosing the goals accurately, determining the pros and cons of the area where the goals will be achieved, the quality of the service at the time of the event, all decisions from the management ability to technical expertise, from media relations to the fundamental characteristics of the target audience, from risk analysis to marketing expertise, as well as all employees should be organized within the plan (Babacan & Göktaş, 2011).

The general strategic planning process of event marketing planning starting with developing the model, purpose, and the goals shows the main stages of a strategic marketing process with a situation analysis including demands of an event and the factors that affect the event organization. Based on goals and situation analysis, event managers should measure the market potential in terms of demand forecasts, segmentation and target market selection and choose an appropriate overall strategy, as they will be guided and influenced by future marketing mix strategies, interactive marketing strategies, and internal marketing strategies (Sun, 2007; Surya, 2018).

Bowdin, O'Toole, Allen, Harris, and McDonnel (2006) state that the strategic event marketing requires a process for completion. The first stage is to determine the mission and the purpose of the event. The basic activities of this stage are to determine a management strategy according to the objectives, to identify what work needs be done and to perform the situation analysis required for the second stage. Along with the situation analysis, the strengths, and weaknesses of the event, as well as opportunities and threats in the external environment are identified. At this stage, what needs to be focused on includes all the needs and characteristics to be satisfied for the event marketing, identifying the target audience, their understanding, attitudes and behaviors, and the state of the market share. With the determination of the management strategy and situation analysis, the resources are identified and the situation of the competitors and the competition in the market is analyzed. In the third stage, dividing the active market into the target market is started. With this stage, the purposes of the event marketing are arranged according to the situation in the market and the fourth stage which is the marketing strategy stage starts. With the special marketing strategies for the event, the product, price, location, positioning and announcement to the target audiences, the integrated marketing activities, that is, the creation of a marketing mix starts. The last stage of the event marketing process is the analysis of the effects of event marketing, obtaining marketing research results, receiving feedback from participants and measuring their satisfaction levels.

Events by Size

Many authors classified events into different categories according to their size (Hall, 1989; Bowdin, et al., 2006; Getz, 2008; Van der Wagen, 2010; Smith, 2012; Müller, 2015a). For example, Hall (1989) classified large-scale events into four groups: mega, private, hallmark, and social. Bowdin et al. (2006) categorized events in four classes according to their size as local or social events, major events, hallmark, and mega events. Getz (2008) categorized events in four groups as mega, hallmark, regional and local events. Van der Wagen (2010) also categorized large-scale events in four groups. Accordingly, events are mega, hallmark, major and minor events. Smith (2012) and Müller (2015a) classified the events into three groups, different from other authors. According to Smith (2012), events are divided into mega, major, and special events, while Müller (2015a) classifies events as giga, mega and major. The common point in the above approaches to large-scale event groupings in the literature is that the events are mega, major, hallmark and social in nature.

"Mega events" are events that take place at the international level and under the leadership of the state (Hall, 1989). The frequency of the organization takes place once a year, once every two years or

every four years, and such events have high-value events such as high tourist demand and growth potential, quality, image development, environmental values, economic support, etc. (Getz, 2008). Olympic games, Paralympic Games, FIFA World Cup and Superbowl are large-scale events that can be shown as examples of mega events (Hall, 1989; Bowdin et al., 2006; Getz, 2008; Van der Wagen, 2010; Rodrigues & Brandao, 2017; Gold & Gold, 2018).

"Major events" are events with broad visitor participation due to their large scale and media attention. These kinds of events attract more and more participants with their widespread media coverage. Thus, major activities can create more economic contributions to the region and local people (Bowdin, et al., 2006). Formula 1 Grand Prix, Chinese New Year, Commonwealth Games and Pan American Games organized in England can be cited as examples of major events (Bowdin et al., 2006; Van der Wagen, 2010; Smith, 2012).

"Hallmark events" are events that are identified with the city, town or region where they are organized, that raise awareness about the city, town or region in which the event is organized and play an important role in promotion. In Hallmark events, it can be said that there is a very strong connection between the host city and the event, and after a while, the cities start to be remembered in connection with those events. Carnival held in Rio, Oktoberfest in Munich, Tour de France and Melbourne Cup, Australia are examples of hallmark events (Bowdin, et al., 2006; Getz, 2008; Van der Wagen, 2010).

"Local events" can be defined as events where the people living in the region can participate for socializing and entertainment purposes. In addition to offering a different experience, such events are important in terms of increasing the loyalty of the local people to each other and to the region (Bowdin et al., 2006). The effects of such events are generally seen at a regional scale (Getz, 2008). Regional wine festivals and soccer activities organized at universities are examples of social events (Gibson, Willming & Holdnak, 2003; Getz, 2008).

EMITT Fair (Eastern Mediterranean International Tourism and Travel Fair)

The Eastern Mediterranean International Tourism and Travel Fair (EMITT) is one of the world's five largest tourism fairs (Berlin ITB, London WTM, Madrid FITUR, Istanbul EMITT, Milan BIT and Moscow MITT). Every year, the event hosts over 40,000 industry professionals and tourists who want to take advantage of new and exciting travel opportunities offered by holiday destinations and travel companies around the world (Emittistanbul, 2020). Tourism professionals, municipalities, countries, and groups such as independent participants also participate in the EMITT Fair, the first of which was held in 1996 (Şengel, Zengin & Işkın, 2017). The Eastern Mediterranean International Tourism and Travel Exhibition EMITT, which is a leader in its region and one of the five largest tourism exhibitions in the world, has been seen as a tourism summit that offers new business and cooperation opportunities to the sector for the last 24 years. The fair contributes to the growth of the sector by increasing the number of participants and visitors in the region every year (Emittistanbul, 2020).

EMITT Fair is held in Istanbul Beylikdüzü TÜYAP Fair meeting and congress center. The fair and congress center has 21 halls and a capacity of 30,000 people. TÜYAP, whose largest hall hosts 10,000 people, has a total area of 42,000 square meters (Baytok, Soybalı & Emir, 2010). EMITT will open its doors to its visitors for the 25th time in 2022. It is supported by the Trade, Culture and Tourism Ministry, TOBB (Turkish Union of Chambers and Exchange Commodities), Turkish Airlines and the Istanbul Metropolitan Municipality (Emittistanbul, 2020). The number of visitors, exhibitors, and countries for the EMITT 2016-2020 periods are shown in Table 1. According to the table, it was revealed that there was a decrease in the EMITT Fair in 2017 and 2020, and the number of visitors hosted in other years were similar.

Theoretical Framework

Table 1. EMITT Number of Visitors During 2016-2020

	2016	2017	2018	2019	2020
Visitor number	56.124	46.470	54.364	57.470	44.321
Participant Number	882	685	1065	1201	842
Country Number	70	80	85	94	103

Source: Adapted from EMITT Istanbul official website.

The effectiveness of e-marketing tools in proactive marketing communications is important for the preparation of large-scale event management. Some of these marketing tools include website and brochure resources, internet advertising, internet public relations, e-mail marketing, e-viral marketing, internet communities, database marketing, mobile telecommunications, and digital television and radio. In addition to these tools, blogs and blogging concepts and their use have also developed and gained importance in creating forums and sharing ideas. Within the scope of the research, since effective website marketing of large-scale events is examined, only web marketing of events will be mentioned under this heading.

Web Marketing of Events

Werthner and Klein (2002) state that consumer behavior is changing in the tourism industry as in other industries. Within the general trend, tourists; (1) demand better service, (2) require more specific presentations in terms of both content and general regulations, (3) demand more qualified information about the product itself as well as general regulations, (4) are more mobile and critical but they become less loyal, (5) are more price sensitive and compare more and more offers, (6) tend to have more but shorter vacations, (7) shorten the time interval between booking and consumption by making the decision later.

One of the most important ways to respond to the changing behavior of consumers mentioned above is websites. The main purpose of websites is to provide information. This information is categorized under three groups: commercial/non-commercial information, information about transaction-related activities and entertainment information. The first group of information is commercial and non-commercial information provided by businesses. Commercial information consists of information about the business such as the mission statement regarding the past of the business, financial indicators, and defined projects. Including such information on the website is of great importance in introducing businesses to customers. Like general information about the business, information about the product, features, definitions, pictures, prices that support the sales activities of the business and that are geared towards establishing relationships with customers are also commercial information. Non-commercial information on websites is information that is thought to be relevant to the business. Information about the region where the business operates, the place of residence and the weather can be listed among the non-commercial information (Huizing, 2000). For example, when considered for the tourism sector, the information provided on subjects such as festivals and handicrafts about the region is non-commercial information. However, since it is the service industry, it would be appropriate to state that information about the region, festivals and handicrafts can also turn into commercial information.

The second group of information includes the activities in relation to the transaction (Huizing, 2000). For example, online reservations, all interactive activities between the customer and the operator fall into this group. Many studies in the literature also show that customers attach importance to this second group of information and that this information group affects their decisions (Huizing, 2000; Park & Kim, 2003). Lohse and Spiller (1998) emphasized the importance of information including interactive activities that customers want careful and continuous communication despite geographical obstacles and distances, and therefore, a customer service section should be created on websites. In the section related to customer service, sections such as frequently asked questions, credits, payment policies, online communication should be included (Park & Kim, 2003). In addition, if access to the website is easy, if the search engine and site map are provided, if the site is understood, this becomes an attraction for touristic consumers and increases the use of the website (Park & Kim, 2003). Additionally, it is stated that clearly stating the trust and privacy policies on websites will increase the trust of the consumer in the website and motivate the consumer to use the website (Park & Kim, 2003; Hummer, Kretschmer & Hofman, 2005). Yeung and Law (2006) highlighted the importance of the customer's trust in the website and stated that the customer's purchase of the service using internet channels can only be achieved when they have trust in the relevant website (Yeung & Law, 2006).

The third group of information is related to whether the website of the business is entertaining or not. Although the primary purpose of websites is to present information, it is also important to present information in an entertaining way, rather than simply presenting written information in order to attract the attention of the user (Huizing, 2000). Therefore, websites should be designed as easy-to-access, colorful catalogs that present the product/service to the user with various animations, videos, and photographs. Many researchers also stated that the purchase of the service by touristic consumers depends mainly on the appearance of the product in the virtual environment, separate from the experience, such as pictures, images, information, video clips (Lohse & Spiller, 1998; Kolesar & Galbraith, 2000). The ease of use of the website may not provide entertainment for the customer. Therefore, while increasing the use of the site, the user will be discouraged from staying in an environment that is not fun or interesting. The usability of a website is simply defined as the ability of a customer to use the website without technical or formal training, interacting with the website and information system (Benbunan-Fich, 2001), with the least mental effort while the user performs the desired action in the shortest time (Krug, 2000). The usefulness of the website is classified as (a) user interface, (b) information quality and (c) online server quality (Wan, 2002). The user interface is related to the layout of the website, the routing order, the suitability of information search system (Wan, 2002).

In the 21st century, as the internet continues to gain importance, marketing activities on the internet have begun to develop in all business areas, including the event industry. Websites for the events industry cater to a wide range of stakeholders who expect different services from them; exhibitors or visitors need detailed information about the event; promoters look for historical data and information regarding facilities and locations; and the media researches press releases and sponsors. Masterman and Wood (2006) define the most important aspect of internet marketing communications as ensuring that correct information about the event is presented in all relevant websites in a useful and consistent format. Hence, Hoyle (2002) lists the advantages of web marketing for an event as follows: brand building, direct marketing by increasing the level of knowledge on the event, online sales by reducing mailing and printing costs and allowing rapid changes and individual messages, customer support with fast transactions, content publishing services by answering questions quickly, marketing research, getting information about the customer, and to allow company information to reach a wide audience. Masterman and Wood (2006) also state that today websites are useful communication mediums due to the following advantages: an inexpensive way to reach the target audience, for example, easy measurement of efficiency such as the ease of counting the number of site visitors or the ease of understanding from which sites visitors are coming and which sites they go to; allow easy collection of data on visitors thanks to a registration link, enabling visitors to access up-to-date information with rapid content changes. The fact that websites create a much more interactive communication environment when compared to other marketing channels create this advantage.

It is clear that the marketing communication activities implemented in the field of event marketing are carried out to reach existing and potential event audiences in order to motivate them to participate in the planned event. Websites are considered as powerful tools due to their multifunctional nature. Websites also have certain disadvantages, such as the need to promote the website and the lack of control over the information provided, causing visitors to start thinking that the information provided is misleading. Hoyle (2002) provides the website marketing guidelines as follows:

- Listing the web address of the event in high-traffic engines and directories,
- Listing in meeting and event calendars,
- Considering the exchange of links, sponsorships or advertisements with other websites,
- Online distribution of news bulletins,
- Inclusion of the event web address everywhere,
- Identifying e-mail discussion groups or lists related to your industry and being an active participant,
- Using signature files at the end of e-mails to provide contact information and event information,
- Sharing the links with exhibitors so that customers can get information about the event.

In addition, many researchers, considering the above-mentioned features of websites, generally examine websites using two factors, which are content and design (Liu, Arnett, Capella & Beatty, 1997; Robbins, Stylianou, 2003; Scharl, Wöber & Bauer, 2004). In line with this, the features that should be in an event website can be expressed as follows. The first one is the content features dimension which contains information about the event website, and the other factor is the dimension of the design feature of the event site. Within the scope of the content features, five sub-dimensions of the event were developed, which are; communication-customer support, general information about the event, related services, information about culture (festival, handicrafts, world heritage, etc.) and the security level of the site. Under the main heading of contact/customer support, sub-headings developed include the address, telephone and fax numbers, e-mail address of the event, a map of the event, whether there is a frequently asked questions section, online communication opportunity, reservation, information about the culture of the region, information about the city, city map, weather conditions, climate, transportation facilities, important telephone numbers and important addresses to be reached when needed, local handicrafts, festivals, celebrations, concerts in the region. Under general information about the activity, photographs of the event, leisure activities, information about the services offered, the distance of the event to important centers, and the price were included while excursions, tour programs, guidance, car rental services are addressed under the heading of related services. Whether the sites give importance to security and privacy issues, whether they indicate personal information or credit card information is secured or not are addressed under the security heading of the model. In addition, the information section on world heritage is included in the content features section of the model in order to determine whether the information and data regarding the world heritage are addressed in the relevant websites, considering that it will be suitable for the study structure.

The second main dimension of the event websites is the design features section of the websites. The design features section of the established model consists of four factors which are: the presentation of the site to users, the available language options, routing features and off-page instant advertisements (traps). The presentation section includes whether animation, graphics, music, video images and photographs are included in the relevant website, the language options section includes how many languages the site is prepared in while in the redirecting heading, whether the site provides links to other sites, whether its content is protected, whether there are features such as search engine, sitemap and whether there are traps on the page of the relevant site are included.

MAIN FOCUS OF THE CHAPTER

A comprehensive literature search on the subject was conducted. However, the literature search did not yield any studies examining the effectiveness of any website in large-scale event marketing. A well-prepared website is of paramount importance to the event industry in today's world. Participation in events that have the potential and capacity to draw attention both nationally and internationally usually occurs through the examination of the websites that are prepared for the event by visitors. This study is also significant as its purpose is to examine the effectiveness of the website of the Eastern Mediterranean International Tourism and Travel Fair.

METHODOLOGY

Sample, Implementation and Measurement

The sample included in this study is the web page of the 2022 Eastern Mediterranean International Tourism and Travel (EMITT) Fair.

The implementation in this study was conducted to measure the effectiveness of the website features of the 2022 Eastern Mediterranean International Tourism and Travel (EMITT) Fair. In alignment with this purpose, the features of the website of the 2022 Eastern Mediterranean International Tourism and Travel (EMITT) Fair were examined with content analysis.

Data were collected on the internet and the EMITT Fair website. During the examination of the website features, a review was performed on the website by taking into consideration the characteristics of the websites of the convention offices determined by İnan and Olcer (2010) and, Wang and Fesenmaier (2006), but adhering to a new classification developed by considering the differences found in the event industry.

Findings

EMITT Fair, which will be held for the 25th time in 2022, is in the process of preparing to host national and international industry professionals and thousands of tourists who want to take advantage of the new and exciting travel opportunities offered by holiday destinations and travel companies from all over the world. EMITT Fair will open its doors to visitors for the 25th time in 2022.

A well-prepared website is of paramount importance to the event industry in today's world. EMITT Fair is one of the mega events shown among large-scale events. Participation in events that can result in national and international attention is usually begun with visitors examining the prepared for the event. In this sense, Table 2 presented below reveals the features of the website prepared for the 25th EMITT Fair.

Table 2. Evaluation of 2022 EMITT Fair Website Features

No.	Website Feature	2022 EMITT Fair Website: emittistanbul.com
1	Activities / Attraction Information	1
2	Banner advertisements	0
3	Fair catalog/brochure	1
4	Event Calendar	1
5	Frequently asked questions	1
6	Information about EMITT	1
7	History of EMITT	0
8	Information about Istanbul	0
9	Links to city websites	0
10	Maps	1
11	Online participant reservation	1
12	Online visitor entry form, ticket	1
13	Fair result reports	1
14	Organizer information	1
15	Photo gallery	1
16	Video gallery	1
17	Social media sites	0
18	Feedback surveys	0
19	Contact information	1
20	Accommodation and transportation info	1
21	Information about sponsors	1
22	Fair statistics	1

1= includes 0=does not include

According to the table, activities/attraction information, fair catalog/brochure, event calendar, frequently asked questions, information about EMITT, maps, online exhibitor reservation, online visitor entry form and ticket, fair result reports, organizer information, photo gallery, video gallery, contact information, accommodation and transportation information, information about sponsors and fair statistics are available on the 2022 EMITT Fair web page. On the other hand, banner advertisements, EMITT's history, information about Istanbul, city pages links, social media pages and feedback surveys are not available on the 2022 EMITT Fair website.

The table clearly shows that the 2022 Eastern Mediterranean International Tourism and Travel Fair EMITT website has been prepared in a very detailed way, satisfying the visitors doing research on the web.

Google assigns a numerical weight value in the range of 0 - 10 to each web page on the internet and this page rank value indicates the importance of a site, according to Google. Page rank is derived from a theoretical probability value that depends on a logarithmic scale such as the Richter scale. The page rank value of a given page depends roughly on the number of inbound links, as well as the page rank value of the linked pages. In addition, it is known that other factors such as the relevance of search words and actual visits to the page as reported by Google Toolbar affect the value of the page rank (İnan & Olcer, 2010). Since this very important ranking regarding the importance and effectiveness of the websites was terminated as of 2014, a page ranking value for the website of the 2022 Eastern Mediterranean International Tourism and Travel (EMITT) Fair cannot be given here.

SOLUTIONS AND RECOMMEDATIONS

With globalization, competition is increasing day by day in all sectors. In the global competitive environment where communication technologies are increasingly developing, websites that are considered effective and interactive can make significant contributions to the marketing efforts of the event industry. In addition to presenting written content to visitors, websites also appeal to their visual and auditory senses. An effectively designed website is of great importance in terms of quality service delivery and competitive ability (Ateş & Boz, 2015).

EMITT being considered as the most important tourism fair in Turkey, the fair's great importance on promotion, public relations, and marketing cannot be disputed. Therefore, it would be beneficial to summarize the findings and criticisms addressed in this study evaluating the mega scale fair's website effectiveness in terms of marketing strategies, website design, management, and perceptions:

In order to determine the effectiveness of the website of the 2022 Eastern Mediterranean International Tourism and Travel (EMITT) Fair, an e-mail was sent out to the entire exhibition team listed in the communication section of the EMITT Fair website on August 23, 2020 to obtain the necessary permission for the research. On August 24, 2020, a response to the email from the EMITT Fair Marketing Regional Director was received and the request for work was deemed appropriate. The fact that a response to the email was sent one day later shows that the website is active and interactive.

When the EMITT Fair, which is evaluated within the scope of the mega-scale event industry, is considered in terms of the web marketing of the industry, it is seen that the website is realized for a specific purpose in the context of tourism in question. As a result of the examination performed in 22 items considering the content features of the website, it was observed that the virtual communication and marketing of the site are carried out effectively, the content information that the customer may need in virtual environment is presented in a sufficient, attractive and complete manner, and this information is effectively communicated to the customer.

FUTURE RESEARCH DIRECTIONS

The fact that the evaluation of the EMITT Fair website was performed in a short period of time (2-31 August 2020) can be shown as the most significant limitation of the study. Considering the speed of operation and updating of the website, the updates made after this date could not be taken into account. Due to the dynamic nature of websites and the constant changes made, the changes can be better monitored, and periodic comparisons can be made with evaluations to be made at certain intervals closer to the date of the fair.

In this study, the EMITT Fair website was generally evaluated by considering its content features. However, the evaluation of the fair's website, examining the effectiveness of the website from the consumers' perspective, re-organization and even doing comparative assessments on all fairs that are held regularly every year and considered within mega events like the EMITT fair in Turkey can produce important results that may guide practitioners and future researchers.

CONCLUSION

Large-scale mega events are more easily noticed by the participants through the effectiveness of web marketing. The effectiveness of web marketing in the perspectives of the participants of the event becomes an important element and positively affects the preferences of the visitors.

Thus, the institutions and organizations that carry out the event gain an advantage in competitive conditions by creating awareness. In this study, when taking into consideration the 22 items that were used in examining the web site content, it is concluded that the website satisfies the visitors who will participate in the event. Thus, it will be highly probable that the positive pre-evaluations of the participants before participating in the event will contribute to the image of the event.

Especially, receiving a response within one day to the e- mail that was sent to all the staff members to get necessary permissions in order to identify the effective use of the EMITT Fair website indicates that the website is active and interactive which is considered as an important result.

REFERENCES

Ateş, U., & Boz, M. (2015). Konaklama işletmelerinin web sitelerinin değerlendirilmesi: Çanakkale örneği. *Ekonomi İşletme Siyaset ve Uluslararası İlişkiler Dergisi*, *1*(1), 63–84.

Babacan, E., & Göztaş, A. (2011). *Etkinlik Yönetimi*. Detay Yayıncılık.

Bastida, U., & Huan, T. C. (2014). Performance evaluation of tourism websites' information quality of four global destination brands: Beijing, Hong Kong, Shanghai, and Taipei. *Journal of Business Research*, *67*(2), 167–170. doi:10.1016/j.jbusres.2012.10.008

Baytok, A., Soybalı, H. H., & Emir, O. (2010). Destinasyonların toplantı turizmi amaçlı pazarlanmasında kongre ve ziyaretçi bürolarının rolü: İstanbul kongre ve ziyaretçi bürosu örneği. *Selçuk Üniversitesi Sosyal Bilimler Enstitüsü Dergisi*, *23*, 9–22.

Benbunan-Fich, R. (2001). Using protocol analysis to evaluate the usability of a commercial web site. *Information & Management*, *39*(2), 151–163. doi:10.1016/S0378-7206(01)00085-4

Bowdin, G., O'Toole, W., Allen, J., Harris, R., & McDonnell, I. (2006). *Events management*. Routledge. doi:10.4324/9780080457154

Çakıcı, C. (2009). *Toplantı yönetimi. Kongre, konferans seminer ve fuar organizasyonları*. Detay Yayıncılık.

Chen, Y. F., & Mo, H. E. (2012). Attendees' perspectives on the service quality of an exhibition organizer: A case study of a tourism exhibition. *Tourism Management Perspectives*, *1*, 28–33. doi:10.1016/j.tmp.2011.12.004

Emittistanbul.com. (2020). *Emitt hakkında*. Retrieved from https://emittistanbul.com/Sayfa/emitt-hakkinda

Fan, Y., & Pfitzenmaıer, N. (2002). Event sponsorship in China. *Corporate Communications*, *7*(2), 110–116. doi:10.1108/13563280210426179

Getz, D. (1997). Trends and issues in sport event tourism. *Tourism Recreation Research*, *22*(2), 61–62. doi:10.1080/02508281.1997.11014804

Getz, D. (2008). Event tourism: Definition, evolution, and research. *Tourism Management*, *29*(3), 403–428. doi:10.1016/j.tourman.2007.07.017

Gibson, H. J., Willming, C., & Holdnak, A. (2003). Small-scale event sport tourism: Fans as tourists. *Tourism Management*, *24*(2), 181–190. doi:10.1016/S0261-5177(02)00058-4

Gold, J. R., & Gold, M. M. (2018). *Urban segments and event spaces: World's fairs and olympic sites. The Routledge Handbook of Planning History*. Routledge.

Hall, C. M. (1989). The definition and analysis of hallmark tourist events. *GeoJournal*, *19*(3), 263–268. doi:10.1007/BF00454570

Hoyle, L. H. (2002). *Event marketing. How to successfully promote events, festivals, conventions, and expositions*. John Wiley.

Hsu, A. C., & Wang, F. K. (2009). Study on the key element of the religion type event marketing-"Franklin Graham Festival in Taipei" as a case. *Symposium conducted at the meeting of Chinese Communication Society*.

Huizing, E. (2000). The content and design of web sites: An empirical study. *Information & Management*, *37*(1), 123–124. doi:10.1016/S0378-7206(99)00044-0

Hummer, M., Kretschmer, D., & Hofmann, B. (2005). User-centered requirements engineering: Usability ıssue for websites of tour operators. In Information and Communication Technologies in Tourism. Wien: Springer Verlag.

Hung, K., & Law, R. (2011). An overview of Internet-based surveys in hospitality and tourism journals. *Tourism Management, 32*(4), 717–724. doi:10.1016/j.tourman.2010.05.027

İnan, E., & Ölçer, C. (2010). Büyük ölçekli etkinlik yönetiminde e-pazarlama çalışmaları: İstanbul Avrupa kültür başkenti örneği. *Erciyes İletişim Dergisi, 1*(4).

Kolesar, M. B., & Galbraith, R. W. (2000). A services- marketing perspective on e-retailing: Implications for e-retailers and directions for further research. *Internet Research, 10*(5), 424–438. doi:10.1108/10662240010349444

Krug, S. (2000). *Don't Make me Think! A Common Sense Approach to Web Usability*. New Riders.

Krugman, C., & Wrıght, P. R. (2007). *Global meetings and exhibitions*. John Wiley & Sons, Inc.

Lee, S., Close, A. G., & Love, C. (2010). How information quality and market turbulence impact convention and visitors bureaus' use of marketing information: Insights for destination and event marketing. *Journal of Convention & Event Tourism, 11*(4), 266–292. doi:10.1080/15470148.2010.530541

Liu, C., Arnett, K. P., Capella, L. M., & Beatty, R. C. (1997). Web sites of the fortune 500 companies: Facing customers through home pages. *Information & Management, 31*(1), 335–345. doi:10.1016/S0378-7206(97)00001-3

Liu, L., & Arnett, P. (2000). Exploring the factors associated with website success in the context of electronic commerce. *Information & Management, 38*(1), 23–33. doi:10.1016/S0378-7206(00)00049-5

Liu, L., Zhang, J., & Keh, H. T. (2018). Event-marketing and advertising expenditures: The differential effects on brand value and company revenue. *Journal of Advertising Research, 58*(4), 464–475. doi:10.2501/JAR-2017-043

Liu, Y., Liu, A., Liu, X., & Huang, X. (2019). A statistical approach to participant selection in location-based social networks for offline event marketing. *Information Sciences, 480*, 90–108. doi:10.1016/j.ins.2018.12.028

Lohse, G. L., & Spiller, P. (1998). Electronic Shopping. *Communications of the ACM, 41*(7), 81–90. doi:10.1145/278476.278491

Masterman, G., & Wood, E. H. (2006). *Innovative marketing communications: Strategies for the events industry*. Elsevier Butterworth Heinemann.

Müller, M. (2015a). What makes an event a mega-event? Definitions and sizes. *Leisure Studies, 34*(6), 627–642. doi:10.1080/02614367.2014.993333

Müller, M. (2015b). The mega-event syndrome: Why so much goes wrong in mega-event planning and what to do about it. *Journal of the American Planning Association, 81*(1), 6–17. doi:10.1080/01944363.2015.1038292

Park, C. H., & Kim, Y. G. (2003). Identifying key factors affecting consumer purchase behavior in an online shopping context. *International Journal of Retail & Distribution Management, 31*(1), 16–29. doi:10.1108/09590550310457818

Pira, A. (2004). *Etkinlik yönetimi*. MediaCat Yayıncılık.

Robbins, S. S., & Stylianou, A. C. (2003). Global corporate web sites: An empirical ınvestigation of content and design. *Information & Management, 40*(1), 205–212. doi:10.1016/S0378-7206(02)00002-2

Rodrigues, P., & Brandao, A. (2017). Sports events in the attitude toward the brand: Involvement and emotıons of consumer. In *5th International Consumer Brand Relationships Conference*. University of Porto.

Scharl, A., Wober, W. K., & Bauer, C. (2004). An ıntegrated approach to measure web site effectiveness in the European hotel ındustry. *Information Technology & Tourism, 6*(1), 257–271.

Şengel, Ü., Zengin, B., Şengel, T., & Işkın, M. (2017). Kongre ve fuar organizasyonlarının turizm sektörüne etkileri: EMITT örneği. *Turizm ve Araştırma Dergisi, 7*(1), 4–20.

Smith, A. (2012). *Events and urban regeneration: The strategic use of events to revitalise cities*. Routledge. doi:10.4324/9780203136997

Sun, H. (2007). *Destination and event marketing: A case study in the 2007 c&d xiamen ınternational marathon*. Xiamen, China, Master's Thesis, University Of Waterloo.

Surya, E. D. (2018). The Effect of Advertising, Exhibition and Event Marketing to Improve Awareness Awareness and its Impact on Intereststo Visit to Destination Religi Tour in Padang City (Case Study of Muslim Tourists from Malaysia). *International Conference of ASEAN Prespective and Policy, 1*(1), 226-231.

Tierney, P. (2000). Internet-based evaluation of tourism web site effectiveness: Methodological issues and survey results. *Journal of Travel Research, 39*(2), 212–219. doi:10.1177/004728750003900211

Tığlı, M. (2008). *Güncel pazarlama yaklaşımlarından seçmeler*. Detay Yayıncılık.

Tolan, D. (2014). *Spor endüstrisinde etkinlik pazarlaması: Galatasaray spor kulübü örneği. Yayımlanmamış yükseklisans tezi*. Maltepe Üniversitesi.

Tuckwell, K. J. (1991). *Canadian Marketing in Action*. Pearson Education.

Turco, D. M. (1997). Host residents' perceived social costs and benefits toward a staged tourist attraction. *Journal of Travel & Tourism Marketing, 7*(1), 21–30. doi:10.1300/J073v07n01_02

Van der Wagen, L. (2010). *Event management*. Pearson Higher Education AU.

Wan, C. S. (2002). The web sites of ınternational tourist hotels and tour wholesalers in Taiwan. *Tourism Management, 23*(2), 155–160. doi:10.1016/S0261-5177(01)00048-6

Wang, Y., & Fesenmaier, D. R. (2006). Identifying the success factors of web-based marketing strategy: An investigation of convention and visitors bureaus in the United States. *Journal of Travel Research, 44*(3), 44. doi:10.1177/0047287505279007

Werthner, H., & Klein, S. (2002). *Information technology and tourism-a challenging Relationship*. Springer-Verlag Wien.

Wohlfeil, M., & Whelan, S., (2005). *Event-marketing: When brands become "Real- Lived"*. Academic Press.

Wood, E. H., & Masterman, G. (2008). *Event marketing: Measuring an experience.* In *7th International Marketing Trends Congress*, Venice.

Yeung, T. A., & Law, R. (2006). Evaluation of usability: A study of hotel web sites in Hong Kong. *Journal of Hospitality & Tourism Research (Washington, D.C.), 30*(4), 452–473. doi:10.1177/1096348006290115

Zamzuri, N. H., Awang, K. W., & Samdin, Z. (2011). Environmental issues in meeting, incentive, convention and exhibition (MICE) tourism sector. *2nd international conference on business, economics and tourism management, 24*, 98-101.

Zhao, Z., & Gutierrez, J. (2001). The Fundamental Perspectives in E-Commerce. In *E-Commerce Diffusion: Strategies And Challenges*. Heidelberg Press.

Zou, J. Y., & Ap, J. (2009). Residents' perceptions towards the impacts of the Beijing 2008 Olympic Games. *Journal of Traver Research,* 48-78.

ADDITIONAL READING

Cobos, L. M., Wang, Y., & Okumus, F. (2009). Assessing the web-based destination marketing activities: A relationship marketing perspective. *Journal of Hospitality Marketing & Management, 18*(4), 421–444. doi:10.1080/19368620902799643

Coyle, J. R., & Thorson, E. (2001). The effects of progressive levels of interactivity and vividness in web marketing sites. *Journal of Advertising, 30*(3), 65–77. doi:10.1080/00913367.2001.10673646

Devine, A., Bolan, P., & Devine, F. (2010). Online destination marketing: Maximising the tourism potential of a sports event. *International Journal of Sport Management and Marketing, 7*(1-2), 58–75. doi:10.1504/IJSMM.2010.029712

Doolin, B., Burgess, L., & Cooper, J. (2002). Evaluating the use of the Web for tourism marketing: A case study from New Zealand. *Tourism Management, 23*(5), 557–561. doi:10.1016/S0261-5177(02)00014-6

Kim, Y. H., Yuan, J., Goh, B. K., & Antun, J. M. (2009). Web marketing in food tourism: A content analysis of web sites in West Texas. *Journal of Culinary Science & Technology, 7*(1), 52–64. doi:10.1080/15428050902788352

Martensen, A., Grønholdt, L., Bendtsen, L., & Jensen, M. J. (2007). Application of a model for the effectiveness of event marketing. *Journal of Advertising Research, 47*(3), 283–301. doi:10.2501/S0021849907070316

Perner, P., & Fiss, G. (2002). Intelligent E-marketing with web mining, personalization, and user-adpated interfaces. In *Advances in data mining* (pp. 37–52). Springer. doi:10.1007/3-540-46131-0_3

Sterne, J. (2002). *World Wide Web marketing: Integrating the Web into your marketing strategy.* John Wiley & Sons.

Wang, Y., & Fesenmaier, D. R. (2006). Identifying the success factors of web-based marketing strategy: An investigation of convention and visitors bureaus in the United States. *Journal of Travel Research*, *44*(3), 239–249. doi:10.1177/0047287505279007

Yu, Z., Zhang, D., Yu, Z., & Yang, D. (2015). Participant selection for offline event marketing leveraging location-based social networks. *IEEE Transactions on Systems, Man, and Cybernetics. Systems*, *45*(6), 853–864. doi:10.1109/TSMC.2014.2383993

KEY TERMS AND DEFINITIONS

Berlin ITB: International Travel Trade Show Berlin is one of the world's largest tourism fairs. The companies represented at the fair include hotels, tourist boards, tour operators, system providers, airlines, and car rental companies. ITB Berlin is held in Messe Berlin every year in March.

Istanbul EMITT: Eastern Mediterranean International Tourism and Travel Fair EMITT is one of the most important tourism fairs in the world. Each year, the event welcomes over 40,000 industry professionals and tourists who want to take advantage of the new and exciting travel opportunities offered by resorts and travel companies around the world.

London WTM: London World Travel Market Fair is held every year in ExCeL London. The World Travel Market London, which was first held in 1980, is an annual business-to-business fair for travel industry professionals. Travel and tourism product suppliers showcase the latest developments in the travel industry. The WTM brings together the largest global industry meeting of tour operators, hotels, airlines, technology, and online travel services under one roof and covers a variety of sectors in the travel and tourism industry.

Madrid FITUR: FITUR (Feria Internacional de Turismo) is the first gathering of the year for the world's tourism professionals and the leading trade fair for inbound and outbound markets in Latin America. This year, Turkey has participated in the 40th international tourism fair held in Madrid, the capital of Spain, with the theme of "Göbeklitepe."

Milan BIT: BIT (Borsa Internazionale del Turismo) is an International Travel Fair which brings together the Industry Professionals, Tourism Boards, Promotion and Services Agencies from across the globe.

Moscow MITT: Moscow International Travel and Tourism Exhibition is the largest B2B (business to business) travel & tourism trade show held in Russia which attracts representatives of the tourism industry from Russia, other regions, and all over the world.

Three Es: In event marketing, the three E's refer to entertainment, excitement, and enterprise.

TOBB: The Union of Chambers and Commodity Exchanges of Turkey is a professional institution in the nature of public institution established with a special statue that has a special legal entity as a result of the merger of Chambers of Commerce, Chambers of Industry, Chambers of Trade and Industry, Chamber of Marine Commerce and the Commodity Exchange Markets.

TÜYAP: TÜYAP which was founded under the name of Tüm Fuarcılık Yapım Incorporated Company by Bülent Ünal on June 28, 1979 in Istanbul, continues to operate on fair organizations.

Compilation of References

7ways-to-measure-social-mediaeffectiveness. (2011). Retrieved from before it's news web site: http://www.sitepronews.com/2011/09/06/7-ways-to-measure-social-mediaeffectiveness-for-your-company-a-spn-exclusive-article/

8 Great Examples of Social Media Event Marketing. (2016). Retrieved from https://www.eventbrite.co.uk/blog/social-media-event-marketing-ds00/

Abad, P., Franco, M., Castillón, R., Alonso, I., Cambra, A., Sierra, J., Riozuelo, L., Montano, L., & Murillo, A. C. (2017, November). Integrating an autonomous robot on a dance and new technologies festival. In *Iberian robotics conference* (pp. 75–87). Springer.

Abdüsselam, M. S., & Karal, H. (2012). Fizik öğretiminde artırılmış gerçeklik ortamlarının öğrenci akademik başarısı üzerine etkisi: 11. Sınıf manyetizma konusu [The effect of augmented reality environments on student academic achievement in physics teaching: 11th grade magnetism topic]. *Eğitim ve Öğretim Araştırmaları Dergisi, 1*(4), 170–182.

Accelevents. (2020). *The Top 8 Event Technology Trends to Watch in 2020.* https://www.accelevents.com/top-8-event-technology-trends-2020/

Ahas, R., Aasa, A., Roose, A., Mark, U., & Silm, S. (2008). Evaluating Passive Mobile Positioning Data for Tourism Surveys: An Estonian Case Study. *Tourism Management, 29*(3), 469–486. doi:10.1016/j.tourman.2007.05.014

Ahmed, R. (2017). *4 Famous restaurants that use 3D printers.* Retrieved August 2, 2020, from https://3dprinting.com/food/4-famous-restaurants-that-use-3d-printers/

Ak, A. (2013). Dijital sanat, Akademik Bilişim. XV. Akademik Bilişim Konferansı Bildirileri 23-25 Ocak 2013, Akdeniz Üniversitesi, Antalya.

Akar, E. (2010). *Sosyal medya pazarlaması [Social media marketing].* Efil Yayınevi.

Akar, E. (2010). *Sosyal medya pazarlaması.* Efil Publishing.

Akar, E. (2011). *Sosyal medya pazarlaması: Sosyal Web'te pazarlama stratejileri.* Efil Yayınevi.

Akay, R. A. (2014). Creative competition event management practices and social media integration. *The Turkish Online Journal of Design. Art and Communication, 4*(4), 55–70.

Akay, R. A. (2014). Etkinlik Yönetimi Uygulamalarında Yaratıcı Rekabet ve Sosyal Medyanın Entegrasyonu, *The Turkish Online Journal of Design. Art and Communication, 4*(4), 55–70.

Akbayır, Z. (2016). Bana bir hikâye anlat: Marka iletişiminde hikâyeleştirme ve internet [Tell me a story: Storytelling and internet in brand communication]. *Karadeniz Teknik Üniversitesi İletişim Araştırmaları Dergisi, 3*(12), 67–84.

Akçay, E. (2019). *Dünyanın ilk dijital sanat müzesi: MORI*. Retrieved from https://www.sophosakademi.org/dunyanin-ilk-dijital-sanat-muzesi-mori/

Akgül, D. T. (2020). *Ziyafet servisi yönetimi*. Retrieved August 27, 2020, from https://obs.yasar.edu.tr/oibs/akademik/shr_files/FILE_zou07jrmmfn43fv12zofexnx5hnw3_duyuru.PDF

Akiyama, T., Murata, S., Tsuchiya, K., Yokoyama, T., Maggio, M., Ciulla, G., Santana, J. R., Zhao, M., Nascimento, J. B., & Gürgen, L. (2017). Festival: Design and implementation of federated interoperable smart ICT services development and testing platform. *Journal of Information Processing*, *25*(0), 278–287. doi:10.2197/ipsjjip.25.278

Akram, W., & Kumar, R. (2017). A study on role and applications of augmented reality in tourism: Its challanges and future prospects. *International Journal of Advanced Research in Computer Science*, *8*(8), 168–172. doi:10.26483/ijarcs.v8i8.4633

Aksentyeva, N., Aminov, D.-S., Cayenne, J., Foo, J., Kammogne, G., Lum, A., & Zhou, H. (2020). *Technology Use in Meetings*. https://theirf.org/am-site/media/technology-in-offsite-meetings-and-incentive-events-full-paper.pdf

Aksoy, M., & Akbulut, B. A. (2017). Restoranlardaki teknolojik yeniliklerin deneyim pazarlaması açısından değerlendirilmesi. In *International Congress on Cultural Herigate and Tourism (ICCHT)* (pp. 19-21). Academic Press.

Aksoy, T. (2011). Deneyimsel Pazarlama. [https://www.myfikirler.org/deneyimsel-pazarlama.html]. Access date: January, 2020.

Aksoy, S. (2017). Değişen Teknolojiler ve Endüstri 4.0: Endüstri 4.0'ı Anlamaya Dair Bir Giriş. *SAV Katkı*, *4*, 34–44.

Aktan, E., & Çakmak, V. (2015). Halkla ilişkiler öğrencilerinin sosyal medyadaki siber zorbalık duyarlılıklarını ölçmeye ilişkin bir araştırma. *Gümüşhane Üniversitesi İletişim Fakültesi Elektronik Dergisi*, *3*(2), 159–176.

Aktan, E., & Koçyiğit, M. (2016). A theoretical analysis for role of social media on tourism activities. *Journal of Social Sciences*, 62–73.

Akten, Z. (2008). Gelişen Teknolojilerin Dijital Sanat Alanında Oluşturduğu Yeni Temalar ve Mimarlığa Katkıları. İstanbul Teknik Üniversitesi, Fen Bilimleri Enstitüsü yayınlanmamış yüksek lisans tezi, İstanbul.

Alan, A. K., Kabadayı, E. T., & Erişke, T. (2018). The new face of communication: Digital marketing and social media marketing. *Electronic Journal of Social Sciences*, *17*(66), 493–504.

Alikılıç, I., & Özkan, B. (2018). Bir sosyal medya pazarlama trendi, hatırlı pazarlama ve etkileyiciler: Instagram fenomenleri üzerine bir araştırma [A social media marketing trend, influencer marketing and influencers: A study on Instagram phenomena]. *Uluslararası Sosyal Bilimler Dergisi*, *1*(2), 43–57.

Allen, J., O'Toole, W., McDonnell, I., & Harris, R. (2005). Festival and special event management. Milton, Qld: John Wiley.

Altındal, M. (2013). Brand management and effects of social media in digital marketing. Academic Informatics 2013, 1-6.

Altunbas, H. (2008). Pazarlama iletişimi ve etkinlik (event) pazarlaması 'müzik eğlence etkinliğinin marka iletişimine etkisi'. Istanbul University Faculty of Communication Journal, (34), 23-36.

Altunbaş, H. (2011). Pazarlama İletişimi ve Etkinlik (Event) Pazarlaması 'Müzik Eğlence Etkinliğinin Marka İletişimine Etkisi'. *İstanbul Üniversitesi İletişim Fakültesi Dergisi*, *34*, 23-35.

American Express Meetings & Events. (2018). *Global Meetings and Events Forecast, 2018*. Retrieved July 8, 2020. https://www.amexglobalbusinesstravel.com/content/uploads/2017/12/2018-Global-Meetings-Forecast-US.pdf

American Express Meetings & Events. (2020). *Global Meetings and Events Forecast, 2020.* Retrieved July 23, 2020 https://www.amexglobalbusinesstravel.com/content/uploads/2019/09/2020-Global-Meetings-Forecast-Final-US.pdf

American Marketing Association. (2017). *Definition of Marketing.* https://www.ama.org/AboutAMA/Pages/Definition-of-Marketing.aspx

Anil, N. K. (2012). Festival visitors' satisfaction and loyalty: An example of small, local, and municipality organized festival. *Turizam: znanstveno-stručni časopis, 60*(3), 255-271.

Arapoğu, F. (2012). Dijital Sanat Üzerine. *Artam Global Art & Design,* (16), 48-52.

Arcodia, C. & Robb, A. (2000). A future for event management: A taxonomy of event management terms. In J. Allen, R. Harris, L. K. Jago, & A. J. Veal (Eds.), *Events beyond 2000: Setting the agenda, proceedings of conference on event evaluation, research and education.* Sydney: Australian Centre for Event Management School of Leisure, Sport and Tourism, University of Technology.

Arcodia, C. (2009). Event Management Employment in Australia: A Nationwide Investigation of Labour Trends in Australian Event Management. In T. Baum, M. Deery, & C. Hanlon (Eds.), People and Work in Events and Conventions: A Research Perspective. CABI. doi:10.1079/9781845934767.0017

Arcodia, C., & Whitford, M. (2006). Festival attendance and the development of social capital. *Journal of Convention & Event Tourism, 8*(2), 1–18. doi:10.1300/J452v08n02_01

Argan, M. (2007). *Eglence pazarlamasi.* Detay Yayincilik.

Argan, M. T. (2008). Pazarlamada sanal topluluklar (Virtual communities in marketing). In İ. Varinli & K. Çatı (Eds.), *Güncel pazarlama yaklaşimlarindan seçmeler* (pp. 305–332). Detay Yayıncılık.

Argyropoulou, A., Dionyssopoulou, P., & Miaoulis, G. (2011). Tourist destination marketing and management using advanced ICTs technologies. *Advances on Information Processing and Management,* 365-369.

Arıca, L. A. (2016). Deneyimsel Pazarlama ve Başarılı Örnekler. [https://www.dijitalajanslar.com/deneyimsel-pazarlama-ve-basarili-ornekler/]. Access date: January, 2020.

Armstrong, A., & Hagel, J. III. (1996). The Real Value of On-Line Communities. *Harvard Business Review, 74,* 134–141.

Arnold, A. (2019). *How AI is transforming the event planning space one conservation at time.* Retrieved from https://www.forbes.com/sites/andrewarnold/2019/02/25/how-ai-is-transforming-the-event-planning-space-one-conversation-at-a-time/#4f28510210b3

Arnold, A. (2019). *How AI is Transforming the Event Planning Space One Conversation at a Time.* Retrieved February 1, 2020, from https://www.forbes.com/sites/andrewarnold/2019/02/25/how-ai-is-transforming-the-event-planning-space-one-conversation-at-a-time/#303aa94510b3

ars.electronica.art. (2019). *What is Ars Electronica?* Retrieved from https://ars.electronica.art/about/en/

ArtJaws. (2017). *The Ars Electronica Festival explores the realities and visions of artificial intelligence from september 7th to 11th in Linz.* https://www.artjaws.com/en/the-ars-electronica-festival-explores-the-realities-and-visions-of-artificial-intelligence-from-7-to-11-september-in-linz/

Artug, E. (2019). *4 Examples of Successful Real-Time Marketing.* Retrieved from: https://medium.com/better-marketing/4-examples-of-successful-real-time-marketing-4b55c089adac

Ashforth, B. E., & Mael, F. (1989). Social identity theory and the organization. *Academy of Management Review, 14*(1), 20–39. doi:10.5465/amr.1989.4278999

Ashraf, S. (2018). *7 Incredible Examples of Brand Storytelling on Social Media*. Retrieved from: https://locowise.com/blog/7-incredible-examples-of-brand-storytelling-on-social-media

Atalay, M., & Çelik, E. (2017). Artificial Intelligence and Machine Learning Applications in Big Data Analysis. *Mehmet Akif Ersoy Üniversitesi Sosyal Bilimler Enstitüsü Dergisi*, *9*, 155–172. doi:10.20875/makusobed.309727

Atan, A., Uçan, B., & Bilsel, Ç. (2015). Dijital Sanat Uygulamaları Üzerine Bir İnceleme. *İstanbul Aydın Üniversitesi Dergisi, 7*(26).

Atçeken, K., Doğrul, Ü., & Çabuk, S. (2018). Tutundurmada Sosyal Medyanın Önemi: 5. Mersin ULuslararası Narenciye Festivali Örneği. *Akademik Araştırmalar ve Çalışmalar Dergisi*, *10*(18), 146–157. doi:10.20990/kilisiibfakademik.428624

Atçı, D., Unur, K., & Gürsoy, D. (2016). The impacts of hosting major sporting events: Resident's perceptions of the mediterranean games 2013 in Mersin. *International Review of Management and Marketing*, *6*(1), 139–145.

Ateş, U., & Boz, M. (2015). Konaklama işletmelerinin web sitelerinin değerlendirilmesi: Çanakkale örneği. *Ekonomi İşletme Siyaset ve Uluslararası İlişkiler Dergisi*, *1*(1), 63–84.

Atmaca, A. E. (2011). Modern Sanat Ve Bilgisayar Destekli Sanat Çalışmaları (Dijital Art). *Elektronik Sosyal Bilimler Dergisi*, *10*(37), 293–302.

Avcı, E. (2013). *Dijital Sanat Bağlamında Dijital Teknolojilerin Güzel Sanatlar Eğitimine Entegrasyonu: Bir Eylem Araştırması*. Anadolu Üniversitesi Eğitim Bilimleri Enstitüsü Yayınlanmamış Yüksek Lisans Tezi.

Aventri. (2019). *The future of Event Marketing* (2nd ed.). Norwalk: Event.

Aventri. (2020). *The 2020 event technology guide*. https://www.aventri.com/strategy/onsite-event-technology#

Aydın, N. (2016). *Moore yasası ve geleceği*. Retrieved December 2, 2020, from https://www.endustri40.com/moore-yasasi-ve-gelecegi/

Ayob, N. (2003). An analysis of event tourism in Malaysia. *ASEAN Journal on Hospitality and Tourism*, *2*, 92–102.

Azuma, R. (1993). Tracking requirements for augmented reality. *Communications of the ACM*, *36*(7), 50–51. doi:10.1145/159544.159581

Babacan, E., & Göztaş, A. (2011). *Etkinlik Yönetimi*. Detay Yayıncılık.

Backman, K. F. (2018). Event management research: The focus today and in the future. *Tourism Management Perspectives*, *25*, 169–171. doi:10.1016/j.tmp.2017.12.004

Baglietto, M. (2019). *What Brands Can Learn From Coachella's Social Media Marketing Mastery*. Retrieved from netbasequid.com web site: https://netbasequid.com/blog/coachellas-social-media-marketing-mastery/

Bagozzi, R. P., & Dholakia, U. M. (2002). Intentional social action in virtual communities. *Journal of Interactive Marketing*, *16*(2), 2–21. doi:10.1002/dir.10006

Balkır, B. (2018). Sanayi 4.0 Üzerine Görüşler. *İktisat ve Toplum Dergisi*, *92*, 77-82.

Baloglu, S., & Love, C. (2005). Association meeting planners' perceptions and intentions for five major US convention cities: The structured and unstructured images. *Tourism Management*, *26*(5), 743–752. doi:10.1016/j.tourman.2004.04.001

Banks, N. (2019). *Man And Machine: New Rolls-Royce Artwork By Refik Anadol Uses Complex Data To Provoke Dialogues*. Retrieved from https://www.forbes.com/sites/nargessbanks/2019/09/09/rolls-royce-art-refik-anadol/#56debf8733b5

Barron, P., & Ali-Knight, J. (2017). Aspirations and progression of event management graduates: A study of career development. *Journal of Hospitality and Tourism Management, 30*, 29–38. doi:10.1016/j.jhtm.2017.01.005

Bartodziej, C. J. (2017). The concept industry 4.0. In *The concept industry 4.0* (pp. 51–77). Springer Gabler. doi:10.1007/978-3-658-16502-4_4

Barutçu, S. (2011). Mobil Viral Pazarlama. *İnternet Uygulamaları ve Yönetimi Dergisi, 2*(1), 5-14.

Barutçu, S., & Tomaş, M. (2013). Sürdürülebilir Sosyal Medya Pazarlaması ve Sosyal Medya Pazarlaması Etkinliğinin Ölçümü. *Journal of Internet Applications and Management*, 5-24.

Barutçu, S., & Toma, M. (2013). Sustainable social media marketing and measuring effectiveness of social media marketing. *Journal of Internet Applications & Management, 4*(1), 5–23. doi:10.5505/iuyd.2013.69188

Başöz, İ. (2017). *Geleceğin robot mutfak şefleri.* Retrieved August 2, 2020, from https://www.itohaber.com/haber/teknoloji/205713/gelecegin_robot_mutfak_sefleri.html

Bastida, U., & Huan, T. C. (2014). Performance evaluation of tourism websites' information quality of four global destination brands: Beijing, Hong Kong, Shanghai, and Taipei. *Journal of Business Research, 67*(2), 167–170. doi:10.1016/j.jbusres.2012.10.008

Bayram, A. T. (2012). *Importance of social media that is a current element of marketing database in hotel marketing* (Unpublished Master's Thesis). Gazi University, Ankara.

Baytok, A., Soybalı, H. H., & Emir, O. (2010). Destinasyonların toplantı turizmi amaçlı pazarlanmasında kongre ve ziyaretçi bürolarının rolü: İstanbul kongre ve ziyaretçi bürosu örneği. *Selçuk Üniversitesi Sosyal Bilimler Enstitüsü Dergisi, 23*, 9–22.

Bazarcı, S. (2017). *Dijital çağda yeni bir pazarlama yaklaşımı olarak gerçek zamanlı pazarlama: Türkiye'de markaların sosyal medya paylaşımları üzerine bir inceleme* [Real-time marketing as a new marketing approach in the digital age: A review on social media sharing of brands in Turkey] (Unpublished master's thesis). İzmir Ege University, Social Science Institute, Turkey.

Bazarcı, S., & Mutlu, B. (2017, April). *Yeni bir pazarlama iletişimi yaklaşımı olarak gerçek zamanlı pazarlama: Markaların sosyal medyadaki paylaşımları üzerine bir inceleme* [Real-time marketing as a new marketing communication approach: A review of brands' shares on social media]. Paper presented at the meeting of the 1. Uluslararası İletişimde Yeni Yönelimler Konferansı, İstanbul, Turkey.

BBC. (2016). *Dancing robots break world record.* https://www.bbc.com/news/av/world-asia-china-37019690/dancing-robots-break-world-record

BBC. (2018). *Future article.* Retrieved September 3, 2020, from https://www.bbc.com/future/article/20181204-the-chef-making-fast-food-even-faster

BBC. (2019). *A German Circus Uses Holograms instead of Animals and it Looks Amazing!* https://www.bbc.co.uk/newsround/48543263

Becker, H., Naaman, M., & Gravano, L. (2009). *Event identification in social media.* Paper Presented at the *2009 ACM International Conference on Web Search and Data Mining (WSDM 2009).*

Beck, J., Rainoldi, M., & Egger, R. (2019). Virtual reality in tourism: A state-of-the-art review. *Tourism Review, 74*(3), 586–612. doi:10.1108/TR-03-2017-0049

Behrer, M., & Larsson, A. (1998). *Event marketing att använda evenemang som strategisk resurs i marknadsföringen*. IHM Förlag AB.

Belch, G. E., & Belch, M. A. (2004). *Advertising and promotion: An integrated marketing communications perspective*. McGraw-Hill.

Bellis, S., & Harris, C. G. (2009). *A Mobile Augmented Reality System to Enhance Live Sporting Events*. https://dl.acm.org/doi/pdf/10.1145/2735711.2735836

Benbunan-Fich, R. (2001). Using protocol analysis to evaluate the usability of a commercial web site. *Information & Management*, *39*(2), 151–163. doi:10.1016/S0378-7206(01)00085-4

Benson, A. M., Dickson, T. J., Terwiel, F. A., & Blackman, D. A. (2014). Training of Vancouver 2010 volunteers: A legacy opportunity? *Contemporary Social Science*, *9*(2), 210–226. doi:10.1080/21582041.2013.838296

Berridge, G. (2007). *Events design and experience*. Routledge. doi:10.4324/9780080468112

Berryman, D. R. (2012). Augmented Reality: A Review. *Medical Reference Services Quarterly*, *31*(2), 212–218. doi:10.1080/02763869.2012.670604 PMID:22559183

Berthon, P. R., Pitt, L. F., Plangger, K., & Shapiro, D. (2012). Marketing meets web 2.0, social media, and creative consumers: Implications for international marketing strategy. *Business Horizons*, *55*(3), 261–271. doi:10.1016/j.bushor.2012.01.007

Bessenoff, G. R. (2006). Can the media affect us? Social comparison, self-discrepancy, and then ideal. *Psychology of Women Quarterly*, *30*(3), 239–251. doi:10.1111/j.1471-6402.2006.00292.x

Bethapudi, A. (2013). The role of ICT in the tourism industry. *Journal of Applied Economics and Business*, *1*(4), 67–79.

Bethapudi, A. (2013). The Role of ICT in Tourism Industry. *Journal of Applied Economics and Business*, *1*(4), 67–79.

Bhe, T., Glasmacker, P., Meckwood, J., Pereira, G. & Wallace, M. (2004). *Event management and best practices*. IBM.

Bierman, J. (2010, Nov.). Tell me a story. *NZ Business*, 40-42.

Bilgen, İ. (2011). *Tüketici davranışlarında durumsal faktörlerin satın alma niyeti ve memnuniyet üzerinedeki etkisi ve bir araştırma* [The effect of situational factors in consumer behavior on purchasing intention and satisfaction and a study] (Unpublished master's thesis). Marmara University, Social Science Institute, Turkey.

Billetto. (2020). *9 ways to use augmented and virtual reality for events*. https://billetto.co.uk/blog/augmented-virtual-reality-events/

Bingöl, D. (2016). *İnsan Kaynakları Yönetimi*. Beta Yayınevi.

Birer, C. G. (2018). Yapay Zeka Temel Kavramlar. *TÜBİTAK Bilim ve Teknik. Ocak, 2018*, 2–11.

Bissola, R., & Imperatori, B. (2014). The unexpected side of relational e-hrm: Developing trust in the hr department. *Employee Relations*, *36*(4), 376–397. doi:10.1108/ER-07-2013-0078

Bitner, M. J. (1992). Servicescape: The impact of physical surroundings on customers and employees. *Journal of Marketing*, *56*(2), 57–71. doi:10.1177/002224299205600205

Bizzabo. (2019). *Event Marketing 2019 Benchmarks and Trends Report*. Retrieved from https://welcome.bizzabo.com/hubfs/White-Papers-and-Ebooks/Event-Marketing-2019.pdf

Bizzabo. (2019). *Event Marketing 2019. Benchmarks and Trends Report*. Retrieved from https://welcome.bizzabo.com/hubfs/White-Papers-and-Ebooks/Event-Marketing-2019.pdf. 20.02.2020.

Blackshaw, P., & Nazzaro, M. (2006). *Consumer-generated media (CGM) 101: Wordof-mouth in the age of the web-fortified consumer*. Nielsen Buzz Metrics.

Bladen, C., & Kennell, J. (2014). Educating the 21st century event management graduate: Pedagogy, practice, professionalism, and professionalization. *Event Management*, *18*(1), 5–14. doi:10.3727/152599514X13883555341724

Bladen, C., Kennell, J., Abson, E., & Wilde, N. (2012). *Events Management*. Routledge. doi:10.4324/9780203852972

Blaisdell, R. (2018). *Is artificial intelligence goodfor the event industry?* Retrieved from September 5. https://rickscloud.com/is-artificial-intelligence-good-for-the-event-industry/

Bondarouk, T., & Furtmueller-Ettinger, E. (2012, August). Electronic human resource management: four decades of empirical evidence. *72nd academy of management annual meeting 2012*. 10.5465/AMBPP.2012.245

Bondarouk, T., Harms, R., & Lepak, D. (2015). Does e-hrm lead to better hrm service? *International Journal of Human Resource Management*, *28*(9), 1–32.

Bosnalı, C. (2019a). *Dünyanın İlk Dijital Sanat Müzesi: teamLab Borderless*. Retrieved from https://www.Oggusto .com/blog/detay/1750/dunyanin-ilk-dijital-sanat-muzesi-teamlab-borderless.html

Bosnalı, C. (2019b). *Van Gogh'un Dijital Sergisi Fransa'da*. Retrieved from https://www.oggusto.com/blog/detay/1833/van-gogh-39-un-dijital-sergisi-fransa-39-da.html

Boudet, A. (2017). *EnItalie, un robot chef d'orchestre a dirigé son premier concert* [In Italy, a robot conductor conducted his first concet]. https://www.numerama.com/tech/288927-en-italie-un-robot-chef-dorchestre-a-dirige-son-premier-concert.html

Bowdin, G. A., Allen, J., O'Toole, W., Harris, R., & McDonell, I. (2006). *Events management* (2nd ed.). Publishing House Elsevier. doi:10.4324/9780080457154

Boyd, D. M., & Ellison, N. B. (2008). Social network sites: Definition, history, and scholarship. *Journal of Computer-Mediated Communication*, *13*(1), 210–230. doi:10.1111/j.1083-6101.2007.00393.x

Bozkurt, İ. (2002). Bütünleşik pazarlama iletişimi sürecinde halkla ilişkilerin rolü. *Gazi Üniversitesi İletişim Fakültesi Dergisi*, (16), 139-154.

Brake, D., & Safko, L. (2009). *The social media bible*. John Wiley and Sons, Inc.

Bramwell, B. (1997). Strategic planning before andafter a mega-event. *Tourism Management*, *18*(3), 167–176. doi:10.1016/S0261-5177(96)00118-5

Breukel, A., & Go, F. M. (2009). Knowledge-based network participation in destination and event marketing: A hospitality scenario analysis perspective. *Tourism Management*, *30*(2), 184–193. doi:10.1016/j.tourman.2008.05.015

Briodagh, K. (2013). *3M Posts its Technical Chops in Interactive Lounge at SXSW*. Retrieved July 23, 2020. https://www.eventmarketer.com/article/sxsw-3m/

Brite, E. (2020). *10 Event Technology Trends for 2020*. https://www.eventbrite.co.uk/blog/10-event-technology-trends-2020-ds00/

Brittow, R. (2018). *Digital dining: Is this the way forwardfor the restaurant industry?* RetrievedSeptember 5, 2020, from https://www.food24.com/News-and-Guides/News-and-Trends/digital-dining-is-this-the-way-forward-for-the-restaurant-industry-20180911

Brooks, R. (2020). *12 Ways to Market Your Event With Social Media.* Retrieved from https://www.socialmediaexaminer.com/12-ways-to-market-your-event-with-social-media/

Brown, A. E., Donne, K., Fallon, P., & Sharpley, R. (2019). From headliners to hangovers: Digital media communication in the British rock music festival experience. *Tourist Studies*. Advance online publication. doi:10.1177/1468797619885954

Brown, D., & Fiorella, S. (2013). *Influence marketing*. Que Publishing.

Brown, D., & Hayes, N. (2008). *Influencer marketing, who really influences your customers?* Elsevier Ltd.

Brown, J., Broderick, A. J., & Lee, N. (2007). Word of mouth communication within online communities: Conceptualizing the online social network. *Journal of Interactive Marketing*, *21*(3), 2–20. doi:10.1002/dir.20082

Brown, S., & James, J. (2004). Event design and management: ritual sacrifice? In *Festival and Events Management:Ritual Sacrifice*. doi:10.1016/B978-0-7506-5872-0.50009-0

Bruckheimer, E., & Rotschild, C. (2019). Holography in Congenital Heart Disease: Diagnosis and Transcatheter Treatment. In G. Butera, M. Chessa, A. Eicken, & J. Thomson (Eds.), *Atlas of Cardiac Catheterization for Congenital Heart Disease* (pp. 383–386). Springer. doi:10.1007/978-3-319-72443-0_44

Bryman, H. (2018). *Bubble Lab Launching Drop Milk Dispenser and Drip Pourover Arm*. Retrieved July 28, 2020. https://dailycoffeenews.com/2018/08/15/bubble-lab-launching-drop-milk-dispenser-and-drip-pourover-arm/

Buhalis, D. (2003). eTourism: Information technology for strategic tourism management. Pearson Education.

Buhalis, D. (1998). Strategic use of information technologies in the tourism industry. *Tourism Management*, *19*(5), 409–421. doi:10.1016/S0261-5177(98)00038-7

Buhalis, D. (2019). Technology in tourism-from information communication technologies to eTourism and smart tourism towards ambient intelligence tourism: A perspective article. *Tourism Review*, *75*(1), 267–272. Advance online publication. doi:10.1108/TR-06-2019-0258

Buhalis, D., & Amaranggana, A. (2013). Smart tourism destinations. In *Information and communication technologies in tourism 2014* (pp. 553–564). Springer. doi:10.1007/978-3-319-03973-2_40

Buhalis, D., Harwood, T., Bogievic, V., Viglia, G., Beldona, S., & Hofacker, C. (2019). Technological disruptions in services: Lessons from tourism and hospitality. *Journal of Service Management*, *30*(4), 484–506. doi:10.1108/JOSM-12-2018-0398

Buhalis, D., & Kaldis, K. (2008). eEnabled internet distribution for small and medium sized hotels: The case of Athens. *Tourism Recreation Research*, *33*(1), 67–81. doi:10.1080/02508281.2008.11081291

Buhalis, D., & Law, R. (2008). Progress in information technology and tourism management: 20 years on and 10 years after the Internet—The state of eTourism research. *Tourism Management*, *29*(4), 609–623. doi:10.1016/j.tourman.2008.01.005

Buhalis, D., & O'Connor, P. (2005). Information communication technology revolutionizing tourism. *Tourism Recreation Research*, *30*(3), 7–16. doi:10.1080/02508281.2005.11081482

Bulunmaz, B. (2016). Gelişen Teknolojiyle Birlikte Değişen Pazarlama Yöntemleri ve Dijital Pazarlama. *Trt Akademi*, *1*(2), 348–365.

Bulut, E. (2012). *Pazarlama iletişiminde yeni yaklaşimlar kapsaminda sosyal medya uygulamalari ve etkili kampanya örnekleri* [Social media applications and examples of effective campaigns within the scope of new approaches in marketing communication] (Unpublished master's thesis). Istanbul Kültür University, Social Science Institute, Turkey.

Bulut, E. (2012). *Pazarlama İletişiminde Yeni Yaklaşımlar Kapsamında Sosyal Medya Uygulamaları ve Etkili Kampanya Örnekleri*. İstanbul: Unpublished masters thesis.

Bulut, E., & AKÇACI, T. (2017). Endüstri 4.0 ve inovasyon göstergeleri kapsaminda Türkiye analizi. *ASSAM Uluslararası Hakemli Dergi, 4*(7), 55-77.

Burçoğlu, Z. (2018). *Binaların İnsanlarla İletişim Kurma Biçimi ve Refik Anadol*. Retrieved from http://aura-istanbul.com/index.php/2018/11/16/binalarin-insanlarla-iletisim-kurma-bicimi-ve-refik-anadol/

Burgess, S., Sellitto, C., Cox, C., & Buultjens, J. (2009). User-generated content (UGC) in tourism: Benefits and concerns of online consumers. *Proceedings of the 17th European Conference on Information Systems*, 1–14.

Buswell, J. (2004). Sport and leisure service encounter. In Sport and Leisure Operations Management. Thomson.

Büyükkalaycı, G., & Karaca, H. M. (2019). Pazarlama 4.0: Nesnelerin İnterneti. *Üçüncü Sektör Sosyal Ekonomi Dergisi, 54*(1), 463-477.

Büyükşener, E. (2009). Türkiye'de Sosyal Ağların Yeri ve Sosyal Medyaya Bakış. In *XIV. Türkiye'de İnternet Konferansı Bildirileri (12-13 Aralık 2009)* (s. 39-43). Bilgi Üniversitesi, İstanbul: inet-tr'09.

Cain, L. N., Thomas, J. H., & Alonso, M. Jr. (2019). From sci-fi to sci-fact: The state of robotics and AI in the hospitality industry. *Journal of Hospitality and Tourism Technology, 10*(4), 624–650. doi:10.1108/JHTT-07-2018-0066

Çakaloğlu, M., & Çağatay, S. (2015). *Coğrafi İşaretler ve Değişen Tüketici Algısı: Finike Portakalı ve Antalya Tavşan Yüreği Zeytini Örnekleri*. Antalya: Yüksek Lisans Tezi. Akdeniz Üniversitesi Sosyal Bilimler Enstitüsü.

Çakıcı, C. (2009). *Toplantı yönetimi. Kongre, konferans seminer ve fuar organizasyonları*. Detay Yayıncılık.

Çakır, Ö. (2020). *Yapay Zeka ve Kullanım Alanları*. Retrieved July 20, 2020 https://www.yapayzekatr.com/2020/01/06/yapay-zeka-ve-kullanim-alanlari/

Çakırkaya, M. (2019). The effect of digital content marketing applications on perceived quality. *Journal of Turkish Studies, 14*(5), 19–35.

Çakmak, A. (2011). *Doğrudan satış ve şebeke yoluyla pazarlama sistemi [Direct selling and network marketing system]*. Türkmen Kitabevi.

Çalık, M., Altunışık, R., & Sütütemiz, N. (2013). Bütünleşik pazarlama iletişimi, marka performansi ve pazar performansi ilişkisinin incelenmesi [Integrated marketing communications, brand performance and market performance analysis]. *Uluslararası Yönetim İktisat ve İşletme Dergisi, 9*(19), 137–161.

Cankül, D., Doğan, A., & Sönmez, B. (2018). Yiyecek-içecek işletmelerinde inovasyon ve artırılmış gerçeklik uygulamaları. *Journal Of Business Research-Turk, 10*(3), 576–591.

Cardoso, J., Voigt, K., & Winkler, M. (2008). Service engineering for the internet of services. *International Conference on Enterprise Information Systems*, 15-27.

Carreirão, P. (2019). *Top 10 self-service technologies that we all love to use!* https://asksuite.com/blog/top-10-self-service-technologies/

Çatalkaya, Y. (2020). *Ziyafet ve ikram hizmetlerinde yönetim*. Retrieved August 25, 2020, from https://avys.omu.edu.tr/storage/app/public/yusuf.catalkaya/134619/Z%C4%B0YAFET%20H%C4%B0ZMETLER%C4%B0%20Y%C3%96NET%C4%B0M%C4%B0%20HAFTA%202.pdf

Çelen, S. (2018). *A research on the use and efficiency of social media in food marketing* (Unpublished Master's Thesis). Ege University, İzmir.

Çelik, S. (2014). Sosyal medyanın pazarlama iletişimine etkisi [The effect of social media on marketing communications]. *Erciyes İletişim Dergisi*, *3*(3), 28–42.

Çelikten, M. (2005). Neden İş Analizi Yapılmalı? *Erciyes Üniversitesi Sosyal Bilimler Enstitüsü Dergisi*, *1*(18), 127–135.

Çeltek, E., & İlhan, İ. (2020). Big Data, Artificial Intelligence, and Their Implications in the Tourism Industry. In E. Çeltek (Ed.), *Handbook of Research on Smart Technology Applications in the Tourism Industry* (pp. 115–130). IGI Global. doi:10.4018/978-1-7998-1989-9.ch006

Çetinkaya, F. Ö. (2019). Sosyal Medya ve Turizm. In Turizm 4.0 Dijital Dönüşüm (pp. 173-184). Ankara: Detay Yayıncılık.

Chacko, H., & Schaffer, J. (1993). The evolution of a festival: Creole Christmas in New Orleans. *Tourism Management*, *14*(6), 475–482. doi:10.1016/0261-5177(93)90100-Y

Chalip, L. (1992). The construction anduse of polysemic structures: Olympic lessons for sport marketing. *Journal of Sport Management*, *6*(2), 87–98. doi:10.1123/jsm.6.2.87

Chalip, L. (2006). Towards social leverage of sport events. *Journal of Sport & Tourism*, *11*(2), 109–127. doi:10.1080/14775080601155126

Chalip, L., Green, C., Taks, M., & Misener, L. (2017). Creating sport participation from sport events: Making it happen. *International Journal of Sport Policy and Politics*, *9*(2), 257–276. doi:10.1080/19406940.2016.1257496

Chan, H. (2018). *5 Tips: How to Use Experience Design to Create a Memorable Event*. Eventmobi. Retrieved from https://www.eventmobi.com/blog/5-tips-use-experience-design-create-memorable-event/

Chan, G. (2015). Part-Time Event Management Employee Expected Quality of Work Life. *International Journal of Business and Management*, *10*(5). Advance online publication. doi:10.5539/ijbm.v10n5p233

Chappuis, B., Gaffey, B., & Parvizi, P. (2011). *Are your customers becoming digital junkies?* Academic Press.

Chathoth, P. K., Ungson, G. R., Harrington, R. J., & Chan, E. S. (2016). Co-creation and higher order customer engagement in hospitality and tourism services. *International Journal of Contemporary Hospitality Management*, *28*(2), 222–245. doi:10.1108/IJCHM-10-2014-0526

Cheng, K. H., & Tsai, C. C. (2013). Affordances of augmented reality in Science learning: Suggestions for future search. *Journal of Science Education and Technology*, *22*(4), 449–462. doi:10.100710956-012-9405-9

Chen, M., Mao, S., & Liu, Y. (2014). Big Data: A Survey. *Mobile Networks and Applications*, *19*(2), 171–209. doi:10.100711036-013-0489-0

Chen, S., Zheng, J., & Dickson, G. (2018). Volunteering for sports mega events: A non-host region perspective. *Managing Sport and Leisure*, *23*(3), 189–203. doi:10.1080/23750472.2018.1530609

Chen, Y. F., & Mo, H. E. (2012). Attendees' perspectives on the service quality of an exhibition organizer: A case study of a tourism exhibition. *Tourism Management Perspectives*, *1*, 28–33. doi:10.1016/j.tmp.2011.12.004

Chinadaily. (2017). *53-finger robot plays piano with Italian pianist in Tianjin*. https://www.chinadaily.com.cn/china/2017-06/05/content_29614677.htm

Choi, R. I. (2011). A multiple regression analysis on developing the profitability model of local cultural festivals. *Journal of The Korea Society of Computer and Information*, *16*(10), 229–239. doi:10.9708/jksci.2011.16.10.229

Chong, C. W., Holden, T., Wilhelmij, P., & Schmidt, R. A. (2000). When does konowledge management add value? *Journal of Intellectual Capital, 1*(4), 366–380. doi:10.1108/14691930010359261

Chowdhury, T., Adafin, J., & Wilkinson, S. (2019). Review of digital technologies to improve productivity of New Zealand construction industry. *Journal of Information Technology in Construction, 24*(2019VMAR), 569–587. doi:10.36680/j.itcon.2019.032

Chu, S. C., & Kim, Y. (2017). The ınfluence of perceived interactivity of social media advertising and voluntary self-disclosure on attitudes and intentions to pass-along. In Advertising and Branding: Concepts, Methodologies, Tools, and Applications (pp.1388-1405). IGI Global. doi:10.4018/978-1-5225-1793-1.ch064

Chung, N., Han, H., & Joun, Y. (2015). Tourists' intention to visit a destination: The role of augmented reality (AR) application for a heritage site. *Computers in Human Behavior, 50*, 588–599. doi:10.1016/j.chb.2015.02.068

Ciderol, M. (2020). *Evaluation of event tourism from local perspective and its role on destination marketing: International Manisa Mesir Macunu Festival case* (Unpublished Master's Thesis). Selçuk University, Konya.

Çifterler, Ö. (2013). *Elektronik Pazarlamada İnternet Reklamcılığı: Özel Alışveriş Siteleri Üzerine Bir İnceleme*. İstanbul: Yüksek Lisans Tezi. Marmara Üniversitesi Sosyal Bilimler Enstitüsü.

Cimbaljević, M., Stankov, U., Demirović, D., & Pavluković, V. (2019). Nice and smart: Creating a smarter festival–the study of EXIT (Novi Sad, Serbia). *Asia Pacific Journal of Tourism Research*, 1–13. doi:10.1080/10941665.2019.1596139

City of Gold Coast. (2019). *Volunteering Legacy Action Plan*. Retrieved from https://www.goldcoast.qld.gov.au/documents/bf/volunteering-legacy-action-plan.pdf

Çizgen, G. (2007). *Sanat Köprüsü Sırat Köprüsü*. Arkeoloji Sanat Yayınları.

Clark, H., Dimanche, F., Cotter, R., & Lee-Rosen, D. (2017). Human capital challenges in the events industry of Canada: Finding innovative solutions. *Worldwide Hospitality and Tourism Themes, 9*(4), 424–432. doi:10.1108/WHATT-04-2017-0018

Clement, J. (2020). *Instagram accounts with the most followers worldwide 2020*. Retrieved from Statista web site: https://www.statista.com/statistics/421169/most-followers-instagram/

Clement, J. (2020). *Selected global media and sporting events with the most Facebook interactions as of May 2017*. Retrieved from Statitas: https://www.statista.com/statistics/477371/facebook-sporting-events-interactions/

Clement, J. (2020). *Twitter accounts with the most followers worldwide 2020*. Retrieved from Sttista web site: https://www.statista.com/statistics/273172/twitter-accounts-with-the-most-followers-worldwide/

Close, A. G., Finney, R. Z., Lacey, R. Z., & Sneath, J. Z. (2006). Engaging the consumer through event marketing: Linking attendees with the sponsor, community, and brand. *Journal of Advertising Research, 46*(4), 420–433.

Close, A. G., Finney, R. Z., Lacey, R. Z., & Sneath, J. Z. (2006). Engaging the consumer through event marketing: Linking attendees with the sponsor, community, and brand. *Journal Of Advertısıng Research, New York, 46*(4), 420–433. doi:10.2501/S0021849906060430

Close, A. G., Krishen, A. S., & Latour, M. S. (2009). The event is me! How consumer event selfcongruity leverages sponsorship. *Journal of Advertising Research, 49*(3), 271–284. doi:10.2501/S0021849909090412

Coates, G. (1992). *Invisible site-a virtual sho*. Siggraph.

Cohen, H. (2011). *30 social media definitions. Posted by Heidi Cohen on May 9, 2011 in actionable marketing social media, 101*. http://heidicohen.com/ social-media-definition/

Çokokumuş, B. (2012). Art And Culture On Dıgıtal Medıa, International Journal of New Trends in Arts, Sports &. *Science Education, 1*(3).

Cole, S. T., & Chancellor, H. C. (2009). Examining the festival attributes that impact visitor experience, satisfaction and re-visit intention. *Journal of Vacation Marketing, 15*(4), 323–333. doi:10.1177/1356766709335831

Cole, S. T., & Illum, S. F. (2006). Examining the mediating role of festival visitors' satisfaction in the relationship between service quality and behavioral intentions. *Journal of Vacation Marketing, 12*(2), 160–173. doi:10.1177/1356766706062156

Cooper, K. (2018). *AI for Events: The Future is Here.* Retrieved February 3, 2020, from https://helloendless.com/ai-for-events/

Corbinball. (2020). *The Rise and Benefits of Text Apps and Chatbots for Events.* Retrieved July 23, 2020. https://www.corbinball.com/article/36-mobile-and-wireless-technology/212-rise-of-text-apps-and-chatbots-for-events

Cory, J. (1991). Niche marketing: What it is and how it works. *Chilton's Hardware Age, 228*(8), 239–245.

Costa, C., Chalip, L., Green, C., & Simes, C. (2006). Reconsidering the Role of Training in Event Volunteers' Satisfaction. *Sport Management Review, 9*(2), 165–182. doi:10.1016/S1441-3523(06)70024-9

Coulton, P. (2015). Playful and gameful design for the internet of things. In More playful user interfaces (pp. 151-173). Springer. doi:10.1007/978-981-287-546-4_7

Cova, B., & Cova, V. (2002). Tribal marketing: The tribalisation of society and its impact on the conduct of marketing. *European Journal of Marketing, 36*(5/6), 595–620. doi:10.1108/03090560210423023

Cox, C., Burgess, S., Sellitto, C., & Buultjens, J. (2009). The role of user-generated content in tourists' travel planning behavior. *Journal of Hospitality Marketing & Management, 18*(8), 743–764. doi:10.1080/19368620903235753

CRM. (2019). *Otelcilik sektöründe 2019 dijital pazarlama trendleri nelerdir?* https://www.crmturizm.com/otelcilik-sektorunde-2019-dijital-pazarlama-trendleri-nelerdir/

Crompton, J. L., & McKay, S. L. (1997). Motives of visitors attending festival events. *Annals of Tourism Research, 24*(2), 425–439. doi:10.1016/S0160-7383(97)80010-2

Crowther, P. (2011). Marketing event outcomes: From tactical to strategic. *International Journal of Event and Festival Management, 2*(1), 68–82. doi:10.1108/17582951111116623

Crowther, P., & Donlan, L. (2011). Value-creation space: The role of events in a service-dominant marketing paradigm. *Journal of Marketing Management, 27*(13-14), 1444–1463. doi:10.1080/0267257X.2011.626786

Cruceru, A. F., & Moise, D. (2014). Customer relationships through sales forces and marketing events. *Procedia: Social and Behavioral Sciences, 109*, 155–159.

Culturespaces.com. (2019). *Venues.* Retrieved from https://www.culturespaces.com/en/venues

Cvent. (2017). *Second Annual Global Event Industry Benchmarks Study.* https://nsw.tourismaccommodation.com.au/files/2017/05/2nd-annual-global-event-industry-benchmarks-study.pdf

Cvent. (2019). *The Future of Augmented Reality at Events.* https://www.cvent.com/en/blog/events/the-future-of-augmented-reality-at-events

CWT Meetings&Events. (2019). *2019 Meetings & Events Future Trends.* Retrieved from https://www.levenement.org/wp-content/uploads/2018/12/Future-Trends-Report-2019-CWT-ME-Base-doc-%C3%A9tude.pdf

Dadanizm. (2019). *Refik Anadol ve Hislerimizin Heykelleri*. Retrieved from https://kolektifhouse.co/komag/refik-anadol-ve-hislerimizin-heykelleri/

Daily News. (2013). https://www.nydailynews.com/life-style/eats/drone-drops-beers-not-bombs-south-africa-article-1.1422617

Daley, D. (2019). *Rise of the Event Drones*. https://www.avixa.org/insight/whitepapers/Details/rise-of-the-event-drones/

Dalgıç, A. (2018). *Festival ziyaretçilerinin sadakatlerini etkileyen faktörlerin analizi: Adana Portakal Çiçeği Festivali örneği* (Doctoral dissertation). Mersin University.

Dalgıç, A., & Birdir, K. (2017). Otel işletmeciliğinde yeni trendler. In Y. Akgündüz (Ed.), *Otel İşletmeciliği* (pp. 311–328). Paradigma Akademi.

Dalgıç, A., & Birdir, K. (2019). Festival Anahtar Başarı Faktörlerinin Festival Sadakati Üzerine Etkisi: Portakal Çiçeği Festivali Örneği. *Journal of Tourism and Gastronomy Studies*, *7*(4), 2718–2738.

Dalgic, A., & Birdir, K. (2020). Smart hotels and technological applications. In *Handbook of Research on Smart Technology Applications in the Tourism Industry* (pp. 323–343). IGI Global. doi:10.4018/978-1-7998-1989-9.ch015

Dalgiç, A., & Birdir, K. (2020). The effect of key success factors on loyalty of festival visitors: The mediating effect of festival experience and festival image. *Tourism & Management Studies*, *16*(1), 28–38. doi:10.18089/tms.2020.160103

Daly, I. (2010). *Just like Mombot used to make*. https://www.nytimes.com/2010/02/24/dining/24robots.html

Daniel, M., Bogdan, G., & Daniel, Z. (2012). The use of event marketing management strategies. *Procedia: Social and Behavioral Sciences*, *46*, 5409–5413. doi:10.1016/j.sbspro.2012.06.448

Dankar, I., Haddarah, A., Omar, F. E. L., Sepulcre, F., & Pujolà, M. (2018). 3D printing technology: The new era for food customization and elaboration. *Trends in Food Science & Technology*, *75*, 231–242. doi:10.1016/j.tifs.2018.03.018

Davidson, R., & Rogers, T. (2006). *Marketing Destinations and Venues for Conferences, Conventions and Business Events*. Publishing House Elsevier.

Davis Mersey, R., Malthouse, E. C., & Calder, B. J. (2010). Engagement with online media. *Journal of Media Business Studies*, *7*(2), 39–56. doi:10.1080/16522354.2010.11073506

De Lira, V. M., Macdonald, C., Ounis, I., Perego, R., Renso, C., & Times, V. C. (2019). Event attendance classification in social media. *Information Processing & Management*, *56*(3), 687–703. doi:10.1016/j.ipm.2018.11.001

Del Río, A. B., Vázquez, R., & Iglesias, V. (2001). The Effects of Brand Associations on Consumer Response. *Journal of Consumer Marketing*, *18*(5), 410–425. doi:10.1108/07363760110398808

Delamere, T. A., Wankel, L. M., & Hinch, T. D. (2001). Development of a scale to measure resident attitudes toward the social impacts of community festivals, part 1: Item generation and purification of the measure. *Event Management*, *7*(1), 11–24. doi:10.3727/152599501108751443

Démeijer, D. (2017). *Making digital hrm work: A study in changes in perceived consequences of e-hrm in the past decade* (Master's thesis). University of Twente.

Demirci, S. (2018). Giyilebilir Teknolojilerin Sağlık Hizmetlerine ve Sağlık Hizmet Kullanıcılarına Etkileri. *Anemon Muş Alparslan Üniversitesi Sosyal BilimlerDergisi*, *6*(6), 985–992.

DePhillips, H. III. (2007). Initiatives and Barriers to Adopting Health Information Technology. *Disease Management & Health Outcomes*, *15*(1), 1–6. doi:10.2165/00115677-200715010-00001

Derret, R. (2011). Festivals, Events and The Destination. In *Festival and events management an international arts and cultural perspective*. Routledge Taylor&Francis Group.

Derrett, R. (2004). Making sense of how festivals demonstrate a community's sense of place. *Event Management*, *8*(1), 49–58. doi:10.3727/152599503108751694

Desai, P. R., Desai, P. N., Ajmera, K. D., & Mehta, K. (2014). A review paper on oculus rift-a virtual. *Int. J. Eng. Trends Technol*, *13*(4), 175–179. doi:10.14445/22315381/IJETT-V13P237

Deshwal, P. (2015). Role of e-hrm in organizational effectiveness and sustainability. *IJAR*, *1*(12), 605–609.

Deyan, G. (2020). *29+ Augmented Reality Stats to Keep your Sharp in 2020*. https://techjury.net/blog/augmented-reality-stats/?_ga=2.178951265.433351076.1602176151-113602177.1602176151

Dholakiya, P. (2015). *Content Marketing Done Right: 8 Examples You Can Learn From*. Retrieved from: https://marketingland.com/content-marketing-done-right-8-examples-can-learn-149088

Dictonary.com. (n.d.). *Definition of Virtual reality*. Retrieved December 15, 2019, from https://www.dictionary.com/browse/virtual-reality

Dieguez, V. S. (2015). *Are You Overlooking the Most Valuable Real-Time Marketing Strategy?* Retrieved from http://www.convinceandconvert.com/digital-marketing/are-you-overlooking-the-most-valuable- real-time-marketing-strategy/

Dodd, K. (2017). *Using Drones at your Events*. https://www.eventtechsoftware.com/blog/using-drones-at-your-event

Doğan, M., Pekiner, A., & Karaca, E. (2018). The effect of social media on tourism and tourist choices: Case of Kars-Doğu Express. *Journal of Travel and Hotel Management*, *15*(3), 669–683.

Dorn, L. (2016). *The Dali Museum Offers an Immersive Virtual Reality Tour Inside One of Dali's Most Famous Paintings*. Retrieved from https://laughingsquid.com/dali-museum-dreams-of-dali/

Doyduk, H. B. B., & Tiftik, C. (2017). Internet of things: Future projections and business opportunities. *Third Sector Social Economic Review*, *52*(3), 127–147.

Drengner, J., Gaus, H., & Jahn, S. (2008). Does flow influence the brand image in event marketing? *Journal of Advertising Research*, *48*(1), 138–147. doi:10.2501/S0021849908080148

Duğan, Ö., & Aydın, B. (2018). Publicity Aimed Usage of Social Media in Tourism: Sample of TR Ministry of Culture and Tourism. *International Journal of Turkic World Tourism Studies*, *3*(1), 1–13. https://dergipark.org.tr/tr/pub/tdtad/issue/38069/347607

Dunleavy, M., Dede, C., & Mitchell, R. (2009). Affordances and limitations of immersive participatory augmented reality simulations for teaching and learning. *Journal of Science Education and Technology*, *18*(1), 7–22. doi:10.100710956-008-9119-1

Durge, M. R., & Jagtap, H. P. (2016). 7D Holographic Technology. *International Journal on Recent and Innovation Trends in Computing and Communication*, *4*(1), 67–70.

Dwyer, L., Mellor, R., Mistilis, N., & Mules, T. (2000). A framework for evaluating and forecasting the ımpacts of special events. In J. Allen, R. Harris, L. K. Jago, & A. J. Veal (Eds.), *Events beyond 2000: Setting the agenda* (pp. 31–45). Australian Centre for Event Management.

E2m.live. (2020). *E2m Event Chatbot Industry-First Chatbot for Event Apps*. Retrieved July 23, 2020 https://e2m.live/chatbots

EBSO. (2015). *Sanayi 4.0: Uyum sağlamayan kaybedecek.* https://www.inovasyon.org/pdf/EBSO.Sanayi4.0_Raporu.Ekim.2015.pdf

Eckerstein, A. (2002). *Evaluation of event marketing* (Unpublished master's thesis). Göteborg University, Graduate Business School, School of Economics and Commercial Law, Swedish.

Eckerstein, A. (2002). *Evaluation of event marketing important indicators to consider when evaluating event marketing* (Master thesis). Graduate Business School School of Economics and Commercial Law, Göteborg University.

Eckerstein, A. (2009). Evaluation of event marketing. Important indicators to consider when evaluating event marketing. Käsikirjaline magistritöö. Graduate Business School, Göteborg University, Göteborg.

Eker, M., Bayindir, M., Büktel, S., & Yilmaz, K. (2017). Influencer'ın hatırı kaç yıl sürer? [How many years does the Influencer respect?]. *Campaign Dergisi*, *69*, 22–24.

Ellison, H. (2017). *Event tech: Robots.* https://www.campaignlive.co.uk/article/event-tech-robots/1421036

Emery, P. (2010). Past, present, future major sport event management practice: The practitioner perspective. *Sport Management Review*, *13*(2), 158–170. doi:10.1016/j.smr.2009.06.003

Emittistanbul.com. (2020). *Emitt hakkında.* Retrieved from https://emittistanbul.com/Sayfa/emitt-hakkinda

Engelking, C. (2015). *Beyond Tupac, Can Hologram Concerts Take Off?* https://www.discovermagazine.com/the-sciences/beyond-tupac-can-hologram-concerts-take-off

Erciş, M. S. (2010). *Pazarlama iletişiminde temel yaklaşımlar [Basic approaches in marketing communication].* Nobel Yayıncılık.

Erdem, A. (2009). Firmalarda bütünleşik pazarlama iletişim stratejilerinin belirlenmesinde tüketici davranışlarının önemi [The importance of consumer behaviors in determining integrated marketing communication strategies in companies]. *Erciyes Üniversitesi İktisadi ve İdari Bilimler Fakültesi Dergisi*, 42-64.

Erdil, E. (2018). Dijital Dönüşüm/Endüstri 4.0 ve Türkiye. *İktisat ve Toplum Dergisi*, *92*, 57-61.

Erdoğan, Y. (2020). *Sales effect of digital marketing in small and medium-sized accommodation enterprises in core Cappadocia* (Unpublished Master's Thesis). Nevşehir Hacı Bektaşi Veli University, Nevşehir.

Eröz, S. S., & Doğdubay, M. (2012). Turistik Ürün Tercihinde Sosyal Medyanın Rolü ve Etik İlişkisi. *Dokuz Eylül Üniversitesi İktisadi İdari Bilimler Fakültesi Dergisi*, *27*(1), 133–157.

Ertuğrul, İ., & Deniz, G. (2018). 4.0 Dünyası: Pazarlama 4.0 ve Endüstri 4.0. *Bitlis Eren Üniversitesi Sosyal Bilimler Enstitüsü Dergisi*, *7*(1), 143–170.

Eryılmaz, B. & Zengin, B. (2014). Sosyal medyada konaklama işletmelerine yönelik tüketici yaklaşımları üzerine bir araştırma. *İşletme Bilimi Dergisi*, 147-167.

Eryılmaz, B., & Zengin, B. (2014). A research on the botique hotels'social media use: Facabook Sample. *Journal of Kastamonu University Economics and Administrative Sciencies*, *14*(2), 42–59.

Esu, B. B., & Arrey, V. M. E. (2009). Tourists' satisfaction with cultural tourism festival: A case study of Calabar Carnival Festival, Nigeria. *International Journal of Business and Management*, *4*(3), 116. doi:10.5539/ijbm.v4n3p116

Etkinlik Nasıl Pazarlanır. (2020). https://blog.adgager.com/etkinlik-nasil-pazarlanir-9-adimda-etkinlik-pazarlama/

Evans, D. (2008). *Social media marketing an hour a day.* Wiley Publishing Inc.

Evans, D. (2010). *Social media marketing: the next generation of business engagement*. John Wiley & Sons.

Event, M. B. (2019). *100 Event Statistics (2020 Edition)*. https://www.eventmanagerblog.com/event-statistics

Eventbride. (2019). *Tip #3: newest technology trends to spruce up your festival*. https://www.eventbrite.com/blog/academy/festival-newest-technology-trends/

Eventbrite. (2013). *New trends impacting festival and consumer events*. Retrieved from https://eventbrites3.s3.amazonaws.com/marketing/britepapers/Britepaper_6newtrends_webVersion.pdf

Eventmb Studio Team. (2019). *5 Trends In Virtual Reality For Events*. Retrieved from https://www.eventmanagerblog.com/virtual-reality-trends-events

Eventsforce. (2016a). *5 ways you could use virtual and augmented reality at events*. https://www.eventsforce.com/blog/5-ways-you-could-use-virtual-augmented-reality-at-events/

Eventsforce. (2016b). *6 technology trends from experts at Europe's largest event tech show*. https://www.eventsforce.com/blog/6-technology-trends-from-experts-at-europes-largest-event-tech-show/

Experenti. (2016). *Augmented and virtual reality hit Sundance Film Festival*. https://www.experenti.eu/ar/augmented-and-virtual-reality-hit-sundance-film-festival/

Expert System. (2020). *Chatbot: What is a Chatbot? Why are Chatbots Important?* https://expertsystem.com/chatbot/

Fan, Y., & Pfitzenmaıer, N. (2002). Event sponsorship in China. *Corporate Communications*, *7*(2), 110–116. doi:10.1108/13563280210426179

Farazad, K. (2020). *The Recovery Period Time for Hospitality Sector*. https://www.hospitalitynet.org/opinion/4101168.html

Feiner, S. (2002). Augmented reality: A new way of seeing. *Scientific American*, *286*(4), 48–55. doi:10.1038cientificamerican0402-48

Feng, Z., González, V. A., Amor, R., Lovreglio, R., & Cabrera-Guerrero, G. (2018). Immersive virtual reality serious games for evacuation training and research: A systematic literature review. *Computers & Education*, *127*, 252–266. doi:10.1016/j.compedu.2018.09.002

Ferdinand, N., & Kitchin, P. (2012). *Events Management: An International Approach*. Sage.

Financial Times. (2017). *World*. Retrieved August 2, 2020, from https://www.ft.com/content/9b72c5a6-d680-11e6-944b-e7eb37a6aa8e

Finin, T., Ding, L., Zhou, L., & Joshi, A. (2005). Social networking on the semantic web. *The Learning Organization*, *12*(5), 418–435. doi:10.1108/09696470510611384

Finkelstein, N., Perkins, K., & Adams, W. (2005). Can computer simulations replace real equipment in undergraduate laboratories? In *Physics Education Research Conference* (vol.790, pp. 101-104). New York: American Institute of Physics Conference Proceedings. 10.1063/1.2084711

Fırat, S. Ü., & Fırat, O. Z. (2017). Gıda ve İçecek Sektöründe Endüstri 4.0 Devrimi: Otomasyon ve Robotlar. *ST Robot Yatırımları, Robot Ürün ve Sistemleri, Ekim*, 214-220.

Fırat, S. Ü., & Fırat, O. Z. (2017). Sanayi 4.0 Devrimi Üzerine Karşılaştırmalı Bir İnceleme: Kavramlar, Küresel Gelişmeler ve Türkiye. *Toprak İşveren Dergisi*, *114*, 10–23.

Fischer, E., & Reuber, A. R. (2011). Social interaction via new social media: (How) can interactions on twitter affect effectual thinking and behavior? *Journal of Business Venturing*, *26*(1), 1–18. doi:10.1016/j.jbusvent.2010.09.002

Flynn, N. (2012). *The social media handbook: Rules, policies and best practices to successfully manage your organization's social media presence, posts and potential risks.* Pfeiffer Publishing.

Fotis, J., Buhalis, D., & Rossides, N. (2012). Social media use and impact during the holiday travel planning process. In Information and Communication Technologies in Tourism. Springer. doi:10.1007/978-3-7091-1142-0_2

Fotis, J., Buhalis, D., & Rossides, N. (2011). Social media impact on holiday travel planning: The case of the Russian and the FSU markets. *International Journal of Online Marketing*, *1*(4), 1–19. doi:10.4018/ijom.2011100101

Fredline, E., & Faulker, B. (2000). Host community reactions a cluster analysis. *Annals of Tourism Research*, *27*(3), 763–784. doi:10.1016/S0160-7383(99)00103-6

Friedman, F. (2016). *Future trends impacting the exhibitions and events industry 2016 update.* International Association of Exhibitions and Events. Retrieved from http://www.iaee.com/wp-content/uploads/2016/04/2016-IAEE-Future-Trends-Impacting-the-Exhibitions-and-Events-Industry-White-Paper.pdf

Fuchs, C. (2014). *Social Media a Critical Introduction.* Sage Publication Inc. doi:10.4135/9781446270066

Gallo, P. (2014). *Michael Jackson Hologram Rocks Billboard Music Awards: Watch & Go Behind the Scenes.* https://www.billboard.com/articles/events/bbma-2014/6092040/michael-jackson-hologram-billboard-music-awards

Gani, R., & Anjum, D. (2017). E-human resource management (e-hrm). *International Journal of Emerging Research in Management &Technology*, *6*(6), 184–188.

Garcia, M. F. L., Lansley, G., & Calnan, B. (2017). Modelling Spatial Behaviour in Music Festivals Using Mobile Generated Data and Machine Learning. *GISRUK 2017 Conference.*

Gardner, M., & Shuman, P. (1987). Sponsorship: An important component of the promotions mix. *Journal of Advertising*, *16*(1), 11–17. doi:10.1080/00913367.1987.10673055

Gaziantep Uluslararası Gastronomi Festivali. (2020). https://www.facebook.com/GastroAntepFest/?__tn__=%2Cd%2CPR&eid=ARA0Y4KSs3RnjPx3yI7fTNjYQwA1oZEQiKe_y2tqdLIULhG25IAHEmz1GhqBpY2S8EsW9_lTWbvDlbr8

Genc, S. (2018). Turkey's proceed on industry 4.0. *Sosyoekonomi*, *26*(36), 235–243. doi:10.17233osyoekonomi.2018.02.14

Gentile, C., Spiller, N., & Noci, G. (2007). How to sustain the customer experience? *European Management Journal*, *25*(5), 395–410. doi:10.1016/j.emj.2007.08.005

George, J., Meyers, A. & Chasalow, B. (2012). *How It Works: Chris Milk's The Treachery Of Sanctuary.* Retrieved from https://www.vice.com/en_us/article/3dpg9v/how-it-works-chris-milks-ithe-treachery-of-sanctuaryi

Geraghty, G., & Conway, A. (2016). *The Study of Traditional and Non-traditional Marketing Communications: Target Marketing in the Events Sector.* Paper presented at the 12th Annual Tourism and Hospitality Research in Ireland Conference, THRIC 2016, 16th and 17th June, Limerick Institute of Technology.

Gervautz, M., & Schmalstieg, D. (2012). Anywhere Interfaces Using Handheld Augmented Reality. *Computer*, *45*(7), 26–31. doi:10.1109/MC.2012.72

Getz, D. (1991). *Festivals, special events and tourism.* Van Nostrand Reinhold.

Getz, D. (1993). Festivals and special events. In M. A. Khan, M. D. Olsen, & T. Var (Eds.), *Encyclopedia of hospitality and tourism* (pp. 789–810). Van Nostrand Reinhold.

Getz, D. (1997). *Event management & event tourism.* Cognizant Communication Corporation.

Getz, D. (1997). *Event Management & Event Tourism.* Cognizant Communication Corporation.

Getz, D. (1997). *Event management and event tourism.* Cognizant Communication.

Getz, D. (1997). Trends and issues in sport event tourism. *Tourism Recreation Research, 22*(2), 61–62. doi:10.1080/02508281.1997.11014804

Getz, D. (2005). *Event Management and Event Tourism.* Cognizant.

Getz, D. (2007). *Event studies: theory, research and policy for planned events.* Elsevier.

Getz, D. (2008). Event tourism: Definition, evolution, and research. *Tourism Management, 29*(3), 403–428. doi:10.1016/j.tourman.2007.07.017

Getz, D. (2012). Event Studies: Discourses and Future Directions. *Event Management, 16*(2), 171–187. doi:10.3727/152599512X13343565268456

Getz, D., Anderssen, T., & Larson, M. (2007). Festival Stakeholder Roles: Concepts and Case Studies. *Event Management, 10*(2–3).

Getz, D., & Page, S. (2020). *Event Studies: Theory, Research and Policy for Planned Events* (4th ed.). Routledge.

Getz, D., & Page, S. J. (2016). Progress and prospects for event tourism research. *Tourism Management, 52*, 593–631. doi:10.1016/j.tourman.2015.03.007

Ghazali, A., & Ramli, N. (2014). The Relationship Between Social Media Uzage and Event Attendees Satisfaction At Carnival Event. In *Proceedings of the Australian Academy of Business and Social Sciences Conference* (pp. 1-10). Dubai: Australian Academy of Business and Social Sciences.

Gibson, M. (2015). *Meet the robot chef that can prepare your dinner.* Retrieved August 2, 2020, from https://time.com/3819525/robot-chef-moley-robotics/

Gibson, H. J., Willming, C., & Holdnak, A. (2003). Small-scale event sport tourism: Fans as tourists. *Tourism Management, 24*(2), 181–190. doi:10.1016/S0261-5177(02)00058-4

Gilbert, B. (2016). *540 robots dancing in sync looks just as insane as you'd think.* https://www.businessinsider.com/this-is-540-robots-dancing-in-sync-2016-2

Gilbert, E., & Karahalios, K. (2009). Predicting tie strength with social media. In *Proceedings of the SIGCHI Conference on Human Factors in Computing Systems* (pp. 211-220). ACM.

Giomelakis, D., & Veglis, A. (2016). Investigating search engine optimization factors in media websites: The case of Greece. *Digital Journalism, 4*(3), 379–400. doi:10.1080/21670811.2015.1046992

Girgin, F. A., & Tasci, O. E. (2019). Mega-Event Organization Considering Safety, Security and Resilience. *TeMA - Journal of Land Use. Mobility and Environment, 12*(3), 249–264. doi:10.6092/1970-9870/6269

Glastonbury, Tomorrowland, Sziget & More: How Top European Music Festivals Use Social Media. (2020). Retrieved from Ticketbooth web site: https://www.ticketbooth.com.au/ticketing/blog/glastonbury-tomorrowland-sziget-more-how-top-european-music-festivals-use-social-media/

Glion. (2020). *Why events are so important to the hospitality industry.* https://www.glion.edu/magazine/events-important-hospitality-industry/

Go, F. M., Lee, R. M., & Russo, A. P. (2003). E-heritage in the globalizing society: Enabling cross-cultural engagement through ICT. *Information Technology & Tourism, 6*(1), 55–68. doi:10.3727/109830503108751225

Göktaş, B., & Kulga, C. E. (2017). Tüketicilerin Etkinlik Pazarlaması Faaliyetlerine ve Düzenleyen Markalara Bakış Açısına Yönelik Bir Araştırma. *Global Journal of Economics and Business Studies*, *6*(11), 85–97.

Goldblatt, J. (2005). *Special Events: Event leadership for a New World* (4th ed.). John Wiley & Sons.

Goldblatt, J. (2011). *Special events: a new generation and the next frontier*. John Wiley & Sons.

Goldblatt, J. (2013). *Special events: creating and sustaining a new world for celebration*. Wiley Global Education.

Gold, J. R., & Gold, M. M. (2018). *Urban segments and event spaces: World's fairs and olympic sites. The Routledge Handbook of Planning History*. Routledge.

Goldstein, J. (2013). Content marketing: The smart way to grab attention. *Bank Marketing*, 26–29.

Goodyear, S. (2020). *These hyper-realistic robot dolphins could replace live animals at aquariums*. https://www.cbc.ca/radio/asithappens/as-it-happens-monday-edition-1.5647594/these-hyper-realistic-robot-dolphins-could-replace-live-animals-at-aquariums-1.5647597

Gradinaru, A., Moldoveanu, A., & Moldoveanu, F. (2018). Designing a virtual reality learning management system. *ELearning & Software for Education*, *2*, 11–17. doi:10.12753/2066-026X-18-072

Graham-McLay, C. (2020). *Robot dolphins: The Cruelty-free 20m animal you can't tell from the real thing*. https://www.theguardian.com/environment/2020/jul/13/robot-dolphins-the-cruelty-free-20m-animal-you-cant-tell-from-the-real-thing

Grate, R. (2020). *Event Marketing 101: How to Keep Attendees Engaged Before, During and After Your Event*. Retrieved from Buffer LİbraryWeb Site: https://buffer.com/library/social-media-event-marketing/

Green, R. (2018). *How technology is drastically shaking up the events industry*. Retrieved from September 10. https://www.verdict.co.uk/technology-events-industry/

Groenli, T. M., Flesch, B., Mukkamala, R., Vatrapu, R., Klavestad, S., & Bergner, H. (2018, December). Internet of Things Big Data Analytics: The Case of Noise Level Measurements at the Roskilde Music Festival. In *2018 IEEE International Conference on Big Data (Big Data)* (pp. 5153-5158). IEEE.

Groot, T. (2017). *AI in 2019: How Artificial Intelligence Is Impacting Events*. Retrieved February 22, 2020, from https://www.eventbrite.com/blog/ai-in-2018-artificial-intelligence-events-ds00/

Gubbi, J., Buyya, R., Marusic, S., & Palaniswami, M. (2013). Internet of Things (IoT): A vision, architectural elements, and future directions. *Future Generation Computer Systems*, *29*(7), 1645–1660. doi:10.1016/j.future.2013.01.010

Guinness World Records. (2020). *First restaurant with robot waiting staff*. Guinness World Records. Retrieved August 26, 2020, from https://www.guinnessworldrecords.com

Gülal, S. (2019). *Seyahatlerinizi kolaylaştıracak 20 mobil uygulama*. https://www.turizmgunlugu.com/2019/01/05/en-iyi-20-seyahat-uygulamasi/

Güler, O., Akdağ, G., Çakıcı, A. C., & Benli, S. (2015). Turizmi değiştiren 100 yenilik. (U. Gökovalı, Dü.). *Anatolia: Turizm Araştırmaları Dergisi*, *26*(2), 290–317.

Gümüş, F. (2019). *Müzelerde Yapay Zeka Uygulamalari, Etkileri ve Geleceği* (Unpublished master dissertation). İstanbul Üniversitesi Sosyal Bilimler Enstitüsü, İstanbul.

Gunelius, S. (2011). *30-Minute social media marketing*. McGraw-Hill.

Gunelius, S. (2011). *30-minute social media marketing: Step-by-step techniques to spread the word about your business*. McGraw-Hill.

Gupta, S. (2003). Event marketing: Issues and challenges. *IIMB Management Review*, *15*(2), 87–96.

Gursoy, D., & Kendall, K. W. (2006). Hosting mega events-modelling locals' support. *Annals of Tourism Research*, *33*(3), 603–623. doi:10.1016/j.annals.2006.01.005

Güven, M. (2017). *Internet of things (nesnelerin interneti) nedir?* Retrieved August 2, 2020, from http://www.teknolojivetasarim.org/internet-of-things-nesnelerin-interneti-nedir/

Hahn, G. J. (2019). Industry 4.0: A supply chain innovation perspective. *International Journal of Production Research*, 1–17.

Hall, C. M. (1989). The definition and analysis of hallmark tourist events. *GeoJournal*, *19*(3), 263–268. doi:10.1007/BF00454570

Hall, C. M. (1992). *Hallmark tourist events – Impacts, management and planning*. Belhaven Press.

Hamilton, C. A., Alici, G., & Panhuis, M. (2018). 3D printing vegemite and marmite: Redefining "Breadboards.". *Journal of Food Engineering*, *220*, 83–88. doi:10.1016/j.jfoodeng.2017.01.008

Hanan, H., & Karim, S. A. (2015). Influence of social media in food festival destination image. In *Proceeding of International conference on tourism and ethnicity in ASEAN and beyond* (pp. 15-16). Academic Press.

Handley, A., & Chapman, C. (2012). *Dijital çağda içerik yönetiminin kuralları [Content management rules in the digital age]*. Kapital Medya Hizmetleri.

Hanlon, A. (2019). *Digital marketing: Strategic planning & integration*. SAGE Publications.

Hanna, R., Rohm, A., & Crittenden, V. L. (2011). We're all connected: The power of the social media ecosystem. *Business Horizons*, *54*(3), 265–273. doi:10.1016/j.bushor.2011.01.007

Hannon, K. (2018). *Artechouse Lights Up Washington's Museum Scene*. Retrieved from https://www.nytimes.com/2018/03/14/arts/artechouse-washington-dc-museum.html

Hao, L., Mellor, S., Seaman, O., Henderson, J., Sewell, N., & Sloan, M. (2010). Material characterisation and process development for chocolate additive layer manufacturing. *Virtual and Physical Prototyping*, *5*(2), 57–64. doi:10.1080/17452751003753212

Harb, A. A., Fowler, D., Chang, H. J. J., Blum, S. C., & Alakaleek, W. (2019). Social media as a marketing tool for events. *Journal of Hospitality and Tourism Technology*, *10*(1), 28–44. doi:10.1108/JHTT-03-2017-0027

Hatch, K. (2017). *The Who, What, and Why of Chatbots for Events*. Retrieved July 23, 2020 https://meetingpool.net/the-who-what-and-why-of-chatbots-for-events/

Hayes-Peirce, S. (2017). *Social Media Strategies for Sparking Event Conversations in 2018*. Retrieved from Mpi web site: https://www.mpi.org/chapters/southern-california/chapter-news/single-blog/article/social-media-strategies-for-sparking-event-conversations-in-2018

Hays, S., Page, S. J., & Buhalis, D. (2013). Social media as a destination marketing tool: Its use by national tourism organisations. *Current Issues in Tourism*, *16*(3), 211–239. doi:10.1080/13683500.2012.662215

Hede, A.-M., & Kellett, P. (2012). Building online brand communities: Exploring the benefits, challenges and risks in the Australian event sector. *Journal of Vacation Marketing*, *18*(3), 239–250. doi:10.1177/1356766712449370

Heraldkeepers. (2020). *MICE (Meetings, Incentives, Conferencing, Exhibitions) Market Size To Worth USD 1546.69 Billion by 2025 ndustry Analysis, Business Outlook, Current and Future Growth By 2025*. Retrieved from Marketwatch Web Sitesi: https://www.marketwatch.com/press-release/mice-meetings-incentives-conferencing-exhibitions-market-size-to-worth-usd-154669-billion-by-2025-industry-analysis-business-outlook-current-and-future-growth-by-2025-2020-08-17

Higham, J., & Hinch, T. (2002). Tourism, sport and seasons: The challenges and potentials of overcoming seasonality in the sport and tourism sectors. *Tourism Management*, *23*(2), 175–185. doi:10.1016/S0261-5177(01)00046-2

Hill, R. A. (2015). *How Drones may Propel your Event*. https://www.meetingstoday.com/magazines/article-details/articleid/26406/title/how-drones-may-propel-your-event

Hiller, H. H. (1998). Assessing the impact of mega-events: A linkage model. *Current Issues in Tourism*, *1*(1), 47–57. doi:10.1080/13683509808667832

Hindman, B. (2018). The event marketing evolution an era of data, technology, and revenue impact. *Harvard Business Review Analytic Services Research Report/Splash*. Retrieved from https://hbr.org/sponsored/2018/09/the-event-marketing-evolution

Hive, D. (2019). *How drones enhance events and event planning*. https://dronehive.com.au/news/26_how-drones-enhance-events-and-event-planning

Hoffman, D. L., & Fodor, M. (2010). Can You Measure the ROI of Your Scial Media Marketing. *MIT Sloan Management Review*, *52*(1), 41–49.

Hoffman, D. L., & Fodor, M. (2010). Can you measure the ROI of your social media marketing? *MIT Sloan Management*, *52*(1), 41–49.

Hoffman, D. L., & Novak, T. P. (2009). Flow online: Lessons learned and future prospects. *Journal of Interactive Marketing*, *23*(1), 23–34. doi:10.1016/j.intmar.2008.10.003

Hoffman, D. L., Novak, T. P., & Chatterjee, P. (1995). Commercial scenarios for the web: Opportunities and challenges. *Journal of Computer-Mediated Communication*, *1*(3), 0. doi:10.1111/j.1083-6101.1995.tb00165.x

Hoffman-Riem, H., Biber-Klemm, S., Grossenbacher-Mansuy, W., Hirsch Hadorn, G., Joye, D., Pohl, C., Wiesmann, U., & Zemp, E. (2008). Idea of the Handbook. In G. Hirsch Hadorn, H. Hoffman-Riem, S. Biber-Klemm, W. Grossenbacher-Mansuy, D. Joye, C. Pohl, U. Wiesmann, & E. Zemp (Eds.), Handbook of Transdisciplinary Research (pp. 3-18). Bern, Switzerland: Springer.

Hofmann, E., & Rüsch, M. (2017). Industry 4.0 and the current status as well as future prospects on logistics. *Computers in Industry*, *89*, 23–34. doi:10.1016/j.compind.2017.04.002

Hogan, J. E., Lemon, K. N., & Libai, B. (2004). Quantifying the ripple: Word-of-mouth and advertising effectiveness. *Journal of Advertising Research*, *44*(3), 271–280. doi:10.1017/S0021849904040243

Hoksbergen, E., & Insch, A. (2016). Facebook as a platform for co-creating music festival experiences. *International Journal of Event and Festival Management*, *7*(2), 84–99. doi:10.1108/IJEFM-02-2016-0012

Holbrook, M., & Hirschman, E. (1982). The experiential aspects of consumption. *The Journal of Consumer Research*, *9*(2), 132–140. doi:10.1086/208906

Holland, S., Foster, T., MacNaughtan, W., & Tuck, C. (2018). Design and characterisation of food grade powders and inks for microstructure control using 3D printing. *Journal of Food Engineering*, *220*, 12–19. doi:10.1016/j.jfoodeng.2017.06.008

Horo, S. (2015). *The Role of Social Media on Event Marketing* (Master's Thesis). The Republic of Turkey Bahcesehir University, Istanbul.

Horo, S. (2015). *The role of social media on event marketing* (Unpublished master's thesis). Bahcesehir University, Social Science Institute, Turkey.

HospitalityNet. (2018). *Millennium hotels and resorts deploys robotic solutions to ıts singapore properties*. Retrieved August 2, 2020, from https://www.hospitalitynet.org/news/4090560.html

Hoyle, L. H. CAE., & CMP. (2002). Event marketing: How to successfully promote events, festivals, conventions, and expositions, John Wiley & Sons, Inc.

Hoyle, H. L. (2002). *Event Marketing. How to Successfully Promote Events, Festivals, Conventions and Expositions*. John Wiley & Sons, Inc.

Hoyle, L. (2002). *Event marketing: How to successfully promote events, festivals, conventions and expositions*. John Wiley and Sons.

Hoyle, L. H. (2002). *Event marketing. How to successfully promote events, festivals, conventions, and expositions*. John Wiley.

Hoyle, L. H. (2012). *How to successfully promote events, festivals, conventions, and expositions*. John Wiley & Sons.

Hsu, A. C., & Wang, F. K. (2009). Study on the key element of the religion type event marketing-"Franklin Graham Festival in Taipei" as a case. *Symposium conducted at the meeting of Chinese Communication Society*.

http://www.brandlifemag.com/. (2019). *Işıktan Tabloların İçinde Kaybolun*. Retrieved from http://www.brandlifemag.com /isiktan-tablolarin-icinde-kaybolun/

https://borderless.teamlab.art. (2019). *MORI Mueum*. Retrieved from https://borderless.teamlab.art/

Huang, Y., Basu, C., & Hsu, M. K. (2010). Exploring motivations of travel knowledge sharing on social network sites: An empirical investigation of US college students. *Journal of Hospitality Marketing & Management*, *19*(7), 717–734. doi:10.1080/19368623.2010.508002

Hudson, S., & Hudson, R. (2013). Engaging with consumers using social media: A case study of music festivals. *International Journal of Event and Festival Management*, *4*(3), 206–223. doi:10.1108/IJEFM-06-2013-0012

Hudson, S., Roth, M. S., Madden, T. J., & Hudson, R. (2015). The effects of social media on emotions, brand relationship quality, and word of mouth: An empirical study of music festival attendees. *Tourism Management*, *47*, 68–76. doi:10.1016/j.tourman.2014.09.001

Huizing, E. (2000). The content and design of web sites: An empirical study. *Information & Management*, *37*(1), 123–124. doi:10.1016/S0378-7206(99)00044-0

Hummer, M., Kretschmer, D., & Hofmann, B. (2005). User-centered requirements engineering: Usability ıssue for websites of tour operators. In Information and Communication Technologies in Tourism. Wien: Springer Verlag.

Hung, K., & Law, R. (2011). An overview of Internet-based surveys in hospitality and tourism journals. *Tourism Management*, *32*(4), 717–724. doi:10.1016/j.tourman.2010.05.027

Hussain, M., & Manhas, J. (2016). Artificial Intelligence for Big Data: Potential and Relevance. *International Acadmey of Engineering and Medical Research*, *1*(1), 1–5.

Hvass, K. A., & Munar, A. M. (2012). The takeoff of social media in tourism. *Journal of Vacation Marketing, 18*(2), 93–103. doi:10.1177/1356766711435978

Hwaya, K. (2019). *Augmented reality dragon wows baseball fans on opening day.* http://www.korea.net/NewsFocus/Sci-Tech/view?articleId=169492

İbiş, S. (2019). Turizm Endüstrisinde Robotlaşma. *Türk Turizm Araştırmaları Dergisi, 3*(3), 403–420. doi:10.26677/TR1010.2019.169

Ibis, S. (2019). Turizmde robotlaşma [Robotics in the Tourism Industry]. *Türk Turizm Araştırmaları Dergisi, 3*(3), 403–420.

İçten, T and Bal, G. (2017). Artırılmış gerçeklik üzerine son gelişmelerin ve uygulamaların incelenmesi [Examining the latest developments and applications on augmented reality]. *GU J Sci, Part C, 5*(2), 111-136.

Ideausher. (2020). *How can Artificial Intelligence (AI) benefit the events industry in 2020?* https://ideausher.com/blog/artificial-intelligence/how-can-artificial-intelligence-ai-benefit-the-events-industry-in-2020/

Illum, M. (2018). *How IoT could transform the experience for Dubai Shopping Festival season.* https://www.iotevolutionworld.com/iot/articles/436340-how-iot-could-transform-experience-dubai-shopping-festival.htm

İmre, N. (2020). An evaluation of using social media in tourism sector. *Journal of Turkısh Tourism Resarch, 4*(2), 1655–1670.

İnan, E., & Ölçer, C. (2010). Büyük ölçekli etkinlik yönetiminde e-pazarlama çalışmaları: İstanbul Avrupa kültür başkenti örneği. *Erciyes İletişim Dergisi, 1*(4).

Innovation, B. C. C. (2019). *Lab-e digital gastronomy lab.* Retrieved September 3, 2020, from https://innovation.bculinary.com/en/portfolio/labe-digital-gastronomy-lab/

International Telecommunication Union. (2019). *United Nations Activities on Artificial Intelligence (AI) 2019.* International Telecommunication Union.

İq-mag. (2016). *The internet of things: The future of event tech.* https://www.iq-mag.net/2016/10/internet-of-things-future-event-tech/#.XiALmpIzYdU

Ivanov, S., & Webster, C. (2017). *Adoption of Robots, Artificial Intelligence and Service Automation by Travel, Tourism and Hospitality Companies – A Cost – Benefit Analysis.* International Scientific Conference "Contemporary Tourism – Traditions and Innovations", Sofia University.

Ivanov, S., Webster, C., & Berezina, K. (2020). Robotics in tourism and hospitality. In *Handbook of e-Tourism.* Springer. https://link.springer.com/content/pdf/10.1007/978-3-030-05324-6_112-1.pdf

Ivanov, S., Gretzel, U., Berezina, K., Sigala, M., & Webster, C. (2019). Progress on Robotics in Hospitality and Tourism: A Review of the Literature. *Journal of Hospitality and Tourism Technology, 10*(4), 489–521. doi:10.1108/JHTT-08-2018-0087

Ivanov, S., Webster, C., & Berezina, K. (2017). Adoption of Robots and Service Automation by Tourism and Hospitality Companies. *Revista Turismo & Desenvolvimento, 27*(28), 1501–1517.

Jabreel, M., Moreno, A., & Huertas, A. (2017). Semantic comparison of the emotional values communicated by destinations and tourists on social media. *Journal of Destination Marketing & Management, 6*(3), 170–183. doi:10.1016/j.jdmm.2016.03.004

Jackson, N. (2013). *Promoting and marketing events: Theory and practice.* Routledge. doi:10.4324/9780203583166

Jago, L., Veal, A. J., Allen, J., & Harris, R. (2000). Events beyond 2000: setting the agenda: proceedings of conference on event evaluation, research and education. Australian Centre for Event Management.

Jago, L., Veal, A. J., Allen, J., & Harris, R. (2000). *Events beyond 2000: setting the agenda: proceedings of conference on event evaluation, research and education*. Australian Centre for Event Management.

Janiskee, R. L. (1996). Historic houses and special events. *Annals of Tourism Research*, *23*(2), 398–414. doi:10.1016/0160-7383(95)00069-0

Jara, A. J., Parra, M. C., & Skarmeta, A. F. (2012, July). Marketing 4.0: A new value added to the Marketing through the Internet of Things. In *2012 Sixth International Conference on Innovative Mobile and Internet Services in Ubiquitous Computing* (pp. 852-857). IEEE. 10.1109/IMIS.2012.203

Javalgi, R. G., Traylor, M. B., Gross, A. C., & Lampman, E. (1994). Awareness of sponsorship and corporate image: An empirical investigation. *Journal of Advertising*, *23*(4), 47–58. doi:10.1080/00913367.1943.10673458

Javornik, A. (2016). Augmented reality: Research Agenda for Studying the Impact of Its Media Characteristics on Consumer Behaviour. *Journal of Retailing and Consumer Services*, *30*, 252–261. doi:10.1016/j.jretconser.2016.02.004

Jeong, G. H., & Faulkner, B. (1996). Resident perceptions of mega-event impacts: The Taejon International Exposition Case. *Festival Management & Event Tourism*, *4*(1-2), 3–11. doi:10.3727/106527096792232388

Johnson, R. D., Lukaszewski, K. M., & Stone, D. L. (2016). The evolution of the field of human resource ınformation systems: co-evolution of technology and hr processes. CAIS, 38, 28.

Jordan, E. (2019). *ARTECHOUSE: A Technology-Based Museum Shakes up D.C., Miami, and New York*. Retrieved from https://www.whitewall.art/art/artechouse-technology-based-museum-shakes-d-c-miami-new-york

Junek, O., Lockstone, L., & Mair, J. (2009). Two perspectives on event management employment: Student and employer insights into the skills required to get the job done! *Journal of Hospitality and Tourism Management*, *16*(1), 120–129. doi:10.1375/jhtm.16.1.120

Jyh-Hwa, T., & Kuo, S., L. (2008). The Development of the Restaurant Service Mobile Robot with a Laser Positioning System. *Chinese Control Conference*, 662-666.

Kabaklarlı, E. (2016). *Endüstri 4.0 ve dijital ekonomisi: Dünya ve Türkiye ekonomisi için fırsatlar, etkiler ve tehditler*. Nobel Bilimsel Eserler.

Kagermann, H., Wahlster, W., & Helbig, J. (Eds.). (2013). Recommendations for implementing the strategic initiative industrie 4.0: Final report of the industrie 4.0 working group. Academic Press.

Kansakar, P., Munir, A., & Shabani, N. (2017). *Technology in hospitality industry: Prospects and challenges*. arXiv preprint arXiv:1709.00105

Kaplan, A. M., & Haenlein, M. (2009). The fairyland of Second Life: Virtual social worlds and how to use them. *Business Horizons*, *52*(6), 563–572. doi:10.1016/j.bushor.2009.07.002

Kaplan, A. M., & Haenlein, M. (2010). Users of the world, unite! The challenges and opportunities of Social Media. *Business Horizons*, *53*(1), 59–68. doi:10.1016/j.bushor.2009.09.003

Kaplan, A., & Haenlein, M. (2012). Social media: Back to the roots and back to the future. *Journal of Systems and Information Technology*, *14*(2), 101–105. doi:10.1108/13287261211232126

Karjaluoto, H., Ulkuniemi, P., & Hänninen, N. (2015). The role of digital channels in industrial marketing communications. *Journal of Business and Industrial Marketing*, *30*(6), 703–710. doi:10.1108/JBIM-04-2013-0092

Karkar, A. (2016). Değer ve güven ağlarının yükselişinde içerik pazarlaması [Content marketing in the rise of value and trust networks]. *International Journal of Social Sciences and Education Research*, *2*(1), 274–285. doi:10.24289/ijsser.279104

Karpinska-Krakowiak, M. (2015). Marketing events in a digital era–a comparative analysis of new and traditional events in terms of branding effectiveness. *Conference Proceedings, 11 Annual International Bata Conference*, 239-255.

Kaspar, R. (2014). The dimensions of events management. In The business of events management. Pearson Higher Ed.

Katiyar, A., Kalra, K., & Garg, C. (2015). Marker based augmented reality. *Advances in Computer Science and Information Technology*, *2*(5), 441–445.

Kaur, A., & Sandhu, G. (2017). Opportunities and challenges to digital marketing in developing countries. *International Journal of Science Technology & Management*, *6*(1).

Kaya, İ. (2015). *Pazarlama bitanedir: Bir pazarlama ansiklopedisi [Marketing is solidarity: An encyclopedia of marketing]*. Babıali Kültür.

Kaynak, S., & Koç, S. (2015). Telif hakları hukuku'nun yeni macerası: Sosyal medya. *Folklor/Edebiyat, 21*(83), 389-410.

Kehinde, O. J. (2009). *Integrated marketing communications and consumers patronage of Nigerian beverage products* (Unpublished doctoral dissertation). Covenant University, College of Business and Social Sciences, Nigeria.

Keller, L. K. (2013). *Strategic Brand Management: Building, Measuring, and Managing Brand Equity*. Pearson Education Limited.

Kemp, S. (2020). *Digital 2020: 3.8 Billion People Use Social Media*. https://wearesocial.com/blog/2020/01/digital-2020-3-8-billion-people-use-social-media

Kerns, C. (2014). *Trendology: Building an advantage through data-driven real-time marketing*. New York: MacMillan Press.

Khan, S. (2012). *Tupac's rise from the dead was, sadly, not holography*. https://theconversation.com/tupacs-rise-from-the-dead-was-sadly-not-holography-6641

Kharouf, H., Biscaia, R., Garcia-Perez, A., & Hickman, E. (2020). Understanding online event experience: The importance of communication, engagement and interaction. *Journal of Business Research*. Advance online publication. doi:10.1016/j.jbusres.2019.12.037

Khosla, S. (2019). *Watch: Robots serve food at east India's first-of-its-kind high-tech restaurant in Odisha; Twitter Reacts*. Retrieved April 3, 2020, from https://food.ndtv.com/news/watch-robots-serve-food-at-east-indias-first-of-its-kind-high-tech-restaurant-in-odisha-twitter-reac-2118340

Khotimah, K., Sari, D., & Kaltum, U. (2016). Event marketing and experiential marketing towards the formation of net marketing contribution margin (NMCM)(study at pt. garuda indonesia, tbk). *Procedia: Social and Behavioral Sciences*, *219*, 431–439. doi:10.1016/j.sbspro.2016.05.017

Kietzmann, J. H., Hermkens, K., McCarthy, I. P., & Silvestre, B. S. (2011). Social media? Get serious! Understanding the functional building blocks of social media. *Business Horizons*, *54*(3), 241–251. doi:10.1016/j.bushor.2011.01.005

Kılıçhan, R. (2015). *Ziyafet/banket organizasyonu menü çeşitleri, tanzimi ve takdimi kahvaltı çeşitleri oda servisi*. RetrievedAugust 23, 2020, fromhttp://www.gastronomi-mutfaksanatlari.com/FileUpload/ks241201/File/ziyafet-menu-kahvalti-oda_servisi.pdf

Kılıçhan, R. (2018). *Ziyafet organizasyonu ve yönetimi.* Retrieved August 25, 2020, from http://www.gastronomi-mutfaksanatlari.com/

Kim, A. J., & Ko, E. (2010). Impacts of luxury fashion brand's social media marketing on customer relationship and purchase intention. *Journal of Global Fashion Marketing, 1*(3), 164–171. doi:10.1080/20932685.2010.10593068

Kim, B. (2015). What facilitates a festival tourist? Investigating tourists' experiences at a local community festival. *Asia Pacific Journal of Tourism Research, 20*(9), 1005–1020. doi:10.1080/10941665.2014.957222

Kim, N. S., & Chalip, L. (2004). Why travel to the FIFA World Cup? Effects of motives, background, interest, and constraints. *Tourism Management, 25*(6), 695–707. doi:10.1016/j.tourman.2003.08.011

Kiran, S., Yilmaz, C., & Emre, I. E. (2019). Instagram'daki influencer'larin takipçiler üzerindeki etkisi [Influence of Instagram influencers on followers]. *Uluslararası Yönetim Bilişim Sistemleri ve Bilgisayar Bilimleri Dergisi, 3*(2), 100–111. doi:10.33461/uybisbbd.637155

Kocabaş, B. (2020). *Sosyal Medya Yönetiminin Olmazsa Olmazları.* http://www.sosyalmedya.co/sosyal-medya-yonetimi

Koçyiğit, M. (2015). *Sosyal ağ pazarlaması marka bağlılığı oluşturmada bir pazarlama stratejisi.* Eğitim Yayınevi.

Koh, K. Y., & Jackson, A. A. (2006). Special events marketing. *Journal of Convention & Event Tourism, 8*(2), 19–44. doi:10.1300/J452v08n02_02

Köksal, Y., & Özdemir, Ş. (2013). Bir iletişim araci olarak sosyal medya'nin tutundurma karmasi içerisindeki yeri üzerine bir inceleme [A review on the place of social media as a communication tool in the promotional mix]. *Süleyman Demirel Üniversitesi İktisadi ve İdari Bilimler Fakültesi Dergisi, 18*(1), 323–337.

Kolesar, M. B., & Galbraith, R. W. (2000). A services- marketing perspective on e-retailing: Implications for e-retailers and directions for further research. *Internet Research, 10*(5), 424–438. doi:10.1108/10662240010349444

Kondo, A. (2018). *Rice-serving robot dishes up sales.* Retrieved August 2, 2020, from https://asia.nikkei.com/Editor-s-Picks/Japan-Update/Rice-servingrobot-dishes-up-sales

Kong, Y. (2015). *Understanding group cohesion of festival and events attendees satifaction and intention to revisit* (Unpublished doctoral dissertation). Clemson University, Güney Carolina.

Köse, N. & Yengin, D. (2018). Dijital pazarlamadan fijital pazarlamaya geçişe örnek olarak artirilmiş gerçeklik ve sanal gerçeklik uygulamalarinin pazarlama üzerindeki katkilarinin incelenmesi [Examining the contribution of augmented reality and virtual reality applications on marketing as an example of the transition from figital marketing to digital marketing]. *İstanbul Aydın Üniversitesi Dergisi, 10*(1), 77-111.

Köse, G., & Çakır, S. Y. (2019). Markaların dijital pazarlama çağında tüketicileri etkileşime ikna etme yolları: Influencer pazarlama ve içerik pazarlamasına ilişkin kavramsal bir çalışma [Ways to convince consumers to interact with brands in the digital marketing era: A conceptual study on influencer marketing and content marketing]. *KOSBED, 38*, 205–222.

Kotler, P., Kartajaya, H., & Setiawan, I. (2010). *Welcome to marketing 3.0.* John Wiley & Sons, Inc. doi:10.1002/9781118257883.ch1

Kotler, P., & Keller, K. (2006). *Marketing management* (12th ed.). Pearson Prentice Hall.

Kounavis, C. D., Kasimati, A. E., & Zamani, E. D. (2012). Enhancing the tourism experience through mobile augmented reality: Challenges and prospects. *International Journal of Engineering Business Management, 4*(10), 1–6. doi:10.5772/51644

Kozinets, R. V., De Valck, K., Wojnicki, A. C., & Wilner, S. J. (2010). Networked narratives: Understanding word-of-mouth marketing in online communities. *Journal of Marketing*, *74*(2), 71–89. doi:10.1509/jm.74.2.71

Krishnan, A. (2019). *Quora, what are the basic features of digital marketing?* https://www.quora.com/What-are-the-basic-features-of-digital-marketing

Krugman, C., & Wrıght, P. R. (2007). *Global meetings and exhibitions*. John Wiley & Sons, Inc.

Krug, S. (2000). *Don't Make me Think! A Common Sense Approach to Web Usability*. New Riders.

Küçüksaraç, B., & Sayımer, İ. (2016). Deneyimsel pazarlama aracı olarak arttırılmış gerçeklik: Türkiye'deki marka deneyimlerinin etkileri üzerine bir araştırma [Augmented reality as an experiential marketing tool:A study on the effects of brand experience in Turkey]. *İstanbul Üniversitesi İletişim Fakültesi Dergisi*, 73-95.

Kumar, R. (1997). The role of affect in negotiations: An integrative overview. *Journal of Behavioural Science*, *33*(1), 84–100. doi:10.1177/0021886397331007

Kunreuther, H., & Michel-Kerjan, E. (2004). *Dealing with extreme events: new challenges for terrorism risk coverage in the US. Center for Risk Management and Decision Processes*. Wharton School, University of Pennsylvania.

Kurgun, O. A. (2019). Kuresel Turizm Ekosistemi ve Turizm 4.0 [Global Tourism Ecosystem and Tourism 4.0]. In H. Kurgun & O. A. Kurgun (Eds.), *Turizm 4.0: Kavramlar ve Uygulamalar* [Tourism 4.0: Concepts and Applications]. Detay Yayincilik.

Kurum, B. (2020). *Pazarlama 4.0: Gelenekselden Dijitale Geçiş*. https://medium.com/türkiye/pazarlama-4-0-geleneksel-den-dijitale-gecis-e2a4cabea825

Lade, C., & Jackson, J. (2004). Key success factors in regional festivals: Some Australian experiences. *Event Management*, *9*(1), 1–11. doi:10.3727/1525995042781066

Lamasatech. (2019). *5 innovative self-service technology examples*. https://www.lamasatech.com/blog/5-innovative-self-service-technology-examples/

Lambert, J. (2013). *Digital storytelling* (4th ed.). Routledge. doi:10.4324/9780203102329

Laurell, C., & Björner, E. (2018). Digital festival engagement: On the interplay between festivals, place brands, and social media. *Event Management*, *22*(4), 527–540. doi:10.3727/152599518X15300559276930

Law, R., Buhalis, D., & Cobanoglu, C. (2014). Progress on information and communication technologies in hospitality and tourism. *International Journal of Contemporary Hospitality Management*, *26*(5), 727–750. doi:10.1108/IJCHM-08-2013-0367

Le Tohic, C., O'Sullivan, J. J., Drapala, K. P., Chartrin, V., Chan, T., Morrison, A. P., Kerry, J. P., & Kelly, A. L. (2018). Effect of 3D printing on the structure and textural properties of processed cheese. *Journal of Food Engineering*, *220*, 56–64. doi:10.1016/j.jfoodeng.2017.02.003

Lee, E. A. (2008). Cyber physical systems: Design challenges. *2008 11th IEEE International Symposium on Object and Component-Oriented Real-Time Distributed Computing (ISORC)*, 363-369.

Lee, J. (2019). *6 Amazing Use Cases for AR/VR Technology within the Events Industry*. Retrieved from: https://www.virtualimmersive.com.au/post/6-amazing-use-cases-for-ar-vr-technology-within-the-events-industry

Lee, S. S., Boshnakova, D., & Goldblatt, J. (2017). *The 21st Century Meeting and Event Technologies Powerful Tools for Better Planning, Marketing, and Evaluation*. Oakville: Taylor & Francis Group.

Lee, E. A. (2008). Cyber physical systems: Design challenges. *11th IEEE International Symposium on Object and Component-Oriented Real-Time Distributed Computing (ISORC)* (pp. 363-369). IEEE. 10.1109/ISORC.2008.25

Leeflang, P. S., Verhoef, P. C., Dahlström, P., & Freundt, T. (2014). Challenges and solutions for marketing in a digital era. *European Management Journal*, *32*(1), 1–12. doi:10.1016/j.emj.2013.12.001

Lee, K. (2012). Augmented reality in education and training. *TechTrends*, *56*(2), 13–21. doi:10.100711528-012-0559-3

Leenders, M. A., Go, F. M., & Bhansing, P. V. (2015). The importance of the location in hosting a festival: A mapping approach. *Journal of Hospitality Marketing & Management*, *24*(7), 754–769. doi:10.1080/19368623.2014.934981

Leenders, M. A., van Telgen, J., Gemser, G., & Van der Wurff, R. (2005). Success in the Dutch music festival market: The role of format and content. *International Journal on Media Management*, *7*(3-4), 148–157. doi:10.1080/1424127 7.2005.9669431

Lee, S. (2011). To tweet or not to tweet: An exploratory study of meeting professionals' attitudes toward applying social media for meeting sessions. *Journal of Convention & Event Tourism*, *12*(4), 271–289. doi:10.1080/15470148.2011.621586

Lee, S. Y., Petrick, J. F., & Crompton, J. (2007). The roles of quality and intermediary constructs in determining festival attendees' behavioral intention. *Journal of Travel Research*, *45*(4), 402–412. doi:10.1177/0047287507299566

Lee, S., Shin, H. H., & Jeong, M. (2019). Are Students Ready for Their Future Career in the Event and Meeting Industry? Lessons from a Comparative Study between Students and Event and Meeting Professionals. *Journal of Hospitality & Tourism Education*, 1–11. doi:10.1080/10963758.2019.1654886

Lee, S., Close, A. G., & Love, C. (2010). How information quality and market turbulence impact convention and visitors bureaus' use of marketing information: Insights for destination and event marketing. *Journal of Convention & Event Tourism*, *11*(4), 266–292. doi:10.1080/15470148.2010.530541

Lee, T. H., & Chang, P. S. (2017). Examining the relationships among festivalscape, experiences, and identity: Evidence from two Taiwanese aboriginal festivals. *Leisure Studies*, *36*(4), 453–467. doi:10.1080/02614367.2016.1190857

Lee, W., Tyrrell, T., & Erdem, M. (2013). Exploring the behavioral aspects of adopting technology. *Journal of Hospitality and Tourism Technology*, *4*(1), 6–22. doi:10.1108/17579881311302329

Lee, W., Xiong, L., & Hu, C. (2012). The effect of Facebook users' arousal and valence on intention to go to the festival: Applying an extension of the technology acceptance model. *International Journal of Hospitality Management*, *31*(3), 819–827. doi:10.1016/j.ijhm.2011.09.018

Lee, Y. K., Lee, C. K., Lee, S. K., & Babin, B. J. (2008). Festivalscapes and patrons' emotions, satisfaction, and loyalty. *Journal of Business Research*, *61*(1), 56–64. doi:10.1016/j.jbusres.2006.05.009

Leigh, J., Lamont, M., & Cairncross, G. (2013). Towards a Process Model of Induction and Training for Young Event Volunteers. *International Journal of Event Management Research*, *8*(1), 1–20. www.ijemr.org

Lengnick-Hall, M. L., & Moritz, S. (2003). The impact of e-hr on the human resource management function. *Journal of Labor Research*, *24*(3), 365–379. doi:10.100712122-003-1001-6

Leonard, H. H. (2002). *Event marketing. how to successfully promote events, festivals, conventions and expositions* (Vol. J). Wiley.

Lepak, D. P., & Snell, S. A. (1998). Virtual hr: Strategic human resource management in the 21st century. *Human Resource Management Review*, *8*(3), 215–234. doi:10.1016/S1053-4822(98)90003-1

Leung, D., Law, R., Van Hoof, H., & Buhalis, D. (2013). Social media in tourism and hospitality: A literature review. *Journal of Travel & Tourism Marketing*, *30*(1-2), 3–22. doi:10.1080/10548408.2013.750919

Levine, J., Schutz, S., & Epstein, D. (2018). *Virtual and Augmented Reality: What Event Organizers must Know*. Retrieved from https://blog.bizzabo.com/virtual-and-augmented-reality-for-event-organizers

Li, D., & Yang, Y. (2017). GIS Monitoring of Traveler Flows Based on Big Data. In Analytics in Smart Tourism Design Concepts and Methods. (pp. 111-128). Springer. doi:10.1007/978-3-319-44263-1_7

Light, D. (1996). Characteristics of the audience for "events" at a heritage site. *Tourism Management*, *17*(3), 183–190. doi:10.1016/0261-5177(96)00005-2

linztourismus.at. (2019). *Ars Electronica Center*. Retrieved from https://www.linztourismus.at/en/leisure/discover-linz/museums-and-exhibitions/ars-electronica-center/. Access 15.09.2019

Lipton, J. I., Cutler, M., Nigl, F., Cohen, D., & Lipson, H. (2015). Additive manufacturing for the food industry. *Trends in Food Science & Technology*, *43*(1), 114–123. doi:10.1016/j.tifs.2015.02.004

Lipton, J., Arnold, D., Nigl, F., Lopez, N., Cohen, D. L., & Norén, N., & Lipson, H. (2010, August). Multi-material food printing with complex internal structure suitable for conventional post-processing. *Solid Freeform Fabrication Symposium*, 809-815.

Litvin, S. W., Goldsmith, R. E., & Pan, B. (2008). Electronic word-of-mouth in hospitality and tourism management. *Tourism Management*, *29*(3), 458–468. doi:10.1016/j.tourman.2007.05.011

Liu, C., Arnett, K. P., Capella, L. M., & Beatty, R. C. (1997). Web sites of the fortune 500 companies: Facing customers through home pages. *Information & Management*, *31*(1), 335–345. doi:10.1016/S0378-7206(97)00001-3

Liu, L., & Arnett, P. (2000). Exploring the factors associated with website success in the context of electronic commerce. *Information & Management*, *38*(1), 23–33. doi:10.1016/S0378-7206(00)00049-5

Liu, L., Zhang, J., & Keh, H. T. (2018). Event-marketing and advertising expenditures: The differential effects on brand value and company revenue. *Journal of Advertising Research*, *58*(4), 464–475. doi:10.2501/JAR-2017-043

Liu, Y. (2006). Word of mouth for movies: Its dynamics and impact on box office revenue. *Journal of Marketing*, *70*(3), 74–89. doi:10.1509/jmkg.70.3.074

Liu, Y., Liu, A., Liu, X., & Huang, X. (2019). A statistical approach to participant selection in location-based social networks for offline event marketing. *Information Sciences*, *480*, 90–108. doi:10.1016/j.ins.2018.12.028

Liu, Z., Zhang, M., Bhandari, B., & Yang, C. (2018). Impact of rheological properties of mashed potatoes on 3D printing. *Journal of Food Engineering*, *220*, 76–82. doi:10.1016/j.jfoodeng.2017.04.017

Li, X., & Duan, B. (2018). Organizational microblogging for event marketing: A new approach to creative placemaking. *International Journal of Urban Sciences*, *22*(1), 59–79. doi:10.1080/12265934.2017.1343155

Li, Y., & Liu, C. (2019). Applications of multirotor drone technologies in construction management. *International Journal of Construction Management*, *19*(5), 401–412. doi:10.1080/15623599.2018.1452101

Lockstone-Binny, L., & Ong, F. (2019). Event studies: Progression and future in the field. In S. Beeton & A. Morrison (Eds.), *The Study of Food, Tourism, Hospitality and Events* (pp. 37–46). Springer. doi:10.1007/978-981-13-0638-9_4

Lohse, G. L., & Spiller, P. (1998). Electronic Shopping. *Communications of the ACM*, *41*(7), 81–90. doi:10.1145/278476.278491

Lom, M., Pribyl, O., & Svitek, M. (2016, May). Industry 4.0 as a part of smart cities. In *2016 Smart Cities Symposium Prague (SCSP)* (pp. 1-6). IEEE. 10.1109/SCSP.2016.7501015

Lundmark, M. (1998). Lys upp marknaden med Event Marketing. *Sälj och marknadsstrategi, 8*, 50-57.

Luo, W. (2014). Germany industrial 4.0 strategic enlightenment to China's industrial transformation. *Fiber Reinforced Plastics/Composites*, 125-128.

Luttorp, E. (1997). Event marketing. *Ansikte Mot Ansikte Med Målgruppen,* 45-47.

Luty, J. (2020). *Direct spending in the events sector in the United Kingdom (UK) as of 2017, by event type*. Retrieved from Statista Web Sitesi: https://www.statista.com/statistics/426464/direct-spending-in-the-events-sector-in-the-united-kingdom/

Lyons, K. (2020). *A restaurant in the Netherlands is using creepy robot waiters for social distancing*. The Verge. Retrieved August 26, 2020, from https://www.theverge.com/2020/5/31/21276318/restaurant-netherlands-robot-waiters-social-distancing-pandemic

MacKay, K., Barbe, D., Van Winkle, C. M., & Halpenny, E. (2017). Social media activity in a festival context: Temporal and content analysis. *International Journal of Contemporary Hospitality Management, 29*(2), 669–689. doi:10.1108/IJCHM-10-2015-0618

Mackellar, J. (2008). Conventions, festivals and tourism. *Journal of Convention & Event Tourism, 8*(2), 45–56. doi:10.1300/J452v08n02_03

Macy, B., & Thompson, T. (2011). *The power of real-time social media marketing*. Mc Graw Hill Press.

Mair, J., & Weber, K. (2019). Editorial Event and festival research: A review and research directions. *International Journal of Event and Festival Management, 10*(3), 209–216. doi:10.1108/IJEFM-10-2019-080

Mair, J., & Whitford, M. (2013). An exploration of events research: Event topics, themes and emerging trends. *International Journal of Event and Festival Management, 4*(1), 6–30. doi:10.1108/17582951311307485

Malhotra, Y. (2001). *Enabling next generation e-business architectures: balancing integration and flexibility for managing business transformation.* Intel e-Strategy White Paper. www. brint. net/members/01060524/intelebusiness.pdf

Mallen, C. (2008). The concept of knowledge in event management. In C. Mallen & L. Adams (Eds.), Sport, Recreation and Tourism Event Management (pp. 9–24). Butterworth-Heinemann. doi:10.1016/B978-0-7506-8447-7.00002-X

Mamoudou, S. E. Y. N. I., & Joshi, G. P. (2014). Impact of ınformation technology in human resources management. *Global Journal of Business Management and Information Technology, 4*(1), 33–41.

Mangold, W. G., & Faulds, D. J. (2009). Social media: The new hybrid element of the promotion mix. *Business Horizons, 52*(4), 357–365. doi:10.1016/j.bushor.2009.03.002

Manners, B., Kruger, M., & Saayman, M. (2012). Managing the beautiful noise: Evidence from the Neil Diamond Show! *Journal of Convention & Event Tourism, 13*(2), 100–120. doi:10.1080/15470148.2012.679612

Marais, M. (2009). *Key success factors in managing the Wacky Wine Festival* (Unpublished doctoral dissertation). North-West University, Potchefstroom.

Maritz Global Events. (n.d.). *Evolving Trends in the Event Industry*. Retrieved from https://cdn2.hubspot.net/hubfs/2186839/trendswhitepaper11.17-1.pdf?t=1528340918401

Marshall, C. (2016). *Walk Inside a Surrealist Salvador Dalí Painting with This 360º Virtual Reality Video*. Retrieved from http://www.openculture.com/2016/02/walk-inside-a-salvador-dali-surrealist-painting-with-this-360o-virtua l-reality-video.html

Martensen, A., & Grønholdt, L. (2008). How events work: Understanding consumer responses to event marketing. *Innovative Marketing*, *4*(4), 44–56.

Martensen, A., Grønholdt, L., Bendtsen, L., & Jensen, M. J. (2007). Application of a model for the effectiveness of event marketing. *Journal of Advertising Research*, *47*(3), 283–301. doi:10.2501/S0021849907070316

Masiello, B., Bonetti, E., & Izzo, F. (2020). Multiple identities of a festival. *International Journal of Contemporary Hospitality Management, 32*(2), 749-768.

Mason, M. C., & Paggiaro, A. (2012). Investigating the role of festivalscape in culinary tourism: The case of food and wine events. *Tourism Management*, *33*(6), 1329–1336. doi:10.1016/j.tourman.2011.12.016

Masterman, G., & Wood, E. (2007). *Innovative marketing communications*. Routledge.

Masterman, G., & Wood, E. H. (2006). *Innovative marketing communications: Strategies for the events industry*. Elsevier Butterworth Heinemann.

Mathews, R., & Wacker, W. (2007). Senin hikayen ne? [What's your story?] (A. Özer, Trans.). İstanbul: MediaCat Press.

Mathwick, C., Malhotra, N., & Rigdon, E. (2001). Experiential value: Conceptualization, measurement and application in the catalog and internet shopping environment. *Journal of Retailing*, *77*(1), 39–56. doi:10.1016/S0022-4359(00)00045-2

Mayfield, A. (2020). *What is Social Media*. Retrieved from icrossing Web sitesi: https://www.icrossing.com/uk/sites/default/files_uk/insight_pdf_files/What%20is%20Social%20Media_iCrossing_ebook.pdf

McCarthy, J., Minsky, L. M., Rochester, N., & Shannon, E. C. (1955). *A Proposal for the Dartmouth Summer Research Project on Artificial Intelligence. August 31*. Retrieved February 1, 2020, from http://jmc.stanford.edu/articles/dartmouth/dartmouth.pdf

McCarthy, E. J. (1960). *Basic marketing: A managerial approach*. R.D. Irwin, Indiana University.

McDonnel, I., Allen, J., & O'Toole, W. (1998). *Festival and special event management*. John Wiley & Sons.

McDonnell, I., Allen, J., & O'Toole, W. (1999). *Festival and Special Event Management*. John Wiley and Sons.

McDowall, S. (2011). The festival in my hometown: The relationships among performance quality, satisfaction, and behavioral intentions. *International Journal of Hospitality & Tourism Administration*, *12*(4), 269–288. doi:10.1080/15256480.2011.614528

McDrury, J., & Alterio, M. (2001). Achieving reflective learning using storytelling pathways. *Innovations in Education and Teaching International*, *38*(1), 63–73. doi:10.1080/147032901300002864

Mediaclick. (2020). *İçerik Pazarlaması Nedir?* https://www.mediaclick.com.tr/tr/blog/icerik-pazarlamasi-nedir

Medium. (2018). *The 10 most tech-forward music festivals of 2018*. https://medium.com/singulardtv/the-10-most-tech-forward-music-festivals-of-2018-44a3189f33fe

Mehrotra, A., & Lobo, J. (2020). Technology Driving Event Management Industry to the Next Level. *8th International Conference on Reliability, Infocom Technologies and Optimization (Trends and Future Directions) (ICRITO)*. https://doi:10.1109/icrito48877.2020.9198025

Meisenzahl, M. (2020). *These $26 million robotic dolphins are coming to a Chinese aquarium soon and they look exactly like the real thing*. https://www.businessinsider.com/robot-dolphins-coming-to-chinese-aquarium-2020-7

Mert, Y. L. (2018). Dijital pazarlama ekseninde influencer marketing uygulamaları [Influencer marketing applications on the digital marketing axis]. *Gümüşhane Üniversitesi İletişim Fakültesi Elektronik Dergisi*, *6*(2), 1299–1328.

Meyer, E. (2014). *Tupac's hologram ushers change in live concerts*. https://roundup.brophyprep.org/index.php/2012/05/tupacs-hologram-ushers-change-in-live-concerts/

Miley, J. (2019). *German Circus Replaces Animals with Stunning Holograms*. https://interestingengineering.com/german-circus-replaces-animals-with-stunning-holograms

Milgrom, J. (2002). *Two decades of event marketing and sponsorship, I have good and bad news. In Event Marketing Strategies*. EMS.

MilkC. (2019). *Bio*. Retrieved from http://milk.co/bio

Miller, J. (2015). Case study; Exococand the future of storytelling. *Interaction*, (January- February), 30–47.

Miller, K. D., Fabian, F., & Lin, S.-J. (2009). Strategies for online communities. *Strategic Management Journal*, *30*(3), 305–322. doi:10.1002mj.735

Milman, A. (2010). The global theme park industry. *Worldwide Hospitality and Tourism Themes*, *2*(3), 220–237. doi:10.1108/17554211011052177

Mintel. (2013). Music festival tourism worldwide. *Travel and Tourism Analyst, 10*. London: Mintel Group Ltd.

Mobil Pazarlama Nedir? (n.d.). https://www.dijitalfakulte.com/mobil-pazarlama-nedir/

Moise, D., & Cruceru, A. F. (2014). An empirical study of promoting different kinds of events through various social media networks websites. *Procedia: Social and Behavioral Sciences*, *109*, 98–102. doi:10.1016/j.sbspro.2013.12.426

Moliner, M., Sanchez, J., Rodriguez, R. M., & Callarisa, L. (2007). Relationship quality with a travel agency: The influence of the post-purchased perceived value of a tourism package. *Tourism and Hospitality Research*, *7*(3/4), 194–211. doi:10.1057/palgrave.thr.6050052

Moon, M., & Millison, D. (2003). Ateşten markalar [Fiery Brands] (Ş. T. Kalkay, Trans.). İstanbul: MediaCat Press.

Morarji, B., & Sharma, V. N. (2015). A study on job stress in event management organizations with reference to Thrissur District, Kerala. *International Journal of Advanced Research*, *7*(4), 51–58.

Morgan, M. (2008). What makes a good festival? Understanding the event experience. *Event Management*, *12*(2), 81–93. doi:10.3727/152599509787992562

Morozova, A. (2020). *How event organizers can apply virtual reality in the event industry*. https://jasoren.com/how-event-organizers-can-apply-virtual-reality-in-the-event-industry/

Morph.ai. (2020). *Events. Create a Chatbot for Your Event in Minutes without Coding*. Retrieved July 23, 2020 https://morph.ai/events

Mount, J., & Niro, B. (1995). Sponsorship: An empirical study of its application to local business in a small town setting. *Festival Management & Event Tourism*, *2*(3-4), 167–175. doi:10.3727/106527095792315576

Mucuk, İ. (2010). *Pazarlama İlkeleri*. Türkmen Kitabevi.

Mucuk, İ. (2012). *Pazarlama ilkeleri [Marketing principles]*. Türkmen Kitapevi.

Mulhern, F. (2009). Integrated marketing communications: From media channels to digital connectivity. *Journal of Marketing Communications*, *15*(2-3), 85–101. doi:10.1080/13527260902757506

Müller, M. (2015a). What makes an event a mega-event? Definitions and sizes. *Leisure Studies*, *34*(6), 627–642. doi:10.1080/02614367.2014.993333

Müller, M. (2015b). The mega-event syndrome: Why so much goes wrong in mega-event planning and what to do about it. *Journal of the American Planning Association*, *81*(1), 6–17. doi:10.1080/01944363.2015.1038292

Munar, A. M., & Jacobsen, J. K. S. (2014). Motivations for sharing tourism experiences through social media. *Tourism Management*, *43*, 46–54. doi:10.1016/j.tourman.2014.01.012

Murphy, J., Hofacker, C., & Gretzel, U. (2017). Dawning of the age of robots in hospitality and tourism: Challenges for teaching and research. *European Journal of Tourism Research*, *11*, 104–111.

Murphy, P. E., & Carmichael, B. A. (1991). Assesing the tourism benefits of an open access sports tournament: The 1989 B. C. Winter Games. *Journal of Travel Research*, *29*(32), 32–36. doi:10.1177/004728759102900305

Murphy, S. V., & Atala, A. (2014). 3D bioprinting of tissues and organs. *Nature Biotechnology*, *32*(8), 773–785. doi:10.1038/nbt.2958 PMID:25093879

Muskat, B., & Mair, J. (2019). Knowledge Sharing and Power in the Event Workforce. *Event Management*. Advance online publication. doi:10.3727/152599519X15506259856228

Mutch, A. (1995). IT and small tourism enterprises: A case study of cottage-letting agencies. *Tourism Management*, *16*(7), 533–539. doi:10.1016/0261-5177(95)00056-T

Myers, B. (2020). *What self-service technology means for the future of events*. https://pheedloop.com/blog/self-service-technology-the-future-of-events

Nagasawa, S. (2008). Customer experience management influencing on human kansei to management of technology. *The TQM Journal*, *20*(4), 312–323. doi:10.1108/17542730810881302

Nardi, B. A., Schiano, D. J., & Gumbrecht, M. (2004). Blogging as social activity, or, would you let 900 million people read your diary? CSCW'04, 222-231.

Nayyar, A., Mahapatra, B., Le, D. N., &Suseendran, G. (2018). Virtual Reality (VR) & Augmented Reality (AR) technologies for tourism and hospitality industry. *International Journal of Engineering & Technology, 7*(2.21), 156-160.

Ndou, V. (2004). E–Government for developing countries: Opportunities and challenges. *The Electronic Journal on Information Systems in Developing Countries*, *18*(1), 1–24. doi:10.1002/j.1681-4835.2004.tb00117.x

Neirotti, L. D., Bosetti, H. A., & Teed, K. C. (2001). Motivation to attend the 1996 Summer Olympic Games. *Journal of Travel Research*, *39*(3), 327–331. doi:10.1177/004728750103900315

Nenwani, P. J., & Raj, M. D. (2013). E-hrmprospective in present scenario. *International Journal (Toronto, Ont.)*, *1*(7).

Neuhofer, B., Buhalis, D., & Ladkin, A. (2014). A typology of technology-enhanced tourism experiences. *International Journal of Tourism Research*, *16*(4), 340–350. doi:10.1002/jtr.1958

Neuhofer, B., Magnus, B., & Celuch, K. (2020). The Impact of Artificial Intelligence on Event Experiences: A Scenario Technique Approach. *Electronic Markets*. Advance online publication. doi:10.100712525-020-00433-4

Ngernyuang, K., & Wu, P. (2020). Using Social Media as A Tool for Promoting Festival Tourism. *International Journal of Computer Science & Information Technology*, *12*(3), 17–32. doi:10.5121/ijcsit.2020.12302

Nguyen, C. (2016). *Restaurants in China are replacing waiters with robots*. Retrieved August 26, 2020, from https://www.businessinsider.com/chinese-restaurant-robot-waiters-2016-7

Nicholson, R., & Pearce, D. G. (2000). Who goes to events: A comparative analysis of the profile characteristics of visitors to four South Island events in New Zealand. *Journal of Vacation Marketing*, *6*(3), 236–253. doi:10.1177/135676670000600304

Nicoletti, B. (2018). The Future: Procurement 4.0. In Agile Procurement (pp. 189–230). doi:10.1007/978-3-319-61085-6_8

Nilbe, K., Ahas, R., & Silm, S. (2014). Evaluating the Travel Distances of Events Visitors and Regular Visitors Using Mobile Positioning Data: The Case of Estonia. *Journal of Urban Technology*, *21*(2), 91–107. doi:10.1080/10630732.2014.888218

Nisancioglu, B. (2020). *Coachella Highlights: Tupac Hologram in 2012*. https://festileaks.com/2020/04/coachella-highlights-tupac-hologram-in-2012/

Novak, M. (2017). *Robots and Event Planning*. Retrieved February 22, 2020, from https://www.seebtm.com/en/robots-and-event-planning/

NTV. (2015). *Konya'daki bu kafede çay servisini robot yapıyor*. Retrieved August 25, 2020, from https://www.ntv.com.tr/teknoloji/caylar-robot-adadan,qa4oUOCklUGMjOeuU4Q6Sw

O'Connor, E., & Domingo, J. (2017). A Practical Guide, With Theoretical Underpinnings, for Creating Effective Virtual Reality Learning Environments. *Journal of Educational Technology Systems*, *45*(3), 343–364. doi:10.1177/0047239516673361

Obe, M. (2018). *Business trends*. Retrieved August 2, 2020, from https://asia.nikkei.com/Business/Business-trends/Nestle-serves-up-robots-in-Japan-to-woo-Chinese-customers

Odabaşı, Y., & Oyman, M. (2002). *Pazarlama iletişimi yönetimi [Marketing communication management]*. Mediacat Kitapları.

Ogle, A., & Lamb, D. (2019). The Role of Robots, Artificial Intelligence, and Service Automation in Events. In S. Ivanov & C. Webster (Eds.), *Robots, Artificial Intelligence, and Service Automation in Travel, Tourism and Hospitality* (pp. 255–269). Emerald Publishing Limited. doi:10.1108/978-1-78756-687-320191012

Okay, H. (2017). Helikopter Bakışı. [https://www.dunya.com/kose-yazisi/deneyimsel-pazarlama/345266]. Access date: January, 2020.

Öksüz, B. (2012). E-İşe Alım Sürecinde Kurumsal Web Sitelerinin Kullanımı ve Konu Üzerine Bir Araştırma. *Uluslararası Yönetim İktisat ve İşletme Dergisi*, *7*(14), 267–283.

Oliver, R. W., Roland, T. R., & Sanjeev, V. (1998). Real-time marketing. *Marketing Management*, *7*(Fall), 28–37.

Ong, T. (2017). *YuMi the robot makes debut as orchestra conductor in Italy*. https://www.theverge.com/2017/9/14/16306528/yumi-robot-abb-debut-orchestra-conductor-italy

Onishi, H., & Manchanda, P. (2012). Marketing activity, blogging and sales. *International Journal of Research in Marketing*, *29*(3), 221–234. doi:10.1016/j.ijresmar.2011.11.003

Ozawa, T., Sekiguchi, A., & Tsuda, K. (2017). A method for the construction of customer behavioral modeling knowledge for B2B event marketing strategy. *Procedia Computer Science*, *112*, 1353–1360. doi:10.1016/j.procs.2017.08.027

Özçit, H. (2015). *The implementation of content marketing in the hotel industry: The example of hotels in İstanbul* (Unpublished Master's Thesis). İstanbul University, İstanbul.

Özdemir, G., & Çulha, O. (2009). Satisfaction and loyalty of festival visitors. *Anatolia*, *20*(2), 359–373. doi:10.1080/13032917.2009.10518914

Özel, C., & Uluyol, Ç. (2016). Development of an augmented reality application and students' opinions. *Turkish Journal of Social Research.*, *20*(3), 793–823.

Özgen, E., & Doymuş, H. (2013). A communicational approach to content management concepts as a differentiating factor in social media marketing. *Online Academic Journal of Information Technology*, *4*(11), 91–103.

Özgüner Kılıç, H. (2017). Giyilebilir Teknoloji Ürünleri Pazarı ve Kullanım Alanları [Wearable Technology Products Market and Usage Areas]. *Aksaray Üniversitesi İİBF Dergisi*, *9*(4), 99–112.

Özgüneş, R. E., & Bozok, D. (2017). Turizm sektörünün sanal rakibi(mi?): Arttırılmış gerçeklik. *Uluslararası Türk Dünyası Turizm Araştırmaları Dergisi*, *2*(2), 146–160.

Özsoylu, A. F. (2017). Endüstri 4.0. *Çukurova Üniversitesi İktisadi ve İdari Bilimler Fakültesi Dergisi*, *21*(1), 41-64.

Öztel, T., & Öymen, G. (2019). Duygusal pazarlamada slogan kullanımının önemi: Pandora reklamları üzerine bir inceleme [The importance of using slogans in emotional marketing: A review on Pandora ads]. *Halkla İlişkiler ve Reklam Çalışmaları E-Dergisi*, *2*(2), 31–53.

Pallottino, F., Hakola, L., Costa, C., Antonucci, F., Figorilli, S., Seisto, A., & Menesatti, P. (2016). Printing on food or food printing: A review. *Food and Bioprocess Technology*, *9*(5), 725–733. Advance online publication. doi:10.100711947-016-1692-3

Pamukçu, H., & Tanrısever, C. Y. (2019). Turizm Endüstrisinde Dijital Dönüşüm. In Turizm 4.0 Dijital Dönüşüm (pp. 2-29). Ankara: Detay Yayıncılık.

Parent, M. (2008). Evolution and Issue Patterns for Major-Sport-Event Organizing Committees and Their Stakeholders. *Journal of Sport Management*, *22*(2), 135–164. doi:10.1123/jsm.22.2.135

Paris, C. M., Lee, W., & Seery, P. (2010). The role of social media in promoting special events: acceptance of Facebook 'events. In ENTER2010 eTourism Conference, Lugano, Switzerland.

Paris, C. M., Lee, W., & Seery, P. (2010). *The Role of Social Media in Promoting Special Events: Acceptance of Facebook 'Events'. In Information and Communication Technologies in Tourism 2010* (pp. 531-541). Lugano: Springer-Verlag/Wien.

Park, C. H., & Kim, Y. G. (2003). Identifying key factors affecting consumer purchase behavior in an online shopping context. *International Journal of Retail & Distribution Management*, *31*(1), 16–29. doi:10.1108/09590550310457818

Parker, R. (2018). *Internet of things in events: What's in it for event planners.* https://readwrite.com/2018/03/18/internet-things-events-whats-event-planners/?__cf_chl_jschl_tk__=88d032fbae466d085c6f3c21bd4605f8c266fe93-1597857303-0-AZAJqw3s2ph3LFX-mKqK85rPsPPSJsypJ9ESxGWN_UeYGr5BGpSV8Bvv7dbF1iLj7eLe4t-Fk5hfihM32ASFe_T7qpyTScMQ8KFjl8_AOgCHGy1HcJZVkTTP-b5QWaVoOdH4XHPHhYeBNgX4cTBhTV-lxJGFZHBLhJAX3k3V5oCApoN_wEgwVF0BImeTZhMko3PY96d45RPXEIQW9AuDtsETWHQc_yH9Z3BY3aEx-5ZU5Q_TGpE_TBTj0lZrmaCn7UVf3vtnfrMG02UFFh27l_yZslI18Q4kl7YcDez6Ug6HIghGmeVROpCQHKzD1l6TY-I21mcxjoHZz3r3e6Pqdj2e9LVsWDucEk1RH1R7laj4mk3IA3rzTkoaw9Lb4yuyfQsW0cWwm9hxQDkeEXIFNmq81FY

Park, K., & Park, S. (2016). Topic trend of event management research. *Event Management*, *20*(1), 109–115. doi:10.3727/152599516X14538326024991

Parra-López, E., Bulchand-Gidumal, J., Gutiérrez-Taño, D., & Díaz-Armas, R. (2011). Intentions to use social media in organizing and taking vacation trips. *Computers in Human Behavior*, *27*(2), 640–654. doi:10.1016/j.chb.2010.05.022

Pavlik, J. V., & Bridges, F. (2013). The emergence of augmented reality (AR) as a storytelling medium in journalism. *Journalism & Communication Monographs, 15*(1), 4–59. doi:10.1177/1522637912470819

Peltz, P., Junek, O., & De Ross, J. (2018). Virtual Reality: The white knight of festival management education? In J. Mair (Ed.), *The Routledge Handbook of Festivals* (pp. 397–405). Routledge.

Peng, T. (2018). *China's Lunar New Year's Gala wowed Watchers with AI Innovations*. https://syncedreview.com/2018/02/16/chinas-lunar-new-years-gala-wowed-watchers-with-ai-innovations/

Penpece, D. (2013). *Dijital içerik pazarlaması [Digital content marketing]*. Karahan Kitabevi.

Periard, D., Schaal, N., Schaal, M., Malone, E., & Lipson, H. (2007). Printing food. *Proceedings of the 18th solid free-form fabrication symposium*, 564-574.

Petkov, A. (2019). *A robot plays Jenga, physics enters the graphic novel, and London hosts a chemistry festival*. https://physicsworld.com/a/a-robot-plays-jenga-physics-enters-the-graphic-novel-and-london-hosts-a-chemistry-festival/

Phua, J., Jin, S. V., & Kim, J. (2017). Gratifications of using facebook, twitter, instagram, or snapchat to follow brands: The moderating effect of social comparison, trust, tie strength, and network homophily on brand identification, brand engagement, brand commitment, and membership intention. *Telematics and Informatics, 34*(1), 412–424. doi:10.1016/j.tele.2016.06.004

Pickton, D., & Broderick, A. (2005). *Integrated marketing communications*. Pearson Education Limited.

Pimental, K., & Teixeira, K. (1993). *Virtual reality through the new looking glass* (2nd ed.). McGraw-Hill.

Pine, B. J., Pine, J., & Gilmore, J. H. (1999). *The experience economy: work is theatre & every business a stage*. Harvard Business Press.

Pine, B. J., Pine, J., & Gilmore, J. H. (1999). *The experience economy: Work is theatre & every business a stage*. Harvard Business Press.

Piñeiro-Oter, T., & Martínez-Rolán, X. (2016). *Understanding digital marketing-basics and actions*. Springer. doi:10.1007/978-3-319-28281-7_2

Pinillos, R., Marcos, S., Feliz, R., Zalama, E., & Bermejo, G. G. J. (2016). Long-term Assessment of a Service Robot in a Hotel Environment. *Robotics and Autonomous Systems, 79*, 40–57. doi:10.1016/j.robot.2016.01.014

Pinker, A. (2017). *Virtual Reality in Event Management*. Retrieved from https://medialist.info/en/2017/10/17/virtual-reality-in-event-management/

Pino, G., Peluso, A. M., Del Vecchio, P., Ndou, V., Passiante, G., & Guido, G. (2019). A methodological framework to assess social media strategies of event and destination management organizations. *Journal of Hospitality Marketing & Management, 28*(2), 189–216. doi:10.1080/19368623.2018.1516590

Pira, A. (2004). *Etkinlik yönetimi*. MediaCat Yayıncılık.

Pitman, L. (2019). *Internet of Things – the Newest Wrinkle in Event Management*. Retrieved from https://datafloq.com/read/internet-of-things-newest-wrinkle-event-management/6431

Pope, N. K., & Voges, K. E. (2000). The Impact of Sport Sponsorship Activities, Corporate Image, and Prior Use on Consumer Purchase Intention. *Sport Marketing Quarterly, 9*(2), 96–102.

Potter, B. (2018). *The Impact of Social Media on Meetings and Events*. Retrieved from Mpi Web site: https://www.mpi.org/blog/article/the-impact-of-social-media-on-meetings-and-events

Powell, M. (2016). *IoT in action...at a music festival.* https://www.plant.ca/insights/162614/

Preston, C. (2012). *How to Successfully Promote Events, Festivals, Conventions, and Expositions.* Wiley Press.

Pulizzi, J., & Barrett, N. (2009). *Get content- Get customers.* McGraw Hill.

Purves, T. (2005). *What We Want Is Free.* State University of New York Press.

Rajesh, R. (2014). Issues and Trends of Event Tourism Promotion in destination Puducherry- An Empirical Study. *International Journal of Safety and Security in Tourism, 6,* 25–41.

Raj, R., & Musgrave, J. (2009). *Event management and sustainability.* CABI. doi:10.1079/9781845935245.0000

Ravald, A., & Gronoos, C. (1996). The value concept and relationship marketing. *European Journal of Marketing, 30*(2), 19–30. doi:10.1108/03090569610106626

Rayna, T., & Striukova, L. (2016). From rapid prototyping to home fabrication: How 3D printing is changing business model innovation. *Technological Forecasting and Social Change, 102,* 214–224. doi:10.1016/j.techfore.2015.07.023

Regalix Research. (2019). *Event Marketing.* Retrieved from https://www.regalix.com/wp-content/uploads/2019/05/CMO_Guide_Event_Marketing_2019.pdf

Reid, S., & Ritchie, B. (2011). Risk management: Event managers' attitudes, beliefs, and perceived constraints. *Event Management, 15*(4), 329–341. doi:10.3727/152599511X13175676722528

Restaurants, F. (2019). *Bareburger's augmented reality strategy: AR menus.* Retrieved May 1, 2020, from https://restaurants.wbresearch.com/blog/bareburger-augmented-reality-technology-strategy-to-menus

Rheingold, H. (1993). *The virtual community: Homestanding on the electronic frontier.* Harper Collins.

Richards, G., & Palmer, R. (2010). *Eventful cities: Cultural management and urban revitalization.* Butterworth-Heinemann.

Richards, G., & Wilson, J. (2004). The impact of cultural events on city image: Rotterdam, Cultural Capital of Europe 2001. *Urban Studies (Edinburgh, Scotland), 41*(10), 1931–1951. doi:10.1080/0042098042000256323

Rigby, B. (2008). *Mobilizing generation 2.0: A practical guide to using web 2.0 technologies to recruit, organize, and engage youth.* Jossey-Bass.

Ritchie, J. R. B. (1984). Assessing the impact of hallmark events: Conceptual and research issues. *Journal of Travel Research, 23*(1), 2–11. doi:10.1177/004728758402300101

Ritchie, J. R. B., & Beliveau, D. (1974). The impact of a mega-event on host region awareness: A longitudinal study. *Journal of Travel Research, 13*(2), 14–20. doi:10.1177/004728757401300202

Robakowska, M., Tyranska-Fobke, A., Nowak, J., Slezak, D., Zuratynski, P., Robakowski, P., Nadolny, K., & Ładny, J. R. (2017). The Use of Drones during Mass Events. *Disaster and Emergency Medicine Journal, 2*(3), 129–134. doi:10.5603/DEMJ.2017.0028

Robbins, S. S., & Stylianou, A. C. (2003). Global corporate web sites: An empirical ınvestigation of content and design. *Information & Management, 40*(1), 205–212. doi:10.1016/S0378-7206(02)00002-2

Robertson, M., Hutton, A., & Brown, S. (2018). Event design in outdoor music festival audience behavior (A critical transformative research note). *Event Management, 22*(6), 1073–1081. doi:10.3727/152599518X15346132863157

Robertson, M., Yeoman, I., Smith, K. A., & Mcmahon-Beattie, U. (2015). Technology, society, and visioning the future of music festivals. *Event Management, 19*(4), 567–587. doi:10.3727/152599515X14465748774001

Roblek, V., Meško, M., & Krapež, A. (2016). A complex view of industry 4.0. *Sage Open, 6*(2), 1-11.

Robotex. (2019). *Event information.* https://robotex.international/information/

Robotfilmfestival. (2019). *Robot film festival.* http://robotfilmfestival.com/

Rodrigues, P., & Brandao, A. (2017). Sports events in the attitude toward the brand: Involvement and emotıons of consumer. In *5th International Consumer Brand Relationships Conference*. University of Porto.

Rogers, T., & Davidson, R. (2006). *Marketing destinations and venues for conferences, conventions and business events.* Butterworth-Heinemann. Routledge.

Roig, E. M., Fuentes, E. M., & Ramon, N. D. (2017). User-Generated Social Media Events in Tourism. *Sustainability*, 1–23.

Rojko, A. (2017). Industry 4.0 concept: Background and overview. *International Journal of Interactive Mobile Technologies, 11*(5), 77–90. doi:10.3991/ijim.v11i5.7072

Romm, C., & Plinskin, N. (1997). Virtual communities and society: Toward an integrative three phase model. *International Journal of Information Management, 17*(4), 261–270. doi:10.1016/S0268-4012(97)00004-2

Rosete, A., Soares, B., Salvadorinho, J., Reis, J., & Amorim, M. (2020). Service robots in the hospitality industry: An exploratory literature review. In H. Nóvoa, M. Drăgoicea, & N. Kühl (Eds.), *Exploring Service Science. IESS 2020. Lecture Notes in Business Information Processing, 377.* Springer. doi:10.1007/978-3-030-38724-2_13

Rozgonyi, B. (2019). *New Social Media Rules for Engaging Event Design.* Retrieved from Mpi.org web site: https://www.mpi.org/chapters/chicago-area/chapter-news/single-blog/c-c-articles/2019/08/06/new-social-media-rules-for-engaging-event-design

Ruël, H., Bondarouk, T., & Looise, J. K. (2004). E-hrm: Innovation or irritation. An explorative empirical study in five large companies on web-based hrm. *Management Review*, 364–380.

Ruël, H., Magalhães, R., & Chiemeke, C. C. (2011). *Human resource ınformation systems: an ıntegrated research agenda. In electronic hrm in theory and practice.* Emerald Group Publishing Limited.

Ryan, D. (2016). *Dijital pazarlama: Dijital kuşağa seslenmek için pazarlama stratejileri [Digital marketing: Marketing strategies to address the digital generation]* (M. M. Kemaloğlu, Trans.). Türkiye İş Bankası Kültür Yayınları.

Saayman, M., Kruger, M., & Erasmus, J. (2012). Finding the key to success: A visitors' perspective at a National Arts Festival. *Acta Commercii, 12*(1), 150–172. doi:10.4102/ac.v12i1.142

Sabuncuoğlu, Z., & Gümüş, M. (2008). *Örgütlerde iletişim.* Arıkan Publishing.

Safko, L. (2010). *The social media bible: tactics, tools, and strategies for business success.* John Wiley & Sons.

Saget, A. (2006). *The Event Marketing Handbook.* Dearborn Trade.

Saget, A. (2006). *The event marketing handbook: beyond logistics and planning.* Kaplan Publishing.

Sağlamtimur, Z. Ö. (2010). Dijital Sanat. *Anadolu Üniversitesi Sosyal Bilimler, 10*(3), 213–238.

Sağlamtimur, Z., Ö. (2017). Yeni Medya Sanatı ve Fotoğraf. *Anadolu Üniversitesi Sanat & Tasarım Dergisi, 7*(2).

Saldamlı, A. (2008). İnsan Kaynakları Yönetiminde Bilişim Teknolojisinin Kullanımına Yönelik Bir Araştırma. *Tekirdağ Örneği, İstanbul Ticaret Üniversitesi Sosyal Bilimler Dergisi, 7*(13), 239–263.

Saleh, F., & Ryan, C. (1993). Jazz and knitwear: Factors that attract tourists to festivals. *Tourism Management, 14*(4), 289–297. doi:10.1016/0261-5177(93)90063-Q

Sample, I. (2019). *What is Facial Recognition – and How Sinister is it?* https://www.theguardian.com/technology/2019/jul/29/what-is-facial-recognition-and-how-sinister-is-it

Sanay, G. Y. (2017). *Current approaches in electronic tourism marketing and analysis of the effects of social media on tourists' destination selection* (Unpublished Master's Thesis). Haliç University, Istanbul.

Saravanakumar, M., & Suganthalakshmi, T. (2012). Social media marketing. *Life Science Journal, 9*(4), 4444–4451.

Sarıtaş, A. (2018). İçerik pazarlamasına yönelik bir literatür taraması [A literature review on content marketing]. *Sosyal Araştırmalar ve Davranış Bilimleri Dergisi, 4*(6), 232–239.

Sari, Y., & Kozak, M. (2005). Turizm pazarlamasına internetin etkisi: Destinasyon web siteleri için bir model önerisi. *Akdeniz İİ BF Dergisi, 9*, 248–271.

Saruhan, O. (2018). Sosyal medya canavarı olmak ister misin? [Do you want to be a social media monster?]. İstanbul: MediaCat Press.

Saxena, P. (2016). *The advantages and disadvantages of Internet of Things.* https://e27.co/advantages-disadvantages-internet-things-20160615/

Saylı, H., & Kızıldağ, D. (2007). Yönetsel Etik Ve Yönetsel Etiğin Oluşmasında İnsan Kaynakları Yönetiminin Rolünü Belirlemeye Yönelik Bir Analiz. *Afyon Kocatepe Üniversitesi Sosyal Bilimler Dergisi, 9*(1), 231–251.

Schachter, H. (n.d.). *20 Killer Exanples of Influencer Marketing.* Retrieved from: https://www.travelmindset.com/20-influencer-marketing-examples/

Scharl, A., Wober, W. K., & Bauer, C. (2004). An ıntegrated approach to measure web site effectiveness in the European hotel ındustry. *Information Technology & Tourism, 6*(1), 257–271.

Schatz, L. (2019). *Roy Orbison and Buddy Holly holograms are going on tour together.* https://consequenceofsound.net/2019/03/roy-orbison-buddy-holly-hologram-rock-roll-dream-tour-dates/

Schikowitz, A. (2020). Creating relevant knowledge in transdisciplinary research projects – Coping with inherent tensions. *Journal of Responsible Innovation, 7*(2), 217-237.

Schmidt, R. (2020). *What is Facedeals?* http://shebytes.com/what-is-facedeals/#:~:text=Facedeals%20is%20a%20face%2Drecognition,sends%20you%20a%20customized%20deal.&text=Facedeals%2C%20which%20is%20a%20retail,connects%20data%20from%20social%20networks

Schmitt, B. H. (1999). *Experiential marketing.* The Free Press.

Schmitt, B. H. (1999). *Experiential Marketing.* The Free Press.

Schmitt, B. H. (1999). *Experiential Marketing: How to Get Customers to Sense. Feel, Think, Act, and Relate to Your Company and Brands.* The Free Press.

Schmitt, B. H. (2003). *Competitive advantage through the customer experience.* The EX Group.

Scott, D. M. (2009). *The new rules of marketing and PR: how to use social media, blogs, news releases, online video, and viral marketing to reach buyers directly.* John Wiley & Sons.

Scott, D. M. (2011). *Gerçek zamanlı pazarlama ve halkla ilişkiler [Real time marketing and public relations]* (A. Özer, Trans.). MediaCat Press.

Scott, S. V., & Orlikowski, W. J. (2012). Reconfiguring relations of accountability: Materialization of social media in the travel sector. *Accounting, Organizations and Society, 37*(1), 26–40. doi:10.1016/j.aos.2011.11.005

Selvan, V. T. (2015). Study on role of technology in human resource management. *International Journal Of Applied Research, 1*(7), 472–475.

Şener, S. (2019). *Yapay Zeka, Makine Öğrenimi ve Derin Öğrenme Arasındaki Farklar.* Retrieved February 22, 2020, from https://www. endustri40.com/yapay-zeka-makine-ogrenimi-ve-derin-ogrenme-arasindaki-farklar/

Şengel, Ü., Zengin, B., Şengel, T., & Işkın, M. (2017). Kongre ve fuar organizasyonlarının turizm sektörüne etkileri: EMITT örneği. *Turizm ve Araştırma Dergisi, 7*(1), 4–20.

Sertalp, E. (2017). Müzelerin tanıtım kitaplarında artırılmış gerçeklik (ag) teknolojisi kullanımı: Ankara Anadolu Medeniyetleri Müzesi kitabı örneği [The use of augmented reality (ag) technology in the promotional books of museums: An example of the Ankara Anatolian Civilizations Museum book]. *Hacettepe Üniversitesi Güzel Sanatlar Fakültesi Sanat Yazıları, 36*(May), 107–120.

Severini, C., Derossi, A., & Azzollini, D. (2016). Variables affecting the printability of foods: Preliminary tests on cereal-based products. *Innovative Food Science & Emerging Technologies, 38*, 281–291. doi:10.1016/j.ifset.2016.10.001

Severt, K., Fjelstul, J., & Breiter, D. (2013). Information Communication Technologies: Usages and Preferences of Generation Y Students and Meeting Professionals. *Journal of Convention & Event Tourism, 14*(2), 124–143. doi:10.1080/15470148.2013.781487

Seyfi, M. (2017). *Halkla ilişkiler perspektifinde dijital etkinlik yönetimi.* Der Yayınları.

Sezer, A. A., & Bröchner, J. (2019). Site managers' ICT tools for monitoring resources in refurbishment. *Engineering, Construction, and Architectural Management, 27*(1), 109–127. doi:10.1108/ECAM-02-2018-0074

Sezgin, S. (2016). Eğitimde Giyilebilir Teknolojiler: Fırsatlar ve Eğilimler [Wearable Technologies in Education: Opportunities and Trends]. *Mehmet Akif Ersoy Üniversitesi Eğitim Fakültesi Dergisi, 40*, 405–418.

Sharp, B., & Wind, Y. J. (2009). Today's Advertising Laws: Will They Survive the Digital Revolution? *Journal of Advertising Research, 49*(2), 120–126. doi:10.2501/S002184990909014X

Shaw, T. (2019). *23 Event Marketing Statistics You Need to Know.* https://www.aventri.com/blog/23-event-marketing-statistics-you-need-to-know#:~:text=Engagement%20and%20Event%20Tech&text=An%20overwhelming%20majority%20of%20event,the%20success%20of%20their%20events.&text=90%25%20of%20event%20technology%20adopters,65%25%20of%20non%2Dadopters

Shaw, T. (2019). *How Social Media is Appealing to the Events Industry.* Retrieved from https://www.aventri.com/blog/how-social-media-is-appealing-to-the-events-industry

Sherlock, J., & O'Connor, N. (2015). Research into the Impact of Technology in the Events Industry. *International Hospitality and Tourism Student Journal, 7*(1), 88–102.

Shih, C. (2009). *The Facebook Era: Tapping Online Social Networks to Build Better Products, Reach New Audiences, and Sell More Stuff.* Prentice Hall Direct.

Shim, J., Avital, M., Dennis, A. R., Sheng, O., Rossi, M., & Sørensen, C. (2017). Internet of things: Opportunities and challenges to business, society, and is research. *Proceedings of the 38th International Conference on Information Systems.*

Shone, A., & Parry, B. (2004). *Successful event management: a practical handbook.* Cengage Learning EMEA.

Silvers, J. R. (2009). *Risk management for meetings and events.* Routledge.

Silvers, J. R. (2012). *Professional event coordination* (Vol. 62). John Wiley & Sons.

Singh, S., & Diamond, S. (2012). Social media marketing for dummies (2nd ed.). John Wiley and Sons, Inc.

Sitapara, J. (2017). *8 Event Technologies Every Organiser must Embrace.* https://medium.com/hubilo-officil-blog/8-technologies-all-event-planners-must-embrace-2910b1371ebf

Smart Hotel Technology Guide (2018). *Using technology to navigate the guest experience journey.* https://sha.org.sg/userfiles/ckeditor/Files/Smart%20Hotel%20Technology%20Guide%202018.pdf

Smilansky, S. (2009). *Experiential marketing: A practical guide to interactive brand experiences.* Kogan Page Publishers.

Smith, A. (2008). *Using major events to promote peripheral urban areas: Deptford and the 2007 Tour de France. In International perspectives of festivals and events: Paradigms of analysis.* Elseveir.

Smith, A. (2012). *Events and urban regeneration: The strategic use of events to revitalise cities.* Routledge. doi:10.4324/9780203136997

Smith, J. B., & Colgate, M. (2007). Customer value creation: A practical framework. *Journal of Marketing Theory and Practice*, *15*(1), 7–23. doi:10.2753/MTP1069-6679150101

Smith, W. A. (2006). Social marketing: An overview of approach and effects. *Injury Prevention*, *12*(1, suppl_1), 38–43. doi:10.1136/ip.2006.012864 PMID:16788110

Sneath, J. Z., Finney, R. Z., & Close, A. G. (2005). An IMC approach to event marketing: The effects of sponsorship and experience on customer attitudes. *Journal of Advertising Research*, *45*(4), 373–381. doi:10.1017/S0021849905050440

Social Tables. (2020). *15 Tactics to Sell More Event Tickets Today.* Retrieved from Socialtables web site: https://www.socialtables.com/blog/social-media/drive-event-ticket-sales/

Soft, A. (2019). *Mini Ada Expertika Açılış Organizasyonunda* [Mini Ada at the opening ceremony of Expertika]. https://www.akinsoft.com.tr/medya-merkezi/request.php?q=mini-ada-expertika-acilis-organizasyonunda-7097

Softjourn. (2020). *How to Elevate your Event with Augmented Reality.* https://softjourn.com/insights/how-to-elevate-your-event-with-augmented-reality

Sohn, D. (2005). *Interactive media and social exchange of market information* (Unpublished doctoral dissertation). The University of Texas.

Solaris, J. (2018). *Social Media For Events (2019 Edition): A Complete Guide To Marketing Your Events Using Social Media.* https://www.eventmanagerblog.com/social-media-events

Solaris, J. (2020). *10 events trend for 2020.* Retrieved from eventmanagerblog web site: https://www.eventmanagerblog.com/10-event-trends

Solaris, J. (2020). *Event Technology: Trends and Strategy for 2020.* https://www.eventmanagerblog.com/event-technology

Solutions, S. M. A. C. A. R. (2018). *Augmented reality case study for restaurants.*Retrieved February 15, 2020, from https://smacar.com/augmented-reality-case-study-restaurants-case-study-restaurants/

Song, H., & Liu, H. (2017). Predicting Tourist Demand Using Big Data. In Analytics in Smart Tourism Design Concepts and Methods. (pp. 13-30). Springer. doi:10.1007/978-3-319-44263-1_2

Sönmez, H. (2020). *Proposal of a common tourism portal model in Turkic World countries* (Unpublished Master's Thesis). Kastamonu University, Kastamonu.

Sorrells, M. (2013). *5 ways robots are being used at events*. https://www.bizbash.com/production-strategy/event-management-tech-tools/media-gallery/13479962/5-ways-robots-are-being-used-at-events

Sorrells, M. (2013). *5 Ways Robots are being Used at Events*. https://www.bizbash.com/production-strategy/event-management-tech-tools/media-gallery/13479962/5-ways-robots-are-being-used-at-events

Sorrels, M. (2013). *5 Ways Robots Are Being Used at Events*. Retrieved July 28, 2020 https://www.bizbash.com/production-strategy/event-management-tech-tools/media-gallery/13479962/5-ways-robots-are-being-used-at-events

Soucy, C. (2020). *Stay Connected with Virtual Community Events*. Retrieved From: https://wiredimpact.com/blog/virtual-community-events-stay-connected/

Sparks, B. A., & Browning, V. (2011). The impact of online reviews on hotel booking intentions and perception of trust. *Tourism Management*, *32*(6), 1310–1323. doi:10.1016/j.tourman.2010.12.011

Spiro, R. S., & Weitz, B. A. (1990). Adaptive selling: Conceptualization, measurement, and nomological validity. *JMR, Journal of Marketing Research*, *27*(1), 61–69. doi:10.1177/002224379002700106

Stanfield, J. (2017). *5 Ways to Harness the Power of Storytelling at Events*. Retrieved from: https://www.eventmanagerblog.com/the-power-of-storytelling-at-events

Stapleton, C. B., & Hughes, C. E. (2006). Making memories of a lifetime. In M. Haller, M., Billinghurst, & B. H. Thomas (Eds.), Emerging Technologies of Augmented Reality: Interfaces & Design (pp. 329-351). London: IDEA Group Inc.

Stek, T. D. (2016). Drones over Mediterranean Landscapes. The Potential of Small UAV's (Drones) for Site Detection and Heritage Management in Archaeological Survey Projects: A Case Study from le Pianelle in the Tappino Valley, Molise (Italy). *Journal of Cultural Heritage*, *22*, 1066–1071. doi:10.1016/j.culher.2016.06.006

Stevens, R. P. (2005). *Trade show and event marketing*. Thomson.

Střelák, D. (2016). *Augmented reality tourist guide* (Master's Thesis). Masarykova Univerzita Fakulta Informatiky. Czechia.

Strickland, P., Williams, K. M., Laing, J., & Frost, W. (2016). The Use of Social Media in the Wine Event Industry. A Case Study of the High-Country Harvest in Australia. In G. Szolnoki, L. Thach, & D. Kolb (Eds.), *Successful Social Media and eCommerce Strategies in the Wine Industry*. Palgrave Macmillan. doi:10.1057/9781137602985_5

Strohmeier, S., & Kabst, R. (2014). Configurations of e-hrm–an empirical exploration. *Employee Relations*, *36*(4), 333–353. doi:10.1108/ER-07-2013-0082

Sui, Y., Geng, D., Allen, C. R., Burn, D., Bell, G. D., & Rowland, R. (2001). Three-dimensional motion system ("data-gloves"): Application for Parkinson's disease and essential tremor. In *IEEE International Workshop on Virtual and Intelligent Measurement Systems* (pp.28-33). Budapest, Hungary: IEEE. 10.1109/VIMS.2001.924896

Sun, H. (2007). *Destination and event marketing: A case study in the 2007 c&d xiamen ınternational marathon*. Xiamen, China, Master's Thesis, University Of Waterloo.

Surya, E. D. (2018). The Effect of Advertising, Exhibition and Event Marketing to Improve Awareness Awareness and its Impact on Intereststo Visit to Destination Religi Tour in Padang City (Case Study of Muslim Tourists from Malaysia). *International Conference of ASEAN Prespective and Policy*, *1*(1), 226-231.

Tables, S. (2020). Top Event Technology Trends: 14 most-know. *Innovations: Technology, Governance, Globalization*. https://www.socialtables.com/blog/event-technology/event-technology-trends/

Tafesse, W. (2016). Conceptualization of Brand Experience in an Event Marketing Context. *Journal of Promotion Management*, *22*(1), 34–48. doi:10.1080/10496491.2015.1107007

Tafesse, W., Narui, J., & Korneliussen, T. (2014). Branding goals and strategies at international auto shows. *International Journal of Marketing Studies*, *6*(4), 23–34. doi:10.5539/ijms.v6n4p23

Tarabasz, A. (2013). The reevaluation of communication in customer approach-towards marketing 4.0. *International Journal of Contemporary Managament*, *12*(4), 124–134.

Tasner, M. (2011). *Anında pazarlama, web 3.0 pazarlama kılavuzu [Instant marketing, web 3.0 marketing guide]* (A. Özer, Trans.). MediaCat Press.

Tassiopoulos, D. (2005). *Event management: A professional and developmental approach* (2nd ed.). Juta Academic.

Tassiopoulus, D. (2005). *Events – an introduction. In Event Management: A Professional and Developmental Approach.* Juta Academic.

Tatar, Ş. B., & Eren-Erdoğmuş, İ. (2016). The effect of social media marketing on brand trust and brand loyalty for hotels. *Information Technology & Tourism*, *16*(3), 249–263. doi:10.100740558-015-0048-6

Tatulli, K. (2019). *The Top 9 Meeting & Event Technology Trends for 2020.* https://www.aventri.com/blog/meeting-and-event-technology-trends

Tavakoli, R., & Wijesinghe, S. N. R. (2020). Digital Art and Virtual Tourism Mobility: A Critical Discussion in Contemporary Asian Artistic Expressions and Tourism (P. Mura, K. H. T. Keith, C. W. Choy, & S. Singapore, Eds.). Academic Press.

Taylor, R., & Shanka, T. (2008). Cause for event: Not-for-profit marketing through participant sports events. *Journal of Marketing Management*, *24*(9-10), 945–958. doi:10.1362/026725708X381984

Taylor, S. F., & Cunningham, P. H. (1999). *"Event Marketing" The Advertising Business.* Sage Publications.

Thackeray, R., Neiger, B. L., Hanson, C. L., & McKenzie, J. F. (2008). Enhancing promotional strategies within social marketing programs: Use of Web 2.0 social media. *Health Promotion Practice*, *9*(4), 338–343. doi:10.1177/1524839908325335 PMID:18936268

Theocharis, N. (2008). *Event Tourism: Examining the management of sports events from a physical approach.* Synenergy Forum, Athens.

TheStar. (2020). *World's first robot-operated Chinese eatery opens in South China.* Retrieved February 8, 2020, from https://www.thestar.com.my/news/regional/2020/01/14/world039s-first-robot-operated-chinese-eatery-opens-in-south-china

Thevenot, G. (2007). Blogging as a social media. *Tourism and Hospitality Research*, *7*(3/4), 287–289. doi:10.1057/palgrave.thr.6050062

Thompson, J. B. (2013). *Media and modernity: A social theory of the media.* John Wiley & Sons.

Thornley-Brown, A. (2018). *5 Ways to Use Drones in the Event Industry.* https://www.mpi.org/blog/article/5-ways-to-use-drones-in-the-event-industry

Tierney, P. (2000). Internet-based evaluation of tourism web site effectiveness: Methodological issues and survey results. *Journal of Travel Research*, *39*(2), 212–219. doi:10.1177/004728750003900211

Tığlı, M. (2008). *Güncel pazarlama yaklaşımlarından seçmeler.* Detay Yayıncılık.

Tığlı, M. (2010). *Pazarlama iletişimde şöhret figürü [Fame figure in marketing communications].* Beta Basım.

Timur, N., M., Çevik, S. & Kıcır, K., G. (2014). Etkinlik Turizmi: Kültür Başkenti Etkinliklerinin Başarı Unsurları Üzerine Bir Değerlendirme. *Akademik Sosyal Araştırmalar Dergisi*, *2*(2/1), 56-83.

Timur, M. N., Çevik, S., & Kıcır, G. K. (2014). Event Tourism: An Evaluation on Success Components of Capital of Culture Events. *The Journal of Academic Social Science*, *2*(1), 56–83.

Tinnish, S. M., & Mangal, S. M. (2012). Sustainable event marketing in the MICE industry: A theoretical framework. *Journal of Convention & Event Tourism*, *13*(4), 227–249. doi:10.1080/15470148.2012.731850

Toker, K. (2018). Endüstri 4.0 ve Sürdürülebilirliğe Etkileri. *Institute of Business Administration-Management Journal/ İşletme İktisadi Enstitüsü Yönetim Dergisi*, *29*(84), 51-64.

Tokyo 2020. (2020). Retrieved from Tokyo 2020 Facebook page: https://www.facebook.com/tokyo2020/about/?ref=page_internal

Tolan, D. (2014). *Spor endüstrisinde etkinlik pazarlaması: Galatasaray spor kulübü örneği. Yayımlanmamış yükseklisans tezi*. Maltepe Üniversitesi.

Tolan, S. (2014). *Spor Endüstrisinde Etkinlik Pazarlaması: Galatasaray Spor Kulübü Örneği*. Yüksek Lisans Tezi. Maltepe Üniversitesi Sosyal Bilimler Enstitüsü.

tom Dieck, M. C., & Hyungsoo Jung, T. (2017). Value of Augmented Reality at Cultural Heritage Sites: A Stakeholder Approach. *Journal of Destination Marketing & Management*, *6*(2), 110–117. doi:10.1016/j.jdmm.2017.03.002

Toner, L. & Walker, M. (2014). *The new age of event marketing: Increase event attendance and engagment with an inbound marketing strategy*. Https://cdn2.hubspot.net/hub/53/file-1298172927pdf/The_New_Age_of_Event_Marketing.pdf

Tontuş, Ö. (2019). *Etkinlik Yönetimi*. Retrieved August 8, 2020. file:///C:/Users/dogan/Downloads/EtkinlikYonetimi2.pdf

Topsakal, Y., Yüzbasıoglu, N., Celik, P., & Bahar, M. (2018). Tourism 4.0 - tourist 5.0: Why the human revolution is one number bigger than industrial revolutions? *Journal Of Tourism Intelligence And Smartness*, *1*(2), 1–11.

Toros, S. (2016). Reklam iletişiminde dönüşümler: Çevrimiçi reklam ve tüketiciler. *Journal of Economy and Society*, *71*, 30–36.

Toy, E. (2017). *Görsel İletişim Tasarımı ve Animasyon*. İçinde İnteraktif Sanatın Oluşum Süreci ve Günümüzdeki Durumu, Pegem Akademi.

TozlumikrofonB. G. E. N. (2020). https://www.tozlumikrofon.com/boyutlarina-gore-etkinlikler-nelerdir-etkinlikler-kaca-ayrilir/

Tremaud, J. (2017). *Augmented Reality in Events: Examples and Benefits*. https://esculturaeventos.com/en/posts/augmented-reality-in-events/

Tsukayama, H. (2012). *How the Tupac Hologram works*. https://www.washingtonpost.com/business/technology/how-the-tupac-hologram-works/2012/04/18/gIQA1ZVyQT_story.html

TUBITAK. (2016). *Yeni sanayi devrimi, akıllı üretim sistemleri, teknoloji yol haritası*. https://www.tubitak.gov.tr/sites/default/files/akilli_uretim_sistemleri_tyh_v27aralik2016.pdf

Tuckwell, K. J. (1991). *Canadian Marketing in Action*. Pearson Education.

Tunçalp, O., & İrge, N. T. (2018). The customer reviews and scoring system effects for sales price of choice hotels in online site of tourism marketing. *International Journal of Global Tourism Research*, *2*(1), 43–57.

Turco, D. M. (1997). Host residents' perceived social costs and benefits toward a staged tourist attraction. *Journal of Travel & Tourism Marketing*, *7*(1), 21–30. doi:10.1300/J073v07n01_02

Türen, U., Gökmen, Y., & Tokmak, İ. (2013). İnsan Kaynakları Yönetimi Uygulamalarının İşletme Performansına Etkisi: İşletmelerin Sahip Oldukları Bilgi ve İletişim Teknolojileri Kabiliyetlerinin Aracılık Rolü. *Business and Economics Research Journal, 4*(4), 103.

Türk Dil Kurumu. (2020). Etkinlik. *Sözlük maddesi.* Retrieved August 15, 2020, from https://sozluk.gov.tr/

Türk, C. N. N. (2019). *İstanbul'da robot garsonlar işe başladı.* Retrieved August 26, 2020, from https://www.cnnturk.com/turkiye/istanbulda-robot-garsonlar-ise-basladi

Türker, İ.H. (2011). Tuvalden Sayısala, Anadolu Üniversitesi Sanat ve Tasarım Dergisi. *Güzel Sanatlar Enstitüsü Yayınları, 2419*(1).

Türkiye, E. Y. (2019). *Turizm Sektörü Dijitalleşme Yol Haritası Seyahat Acentaları Dijital Dönüşüm Raporu.* TÜRSAB & TBV.

Turner, A. (2019). *Trends Watch Report 2019.* https://www.ibtmworld.com/RXUK/RXUK_EIBTM/IBTM-World-2019/PDFs/13409_IBTM_TRENDS_WATCH_REPORT_2019_FINAL.pdf?v=637096812923316749

Tuten, T. L. (2008). *Advertising 2.0: Social media marketing in a web 2.0 world.* ABC-CLIO.

TUYED. (2020). *Turizm Sektörüne 5 Yapay Zeka Uygulaması.* Turizm Yazarları ve Gazeteleri Derneği. Retrieved August 20, 2020, from http://www.tuyed.org.tr/turizm-sektorune-5-yapay-zeka-uygulamasi/

Uçar, P. (2019). Elektronik İnsan Kaynakları Yönetimi: Kavramsal Bir Çerçeve. *Yönetim. Ekonomi ve Pazarlama Araştırmaları Dergisi, 3*(5), 182–191.

Uludağ İhracatçı Birlikleri Genel Sekreterliği AR&GE Şubesi. (2017). *Yapay Zeka ve Yeni Teknolojiler.* Retrieved August 23, 2020. file:///C:/Users/dogan/Downloads/Yapay%20zeka%20ve%20yeni%20teknolojiler.pdf.

Ulusoy, G. (2018). İmalat Sektöründe Endüstri 4.0 Dönüşüm Çabaları. *Bazı Gözlemler, İktisat ve Toplum Dergisi, 92,* 63–65.

Uraltaş, N. T. (2012). lektronik Perakendecilik ve Bir reklam Mecrası Olarak Sosyal Ağ Siteleri. In Sosyal Medya - Akademi (pp. 21-56). İstanbul: Beta Yayınları.

Urry, J. (1990). The consumption'of tourism. *Sociology, 24*(1), 23–35. doi:10.1177/0038038590024001004

Valck, K. D., & Bruggen, G. H. V. (2009). Virtual communities: A marketing perspective. *Decision Support Systems, 47*(3), 185–203. doi:10.1016/j.dss.2009.02.008

Vallee, R., & Westcott, M. (2002). *Trends in Event Marketing. The George P.* Johnson Company.

Valos, M. J., Hajı Habıbı, F., Casıdy, R., Drıesener, C. B., & Maplestone, V. L. (2016). Exploring the integration of social media within integrated marketing communication frameworks: Perspectives of services marketers. *Marketing Intelligence & Planning, 34*(1), 19–40. doi:10.1108/MIP-09-2014-0169

Van der Wagen, L. (2005). *Event management for tourism, cultural, business and sporting events* (2nd ed.). Pearson Education Australia.

Van der Wagen, L. (2007). *Human Resource Management for Events: Managing the Event Workforce.* Butterworth-Heinemann.

Van der Wagen, L. (2009). *Human resource management for events.* Routledge.

Van der Wagen, L. (2010). *Event management.* Pearson Higher Education AU.

Van der Wagen, L., & White, L. (2010). *Event management: for tourism, cultural, business and sporting events* (4th ed.). Pearson Pub.

Van Winkle, C., Bueddefeld, J., Halpenny, E., & MacKay, K. (2019). The unified theory of acceptance and use of technology 2: Understanding mobile device use at festivals. *Leisure Studies*, *38*(5), 634–650. doi:10.1080/02614367.2019.1618895

Vargo, S. L., & Lusch, R. F. (2006). Service-dominant logic: What it is, what it is not, what it might be. In R. F. Lusch & S. L. Vargo (Eds.), *The service-dominant logic of marketing: Dialog, debate and directions* (pp. 43–56). M.E Sharpe, Inc.

Veirman, D. M., Cauberge, V., & Hudders, L. (2017). Marketing through Instagram influencers: The impact of number of followers and product divergence on brand attitude. *International Journal of Advertising*, *36*(5), 798–828. doi:10.1080/02650487.2017.1348035

Versichele, M., Neutens, T., Delafontaine, M., & Van deWeghe, N. (2012a). The Use of Bluetooth for Analyzing Spatiotemporal Dynamics of Human Movement at Mass Events: A Case Study of the Ghent Festivities. *Applied Geography (Sevenoaks, England)*, *32*(2), 208–220. doi:10.1016/j.apgeog.2011.05.011

Versichele, M., Neutens, T., Goudeseune, S., Bossche, F., & Weghe, N. (2012b). Mobile Mapping of Sporting Event Spectators Using Bluetooth Sensors: Tour of Flanders. *Sensors (Basel)*, *12*(10), 14196–14213. doi:10.3390121014196 PMID:23202044

Vincent, J. (2019). *Security robots are mobile surveillance devices, not human replacements*. https://www.theverge.com/2019/11/14/20964584/knightscope-security-robot-guards-surveillance-devices-facial-recognition-numberplate-mobile-phone

Vural, Z. B., & Bat, M. (2010). Yeni bir iletişim ortamı olarak sosyal medya: Ege Üniversitesi İletişim Fakültesine yönelik bir araştırma. *Journal of Yasar University*, *5*(20), 3348–3382.

Wahlster, W., Grallert, H. J., Wess, S., Friedrich, H., & Widenka, T. (Eds.). (2014). *Towards the internet of services: The THESEUS research program*. Springer. doi:10.1007/978-3-319-06755-1

Wan, C. S. (2002). The web sites of ınternational tourist hotels and tour wholesalers in Taiwan. *Tourism Management*, *23*(2), 155–160. doi:10.1016/S0261-5177(01)00048-6

Wang, C. P., & Tsai, C. H. (2019, February). Application of virtual reality to the study of festival culture in aboriginal literature. In *Proceedings of the 2nd International Conference on Image and Graphics Processing* (pp. 136-139). 10.1145/3313950.3313975

Wang, D., Park, S., & Fesenmaier, D. R. (2012). The role of smartphones in mediating the touristic experience. *Journal of Travel Research*, *51*(4), 371–387. doi:10.1177/0047287511426341

Wang, F. Y., Carley, K. M., Zeng, D., & Mao, W. (2007). Social computing: From social informatics to social intelligence. *IEEE Intelligent Systems*, *22*(2), 79–83. doi:10.1109/MIS.2007.41

Wang, W. T., & Li, H. M. (2012). Factors influencing mobile services adoption: A brand-equity perspective. *Internet Research*, *22*(2), 142–179. doi:10.1108/10662241211214548

Wang, Y., & Fesenmaier, D. R. (2006). Identifying the success factors of web-based marketing strategy: An investigation of convention and visitors bureaus in the United States. *Journal of Travel Research*, *44*(3), 44. doi:10.1177/0047287505279007

Wan, Y. K. P., & Chan, S. H. J. (2013). Factors that affect the levels of tourists' satisfaction and loyalty towards food festivals: A case study of Macau. *International Journal of Tourism Research*, *15*(3), 226–240. doi:10.1002/jtr.1863

Watkin, H. (2016). *World's first 3d printing restaurant opens in london.* Retrieved May 5, 2020, from https://all3dp.com/worlds-first-3d-printing-restaurant-coming-london/

we are social. (2020). *Digital 2020: Global Digital Yearbook.* Retrieved from Hootsuite Web Site: https://datareportal.com/reports/digital-2020-july-global-statshot

We Are Social-Hootsuite. (2018). *Digital In 2018.* Hootsuite. http://www.mediacatonline.com/wp-content/uploads/2018/05/we-are-social-digital-in-2018.pdf

Weaver, G. R., & Treviño, L. K. (2001). The role of human resources in ethics/compliance management: A fairness perspective. *Human Resource Management Review, 11*(1-2), 113–134. doi:10.1016/S1053-4822(00)00043-7

Weijman, J. (2014). *AGT leveraged the internet of things to improve attendees' experience at Tomorrowland.* https://www.agtinternational.com/agt-leveraged-the-internet-of-things-to-improve-attendees-experience-at-tomorrowland-2/

Weinberg, T. (2009). *The new community rules: Marketing on the social web.* O'Reilly Media.

Werthner, H., & Klein, S. (2002). *Information technology and tourism-a challenging Relationship.* Springer-Verlag Wien.

What is an Influencer? (2020). Retrieved from influencermarketinghub.com web site: https://influencermarketinghub.com/what-is-an-influencer/

Whiting, A., & Deshpande, A. (2016). Towards greater understanding of social media marketing: A review. *Journal of Applied Business and Economics, 18*(4), 82–91.

Williams, J., & Chinn, S. J. (2010). Meeting relationship-marketing goals through social media: A conceptual model for sport marketers. *International Journal of Sport Communication, 3*(4), 422–437. doi:10.1123/ijsc.3.4.422

Wilson, A. (2010). *Hajime robot restaurant.* Live Less Ordinary. Retrieved August 25, 2020, from https://www.live-less-ordinary.com/hajime-robot-restaurant-in-bangkok-yakiniku/

Wilson, C. (2019). *Artificial Intelligence is Changing the Event Industry – Here's How.* Retrieved July 23, 2020. https://blog.swapcard.com/artificial-intelligence-and-events

Wilson, C. (2019). *Artificial intelligence is changing the event industry — Here's how.* https://blog.swapcard.com/artificial-intelligence-and-events

Winer, R. S. (2009). New communications approaches in marketing: Issues and research directions. *Journal of Interactive Marketing, 23*(2), 108–117. doi:10.1016/j.intmar.2009.02.004

Wired. (2019). *How artificial intelligence is influencing creativity at this year's Sónar Festival.* https://www.wired.co.uk/article/artificial-intelligence-creativity-sonar-festival

Wirtz, J., Patterson, P., Kunz, W., Gruber, T., Lu, V. N., Paluch, S., & Martins, A. (2018). Service Robots in the Front Line: Will it be a Brave New World. *Journal of Service Management, 29*(5), 907–931. doi:10.1108/JOSM-04-2018-0119

Wohlfeil, M., & Whelan, S., (2005). *Event-marketing: When brands become "Real- Lived".* Academic Press.

Wohlfeil, M., & Whelan, S. (2005a). Consumer Motivations to Participate in Marketing-Events: the Role of Predispositional Involvement. In K. M. Ekstrom & H. Brembeck (Eds.), *E - European Advances in Consumer Research* (Vol. 7, pp. 125–130). Association for Consumer Research.

Wohlfeil, M., & Whelan, S. (2005b). Event-marketing as innovative marketing communications: Reviewing the German experience. *Journal of Customer Behaviour, 4*(2), 181–207. doi:10.1362/1475392054797214

Wohlfeil, M., & Whelan, S. (2006). Consumer motivations to participate in event-marketing strategies. *Journal of Marketing Management*, *22*(5-6), 643–669. doi:10.1362/026725706777978677

Wolf, W. (2009). Cyber-physical systems. *Computer*, *42*(3), 88–89. doi:10.1109/MC.2009.81

Wolters, C. (2019). *Holographic Elephants Shine New Light on Tradition—and Other Innovations*. https://www.nationalgeographic.com/science/2019/11/holographic-circus-elephants-naked-man-orchid-and-more-breakthroughs/#close

Wong, J. W. C., Lai, I. K. W., & Tao, Z. (2020). Sharing memorable tourism experiences on mobile social media and how it influences further travel decisions. *Current Issues in Tourism*, *23*(14), 1773–1787. doi:10.1080/13683500.2019.1649372

Wood, B. (2019). *TeamLab launches the world's first digital art museum in Tokyo*. Retrieved from https://thespaces.com/teamlab-launches-the-worlds-first-digital-art-museum-in-tokyo/

Wood, E. H. (2009). Evaluating event marketing: Experience or outcome? *Journal of Promotion Management*, *15*(1-2), 247–268. doi:10.1080/10496490902892580

Wood, E. H., & Masterman, G. (2008). *Event marketing: Measuring an experience*. In *7th International Marketing Trends Congress*, Venice.

World Economic Forum. (2016). The future of jobs. [http://www3.weforum.org/docs/WEF_FOJ_Executive_Summary_Jobs.pdf]. Access date: January, 2020.

Wright, P. M., & Dyer, L. (2000). *People in the e-business: new challenges. new solutions*. Working paper 00-11, Center for Advanced Human Resource Studies, Cornell University.

Wu, D., Rosen, D. W., Wang, L., & Schaefer, D. (2014). Cloud-based manufacturing: Old wine in new bottles? *Procedia CIRP*, *17*, 94–99. doi:10.1016/j.procir.2014.01.035

Wu, H. C., Wong, J. W. C., & Cheng, C. C. (2014). An empirical study of behavioral intentions in the food festival: The case of Macau. *Asia Pacific Journal of Tourism Research*, *19*(11), 1278–1305. doi:10.1080/10941665.2013.844182

Wu, S. I. (2016). Competing Model of Event Marketing Activities. *International Journal of Marketing Studies*, *8*(4), 52–66. doi:10.5539/ijms.v8n4p52

www.abdiibrahim.com.tr/en. (2020). *Van Gogh Alive Digital Art Exhibit*. Retrieved from https://www.abdiibrahim.com.tr/en/responsibility/social-responsibility-at-abdi-ibrahim/van-gogh-alive-digital-art-exhibit

www.architecturelab.net. (2019). *15 Types of Digital Art to Consider.* Retrieved from https://www.architecturelab.net/types-of-digital-art/

www.carrieres-lumieres.com. (2019). *The Hıstory Of The Carrıères De Lumıères*. Retrieved from https://www.carrieres-lumieres.com/en/venue/history-carrieres-lumieres

www.superevent.com. (n.d.). How Big Data Is Revolutionizing the Event Industry. Retrieved from https://superevent.com/blog/how-big-data-is-revolutionizing-the-event-industry/

Xiang, Z., & Fesenmaier, R. D. (2017). Analytics in Tourism Design. In Analytics in Smart Tourism Design Concepts and Methods (pp. 1-12). Springer. doi:10.1007/978-3-319-44263-1_1

Xiang, Z., & Gretzel, U. (2010). Role of social media in online travel information search. *Tourism Management*, *31*(2), 179–188. doi:10.1016/j.tourman.2009.02.016

Xiang, Z., Wöber, K., & Fesenmaier, D. R. (2008). Representation of the online tourism domain in searchengines. *Journal of Travel Research*, *47*(2), 137–150. doi:10.1177/0047287508321193

Xu, M., David, J. M., & Kim, S. H. (2018). The fourth industrial revolution: Opportunities and challenges. *International Journal of Financial Research*, *9*(2), 90–95. doi:10.5430/ijfr.v9n2p90

Yalcin Kayikci, M., & Kutluk Bozkurt, A. (2018). Dijital Çağda Z ve Alpha Kusagi, Yapay Zeka Uygulamalari ve Turizme Yansimalari [Generation Z and Alpha in Digital Age, Artificial Intelligence and Reflections on Tourism]. *Sosyal Bilimler Metinleri*, *1*, 54–64.

Yalçın, F. G. (2017). DijitalAge. [https://digitalage.com.tr/tum-yonleriyle-etkinlik-pazarlamasi-ve-etkinlik-pazarlamasinda-son-trendler/]. Access date: January, 2020.

Yalçın, F. G. (2017). *Tüm yönleriyle etkinlik pazarlaması ve etkinlik pazarlamasında son trendler*. Retrieved from Digitalage Web site: https://digitalage.com.tr/tum-yonleriyle-etkinlik-pazarlamasi-ve-etkinlik-pazarlamasinda-son-trendler/

Yang, L., Henthorne, T. L., & George, B. (2020). Artificial Intelligence and Robotics Technology in the Hospitality Industry: Current Applications and Future Trends. In Digital Transformation in Business and Society (pp. 211-228). Palgrave Macmillan. doi:10.1007/978-3-030-08277-2_13

Yang, F., Zhang, M., & Bhandari, B. (2017). Recent development in 3D food printing. *Critical Reviews in Food Science and Nutrition*, *57*(14), 3145–3153. doi:10.1080/10408398.2015.1094732 PMID:26479080

Yavuz, B. (2011). *Investigation of electronic marketing methods: A research made through surveying on three, four- and five-star hotels in Antalya region* (Unpublished Master's Thesis). Gazi University, Ankara.

Yaylagül, Ş. (2017). Sosyal Medya Fenomenlerine Bağlanmışlığın Belirlenmesi: Yükseköğretim Öğrencileri Üzerine Bir Uygulama. *Adnan Menderes Üniversitesi Sosyal Bilimler Enstitüsü Dergisi*, *4*(3), 219–235. doi:10.30803/adusobed.349934

Yen, T.-H., Wey, P.-S., & Sullivan, K. (2016). Classification of Event and Meeting Technology. *IIBA International Interdisciplinary Business-Economics Advancement Conference.* https://core.ac.uk/download/pdf/216960107.pdf#page=94

Yeung, T. A., & Law, R. (2006). Evaluation of usability: A study of hotel web sites in Hong Kong. *Journal of Hospitality & Tourism Research (Washington, D.C.)*, *30*(4), 452–473. doi:10.1177/1096348006290115

Yıldız, A., & Karagöz, Ş. (2018). İçerik pazarlaması. In Değişen Pazarlama Anlayışı. Gazi Publishing.

Yıldız, A. (2018). Endüstri 4.0 ve akıllı fabrikalar. *Sakarya Üniversitesi Fen Bilimleri Enstitüsü Dergisi*, *22*(2), 546–556.

Yıldız, A. (2018). Endüstri 4.0 ve Akıllı Fabrikalar. *Sakarya Üniversitesi Fen Bilimleri Enstitüsü Dergisi*, *22*(2), 546–556.

Yıldız, A., & Karagöz, Ş. (2018). İçerik pazarlaması (Content marketing). In Y. Akçi (Ed.), *Değişen pazarlama anlayışı- Yeni pazarlama yaklaşımları [Changing marketing understanding - New marketing approaches]* (pp. 75–102). Gazi Kitapevi.

Yildiz, S. (2019). Turist Rehberligi Mesleginde Robot Rehberlerin Yukselisi [The Rise of Robot Guides in Tourist Guidance Profession]. *Vizyoner Dergisi*, *10*(23), 164–177. doi:10.21076/vizyoner.481225

Yılmaz, Y. (2007). İnsan Kaynakları Yönetiminde E-Dönüşüm. *İktisadi ve İdari Bilimler Fakültesi Dergisi*, *9*(1).

Yin, Y., Stecke, K. E., & Li, D. (2018). The evolution of production systems from Industry 2.0 through Industry 4.0. *International Journal of Production Research*, *56*(1-2), 848–861. doi:10.1080/00207543.2017.1403664

Yoo, K. H., & Gretzel, U. (2011). Influence of personality on travel-related consumer-generated media creation. *Computers in Human Behavior*, *27*(2), 609–621. doi:10.1016/j.chb.2010.05.002

Yoon, S., Spencer, D. M., Holecek, D. F., & Kim, D. K. (2000). A profile of Michigan's festival and special event tourism market. *Event Management*, *6*(1), 33–44.

Yoon, Y. S., Lee, J. S., & Lee, C. K. (2010). Measuring festival quality and value affecting visitors' satisfaction and loyalty using a structural approach. *International Journal of Hospitality Management, 29*(2), 335–342. doi:10.1016/j.ijhm.2009.10.002

Yorkfestival. (2019). *About the festival.* http://yorkfestivalofideas.com/about/

Yovcheva, Z., & Buhalis, D. (2013). Augmented reality in tourism: 10 unique applications explained. *Digital Tourism Think Tank,* 1-12.

Yuan, J., & Jang, S. (2008). The effects of quality and satisfaction on awareness and behavioral intentions: Exploring the role of a wine festival. *Journal of Travel Research, 46*(3), 279–288. doi:10.1177/0047287507308322

Yu, H., & Ko, H. T. (2012). Integrating Kano model with strategic experiential modules in developing ICT-enabled services: An empirical study. *Management Decision, 50*(1), 7–20. doi:10.1108/00251741211194840

Yüksekbilgili, Z., & Çevik, G. Z. (2018). Endüstri 4.0 Bağlamında Türkiye'nin Yerine İlişkin Güncel ve Gelecek Eksenli Bir Analiz. *Finans Ekonomi ve Sosyal Araştırmalar Dergisi, 3*(2), 422–436.

Yürük, P. (2015). Etkinlik pazarlamasında sosyal etki algılamasının etkinliğe katılım, tatmin ve sadakat üzerine etkisi: Kırkpınar festivali örneği (Doktora tezi). Trakya Üniversitesi Sosyal Bilimler Enstitüsü, İşletme A.B.D., Edirne.

Yürük, P. (2015). *Etkinlik pazarlamasinda sosyal etki algilamasinin etkinliğe katilim, tatmin ve sadakat üzerine etkisi: Kirkpinar festivali örneği* [The effect of social impact perception in event marketing on participation, satisfaction and loyalty: The example of the Kirkpinar festival] (Unpublished doctoral dissertation). Trakya University, Social Science Institute, Turkey.

Zachary, W., Ryder, J., Hicinbothom, J., & Bracken, K. (1997). The Use of executable cognitive models in simulation-based intelligent embedded training. In *Proceedings of Human Factors Society 41st Annual Meeting* (pp. 1118-1122). Santa Monica, CA: Human Factor Society. 10.1177/107118139704100287

Zamzuri, N. H., Awang, K. W., & Samdin, Z. (2011). Environmental issues in meeting, incentive, convention and exhibition (MICE) tourism sector. *2nd international conference on business, economics and tourism management, 24,* 98-101.

Zarantonello, L., & Schmitt, B. H. (2013). The impact of event marketing on brand equity: The mediating roles of brand experience and brand attitude. *International Journal of Advertising, 32*(2), 255–280. doi:10.2501/IJA-32-2-255-280

Zeleny, P., & Ruzicka, V. (2017). The design of the 3d printer for use in gastronomy. *Modern Machinery (MM). Science Journal, 1744-1747.* Advance online publication. doi:10.17973/mmsj.2017_02_2016187

Zeng, B., & Gerritsen, R. (2014). What do we know about social media in tourism? A review. *Tourism Management Perspectives, 10,* 27–36. doi:10.1016/j.tmp.2014.01.001

Zhang, M. (2019). *Couple hires robot photographer for their wedding.* https://petapixel.com/2019/04/11/this-robot-photographer-just-shot-her-first-wedding/

Zhao, Z., & Gutierrez, J. (2001). The Fundamental Perspectives in E-Commerce. In *E-Commerce Diffusion: Strategies And Challenges.* Heidelberg Press.

Zhou, K., Liu, T., & Zhou, L. (2015, August). Industry 4.0: Towards future industrial opportunities and challenges. In *2015 12th International conference on fuzzy systems and knowledge discovery (FSKD)* (pp. 2147-2152). IEEE.

Ziewitz, M., & Brown, I. (2013). A prehistory of internet governance. In *Research Handbook on Governance of the Internet.* Edward Elgar Publishing. doi:10.4337/9781849805049.00008

Ziyadin, S., Koryagina, E., Grigoryan, T., Tovma, N., & Zharaskyzy Ismail, G. (2019). Specificity of Using Information Technologies in the Digital Transformation of Event Tourism. *International Journal of Civil Engineering and Technology, 10*(1), 998–1010.

Zou, J. Y., & Ap, J. (2009). Residents' perceptions towards the impacts of the Beijing 2008 Olympic Games. *Journal of Traver Research,* 48-78.

Zsarnoczky, M. (2017). How does Artificial Intelligence affect the Tourism Industry? *Journal of Management, 31*(2), 85–90.

Zumstein, D. & Hundertmark, S. (2017). Chatbots-An Interactive Technology for Personalized Communication, Transactions and Services. *IADIS International Journal on WWW/Internet, 15*(1), 96-109.

About the Contributors

Ali Dalgic was born in Antalya, Turkey in 1987. He is a research assistant in the Department of Tourism Management at Mersin University. He completed his MSc degree in Management at Adnan Menderes University, Aydin/Turkey in December 2013. He got PhD in Tourism Management at Mersin University. He is working at Isparta University of Applied Sciences Faculty of Tourism as an assistant professor. His research interests include event management, alternative tourism and strategic management.

* * *

Gökhan Akel is a Research Assistant of Management Information Systems at the University of Antalya AKEV University, Turkey. He is a Ph.D. student in Business Administration at the University of Aydın Adnan Menderes, Turkey. Currently, he serves as a foreign language editor for the Business Economics and Management Research Journal. Gökhan Akel has an interest in consumer behavior and tourism marketing research.

Kemal Birdir was born in Adana, Turkey in 1967. He completed his bachelors degree in 1989 in Çukurova University, received MBA from Hawaii Pacific University in 1994 and completed his PhD in Purdue University in 1998. He is currently working at Mersin University Faculty of Tourism as a full-time professor.

Mısra Çakaloğlu completed her undergraduate education in Economics at Anadolu University in 2012, and her master's degree at Akdeniz University, Institute of Social Sciences, Department of Economics in 2015. In 2016, she started her PhD at Akdeniz University, Institute of Social Sciences, Department of Economics. Currently, she is a Lecturer of Banking and Insurance Program at Antalya AKEV University.

İpek Itır Can is a first-year PhD student and a full-time faculty member (a research assistant) in the Department of Tourism Management at Anadolu University. She obtained her BA and MA in Tourism Management at Istanbul University. Her research interests centre around the intersection of tourism marketing, destination management, tourist behaviours and digital technology. Since she started her academic career, she has written 4 articles, 11 papers and a book in the last 3 years.

Evrim Çeltek obtained her master of science in tourism business administration from Sakarya University (Turkey) and she obtained her PhD in tourism and hotel management from Anadolu University (Turkey). Her researches focused on tourism marketing. She has several articles, books and book chapters about, mobile marketing, e-commerce, mobile commerce, advergame, digital marketing, augmented reality, virtual reality, gamification, electronic customer relationship management, big data, artificial intelligence and rural tourism.

Dilaysu Cinar was born in 1986 in Bursa, Turkey. In 2008, she graduated from Muğla Sıtkı Koçman University, Faculty of Economics and Administrative Sciences, Department of Business Administration. Simultaneously, she also completed the Public Administration Department with the Double Major Program. In 2011, she received her master's degree from the Department of MBA at Dokuz Eylül University. In 2017, she completed her Ph.D. in Business Administration Program at Yıldız Technical University. Since 2012, Cinar has been working as an academician at Beykent University.

Cihan Cobanoglu is the McKibbon Endowed Chair Professor of the School of Hospitality and Tourism Management (SHRM) in the Muma College of Business at the University of South Florida (USF), who also serves as the Director of the M3 Center for Hospitality Technology and Innovation and Coordinator of International Programs for the School of Hospitality and Tourism Management. He is a renowned hospitality and tourism technology expert. Dr. Cobanoglu is a Fulbright Specialist commissioned by the Fulbright Commission which is part of the U.S. Department of State's Bureau of Educational and Cultural Affairs (ECA) and World Learning (2018-2021). He is a Certified Hospitality Technology Professional (CHTP) commissioned by Hospitality Financial & Technology Professionals (HFTP) and Educational Institute of American Hotel & Lodging Association (AHLA). He is the Editor of the Journal of Hospitality and Tourism Technology (JHTT)(Indexed in SSCI IF=2.796), editor of Journal of Global Business Insights (JGBI), Journal of Global Hospitality and Tourism, associate editor of Tourism Review (SCCI IF=2.908) and a co-author of six books and ten conference proceedings. He is also currently serving as the President of Association of North America Higher Education International (ANAHEI).

Seda Derinalp Çanakçi was born in 1983 in Adana- Turkey. She earned her bachelor degree from School of Tourism and Hotel Management of Mersin University in 2007. She received her Master's and PhD degree in Department of Hotel Management of Mersin University. Much of her research focused on Gastronomy Tourism. Currently, she is an assistant professor in Gastronomy and Culinary Arts at Sarikamis Tourism Faculty in Kafkas University.

Rebecca Dodds-Gorman is a recent graduate of Griffith University with industry experience in event volunteer management.

Seden Dogan who is an Assistant Professor at the Faculty of Tourism at the Ondokuz Mayis University in Turkey earned her masters and Ph.D. degrees from Akdeniz University. She worked at different 5-star hotels and OTA (online travel agency) between 1998-2013. She decided to continue her career in academia and became a lecturer at Adnan Menderes University in 2013 and transferred to Ondokuz Mayis University in 2017. She conducted her post doctoral research at the University of South Florida between the years 2019-2020. She published 32 journal articles and 12 book chapters. Her area of interest is technology in the hospitality and tourism industry. She serves as Assistant Editor at the Journal of Hospitality and Tourism Technology which is an SSCI journal and General Secretary at the IFITT (International Federation for IT and Travel & Tourism) Turkey Chapter.

Remziye Ekici graduated from Balıkesir University in 2010. She graduated from Akdeniz University Tourism Business Management Department in 2013. In 2018, she completed her PhD. education in Akdeniz University Tourism Business Management Program. Ekici has been working as an academician at Isparta University of Applied Sciences since 2019.

Kemal Enes is an academician and he is studying on the Tourism and Gastronomy. Besides these he is a chef and working on the Gastronomy and the Culinary Arts. He is lecturing Culinary Art since 2010 and also he has worked at the kitchens of various organization firms and otels since he was 16. His education status, he is graduated master programme in the Tourism and he is writing a PHD thesis in tourism programme. He has got several international experiences, between October 28 and 09 November 2014 he has been invited by Bangladesh Turkish Embassy to present a Turkish Local Cuisine. He managed a team in Radisson Blue Garden hotel and honored with a certificate of appreciation by the Turkish embassy. In April 2012, within the scope of Erasmus Teaching Mobility, he gave a 10-hour Practice Course on Local Turkish Cuisine at Saimaa University in Finland, In March 2016, he was a guest lecturer at the University of Antwerp in Belgium as part of International Week . he explained the Turkish cuisine within the scope of UNESCO cultural heritage. lastly summer of 2019 he was invited by the Kazakhstan government as a specialist to improve the quality of restaurant business within the scope of the Kazakhstan horizon project. He has got several Academik publication Book chapter, Articles and reports. He is married to Esra enes, an academician who studies fashion design, and has a baby.

Fatma Doğanay Ergen graduated from Tourism Management and Hotel Applied Sciences of Abant İzzet Baysal University in 2010. She completed her master's degree in Tourism and Hotel Management at Afyon Kocatepe University in June 2013. In 2014, Ergen started to work as a lecturer and as the head of Tourism and Hotel Management program at Nisantasi University. She completed her PhD in Tourism and Hotel Management at Balıkesir University. After completing her PhD's, she was appointed as assistant professor to the Department of Tourism Guidance at Nişantaşı University and continued working at Nişantaşı University. In 2019, she was appointed as a professor assistant and head of the Department of Tourism Guidance at Isparta University of Applied Sciences. She is currently working at Isparta University of Applied Sciences. She works on alternative tourism types, health tourism and tourism management.

Andrew Goldston is Director of Operations at Real Serious Games. Mr Goldston has extensive experience in Extended Reality technologies and large-scale infrastructure projects.

Nurhayat İflazoğlu is a lecturer in the Department of Gastronomy and Culinary Arts at Hatay Mustafa Kemal University, School of Hotel and Tourism Management. İflazoğlu holds a bachelor's degree in Gastronomy and Culinary Arts from Gazi University and a master's degree in Gastronomy and Culinary Arts from Mersin University. She continues her Ph.D. studies at Ankara Hacı Bayram Veli University, Department of Gastronomy and Culinary Arts. She worked as a chef in hotels and restaurants such as Hilton, Rixos, Marriott in Turkey; NH Hotel in Germany; Inlet Tower, Hilton, Marriott and Kincaid Grill in United States. She has some studies and researches on topics such as Mevlevi culinary culture, cookery history, olive oil, geographical marking, gastronomy, gastronomy tourism, local cuisines, food neophobia, destination image, Unesco gastronomic cities, behavioral intention, HACCP and conspicuous consumption on social media.

Betül Kodaş is assistant professor of department of tourism management in the Faculty of Tourism, Mardin Artuklu University, Turkey. She hold Bachelor's degree from School of Tourism and Hotel Management in Adnan Menderes University (Aydın/Turkey), Master's degree from Dokuz Eylül University and Ph.D. from Eskişehir Osmangazi University, Turkey. Her research interests are tourism management, organizational behaviour, destination management and marketing, travel management.

Ingrid Proud, with over 20 years experience in the Sport, Venue and Major Event Industry across Australia, United Kingdom, Middle East, and Asia, has developed a hightened awareness of cross cultural interaction, collaboration processes, legacy development and strategic planning to achieve an optimum operational environment. Ingrid's career has provided her an opportunity to plan and operate major world events from various cross agency positions enabling a better understanding and view of the intricacies and objectives all parties set out to achieve. Her career portfolio expands across Olympic Games, Commonwealth Games, Asian Games, Rugby World Cup, Stadium operations, International and National Sporting Events, Cultural and Entertainment Events, Host City Operations and Public Domain Management.

Asım Saldamlı received his bachelor's degree in Tourism Management and graduate education in The Department of Business Administration. He received the title of doctor in 1999, associate professor in 2010 and professor in 2015. He started his academic career in 1992. To date, he has worked at four different universities. During this period, he has held administrative duties such as head of the tourism department, dean and vice-chancellor. He currently serves as dean of Faculty of Tourism at Bolu Abant Izzet Baysal University. He has articles published in numerous national and international journals, has presented papers at scientific meetings, written book chapters and completed editorial work. Prof. Dr. Asım Saldamlı is a member of the advisory board and scientific board in national and international activities in the field of tourism and has refereeing duties in scientific journals. He also lectures on management science, research methods and tourism management in both the undergraduate and graduate programs. He speaks German, English and Turkish.

Serap Serin Karacaer completed her bachelors degree in 1999 in Anadolu University, Tourism and Hotel Management. She received MBA from Aksaray University, Management in 2012. She completed her PhD in Gazi University, Tourism Management in 2019.

Alana Thomson is Lecturer in Management at Federation Business School. Dr Thomson's research focuses on event management and event legacies.

Derya Toksoz graduated from Ege University, Department of Hospitality Management in 2012. She completed her MSc degree and PhD in the field of Tourism Management at Mersin University. She has been working as a research assistant at Mersin University Faculty of Tourism since 2014. Her research interests are mainly focused on tourism planning, cultural heritage management, visitor management, and tour guiding.

Cigdem Unurlu is a lecturer at Trakya University in the department of Tourism and Hotel Management. She holds a Bachelor's Degree in Tourism and Hotel Management from Abant İzzet Baysal

University and a masters and Ph.D. in business administration from Trakya University. Her research interests include consumer behavior, destination marketing and branding.

Pınar Uçar completed Pamukkale University Business Administration Department in 2014. Then, in 2016, she completed the master's degree with Pamukkale University Management and Organization thesis. She continue to the Akdeniz University General Management doctorate program that started in 2018. Also, she is currently working as a lecturer in Antalya AKEV University Banking and Insurance Program, which started in 2017.

Gülser Yavuz completed her PhD in Mersin University in 2015. She works as an assistant professor at Mersin University and is responsible for Communication Technics, Health Tourism, Business Ethics, Introduction to Business, Management, Management and Organization, Strategic Management, Entrepreneurship courses. Her research interests such as events, gastronomy, tourism education, social media and entrepreneurship.

Mehtap Yücel Güngör completed her master's degree at Gazi University, Institute of Social Sciences, Department of Tourism Management Education. She completed her doctorate at Adnan Menderes University, Institute of Social Sciences, Department of Tourism Management. She started his academic career in 2009 as a Lecturer. She is currently working as an Assistant Professor at Anadolu University, Faculty of Tourism, Department of Gastronomy and Culinary Arts. Her research interests are digitalization in tourism, social media, food and beverage marketing and gastronomy.

Index

F

G

H

I

J

L

M

www.ingramcontent.com/pod-product-compliance
Lightning Source LLC
LaVergne TN
LVHW060412300926
849162LV00006B/1404